A BIG YEAR FOR
RECORD-BREAKING AT GUINNESS!

WHO IS THE WEALTHIEST MAN? He lives in a 1,788-room palace with a 110-car garage. His home is valued at $422 million, and he earns $3.78 billion a year with $14 billion in reserves!

WHO IS THE BIGGEST THIEF? He has stolen up to $10 billion!

WHICH IS THE POOREST COUNTRY? Its per-capita income is only $80.00 per year!

WHO broke the underwater pogo-stick-jumping record?

WHAT DUCK broke the egg-laying record?

WHAT LUCK! Who set the record for the luckiest find (a bag of diamonds!)?

WHO caught 120 million fish—with a single throw of the net?

WHO holds the oldest record in *Guinness*?

WHO set a record for the most *Guinness* records held by one person?

A GALA FEAST OF
FACTS AND ENTERTAINMENT

Bantam Books in the Guinness Series

GUINNESS BOOK OF WORLD RECORDS 1985
GUINNESS BOOK OF WORLD RECORDS 1986
GUINNESS BOOK OF WORLD RECORDS 1987

1987
GUINNESS
BOOK OF
WORLD RECORDS

ALAN RUSSELL, Editor-in-Chief
NORRIS McWHIRTER, Consulting Editor

DAVID A. BOEHM, *American Editor-in-Chief*
CYD SMITH, *Assistant Editor*
JIM BENAGH, *Sports Editor*
GENE JONES, *Associate Editor*

BANTAM BOOKS
TORONTO • NEW YORK • LONDON • SYDNEY • AUCKLAND

This low-priced Bantam Book has been completely reset in a type face designed for easy reading, and was printed from new plates. It contains the complete text of the original hard-cover edition. NOT ONE WORD HAS BEEN OMITTED.

GUINNESS BOOK OF WORLD RECORDS 1987
*A Bantam Book / published by arrangement with
Sterling Publishing Co., Inc.*

PRINTING HISTORY
*American Guinness edition published October 1956
Bantam edition / October 1963
Revised Bantam edition April 1964
Revised and enlarged Bantam Special edition / June 1966
Revised and enlarged new Bantam edition / March 1968
Revised and enlarged new Bantam edition / May 1970
Revised and enlarged new Bantam edition / April 1971
Revised and enlarged new Bantam edition / March 1973
Revised and enlarged new Bantam edition / February 1974
Revised and enlarged new Bantam edition / February 1975
Revised and enlarged new Bantam edition / March 1976
Revised and enlarged new Bantam edition / January 1977
Revised and enlarged new Bantam edition / March 1978
Revised and enlarged new Bantam edition / March 1979
7 printings through October 1979
Revised and enlarged new Bantam edition / March 1980
9 printings through October 1980
Revised and enlarged new Bantam edition / March 1981
4 printings through October 1981
Revised and enlarged new Bantam edition / March 1982
5 printings through August 1982
Revised and enlarged new Bantam edition / April 1983
4 printings through October 1983
Revised and enlarged new Bantam edition / April 1984
3 printings through July 1984
Revised and enlarged new Bantam edition / April 1985
3 printings through August 1985
Revised and enlarged new Bantam edition / April 1986
4 printings through October 1986
Revised and enlarged new Bantam edition / April 1987*

World rights reserved.
Revised American editions copyright © 1986, 1985, 1984, 1983, 1982, 1981, 1980, 1979, 1978, 1977, 1976, 1975, 1974, 1973, 1972, 1971, 1970, 1969, 1968, 1966, 1965, 1964, 1963, 1962, 1960 by Guinness Superlatives Ltd.

CONTENTS

THE STORY BEHIND
THE GUINNESS BOOK

On September 12, 1954, Sir Hugh Beaver invited Norris and Ross McWhirter to see if their fact and figure agency in London could help settle arguments about records. An office was set up at 107 Fleet Street, London, and work began on the first 198-page book. The printers bound the first copy on August 27, 1955. Before Christmas the *Guinness Book* was No. 1 on the best-sellers list. It has occupied this position every year since except 1957 and 1959 when it was not republished.

The first US edition appeared in New York in 1956 followed by editions in French (1962) and German (1963). In 1967 there were first editions in Japanese, Spanish, Danish and Norwegian, while the following year editions were published in Swedish, Finnish and Italian. In the seventies there followed Dutch (1971); Portuguese (1974); Czechoslovak (1976); Hebrew, Serbo-Croat and Icelandic (all in 1977) and Slovenian (1978). In the 1980s translations into Greek, Indonesian, Chinese, Turkish, Hindi, Malay, Polish and Arabic brought the total to 220 editions in 25 languages.

By 1974 the *Guinness Book* earned its own place in the *Guinness Book*. It had become the top-selling copyright book in publishing history. By 1986 the global sales had risen to more than 53 million, which is equivalent to 118 stacks, each as high as Mount Everest.

On March 31, 1986, having edited the book for 32 years, Norris McWhirter handed over the chief editorship to Alan Russell, who had been the television producer of the "Record Breakers" program in Great Britian.

October 1986

Iveagh
[BENJAMIN GUINNESS]
EARL OF IVEAGH, Chairman
Guinness, PLC

PREFACE

This 25th US edition has been brought up to date by the compilers and editors and provided with new photos. About a quarter of the many thousands of records listed have to be changed from one edition to the next.

In this edition we have devoted more attention to American events that led to world records.

We wish to thank correspondents from the many countries of the world for raising and settling various editorial points. Strenuous efforts have been made to improve the value of the material presented and this policy will be continued in future editions.

Sterling Publishing Co., Inc.
Two Park Ave., New York, NY 10016

IS IT A RECORD?

Categories

We are *likely* to publish only those records which improve upon previously published records or which are newly significant in having become the subject of widespread and, preferably, worldwide competition. Records in our sense essentially have to be both measurable and comparable to other performances in the same category.

It should be stressed that unique occurrences, interesting peculiarities and the collecting of everyday objects, are not themselves necessarily records. Records which are *qualified* or limited in some way—for example, by age, handicap, day of the week, etc.—cannot be accommodated in a reference work so general as the *Guinness Book of World Records.*

We do not publish records in gratuitously hazardous categories, such as the lowest starting height for a handcuffed, free-fall parachute jump, or the thinnest burning rope suspending a man in a straitjacket from a helicopter. World records claimed on TV specials are not always set according to Guinness rules. Certain innately dangerous but historically significant activities, such as tightrope walking, are included but are best left to professionals. Other categories which have reached the limits of safety, such as sword swallowing and Volkswagen stuffing, have been retired and either are so marked or have been deleted. No further claims will be considered for publication.

We reserve the right to determine in our sole discretion the record to be published and the use of the name of the record holder for purposes of inclusion in the book.

Rules and Procedures

A record attempt should compete *exactly* with the record in the book and the conditions under which it was set. Where there is doubt about the rules, it is recommended that the strictest interpretation be adopted. Contact with the Guinness editorial offices at 2 Cecil Court, London Road, Enfield, Middlesex, England (01-441-367-4567) for clarification should be made well in advance of a planned attempt.

If there is a recognized world or national governing body for an activity, that body should be consulted for rules and one of its representatives, whenever possible, should be involved in officiating. For any attempt, expert officiating by impartial witnesses is desirable.

In marathon events, five-minute rest intervals are permitted, but only AFTER each *completed* hour, except for a few "non-stop" categories in which minimal intervals may be taken only for purposes other than for resting. These rest breaks are optional and may be accumulated (for example, 3 hours of activity earns 15 minutes of rest time, etc.). Violation of the rest-interval rules will disqualify an attempt. The accepted record will be the gross time (that is, the total elapsed time, including rest intervals, from start to finish). However, unused accumulated rest break time cannot be added to the final figure.

In recent years there has been a marked increase in efforts to establish records for sheer endurance in many activities. In the very nature of record-breaking, the duration of such "marathons" will tend to be pushed to greater and greater extremes, and it should be stressed that marathon attempts are not without possible dangers. Those responsible for marathon events would be well counseled to seek medical advice before, and surveillance during, marathons which involve extended periods with little or no sleep.

Documentation and Verification

■ We do *not* normally supply personnel to monitor, invigilate or observe record attempts, but reserve the right to do so. In any case, the burden of proof rests with the claimant. No particular form is required, and no entry fee is payable. Guidelines for documentation are provided below. We cannot accept as accurate any claim that is insufficiently documented.

■ Claimants should obtain independent corroboration in the form of local or national newspaper, radio or TV coverage. Newspaper clippings must be annotated with the name of the newspaper, its place of publication and the date of the issue in which the article appeared. When possible, the name of the reporter and black-and-white and/or color action photographs should also be supplied. Videotapes and audio cassettes should not be sent, but held in reserve in the event further documentation is requested.

■ Claimants should send signed authentication by independent, impartial adult witnesses or representatives of organizations of standing in their community. Where applicable, a signed document showing ratification by a governing body should be supplied (see above). A claim is naturally enhanced by a witness with a high degree of expertise in the area of endeavor.

■ Signed log books should show there has been unremitting surveillance in the case of endurance events. These log books must include, in chronological order, the times of activity and the times and durations of all rest breaks taken. The log books must be legible and readily decipherable. They must include signatures of witnesses with times of entering and leaving (at least two *independent* witnesses must be on hand at all times). Where applicable, score sheets must be kept to demonstrate a satisfactory rate of play.

All submissions become the property of the publishers. The publishers will consider, but not guarantee, the return of material, only if a self-addressed stamped envelope or wrapper is supplied *with sufficient postage.*

Revisions

Notwithstanding the best efforts of the editors, errors in the book, while rare, may occur. In the event of such errors, the sole responsibility of the publishers will be to correct such errors in subsequent editions of the book.

If there are discrepancies between entries in one edition and another, it may be generally assumed that the *later* entry is the product of up-to-date research.

Editorial Offices

Please consult the latest edition of the book before phoning or writing the editorial offices, which are primarily concerned with maintaining and improving the quality of each succeeding edition. **We do not offer advice on choosing a record for anyone to attempt breaking.** Also, we are unable to perform the function of a free general information bureau for quiz competitions and the like. However, we are always happy to hear about new record attempts.

From the American Editors of *Guinness*

GUINNESS
WORLD
RECORDS
EXHIBIT HALL

EMPIRE STATE OBSERVATORY
tickets are also on sale at the Guinness ticket
booth along with EXHIBIT HALL tickets.

ADMISSION
$3.00 general admission
$2.00 for age 12 or under
Family rate—$7.50 for 2 adults and 1 child
$1.50 each for additional child
Group rate—Special rate for groups of
10 or more
HOURS: Open daily 9:30 A.M.–6:00 P.M.
(July and August to 8:00 P.M.)

A ROYAL VISIT TO
NEW YORK'S GUIN-
NESS EXHIBIT HALL:
Queen Sofia of Spain
(right) and Prince Fe-
lipe are watching domi-
noes tumble on the
video screen. The man in
the middle is Marvin
Reiter, managing direc-
tor of the Guinness Mu-
seums.

Chapter 1

The Human Being

1. DIMENSIONS

Tallest Giants

The true height of human giants is frequently obscured by exaggeration and commercial dishonesty. The only really admissible evidence on the actual height of giants is that collected in this century under impartial medical supervision. Unfortunately, medical papers themselves are not guiltless in including fanciful, as opposed to measured, heights.

The assertion that Goliath of Gath (*c.* 1060 BC) stood 6 cubits and a span (9 ft 6½ in) suggests a confusion of units or some over-enthusiastic exaggeration by the Hebrew chroniclers. The Hebrew historian Flavius Josephus (b 37 or 38 AD, d after 93 AD) and some of the manuscripts of the Septuagint (the earliest Greek translation of the Old Testament) attribute to Goliath the wholly credible height of 4 Greek cubits and a span (6 ft 10 in).

Modern opinion is that the tallest recorded man of whom there is irrefutable evidence was the pre-acromegalic giant Robert Pershing Wadlow, born at 6:30 a.m. in Alton, Ill, on Feb 22, 1918. He was born to Harold F. and Addie Mae Wadlow (1896–1980) and weighed 8½ lb. His abnormal growth started at the age of 2, following a double hernia operation.

Dr C. M. Charles, Associate Professor of Anatomy at Washington University School of Medicine, in St Louis, and Dr Cyril MacBryde measured him at 8 ft 11.1 in, on June 27, 1940. He died 18 days later, at 1:30 a.m. on July 15, 1940, in Manistee, Mich, as a result of cellulitis (inflammation of cellular tissue) of the right ankle aggravated by a brace, which had been poorly fitted only a week earlier. He was buried in Oakwood Cemetery, Alton, Ill, in a coffin measuring 10 ft 9 in long, 32 in wide, and 30 in deep.

His greatest recorded weight was 491 lb on his 21st birthday. He weighed 439 lb at the time of death. His shoes were size 37AA (18½ in long) and his hands measured 12¾ in from the wrist to the top of the middle finger. His arm span was 9 ft 5¾ in and he consumed 8,000 calories daily. He wore a size 25 ring.

At the age of 9 he was able to carry his father, Harold (d Sept 1967), later mayor of Alton, who stood 5 ft 11 in tall and weighed 170 lb, up the stairs of the family home. His last words were, "The doctor says I won't get home for the . . . celebrations" (a reference to his paternal grandparents' golden wedding anniversary).

TALLEST HUMAN EVER: Robert Wadlow, the 8-ft-11.1-in son of the mayor of Alton, Ill, towers over police officer Robert Galloway, who is himself 6 ft 2 in. (*Alton Telegraph*)

His height progressed as follows:

Age in Years	Height ft	in	Weight in lb	Age in Years	Height ft	in	Weight in lb
5	5	4	105	15	7	8	355
8	6	0	169	16	7	10½	374
9	6	2½	180	17	8	0½	315*
10	6	5	210	18	8	3½	—
11	6	7	—	19	8	5½	480
12	6	10½	—	20	8	6¾	—
13	7	1¾	255	21	8	8¼	491
14	7	5	301	22.4†	8	11.1	439

* Following severe influenza and infection of the foot.
† He was still growing during his terminal illness.

The only other men for whom heights of 8 ft or more have been reliably reported are listed on page 47. In seven cases gigantism was followed by acromegaly, a disorder which causes an enlargement of the nose, lips, tongue, lower jaw, hands and feet, due to renewed activity by an already swollen pituitary gland, which is located at the base of the brain.

Giants exhibited in circuses and exhibitions are routinely under contract not to be measured and are, almost traditionally, billed by their promoters at heights up to 18 in in excess of their true heights. Notable examples of such exaggeration were listed in the 1982 *Guinness Book of World Records*. The acromegalic giant Eddie Carmel (b Tel Aviv, Israel, 1938), formerly "The Tallest Man on Earth" of Ringling Bros. and Bar-

HEIGHT MADE WADLOW A CELEBRITY: When he visited St Louis in 1939, the crowds found his height of almost 9 feet hard to believe.

num & Bailey's Circus (1961–8), was allegedly 9 ft 0⅝ in tall (weighing 535 lb), but photographic evidence suggests that his true height was about 7 ft 6⅝ in. He died in NYC on Aug 14, 1972, when his standing height, due to severe kyphoscoliosis (two-dimensional spinal curvature), was *c.* 7 ft.

Tallest Living Man

Muhammad Aalam Channa (b Sehwan, Pakistan, 1956), who works as an attendant at the shrine of Lal Shahbaz Qalandar in Pakistan assumed the role of the world's tallest man in 1981 with the death of Don Koehler (see table). A height of 8 ft 2¾ is attributed to him by news agencies and the international press was proved in 1984 to be exaggerated reducing his height to 7 ft 10 in. The tallest living humans are thus Monjane and Nashnush (see table).

The tallest teenage giant still growing is Kazim Hussein (b 1968) of Baghdad, Iraq, who was 7 ft 5 in in Feb 1985. He had grown 3 in in the previous 12 months.

Tallest Twins

The tallest (identical) twins ever recorded are Michael and James Lanier (b Nov 27, 1969) of Troy, Mich, who both measure 7 ft 4 in.

Tallest Living Woman

The tallest living woman is Sandy Allen (b June 18, 1955, in Chicago), who lives now in Niagara Falls, Canada. On July 14, 1977, she measured 7 ft 7¼ in at age 22, when she underwent a pituitary gland operation to inhibit further growth. A 6½-lb baby, her acromegalic growth began soon after birth. She now weighs about 462 lb and takes a size 16EEE shoe.

Tallest Giantesses

Giantesses are rarer than giants but their heights are still spectacular. The tallest woman in history was the acromegalic giantess Zeng Jinlian

TALLEST PEOPLE

		ft	in
John F. Carroll (1932–69) of Buffalo, NY	(a)	8	7¾
John William Rogan (1871–1905) of Gallatin, Tenn	(b)	8	6
Väinö Myllyrinne (1909–63) of Helsinki, Finland	(f)	8	3
Don Koehler (1925–81) of Denton, Mont, later Chicago	(d)	8	2
Bernard Coyne (1897–1921) of Anthon, Iowa	(e)	8	2
Patrick Cotter O'Brien (1760–1806) of Kinsale, County Cork, Ireland	(g)	8	1
"Constantine" (1872–1902) of Reutlingen, W. Germany	(h)	8	0.8
Gabriel Estevao Monjane (b 1944–fl. 1986) of Monjacaze, Mozambique	(j)	8	0.75
Sulaiman 'Ali Nashnush (b 1943–fl. 1986) of Tripoli, Libya	(i)	8	0.4

(a) Carroll was a victim of severe kypho-scoliosis (two-dimensional spinal curvature). The figure represents his height with assumed normal spinal curvature, calculated from a standing height of 8 ft 0 in, measured Oct 14, 1959. His standing height was 7 ft 8¾ in shortly before his death.

(b) Measured in a sitting position. Unable to stand owing to ankylosis (stiffening of the joints through the formation of adhesions) of the knees and hips. Weighed only 175 lb.

(d) Spinal curvature reduced his standing height to 7 ft 10 in. Abnormal growth started at age 10. He had a twin sister who is 5 ft 9 in tall. His father was 6 ft 2 in tall, his mother 5 ft 10 in.

(e) Eunuchoidal giant ("daddy-longlegs" syndrome). He was rejected by the US Army in 1918 when he stood 7 ft 9 in.

(f) Stood 7 ft 3½ in at the age of 21. Experienced a second phase of growth in his late thirties and measured 8 ft 1.2 in at the time of his death.

(g) Revised height based on skeletal remeasurement in 1975.

(h) Height estimated, as both legs were amputated after they turned gangrenous. He claimed a height of 8 ft 6 in. Eunuchoidal.

(i) Operation in Rome in 1960 to correct abnormal growth was successful.

(j) Measured 7 ft 5 in at age of 16, and 7 ft 10 in Dec 1965. Eunuchoidal. Has not been anthropometrically assessed since joining a Portuguese circus, billed as 8 ft 8⅓ in.

(pronounced San Chung Lin) (b June 26, 1964) of Yujiang village in the Bright Moon Commune, Hunan Province, central China. She could not stand erect, due to scoliosis, but was 8 ft 1¼ in long when she died on Feb 13, 1982. She began to grow abnormally from the age of 4 months and stood 5 ft 1½ in before her 4th birthday and 7 ft 1½ in when she was 13. Her hands measured 10 in and her feet 14 in in length. Her parents are 5 ft 4 in and 5 ft 1½ in while her brother was 5 ft 2 in tall at age 18.

Tallest Couple

Anna Haňen Swan (1846–88) of Nova Scotia, Canada, was billed at 8 ft 1 in but actually measured 7 ft 5½ in. In London, June 17, 1871, she married Martin van Buren Bates (1845–1919), of Whitesburg, Letcher County, Ky, who stood 7 ft 2½ in, making them the tallest married couple on record.

Shortest Little People

The strictures which apply to giants apply equally to dwarfs, except that exaggeration gives way to understatement. In the same way 9 ft may be regarded as the limit toward which the tallest giants tend, so 23 in must be regarded as the limit toward which the shortest mature dwarfs tend (*cf.* the average length of new-born babies is 18 to 20 in). In the case of child dwarfs their *ages* are often enhanced by their agents or managers.

There are many forms of human dwarfism, but those suffering from ateliosis (midgets) are generally the shortest. They have essentially normal proportions but suffer from growth hormone deficiency. Such dwarfs tended to be even shorter at a time when human stature was generally shorter due to lower nutritional standards.

The shortest mature human of whom there is independent evidence was Pauline Musters ("Princess Pauline"), a Dutch midget. She was born at Ossendrecht Feb 26, 1876, and measured 11.8 in at birth. At the age of 9 she was 21.65 in tall and weighed only 3 lb 5 oz. She died, at the age of 19, of pneumonia, with meningitis, in New York City on Mar 1, 1895. Although she was billed at 19 in, she had earlier been medically measured and found to be 23.2 in tall. A *post mortem* examination showed her to be exactly 24 in (there was some elongation after death). Her mature weight varied from 7½ lb to 9 lb and her "vital statistics" were 18½–19–17, which suggests she was overweight.

In 1938 a height of 19 in was attributed to Paul Del Rio (b Madrid, Spain, 1920) by *Life Magazine* when he visited Hollywood, but the fact that he created no "fuss" in the film capital and weighed as much as 12 lb suggests he was closer to 26 in tall.

In 1979 a height of 19.68 in and a weight of 4 lb 6 oz were reported for a 9-year-old Greek girl named Stamatoula (b Sept 1969). She measured 5.9 in at birth. When she died on Aug 22, 1985, at the Lyrion Convent, Athens, she measured 26.4 in and weighed 11 lb. The child, believed to be the survivor of twins, suffered from Seckel's "bird-face" syndrome.

TALLEST MARRIED COUPLE: The Canadian giantess Anna Hanen Swan, 7 ft 5½ in tall, married Martin van Buren Bates (not shown here) in London in 1871. Bates was only 3 in shorter than his wife. (*Gary Doidge*)

SHORTEST LIVING ADULT (left): Antonio Ferreira of Arcozelo, Portugal (b 1943), is a drummer. Here he shows his "entire" 29½-in height. (*Gamma Presse Agence*).

CLAIMANT FOR SHORTEST LIVING MAN (below): "Nelson, the Little Man" poses in the indoor market place in his home town, Santo Domingo, Dominican Republic, with American "amigo," Richard L. Finkler. He is said to be 30–32 years old and to measure 24–26 in in height, but this is not certain.

FAMOUS MIDGET (above left), "General" Tom Thumb, who stood 3 ft 4 in high at his tallest, at the age of 25, married Lavinia Warren (2 ft 8 in) on Feb 10, 1863 while they were in P. T. Barnum's Circus. Two thousand people attended the wedding at NYC's Grace Episcopal Church. At the hotel reception that followed, the bridal couple stood on top of a piano to greet the guests, then cut into a wedding cake that weighed more than they did together. Later President Lincoln gave a reception for them at the White House, and they went on to 20 years of married life.

SHORTEST AND LIGHTEST GIRLS: (Above left) The little Greek girl, Stamatoula, photographed at age 9. In this picture, she weighed 4 lb 4 oz. (Left) Lucia Zarate of Mexico weighed 4.7 lb at age 17, after weighing 2½ lb at birth in 1863. (Above right) "Princess Pauline" Musters, a Dutch midget, weighed 9 lb at her heaviest and reached 23.2 in at age 19.

Shortest Males

The shortest recorded adult male dwarf was Calvin Phillips, born in Bridgewater, Mass, Jan 14, 1791. He weighed 2 lb at birth and stopped growing at the age of 5. When he was 19 he measured 26½ in tall and weighed 12 lb with his clothes on. He died two years later, in Apr 1812, from progeria, a rare disorder characterized by dwarfism and premature senility.

The most famous midget in history was Charles Sherwood Stratton, *alias* "General Tom Thumb," born Jan 4, 1838. When he came into the clutches of the circus proprietor P. T. Barnum, his birth date was changed to Jan 4, 1832, so that when he was billed as standing 30½ in at the age of 18 he was in fact only 12 years old. He died of apoplexy on July 15, 1883 in his birthplace of Bridgeport, Conn, aged 45 (not 51), and was then 3 ft 4 in tall.

William E. Jackson, *alias* "Major Mitc" (b Oct 2, 1864, Dunedin, New Zealand), measured 9 in long and weighed 12 oz at birth. In Nov 1880, he stood 21 in and weighed 9 lb. He died in NYC, on Dec 9, 1900, when he measured 27 in.

The shortest known mobile living adult human is Antonio Ferreira (b Arcozelo, Portugal, 1943), a rachitic dwarf drummer, who measures 29¼ in tall. In July 1982 an unconfirmed height of 28 in was reported for a chicken farmer named Ghucam Ahmed Dar living near Srinagar in Kashmir, India.

SHORTEST LIVING TWINS: The Rice brothers, John and Greg, of Maitland, Fla, 34-in tall, love their special-size motorcycles.

Shortest Twins

The shortest twins ever recorded were the primordial dwarfs Matjus and Bela Matina (b 1903–*fl.* 1935) of Budapest, Hungary, who later became naturalized Americans. They both measured 30 in. The world's shortest living twins are John and Greg Rice (b Dec 1951) of Maitland, Fla, who both measure 34 in.

Oldest Little People

There were only two centenarian dwarfs on record. The first was Miss Anne Clowes of Matlock, Derbyshire, England, who died Aug 5, 1784, at the age of 103. She was 3 ft 9 in tall and weighed 48 lb. Hungarian-born Susanna Bokoyni ("Princess Susanna") of Newton, NJ, died, aged 105 years, on Aug 24, 1984. She was 3 ft 4 in tall and weighed 37 lb.

Most Variable Stature

Adam Rainer, born in 1899 in Graz, Austria, measured 3 ft 10.45 in at the age of 21. But then he suddenly started growing at a rapid rate, and by 1931 he had reached 7 ft 1¾ in. He became so weak as a result that he was bedridden for the rest of his life. He measured 7 ft 8 in when he died on March 4, 1950, aged 51, and was the only person in medical history to have been both a dwarf and a giant.

Most Disparate Couple

Nigel Wilksi (6 ft 6 in) of Kingston-upon-Hull, Eng, married Beverly Russell (4 ft), both aged 21, on June 30, 1984. Their son, Daniel, was 9 lb 5 oz, when born on Mar 22, 1986.

Tallest Tribes

The tallest major tribe is the Tutsi (also called Watutsi), Nilotic herdsmen of Rwanda and Burundi, Central Africa, where the average adult height of the males is more than 6 ft. The Tehuelches of Patagonia, long regarded as of gigantic stature (7–8 ft average) have in fact an average adult male height of 5 ft 10 in. The same height is reported for the Montenegrins of Yugoslavia.

Shortest Tribes

The smallest pygmies are the Mbuti, with an average height of 4 ft 6 in for men and 4 ft 5 in for women, with some groups averaging only 4 ft 4 in for men and 4 ft 1 in for women. They live in the forests near the river Ituri in Zaïre, Africa.

WEIGHT

Lightest Humans

The lightest adult human on record was Lucia Zarate (b San Carlos, Mexico, Jan 2, 1863, d Oct 1889), an emaciated ateliotic dwarf of 26½ in who weighed 4.7 lb at the age of 17. She "fattened up" to 13 lb by her 20th birthday. At birth she had weighed 2½ lb.

The thinnest recorded adults of normal height are those suffering from Simmonds' disease (hypophyseal cachexia). Losses up to 65% of the original body weight have been recorded in females, with a "low" of 45 lb in the case of Emma Shaller (b St Louis, Mo, July 8, 1868, d Oct 4, 1890) who stood 5 ft 2 in tall.

Edward C. Hagner (1892–1962), *alias* Eddie Masher, is alleged to have weighed only 48 lb at a height of 5 ft 7 in. He was also known as "the Skeleton Dude." In Aug 1825 the biceps measurement of Claude-Ambroise Seurat (b Apr 10, 1797, d Apr 6, 1826), of Troyes, France, was 4 in and the distance between his back and his chest was less than 3 in. According to one report, he stood 5 ft 7½ in and weighed 78 lb, but in another account was described as 5 ft 4 in and only 36 lb.

It was recorded that the American exhibitionist Rosa Lee Plemons (b 1873) weighed 27 lb at the age of 18.

HEAVIEST MEN

	lb
Jon Brower Minnoch (1941–83) US	1,400
Michael Walker (*né* Francis Lang) (b 1934) US 6 ft 2 in	1,187 (1)
Robert Earl Hughes (1926–58) US 6 ft ½ in	1,069
Mohamed Naaman (b 1946) Kenya 6 ft	1,055 (2)
Mills Darden (1798–1857) US 7 ft 6 in	1,020
John Hanson Craig (1856–94) US 6 ft 5 in	907 (3)
Arthur Knorr (1914–60) US 6 ft 1 in	900 (4)
T. J. Albert Jackson (b 1941) Canton, Miss 6 ft 4 in	891 (5)
Albert Pernitsch (b 1956) Grafkorn, Austria 5 ft 9 in	880 (6)
Toubi (b 1946) Cameroon	857½
T. A. Valenzuela (1895–1937) Mexico 5 ft 11 in	850

1. Estimated weight 1971. Reduced to 369 lb by Feb 1980.
2. Reported to have reduced to 770 lb by Aug 1984.
3. Won $1,000 in "Bonny Baby" contest in NYC in 1858.
4. Gained 300 lb in last 6 months of his life.
5. Born Kent Nicholson, 22 lb, now heaviest living man.
6. His left arm is tattooed "Nobody is perfect." Girth 78¾ in in July 1984.

Heaviest Men

The heaviest human in medical history was alleged to be Jon Brower Minnoch (1941–83) of Bainbridge Island, Wash, who was carried on planking by a rescue team into University Hospital, Seattle, in March 1978. Dr Robert Schwartz, the endocrinological consultant, estimated by extrapolating his intake and elimination rates that he was "probably more" than 1,400 lb. His highest actually recorded body weight was 975 lb in Sept 1976. It took 13 attendants to roll him over in his hospital bed. After nearly 2 years on a 1200-calorie-per-day diet he was discharged at 476 lb. He had to be readmitted in Oct 1981 having reportedly gained 200 lb in 7 days. This former taxicab driver stood 6 ft 1 in tall. He was 400 lb in 1963; 700 lb in 1966; and about 975 lb in late 1976. When Minnoch died in Sept 1983, he had to be rolled in his hospital bed to the funeral home and buried in a double-size wooden casket that took up two cemetery plots.

Francis John Lang (b 1934), *alias* Michael Walker of Clinton, Iowa, was attributed a weight of 1187 lb. He could not be admitted for treatment for inflammation of the gall bladder to the Veterans Administration Hospital, Houston, Tex because of the impossibility of getting him through the doors. He was treated in a trailer in the car park and discharged Jan 5, 1972 unweighed but estimated to be between 900 and 1000 lb. The more precise weight above was claimed for him while he was suffering from drug-induced bulimia, in the summer of 1971 when he was working with the Christian Farms of Killeen, Tex. There is, however, no independent corroboration for the precise upper weight quoted, although photographic evidence suggests the weight was possibly reliable. By Feb 1980 Lang had reduced to 369 lb.

The highest precisely measured weight for a human is 1069 lb in Feb 1958 for 6-ft-0½-in-tall Robert Earl Hughes (b June 4, 1926), Monticello, Mo. An 11¼-lb baby, he weighed 203 lb at 6 years, 378 lb at 10 years, 546 lb at 13 years, 693 lb at 18 years, 896 lb at 25, and 945 lb at 27. He weighed 1041 lb at the time of his death. His claimed waist of 122 in, his chest of 124 in and his upper arm of 40 in were the greatest on record. Hughes died of uremia (condition caused by retention of urinary matter in the blood) in a trailer at Bremen, Ind, July 10, 1958, aged 32, and was buried in Binville Cemetery, near Mt Sterling, Ill. His coffin, as large as a piano case measuring 7 ft by 4 ft 4 in and weighing more than 1100 lb, had to be lowered by crane. It was once claimed by a commercial interest that Hughes had weighed 1500 lb—a 40% exaggeration.

Heaviest Twins

The heaviest were the performers Billy Leon and Benny Loyd McCrary, *alias* Billy and Benny McGuire (b Dec 7, 1946) of Hendersonville, NC. In Nov 1978, they were weighed at 743 lb (Billy) and 723 lb (Benny) and had 84-in waists. As professional tag wrestling performers, they were *billed* at weights up to 770 lb. Billy died of heart failure on July 13, 1979, in Niagara Falls, Canada, after falling from his mini-bike. He was buried in a cubic coffin with a total weight of over 1000 lb in Hendersonville. A hydraulic lift was needed to lower the coffin to its final resting place. After one 6-week slimming course in a hospital, they emerged weighing 5 lb more each.

Heaviest Women

The heaviest ever recorded was the late Mrs Percy Pearl Washington (b Louisiana, 1926) who died in a hospital in Milwaukee, Wis, Oct 9, 1972. The hospital scales registered only up to 800 lb, but she was believed to weigh about 880 lb. The previous weight record for a woman was set 84 years earlier at 850 lb although a wholly unsubstantiated report exists of a woman, Mrs Ida Maitland (1898–1932) of Springfield, Miss, who reputedly weighed 911 lb.

A more reliable and better documented case was that of Mrs Flora Mae (or May) Jackson (*née* King), a 5-ft-9-in black woman born in 1930 at Shuqualak, Miss. She weighed 10 lb at birth; 267 lb at the age of 11; 621 lb at 25; and 840 lb shortly before her death in Meridian, Miss, on Dec 9, 1965. She was known in show business as "Baby Flo."

Greatest Weight Differential

The greatest recorded for a married couple is *c.* 1,300 lb in the case of Jon Brower Minnoch (see pages 11 and 14) and his 110-lb wife Jeannette in Mar 1978. She bore him two sons.

Slimming

The greatest recorded slimming feat was that of William J. Cobb (b 1926), *alias* "Happy Humphrey," a professional wrestler of Augusta, Ga. It was reported in July 1965 that he had reduced from 802 lb to 232 lb, a loss of 570 lb, in 2½ years. His waist measurement declined from 101 to 44 in. In Oct 1985, "Happy" reported he was back to a normal 432 lb.

The US circus fat lady Mrs Celesta Geyer (b 1901), *alias* Dolly Dimples, reduced from 553 lb to 152 lb 1950–51, a loss of 401 lb in 14 months. Her vital statistics diminished *pari passu* from 79–84–84 to a svelte 34–28–36. Her book "How I Lost 400 lb" was not a best seller. In Dec 1967, she was reportedly down to 110 lb.

By July 1979, Jon Brower Minnoch (see page 11) had reduced to 476 lb; if the peak weight quoted for him was authentic, this indicates a weight loss of 924 lb in 16 months, a speed record of 14.4 lb per week.

HEAVIEST TWINS (above): Benny and the late Billy McCrary (McGuire) weighed almost 1,500 lb together. They were normal at birth.

HEAVIEST WOMAN (above): Mrs Percy Pearl Washington could have weighed as much as 880 lb but the scale only registered up to 800 lb.

HEAVIEST LIVING MAN (right): T. J. Albert Jackson (b 1941 in Canton, Miss) known as "Fat Albert," whose weight varies between 872 and 891 lb, spends his time being transported as "overweight baggage" from show place to show place, all over the US for Four C Productions, Inc, of Miami. (*Wide World Photos*)

Richard Stephens of Birmingham, Ala, slimmed from 467 lb to 305¾ lb in 157 days from Apr 12 to Sept 1985.

Roly McIntyre (b 1952, N Ireland) reduced from 592 lb to 187 lb between Apr 1983 and Feb 1985, a loss of 405 lb in 22 months, or 18.4 lb per month.

Ron Allen (b 1947) sweated off 21½ lb of his 250-lb frame in Nashville, Tenn in 24 hours in Aug 1984.

Weight Gaining

The reported record for gaining weight was set by Jon Minnoch (see pages 11 and 14) when in Oct 1981 he was readmitted to University Hospital, Seattle, Wash, having re-gained 200 lb in 7 days.

Miss Doris James of San Francisco is alleged to have gained 325 lb in the 12 months before her death in Aug 1965, aged 38, at a weight of 675 lb. She was only 5 ft 2 in tall.

---

2. ORIGINS OF MAN

Man (*Homo sapiens*) is a species in the sub-family Homininae of the family Hominidae of the super-family Hominoidea of the sub-order Simiae (or Anthropoidea) of the order Primates of the infra-class Eutheria of the sub-class Theria of the class Mammalia of the sub-phylum Vertebrata (Craniata) of the phylum Chordata of the sub-kingdom Metazoa of the animal kingdom.

The earliest known primates appeared in the Paleocene period about 69 million years ago. The earliest members of the sub-order Anthropoidea are known from both Africa and South America in the early Oligocene period, 34–30 million years ago.

Earliest Man

Characteristics typical of the Hominidae, such as the large brain and bipedal locomotion, do not appear until much later. The earliest undoubted hominid relic found is an Australopithecine jawbone with two molars 2 in in length found near Lake Baringo, Kenya, in Feb 1984 and dated at 4 million years by associated fossils.

The most complete of the earliest skeletons of *Homo* is that of "Lucy" (40% complete) found by Dr Donald C. Johanson and T. Gray at Locality 162 by the Awash river, Hadar, in the Afr region of Ethiopia on Nov 30 1974. She was estimated to be about 40 years old when she died about 3 million years ago, and she was 3½ ft tall.

Parallel tracks of hominid footprints extending over 80 ft were discovered at Laetoli, Tanzania, in 1978, in volcanic ash dating to 3.5 million years ago. The height of the smallest of the seemingly three beings was estimated to be 4 ft 7 in.

The earliest species of the genus *Homo* is *Homo habilis* or "Handy Man" named by Prof. Raymond A. Dart (b 1893, Australia) in 1964. The greatest age attributed to fossils of this genus is for the skull "1470" discovered by Bernard Ngeneo at Koobi Fora, North Kenya. It is dated to 1.9 million years old and was reconstructed by Dr Meave Leakey (*née* Epps).

The earliest stone tools are abraded core choppers dating from *c.* 2.5 million years. They were found at Hadar, Ethiopia in 1976 by Helene

Roche (France). Finger- (as opposed to fist-) held quartz dicers found by Roche close to the Hadar site by the Gona River are also dated to *c.* 2.5 million years.

The earliest *Homo erectus* (upright man), the species directly ancestral to *Homo sapiens,* was discovered by Kamoya Kimen on the surface at the site of Nariokotome III to the west of Lake Turkana, Kenya, in 1984. The skeleton of a 12-year-old boy is the most complete of this species ever found, only a few small pieces being missing.

The earliest evidence of the use of fire by hominids is from a site found in 1978 at Chesowanja, near Lake Baringo, Kenya, dated to 1.42 million years ago.

The earliest evidence for the presence of man in the Americas could date from at least 50,000 BC or "more probably 100,000 BC" according to the late Dr Louis Leakey after the examination of some hearth stones found in the Mojave Desert, Calif, and announced in Oct 1970. The earliest human relic is a skull found in the area of Los Angeles, dated in Dec 1970 to be from 22,000 BC.

---

3. LONGEVITY

Oldest Centenarian

No single subject is more obscured by vanity, deceit, falsehood and deliberate fraud than the extremes of human longevity. Extreme claims are generally made on behalf of the very aged rather than *by* them. The 1970 US Census disclosed 106,441 self-reported centenarians of whom 100,241 were disallowed by the US Department of Health and Human Services.

Many hundreds of claims throughout history have been made for persons living well into their second century and some, insulting to the intelligence, for people living even into their third. The facts are that centenarians surviving beyond their 110th year are of the extremest rarity and the present absolute limit of proven human longevity does not admit of anyone living to celebrate any birthday after their 120th.

It was announced in Feb 1984 that the 1982 census in China revealed ｏｎｌｙ 7,470 ｃｅｎｔｅｎａｒｉａｎｓ ｏｆ ｗｈｏｍ ｔｗｏ ｔｈｉｒｄｓ ｗｅｒｅ ｗｏｍｅｎ. In the US the mid-1983 figure was 32,000. Birth and death registration, however, became complete only in 1933 and was only 30.9% complete by 1915.

Oldest Authentic Centenarians

The greatest *authenticated* age to which any human has ever lived is a unique 120 years 237 days in the case of Shigechiyo Izumi of Asan, Tokunoshima Island, Japan. He was born on the island on June 29, 1865, and recorded as a 6-year-old in Japan's first census of 1871. He died at his home at 12:15 GMT on Feb 21, 1986 after developing pneumonia.

The oldest living person after Mr Izumi's death probably is 113-year-old Mrs Mamie Eva Keith (*née* Walter) (b Mar 22, 1873) at Anna, Ill.

The National Statistical Service of Greece recorded that Liakou Efdokia (b Jan 4, 1864) died on Jan 17, 1982, aged 118 years 13 days. Birth registration was however admitted to be fragmentary before 1920. If corroborated by census or other checks she would from May 6, 1977 have been the oldest ever female.

AUTHENTICATED NATIONAL LONGEVITY RECORDS

	Years	Days		Born	Died
Japan	120	237	Shigechiyo Izumi	June 29, 1865	fl. Feb. 21, 1986
US (d)	113	273	Fannie Thomas	Apr 24, 1867	Jan 22, 1981
Canada (a)	113	124	Pierre Joubert	July 15, 1701	Nov 16, 1814
UK (c)	113	+	Anna Eliza Williams (Mrs) (née Davies)	June 2, 1873	fl. June 2, 1986
Spain (h)	112	228	Josefa Salas Mateo	July 14, 1860	Feb 27, 1973
France	112	66	Augustine Teissier (Sister Julia)	Jan 2, 1869	Mar 9, 1981
Morocco	112	+	El Hadj Mohammed el Mokri (Grand Vizier)	1844	Sept 16, 1957
Poland	112	+	Roswlia Mielczarak (Mrs)	1868	Jan 7, 1981
Ireland	111	327	The Hon. Katherine Plunket	Nov 22, 1820	Oct 14, 1932
Australia	111	235	Jane Piercy (Mrs)	Sept 2, 1869	May 3, 1981
S. Africa (b)	111	151	Johanna Booyson	Jan 17, 1857	June 16, 1968
Czechoslovakia	111	+	Marie Bernatkova	Oct 22, 1857	fl. Oct 1968
Channel Islands	110	321	Margaret Ann Neve (née Harvey)	May 18, 1792	Apr 4, 1903
Northern Ireland	110	234	Elizabeth Watkins (Mrs)	Mar 10, 1863	Oct 31, 1973
Sweden	110	200	Wilhelmine Sande (Mrs)	Oct 24, 1874	fl. May 12, 1985
Yugoslavia	110	150+	Demitrius Philipovitch	Mar 9, 1818	fl. Aug 1928
Netherlands (f)	110	141	Gerada Hurenkamp-Bosgoed	Jan 5, 1870	May 25, 1980
Greece	110	+	Lambrini Tsiatoura (Mrs)		Feb 19, 1981
USSR (i)	110	+	Khasako Dzugayev	Aug 7, 1860	fl. Aug 1970
Italy	110	+	Diminia Sette (Mrs)	1884	Feb 25, 1985
Norway	109	208	Marie Olsen (Mrs)	May 1, 1850	Nov 24, 1959
Finland	109	182	Andrei Akaki Kuznetsoff	14 Oct 17, 1873	Apr 17, 1983
Tasmania	109	179	Mary Ann Crow (Mrs)	Feb 2, 1836	July 31, 1945

Country	Age	Name	Date of birth	Date of death
Scotland (j)	109	Rachel MacArthur (Mrs)	Nov 26, 1827	Dec 10, 1936
Belgium	108	Mathilda Vertommen-Hellemans	Aug 12, 1868	July 4, 1977
Germany (g)	108	Luise Schwarz	Sept 27, 1849	Feb 2, 1958
Iceland	108	Halldora Bjarndottir	Oct 14, 1873	Nov 28, 1981
Portugal (e)	108	Maria Luisa Jorge	June 7, 1859	fl. July 1967
Austria	108	Female		
Malaysia	106	Hassan Bin Yusoff	Aug 14, 1865	fl. Jan 1972
Luxenbourg	105	Nicholas Wiscourt	Dec 31, 1872	Aug 17, 1978

Note: fl. is the abbreviation for *floruit*, Latin for the (or she) was living at the relevant date.

(a) Mrs Ellen Carroll died in North River, Newfoundland, Canada, Dec 8, 1943, reputedly aged 115 years 49 days.

(b) Mrs Susan Johanna Deporter of Port Elizabeth, South Africa, was reputedly 114 years old when she died Aug 4, 1954.

(c) London-born Miss Isabella Shepheard was allegedly 115 years old when she died at St Asaph, North Wales, Nov 20, 1948, but her actual age was believed to have been 109 years 90 days. Charles Alfred Nunez Arnold died in Liverpool, England, Nov 15, 1941, reputedly 112 years 66 days (based on a baptismal claim in London on Sept 10, 1829). Mrs Elizabeth Cornish (*née* Veale), who was buried at Stratton, Cornwall, March 10, 1691 or 1692, was reputedly baptized on Oct 16, 1578, 113 years 4 months earlier.

(d) Ex-slave Mrs Martha Graham died in Fayetteville, NC, June 25, 1959, reputedly aged 117 or 118. Census researches by Eckler show that she was seemingly born in Dec 1844, and hence aged 114 years 6 months. Mrs Rena Glover Bralsford died in Summerton, SC, Dec 6, 1977, reputedly aged 118 years. Mrs Rosario Vasquez who died in California on Sept 2, 1980 was reputedly born in Sonora, Mexico, on June 3, 1866, which would make her 114 years 93 days. Claim has been made that Arthur Reed died in 1984 at age 123, but no evidence has been produced.

(e) Senhora Jesuina da Conceição of Lisbon was reputedly 113 years old when she died June 10, 1965.

(f) Thomas Peters was recorded to have been born on Apr 6, 1745 in Leeuwarden and died aged 111 years 354 days on Mar 26, 1857 in Arnhem.

(g) Friedrich Sadowski of Heidelberg reputedly celebrated his 111th birthday Oct 31, 1936. Franz Joseph Eder died in Spitzburg May 3, 1911, allegedly aged 116.

(h) Snr Benita Medrana of Avila died on Jan 28, 1979, allegedly aged 114 years 335 days.

(i) There are allegedly 21,700 centenarians in the USSR compared with 7,000 in the US. Of these, 21,000 are ascribed to the Georgian SSR, or one out of every 232 people. In July 1962 it was reported that 128, mostly male, resided in the one village of Medini.

(j) Lachlen MacDonald (d June 7, 1858) in Harris, Outer Hebrides, was recorded as being "110 years" on his death certificate.

OLDEST MAN WHO EVER LIVED: At a verified 120 years 237 days before he died in Feb 1986, Shigechiyo Izumi of Japan is the undisputed record holder. Here, he is holding court with children born after he was 110.

The government of Colombia issued an airmail postage stamp in 1956 in honor of a man named Javier Pereira who died that year after supposedly having been born 167 years previous, in 1789. A skin doctor who examined the man years before he died estimated that the cells of his skin indicated an age of at least 145 years. However, no birth certificate or family Bible exists to establish the date of his birth.

Oldest Mummy

Mummification (from the Persian word *mām*, wax) dates from 2600 BC or the 4th dynasty of the Egyptian pharaohs. The oldest surviving mummy is of *Wati*, a court musician of *c.* 2400 BC from the tomb of Nefer in Saqqara, Egypt found in 1944.

---

4. REPRODUCTIVITY

Most Children

The greatest officially recorded number of children produced by a mother is 69 by the first of the 2 wives of Feodor Vassilyev (b 1707–*fl.* 1782), a peasant from Shuya, 150 miles east of Moscow. In 27 confinements she gave birth to 16 pairs of twins, 7 sets of triplets and 4 sets of quadruplets. The children, of whom almost all survived to their majority, were born in the period *c.* 1725–1765. At least 67 survived infancy. The case was reported to Moscow by the Monastery of Nikolskiy Feb 27, 1782. Empress Ekaterina II (The Great) (1762–96) was reputed to have evinced wonderment.

Currently the world's most prolific mother is reported to be Leontina Albina (*née* Espinosa) (b 1925) of San Antonio, Chile, who in 1981 produced her 55th and last child. Her husband Gerardo Secundo Albina (variously Alvina) (b 1921) states that they were married in Argentina in 1943 and they had 5 sets of triplets (all boys) before coming to Chile.

"Only" 40 (24 boys and 16 girls) survive. Eleven were lost in an earthquake, thus indicating that she had more than those born in Chile.

Septuplets

The only birth of 7 at a time in the US occurred on May 21, 1985, when septuplets were born to Patti Jorgenson (Mrs) Frustaci of Orange, Calif, a 30-year-old English teacher who had been taking a fertility drug. One baby was stillborn. The infants who lived ranged in weight from 1 lb upwards. In the weeks that followed, 3 more babies died, leaving 3 that survived.

Oldest Mother

Medical literature contains extreme but unauthenticated cases of septuagenarian mothers such as Mrs Ellen Ellis, aged 72, of Four Crosses, Clwyd, Wales, who allegedly produced a stillborn 13th child May 15, 1776, in her 46th year of marriage. Many cases are cover-ups for illegitimate grandchildren. The oldest recorded mother of whom there is certain evidence (provided by the doctor who attended her) was Mrs Ruth Alice Kistler (*née* Taylor), formerly Mrs Shepard, of Portland, Ore. She was born in Wakefield, Mass, June 11, 1899, and gave birth to a daughter, Suzan, in Glendale, Calif, Oct 18, 1956, when her age was 57 years 129 days. After her death (1982), a person purporting to be a relative alleged that Mrs Kistler had "changed the birth date."

Multiple Births

It was announced by Dr Gennaro Montanino of Rome that he had removed the fetuses of 10 girls and 5 boys from the womb of a 35-year-old housewife July 22, 1971. A fertility drug was responsible for this unique and unsurpassed instance of quindecaplets.

"Siamese" Twins

Conjoined twins derived the name "Siamese" from the celebrated Chang and Eng Bunker (known in Thailand as Chan and In) born at Meklong, on May 11, 1811 of Chinese parents. They were joined by a cartilaginous band at the chest and married in Apr 1843 the Misses Sarah and Adelaide Yates of Wilkes County, NC, and fathered 10 and 12 children, respectively. They died within three hours of each other on Jan 17, 1874, aged 62.

Multiple Great-Grandparents

The report in 1983 that Jane Kau Pung (1877–1982) had left 4 great-great-great-great-grand-children has proved to be incorrect. She in fact proved to be one of many cases of great-great-great-grandparents. Of these cases the youngest person to learn that their great-granddaughter had become a grandmother was Mrs Ann V. Weirick (1888–1978) of Paxtonville, Pa, who received news of her great-great-great-grandson Matthew Stork (b. Sept 9 1976) when aged only 88. She died on Jan 6 1978.

Lightest Twins

The lightest recorded birth weight for surviving twins is 2 lb 3 oz in the case of Mary (16 oz) and Margaret (19 oz) born to Mrs Florence Stimson of Peterborough, England, delivered by Dr Macaulay, Aug 16, 1931. Margaret is now Mrs M. J. Hurst.

Descendants

In polygamous countries, the number of a person's descendants soon becomes incalculable. The last Sharifian Emperor of Morocco, Moulay Ismail (1672–1727), known as "The Bloodthirsty," was reputed to have fathered a total of 525 sons and 342 daughters by 1703, and a 700th son in 1721.

In April 1984 the death was reported of Adam Borntrager, aged 96, of Medford, Wis, who had had 707 direct descendants of whom all but 32 were living. The total comprised 11 children, 115 grand, 529 great-grand and 20 great-great grandchildren. The family is of the Amish sect who eschew cars, telephones, electric light, jewelry and higher education.

Family Immortality

Mr and Mrs Thomas E. Eide of Estherville, Iowa, have 141 descendants without a single death in the family (or their spouses) in 61 years of marriage, 1925–Mar 31, 1986 (and still going). Beatrice Eide (b 1905) has 8 children, 34 grandchildren, 59 great-grandchildren, 3 great-great-grandchildren, who, with 37 spouses and ex-spouses, have survived without incurring killing diseases or having accidents.

Most Living Ascendants

Megan Sue Austin (b May 16, 1982) of Bar Harbor, Maine, had a full set of grandparents and great-grandparents and five great-great-grand-parents making 19 direct ascendants.

Oldest Twins

The chances of identical twins both reaching 100 are said to be one in 500 million. The oldest recorded twins were Eli and John Phipps, born Feb 14, 1803, in Affinghton, Virginia. Eli died at the age of 108 years 9 days Feb 23, 1911, in Hennessey, Okla, at which time John was still living, in Shenandoah, Iowa. Identical twins Mildred Widman Philippi and Mary Widman Franzini, born in St Louis, Mo, missed reaching their 105th birthday together, by 44 days, when Mildred died on May 4, 1985.

LIGHTEST TWINS
(below) · Weighing a total of
only 2 lb 3 oz together at
birth, the twin girls born to
Mrs Florence Stimson of
England set a record in 1931.

OLDEST MOTHER
(above): When she was
more than 57 years old, Mrs
Ruth Kistler bore daughter
Suzan. (*"Family Doctor"
magazine (IPC)*)

SEXTUPLETS: All girls, the Walton-six, born healthy on Nov 18, 1983
to Mrs. Janet Walton of Liverpool, England, are here celebrating
Christmas 1984 at home. (*Robert Ettinger*)

MULTIPLE BIRTHS

Highest number reported at single birth (Decaplets): 10 (2 male, 8 female), Bacacay, Brazil, Apr 22, 1946 (also report from Spain, 1924, and China, May 12, 1936).

Highest number medically recorded (Nonuplets): 9 (5 male, 4 female), to Mrs Geraldine Brodrick at Royal Hospital, Sydney, Australia, June 13, 1971. 2 males were stillborn. Richard (12 oz) survived 6 days. 9 (all died), to patient at University of Penn, Philadelphia, May 29, 1972. 9 (all died), reported from Bagerhat, Bangladesh, *c.* May 11, 1977, to 30-year-old mother.

Highest number and percent surviving: 6 out of 6 sextuplets (3 males, 3 females), to Mrs Susan Jane Rosenkowitz (*née* Scoones) (b Colombo, Sri Lanka, Oct 28, 1947) at Mowbray, Cape Town, South Africa, Jan 11, 1974. In order of birth they were: David, Nicolette, Jason, Emma, Grant and Elizabeth; 24 lb 1 oz. was their total weight. 6 out of 6 (4 males, 2 females) to Mrs Rosanna Giannini (b 1952) at Careggi Hospital, Florence, Italy, on Jan 11, 1980. They are Francesco, Fabrizio, Giorgio, Roberto, Letizia and Linda. 6 out of 6 (all female) to Mrs Janet Walton (b 1952) at Liverpool Maternity Hospital, England, Nov 18, 1983.

Quintuplets (Heaviest): 25 lb to Mrs Lui Saulien, Chekiang, China, June 7, 1953. 25 lb to Mrs Kamalammal, Pondicherry, India, Dec 30, 1956. (Most sets): No recorded case of more than a single set.

Quadruplets (Heaviest): 22 lb 13 oz to Mrs Ayako Takeda, Tsuchihashi Maternity Hospital, Kagoshima, Japan, Oct 4, 1978 (4 girls). (Most sets): 4, to Mme Feodor Vassilyev (d *ante* 1770), of Shuya, Russia.

Triplets (Heaviest): 26 lb 6 oz (unconfirmed), Iranian case (2 male, 1 female), March 18, 1968. (Most sets): 15, to Maddalena Granata (1839–*fl.* 1886), Nocera Superiore, Italy. Mrs Anna Steynvaait of Johannesburg, South Africa, produced 2 sets within 10 months in 1960.

Twins (Heaviest): 27 lb 12 oz (surviving), 14 lb and 13 lb 12 oz, to Mrs J. P. Haskin, Fort Smith, Ark, Feb 20, 1924. (Most sets); 16, to Mme Vassilyev (*see p 16*), 15, to Mrs Mary Jonas (d Dec 4, 1899), of Chester, England—all sets were boy and girl. Mrs Barbara Zulu of Barbeton, South Africa, bore 3 sets of girls and 3 mixed sets in 7 years (1967–73).

LARGEST MEETING OF TWINS: 1,181 sets met at Twinsberg, Ohio, Aug 3–4, 1985. This photo shows less than one-quarter of the total group. (*Ellen Palmer*)

LIVING ASCENDANTS (5): Baby Matthew Stark with his mother, grandmother, great grandmother, great-great-grandmother, and great-great-great-grandmother, Mrs. Ann Weirick, who was only 88 when he was born. This is still not a record family—Megan Sue Austin (b 1982) (not shown) has 5 great-great grandparents and 19 direct living ascendants in all.

Most Twins, Geographically

In Chungchon, South Korea, it was reported in Sept 1981 that there were unaccountably 38 pairs in only 275 families—the highest ratio ever recorded.

Birth After Death

A woman who had been kept alive by breathing mechanically gave birth to a 3-lb 11-oz baby girl 84 days after she had had a seizure, the longest time a fetus has been carried in a brain-dead mother and survived. The event occurred in Roanoke (Va) Memorial Hospital July 5, 1983.

The longest recorded interval in a post-mortem birth was one of at least 80 min in Magnolia, Miss. Dr Robert E. Drake found Fanella Anderson, aged 25, dead in her home at 11:40 p.m., Oct 15, 1966, and he delivered her of a son weighing 6 lb 4 oz by Caesarean operation in the Beacham Memorial Hospital at 1 a.m. Oct 16, 1966.

Oldest Quadruplets

The world's oldest quads are the Ottman quads of Munich, W Germany—Adolf, Anne-Marie, Emma and Elisabeth. They celebrated their 74th birthday on May 5, 1986.

Oldest Triplets

The longest-lived triplets on record were Faith, Hope, and Charity Caughlin, born Mar 27, 1868, in Marlboro, Mass. Mrs (Ellen) Hope Daniels was the first to die, Mar 2, 1962, when 93.

Fastest Triplet Birth

The fastest recorded natural birth of triplets has been 2 minutes in the case of Mrs James E. Duck of Memphis, Tenn (Bradley, Christopher and Carmon) March 21, 1977.

Longest Pregnancy

Claims up to 413 days have been widely reported, but accurate data are bedevilled by the increasing use of oral contraceptive pills, which can be a cause of amenorrhea. Some women on becoming pregnant erroneously add some preceding periodless months to their pregnancy. In the pre-pill era, English law had accepted pregnancies with extremes of 174 days (1939), and 349 days (1949).

Most Premature Birth

Ernestine Hudgins was born (weighing 17 oz) 18 weeks premature in San Diego, Calif, on Feb 8, 1983, after a pregnancy of about 147 days.

BABIES

Heaviest Babies

The heaviest viable baby on record of normal parentage was a boy of 22 lb 8 oz born to Signora Carmelina Fedele of Aversa, Italy, in Sept 1955. Tying the record at 22 lb 8 oz, a boy named Sithandive was delivered by Caesarean section on May 24, 1982, at Sipetu Hospital, Transkei, S Africa. He weighed 77 lb at 16 months.

Mrs Anna Bates, *née* Swan, the 7-ft-5½-in Canadian giantess (see Tallest Couple), gave birth to a boy weighing 23 lb 12 oz (length 30 in) at her home in Seville, Ohio, on Jan 19, 1879, but the baby died less than 24 hours later. Her first child, an 18-lb girl (length 24 in), was stillborn when she was delivered in 1872.

On Jan 9, 1891, Mrs Florentin Ortega of Buenos Aires, Argentina, produced a stillborn boy weighing 25 lb.

In May 1939 a deformed baby weighing 29 lb 4 oz was born in a hospital at Effingham, Ill, but died two hours later from respiratory problems.

Most Bouncing Baby

The most bouncing baby on record was probably James Weir (1819–21) whose headstone in the Old Parish Cemetery, Wishaw, Strathclyde, Scotland, lists him at 112 lb, 3 ft 4 in in height, and 39 in around the waist at the age of 13 months.

Brazil's "super-baby" Veridiano dos Santos (b 1978) weighed 143 lb aged 5.

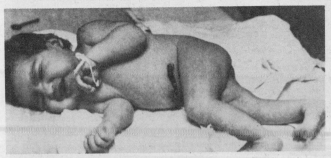

FIRST TEST TUBE BABY (above): Louise Brown weighed 5 lb 12 oz at birth. She was conceived externally in England in 1977.

LEAP-YEAR BABIES (left): The 3 children of the Henriksen family of Andenes, Norway—Heidi (b 1960); Olav (b 1964) and Lief-Martin (b 1968)—all celebrate their birthday infrequently because these all fall on Leap Year Day—Feb 29.

Therese Parentean, who died in Rouyn, Quebec, Canada, aged 9, May 11, 1936, weighed 340 lb (*cf.* 378 lb for Robert Earl Hughes at 10 years of age).

Lightest

The lowest birth weight recorded for a surviving infant, of which there is definite evidence, is 10 oz in the case of Mrs Marion Taggart *née* Chapman, born 6 weeks prematurely on June 5, 1938, in South Shields, northwest England. She was born unattended (length 12¼ in) and was nursed by Dr D. A. Shearer, who fed her hourly for the first 30 hours with brandy, glucose and water through a fountain-pen filler. At three weeks she weighed 1 lb 13 oz and by her first birthday her weight had increased to 13 lb 14 oz. Her weight on her 21st birthday was 106 lb. She died May 31, 1983.

The smallest viable baby reported born in the US has been Jacqueline Benson, who was born in Palatine, Ill, Feb 20, 1936, weighing 12 oz.

A weight of 8 oz was reported on March 20, 1938, for a baby born prematurely to Mrs John Womack, after she had been knocked down by a truck in East St Louis, Ill. The baby was taken alive to St Mary's Hospital, died a few hours later. On Feb 23, 1952, it was reported that a 6 oz baby only 6½ in in length lived for 12 hours in a hospital in Indianapolis. A twin was stillborn.

Earliest Test Tube Baby

Louise Brown (5 lb 12 oz) was delivered by Caesarean section from Lesley Brown, 31, in Oldham General Hospital, Lancashire, England, at 11:47 p.m. July 25, 1978. She was externally conceived on Nov 10, 1977.

First Frozen Embryo Birth

A 5½-lb infant girl named Zoe was reported by the Associated Press on Apr 10, 1984 as having been born in Melbourne, Australia from an embryo that had been frozen. An ovum from the mother had been fertilized in a laboratory with her husband's sperm and then frozen for 2 months, before being implanted in the mother's uterus where it developed normally until delivery by Caesarean section.

Coincidental Birth Dates

While July 4 is celebrated by 225 million Americans, it has special significance for the Williams family of Wilmington, NC. Ralph Bertram Williams IV was born on July 4, 1982, his father (same name, but III) was born on July 4, his grandfather (same name, but Jr) was born on July 4, and his great-grandfather (Sr) was born on July 4, 1876, exactly 100 years after the Declaration of Independence.

The only verified example of a family producing five single children with coincidental birthdays is that of Catherine (1952), Carol (1953), Charles (1956), Claudia (1961) and Cecilia (1966), born to Ralph and Carolyn Cummins of Clintwood, Va, all on Feb 20th. The random odds against five such births occurring singly on the same date would be 1 to 17,797,577,730—almost 4 times the world's population.

Most Southerly Birth

Emilio Marcos Palma (Argentina) born Jan 7, 1978 at the Sargento Cabral Base, Antarctica is the only infant who can claim to be the first born on any continent. The mother was flown from Argentina at governmental expense.

5. PHYSIOLOGY AND ANATOMY

Longest Bones

Excluding a variable number of sesamoids, there are 206 bones in the human body. The thigh bone or *femur* is the longest. It constitutes usually 27½% of a person's stature, and may be expected to be 19¾ in long in a 6-ft-tall man. The longest recorded bone was the *femur* of the German giant Constantine, who died in Mons, Belgium, March 30, 1902, aged 30. It measured 29.9 in. The *femur* of Robert Wadlow, the tallest man ever recorded, measured an estimated 29½ in.

Smallest Waists

Queen Catherine de Medici (1519–89) decreed a standard waist measurement of 13 in for ladies of the French court. This was at a time when females were more diminutive. The smallest recorded waist among women of normal stature in the 20th century is a reputed 13 in in the cases of the French actress Mlle Polaire (1881–1939) and Mrs Ethel Granger (1905–82) of Peterborough, England, who reduced from a natural 22 in over the period 1929–39.

Largest Chest Measurements

The largest chest measurements are among endomorphs (those with a tendency toward globularity). In the extreme case of Robert Earl Hughes of Monticello, Mo (one of the heaviest recorded humans), this was reportedly 124 in, but in the light of his known height and weight a figure of 104 in would be more supportable.

Among muscular subjects (mesomorphs) of normal height *expanded* chest measurements above 56 in are extremely rare. Vasili Alexeyev (b 1942), the 6-ft-1¼-in Russian super-heavyweight weight-lifting champion, had a 60½-in chest at his top weight of 350 lb.

Arnold Schwarzenegger (b 1948, Graz, Austria), the 6-ft-1-in former Mr Universe and "the most perfectly developed man in the history of the world," had a chest measurement of 57 in at his best body weight of 235 lb.

The powerlifter Gary Aprahamian (NYC, 1962–84), the first to achieve a cold (not pumped) biceps measurement over 25 in with 25⅜ in, had a normal chest measurement of 61 in. He weighed 366 lb.

Smallest Brain

The lightest "normal" or non-atrophied brain on record weighed 2 lb 6.7 oz, belonging to a 31-year-old woman. It was reported by Dr P. Davis and Prof E. Wright of King's College Hospital, London, in 1977.

Largest Brains

The brain of an average adult male (*i.e.,* 20–55 years) weighs 3 lb 2.2 oz, falling to 3 lb 1.1 oz. The heaviest non-diseased brain on record was that of Ivan Sergeyvich Turgenev (1818–83), the Russian author. His brain weighed 4 lb 6.9 oz.

Human brains are getting heavier. Examination of post-mortem records shows that the average male brain weight has increased from 3 lb 0.4 oz in 1860 to 3 lb 2.2 oz today. Women's brains have also put on weight, from 2 lb 11.8 oz to 2 lb 12.6 oz, and in recent years have been growing almost as fast as men's.

SMALLEST WAIST (left): Ethel Granger's waist measured 13 in. BIGGEST BICEPS (above): Muscle man Gary Aprahamian of Queens, NYC, showed off his 25⅜-in not-pumped-up biceps ("cold") in 1984. His chest was a normal 61 in.

HUMAN COMPUTER (below): Willem Klein does some mathematical computations faster than a machine. He can extract the 13th root of a 100-digit number in less than 1½ min.

Prof Marian Diamond of the Univ of Calif, at Berkeley, announced on Feb 13, 1985 that the neuron-to-glial-cell ratio in Section 39 of the brain of Albert Einstein (1879–1955) was 1.12 as opposed to the standard 1.936, a difference of 72.8%.

Human Computer

The fastest extraction of a 13th root from a 100-digit number is in 1 min 28.8 sec by Willem Klein (b 1914, Netherlands) on Apr 7, 1981 at the National Laboratory for High Energy Physics (KEK), Tsukuba, Japan.

Mrs Shakuntala Devi of India demonstrated the multiplication of two 13-digit numbers, 7,686,369,774,870 × 2,465,099,745,779, picked at random by the Computer Department of Imperial College, London, on June 18, 1980, in 28 sec. Her correct answer was 18,947,668,177,995,426,-462,773,730.

An eminent mathematical writer has questioned the conditions under which this was apparently achieved and predicts that it would be impossible for her to replicate such a feat under highly rigorous surveillance.

Some experts on calculating prodigies refuse to give credence to the above—largely on the grounds that it is so vastly superior to the calculating feats of any other invigilated prodigy.

Human Memory

Bhandanta Vicitsara recited 16,000 pages of Buddhist canonical texts in Rangoon, Burma, in May 1974. Rare instances of eidetic memory, the ability to reproject and thus "visually" recall material, are known to science.

Creighton Carvello memorized a random sequence of 6 separate packs (312) of cards on a single sighting with only 4 errors including an all correct straight run of 139 cards at the New Marske Institute Club, Cleveland, Eng on Mar 21, 1985. On July 21, 1985, on the Kyoto (Japan) TV *Guinness* program, he achieved the rarer accomplishment of 24 errors with 6 packs shuffled together.

Highest IQ

Intelligence quotients or IQ's comprise the subject's mental age divided by his chronological or actual age multiplied by 100, so that an 8-year-old more gifted than an average 16-year-old would have an IQ of $^{16}/_8 \times 100 = 200$. The highest childhood score has been achieved by Marilyn Mach vos Savant of St. Louis, Mo, who as a 10-year-old achieved a ceiling score for 23-year-olds, thus giving her an IQ of 228.

In adult High IQ clubs, admission requirements are not on IQ points but are gauged in percentiles. An IQ exhibited by 1 person in 10,000 for instance coincides with 158 on the Stanford-Binet scale but 187 on the Cattell scale. The most elite ultra-high IQ Society is the Mega Society with 26 members with percentiles of 99.9999 or 1 in a million. The topmost scorer in the Mega admission test, devised by its founder Ronald K. Hoeflin, has been 46 out of 48 by Marilyn Mach vos Savant superseding the 43 of Jeff Ward.

The 3 members who have scored 197 are Christopher Philip Harding (b Keynsham, England, 1944) of Rockhampton, Australia; Dr Ferris Eugene Alger (b Des Moines, Ia, 1913) of New Hope, Pa, and Dr Johannes Dougles Veldhuis (b Hamilton, Ont, Canada, 1949) of Charlottesville, Va.

The highest IQ published for a national population is 115 for the Japanese born in 1960–61. At least 10 percent of their whole population has an IQ over 130.

Memorizing Pi

All India Radio broadcast in its *Weekly Roundup* on July 5, 1981, part of a recording made earlier that day by Rajan Srinivasen Mahadevan, 23, in the process of reciting π (Pi) from memory (in English) to 31,811 places in 3 hours 49 min (including 26 min of breaks) at the Lion Seva Mandir, Mangalore. His rate was 156.7 digits per minute.

(Note: It is only the *approximation* of π at 22/7 which recurs after its sixth decimal place and can, of course, be recited *ad nauseam*.)

Longest Necks

The maximum measured extension of the neck by the successive fitting of copper coils, as practiced by the Padaung or Kareni people of Burma, is 15¾ in. The neck muscles become so atrophied that the removal of the rings produces asphyxiation.

Longest Finger Nails

The longest known set of nails now belongs to the left hand of Shridhar Chillal (b 1937), of Poona, India. The five nails on his left hand, by Apr 1985, had achieved a measured aggregate length of 143 in (thumb 34½ in) uncut since 1952. Human nails normally grow from cuticle to cutting length in from 117 to 138 days.

Most Fingers and Toes

At an inquest held on a baby at Shoreditch, East London, England, on Sept 16, 1921, it was reported that the boy had 14 fingers and 15 toes.

Fewest Toes

The "lobster claw syndrome" exhibited by the two-toed Kalanga people of the Zimbabwe-Botswana border area is hereditary *via* a single mutated gene.

LONGEST NECKS: The Padaung women of Burma are much admired for the length of their necks. The copper coils, however, make neck turning difficult and the muscles tend to atrophy. (*Planet News*)

Touch Sensitivity

The extreme sensitivity of the fingers is such that a vibration with a movement of 0.02 of a micron can be detected.

Strongest Hair

In a test on BBC-TV *Record Breakers* on Sept 9, 1984 a hair from the head of Miss Pham Thy Lan broke at a strain of 6¼ oz.

Longest Hair

Swami Pandarasannadhi, the head of the Tirudaduturai monastery, Tanjore district, Madras, India, was reported in 1949 to have hair 26 ft in length. From photographs it appears that he was afflicted with the disease Plica caudiformis, in which the hair becomes matted and crusted as

LONGEST FINGER NAILS
(left): Shridhar Chillal of India is proud of his left hand with its nails that total 143 in in length. However, it's a handicap in his job as a photographer, and as for typing, that's impossible. He keeps them covered when he sleeps, too.

LONGEST BEARD (above): Hans Langseth had this picture of his 17½-foot-long beard taken in Barney, ND.

LONGHAIR CONTENDER (left): Georgia Sebrantke of W Germany, with tresses that measured 9 ft 8½ in, may eventually capture the world record for hair length—10 ft 6 in—as her locks continue to grow.

Physiology and Anatomy ▪ 31

a result of neglect. The length of the hair of Miss Skuldfrid Sjorgien (b Stockholm) was reported from Toronto, Canada, in 1927 to have attained twice her height at 10 ft 6 in.

Longest Beard

The longest beard preserved was that of Hans N. Langseth (1846–1927) of Norway, which measured 17½ ft at the time of his burial in Kensett, Iowa, in 1927 after 15 years residence in the US. The beard was presented to the Smithsonian Institution, Washington, DC in 1967.

The beard of the bearded lady Janice Deveree (b Bracken County, Ky, 1842) was measured at 14 in in 1884. The beard of Mlle Helene Antonia of Liège, Belgium, a 17th century exhibitionist, was said to have reached her hips.

Longest Moustache

The longest moustache on record was that of Masuriya Din (b 1908), a Brahmin of the Partabgarh district in Uttar Pradesh, India. It grew to an extended span of 102 in between 1949 and 1962. Karna Ram Bheel (b 1928) was granted permission by a New Delhi prison governor in Feb 1979 to keep his 7-ft-10-in moustache, grown since 1949, during his life sentence. Birger Pellas (b Sept 21, 1934) of Malmö, Sweden, has an 8-ft-8-in moustache grown since 1973.

Most Teeth

Cases of the growth in late life of a third set of teeth have been recorded several times. A reference to an extreme case in France of a fourth dentition known as Lison's case was published in 1896. A triple row of teeth was noted in 1680 by Albertus Hellwigius.

Earliest Dentition

The first deciduous or milk teeth normally appear in infants at 5 to 8 months, these being the mandibular and maxillary first incisors. There are many records of children born with teeth, the most distinguished example being Prince Louis Dieudonné, later Louis XIV of France, who was born with two teeth on Sept 5, 1638. Molars usually appear at 24 months, but in Pindborg's case published in Denmark in 1970, a 6-week premature baby was documented with 8 natal teeth of which 4 were in the molar region.

Most Dedicated Dentist

Brother Giovanni Battista Orsenigo of the Ospedale Fatebenefratelli, Rome, Italy, a religious dentist, conserved all the teeth he extracted in three enormous boxes during the time he exercised his profession from 1868 to 1904. In 1903, the number was counted and found to be 2,000,-744 teeth, indicating an average of 185 a day.

Most Valuable Tooth

In 1816 a tooth belonging to Sir Isaac Newton (1643–1727) was sold in London for £730 (now $1,100). It was purchased by a nobleman who had it set in a ring which he wore constantly.

Most Acute Vision

In Oct 1972, the University of Stuttgart, West Germany reported that their student Veronica Seider (b 1951) possessed a visual acuity 20 times better than average. She could identify people at a distance of more than

HEART TRANSPLANT PIONEER: Dr Christiaan Barnard (left) in 1967 in Cape Town, South Africa, completed the first of his spectacular operations successfully. HEART STOPPAGE VICTIM Vegard Slettmoen (right) at age 5 in Norway fell through river ice, remained 8 ft down for 40 min, but was revived without brain damage.

a mile. The Russians are reputedly working on a new type of lens implant which will give the wearer super-human sight.

Color Sensitivity

The unaided human eye, under the best possible viewing conditions, comparing large areas of color, in good illumination, using both eyes, can distinguish 10,000,000 different color surfaces.

The most extreme form of color blindness, monochromatic vision, is very rare. The highest rate of red-green color blindness exists in Czechoslovakia and the lowest rate among Fijians and Brazilian Indians.

Leading Cause of Death

The leading cause of death in industrialized countries is arteriosclerosis (thickening of the arterial wall), which underlies much coronary and cerebrovascular disease.

Longest Coma

The longest recorded coma was that of Elaine Esposito (b Dec 3, 1934) of Tarpon Springs, Fla. She never stirred after an appendectomy on Aug 6, 1941, when she was six, in Chicago. She died on Nov 25, 1978, aged 43 years 357 days, having been in a coma for 37 years 111 days.

Heart Stoppage

The longest recorded heart stoppage is a minimum of 3 hours 32 min in the case of Miss Jean Jawbone, 20, who was revived by a team of 26, using peritoneal dialysis, in the Health Sciences Centre, Winnipeg, Manitoba, Canada, Jan 18, 1977.

In Feb 1974 Vegard Slettmoen, 5, fell through the ice on the River Nitselv, Norway. He was found 40 min later, 8 ft down, but was revived in Akerhaus Central Hospital without brain damage. "Mammalian diving reflex" can be triggered in humans falling into water cooler than 70° F.

(Also see *Birth After Death,* p. 23)

Heart Transplants

The first human heart transplant operation was performed on Louis Washkansky, aged 55, at the Groote Schuur Hospital, Cape Town, South Africa, between 1:00 and 6:00 a.m. Dec 3, 1967, by a team of 30 headed by Prof Christiaan N. Barnard (b 1922). The donor was Miss Denise Ann Darvall, aged 25. Washkansky died Dec 21, 1967.

The first transplantee to give birth was Betsy Sneith, 23, with a baby girl Sierra (7 lb 10 oz) at Stanford University, Calif on Sept 17, 1984. She had received a donor heart in Feb 1980.

The longest surviving heart transplantee has been Emmanuel Vitria of Marseilles, France (b 1920), who received a heart transplant Nov 27, 1968, and entered the 18th year of his new life in 1985.

The youngest person to have a heart transplant was Hollie Roffey (b July 20, 1984) who underwent a heart transplant at a record age of 10 days in a 5½-hour operation by Mr Magdi Yacoub at the National Heart Hospital, London, Eng on July 30, 1984. She died aged 28 days, on Aug 17.

Artificial Heart

On Dec 1-2, 1982 at the Utah Medical Center, Salt Lake City, Dr Barney B. Clark, 61, of Des Moines, Wis, received an artificial heart. The surgeon was Dr William C. De Vries. The heart was a mark 7 Jarvik 7 designed by Dr Robert Jarvik. Dr Clark died on Mar 23, 1983, 112 days later.

Highest Body Temperature

Sustained body temperatures of much over 109°F are normally incompatible with life, although recoveries after readings of 111°F have been noted. Marathon runners in hot weather attain 105.8°F.

Willie Jones, a 52-year-old black, was admitted to Grady Memorial Hospital, Atlanta, Ga, on July 10, 1980 with heat stroke on a day when the temperature reached 90°F with 44% humidity. His temperature was found to be 115.7°F. After 24 days he was discharged "at prior baseline status."

Lowest Body Temperature

There are two recorded cases of patients surviving body temperatures as low as 60.8°F. Dorothy Mae Stevens (1929–74) was found in an alley in Chicago Feb 1, 1951, and Vickie Mary Davis of Milwaukee, Wis, at age 2 years 1 month was admitted to the Evangelical Hospital, Marshalltown, Iowa, Jan 21, 1956, each with a temperature of 60.8°F. The little girl had been found unconscious on the floor of an unheated house and the air temperature had dropped to −24°F. Her temperature returned to normal (98.4°F) after 12 hours and may have been as low as 59°F when she was first found. People may die of hypothermia with body temperatures of 95°F.

Commonest Diseases

The commonest non-contagious disease is periodontal disease, such as gingivitus, which afflicts some 80% of the US population. In Great Britain 13% of the people have lost all their teeth before reaching 21. During their lifetime few completely escape its effects.

Infestation with pinworm (*Enterobius vermicularis*) approaches 100% in some areas of the world.

The commonest contagious illness in the world is coryza (acute naso-pharyngitis) or the common cold. The case of the person most resistant to being infected by a cold was reported by the Medical Research Council Common Cold Unit, Salisbury, England, to be J. Brophy, who had only one mild reaction after being exposed 24 times.

Highest Mortality

Rabies in humans has been regarded as uniformly fatal when asso-ciated with the hydrophobia symptom. A 25-year-old woman, Candida de Sousa Barbosa of Rio de Janeiro, Brazil, after surgery by Dr Max Karpin, was believed to be the first to survive the disease in Nov 1968, though some sources give priority to Matthew Winkler, 6, who, on Oct 10, 1970, survived a bite by a rabid bat.

Parkinson's Disease

The most protracted case of Parkinson's disease (named after Dr James Parkinson's essay of 1817) for which the earliest treatments were not published until 1946, is 62 years in the case of Frederick G. Humphries (d Feb 23, 1985) of Croydon, London, England, whose symptoms became detectable in 1923.

Most Durable Cancer Patient

The most extreme recorded case of survival from diagnosed cancer is that of Mrs Winona Mildred Melick (née Douglass) (b Oct 22, 1876) of Long Beach, Calif. She had four cancer operations, in 1918, 1933, 1966 and 1968, but she died from pneumonia on Dec 28, 1981, just 67 days after her 105th birthday.

Most Notorious Carriers

The most publicized of all typhoid carriers was Mary Mallon, known as Typhoid Mary, of NYC. She was the source of 9 outbreaks, notably that of 1903. Because of her refusal to leave employment, often under assumed names, involving the handling of food, she was placed under permanent detention from 1915 until her death in 1938. A still anony-mous dairy farmer from Camden, NY, was the source of 409 cases (40 fatal) in Aug 1909.

Most Infectious Disease

The most infectious of all diseases is the pneumonic form of plague, as evidenced by the Black Death of 1347–51. It has a mortality rate of 99.99%.

AIDS (Acquired Immune Deficiency Syndrome) was first recognized in 1978, though it has similarities to an outbreak of African swine fever in Haiti, which has been known since 1909. The virus was first identified in Jan 1983 at the Pasteur Institute, Paris by Luc Montagnier, Francoise Barre-Sinoussi and Jean-Claude Chermann as a human T-lymphotro-phic virus Type III (HTLV III). A US patent was granted to Prof Robert Gallo at the National Cancer Institute, Bethesda, Md, for HTLV III in May 1985.

Leprosy, transmissible by coughing, sneezing or spitting, is the most bacilliferous of communicable diseases. The bacillus is *Mycobacterium leprae* discovered by G. H. A. Hansen (Norway) (1841–1912) in 1871.

Blood Groups

The preponderance of one blood group varies greatly from one locality to another. On a world basis Group O is the most common (46%), but in some areas, for example Norway, Group A predominates.

The rarest blood group on the ABO system, one of 14 systems, is AB. The rarest blood is a type of Bombay blood (sub-type h-h) found so far only in a Czechoslovak nurse in 1961 and in a brother (Rh positive) and sister (Rh negative) named Jalbert in Mass, reported in Feb 1968. The brother has started a blood bank for himself.

Champion Blood Donors and Users

Joe Thomas of Detroit, Mich, was reported in Aug 1970 to have the highest known counts of Anti-Lewis B, the rare blood antibody. A US biological supply firm pays him $1,500 per quart. The Internal Revenue Service regards this income as a taxable liquid asset. He regards his blood as the world's richest natural resource.

Since 1966 Allen Doster, a self-employed beautician, has (to Apr 1986) donated 1,800 US pints at Roswell Park Memorial Institute, NY, as a plasmapheresis donor. The present-day normal limit on donations is 5 pints a year. Warren C. Jyrich, a 50-year-old hemophiliac, required 2,-400 donor units (2,283 pints) of blood when undergoing open heart surgery at the Michael Reese Hospital, in Chicago, in Dec 1970.

Swallowing

The worst reported case of compulsive swallowing was an insane woman, Mrs H., aged 42, who complained of a "slight abdominal pain." She was found to have 2,533 objects in her stomach, including 947 bent pins. They were removed by Drs Chalk and Foucar in June 1927 at the Ontario Hospital, Canada.

The heaviest object ever extracted from a human stomach was a 5-lb 3-oz ball of hair, from a 20-year-old woman at the South Devon and East Cornwall Hospital, England, March 30, 1895.

Sword "Swallowing"

Edward Benjamin, known as Count Desmond (b July 30, 1941, Binghamton, NY), swallowed thirteen 23-in-long blades to below his xiphisternum and injured himself in the process. *This category has now been retired and no further claims will be entertained.*

Pulse Rates

A normal adult pulse rate is 70–72 beats per min at rest for males, and 78–82 for females. Rates increase to 200 or more during violent exercise or drop to as low as 12 in the extreme case of Dorothy Mae Stevens (see *Lowest Body Temperature*) and Jean Hilliard (b 1962) of Fosston, Minn on Dec 20, 1980.

Largest Tumor

The largest tumor ever recorded was Spohn's case of an ovarian cyst weighing 328 lb from a woman in Tex in 1905. She recovered fully.

Largest Stone

The largest stone or vesical calculus reported in medical literature was one of 13 lb 14 oz removed from an 80-year-old woman by Dr Humphrey Arthure at Charing Cross Hospital, London, on Dec 29, 1952.

Fastest Reactions

The fastest reaction times recorded for sprinters at the 1980 Olympic

SWORD-SWALLOWER "Count Desmond" swallowed 13 blades 23 in long to set a final record in this category. (*Franklin Berger photo*)

Games were 120/1000ths of a second for Romy Müller (East Germany) in the women's 200-meter semi-final and 124/1000ths for Wilbert Greaves (GB) in the 110-m hurdles heats. These compare with 11/1000ths for the cockroach (*Periplaneta americana*).

Fastest Nerve Impulses

The results of experiments published in 1966 have shown that the fastest messages transmitted by the human nervous system travel as fast as 180 mph. With advancing age, impulses are carried 15% slower.

Most Alcoholic Person

California University Medical School, Los Angeles reported in Dec 1982 the case of a confused 24-year-old female, who was shown to have a blood alcohol level of 1510 mg per 100 ml—nearly 19 times the normal driving limit and triple the normal lethal limit. After two days she discharged herself.

Pill Taking

The highest recorded total of pills swallowed by a patient is 500,689 from June 9, 1967 to Jan 1, 1986, by C. H. A. Kilner (b 1926) of Bindura, Zimbabwe, following a successful operation to remove a cancerous pancreas on May 26, 1966.

Longest Survival in Iron Lung

The longest recorded survival by an iron lung patient is 37 years 58 days by Mrs Laurel Nisbet (b Nov 17, 1912) of La Crescenta, Calif, who was in an iron lung continuously from June 25, 1948, to her death on Aug 22, 1985.

Earliest Anesthesia

The earliest recorded operation under general anesthesia was for the removal of a cyst from the neck of James Venable by Dr Crawford Williamson Long (1815–78), using diethyl ether ($(C_2H_5)_2O$), in Jefferson, Ga, on Mar 30, 1842.

Fastest Amputation

The shortest time recorded for the amputation of a leg in the pre-anesthetic era was 13 to 15 sec by Napoleon's chief surgeon, Dominique Larrey. There could have been no ligation.

Most Operations by a Doctor

Padmabhushan Dr M. C. Modi, a pioneer of mass eye surgery in India since 1943, has performed 833 cataract operations in a single working day.

Dr Robert B. McClure (b 1901) of Toronto, Canada performed a career total of 20,423 major operations 1924–78.

Oldest Subject Operated On

The greatest recorded age at which a person has been subjected to an operation is 111 years 105 days in the case of James Henry Brett, Jr. (b July 25, 1849, d Feb 10, 1961) of Houston, Tex. He underwent a hip operation Nov 7, 1960.

Longest Operation

The most protracted reported operation for surgical as opposed to medical control purposes was one of 96 hours performed on Mrs Gertrude Levandowski (b 1893) of Burnips, Mich, for removal of a cyst which reduced her weight by 308 lb, Feb 4–8, 1951. The patient suffered from a weak heart and the surgeons had to exercise the utmost caution during the operation.

The "slowest" operation on record is one on the feet of Mrs Doreen Scott of Derby, England, on Nov 20, 1981. She had been waiting since Mar 10, 1952—19 years 8 months.

Earliest Appendectomy

The earliest recorded successful appendix operation was performed in 1736 by Claudius Amyand (1680–1740). He was Serjeant Surgeon to King George II (reigned 1727–60) of Great Britain.

Laryngectomy

On July 24, 1924, John I. Poole of Plymouth, England, then aged 33, after diagnosis of carcinoma, underwent total laryngectomy in Edinburgh, Scotland." He died on June 19, 1979, after surviving 55 years as a "neck-breather." Mr F. B. Harvey of Plymouth, England, has been a neck-breather since 1929.

Earliest Kidney Transplant

R. H. Lawler (b 1895, US) performed the first transplantation of a human kidney in 1950. The longest survival, as between identical twins, has been 20 years.

Most Major Operations

Joseph Ascough (b 1935) of Nottingham, England, underwent his 333rd operation (for the removal of papillomas from his windpipe) on Apr 24, 1986. These wart-like growths which impede breathing first formed when he was 18 months old.

Hiccoughing

The longest recorded attack of hiccoughs is that which afflicted Charles Osborne (b 1894) of Anthon, Iowa, from 1922 for 64 years. He contracted it when slaughtering a hog and hiccoughed about 430 million times in the interim period. He was unable to find a cure, but led a reasonably normal life in which he had two wives and fathered eight children. He did admit, however, that he could not keep in his false teeth. In July 1986, his rate went up to 20–25 times from 10 hics per min in 1985, and an earlier high of 40.

Sneezing

The most chronic sneezing fit ever recorded is that of Donna Griffiths (b 1969) of Pershore, England. She started sneezing on Jan 13, 1981, and surpassed the previous duration record of 194 days on July 27, 1981. She sneezed an estimated million times in the first 365 days. She achieved her first sneeze-free day on Sept 16, 1983—the 978th day.

The highest speed at which expelled particles have been measured to travel is 103.6 mph.

Yawning

In Lee's case, reported in 1888, a 15-year-old female patient yawned continuously for a period of five weeks.

Loudest Snore

The highest measured sound level recorded by any chronic snorer is a peak of 87.5 decibels at Hever Castle, Kent, Eng, in the early hours of June 28, 1984. Melvyn Switzer of Hampshire was 1 ft from the meter. His wife Julie is deaf in one ear. A sagging pharynx is associated with snoring.

Voice

The highest and lowest recorded notes attained by the human voice before this century were a staccato E in *alt-altissimo* (*e″″*) by Ellen Beach Yaw (US, 1869–1947) in Carnegie Hall, New York City, Jan 19, 1896, and an A1 (55 Hz cycles per sec) by Kaspar Foster (1617–73).

Madeleine Marie Robin (1918–60), the French operatic coloratura, could produce and sustain the B flat above high C in the Mad Scene in *Lucia di Lammermoor*.

Since 1950 singers have achieved high and low notes far beyond the hitherto accepted extremes. Notes, however, at the bass and treble extremities of the register tend to lack harmonics and are of little musical value.

Fräulein Marita Günther, trained by Alfred Wolfsohn, has covered the range of the piano from the lowest note A₋ to *c′″″*. Of this range of 7¼ octaves, 6 octaves are considered to be of musical value.

Roy Hart, also trained by Wolfsohn, has reached notes below the range of the piano. Barry Girard of Canton, Ohio, in May 1975 reached the e (4,340 Hz) above the piano's top note.

The highest note put into song is G^{iv} first occurring in *Popoli di Tessaglia* by Mozart.

The lowest vocal note in the classical repertoire is in Mozart's *Il Seraglio* by Osmin who descends to low D (73.4 Hz). Dan Britton reached the 4th E below middle C at 20.6 Hz at Anoka County Fair, Maryland, on July 31, 1984. Stefan Zucker sang A in *alt-altissimo* for 3.8 sec in the

tenor role of Salvini in the world premiere of Bellini's *Adelson e Salvini* in Carnegie Hall, New York City, Sept 12, 1972.

Greatest Range

The normal intelligible outdoor range of the male human voice in still air is 200 yards. The *silbo,* the whistled language of the Spanish-speaking Canary Island of La Gomera, is intelligible across the valleys, under ideal conditions, at 5 miles. There is a recorded case, under freak acoustic conditions, of the human voice being detectable at a distance of 10½ miles across still water at night. It was said that Mills Darden (see *Heaviest Men*) could be heard 6 miles away when he bellowed at the top of his voice.

Shouting

Because of their more optimal frequency, female screams generally register higher readings on decibel meters than male bellows, but the annual World Shouting championship at 112.4 dBA was won by a man, Anthony Fieldhouse, on Sept 9, 1984, at Scarborough, Eng.

The highest scientifically measured emission has been one of 123.2 dBA by the screaming of Neil Stephenson of Newcastle-upon-Tyne, Eng on May 18, 1985.

Lowest Detectable Sound

The intensity of noise or sound is measured in terms of pressure. The pressure of the quietest sound that can be detected by a person of normal hearing at the most sensitive frequency of *c.* 2,750 Hz (cycles per sec) is 2×10^{-5} pascal. One tenth of the logarithm to this standard provides a unit termed a decibel (dBA).

Highest Detectable Pitch

The upper limit of hearing by the human ear has been regarded as 20,-

000 Hz (cycles per sec), although it has been alleged that children with asthma can often detect a sound of 30,000 Hz. Bats emit pulses at up to 90,000 Hz. It was announced in Feb 1964 that experiments in the USSR had conclusively proved that oscillations as high as 200,000 Hz can be heard if the oscillator is pressed against the skull.

Fastest Talker

Extremely few people are able to speak *articulately* at a sustained speed above 300 words per min. The fastest broadcaster has usually been regarded to be Gerry Wilmot (b Oct 6, 1914, Victoria, BC, Canada), the ice hockey commentator in the post-World War II period. Raymond Glendenning (1907–74), the BBC horse-racing commentator, once spoke 176 words in 30 seconds while reporting a greyhound race. In public life the highest speed recorded is a 327-words-per-min burst in a speech made in Dec 1961, by John Fitzgerald Kennedy (1917–63), then President. Tapes of attempts to recite Hamlet's 262-word soliloquy in under 24 sec (655 wpm) have proved indecipherable.

Fasting

Most humans experience considerable discomfort after an abstinence from food for even 12 hours, but this often passes off after 24–48 hours. Records claimed without unremitting medical surveillance are of little value.

The longest period for which anyone has gone without solid food is 382 days by Angus Barbieri (b 1940) of Tayport, Fife, Scotland, who lived on tea, coffee, water, soda water and vitamins from June 1965 to July 1966 in Maryfield Hospital, Dundee, Angus, Scotland. His weight declined from 472 lb to 178 lb.

The longest recorded case of survival without food *and* water is 18 days by Andreas Mihavecz, 18, of Bregenz, Austria, who was put in a holding cell April 1, 1979, in a local government building in Höchst, Austria, but was totally forgotten by the police. On April 18, 1979, he was discovered close to death, having had neither food nor water. He had been a passenger in a car crash.

Hunger Strike

The longest recorded hunger strike was 385 days from June 28, 1972 to July 18, 1973 by Denis Galer Goodwin in Wakefield Prison, W Yorkshire, Eng, protesting his innocence of a rape charge. He was force fed by tube orally.

The longest recorded hunger strike without force feeding was one of 94 days by 9 men in Cork Prison, Ireland, from Aug 11 to Nov 12, 1920. These 9 survivors owed their lives to expert medical attention and an appeal by the nationalist leader, Arthur Griffith.

Extrasensory Perception

The two most extreme published examples of ESP in scientific literature have been those of the Reiss case of a 26-year-old female at Hunter College, NY, in 1936 and of Pavel Stepánek (Czechoslovakia) in 1967–68. The importance which had been attached to their cases was diminished by subsequent developments. The Reiss subject refused to undergo any further tests under stricter conditions. When Stepánek was re-tested at Edinburgh University with plastic cards he "failed to display any clairvoyant ability." Much smaller departures from the laws of prob-

MOST TATTOOS: Rusty Field of England (above left) has 2,500 designs covering almost all of her body. Her husband, who did the tattooing, says he always had designs on her. Wilfred Hardy (above right), also of England, left very little of his body without artistic embellishment. He even has tattoos on his tongue, gums and inner cheeks.

MOTIONLESS CHAMPION: Bill Fuqua can stay absolutely still for 24 hours at a time, and did exactly that to recapture this world record on May 18, 1985 at the Glendale (Calif) Galleria. He had a bodyguard to protect him from being pinched by spectators who couldn't believe he wasn't a dummy.

ability have, however, been displayed in less extreme cases carried out under strict conditions.

Longest Dream

Dreaming sleep is characterized by rapid eye movements (known as REM), discovered in 1953 by William Dement of the University of Chicago. The longest recorded period of REM is 2 hours 23 min, set by Bill Carskadon on Feb 15, 1967, at the Department of Psychology, University of Illinois, Chicago. His previous sleep had been interrupted.

In July 1984 The Sleep Research Centre, Haifa, Israel, recorded nil REM in a 33-year-old male who had a shrapnel brain injury.

Isolation

The longest recorded period for which any volunteer has been able to withstand total deprivation of all sensory stimulation (sight, hearing and touch) is 92 hours, recorded in 1962 at Lancaster Moor Hospital, England.

Most Tattoos

The seeming ultimate in being tattooed is represented by Wilfred Hardy of Huthwaite, Nottinghamshire, England. Not content with a perilous approach to within 4% of totality of his outer skin, he has been tattooed on the inside of his cheek, his tongue, gums and eyebrows.

Walter Stiglitz of N Plainfield, NJ, in Mar 1984 claimed 5,457 separate tattoos by 6 artists.

The most decorated woman is Rusty Field (b 1944) of Aldershot, Hampshire, England, who, after 12 years under the needle of tattoo artist Bill Skuse, has come within 15% of totality. He stated he always had designs on her.

Both the 1980 and 1981 World's Most Beautiful Tattooed Lady Contest in the US were won by Susan James (GB) (b 1959).

Highest Temperature Endured

The highest dry-air temperature endured by naked men in US Air Force experiments in 1960 was 400°F and for heavily clothed men 500°F. (*Steaks require only 325°F.*) Temperatures of 284°F have been found quite bearable in sauna baths.

g Forces

The acceleration due to gravity (g) is 32 ft 1.05 in per sec per sec at sea level at the Equator. A *sustained* force of 25 g was withstood in a dry capsule during astronautic research by Dr Carter Collins of Calif.

The highest g force endured was 82.6 g for 0.04 sec on a water-braked rocket sled by Eli L. Beeding, Jr., at Holloman Air Force Base, NM, May 16, 1958. He was put in the hospital for three days.

A man who fell off a 185-ft cliff survived a *momentary* g force of 209 in decelerating from 68 mph to stationary in 0.015 sec.

In a crash, race car driver David Purley survived a deceleration from 108 mph to zero in 26 in at the Silverstone circuit, Northamptonshire, England, July 13, 1977, which involved a force of 179.8 g. He suffered 29 fractures, 3 dislocations and 6 heart stoppages.

A land diver of Pentecost Island, New Hebrides, dove from a platform 81 ft 3 in high on May 15, 1982 for a TV show. He had liana vines attached to his ankles, his body speed was 50 ft/sec (34 mph) and the force was in excess of 110 g.

Motionlessness

The longest recorded time that anyone was involuntarily made to stand at attention was 132 consecutive hours without food or water while a prisoner of the Japanese in Osaka from 8 a.m. Aug 15 until 8 p.m. Aug 20, 1944, by Everett D. Reamer (b 1923) of Havasu City, Ariz. Whenever he slumped, he was beaten; finally he dropped to the ground.

The longest that anyone has continuously remained motionless is 24 hours by William Fuqua at Glendale, Calif, on May 17–18, 1985 while sitting on a motorcycle.

Electric Shock

People in aircraft in thunder clouds may be at 30 million volts relative to the earth without harm. In some "bare hand" laboratory work in France experimenters in insulated cabins have experienced 5 million volts.

People walking on nylon carpets on dry days may go up to 10,000 volts relative to earth and yet experience only mild shocks. Contacts with exposed high tension power lines with system voltages of 765,000 have occurred in the US. A person in contact with earth via ladders, dinghy masts, crane jibs, etc, normally suffers instant death due to a heavy current arc or flashover flowing through the body. That shocks received from high tension cables by Brian Latasa (230,000 volts in Griffith Park, Los Angeles on Nov 9, 1967) and Harry F. McGrew (340,000 volts in Huntington Canyon, Utah, on Oct 7, 1977) were non-lethal underlines their idiosyncratic nature when compared with the mere 2,500 volts used since 1890 in judicial electrocution.

Underwater Duration

The record for voluntarily staying underwater is 13 min 42.5 sec by Robert Foster, aged 32, an electronics technician of Richmond, Calif, who stayed under 10 ft of water in the swimming pool of the Bermuda Palms at San Rafael, Calif, on March 15, 1959. He hyperventilated with oxygen for 30 min before his descent. *It must be stressed that record-breaking of this kind is extremely dangerous.*

Fire-Walking

The highest temperature recorded by a pyrometer for the coals in any fire-walk is 1,494 °F by "Komar" (Vernon E. Craig) of Wooster, Ohio, at the International Festival of Yoga and Esoteric Sciences, Maidenhead, England, on Aug 14, 1976.

Thirty-five people from the Sawau tribe on the island of Beqa, Fiji, participated in a fire-walk with the temperature over 1,000 °F on May 18, 1982. There is an annual fire-walk during the feast of St Constantine each May in Aghia Eleni, northern Greece.

Fire-Eating

Reg Morris (GB) on Nov 5, 1983, blew a flame from his mouth to a distance of 27 ft igniting a bonfire at the Castle Working Men's Club, Brownhills, Walsall, W Midlands, Eng.

On May 11, 1985, Gerry Mawdsley extinguished 13,115 torches of flame successfully in his mouth in 2 hours at Blackrod, Lancashire, Eng.

Mrs Jean Chapman Leggett successively extinguished 6,607 flaming torches in her mouth in 2 hours (a rate of more than 55 per min) on Feb 13, 1982, in Stoke Poges, Buckinghamshire, England for the female record. *Fire-eating is potentially a highly dangerous activity.*

UNDERWATER LONGEST (above): Robert L. Foster of Calif held his breath for a record 13 min 42½ sec in a swimming pool. Record-breaking of this kind is extremely dangerous.

FIRE-EATERS: Their mothers never told them to stay away from fire. Jean Leggett (right) put out 6,607 flaming torches in her mouth in 2 hours 2 min in 1982. Gerry Mawdsley (below) extinguished almost twice as many—13,115—in 2 hours in 1985. Both are English.

Chapter 2

The Living World

ANIMAL KINGDOM (*ANIMALIA*)

Largest and Heaviest Animal

The largest and heaviest animal is the female blue or sulphur-bottom whale (*Balaenoptera musculus*), also called Sibbald's rorqual. The longest specimen ever recorded was a female landed at the Compania Argentina de Pesca, Grytviken, South Georgia, Falkland Islands, in 1909 which measured 110 ft 2½ in in length. During summer months an average-sized specimen consumes up to 3 million calories per day.

The tongue and heart of the 209-ton female taken by the *Slava* whaling fleet in the South Atlantic Ocean on Mar 20, 1947 weighed 4.72 tons and 1,540 lb, respectively.

The low frequency pulses (whistles) made by blue whales when communicating with each other have been measured up to 188 dB, making them the loudest sounds emitted by any living source. They are detectable 530 miles away.

Longest Animal

The longest animal ever recorded is the ribbon worm *Lineus longissimus*, also known as the "boot-lace worm," which is found in the shallow coastal waters of the North Sea. In 1864 a specimen measuring more than 180 ft was washed ashore at St. Andrews, Fifeshire, Scotland, after a storm.

Tallest Animal

The tallest living animal is the giraffe (*Giraffa camelopardalis*), which is now found only in the dry savannah and semi-desert areas of Africa south of the Sahara. The tallest ever recorded was a Masai bull (*G. camelopardalis tippelskirchi*) named "George," received at Chester Zoo, England, Jan 8, 1959 from Kenya. His "horns" *almost* touched the roof of the 20-ft-high Giraffe House when he was 9 years old. George died July 22, 1969. Less credible heights of up to 23 ft between taxidermist's pegs have been claimed for bulls shot in the field.

Note: For more information about animals, see *Animal Facts and Feats: One of the Guinness Family of Books*. This work treats the dimensions and performances of the Classes of the Animal Kingdom in greater detail, giving also sources and authorities for much of the material in this chapter.

MOST VALUABLE (above): Killer whales like "Orky" of Marineland of the Pacific, Palos Verdes, Calif, are valued at about $2 million per pair.

TALLEST ANIMAL (right): George, the tallest giraffe in captivity, along with his friends, licked the telephone wires that ran past his pen, disrupting the system.

GIANT PANDA, the most costly zoo animal. One cub in the Madrid (Spain) Zoo is valued at $1.4 million. The one pictured below is in the San Diego (Calif) Zoo.

LONGEST OF ALL SNAKES: This 29-ft-long skin was yielded by "Cassius," a female reticulated python from the Knaresborough Zoo in Yorkshire, Eng. Big as it is, it measured less than the world record of 32 ft 9½ in. (*David Roberts*)

Most Valuable Animals

The most valuable animals in cash terms are race horses. *Shareef Dancer* was syndicated for $40 million in Aug 1983 by his owner Sheikh Mohammed al Maktoum when 40 shares were issued at $1 million each. (See *Horse Racing.*) The most valuable zoo exhibit is the giant panda (*Ailuropoda melanoleuca*). "Chu-Lin," (b Sept 1982) of the Madrid Zoo, Spain, the only panda cub in Europe, which has been valued at about $1.4 million. The most valuable marine exhibit is a pair of killer whales (*Orcinus orca*) named "Orky" and "Corky" at Marineland of the Pacific, Palos Verdes, Calif. Their value in 1985 was $2 million.

Longest-Lived Animal

Few non-bacterial creatures live longer than humans.

In 1982, a specimen of an ocean quahog (*Arctica islandica*), a thick-shelled clam, was found in the mid-Atlantic with 220 annual growth rings, indicating an age of 220 years.

Up until 1982 tortoises were regarded as the longest-lived such animals. The greatest authentic age recorded for a tortoise is 152-plus years.

Fastest Flying Animal

The fastest-moving animal is the peregrine falcon (*Falco peregrinus*), which has been timed electronically at 217 mph in Germany while making a stoop at a 45-degree angle of descent. In a vertical fall of 5,000 ft, it has been calculated a stooping peregrine in display could probably reach 230–240 mph, but it usually strikes its prey at about half this velocity. The fastest bird in level flight is the red-breasted merganser (*Mergus serrator*) (US) which attained an air speed of 80 mph in 1960.

Commonest Animal

It is estimated that man shares the earth with 3×10^{33} (3 followed by 33 zeros) other living things. The number of nematode sea-worms has been estimated at 4×10^{25}. The house mouse (*Mus musculus*) is found on all continents.

Largest Concentration of Animal Life

The largest single concentration of animals ever recorded was an enor-

mous swarm of krill (*Euphausia superba*) estimated to weigh 10 million tons tracked by American scientists off Antarctica in Mar 1981. The swarm was so dense it equaled about one-seventh of the world's yearly catch of fish and shellfish.

Highest Altitude Animal

In Apr 1967, NASA reported that bacteria had been discovered at an altitude of 135,000 ft (25.30 miles).

Greatest Size Difference Between Sexes

The largest female marine worms of the species *Bonellia viridis* are at least 100 million times heavier than the smallest males. The female is up to 39.3 in long against the miserable 0.04 in of the male.

Rarest Animal

A number of mammals are known only from a single (holotype) specimen. An example is Garrido's hutia (*Capromys garridoi*) known only from a single specimen collected on the islet of Cayo Maja off southern Cuba in Apr 1967.

A wildlife ranger in Tasmania announced that a Tasmanian wolf (*Thylacine cynocephalus*) had been positively identified in July 1982, after a 21-year void.

In 1979 scientists uncovered the first evidence that the Bali leopard (*Panthera pardus balica*) still existed on the island.

Longest Gestation

The viviparous amphibian Alpine black salamander (*Salamandra atra*) can have a gestation period of up to 38 months at altitudes above 4,600 ft in the Swiss Alps, but this drops to 24–26 months at lower altitudes.

Most Monogamous

Male klipspringers (*Oreotragus oreotragus*), small antelopes of eastern and southern Africa, rarely stray more than 16½ ft from their mate during their lifetime.

Fastest and Slowest Growth

The fastest growth in the animal kingdom is that of the blue whale calf. A barely visible ovum weighing a fraction of a milligram (0.000035 of an ounce) grows to a weight of *c.* 29 tons in 22¾ months, made up of 10¾ months gestation and the first 12 months of life. This is equivalent to an increase of 30,000 millionfold.

The slowest growth in the animal kingdom is that of the deep-sea clam (*Tindaria callistiformis*) of the North Atlantic, which takes an estimated 100 years to reach a length of 0.31 in (8 mm).

Blood Temperatures

The highest average mammalian blood temperature is that of the Xoloitzcuintli or Mexican hairless dog with 104° F. That of the dromedary (*Camelus dromedarius*) reaches 105.8° F at the end of a hot day. The lowest mammalian blood temperature is that of the spiny anteater (echidna), (*Tachyglossus aculeatus*), a monotreme found in Australia and New Guinea, with a normal range of 22.2°–24.4° C. The ice worm of Alaska has an internal temperature of 14° F.

"COOLEST" MAMMAL: The spiny anteater (right), from Australia and New Guinea, has the lowest blood temperature of any mammal. This one is a baby.

Heaviest Brain

The sperm whale (*Physeter macrocephalus*) has the heaviest brain of any living animal. The brain of a 49-ft-long bull processed aboard the Japanese factory ship *Nissin Maru No. 1* in the Antarctic Dec 11, 1949 weighed 9.2 kg (20.24 lb), compared to 6.9 kg (15.38 lb) for a 90-ft blue whale. The heaviest brain recorded for an elephant was an exceptional 16.5 lb in the case of a 2.17-ton Asiatic cow. The normal brain weight for an adult African bull is 9¼–12 lb.

Largest Eye

The giant squid *Architeuthis sp.* has the largest eye of any living animal. The ocular diameter may exceed 15 in, compared to less than 12 in for a 33⅓-rpm long-playing record and 4.72 in for a large blue whale.

Largest Egg

The largest egg laid by any known animal was that of the elephant bird (*Aepyornis maximus*) which lived in southern Madagascar until *c.* 900 AD. One example preserved in the British Museum (Natural History), London, measures 33.7 in around the long axis with a circumference of 28.5 in, giving a capacity of 2.35 gal. It weighed about 27 lb when full.

The largest egg of any living animal is that of the whale shark (*Rhineodon typus*). One egg case measuring 12 in × 5.5 in × 3.5 in was picked up June 29, 1953 at a depth of 186 ft in the Gulf of Mexico, 130 miles south of Port Isabel, Tex. The egg contained a perfect embryo of a whale shark 13.78 in long.

Most Prodigious Eater

The most phenomenal eating machine in nature is the larva of the Polyphemus moth (*Antheraea polyphemus*) of North America which, in the first 48 hours of its life, consumes an amount equal to 86,000 times its own birthweight. In human terms, this would be equivalent to a 7-lb baby taking in 301 tons of nourishment.

Most Acute Sense of Smell

The most acute sense of smell exhibited in nature is that of the male emperor moth (*Eudia pavonia*), which, according to German experiments in 1961, can detect the sex attractant of the virgin female at the almost unbelievable range of 6.8 miles upwind. This scent has been identified as one of the higher alcohols ($C_{16}H_{29}OH$) of which the female carries less than 0.0001 mg.

---

1. MAMMALS (*MAMMALIA*)

Largest and Heaviest Animal

The blue whale (see details on page 37) holds the record.

Blue whales inhabit the colder seas and migrate to warmer waters in winter for breeding. Observations made in the Antarctic in 1947–8 showed that a blue whale can maintain speeds of 20 knots (23 mph) for 10 minutes when frightened. This means a 90-ft blue whale traveling at 20 knots would develop 520 hp. Newborn calves measure 21–28.5 ft long and weigh up to 3.3 tons.

It has been estimated that there were about 12,000 blue whales living throughout the oceans in 1986 as a result of overfishing—compared to a peak estimate of about 220,000 in the past.

The species has been protected *de jure* since 1967 although non-member countries of the International Whaling Commission (*e.g.* Panama and Taiwan) are not bound by this agreement. A worldwide ban on commercial whaling is due to come into effect in 1986, but Iceland and S Korea intend to carry on taking 200 whales annually "for scientific purposes" until 1990, and the Philippines say they will continue whaling until 1988.

Fastest Marine Animal

The fastest is the killer whale (*Orcinus orca*). On Oct 12, 1958, a bull measuring 20–25 ft in length was timed at 30 knots (34.5 mph) in the eastern Pacific. Speeds of up to 30 knots also have been reported for short bursts by Dall's porpoise (*Phocoenoides dalli*).

Deepest Dive

The greatest *recorded* depth to which a whale has dived is 620 fathoms (3,720 ft) by a 47-ft bull sperm whale (*Physeter macrocephalus*) found with his jaw entangled with a submarine cable running between Santa Elena, Ecuador, and Chorillos, Peru, Oct 14, 1955. At this depth he withstood a pressure of 1,680 lb per sq in of body surface.

On Aug 25, 1969, another bull sperm whale was killed 100 miles south of Durban, South Africa, after it had surfaced from a dive lasting 1 hour 52 min, and inside its stomach were found two small sharks which had been swallowed about an hour earlier. These were later identified as *Scymnodon sp.*, a species found only on the sea floor. At this point from land the depth of water is in excess of 1,646 fathoms (10,476 ft) for a radius of 30–40 miles, which now suggests that the sperm whale sometimes may descend to a depth of over 10,000 ft when seeking food, and is limited by pressure of time rather than by pressure of pressure.

Ambergris

The heaviest piece of ambergris (a fatty deposit in the intestine of the sperm whale) on record weighed 1,003 lb and was recovered from a sperm whale (*Physeter macrocephalus*) Dec 24, 1912 by a Norwegian whaling company off Tasmania in Australian waters. The lump was sold in London for £23,000 (then $111,780).

Largest Animal on Land

The largest living land animal is the African bush elephant (*Loxodonta africana*). The average adult bull stands 10 ft 6 in at the shoulder and weighs 6½ tons. The largest specimen ever recorded, and the largest land animal of modern times, was a bull shot 25 miles north-northeast of Mucusso, southern Angola, Nov 7, 1974. Lying on its side this elephant measured 13 ft 8 in in a projected line from the highest point of the shoulder to the base of the forefoot, indicating that its standing height must have been about 13 ft. Other measurements included an overall length of 35 ft (tip of extended trunk to tip of extended tail) and a forefoot circumference of 5 ft 11 in. The weight was computed to be 26,998 lb.

Smallest Mammals

The smallest recorded mammal is the Kitti's hog-nosed bat (*Craseonycteris thonglongyai*) or bumblebee bat, which is now restricted to a few caves near the forestry station at Ban Sai Yoke on the Kwae Noi River, Kanchanaburi, Thailand. A new hydroelectric project is endangering the species. Mature specimens of both sexes have a wing span of about 6.29 in and weigh between 0.062 and 0.071 oz.

The smallest totally marine mammal in terms of weight is probably Commerson's dolphin (*Cephalorhynchus commersoni*) also known as Le Jacobite, which is found in the waters off the southern tip of South America. In one series of six adult specimens the weights ranged from 50.7 lb to 77.1 lb. The sea otter (*Enhydra lutris*) of the north Pacific is of comparable size, weighing from 55 to 81.4 lb, but this species sometimes comes ashore during storms.

Fastest Land Animal

The fastest of all land animals over a short distance (*i.e.* up to 600 yd) is the cheetah or hunting leopard (*Acinonyx jubatus*) of the open plains

SLOWEST MAMMAL: The ai or 3-toed sloth moves on the ground at 6–8 ft per min (or 4 mi per day).

of East Africa, Iran, Turkmenia and Afghanistan, with a probable maximum speed of 60–63 mph over suitably level ground. Speeds of 71, 84 and even 90 mph have been claimed for this animal, but these figures must be considered exaggerated. Tests in London in 1937 showed that on an oval greyhound track over 345 yd a female cheetah's average speed over three runs was 43.4 mph (compared with 43.26 mph for the fastest race horse), but this specimen was not running at its best and had great difficulty negotiating curves.

The fastest land animal over a sustained distance (*i.e.* 1,000 yd or more) is the pronghorn antelope (*Antilocapra americana*) of the western US. Specimens have been observed to travel at 35 mph for 4 miles, at 42 mph for 1 mile and 55 mph for half a mile.

Slowest and Sleepiest Mammal

The slowest-moving land mammal is the ai or three-toed sloth (*Bradypus tridactylus*) of tropical America. The average ground speed is 6–8 ft per min (0.068 to 0.098 mph), but in the trees it can "accelerate" to 15 ft per min (0.170 mph). (Compare these figures with the 0.03 mph of the common garden snail and the 0.17 mph of the giant tortoise.)

The slowest swimming marine mammal is the sea otter (*Enhydra lutris*) which has a top speed of *c.* 6 mph. Some sloths (*Bradypodidae*) sleep up to 20 hours per day.

Longest-Lived Mammal

No other mammal can match the proven age of 120 years attained by man (*Homo sapiens*). It is probable that the closest approach is made by the Asiatic elephant (*Elephas maximus*).

The greatest age that has been verified with absolute certainty is 81 years in the case of Nepal's royal elephant "Prem Prased," who died in Katmandu on Feb 27, 1985.

The longest-lived marine mammal is Baird's beaked whale *(Berardius bairdii)* which has a maximum life-span of *c.* 70 years.

Largest Herds

The largest herds on record were those of the South African springbok *(Antidorcas marsupialis)* during migration across the plains of the western parts of southern Africa in the 19th century. In 1849, Sir John Fraser of Bloemfontein observed a herd that took three days to pass through the settlement of Beaufort West, Cape Province. Another herd seen in the same province in 1888 was estimated to contain 100 million head, although 10 million is probably a more realistic figure. A herd estimated to be 15 miles wide and more than 100 miles long was reported from Karree Kloof, Orange River, South Africa, in July 1896.

The largest concentration of wild mammals found living anywhere in the world today is that of the Mexican free-tailed bat *(Tadarida brasiliensis)* in Bracken Cave, San Antonio, Tex, where up to 20 million animals assemble after migration.

Highest-Living Mammal

The highest-living wild mammal in the world is probably the yak *(Bos grunniens)*, of Tibet and the Szechwanese Alps, China, which occasionally climbs to an altitude of 20,000 ft when foraging.

There are also reliable records of the woolly hare *(Lepus oiostolus)* and the woolly wolf *(Canis lupus chanco)* being seen at 19,800 ft and 19,000 ft respectively on the Tibetan Plateau.

Largest Litter

The greatest recorded number of young born to a *wild* mammal at a single birth is 31 (of which 30 survived), in the case of the tail-less tenrec *(Tenrec ecaudatus)*, found in Madagascar and the Comoro Islands. The normal litter is 12 to 15, although females can suckle up to 24.

Longest and Shortest Gestation Periods

The longest of all mammalian gestation periods is that of the Asiatic elephant *(Elephas maximus)*, with an average of 609 days (or just over 20 months) and a maximum of 760 days, more than 2½ times that of a human. By 1981, only about 35,000 survived.

The gestation periods of the rare water opossum or yapok *(Chironectes minimus)* and the American opossum *(Didelphis marsupialis)* also called the Virginian opossum, both of central and northern South America and the eastern native cat *(Dasyurus viverrinus)* of Australia are all normally 12–13 days, but may also be on occasion as short as 8 days.

Youngest Breeder

The streaked tenrec *(Hemicentetes semispinosus)* of Madagascar is weaned after only 5 days, and females are capable of breeding 3–4 weeks after birth.

Largest Carnivore

The largest living terrestrial carnivore is the Kodiak bear *(Ursus arctos middendorffi)*, which is found on Kodiak Island and the adjacent Afognak and Shuyak islands in the Gulf of Alaska. The average adult male has a nose-to-tail length of 8 ft (tail about 4 in), stands 52 in at the shoulder and weighs 1,050–1,175 lb.

In 1894 a weight of 1,656 lb was recorded for a male shot at English

Bay, Kodiak Island, whose *stretched* skin measured 13 ft 6 in from the tip of the nose to the root of the tail. This weight was exceeded by a "cage-fat" male in the Cheyenne Mountain Zoological Park, Colorado Springs, which scaled 1,670 lb at the time of its death Sept 22, 1955.

In 1981 an unconfirmed weight of over 2,000 lb was reported for an Alaskan brown bear on exhibition at the Space Farms Zoological Park at Beemerville, NJ. Weights in excess of 1,600 lb have also been reported for the polar bear (*Ursus maritimus*), but the average adult male weighs 850–900 lb and measures 7¾ ft nose to tail. In 1960 a polar bear allegedly weighing 2,210 lb before skinning was shot at the polar entrance to Kotzebue Sound, northwest Alaska. The mounted specimen has a standing height of 11 ft 1¼ in.

Smallest Carnivore

The smallest living carnivore is the least weasel (*Mustela rixosa*), also called the dwarf weasel, which is circumpolar in distribution. Four races are recognized, the smallest of which is the *M. r. pygmaea* of Siberia. Mature specimens have an overall length (including tail) of 6.96–8.14 in and weigh between 1¼ and 2½ oz.

Largest Marine Carnivore

The largest toothed mammal ever recorded is the sperm whale (*Physeter macrocephalus*), also called the cachalot. The largest specimen ever to be measured accurately was a bull 67 ft 11 in long captured off the Kurile Islands, in the northwest Pacific, by a USSR whaling fleet in the summer of 1950.

Largest Feline

The largest member of the cat family (Felidae) is the protected long-furred Siberian tiger (*Panthera tigris altaica*), also known as the Amur or Manchurian tiger. Adult males average 10 ft 4 in in length (nose to tip of extended tail), stand 39–42 in at the shoulder, and weigh about 585 lb. A male weighing 846.5 lb was shot in the Sikhote Alin Mountains, Maritime Territory, USSR in 1950. In Nov 1967 an 857-lb Indian tiger (*Panthera tigris tigris*) was shot in northern Uttar Pradesh by David H. Hasinger of Philadelphia. It measured 10 ft 7 in long (between taxidermist's pegs), or 11 ft 1 in over the curves, compared with 9 ft 3 in and 420 lb for the average adult male. It is now on display in the US Museum of Natural History, Smithsonian Institution, Washington, DC.

Smallest Feline

The smallest member of the cat family is the rusty-spotted cat (*Felis rubiginosa*) of southern India and Sri Lanka. The average adult male has an overall length of 25–28 in (tail 9–10 in) and weighs 3 lb.

Largest Pinniped (Seal, Sea Lion, Walrus)

The largest of the 34 known species of pinnipeds is the southern elephant seal (*Mirounga leonina*) which inhabits the sub-Antarctic islands. Adult bulls average 16½ ft in length (tip of inflated snout to the extremities of the outstretched tail flippers), 12 ft in maximum body girth and weigh 5,000 lb. The largest accurately measured specimen on record was a bull killed in Possession Bay, South Georgia, Falkland Islands, South Atlantic, Feb 28, 1913, which measured *c.* 22½ ft in length or 21 ft 4 in after flensing and probably weighed 9,000 lb. There are old records of bulls measuring 25, 30 and even 35 ft, but these figures must be considered exaggerated.

Smallest Pinniped

The smallest pinnipeds are the ringed seal (*Phoca hispida*) of the Arctic and the closely related Baikal seal (*P. sibirica*) of Lake Baikal and the Caspian seal (*P. caspica*) of the Caspian Sea, USSR. Adult specimens (males) measure up to 5 ft 6 in in length and reach a maximum weight of 280 lb. Females are about two-thirds this size.

Fastest and Deepest Pinnipeds

The highest speed measured for a pinniped is a 25-mph spurt for a California sea lion (*Zalophus californianus*). The deepest dive recorded for a pinniped is 2,067 ft by a female northern elephant seal (*Mirounga anguistirostris*) off Ano Nuevo Point, Calif, on Mar 1, 1983. At this depth, the seal withstood a pressure of 919 lb per sq in of body area.

Most Abundant Pinniped

The most abundant species of pinniped is the crabeater seal (*Lobodon carcinophagus*) of Antarctica. In 1978 the total population was believed to be nearly 15 million.

Rarest Pinniped

The last reliable sighting of the Caribbean or West Indian monk seal (*Monachus tropicalis*) was on Serranilla Bank off the coast of Mexico's Yucatan peninsula in 1952. In 1974 two seals were sighted near the southeast Bahamas, but a search in 1979 found nothing. It has been suggested that they may have been California sea lions which had escaped from captivity and have been recorded in the Gulf of Mexico on several occasions.

Longest-Lived Pinniped

A female gray seal (*Halichoerus grypus*) shot at Shunni Wick in the Shetland Islands, Scotland, Apr 23, 1969 was believed to be at least 46 years old, based on a count of dentine rings. The captive record is an estimated 43 years for a bull gray seal "Jacob" held in Skansen (Stockholm Zoo) (1901–42).

Largest and Smallest Bat

The only flying mammals are bats (order Chiroptera), of which there are about 950 living species. The bat with the greatest wing span is the Bismarck flying fox (*Pteropus neohibernicus*) of the Bismarck Archipelago and New Guinea. One specimen preserved in the American Museum of Natural History has a wing spread of 5 ft 5 in, but some unmeasured bats probably reach 6 ft.

The smallest species of bat is the rare Kitti's hog-nosed or bumblebee bat (see page 52).

Highest Detectable Pitch

Because of their ultrasonic echolocation, bats have the most acute hearing of any land animal. Vampire bats (*Desmodontidae*) and fruit bats (*Pteropodidae*) can hear frequencies as high as 120–210 kHz. (Compare with 20 kHz for the adult human limit, but 280 kHz for the common dolphin (*Delphinus delphis*).)

Rarest Bat

At least three species of bat are known only from the holotype specimen. They are: the small-toothed fruit bat (*Neopteryx frosti*) from Tamalanti, West Celebes (1938/39); *Paracoelops megalotis* from Vinh, Vietnam (1945); and *Latidens salimalii* from the High Wavy Mountains, southern India (1948).

Longest-Lived Bat

The greatest age reliably reported for a bat is 31 years 5 months for an Indian flying fox (*Pteropus giganteus*) which died at London Zoo on Jan 11, 1979.

Fastest Bat

Because of great practical difficulties, few data on bat speeds have been published. The greatest velocity attributed to a bat is 32 mph in the

HIGHEST PITCH:
This great vampire bat from Venezuela has an ultrasonic echolocation system that inspired the invention of radar.
(*Stephen Dalton, Oxford Scientific Films*)

case of a Mexican free-tailed bat (*Tadarida brasiliensis*), but this may have been wind-assisted. In one American experiment using an artificial mine tunnel and 17 different kinds of bat, only four of them managed to exceed 13 mph in level flight.

Longest-Lived Primate

The greatest irrefutable age reported for a primate (excluding humans) is *c.* 59 years in the case of a male orangutan (*Pongo pygmaeus*) named "Guas," who was received by the Philadelphia Zoo May 1, 1931, when he was at least 13 years old, and died Feb 9, 1977.

Smallest Living Primate

The smallest known primate is the rare pen-tailed shrew (*Ptilocercus lowii*) of Malaysia, Sumatra and Borneo. Adult specimens have a total body length of 9–13 in, a head and body length of 3.9–5.5 in, a tail of 5.1–7.5 in and weigh 1.23–1.76 oz. The pygmy marmoset (*Cebuella pygmaea*) of the Upper Amazon Basin and the lesser mouse lemur (*Microcebus murinus*) of Madagascar are also of comparable length but heavier, adults weighing 1.76–2.64 oz and 1.58–2.82 oz respectively.

Largest Living Primates

The largest living primate is the mountain gorilla (*Gorilla gorilla berengei*) of the volcanic mountain ranges of W Rwanda, SW Uganda and E Zaire. The average adult male stands 5 ft 9 in tall (including crest) and weighs about 430 lb. The greatest height (top of crest to heel) recorded for a gorilla is 6 ft 4¾ in for a male collected by a German expedition at Alimbongo, N Kivu, Zaire on May 16, 1938.

The heaviest gorilla ever kept in captivity was a male of the mountain race named "N'gagi," who died in the San Diego Zoo, Calif, on Jan 12, 1944, aged 18 years. He scaled 683 lb at his heaviest in 1943, and weighed 636 lb at the time of his death. He was 5 ft 7¾ in tall and boasted a record chest measurement of 78 in.

Rarest Primate

The rarest primate is the hairy-eared dwarf lemur (*Allocebus trichotis*) of Madagascar, which was known, until fairly recently, only from a ho-

---

Most Valuable Furs

The highest-priced animal pelts are those of the sea otter (*Enhydra lutris*), also known as the Kamchatka beaver, which fetched up to $2,700 each before their 55-year-long protection started in 1912. The protection ended in 1967, and at the first legal auction of sea otter pelts in Seattle, Wash, Jan 31, 1968, Neiman-Marcus, the famous Dallas department store, paid $9,200 each for four pelts from Alaska. (The sea otter is the slowest swimming marine mammal.)

In May 1970 a Kojah (mink-sable cross) coat costing $125,000 was sold by Neiman-Marcus to Welsh actor Richard Burton for his then wife, Elizabeth Taylor. In 1983 the most expensive full fur coat in NYC was $100,000 for a Russian lynx on sale at Ben Kahn and Maximilian.

FEMALE GORILLA "Koko," who knows sign language, shows affection for her "baby" adopted kitten. (© *Dr Ronald H. Cohn, The Gorilla Foundation*)

lotype specimen and three skins. However, in 1966 a live one was found on the east coast near Mananara.

Test-Tube Primate

The first non-human primate conceived in a laboratory dish is a female black baboon, born on July 25, 1983, just 6 months after fertilization at the Southwest Foundation for Research and Education in San Antonio, Tex. The date was coincidentally exactly 5 years after the birth of Louise Brown, first human test-tube baby. The baby baboon was named E.T. (for embryo transfer).

Primate Strength

"Boma," a 165-lb male chimpanzee at the Bronx Zoo, NYC, in 1924 recorded a right-handed pull (feet braced) of 847 lb on a dynamometer (compare with 210 lb for a man of the same weight). On another occasion an adult female chimpanzee named "Suzette" (estimated weight 135 lb) at the same zoo registered a right-handed pull of 1,260 lb while in a rage. A record of a 100-lb chimpanzee achieving a two-handed dead lift of 600 lb with ease suggests that a male gorilla could, with training, raise 2,000 lb!

Largest and Smallest Monkeys

The only species of monkey reliably credited with weights of more than 100 lb is the mandrill (*Mandrillus sphinx*) of equatorial West Africa. The greatest reliable weight recorded is 119 lb for a male, but an unconfirmed weight of 130 lb has been reported. Adult females are about half the size of males.

OLDEST LIVING MONKEY: "Bobo," who looks like a pet poodle, celebrated his 50th birthday in 1985. (*Reginald L. Dean*)

The smallest monkey is the pygmy marmoset (*Cebuella pygmaea*) of the Upper Amazon Basin.

Oldest and Rarest Living Monkeys

The oldest living monkey is a male white-throated capuchin (*Cebus capucinus*) called "Bobo" owned by the American Cyanamid Company of Pearl River, NY, who celebrated his 50th birthday in 1985.

The rarest living monkey is the golden lion tamarin of southeastern Brazil. In 1980 there were fewer than 100 left, all of them in the Sao Joao basin in the state of Rio de Janeiro, and the species could well be extinct in the wild by 1990.

Largest Rodent

The largest rodent is the capybara (*Hydrochoerus hydrochaeris*), also called the carpincho or water hog, found in tropical South America. Mature specimens have a head and body length of 3¼–4½ ft and weigh up to 250 lb (cage-fat specimen).

Smallest Rodent

The smallest known rodent is the northern pygmy mouse (*Baiomys taglore*) of central Mexico, southern Ariz and Tex, which measures up to 5.3 in in total length and weighs 0.24–0.35 oz.

Longest-Lived Rodent

The greatest reliable age reported for a rodent is 27 years 3 months for a Sumatran crested porcupine (*Hystrix brachyura*) which died in the National Zoological Park, Washington, DC, on Jan 12, 1965.

Rarest Rodent

The rarest rodent is probably the little earth hutia (*Capromys sanfelipensis*) of Juan Garcia Cay, an islet off southern Cuba. It has not been recorded since its discovery in 1970.

Rarest Antelope

The rarest antelope is the Arabian oryx (*Oryx leucoryx*) which has not been reported in the wild since 1972 when 3 were killed and 4 others captured on the Jiddat-al Harasis plateau, South Oman. On Jan 31, 1982, ten specimens, nine of them born and bred at San Diego Zoo, were released into the open desert in South Oman under the protection of a nomadic tribe. Since then 6 young have been born in the wild and, by Jan 1985, there were 25 animals in the herd. Another release has been carried out in Jordan.

Largest Antelope

The largest of all antelopes is the rare giant eland (*Tragelaphus derbianus*) of West and Central Africa, which may surpass 2,000 lb. The common eland (*T. oryx*) of East and South Africa has the same shoulder height of up to 5 ft 10 in, but is not quite so massive, although there is one record of a 5 ft 5 in bull shot in Nyasaland (now Malawi) in *c.* 1937 which weighed 2,078 lb.

Smallest Antelope

The smallest known antelope is the royal antelope (*Neotragus pygmaeus*) of West Africa. Mature specimens measure only 10–12 in at the shoulder, and weigh only 7–8 lb, which is the size of a large brown hare (*Lepus europaeus*). Salt's dik-dik (*Madoqua saltina*) of northeast Ethiopia and Somalia weighs only 5–6 lb when adult, but this species stands about 14 in at the withers.

Oldest Antelope

The greatest reliable age recorded for an antelope is 25 years 4 months for an addax (*Addax nasomaculatus*) which died in the Brookfield Zoo, Chicago, on Oct 15, 1960.

Oldest Deer

The greatest reliable age recorded for a deer is 26 years 8 months for a red deer (*Cervus elaphus scoticus*), which died in the Milwaukee Zoo, Wis, on June 28, 1954.

Largest Deer and Antler Span

The largest deer is the Alaskan moose (*Alces alces gigas*).
Adult bulls average 6 ft at the shoulder and weigh about 1,100 lb.
A bull standing 7 ft 8 in at the withers and weighing 1,800 lb was shot in Sept 1897 in the Yukon Territory, Canada. Unconfirmed measurements of up to 8½ ft at the withers and 2,600 lb have been claimed. The record antler span or "rack" is 78½ in.

Smallest Deer

The smallest true deer (family Cervidae) is the northern pudu (*Pudu mephistopheles*) of Ecuador and Colombia. Mature specimens measure 13–14 in at the shoulder and weigh 16–18 lb. The smallest ruminant is the lesser Malay chevrotain (*Tragulus javanicus*) of SE Asia, Sumatra and Borneo. Adult specimens measure 8–10 in at the shoulder and weigh 6–7 lb.

Rarest Deer

The rarest deer is Fea's muntjac (*Muntiacus feae*), which until recently was known only from two specimens collected on the borders of Burma and Thailand. In Dec 1977 a female was received at the Dusit Zoo, Bangkok, followed by 2 females in 1981, and 3 males and 3 females from Xizang, Tibet, southwest China, Feb 1982–Apr 1983.

Largest Goat

"Shad," a 352-lb wether male (b May 1978) standing 41 in high at the shoulder, owned by Bill and Mickey Vestle of Modesto, Calif, is said to be the heaviest and largest goat.

Largest Insectivore (Insect-Eating Mammal)

The largest insectivore is the moon rat (*Echinosorex gymnurus*), also known as Raffles' gymnure, found in Burma, Thailand, Malaysia, Sumatra and Borneo. Mature specimens have a head and body length of 10.43–17.52 in, a tail measuring 7.87–8.26 in, and weight up to 3.08 lb. Although the much larger anteaters (family Tachyglossidae and Myrmecophagidae) feed on termites and other soft-bodied insects, they are not insectivores, but belong to the orders Monotremata and Edentata ("without teeth").

Smallest Insectivore

The smallest insectivore is Savi's white-toothed pygmy shrew (*Suncus etruscus*), also called the Etruscan shrew, which is found along the coast of the northern Mediterranean and southwards to Cape Province, South Africa. Mature specimens have a head and body length of 1.32–2.04 in, a tail length of 0.94–1.14 in, and weight of between 0.052 and 0.09 oz.

Longest-Lived Insectivore

The greatest reliable age recorded for an insectivore is 16 years for a lesser hedgehog-tenrec (*Echinops telefairi*), which was born in the Amsterdam Zoo, Netherlands, in 1966 and was later sent to Jersey Zoo. It died on Nov 27, 1982.

Heaviest Tusks

The heaviest recorded tusks are a pair in the British Museum (Natural History), London, which were collected from an aged bull shot by an Arab with a muzzle-loading gun at the foot of Mt Kilimanjaro, Tanzania, in 1897. They originally weighed 240 lb (length 10 ft 2½ in) and 225 lb (length 10 ft 5½ in) respectively, giving a combined weight of 465 lb, but their combined weight today is 440½ lb.

The greatest weight ever recorded for one elephant tusk is 258 lb for a specimen collected in Benin (formerly Dahomey), West Africa, and exhibited at the Paris Exposition in 1900.

Longest Tusks

The longest recorded elephant tusks (excluding prehistoric examples) are a pair from Zaïre preserved in the National Collection of Heads and Horns, kept by the New York Zoological Society, Bronx Park. The right tusk measures 11 ft 5½ in along the outside curve and the left measures 11 ft. Their combined weight is 293 lb. A single tusk of 11 ft 6 in has been reported, but details are lacking. Ivory rose in market price from $2.30 to $34 per lb, 1970–80.

Rarest Marsupial

The rarest marsupial is probably the thylacine (*Thylacinus cynocephalus*), also known as the "Tasmanian wolf." (See page 49.)

Longest Horns

The longest horns grown by any living animal are those of the water buffalo (*Bubalus arnee* = *B. bubalis*) of India. One huge bull shot in 1955 had horns measuring 13 ft 11 in from tip to tip along the outside curve across the forehead. The longest single horn on record was one measuring 81¼ in on the outside curve found on a specimen of domestic Ankole cattle (*Bos taurus*) near Lake Ngami, Botswana, Africa.

The largest spread recorded for a Texas longhorn steer is 9 ft 9 in.

Largest Marsupial

The largest of all marsupials is the red kangaroo (*Macropus rufus*) of southern and eastern Australia. Adult males or "boomers" stand up to 7 ft tall, weigh up to 175 lb and measure up to 9 ft 6 in along the curves of the body.

JUMPERS (left): The Himalayan ibex escapes from hunters by leaping criss-cross down sheer cliffs, momentarily touching its hoofs down on rocky ledges. Movies of the ibex can be seen at the various Guinness Museums.

RAREST MARSUPIAL (below): The carnivorous "Tasmanian wolf" is very possibly extinct since the 1960's, when the last male to be positively identified was accidentally killed

The highest speed recorded for a marsupial is 40 mph for a young female eastern gray kangaroo (*Macropus giganteus*).

Smallest Marsupial

The smallest known marsupial is the very rare Ingram's planigale (*Planigale ingrami*), a flat-skulled mouse found only in northwestern Australia. Adult males have a head and body length of 1.77 in, a tail length of 2 in and weight of about 0.14 oz.

Highest and Longest Marsupial Jump

The greatest measured height cleared by a hunted kangaroo is 10 ft 6 in over a pile of timber. The longest recorded leap was reported in Jan 1951 when, in the course of a chase, a female red kangaroo made a series of bounds which included one of 42 ft. There is an unconfirmed report of an eastern gray kangaroo (*Macropus canguru*) jumping 44 ft 8½ in on the flat.

Longest-Lived Marsupial

The greatest reliable age recorded for a marsupial is 26 years 0 months 22 days for a common wombat (*Vombatus ursinus*) which died in London Zoo Apr 20, 1906.

DOMESTICATED ANIMALS*

Horse Population

The world's horse population is estimated to be 75 million.

Oldest Horse and Pony

The greatest reliable age recorded for a horse is 62 years in the case of "Old Billy" (foaled 1760), believed to be a cross between a Cleveland and an Eastern blood, who was bred by Edward Robinson of Wild Grave Farm in Woolston, Lancashire, England. In 1762 or 1763 he was sold to the Mersey and Irwell Navigation Company and remained with them in a working capacity, marshalling and towing barges, until 1819 when he was retired to a farm, where he died Nov 27, 1822. The skull of this horse is preserved in the Manchester Museum, and his stuffed head (fitted with false teeth) is now on display in the Bedford Museum.

The greatest reliable age recorded for a pony is 54 years for a stallion owned by a farmer in central France which was still alive in 1919.

The greatest age recorded for a thoroughbred racehorse is 42 years in the case of the bay gelding "Tango Duke" (foaled 1935), owned by Mrs Carmen J. Koper of Barongarook, Victoria, Australia. The horse died Jan 25, 1978.

Largest Horse

The largest and heaviest horse ever recorded was "Brooklyn Supreme," a purebred Belgian (Brabant) stallion (foaled Apr 12, 1928) owned by C. G. Good of Ogden, Iowa, which weighed 3,200 lb shortly

---

* For further information on dogs, cats and all pets consult the *Guinness Book of Pet Records* (Sterling)

before his death Sept 6, 1948, aged 20. He stood 19.2 hands (6 ft 6 in) and had a chest girth of 102 in.

In Apr 1973 the Belgian (Brabant) mare "Wilma du Bos" (foaled July 15, 1966), owned by Mrs Virgie Arden of Reno, Nev was reported to weigh 3,218 lb when in foal and being shipped from Antwerp. The mare stood 18.2 hands (6 ft 2 in) and normally weighed about 2,400 lb.

Tallest Horse

The tallest documented horse on record was the shire gelding named "Sampson" (later renamed "Mammoth") bred by Thomas Cleaver of Toddington Mills, Bedfordshire, Eng. This horse (foaled in 1846) measured 21.2½ hands (7 ft 2½ in) in 1850 and was later said to have been 3,360 lb.

Smallest Horse

The smallest breed of horse is the Falabella of Argentina which was developed over a period of 70 years by inbreeding and crossing a small group of undersized horses originally discovered in the southern part of Argentina. Most adult specimens stand less than 30 in and average 80–100 lb. The smallest mature horse bred by Julio Falabella of Recco de Roca before he died in 1981 was a mare which stood 15 in and weighed 26¼ lb.

Dr T. H. Hamison of the Circle Veterinary Center, Spartanburg, SC on Nov 30, 1975 certified that the stallion "Little Pumpkin" (foaled Apr 15, 1973) owned by J. C. Williams Jr. of Della Terra Mini Horse Farm, Inman, SC stood 14 in and weighed 20 lb.

Dog Population

In 1984 there were an estimated 50.2 million dogs in 40.2% of the households in the US.

SMALLEST LIVING HORSE is not much bigger than a pet dog: "Smidget," a full-grown Falabella, stands 20½ in high and weighs 75 lb. (*Ron Kimball*)

In the city of Peking, China, all dogs even Pekingese are now banned because "pet-keeping has an adverse effect on social order and harms environmental sanitation." All pets had to be destroyed by Nov 1, 1983. A century before, Pekingese dogs were encouraged to sit on an emperor's lap and theft of a Pekingese was a crime punishable by death.

Oldest Dogs

Most dogs live between 8 and 15 years and authentic records of dogs living over 20 years are rare. The greatest reliable age recorded for a dog is 29 years 5 months for a Queensland cattle dog named "Bluey," owned by Les Hall of Rochester, Vic, Australia. The dog was obtained as a puppy in 1910 and worked among cattle and sheep for nearly 20 years. He was put to sleep Nov 14, 1939.

Most Popular Dog Breeds

Cocker spaniels continued in 1985 to lead in new registrations (96,396) with the American Kennel Club. Poodles again were second (87,250) but more than 9,000 behind as compared to 2,600 behind in 1983. Labrador retrievers came in third (74,271) far ahead of German shepherds (57,-598), golden retrievers (56,131) and Doberman pinschers (41,532).

Total registrations rose to 1,089,149 in 1985 from 1,071,299 the year before.

Dog Strength and Endurance

The greatest load shifted by a dog was 6,400½ lb of railroad steel pulled by a 176-lb St Bernard named "Ryettes Brandy Bear," at Bothell, Wash, July 21, 1978. The 4-year-old dog, owned by Douglas Alexander of Monroe, Wash, pulled the weight on a four-wheeled carrier across a cement surface for a distance of 15 ft in less than 90 sec. Ten days earlier the same dog had moved 6,600 lb, but was 5 in short of the 15 ft minimum distance when the 90 seconds were up.

The strongest dog in the world in terms of most proportionate weight hauled is "Barbara-Allen's Dark Hans," a 97-lb Newfoundland, who pulled 5,045½ lb (= 52 lb per lb bodyweight) across a cement surface at Bothell, Wash, July 20, 1979. The dog, owned by Miss Terri Dickinson of Kenmore, Wash, was only 12 months old when he made the attempt.

In the annual 1,049 (not 1,135) mile dog sled race from Anchorage to Nome, Alaska, the record time is 11 days 15 hours 6 min by Susan Butcher's team of dogs in the 1986 race. The dogs wear booties to protect their paws from ice.

Heaviest Dog

The heaviest breed of domestic dog (*Canis familiaris*) is the St Bernard. The heaviest recorded example is "Benedictine Jr Schwarzwald Hof," owned by Thomas and Anne Irwin of Grand Rapids, Mich. He was whelped in 1982 and weighed 310 lb on Dec 3, 1984 (height at shoulder 39 in).

Rarest Dog

The rarest breed of dog has been the Tahltan bear dog of western Canada of which a few specimens were said to exist in 1985. The next rarest is the Chinook, a sled dog, of which 76 are said to exist, all in the US, a breed that at the height of its popularity in the early 1900's numbered only 300.

HEAVIEST DOG (above): This St Bernard, weighing 310 lb and standing 39 in at the shoulder, is the heaviest dog on record. Son of a record-holding father, "Benedictine Jr. Schwarzwald Hof" was whelped in 1982 and belongs to Mr and Mrs Irwin of Grand Rapids, Mich. (*Schwarzwald Hof Kennels*)

RAREST BREED (left): A sled dog, the Chinook, from the US Pacific Northwest, with only 76 known, is now the rarest. (*Barbara A. Martin*)

Tallest Dogs

The tallest breeds of dog are the Great Dane and the Irish wolfhound, both of which can exceed 39 in at the shoulder. The extreme recorded example is the Great Dane "Shamgret Danzas" (whelped in 1975), owned by Mr and Mrs Peter Comley of Milton Keynes, Buckinghamshire, England. He stood 41½ in or 42 in when his hackles went up, and weighed 238 lb. He died on Oct 16, 1984.

Smallest Dogs

The smallest breeds of dog are the Yorkshire terrier, the Chihuahua and the toy poodle, *miniature* versions of which have been known to weigh less than 16 oz when adult.

The smallest mature dog on record was a matchbox-sized Yorkshire terrier owned by Arthur F. Marples of Blackburn, Eng, a former editor of the magazine *Our Dogs*. This tiny atom, which died in 1945, aged nearly 2 years, stood 2½ in at the shoulder and measured 3¾ in from the tip of its nose to the root of its tail. Its weight was an incredible 4 oz.

MOST VALUABLE DOG: A half-interest in "Marathon Hound" was sold for $125,000 in Aug 1984. In his career, this greyhound set a world record in winnings of $225,000. (*American Greyhound Track Operators*)

Largest Litter

The largest recorded litter of puppies is one of 23 thrown on June 9, 1944, by "Lena," a foxhound bitch owned by Commander W. N. Ely of Ambler, Pa. All survived. On Feb 6–7, 1975, "Careless Ann," a St Bernard bitch owned by Robert and Alice Rodden of Lebanon, Mo, produced a litter of 23, but only 14 survived.

Most Prolific Dog

The dog who has sired the greatest recorded number of puppies was the greyhound "Low Pressure" nicknamed "Timmy," whelped in Sept 1957 and owned by Mrs Bruna Amhurst of Regent's Park, London. From Dec 1961 until he died in Nov 1969, he had fathered 2,414 registered puppies, with at least 600 others unregistered.

Most Valuable Dogs

Greyhound racing dogs are more highly valued than family dogs. The most highly valued is "Marathon Hound," worth $250,000 based on a sale of a half-interest for $125,000. The hound has won $225,000 in 4 years, and is now retired to stud at $750 per session.

In 1907 Mrs Clarice Ashton Cross of Ascot, Eng turned down an offer of £32,000 (equivalent to $1,380,000 in 1985!) from the American financier J. Pierpont Morgan for her famous Pekingese "Ch. Ch'erh of Alderbourne" (1904–*fl.*1914). Mr Morgan then came back with an "open" cheque, but again she turned him down.

The largest legacy devoted to a dog was by Miss Ella Wendel of NYC who "left" her standard poodle "Toby" $75 million in 1931.

Drug Sniffing

The greatest drug-sniffing dog on record was a golden retriever named "Trep" (whelped 1969), owned by former policeman Tom Kazo of Dade County, Miami, Fla. During the 5-year period 1973–77 "Agent K9–3," as he was also known, sniffed out $63 million worth of narcotics. His

DOG LEAPER: "Young Sabre," a German shepherd belonging to the RAF, scaled a ribbed wall 11 ft 8 in high in England in 1981.

owner said he would retire his pet, who could detect 16 different drugs, when he reached the magic $100 million mark, but it is not known whether Trep achieved this target.

The only drug-sniffing dog with a 100-percent-arrest record was a German shepherd of the US Army called "General." During the period Apr 1974 to Mar 1976, this canine detective and his handler, SP4 Michael R. Harris of the 591st Military Police Company in Fort Bliss, Tex, carried out 220 searches for narcotics, arrested 220 people for possession and uncovered 330 caches of drugs. The German shepherd "Blue" of the Los Angeles Police Department was reported in Jan 1986 to have assisted in apprehending 253 suspected felons.

Guide Dog

The longest period of *active service* reported for a guide dog is 13 years 2 months, in the case of a Labrador retriever bitch named "Polly" (whelped Oct 10, 1956), owned by Rose Resnick of San Rafael, Calif. The dog was put to sleep Dec 15, 1971.

Highest and Longest Dog Jumps

The canine "high jump" record for a leap and a scramble over a smooth wooden wall (without any ribs or other aids) is held by a German shepherd called "Max of Pangoula." He scaled an 11-ft-5⅛-in wall at Chikurubi prison's dog training school near Salisbury, Zimbabwe on Mar 18, 1980. His trainer was Chief Prison Officer Alec Mann.

Another German shepherd dog, "Young Sabre," handled by Cpl David Smith, scaled a ribbed wall with regulation shallow slats to a height of 11 ft 8 in at RAF Newton, Nottinghamshire, England, on July 17, 1981.

The longest recorded canine long jump was one of 30 ft by a greyhound named "Bang," made in jumping a gate in coursing a hare at Brecon Lodge, Gloucestershire, England, in 1849.

Top Dog Trainer

The most successful dog trainer is Mrs Barbara Woodhouse of Rickmansworth, Hertfordshire, England, who has trained 19,000 dogs to obey the basic commands during the period from 1951 to her retirement in 1985.

The fastest dog trainer is Armand Rabuttinio of Aston, Pa. His highest total for a single day (9 am–6 pm) is 132 dogs at a training marathon held at Upland, Pa, on June 12, 1982.

Top Show Dog

The greatest number of "Best-in-Show" awards won by any dog in all-breed shows is the 203 compiled by the Scottish terrier bitch "Ch. Braeburn's Close Encounter" (whelped Oct 22, 1978) up to Mar 10, 1985. She is owned by Sonnie Novick of Plantation Acres, Fla.

Dog Tracking

The greatest tracking feat on record was performed by the Doberman "Sauer" trained by Detective-Sergeant Herbert Kruger. In 1925 he tracked a stock thief 100 miles across the Great Karroo, South Africa, by scent alone.

In 1923 a collie named "Bobbie," lost by his owners while they were on vacation in Wolcott, Ind, turned up at the family home in Silverton, Ore, 6 months later, after having covered a distance of close to 2,000 miles. The dog, later identified by people who had cared for him along the route, had apparently wandered back through Ill, Iowa, Neb, and Colo, before crossing the Rocky Mts in the depths of winter, then continuing through Wyo and Idaho.

Cat Population

The estimated cat population in 1985 in the US of 46.3 million is the largest in the world, up from 23 million in 1981. Cats are kept in 27.3% of all households in the US, according to the Pet Food Institute in Wash, DC.

Oldest Cats

Cats are generally longer-lived animals than dogs. Information on this subject is often obscured by two or more cats bearing the same nickname in succession. The oldest cat ever recorded was probably the tabby "Puss," owned by Mrs T. Holway of Clayhidon, Devon, England, who celebrated his 36th birthday on Nov 28, 1939 and died the next day.

A more recent and better-documented case was that of the female tabby "Ma," owned by Mrs Alice St George Moore of Drewsteignton, Devon, Eng. This cat was put to sleep on Nov 5, 1957, aged 34.

Heaviest and Longest Cats

In the majority of domestic cats (*Felis catus*), the average weight of males (toms) at maturity is 6.2 lb compared to females (queens) averaging 5.4 lb. Neuters and spays average out somewhat heavier.

The heaviest weight for a domestic cat was recorded as 46 lb 15¼ oz on Jan 14, 1986, for a 10-year-old neutered male tabby named "Himmy," owned by Thomas Vyse of Cairns, Australia. His measurements were neck 15 in, waist 33 in, length 38 in.

The largest of the 330 cat breeds is the ragdoll, with males weighing 15–20 lb.

Smallest Cats

The smallest breed of domestic cat is the Singapura or "Drain Cat" of

Singapore. Adult males average 6 lb in weight and adult females 4 lb. In extreme cases of feline dwarfism weights of under 3 lb have been reliably reported. A male Siamese cross named "Ebony-Eb-Honey Cat," owned by Angelina Johnston of Boise, Idaho, tipped the scales at only 1 lb 12 oz in Feb 1984, when aged 23 months.

Largest Cat Litter

The largest litter ever recorded was one of 19 kittens (4 stillborn) delivered by Caesarean section to "Tarawood Antigone," a 4-year-old brown Burmese, on Aug 7, 1970. Her owner, Mrs Valerie Gane of Kingham, Oxfordshire, England, reported that the litter was the result of mismating with a half-Siamese. Of the 15 survivors, 14 were male.

The largest live litter of which all survived was one of 14 kittens born in Dec 1974 to the Persian cat "Bluebell," owned by Mrs Elenore Dawson of Wellington, Cape Province, South Africa.

Most Prolific Cat

A cat named "Dusty," aged 17, living in Bonham, Tex, gave birth to her 420th kitten June 12, 1952.

Richest Cat

When Mrs Grace Alma Patterson of Joplin, Mo died in Jan 1978, she left her entire estate worth $250,000 to her 18-lb white alley cat "Charlie Chan." When the cat dies, the estate, which includes a three-bedroom house, a 7-acre pet cemetery and a collection of valuable antiques, will be auctioned off and the proceeds donated to humane societies.

Most Valuable Cat

In 1967 Miss Elspeth Sellar of Grafham, England, turned down an offer of 2,000 guineas (then $5,880) from an American breeder for her 2-

HEAVIEST CAT: "Himmy," a 10-year-old tabby of Cairns, Australia, weighs almost 47 lb.

LARGEST PET LITTERS

Animal	Number	Breed	Owner
Cat (1970)	15†	Burmese Siamese	Mrs Valerie Gane, Kingham, Oxfordshire, Eng
Dog (1944)	23	Foxhound	Cdr W. N. Ely, Ambler, Pa
(1975)	23	St Bernard	R. and A. Rodden, Lebanon, Mo
Rabbit (1978)	24	New Zealand White	Joseph Filek, Sydney, Cape Breton, Nova Scotia, Canada
Guinea Pig (1972)	12		Laboratory Specimen.
Hamster (1974)	26*	Golden Hamster	L. and S. Miller, Baton Rouge, La
Mouse (1982)	34‡	House Mouse	Marion Ogilvie, Blackpool, England
Gerbil (1982)	14		Sharon Kirkman, Bulwell, Nottingham, England
(1960's)	15**		George Meares, geneticist-owner, gerbil breeding farm, St Petersburg, Fla.

† 4 stillborn
* 18 killed by mother
‡ 33 survived
** Uses special food formula

CAGED PET LONGEVITY TABLE

The greatest recorded ages for commonly kept pets are as follows:

		Years	Months
Rabbit	"Flopsy" (owner Mrs L. B. Walker, Longford, Tasmania), caught Aug 6, 1964, d. June 29, 1983.	18	10¾
Guinea Pig (*Cavia porcellus*)	"Snowball," Nottinghamshire, Eng. Died 1979	14	10½
Gerbil, Mongolian	Reported from Longford, Tasmania	18	11
House Mouse (*Mus musculus*)	"Fritzy" (owner West House School, Birmingham, Eng) *fl.* Apr 1985	7	6
Rat (*Rattus sp.*)	Philadelphia. Died 1924	5	8
Hamster, Golden	Reported, Cambridge, Eng 1984	19	

year-old international champion copper-eyed white Persian tom, "Coylum Marcus" (b Mar 28, 1965, d Apr 14, 1978).

Mousing Champion

The greatest mouser on record is "Towser," (b Apr 21, 1963), a female tortoiseshell cat owned by Glenturret Distillery Ltd, Scotland, who notched up her 25,716th kill by her 23rd birthday. She averages three mice per day.

Best Climbing Cat

On Sept 6, 1950 a 4-month-old kitten belonging to Josephine Aufdenblatten of Geneva, Switzerland, followed a group of climbers up to the top of the 14,691-ft Matterhorn in the Alps.

Rabbits

The largest breed of domestic rabbit (*Oryctolagus cuniculus*) is the Flemish giant. Adult specimens average 15.4–18.7 lb but weights up to 25 lb have been reliably reported. In Apr 1980 a 5-month-old female French lop weighing 26.45 lb was exhibited at the Reus Fair in northeastern Spain.

The heaviest recorded wild rabbit (average weight 3½ lb) was one of 8 lb 4 oz, killed by Norman Wilkie of Fife, Scotland while ferreting on Nov 20, 1982.

The smallest breeds of domestic rabbit are the Netherlands dwarf and the Polish, both of which reach a maximum of 2–2½ lb at maturity. In 1975, Jacques Bouloc of Coulommiers, France, announced a new cross of the above breeds which weighed 14 oz.

The most prolific domestic breeds are the New Zealand white and the Californian. Does produce 5–6 litters a year during their breeding life, each containing 8–12 young (compare with 5 litters and 3–7 young for the wild rabbit).

Longest Ears

In the lop family (French) ears exceeding 30 in have been measured.

Hares

In Nov 1956 a brown hare (*Lepus europaeus*), weighing a record 15 lb 1 oz, was shot near Welford, Northamptonshire, England. The average adult weight is 8 lb.

---

2. BIRDS (*AVES*)

Largest Bird

The largest living bird is the North African ostrich (*Struthio camelus camelus*) which is found in reduced numbers south of the Atlas Mountains from Upper Senegal and Niger across to the Sudan and central Ethiopia. Male examples of this flightless or ratite subspecies have been recorded up to 9 ft in height and 345 lb in weight.

The heaviest flying bird, or carinate, is the Kori bustard or paauw (*Otis kori*) of East and South Africa. Weights up to 40 lb have been reliably reported for cock birds shot in South Africa. The mute swan (*Cygnus olor*) resident in Britain can also reach 40 lb on occasion, and there is a record from Poland of a cob weighing 49.5 lb which could not fly.

The heaviest bird of prey is the Andean condor (*Vultur gryphus*), which averages 20–25 lb as an adult. A weight of 31 lb has been claimed for an outsize male California condor (*Gymnogyps californianus*) now preserved in the California Academy of Sciences, Los Angeles. This species is appreciably smaller than the Andean condor and rarely exceeds 23 lb.

Longest Bird Flights

The greatest distance covered by a ringed bird during migration is 14,-000 miles by an Arctic tern (*Sterna paradisaea*), which was banded as a nestling July 5, 1955 in the Kandalaksha Sanctuary on the White Sea coast of the USSR, north of Archangel, and was captured alive by a fisherman 8 miles south of Fremantle, W Australia, May 16, 1956. The bird had flown south via the Atlantic Ocean and then circled Africa before crossing the Indian Ocean. It did not survive to make the return journey.

Fastest- and Slowest-Flying Birds

The bird which presents the hunter with the greatest difficulty is the red-breasted merganser (*Mergus serrator*). On May 29, 1960 a specimen flushed from the Kukpuk River, Cape Thompson, northern Alaska, by a light aircraft recorded an air speed of 80 mph in level flight for nearly 13 sec before turning aside. The spur-winged goose (*Plectropterus gambiensis*) has been timed at 88 mph in an escape dive.

The slowest-flying bird is the American woodcock (*Scolopax minor*), which has been timed at 5 mph without sinking.

Fastest and Slowest Wing Beat

The fastest recorded wing beat of any bird is that of the horned sungem (*Heliactin cornuta*) of tropical South America with a rate of 90 beats per sec.

Large vultures (family Vulturidae) sometimes exhibit a flapping rate as low as one beat per sec. Condors can cruise on thermals for 60 miles without beating their wings.

Highest-Flying

The highest acceptable altitude recorded for a bird is just over 27,000 ft for 30 whooper swans (*Cygnus cygnus*) flying from Iceland to winter at N Ireland. They were spotted by an airline pilot over the Outer Hebrides on Dec 9, 1967, and the height was also confirmed by air traffic control in N Ireland after the swans had been picked up on radar.

A vulture known as Ruppell's griffin with an 8-ft wing span was reported to have collided with a plane at 37,000 feet over Abidjan, Ivory Coast, in 1973, but this is doubted by some leading experts. Geese regularly fly over Mt Everest at 30,000 ft.

Rarest Bird

Because of the practical difficulties involved in assessing bird populations in the wild, it is virtually impossible to establish the identity of the rarest living bird. The strongest contenders, however, must be the Ooaa (*Moho braccatus*) of Kauai, Hawaii, which was down to a single pair in 1980, and the protected dusky seaside sparrow (*Ammospiza nigrescens*) of Disneyworld's Discovery Island in Fla, with only 2 males in 1985. The rarest bird of prey is the Calif vulture. In Jan 1986, there were only 7 in the wild plus 20 in captivity.

Smallest Bird

The smallest bird is the bee hummingbird (*Mellisuga helenae*) found in Cuba and the Isle of Pines. Adult males (females are slightly larger) measure 2.24 in in total length, half of which is taken up by the bill and tail. It weighs 0.056 oz, which means it is lighter than a privet-hawk moth (0.084 oz).

The smallest bird of prey is the 1.23-oz white fronted falconet of northwestern Borneo (*Microhierax latifrons*), which is about the size of a sparrow.

The smallest sea bird is the least storm petrel (*Halocyptena microsoma*), which breeds on many of the small islands in the Gulf of Calif, Mexico. Adult specimens average 5½ in in total length and weigh about 1 oz.

Highest g Force in Bird World

Recent American scientific experiments have revealed that the beak of the red-headed woodpecker (*Melanerpes erythrocephalus*) hits the bark of a tree with an impact velocity of 13 mph. This means that when the head snaps back the brain is subject to a deceleration of about 10 g.

Most Airborne Birds

The most airborne of land birds is the common swift (*Apus apus*) which remains aloft for 2–3 years, until it is mature enough to breed. But the sooty tern (*Sterna fuscata*) is the most aerial of all birds. It remains continuously aloft for 3 or 4 years after leaving the nesting grounds before it returns to the breeding grounds.

Longest-Lived Bird

The greatest irrefutable age reported for any bird is 80+ years in the case of a male greater sulphur-crested cockatoo (*Cacatua galerita*) in the London Zoo 1925–82, which was fully mature when acquired.

Largest Wing Span

The wandering albatross (*Diomedea exulans*) of the southern oceans has the largest wing span of any living bird, adult males averaging 10 ft 4 in with wings tightly stretched. The largest recorded specimen was a male measuring 11 ft 11 in caught by members of the Antarctic research ship USNS *Eltanin* in the Tasman Sea on Sept 18, 1965.

The only other bird reliably credited with a wing spread in excess of 11 ft is the vulture-like marabou stork (*Leptoptilus crumeniferus*) of Africa. In 1934, a freakish measurement of 13 ft 4 in was reported for a male shot in Central Africa, but this species rarely exceeds 9 ft.

Largest Nests

The largest bird's nest on record is one 9½ ft wide and 20 ft deep built by a pair of bald eagles (*Haliaeetus leucocephalus*) and possibly their successors near St Petersburg, Fla, reported in 1963. It weighed more than 6,700 lb. The golden eagle (*Aquila chrysaetos*) also constructs huge nests, and one 15 ft deep was reported from Scotland in 1954. It had been in use for 45 years. The incubation mounds built by the mallee fowl (*Leipoa ocellata*) of Australia are much larger, having been measured up to 15 ft in height and 35 ft across, and it has been calculated that the nest site may involve mounding matter weighing 330 tons.

Fastest Swimming and Deepest Diving Birds

The fastest swimmer is the gentoo penguin (*Pygoscelis papua*), which has a maximum burst speed of *c.* 17 mph. This is a respectable flying speed for some birds.

The deepest diver is the emperor penguin (*Aptenodytes forsteri*) of the Antarctic which can reach a depth of 870 ft and remain submerged for as long as 18 min.

SMALLEST BIRD (above): The bee hummingbird (in proportion here) is so tiny, it is smaller than an ostrich's eye.

MOST AIRBORNE (above): The sooty tern remains aloft for 3-4 years.

EGGS: The man (below left) is holding the huge egg of an elephant bird, which is smaller than the record largest egg of the ostrich (below right). The ostrich's is so big—6–8 in long and 4–6 in diameter—and with so strong a shell, it can support the weight of a 280-lb man. It is 352 times as heavy (at 3¾ lb) as the smallest egg, that of the hummingbird (in hand).

Most Abundant Birds

The most abundant species of wild bird is the red-billed quelea (*Quelea quelea*) of the drier parts of Africa south of the Sahara with a population estimated at 10 billion of which a tenth are destroyed each year by pest control units.

The most abundant domesticated bird is the chicken, the domesticated form of the wild red jungle fowl (*Gallus gallus*) of Southeast Asia. In 1984 there were believed to be about 4½ billion in the world, or about one chicken for every member of the human race.

The most abundant sea bird is probably Wilson's storm petrel (*Oceanites oceanicus*) of the Antarctic. No population estimates have been published, but the number must run into hundreds of millions.

Birds with Most Acute Vision

Birds of prey (Falconiformes) have the keenest eyesight in the avian world. Their visual acuity is at least 8–10 times stronger than that of human vision. The golden eagle (*Aquila chrysaetos*) can detect an 18-in-long hare at a range of 2 mi, in good light and against a contrasting background, and a peregrine falcon (*Falco peregrinus*) can detect a pigeon at a range of over 5 mi.

Incubation

The longest incubation period is that of the wandering albatross (*Diomedea exulans*), with a normal range of 75–82 days. There is an isolated case of an egg of the mallee fowl (*Leipoa ocellata*) of Australia taking 90 days to hatch. Its normal incubation period is 62 days. The shortest incubation period is the 10 days of the great spotted woodpecker (*Dendrocopus major*) and the black-billed cuckoo (*Coccyzus erythropthalmus*).

The idlest of cock birds include hummingbirds (family Trochilidae), eider duck (*Somateria mollissuma*) and golden pheasant (*Chrysolophus pictus*), among whom the hen bird does 100% of the incubation, whereas the female common kiwi (*Apteryx australis*) leaves this to the male for 75–80 days.

Largest Bird Eggs

Of living birds, the one producing the largest egg is the ostrich (*Struthio camelus*). The average egg weighs 3.63–3.88 lb, measures 6–8 in in length, 4–6 in in diameter and requires about 40 min for boiling. The shell, though 1/16th in thick, can support the weight of a 280-lb man.

Smallest Bird Eggs

The smallest egg laid by any bird is that of the Vervain hummingbird (*Mellisuga minima*) of Jamaica. Two specimens measuring less than 0.39 in in length weighed 0.0128 oz and 0.0132 oz respectively. The egg of the smallest bird, the bee hummingbird, weighs 0.0176 oz. Eggs emitted from the oviduct before maturity, known as "sports," are not reckoned to be of significance in discussion of relative sizes.

Longest and Most Feathers

The longest feathers grown by any bird are those of the cock long-tailed fowls, or onagadori (a strain of the red jungle fowl *Gallus gallus*), which have been bred in southwestern Japan since the mid-17th century. In 1972 a tail covert measuring 34 ft 9½ in was reported by Masasha Kubota of Kochi, Shikoku. Among flying birds the two central pairs of tail feathers of Reeve's pheasant (*Syrmàticus reevesi*) of central and northern China can exceed 8 ft. They serve as an escape brake.

In a series of "feather counts" on various species of birds, a whistling swan (*Cygnus columbianus*) was found to have 25,216 feathers, 20,177 of which were on the head and neck. The ruby-throated hummingbird (*Archilochus colubris*) has only 940, although hummingbirds have more feathers per area of body surface than any other living bird.

Longest Bill

The longest bill grown by any bird in proportion to its body size is that of the male Toco toucan (*Ramphastos tocs*) of eastern S America, whose bill of 7.87 in compares with its 25.98-in total body length.

Champion Bird-Watcher

The world's leading bird-watcher is Norman Chesterfield (b Mar 8, 1913) of Wheatley, Ont, Canada. By Apr 23, 1986 he had logged 6,220 of the 9,016 known species.

Leading bird-lover Clarence Schilling, ex-math professor at N Dakota State Univ, left his entire estate of $90,000 to feed birds and squirrels.

Heaviest Chicken

The heaviest breed of chicken is the white sully developed by Grant Sullens of West Point, Calif, over a period of 7 years by crossing and recrossing large Rhode Island reds. One monstrous rooster named "Weirdo" reportedly weighed 22 lb in Jan 1973, and was so ferocious that he crippled a dog which came too close and killed two cats.

Chicken Flying

The record distance flown by a chicken is 310 ft 6 in by *"Shorisha"* (means champion) owned by Morimitzu Neura at Hammatzu, Japan Mar 8, 1981. Hens are better flyers than cocks.

Heaviest Turkey

The greatest dressed weight recorded for a turkey (*Meleagris gallopavo*) is 78 lb 14¾ oz for a stag reared by Dale Turkeys of Shropshire, England. It won the annual heaviest turkey competition held in London, Dec 15, 1982.

Most Talkative Bird

The world's most talkative bird is a male African gray parrot (*Psittacus erythacus*) named "Prudle," owned by Mrs Lyn Logue of Golders Green, London, England, which won the "best talking parrot-like bird" title at the National Cage and Aviary Bird Show in London for 12 consecutive years (1965–76) before retiring undefeated. Prudle, who has a vocabulary of nearly 1,000 words, was taken from a nest in a tree about to be felled at Jinja, Uganda, in 1958.

Longest-Lived Domestic Birds

The longest-lived domesticated bird (excluding the ostrich) is the domestic goose which normally lives about 25 years. A gander named "George," owned by Mrs Florence Hull of Lancashire, England, died on Dec 16, 1976, aged 49 years 8 months. He was hatched in Apr 1927. The longest-lived small cage bird is the canary (*Serinus canaria*). The oldest example on record was a 34-year-old cock bird named "Joey," owned by

Mrs K. Ross of Hull, England. The bird was purchased in Calabar, Nigeria, in 1941, and died Apr 8, 1975.

OLDEST BIRD:
"George," a domestic gander, lived for 49 years 8 months though the average age for a goose is 25 years.

3. REPTILES (*REPTILIA*)
(Crocodiles, snakes, turtles, tortoises and lizards)

Largest and Heaviest Reptiles

The largest reptile in the world is the estuarine or salt-water crocodile (*Crocodylus porosus*) of Southeast Asia, northern Australia, New Guinea, Malay Archipelago and the Solomon Islands. Adult males average 14–16 ft in length and scale 900–1,150 lb. A specimen 28 ft 4 in long, weighing *c.* 4,400 lb, was found in the Norman River of Australia in 1957.

Largest Lizards

The largest of all lizards is the Komodo monitor or Ora (*Varanus komodoensis*), a dragon-like reptile found on the Indonesian islands of Komodo, Rintja, Padar and Flores. Adult males average 7 ft 5 in in length and weigh 130 lb. Lengths up to 30 ft (*sic*) have been quoted for this species, but the largest specimen to be accurately measured was a male presented to an American zoologist in 1928 by the Sultan of Bima which taped 10 ft 0.8 in. In 1937 this animal was put on display in the St Louis Zoological Gardens for a short period. It then measured 10 ft 2 in in length and weighed 365 lb.

The longest lizard in the world is the slender Salvadori monitor (*Varanus salvadori*) of New Guinea which has been reliably measured up to 15 ft 7 in long.

Oldest Lizard

The greatest age recorded for a lizard is more than 54 years for a male slow worm (*Anguis fragilis*) kept in the Zoological Museum in Copenhagen, Denmark, from 1892 until 1946.

Largest Chelonians

The largest living chelonian is the Pacific leatherback turtle (*Dermochelys coriacea schlegelii*). The average adult measures 6–7 ft in overall length (length of carapace 4–5 ft) and weighs up to 1,000 lb. The greatest weight reliably recorded is 1,908 lb for a male captured off Monterey, Calif on Aug 29, 1961. Its length was 8 ft 4 in overall.

The largest living tortoise is *Geochelone* (*Testudo*) *gigantea* of the Indian Ocean islands of Aldabra, Mauritius, and the Seychelles (introduced 1874). Adult males in the wild sometimes exceed 450 lb in weight, but much heavier captive specimens have been recorded. A male named "Marmaduke" received at the London Zoo in 1951 recorded a peak weight of 616 lb before his death Jan 27, 1983.

Longest-Lived Chelonians

Tortoises are the longest-lived of all vertebrates. The greatest authentic age is 152+ years for a male Marion's tortoise (*Testudo sumerii*) brought from the Seychelles to Mauritius in 1766, which went blind in 1908, and was accidentally killed in 1918.

When the famous Royal Tongan tortoise "Tu' Malilia" (believed to be a specimen of *Testudo radiata*) died on May 19, 1966, it was reputed to be over 200 years old, having been presented to the king of Tonga by Capt James Cook (1728–79) on Oct 22, 1773, but this record may well be conflated between two (or more) overlapping residents.

The greatest proven age of a continuously observed tortoise is 116+ years for a Mediterranean spur-thighed tortoise (*Testudo graeca*) which died in Paignton Zoo, Devon, England, in 1957.

Slowest-Moving Chelonians

In a recent "speed" test carried out in the Seychelles, in the Indian Ocean, a male giant tortoise (*Geochelone gigantea*) could only cover 5 yd in 43.5 sec (0.23 mph) despite the enticement of a female tortoise.

Smallest Reptiles

The smallest known species of reptile is believed to be *Sphaerodactylus parthenopion,* a tiny gecko found only on the island of Virgin Gorda, one of the British Virgin Islands in the Caribbean. It is known only from 15 specimens, including some gravid females, found between Aug 10 and 16, 1964. The three largest females measured 0.71 in from snout to vent, with a tail of approximately the same length.

It is possible that another gecko, *Sphaerodactylus elasmorhynchus,* may be even smaller. The only specimen ever discovered was an apparently mature female, with a snout-vent length of 0.67 in and a tail of the same length, found March 15, 1966 among the roots of a tree in the western part of the Massif de la Hotte in Haiti.

A species of dwarf chameleon, *Evoluticauda tuberculata,* found in Madagascar, and known only from a single specimen, has a snout-vent length of 0.71 in and a tail length of 0.55 in.

Fastest Reptile

The highest speed measured for any reptile on land is 18 mph by a six-lined race runner (*Cnemidophorus sexlineatus*) pursued by a car near McCormick, SC, in 1941. The highest speed claimed for any reptile in water is 22 mph by a frightened Pacific leatherback turtle (see *Largest Chelonians*).

Rarest Snake

The rarest snake is the keel-sealed boa (*Casarea dussumieri*) of Round Island, western Indian Ocean, which has a total population of 75.

Longest and Heaviest Snakes

The longest of all snakes (average adult length) is the reticulated python (*Python reticulatus*) of Southeast Asia, Indonesia and the Philippines, which regularly exceeds 20 ft. In 1912 a specimen measuring exactly 32 ft 9½ in was shot near a mining camp on the north coast of Celebes in the Malay archipelago.

Lengths of 37½ ft, 42 ft and even 45 ft have been claimed for the anaconda (*Eunectes murinus*) of tropical South America, but these extreme measurements were probably based on stretched skins. The greatest authenticated length (and weight) recorded for an anaconda is 27 ft 9 in for a female killed in Brazil *c.* 1960, weighing 500 lb, and with a girth of 44 in.

The longest (and heaviest) snake ever held in captivity was a female reticulated python (*Python reticulatus*) named "Colossus" who died in Highland Park Zoo, Mifflin, Pa on Apr 15, 1963. She measured 28 ft 6 in and scaled 320 lb at her heaviest.

The longest venomous snake in the world is the king cobra (*Ophiophagus hannah*), also called the hamadryad, of Southeast Asia and the Philippines. A specimen collected near Port Dickson in Malaya in April 1937 grew to 18 ft 9 in in the London Zoo. It was destroyed at the outbreak of war in 1939.

The heaviest venomous snake is the eastern diamondback rattlesnake (*Crotalus adamanteus*) of the southeastern US. One specimen weighed 34 lb and was 7 ft 9 in long.

OLDEST AND SMALLEST SNAKES. Popeye, a common boa constrictor (above) lived for more than 40 years in the Philadelphia Zoo before he had to be euthanased. The tiny thread snake (right) is only 4.7 in long.

Most Venomous Snakes

The most venomous snake is the sea snake *Hydrophis belcheri* which has a venom 100 times as toxic as that of the Australian taipan (*Oxyuranus scutellatus*). The snake abounds around Ashmore Reef in the Timor Sea, off the coast of northwestern Australia.

The most venomous land snake is the 6-ft-long inland taipan snake (*Oxyuranus microlepidotus*) of the drainage bases of Queensland, S Australia, which has a venom 9 times as toxic as that of the tiger snake (*Notechis scutatus*) of S Australia and Tasmania. One specimen yielded

0.00385 oz of venom after milking, a quantity sufficient to kill at least 218,000 mice.

On the Amami Islands in the Ryukyu group, SW Japan, there is an incidence of one snakebite case per 500 people per year from the aggressive Okinawa habu (*Trimeresurus flavavirdes*). With modern treatments mortality is now only 3 percent.

Shortest Snakes

The shortest known snake is the thread snake *Leptotyphlops bilineata*, found on the Caribbean islands of Martinique, Barbados and St. Lucia. It has a maximum recorded length of 4.7 in.

The shortest venomous snake is the spotted dwarf adder (*Bitis paucisquamata*) of Little Namaqualand, SW Africa, with adults averaging 9 in in length.

Longest Fangs

The longest fangs of any snake are those of the Gaboon viper (*Bitis gabonica*), of tropical Africa. In a 6-ft-long specimen, the fangs measured 1.96 in. A Gaboon viper bit itself to death on Feb 12, 1963 in the Philadelphia Zoological Gardens. Keepers found the dead snake with its fangs deeply embedded in its own back.

Most Abundant Snake

The sea snake (*Astrotia stokesii*) is found *en masse* from the Arabian Sea to the southwestern Pacific. In May 1929, a coiled mass in the Malacca Straits measured 60 mi.

---

4. AMPHIBIANS (*AMPHIBIA*)
(Salamanders, toads, frogs, newts, caecilians, etc.)

Largest Amphibian

The largest species of amphibian is the Chinese giant salamander (*Andrias davidianus*), which lives in the cold mountain streams and marshy areas of northeastern, central and southern China. The average adult measures 3 ft 9 in in total length and weighs 55–66 lb. One huge individual collected in Hunan Province in southern China measured 5 ft 11 in in total length and weighed 143 lb. The much rarer Japanese giant salamander (*Andrias japonicus*) is slightly smaller, but one captive specimen weighed 88 lb when alive and 100 lb after death, the body having absorbed water from the aquarium.

Largest Toad

The largest toad is probably the marine toad (*Bufo marinus*) of tropical South America. An enormous female collected on Nov 24, 1965 at Miraflores Vaupes, Colombia, and later exhibited in the reptile house at the Bronx Zoo, New York City, had a snout-vent length of 9.37 in, and weighed 2 lb 11¼ oz at the time of its death in 1967.

This species is also the commonest. The female may ovulate 35,000 eggs in a year.

Largest Frog

The largest known frog is the rare Goliath frog (*Rana goliath*) of Cameroon and Equatorial Guinea. A female weighing 7 lb 4.5 oz was caught in the River Mbia, Equatorial Guinea, on Aug 23, 1960. It had a snout-vent length of 13.38 in and measured 32.08 in overall with legs extended.

Largest Tree Frog

The largest species of tree frog is *Hyla vasta,* found only on the island of Hispaniola (Haiti and the Dominican Republic) in the West Indies. The average snout-vent length is about 3.54 in, but a female collected from the San Juan River, Dominican Republic, in March 1928 measured 5.63 in.

Largest and Smallest Newt

The largest newt is the pleurodele or ribbed newt (*Pleurodeles waltl*), found in Morocco and on the Iberian Peninsula. Specimens measuring up to 15.74 in in total length and weighing over 1 lb have been reliably reported.

The smallest newt is believed to be the striped newt (*Notophthalmus perstriatus*) of the southeastern US. Adult specimens average 2.01 in in total length.

Longest-Lived Amphibian

The greatest authentic age recorded for an amphibian is about 55 years for a male Japanese giant salamander (*Andrias japonicus*) which died in the aquarium at Amsterdam Zoological Gardens June 3, 1881. It was brought to Holland in 1829, at which time it was estimated to be 3 years old.

Rarest Amphibian

The rarest amphibian is the Israel painted frog (*Discoglossus nigriventer*), which has only been recorded from the eastern shore of Israel's Lake Huleh (Hula Lake). Since its discovery in 1940 only 5 specimens have been collected.

Smallest Amphibian

The smallest species of amphibian is believed to be the arrow-poison frog *Sminthillus limbatus,* found only in Cuba. Fully-grown specimens have a snout-vent length of 0.33–0.48 in.

Smallest Tree Frog

The smallest tree frog is the least tree frog (*Hyla ocularis*), found in the southeastern US. It has a maximum snout-vent length of 0.62 in.

Smallest Toad

The smallest toad is the sub-species *Bufo beiranus beiranus,* first discovered *c.* 1906 near Beira, Mozambique, East Africa. Adult specimens have a maximum recorded snout-vent length of 0.94 in.

Highest and Lowest Amphibian

The greatest altitude at which an amphibian has been found is 26,246 ft in the Himalayas for a common toad (*Bufo vulgaris*). This species has also been found at a depth of 1,115 ft in a coal mine.

Most Poisonous Venom

The most active known venom is the batrachotoxin derived from the skin secretions of the golden arrow-poison frog (*Phyllobates terribilis*) of western Colombia, South America, which is at least 20 times more toxic than that of any other known arrow-poison frog. An average adult specimen contains enough poison (0.038 oz) to kill 2,200 people.

Longest Frog Jump

The record for the standard three consecutive leaps is 33 ft 5½ in by a female South African sharp-nosed frog (*Ptychaden oxyrhynchus*) named "Santjie" at a frog derby held at Lurula Natal Spa, Paulpietersburg, Natal, S Africa May 21, 1977. At the annual Calaveras County Jumping Frog Jubilee at Angels Camp, Calif, the record is 21 ft 1½ in set in May 1984, when "Weird Harold," trained and owned by Janet Seiber of Oregon, earned $1,500 for his owner. "Santjie" would have been ineligible at Calaveras because entrants there must measure at least 4 in "stem to stern."

5. FISHES (*AGNATHA, GNATHOSTOMATA*)

Largest Freshwater Fishes

The largest fish which spends its whole life in fresh or brackish water is the rare Pa Beuk or Pla Buk (*Pangasianodon gigas*), a giant catfish found in the deep waters of the Mekong River of Laos and Thailand. Adult males average 8 ft in length and weigh about 360 lb. This size was exceeded by the European catfish or wels (*Silurus glanis*) in earlier times (in the 19th century lengths of up to 15 ft and weights up to 720 lb were reported for Russian specimens from the Dnieper River), but today anything over 6 ft and 200 lb is considered large. The arapaima (*Arapaima glanis*), also called the pirarucu, found in the Amazon and other South American rivers and often claimed to be the largest freshwater fish, averages 6½ ft and 150 lb. The largest "authentically recorded" measured 8 ft 1½ in and weighed 325 lb. It was caught in the Rio Negro, Brazil, in 1836. In Sept 1978 a Nile perch (*Lates niloticus*) weighing 416 lb was netted in the eastern part of Lake Victoria, Kenya.

Largest Sea Fishes

The largest fish is the rare, plankton-feeding whale shark (*Rhincodon typus*) which is found in the warmer areas of the Atlantic, Pacific and Indian Oceans. It is not, however, the largest marine animal, since it is smaller than the larger species of whales (mammals). A whale shark measuring 60 ft 9 in long and weighing an estimated 90,000 lb was caught in a bamboo fish-trap at Koh Chik, in the Gulf of Siam, in 1919.

The largest carnivorous fish (excluding plankton-eaters) is the comparatively rare great white shark (*Carcharodon carcharias*), also called "the man-eater," which ranges from the tropics to temperate-zone waters. Adult specimens (females are larger than males) average 14–15 ft in length and generally scale 1,150–1,700 lb but larger specimens have been recorded.

The heaviest was a 21-ft male caught off Castillo de Cojimar, Cuba in May 1945 which weighed 7,302 lb. A 21-ft-4-in female caught near Hobart, Tasmania in June 1983, was longer but weighed only 4,500 lb.

The longest of the bony or "true" fishes (Pisces) is the Oarfish (*Regalecus glesne*), also called the "King of the Herrings," which has a worldwide distribution. In *c.* 1885 a 25-ft-long example weighing 600 lb was caught by fishermen off Pemaquid Point, Maine. Another oarfish, seen swimming off Asbury Park, NJ by a team of scientists from the Sandy Hook Marine Laboratory on July 18, 1963, was estimated to measure 50 ft in length.

The heaviest bony fish in the world is the ocean sunfish (*Mola mola*), which is found in all tropical, subtropical and temperate waters. On Sept 18, 1908 a huge specimen was accidentally struck by the *SS Fiona* off Bird Island about 40 miles from Sydney, NSW, Australia, and towed to Port Jackson. It measured 14 ft between the anal and dorsal fins and weighed 4,927 lb.

Smallest Sea Fishes

The shortest recorded marine fish—and the shortest known vertebrate—is the dwarf goby (*Trimmatom nanus*) of the Chagos Archipelago, central Indian Ocean. In one series of 92 specimens collected by the

1978–9 Joint Services Chagos Research Expedition of the British Armed Forces, the adult males averaged 0.338 in in length and the adult females 0.350 in. The lightest of all vertebrates and the smallest catch possible for any fisherman is the dwarf goby (*Schindleria praematurus*) from Samoa which measures 0.47–0.74 in. Mature specimens have been known to weigh only 2 mg, which is equivalent to 17,750 to the oz.

The smallest commercial fish is the now endangered Sinarapan (*Mistichthys luzonensis*), a goby found only in Lake Buhi, Luzon, Philippines. Adult males measure 0.39–0.51 in in length, and a dried 1 lb fish cake contains about 70,000 of them!

The smallest known shark is the long-faced dwarf shark (*Squaliolus laticaudus*) of the western Pacific which does not exceed 5.9 in.

Smallest Freshwater Fish

The shortest and lightest freshwater fish species is the dwarf pygmy goby (*Pandaka pygmaea*), a colorless and nearly transparent species found in streams and lakes on Luzon, the Philippines. Adult males measure only 0.28--0.38 in long and weigh only 4–5 mg (0.00014–0.00017 oz).

Fastest Fishes

The cosmopolitan sailfish (*Istiophorus platypterus*) is generally considered to be the fastest species of fish, although the practical difficulties of measurement make data extremely difficult to secure. A figure of 68 mph (100 yd in 3 sec) has been cited for one off Long Key, Fla. The swordfish (*Xiphias gladius*) has also been credited with very high speeds, but the evidence is based mainly on bills that have been found deeply embedded in ships' timbers. A speed of 50 knots (57.6 mph) has been calculated from a penetration of 22 in by a bill into a piece of timber, but 30–35 knots (35–40 mph) is the most conceded by some experts. A wahoo (*Acanthocybium solandri*) 43 in in length is capable of attaining a speed of 47.8 mph.

The four-winged flying fish (*Cypselurus heterurus*) may also exceed 40 mph during its rapid rush to the surface before take-off (the average speed in the air is about 35 mph). Record flights of 90 sec, 36 ft in altitude and 3,640 ft in length have been recorded in the tropical Atlantic.

Most Abundant Fish

The most abundant species is probably the 3-in-long deep-sea bristlemouth (*Cyclothone elongata*) which has a worldwide distribution.

Deepest Fish

The greatest depth from which a fish has been recovered is 27,230 ft in the Puerto Rico Trench (27,488 ft) in the Atlantic by Dr Gilbert L. Voss of the US research vessel *John Elliott*. The fish was a 6½-in-long *Bassogigas profundissimus* taken in Apr 1970 and was only the fifth such brotulid ever caught.

Longest-Lived Fishes

Aquaria are of too recent origin to be able to establish with certainty which species of fish can fairly be regarded as the longest-lived. Early indications are that it may be the lake sturgeon (*Acipenser fulvescens*) of N America. One specimen found in Lake Winnebago, Wis, lived 82 years, an estimate based on its annuli, 1951–54. In July 1974 a figure of 228 years (*sic*) was attributed by growth ring count to a female Koi fish, a

FAST FISH (above): Measurements are difficult to secure but the striped marlin with a top speed of 35 mph is certainly among the speediest. Claims of 68 mph have been cited for the sailfish. WALKING CATFISH (below): Not only can some species walk but others (from Africa) carry an electric discharge of about 350 volts at 1 amp.

form of fancy carp, named "Hanako" living in a pond in Higashi Shira-kawa, Gifu Prefecture, Japan, but the greatest authoritatively accepted age for this species is "more than 50 years."

The death of an 88-year-old female European eel (*Anguilla anguilla*) named "Putte" in the aquarium at Halsingborg Museum, Sweden was reported in 1948. She was allegedly born in the Sargasso Sea of the North Atlantic in 1860, and was caught in a river as a 3-year-old elver (young eel).

Oldest Goldfish

Goldfish (*Carassius auratus*) have been reported to live for over 40 years in China. A specimen named "Fred," owned by A. R. Wilson of Worthing, Sussex, England, died on Aug 1, 1980, aged 41 years.

Shortest-Lived Fishes

The shortest-lived fishes are probably certain species of the sub-order Cyprinodontei (killifish) found in Africa and South America which normally live about 8 months in the wild.

Most Venomous Fish

The most venomous fish are the stonefish (Synanceidae) of the tropical waters of the Indo-Pacific, and in particular *Synanceja horrida* which has the largest venom glands of any known fish. Direct contact with the spines of its fins, which contain a strong neurotoxic poison, often proves fatal.

Most Valuable Fish

The most valuable fish is the Russian sturgeon (*Huso huso*). One 2,-706-lb female caught in the Tikhaya Sosna River in 1924 yielded 541 lb of best quality caviar, valued at $184,500 in 1986, at the rate of $340 per lb.

Dr Takayaki Hosogi, the owner of "Fujitavo," a 7-year-old, 35-in-long carp which won the All-Japan Koi Championship Mar 1, 1982, refused an offer of $125,000.

Most and Least Fish Eggs

The ocean sunfish (*Mola mola*) produces in a single spawning up to 300 million eggs, each of them measuring about 0.05 in in diameter. The egg yield of the tooth carp *Jordanella floridae* of Florida is only about 20 over a period of several days.

Most Electric Fish

The most powerful electric fish is the electric eel (*Electrophorus electricus*), which is found in the rivers of Brazil, Colombia, Venezuela and Peru. An average-sized specimen can discharge 400 volts at 1 ampere, but measurements up to 650 volts have been recorded.

---

6. STARFISHES (*ASTEROIDEA*)

Largest and Heaviest Starfishes

The largest of the 1,600 known species of starfish in terms of total arm span is the very fragile brisingid *Midgardia xandaros*. A specimen collected by the Texas A & M University research vessel *Alaminos* in the southern part of the Gulf of Mexico in the late summer of 1968 mea-

SMALLEST STARFISH: Off S Australia, these tiny starfishes (3 to the inch) grow in profusion.

sured 54.33 in from tip to tip but the diameter of its disc was only 1.02 in. Its dry weight was only 2.46 oz. The heaviest species of starfish is the five-armed *Thromidia catalai* of the Western Pacific. One specimen, collected off Ilot Amedee, New Caledonia, Sept 14, 1969, and later deposited in the Noumea Aquarium, weighed an estimated 13.2 lb with a total arm span of 24.8 in.

Smallest Starfish

The smallest known starfish is the asterinid sea star (*Patiriella parvivipara*) discovered by Wolfgang Zeidler on the west coast of the Eyre Peninsula, S Australia, in 1975, which has a maximum radius of 0.18 in and a diameter of 0.35 in.

Deepest Starfish

The greatest depth from which a starfish has been recovered is 24,881 ft for a specimen of *Porcellanaster ivanovi*, collected by the Russian research ship *Vityaz* in the Marianas Trench, in the Western Pacific in about 1962.

---

7. ARACHNIDS (*ARACHNIDA*)

Largest and Heaviest Spiders

The largest known spiders in terms of leg-span are the bulky theraphosid spiders of the genera *Lasiodora* and *Grammostola* of Brazil, and *Theraphosa* of NE South America, all of which have been credited with leg-spans in excess of 10 in. In 1973 an enormous female *Lasiodora sp.* with a leg-span of 10.63 in was collected at Puraque, W Brazil, and a measurement of 10.24 in has been reported for a *Grammostola mollicoma.* The heaviest spider is a *Theraphosa blondi*, one specimen of which is owned by Charles Seiderman of NYC with an alleged weight of 4.35 oz, captured in Surinam.

Smallest Spider

The smallest known spider is *Patu marplesi* (family Symphytognathidae) of Western Samoa. The type specimen (a male found in moss at *c.* 2,000-ft altitude near Maloleli, Upolu, in Jan 1956) measures 0.016 in overall—half the size of a printed period (.).

Largest and Smallest Webs

The largest webs are the aerial ones spun by the tropical orb weavers of the genus *Nephila*, which have been measured up to 18 ft 9¾ in in circumference.

The smallest webs are spun by spiders such as *Glyphesis cottonae*, etc. which are smaller than a postage stamp, covering ¾ of a sq in.

Most Venomous Spiders

The most venomous spiders are the Brazilian wandering spiders of the genus Phoneutria and particularly *P. fera*, which has the most active neurotoxic venom of any living spider.

Fastest Spider

The highest speed measured for a spider on a level surface is 1.73 ft per sec (1.17 mph) in the case of a specimen of *Tegenaria atrica*. However, the sun spiders (genus *Solpuga*) of the Middle East and African deserts are said to travel about 10 mph.

Rarest Spider

The most elusive of all spiders are the rare trapdoor spiders of the genus *Liphistius* which are found in Southeast Asia.

Longest-Lived Spider

The longest-lived of all spiders are the primitive *Mygalomorphae* (tarantulas and allied species). One mature female tarantula, collected at Mazatlan, Mexico, in 1935 and estimated to be 12 years old at the time, was kept in a laboratory for 16 years, making a total of 28 years.

---

8. CRUSTACEANS

(Crabs, lobsters, shrimps, prawns, crayfish, barnacles, water fleas, fish lice, wood lice, sand hoppers and krill, etc.)

Largest Crustacean

The largest of all crustaceans (although not the heaviest) is the sanschouo or giant spider crab (*Macrocheira kaempferi*), also called the stilt crab, which is found in deep waters off the southeastern coast of Japan. Mature specimens usually have a 12–14-in-wide body and a claw span of 8–9 ft, but unconfirmed measurements up to 19 ft have been reported. A specimen with a claw span of 12 ft 1½ in weighed 41 lb.

Largest Lobster

The largest species of lobster, and the heaviest of all crustaceans, is the American or North Atlantic lobster (*Homarus americanus*). The largest lobster, a specimen weighing 44 lb 6 oz measuring 3 ft 6 in from the end of the tail-fan to the tip of the largest claw, was caught off Nova Scotia, Canada, on Feb 11, 1977. It was later sold to Steve Karathanos, owner of a Bayville, NY restaurant.

Commonest Crustaceans

In 1985, the standing stock of krill in the ocean was estimated at 715 million tons.

Smallest Crustaceans

The smallest known crustaceans are water fleas of the genus *Alonella*, which may measure less than 0.0098 in long. They are found in northern European waters.

The smallest known lobster is the Cape lobster (*Homarus capensis*) of South Africa which measures 3.9–4.7 in in total length.

The smallest crabs in the world are the aptly named pea crabs (family Pinnotheridae). Some species have a shell diameter of only 0.25 in, including *Pinnotheres pisum*.

Longest-Lived Crustacean

The longest-lived of all crustaceans is the American lobster (*Homarus americanus*). Very large specimens may be as much as 50 years old.

Vertical Distribution

The greatest depth from which a crustacean has been recovered is 34,-450 ft for *live* amphipods from the Challenger Deep, Marianas Trench, West Pacific by the US research vessel *Thomas Washington* in Nov 1980. Amphipods and isopods have also been collected in the Ecuadoran Andes at a height of 13,300 ft.

---

9. INSECTS

Longest Insect

The longest insect in the world is the giant stick-insect *Pharnacia serratipes* of Indonesia, females of which have been measured up to 13 in in body length. The longest beetles known (excluding antennae) are the Hercules beetles (*Dynastes hercules* and *D. Neptunus*) of Central and South America, which have been measured up to 7.48 in and 7.08 in, respectively. More than half the length, however, is taken up by the prothoracic horn.

Smallest Insects

The smallest insects recorded so far are the "hairy winged" beetles of the family Ptiliidae (= Trichopterygidae) and the "battledore-wing fairy flies" (parasitic wasps) of the family Myrmaridae. They measure only 0.008 in in length, and the fairy flies have a wing span of only 0.04 in. This makes them smaller than some of the protozoa (single-celled animals).

The male bloodsucking banded louse (*Enderleinellus zonatus*), ungorged, and the parasitic wasp *Caraphractus cinctus* may each weigh as little as 0.005 mg, or 5,670,000 to an oz. The eggs of the latter each weigh 0.0002 mg or 141,750,000 to an oz.

Heaviest Insects

The heaviest insects are the Goliath beetles (family Scarabaeidae) of equatorial Africa. The largest members of the group are *Goliathus regius* and *Goliathus goliathus* (*giganteus*). In one series of fully grown males the weight ranged from 2.5–3.5 oz.

Toughest Insect

The larva of the chironomid fly *Polypedilum vanderplanki* can tolerate temperatures from 216 °F to −454 °F.

Rarest

It was estimated by Dr Erwin (US) in 1982 that there may be 30 million species of insect—more than all other classes put together. Many are single holotypes.

Commonest Insect

The most numerous of all insects are the springtails (order Collembola), which have a very wide geographical range. It has been calculated that the top 9 in of soil in one acre of grassland contains 230 million springtails or more than 5,000 per sq ft.

HEAVIEST INSECT (left): The Goliath beetle (next to a ladybug) weighs as much as 3½ oz and measures 4¼ in.

MAMMOTH MOTH (below): This rare great owlet moth reputedly had a wing expanse of over 14 in, but the specimen was somehow mislaid.

Fastest-Flying Insects

Experiments have proved that a widely publicized claim by an American entomologist in 1926 that the deer bot-fly (*Cephenemyia pratti*) could attain a speed of 818 mph was wildly exaggerated. If true, it would have generated a supersonic "pop." Acceptable modern experiments have now established that the highest maintainable air speed of any insect, including the deer bot-fly, is 24 mph, rising to a maximum of 36 mph for short bursts. A relay of bees (maximum speed 11 mph) would use only a gallon of nectar in cruising 4 million miles at 7 mph.

Loudest Insects

The loudest of all insects is the male cicada (family Cicadidae). At 7,-400 pulses per min its tymbal (sound) organs produce a noise (officially described by the US Dept of Agriculture as "Tsh-ee-EEEE-e-ou") detectable over a quarter of a mile distance.

Largest Dragonfly

The largest dragonfly is *Megaloprepus caeruleata* of Central and South America, which has been measured up to 7.52 in across the wings and 4.72 in in body length.

Longest-Lived Insects

The longest-lived insects are the splendor beetles (*Buprestidae*), some of which remain in the larvae stage for more than 30 years. On May 27, 1983 a *Buprestis aurulenta* appeared from the staircase timber in the home of Mr W. Euston of Prittlewell, Southend-on-Sea, Eng after 47 years as a larva.

Largest Flea

The largest known flea is *Hystrichopsylla schefferi*, described from a single specimen taken from the nest of a mountain beaver *(Aplodontia rufa)* at Puyallup, Wash in 1913. Females measure up to 0.31 in in length, which is the diameter of a pencil.

Flea Jumps

The champion jumper among fleas is the common flea (*Pulex irritans*). In one American experiment carried out in 1910 a specimen allowed to leap at will performed a long jump of 13 in and a high jump of 7¾ in. In jumping 130 times its own height a flea subjects itself to a force of 200 g. Siphonapterologists recognize 1,830 varieties.

Largest Butterflies and Moths

The largest known butterfly is the protected Queen Alexandra bird-wing (*Ornithoptera alexandrae*) of Papua New Guinea. Females may have a wing span exceeding 11.02 in and weigh over 0.176 oz.

The largest moth (though not the heaviest) is the Hercules moth (*Coscinoscera hercules*) of tropical Australia and New Guinea. A wing area of up to 40.8 sq in and a wing span of 11 in have been recorded. In 1948 an unconfirmed measurement of 14.17 in was reported for a female captured near the post office at the coastal town of Innisfail, Queensland, Australia. The rare owlet moth (*Thysania agrippina*) of Brazil has been measured up to 14 in wing span.

Smallest Butterfly

The smallest of the estimated 140,000 known species of Lepidoptera are the moths *Johanssonia acetosae* (*Stainton*), found in Great Britain, and *Stigmella ridiculosa* from the Canary Islands, which have a wing span of 0.08 in and a similar body length. The smallest known butterfly is the dwarf blue (*Brephidium barberae*) from South Africa. It is 0.55 in from wing tip to wing tip.

Rarest Butterfly

The birdwing butterfly *Ornithopteria* (= *Troides*) *allottei* of Bougainville, Solomon Islands is known from less than a dozen specimens. A male from the collection of C. Rousseau Decelle was auctioned for £750 (then $2,100) in Paris on Oct 24, 1966.

10. CENTIPEDES (*CHILOPODA*)

Longest and Shortest

The longest recorded species of centipede is a large variant of the widely distributed *Scolopendra morsitans,* found on the Andaman Islands, Bay of Bengal, India. Specimens have been measured up to 13 in in length and 1½ in in breadth. The shortest recorded centipede is an unidentified species which measures only 0.19 in.

Most Legs

The centipede with the greatest number of legs is *Himantarum gabrielis* of southern Europe which has 171–177 pairs when adult.

Fastest

The fastest centipede is probably *Scutigera coleoptrata* of southern Europe which can travel at a rate of 19.68 in per sec or 1.1 mph.

---

11. MILLIPEDES (*DIPLOPODA*)

Longest and Shortest

The longest species of millipede known are the *Graphidostreptus gigas* of Africa and *Scaphistostreptus seychellarum* of the Seychelles Islands in the Indian Ocean, both of which have been measured up to 11.02 in in length and 0.78 in in diameter. The shortest millipede in the world is the British species *Polyxenus lagurus,* which measures 0.082–0.15 in in length.

Most Legs

The greatest number of legs reported for a millipede is 375 pairs (750 legs) for *Illacme plenipes* of Calif.

MILLIPEDES have as many as 750 legs (not 1,000), and this giant from the Seychelles Islands is nearly 1 ft long.
(*J. Watson/WWF*)

12. SEGMENTED WORMS (*ANNELIDA*)

Longest and Shortest Earthworms

The longest known species of giant earthworm is *Microchaetus rappi* (= *M. microchaetus*) of South Africa. An average-sized specimen measures 4 ft 6 in in length (25½ in when contracted), but much larger examples have been reliably reported. In *c.* 1937 a giant earthworm measuring 22 ft in length when naturally extended and 0.78 in in diameter was collected in the Transvaal, S Africa.

> ### Worm Charming
>
> The record for attracting (by vibrations) earthworms to the surface of a 10.76-sq-yd plot in 30 min is 511 by Tom Shufflebotham in 1980 at Willaston CP School, Cheshire, Eng.

The shortest segmented worm known is *Chaetogaster annandalei*, which measures less than 0.019 in in length.

13. MOLLUSKS
(Squids, octopuses, snails, shellfish, etc.)

Largest Squid

The largest known invertebrate is the Atlantic giant squid *Architeuthis dux.* On Nov 2, 1878 a specimen measuring 55 ft in total length (head and body 20 ft, tentacles 35 ft) was killed after it ran aground in Thimble Tickle Bay, Newfoundland, Canada. It weighed an estimated 4,400 lb. In Oct 1887 another giant squid (*Architeuthis longimanus*) measuring 57 ft in total length was washed up in Lyall Bay, NZ, but 49 ft of this was tentacle.

Largest Octopus

The largest octopus known to science is *Octopus apollyon* of the coastal waters of the N Pacific which regularly exceeds 12 ft in radial spread and 55 lb in weight. One huge individual caught single-handed by skin diver Donald E. Hagen in Lower Hoods Canal, Puget Sound, Wash, on Feb 18, 1973, had a relaxed 23-ft radial spread and weighed 118 lb 10 oz.

Longest-Lived Mollusk

The longest-lived mollusk is the ocean quahog (*Arctica islandica*), a thick-shelled clam found in the North Atlantic. Study of microscopic rings laid down annually on the tooth holding the shells together indicates that one of this species lived for 220 years. It is the world's longest-lived animal species. (See p. 48).

RECORD-SIZE CLAM SHELL: This giant measures 43.3 in in length, but it took 28 years for its record size to be formally ratified. When collected in 1956 off Okinawa, it weighed 734 lb.

Largest Bivalve Shells

The largest of all existing bivalve shells is the marine giant clam *Tridacna gigas*, found on the Indo-Pacific coral reefs. A specimen measuring 43.3 in in length and weighing 734 lb, collected off Ishigaki Island, Okinawa, was found in 1956 but not formally measured until Aug 1984 by Dr Shomei Shirai.

Smallest Shell

The smallest shell is the univalve *Ammonicera rota,* which measures 0.02 in in diameter, found in British waters.

Most Expensive Shell

Conchologists have offered up to $12,000 for examples of *Conus cypraea.*

Largest Gastropods

The largest known gastropod is the trumpet or baler conch (*Syrinx aruanus*) of Australia. One outsized specimen collected off W Australia in 1979 and now owned by Don Pisor of San Diego, Calif, measures 30.39 in in length and has a maximum girth of 39.37 in. It weighed nearly 40 lb when alive.

The largest known land gastropod is the African giant snail (*Achatina* sp.). An outsized specimen "Gee Geronimo" found by Christopher Hudson (1955–79) of Hove, E Sussex, England, measured 15½ in from snout to tail (shell length 10¾ in) in Dec 1978 and weighed exactly 2 lb. The snail was collected in Sierra Leone in June 1976 where shell lengths up to 14 in have been reliably reported.

Snail Speed

The fastest-moving species of land snail is probably the common garden snail (*Helix aspersa*). According to tests carried out in the US absolute top speed for this snail is 0.0313 mph (or 55 yd per hour) while some species are at full stretch at 0.00036 mph (or 23 in per hour).

14. RIBBON WORMS (*NEMERTINA*)

Longest Worm

The longest of the 550 recorded species of ribbon worms, also called nemertines (or nemerteans), is the "boot-lace worm" (*Lineus longissimus*), found in the shallow waters of the North Sea. A specimen washed ashore at St Andrews, Fife, Scotland, in 1864, after a severe storm, measured more than 180 ft in length, making it easily the longest recorded worm of any variety.

15. JELLYFISHES AND CORALS (*CNIDARIA*)

Largest and Smallest

The largest jellyfish is the Arctic giant jellyfish (*Cyanea capillata arctica*) of the northwestern Atlantic. One specimen washed up in Massachusetts Bay had a bell diameter of 7 ft 6 in and tentacles stretching 120 ft.

Some true jellyfishes have a bell diameter of less than 0.78 of an inch.

Most Venomous

The most venomous cnidarian is the Australian sea wasp (*Chironex fleckerei*), which carries a cardiotoxic venom similar in strength to that found in the Asiatic cobra. These box jellyfish have caused the deaths of at least 66 people off the coast of Queensland, Australia since 1880. Victims die within 1–3 min if medical aid is not available. A most effective defense is wearing ladies' panty hose, outsize versions of which are now worn by Queensland life savers at surf carnivals.

Coral

The world's greatest stony coral structure is the Great Barrier Reef off Queensland, northeast Australia. It stretches 1,260 miles and covers 80,-000 sq mi. The largest reported discrete coral growth is a stony colony of *Galaxea fascicularis* found in Sakiyama Bay off Irimote Island, Okinawa on Aug 7, 1982 by Dr. Shohei Shirai. It measured more than 52½ ft overall.

16. SPONGES (*PORIFERA*)

Largest and Smallest

The largest sponge is the barrel-shaped loggerhead sponge (*Spheciospongia vesparium*), found off the islands of the West Indies and off Fla. Single individuals measure up to 3½ ft high and 3 ft in diameter. Neptune's cup or goblet (*Poterion patera*) of Indonesia grows up to 4 ft in height, but it is a less bulky animal. In 1909, a wool sponge (*Hippospongia canaliculatta*) measuring 6 ft in circumference was collected off the Bahama Islands. When first taken from the water it weighed between 80 and 90 lb, but after it had been dried and relieved of all excrescences it scaled 12 lb. (This sponge is now preserved in the US National Museum, Washington, DC.)

The smallest known sponge is the widely distributed *Leucosolenia blanca,* which measures 0.11 in in height when fully grown.

Deepest Sponges

Sponges have been taken from depths of up to 18,500 ft.

---

17. EXTINCT ANIMALS

In this and future editions, only new discoveries of extinct animals and pictures of them will be published. For a complete section on this subject, see the *1984 Guinness Book of World Records* (Sterling edition).

Dinosaur Deaths

Fossil evidence suggests that dinosaur extinction in western America was a gradual (not sudden) process that began 7 million years before the end of the Cretaceous era. It was not due to the impact of a meteorite 65 million years ago, according to a report from paleontologists from the Univ of Minn writing in *Science,* May 2, 1986.

Longest Dinosaur

A huge diplodocid scapula-coracoid bone measuring 8 ft 10 in in length was found in the Dry Mesa Quarry in western Colorado in 1979. This presupposes a diplodicus from the Middle to Late Jurassic (135–160 million years ago) with an overall length of 147–164 ft and a weight of about 56 tons. It was dubbed the "ultrasaurus." The remains of an Ultrasaurus-type brachiosaurid of comparable size has since been discovered in Korea. Rebbachisaurus with a back vertebrae measuring up to 5 ft from Morocco and Tunisia was probably equally large.

The largest marine reptile, a short-necked pliosaur, may have been 46 ft long, judging by a mandible of 9 ft 10 in found in Oxfordshire, Eng.

Fastest Dinosaurs

Trackways can be used to estimate dinosaur speeds, and one from the Lower Cretaceous of Texas discovered in 1981 indicated that a carnivorous dinosaur had been moving at 25 mph. Some of the Ornithomimids (ostrich dinosaurs) were even faster, and the 220-lb *Dromiceiomimus* could probably outsprint an ostrich, which has a top speed of 45 mph.

Smallest Dinosaurs

The smallest dinosaurs so far recorded are the chicken-sized *Compsognathus* ("pretty jaw") of southern W Germany and southeast France, and an undescribed plant-eating fabrosaurid from Colorado, both of which measured 29.5 in from the snout to the tip of the tail.

Earliest Reptile

A 15-in-long insectivore from south central Kentucky, discovered in 1972, was confirmed on Oct 22, 1984 as dating from 310 million years ago.

PLANT KINGDOM (*PLANTAE*)

The medicinal value of plants was known to Neanderthal man *c.* 60,000 BC. The world's oldest garden has yet to be identified but is probably that of a Chinese temple. The world's oldest Botanical Garden is that at Pisa dating from 1543.

Oldest Living Things

"King Clone," the oldest known clone of the creosote plant (*Larria tridentata*) found in southwestern Calif, was estimated in Feb 1980 by Prof Frank C. Vasek to be 11,700 years old.

It is possible that crustose lichens in excess of 19.6 in in diameter may be as old. In 1981 it was estimated that Antarctic lichens of more than 3.9 in in diameter are at least 10,000 years old. The oldest known pot-plant is the succulent *Fockea crispa* potted by Baron Jacquin (1728–1817) at the Schönbrunn gardens, Vienna *c.* 1801.

Largest Blossoming Plant

The largest blossoming plant is the giant Chinese wisteria at Sierra Madre, Calif. It was planted in 1892 and now has branches 500 ft long. It covers nearly an acre, weighs 252 tons and has an estimated 1,500,000 blossoms during its blossoming period of five weeks, when up to 30,000 people pay admission to visit.

Rarest Plants

Plants thought to be extinct are rediscovered each year and there are thus many plants of which specimens are known in but a single locality. The small pink blossoms of *Presidio manzanita* survive in a single specimen reported in June 1978 at an undisclosed site in Calif.

Pennantia baylisiana, a tree found in 1945 on Three Kings Island, off New Zealand, only exists as a female and cannot fruit. In May 1983, it was reported that there was a sole surviving specimen of the lady's slipper orchid (*Cypripedium calceolus*).

Earliest Flower

The oldest fossil of a flowering plant with palm-like imprints was found in Colorado in 1953 and dated about 65 million years old.

Herbs

Herbs are not botanically defined, but consist of plants whose leaves or roots are of culinary or medicinal value. The most heavily consumed is coriander (*Coriandrum sativum*). It is used in curry powder, confectionery, in bread and in gin.

Largest Inflorescence

The largest known inflorescence is that of *Puya raimondii,* a rare Bolivian plant with an erect panicle (diameter 8 ft) which emerges to a height of 35 ft. Each of these bears up to 8,000 white blooms. In 1974 the flower-spike of an agave in Berkeley, Calif was measured to be 52 ft long. (See also *Slowest-Flowering Plant.*)

FRUITS & VEGETABLES

Most and Least Nutritive Fruits. An analysis of the 38 commonly eaten raw (as opposed to dried) fruits shows that the one with the highest calorific value is the avocado (*Persea americana*) with 741 calories per edible lb. That with the lowest value is cucumber with 73 calories per lb. Avocados probably originated in Central and South America and also contain vitamins A, C, and E and 2.2% protein.

Apple. An apple weighing 3 lb 1 oz was reported by V. Loveridge of Ross-on-Wye, England in 1965. Mr & Mrs Harold Spitler of Arcanum, O, grew 2 Stark apples 17½ in in circumference in 1985.

Beet. A 22-lb-4-oz red beet, 34⅛ in around, was grown by Howard Trivelpiece of Yreka, Calif. A sugar beet weighing 45½ lb was grown in 1974 by Robert Meyer of Brawley, Calif.

Broccoli. A head of broccoli weighing 28 lb 14¾ oz was grown in 1964 by J. T. Cooke of Huntington, W Sussex, England.

Cabbage. In 1865 William Collingwood of The Stalwell, County Durham, England, grew a red cabbage with a circumference of 259 in. It reputedly weighed 123 lb.

Carrot. A carrot weighing 15 lb 7 oz was grown by Miss I. G. Scott of Nelson, NZ, in Oct 1978.

Cauliflower. A record cauliflower weighing 52 lb 11½ oz was also grown by Mr Cooke (see *Broccoli*) in 1966.

Celery. A 35-lb bunch was reported grown by C. Bowcock of Willaston, England in 1973.

Collard. A 35-ft-tall, 59¼-in-wide collard was grown by Bobby Rackley of Rocky Mount, NC, in 1980.

Cucumber. Mrs. Eileen Chappel grew a 37-lb-4-oz monster indoors at Nudgee, Queensland, Australia in the 6 months before it was weighed on Apr 29, 1985.

Eggplant. A 5-lb-5.4-oz eggplant was reported grown in Sept 1984 by brothers John and Jim Charles in Summerville, SC.

Garlic. In 1985, Robert Kirkpatrick of Eureka, Calif, grew an elephant garlic 18½ in in circumference, weighing 2 lb 12 oz.

Gourd. A record gourd of the zucca type measuring 91 in in length was grown in 1984 by Armando D'Amario of Downsview, Ont, Canada. It weighed "about" 38 lb. A gourd weighing 196 lb was reported from J. Leathes of Herringfleet Hall, Suffolk, England in 1846.

Grapefruit. A 6-lb-8½-oz grapefruit was weighed for Joshua and Allison Sosnow in Tucson, Ariz on Dec 21, 1984.

Kohlrabi. A kohlrabi weighing 36 lb was grown in 1979 by Emil Krejci of Mt Clemens, Mich.

Lemon. Mrs D. G. Knutzen of Whittier, Calif, reported in May 1984 a lemon with a circumference of 29½ in, weighing 8½ lb.

LARGEST VEGETABLES: (Below left) Charles Wilber of Crane Hill, Ala has trouble reaching the top of his 4 tomato hybrid plants which produced 1,368 lb of fruit. (*Joyce M. Rodgers*) (Above left) Norman Gallagher of Chelan, Wash, set the pumpkin-growing community on its heels when he grew this 612-lb pumpkin in 1984. (Below right) Mrs. Eileen Chappel of Queensland, Australia, hugs her baby cucumber, all 37¼ lbs. (*Brisbane Telegraph*) (Above right) June Rutherford of Hatch, NM, grew this 13½-in-long prize pepper.

Lettuce. A head of 25 lb was grown by C. Bowcock of Willaston, England in 1974.

Lima Bean. One bean pod measuring 14 in in length was grown by Norma McCoy of Hubert, NC, in 1979.

Melons. A watermelon weighing 260 lb was reported by Grace's Gardens in Sept 1985. The grower was Jason Bright of Hope, Ark. The largest cantaloupe reported was one of 55 lb grown by Gene Daughtridge of Rocky Mount, NC, in 1982.

Mushrooms. See *Fungi,* p. 114.

Okra Stalk. An okra plant 17 ft 6¼ in tall was grown by Charles H. Wilber of Crane Hill, Ala in 1983.

Onion. An onion weighing 7 lb 8 oz was grown by Nelson W. Hope of Cardiff, Calif in 1965. It had a girth of 26 in and was reputedly 8 lb when first picked. An onion of 7 lb 11¾ oz was grown by W. Rodger of Fife, Scotland in 1984.

Orange. The heaviest orange is one weighing 5 lb 8 oz exhibited in Nelspruit, South Africa on June 19, 1981. It was the size of a human head, but was stolen.

Parsnip. A parsnip 60 in long was reported by M. Zaninovich of Waneroo, Western Australia. The heaviest was 10 lb 8½ oz grown by C. Moore of Peacehaven, W. Sussex, England in 1980.

Peanut. Ed Weeks of Tarboro, NC, grew a peanut 3½ in long in 1978.

Pear. A pear weighing 3.09 lb was harvested on May 10, 1979 by K. and R. Yeomans, Armidale, NSW, Australia.

Pepper. A NuMex Big Jim pepper 13½ in long was grown by June Rutherford of Hatch, NM, in 1975. A sweet pepper plant owned by Ralph Savarese of Pascagoula, Miss grew to be 56 in tall, yielding 53 peppers, in 1978.

Pineapple. A pineapple weighing 17½ lb was harvested by Dole Philippines, Inc, at South Cotabato, Philippines, in Nov 1984.

Potato. A potato weighing 18 lb 4 oz was reported dug up by Thomas Seddal in his garden in Chester, England, on Feb 17, 1795. A yield was reported of 515 lb from a 2½-lb parent seed by C. Bowcock of Willaston, England, planted in 1977.

Pumpkin. The largest, grown by Norman Gallagher of Chelan, Wash, in 1984 weighed 612 lb and measured 135 in in girth.

Radish. A radish of 27 lb, 27½ in long, was grown by Ron Whitford in Wollongong, Australia, in Nov 1985.

Squash. A squash weighing 513 lb was grown by Harold Fulp, Jr., at Nineveh, Ind, in 1977.

Strawberry. A single berry weighing 8.17 oz was grown in July 1983 by George Anderson of Folkestone, England.

Sweet Potato. A 40¾ lb sweet potato was produced by Ovid Harrison, Kite, Ga on Oct 18, 1982.

Tomato. A 6-lb-8-oz tomato was grown by Clarence Dailey of Monona, Wis, in Aug 1976. The longest tomato plant is 52 ft, grown by Gordon Graham of Edmond, Okla, in 1984.

The greatest weight was 342 lb

LARGEST APPLES (left): Two of these Stark apples (bigger than a teacup) are 17½ in in circumference. They were grown in 1985 by Mr & Mrs Harold Spitler of Arcanum, O.

FRUIT VINE (right): Record bunch of grapes weighing 20 lb 11½ oz grown by Bozzolo y Perut in Santiago, Chile, in 1984.

WHO GREW THIS MONSTER WATERMELON? (below): The boy on the far left did. He is Jason Bright of Hope, Ark. His father, grandfather and little brother are proudly helping him get the weight accurate—260 lb.

PRIZE PEANUT (above): Ed Weeks shows off the 3½-in-long legume he grew in Tarboro, NC.

2 oz on a tomato hybrid plant grown by Charles H. Wilber of Crane Hill, Ala, in 1985, in a group of 4 plants whose fruit totaled 1,368 lb.

Turnip. A turnip weighing 73 lb was reported in Dec 1768. In modern times the record is 35 lb 4 oz for a turnip grown by C. W. Butler of Nafferton, Humberside, England. A turnip of 51 lb was reported from Alaska in 1981.

Zucchini. A zucchini that weighed 36 lb 3 oz and was 29½ in long was grown by M. M. Ricci of Montreal, Canada in 1982. A "zucca" gourd weighing "about" 38 lb was reported.

GARDEN FLOWERS & PLANTS

Aspidistra. The aspidistra (*Aspidistra elatior*) was introduced as a parlor palm to Britain from Japan and China in 1822. The biggest in the world (*pace* Gracie Fields) is uncertain but Cliff Evans of Kiora, Moruya, NSW, Australia had his measured in Apr 1983 to be 56 in tall.

Begonia. A begonia plant 3 ft 8 in tall was grown by Ellen Cassidy of Richmond, British Columbia, Canada in 1979.

Cactus. The largest of all cacti is the saguaro (*Cereus giganteus* or *Carnegiea gigantea*), found in Ariz, southeastern Calif, and Sonora, Mexico. The green fluted column is surmounted by candelabra-like branches rising to a height of 52 ft 6 in in the case of a specimen measured on the boundary of the Saguaro National Monument, Ariz. They have waxy white blooms which are followed by edible crimson fruit. An armless cactus 78 ft in height was measured in 1978 by Hube Yates in Cave Creek, Ariz.

Fourteen-Leafed Clover. A fourteen-leafed white clover (*Trifolium repens*) grown on one petiole was found by Randy Farland near Sioux Falls, SD, June 16, 1975.

Dahlia. A 16-ft-5-in dahlia was grown by Sam and Pat Barnes of Chattahoochee, Fla, in 1982.

Gladiolus. A gladiolus 8 ft 4½ in high was grown in 1981 by A. Breed of Melrose, Scotland.

Hollyhock. The tallest reported hollyhock (*Althaea rosea*) is one of 24 ft 3 in grown by W. P. Walshe of Eastbourne, E. Sussex, England in 1961.

Petunia. A petunia plant 13 ft 8 in tall was grown by Bert Lawrence of Windham, NY over a 2-year period, 1984–85, indoors in winter and outdoors in summer.

Philodendron. A philodendron 1,114 ft long, and 31 years old, was grown by Prof F. J. Francis of the Univ of Mass. It was dismembered in Dec 1984.

Rhododendron. The largest species of rhododendron is the scarlet *Rhododendron arboreum*, examples of which reach a height of 65 ft on Mt Japfu, Nagaland, India. The cross section of the trunk of a *Rhododendron giganteum*, from Yunnan, China, reputedly 90 ft high, is preserved at Inverewe Garden, Highland, Scotland.

LARGEST ROSE TREE (above): This single "Lady Banks" tree at Tombstone, Ariz, has a trunk 40 in thick and is so big that 150 people can sit under its arbor. LARGEST BLOOM (below right): The stinking corpse lily has a bloom 3 ft across and weighs up to 15 lb. Mottled orange-brown and white, these parasitic plants of southeast Asia attach themselves to vines of the jungle. They got their name from really smelling that way.

SMALLEST PLANT: It takes 5,000 of these "Wolffia"-type flowering plants to fill a thimble. (*Wayne P. Armstrong*)

Rose Tree. A "Lady Banks" rose tree at Tombstone, Ariz, has a trunk 40 in thick, stands 9 ft high and covers an area of 5,380 sq ft, supported by 68 posts and several thousand feet of iron piping. This enables 150 people to be seated under the arbor. The original cutting came from Scotland in 1884.

Sunflower. The record height of 24 ft 2½ in was reached by a sun-flower grown by Marten Heijms of The Netherlands in 1983.

Weeds. The most intransigent weed is the mat-forming water weed *Salvinia auriculata,* found in Africa. It was detected on the filling of Kariba Lake, in May 1959 and within 11 months had choked an area of 77 sq mi, rising by 1963 to 387 sq mi. The worst land weeds are regarded as purple nut sedge, Bermuda grass,

Garden Flowers & Plants ▪ 105

barnyard grass, jungle rice, goose grass, Johnson grass, Guinea grass, cogon grass and lantana.

Hedges. The tallest hedge is the Meikleour beech hedge in Perthshire, Scotland. It was planted in 1746 and has now attained a trimmed height of 85 ft. It is 600 yd long, and some of its trees now exceed 120 ft.

Vines. The largest recorded grape vine was one planted in 1842 at Carpinteria, Calif. By 1900 it was yielding more than 9 tons of grapes in some years, and averaging 7 tons per year. It died in 1920.

A single bunch of grapes (red Thomson seedless) weighing 20 lb 11½ oz was weighed in Santiago, Chile, in May 1984.

Largest Blooms

The mottled orange-brown and white parasitic stinking corpse lily (*Rafflesia arnoldi*) has the largest of all blooms. These attach themselves to the cissus vines of the jungle in southeast Asia. They measure up to 3 ft across and ¾ in thick, and attain a weight of 15 lb.

The spathe and spadix of the less massive green and purple flower of *Amorphophallies titanum* of Sumatra may attain a length of 5 ft.

Most Valuable Flower

The $10,000 prize offered by the Burpee Co. in 1954 for producing the first all-white marigold was won on Aug 12, 1975 by Alice Vonk of Sully, Iowa.

Plants at Highest Altitude

The greatest certain altitude at which any flowering plants have been found is 21,000 ft on Kamet (25,447 ft), India, by N. D. Jayal in 1955. They were *Ermania himalayensis* and *Ranunculus lobatus*.

Champion Plant Collector

Dr Julian A. Steyermark of the Herbario Nacional, Caracas, Venezuela had, by Sept 1985, made an unrivalled total of 137,000 collections, of which 132,000 were solo.

Fastest Growth

The case of a *Hesperogucca whipplei* of the family Liliaceae growing 12 ft in 14 days was reported from Treco Abbey, Isles of Scilly, England, in July 1978.

Deepest and Densest Roots

The greatest reported depth to which roots have penetrated is a calculated 400 ft in the case of a wild fig tree at Echo Caves, near Ohrigstad, East Transvaal, South Africa. A single winter rye plant (*Secale cereale*) has been shown to produce 387 miles of roots in 1.83 cu ft of earth.

Most Spreading Plant

The greatest area covered by a single clonal growth is that of the wild box huckleberry (*Gaylussacia brachyera*), a mat-forming evergreen shrub first reported in 1796. A colony covering 8 acres was discovered in 1845 near New Bloomfield, Pa. Another colony, covering about 100 acres, was "discovered" on July 18, 1920, near the Juniata River in Pa. It has been estimated that this colony began 13,000 years ago.

BIGGEST WREATH: 68 ft 4 in in diameter is the record.

Smallest Plants

The smallest flowering plant is the floating aquatic duckweed *Wolffia angusta* which is only 1/42nd of an inch in length and 1/85th of an inch in width. It weighs 1/190th of an oz; its fruit, resembling a minuscule fig, weighs 400,000 to the oz.

The smallest "plant" is a unicellular alga and is classified under *Protista*.

Slowest-Flowering Plant

The slowest-flowering of all plants is the rare *Puya raimondii,* the largest of all herbs, discovered in Bolivia in 1870. The panicle emerges after about 150 years of the plant's life. It then dies. (See also above under *Largest Inflorescence.*)

Some agaves, erroneously called century plants, first flower after 40 years.

Largest Leaves

The largest leaves of any plant belong to the raffia palm (*Raphia ruffia*) of the Mascarene Islands in the Indian Ocean, and the Amazonian bamboo palm (*R. toedigera*) of South America, whose leaf blades may measure up to 65 ft in length with petioles up to 13 ft.

The largest undivided leaf is that of *Alocasia macrorrhiza,* found in Sabah, East Malaysia. One found in 1966 measured 9 ft 11 in long and 6 ft 3½ in wide, and had an area of 34.2 sq ft on one side.

Seaweed

Claims made that seaweed off Tierra del Fuego, South America, grows to 600 and even 1,000 ft in length have gained currency. More recent and more reliable records indicate that the longest species of seaweed is the Pacific giant kelp (*Macrocystis pyrifera*), which does not exceed 196 ft in length. It can grow 18 in in a day.

The greatest depth at which plant life has been found is 884 ft by Mark and Diane Littler (US) off San Salvador Island, Bahamas, in Oct 1984. These maroon-colored algae survived though 99.9995% of sunlight was filtered out.

Wreath

The largest wreath was constructed on Sept 4, 1982 by The Gothenburg Florists at Liseberg Amusement Park, Sweden, measuring 68 ft 4 in in diameter. It weighed 4,368 lb.

TREES

Oldest Tree

The oldest recorded tree was a bristlecone pine (*Pinus longaeva*) designated WPN-114, which grew at 10,750 ft above sea level on the northeast face of Mt Wheeler in eastern Nevada. During studies in 1963 and 1964 it was found to be about 5,100 years old, but was cut down with a chain saw. The oldest known *living* tree is the bristlecone pine named *Methuselah* at 10,000 ft on the Calif side of the White Mts, with a confirmed age of 4,600 years. In March 1974 it was reported that this tree produced 48 live seedlings. Dendrochronologists estimate the *potential* life span of a bristlecone pine at nearly 5,500 years, but that of a "big tree" (*Sequoiadendron giganteum*) at perhaps 6,000 years. No single cell lives more than 30 years. A report in March 1976 stated that some enormous specimens of Japanese cedar (*Cryptomeria japonica*) had been dated by carbon-14 to 5200 BC.

Largest Forest

The largest afforested areas are the vast coniferous forests of the northern USSR, lying mainly between latitude 55°N. and the Arctic Circle. The total wooded areas amount to 2,700 million acres (25% of the world's forests), of which 38% is Siberian larch. The USSR is 34% afforested.

Earliest Species of Tree

The earliest species of tree still surviving is the maidenhair tree (*Ginkgo biloba*) of Chekiang, China, which first appeared about 160 million years ago, during the Jurassic era. It was "re-discovered" by Kaempfer (Netherlands) in 1690, and reached England *c.* 1754. It has been grown in Japan since *c.* 1100 where it was known as *ginkyo* (silver apricot) and now called *icho*.

Fastest-Growing Tree

Discounting bamboo, which is not botanically classified as a tree, but as woody grass, the fastest rate of growth recorded is 35 ft 3 in in 13 months by an *Albizzia falcata* planted on June 17, 1974, in Sabah, Malaysia. The youngest recorded age for a tree to reach 100 ft is 64 months for one of the species planted on Feb 24, 1975, also in Sabah.

Most Massive Tree

The most massive living thing on earth is a giant sequoia "big tree"

MOST MASSIVE LIVING THING (above): The "General Sherman" tree, a giant sequoia in Calif, stands almost 275 ft tall. It has a girth of 114.6 ft, and has grown for 2,500 years at the slow rate of 1/125th of an inch per year. (*National Park Service*)

MOST ORNATE CHRISTMAS TREE (right): The "National Enquirer" in Lantana, Fla, in 1984 erected this 126-ft-tall fir and put on it 15,100 lights, ½ mile of garland, 1,050 colored balls, 250 snowflakes, 225 red bows, and on top a 6-ft-high illuminated silver star.

THIRTY CHILDREN holding hands just about cover half the girth of the Mexican Tule tree's 117.6-ft circumference. This Montezuma cypress is 135 ft tall.

(*Sequoiadendron giganteum*) named the "General Sherman," standing 274.9 ft tall, in Sequoia National Park, Calif. It has a true girth of 114.6 ft (at 5 ft above the ground). The "General Sherman" has been estimated to contain the equivalent of 600,120 board ft of timber, sufficient to make 5,000 million matches. The foliage is blue-green, and the reddish brown bark may be up to 24 in thick in parts. Estimates (1981) place its weight, including its root system, at 6,720 tons, but the lumber is light (18 lb per cu ft) and a 1985 estimate suggests a weight nearer 2,800 tons. The largest known petrified tree is one of this species with a 295-ft trunk near Coaldale, Nev.

The seed of a "big tree" (sequoia) weighs only 1/6,000th oz. Its growth to maturity may therefore represent an increase in weight of 1,300,000 millionfold.

The tree canopy covering the greatest area is the great banyan *Ficus benghalensis* in the Indian Botanical Garden, Calcutta with 1,775 prop or supporting roots and a circumference of 1,350 ft. It covers overall some 3 acres and dates from before 1787.

Tallest Trees

The tallest known species of tree is the coast redwood (*Sequoia sempervirens*), growing indigenously near the coast of Calif north of Monterey to the Oregon border.

The tallest tree ever measured was a Douglas fir (*Pseudotsuga menziesii*) in Lynn Valley, Brit Columbia, Canada, which in 1902 stood 415 ft tall, according to researches by Dr. A. C. Carder (Canada). The closest measured rivals were:

393 ft—mineral Douglas fir, Wash State, 1905
380 ft—Nisqually fir, Wash State, 1899
375 ft—Cornthwaite mountain ash, Thorpdale, Victoria, Australia, 1880.
367.8 ft—"Tallest Tree" (sequoia) Redwood Creek, Humboldt County, Calif, 1963 (tallest living, crown dying)
367.6 ft—Coast redwood (sequoia), Guerneville, Calif, 1873.

William Ferguson, Inspector of Victoria (Australia) State Forests, reported in Feb 1872 a fallen mountain ash (*Eucalyptus regnans*) 18 ft in diameter at 5 ft above ground level and 435 ft in height.

Trees of Greatest Girth

El Arbol del Tule tree, in the state of Oaxaca, in Mexico, is a 135-ft-tall Montezuma cypress (*Taxodium mucronatum*) with a girth of 117.6 ft at a height of 5 ft above the ground. A figure of 167 ft in circumference was reported for the pollarded European chestnut (*Castanea sativa*) known as the "Tree of the 100 Horses" on the edge of Mt Etna, Sicily, Italy, in 1972 and measurements up to 180 ft have been attributed to baobab trees (*Adansonia digitata*).

Slowest-Growing Trees

The speed of growth of trees depends largely upon conditions, although some species, such as box and yew, are always slow-growing. The extreme is represented by a specimen of Sitka spruce which required 98 years to grow to 11 in tall, with a diameter of less than 1 in, on the Arctic tree-line. The growing of miniature trees or *bonsai* is an Oriental cult mentioned as early as c. 1320.

Tallest Christmas Tree

The tallest cut Christmas tree was a 221-ft Douglas fir erected at Northgate Shopping Center, Seattle, Wash, in Dec 1950.

Most Decorated Christmas Tree

A 126-ft tall Douglas fir erected in Lantana, Fla by the *National Enquirer* in Dec 1984 was decorated with 15,100 lights, ½ mile of garland, 1,050 colored balls, 250 snowflakes, 225 red bows and on top it supported a 6-ft-high illuminated silver star.

Remotest Tree

The tree most distant from any other is believed to be one at an oasis in the Ténéré Desert, Niger Republic. There were no other trees within 31 miles. In Feb 1960 it survived being rammed by a truck being backed up by a French driver. The tree was transplanted and is now in the Museum of Niamey, Niger.

Most Expensive Tree

The highest price ever paid for a tree is $51,000 for a single Starkspur golden delicious apple tree from near Yakima, Wash, bought by a nursery in Missouri in 1959.

Forest Fire

What may be the largest forest fire on record burned 13,500 sq mi in East Kalimantan, the Indonesian part of Borneo, continuing from Feb to June, 1983. The area is bigger than the states of Mass and Conn together.

Heaviest and Lightest Woods

The heaviest of all woods is black ironwood (*Olea laurifolia*), also called South African ironwood, with a specific gravity of up to 1.49, and weighing up to 93 lb per cu ft.

The lightest wood is *Aeschynomene hispida,* found in Cuba, which has a specific gravity of 0.044 and a weight of only 2¾ lb per cu ft. The wood

FASTEST GROWING: Bamboo, botanically a woody grass and not a tree, can reach 100 ft in height in less than 3 months. These are in Hawaii. (*Photo by Alex Hansen*)

of the balsa tree (*Ochroma pyramidale*) is of very variable density—between 2½ and 24 lb per cu ft. The density of cork is 15 lb per cu ft.

Seeds

The largest seed is that of the double coconut or Coco de Mer (*Lodoicea seychellarum*), the single-seeded fruit of which may weigh 40 lb. This grows only in the Seychelles Islands in the Indian Ocean. The smallest seeds are those of *epiphytic* orchids, at 35 million to the oz (*cf.* grass pollens at up to 6,000 million grains per oz). A single plant of the American ragweed can generate 8,000 million pollen grains in 5 hours.

The most protracted claim for the viability of seeds is that made for the Arctic lupin (*Lupinus arcticus*) found in frozen silt at Miller Creek in the Yukon, Canada, in July 1954 by Harold Schmidt. The seeds were germinated in 1966 and dated by the radio-carbon method of associated material to at least 8,000 BC and more probably to 13,000 BC.

Largest Orchids

The largest of all orchids is *Grammatophyllum speciosum,* native to Malaysia. Specimens up to 25 ft high have been recorded. The largest orchid flower is that of *Phragmipedium caudatum,* found in tropical areas of America. Its petals grow up to 18 in long, giving it a maximum outstretched diameter of 3 ft. The flower is, however, much less bulky than that of the stinking corpse lily (see *Largest Blooms*).

Tallest and Smallest Orchids

The tallest free-standing orchid is *Grammatophyllum speciosum* (see above). *Galeola foliata* may attain 49 ft on decaying rainforest trees in Queensland, Australia. The smallest orchid is *Platystele jungermannoides,* found in Central America. Its flowers are 0.04 in across.

Highest-Priced Orchid

The highest price ever paid for an orchid is £1,207.50 (then $6,000), paid by Baron Schröder to Sanders of St Albans for an *Odontoglossum crispum* (variety *pittianum*) at an auction by Protheroe & Morris of Bow Lane, London, England, on March 22, 1906. A cymbidium orchid called "Rosanna Pinkie" was sold in the US for $4,500 in 1952.

Tallest and Fastest-Growing Bamboo

The tallest recorded bamboo was a thorny bamboo culm (*Bambusa arundinacea*) felled at Pattazhi, Travancore, India, in Nov 1904, which measured 121½ ft. Some species of the 45 genera of bamboo have attained growth rates of up to 36 in per day (0.00002 mph), on their way to reaching a height of 100 ft in less than 3 months.

Largest and Smallest Ferns

The largest of all the more than 6,000 species of fern is the tree-fern (*Alsophila excelsa*) of Norfolk Island, in the South Pacific, which attains a height of up to 60 ft. The smallest are *Hecistopteris pumila,* found in Central America, and *Azolla caroliniana,* which is native to the US and has fronds as small as ½ in.

Grasses

The world's commonest grass is *Cynodon ductylon* or Bermuda grass. The "Callie" hybrid, selected in 1966, grows as much as 6 in a day and stolons reach 18 ft in length.

Mosses

The smallest of mosses is the pygmy moss (*Ephemerum*), and the longest is the brook moss (*Fontinalis*), which forms streamers up to 3 ft long in flowing water.

KINGDOM PROTISTA

Protista were first discovered in 1676 by Anton van Leeuwenhoek (1632–1723), a Dutch microscopist. Among Protista are characteristics common to both plants and animals. The more plant-like are termed Protophyta (protophytes), including unicellular algae, and the more animal-like are placed in the phylum Protozoa (protozoans) which includes amoebas and flagellates.

The largest protozoans, in terms of volume, which are known to have existed were calcareous foraminifera (Foraminiferida) belonging to the genus *Nummulites,* a species of which, in the Middle Eocene rocks of Turkey, attained 8.6 in in diameter. The largest existing protozoan, a species of the fan-shaped *Stannophyllum* (Xenophyophorida), can exceed this in length (9.8 in has been recorded) but not in volume.

The smallest of all protophytes is the marine microflagellate alga *Micromonas pusilla,* with a diameter of less than 2 microns or 0.00008 in.

The protozoan *Monas stigmatica* has been measured to move a distance equivalent to 40 times its own length in a sec. No human can cover even seven times his own length in a sec.

The protozoan *Glaucoma,* which reproduces by binary fission, divides as frequently as every 3 hours. Thus in the course of a day it could become a "six greats grandparent" and the progenitor of 510 descendants.

KINGDOM FUNGI

Fungi were once classified in the subkingdom Protophyta of the kingdom Protista.

Martin Mortenson, a science teacher at Dodgeland Jr High, Reeseville, Wis, found a puff ball (*Calvatia gigantea*) 76½ in in circumference in 1985.

A 72-lb example of the edible mushroom *Polyporus frondosus* was reported by Joseph Opple near Solon, Ohio, in Sept 1976. A mushroom of "nearly 100 lb" and 20 in in circumference was reported Oct 3, 1985 from Potenza, Italy.

The largest officially recorded tree fungus was a specimen of *Oxyporus* (*Fomes*) *nobilissimus,* measuring 56 in by 37 in and weighing at least 300 lb found by J. Hisey in Wash State in 1946.

Most Poisonous Toadstool

The yellowish-olive death cup (*Amanita phalloides*) is regarded as the world's most poisonous fungus. From 6 to 15 hours after tasting, the effects are vomiting, delirium, collapse and death. Among its victims was Cardinal Giulio de' Medici, Pope Clement VII (1478–1534).

KINGDOM PROCARYOTA

Earliest Life Form

In June 1980 Prof J. William Schopf announced the discovery of thread-like cellular remnants built by blue-green algae or bacteria-like organisms in calcareous stromatolites dated to 3,500 million years old in the "North Pole" region of northern W Australia.

Largest and Smallest Bacteria

Anton van Leeuwenhoek (1632–1723) was the first to observe bacteria, in 1675. The largest of the bacteria is the sulphur bacterium *Beggiatoa mirabilis,* which is from 16 to 45 microns in width and which may form filaments several millimeters long.

The smallest of all free-living organisms are the pleuro-pneumonia-like organisms (PPLO) of the *Mycoplasma.* One of these, *Mycoplasma laidlawii,* first discovered in sewage in 1936, has a diameter during the early part of its life of only 100 millimicrons, or 0.000004 in. Examples of the strain known as H.39 have a maximum diameter of 300 millimicrons and weigh an estimated 1.0×10^{-16} of a gram. Thus, a blue whale at 177 tons would weigh 1.77×10^{24} times as much.

Fastest Bacteria

The rod-shaped bacillus *Bdellovibrio bacteriovoras,* by means of a polar flagellum rotating 100 times/sec, can move 50 times its own length of 2 μm per second. This would be the equivalent of a human sprinter reaching 200 mph or a swimmer crossing the Channel in 6 min.

Highest Bacteria

In Apr 1967 the US National Aeronautics and Space Administration (NASA) reported that bacteria had been discovered at an altitude of 135,000 ft (25.26 miles).

Longest-Lived Bacteria

The oldest deposits from which living bacteria are claimed to have been extracted are salt layers near Irkutsk, USSR, dating from about 600 million years ago. The discovery was not accepted internationally. The US Dry Valley Drilling Project in Antarctica claimed resuscitated rod-shaped bacteria from caves up to a million years old.

Toughest Bacteria

The bacterium *Micrococcus radiodurans* can withstand atomic radiation of 6,500,000 röntgens or 10,000 times greater than radiation that is fatal to the average man.

In March 1983 John Barras (Univ of Oregon) reported bacteria from sulfurous sea bed vents thriving at 583 °F in the East Pacific rise at Lat 21° N.

Largest and Smallest Viruses

Dmitriy Ivanovsky (1864–1920) first reported filterable objects in 1892, but Martinus Willem Beijerink (1851–1931) first confirmed the nature of viruses in 1898. These are now defined as aggregates of two or more types of chemical (including either DNA or RNA) which are infectious and potentially pathogenic. The longest known is the rod-shaped *Citrus tristezu* virus with particles measuring 200 × 10 nm (1 nanometer = 1×10^{-9}m).

The smallest known viruses are the nucleoprotein plant viruses such as the satellite of tobacco *necrosis virus* with spherical particles 17 nm in diameter. A putative new infectious sub-microscopic organism but without nucleic acid, named a "prion," was announced from the Univ of Calif in Feb 1982.

Viroids (RNA cores without protein coating) are much smaller than viruses. They were discovered by Theodor O. Diener (US) in Feb 1972.

Dr Rohwer of Bethesda, Md, stated in Sept 1984 that scrapie-specific protein was smaller than the concept of a "yet-to-be identified prion."

LARGEST AQUARIUM: On the shores of Monterey Bay, Calif, a new aquarium houses 5,500 specimens of 525 species of marine life from the immediate area. There are several "touch pools" where children can pet and pick up starfish, sea cucumbers, snails and even rays. Seawater for the pools is drawn from the bay at 2,500 gal per min. Besides, there is a walk-through aviary filled with seabirds. (*Kathleen Olson, Monterey Bay Aquarium*) (Below) IN THE TANK at the world's largest aquarium, a diver enters among the smaller fish and vegetation.

PARKS, ZOOS, AQUARIA AND OCEANARIA

Oceanaria

The first oceanarium, opened in 1938, is Marineland of Florida located 18 miles south of St Augustine. Up to 7 million gallons of sea water are pumped daily through two major tanks, one rectangular (100 ft long by 40 ft wide by 18 ft deep) containing 450,000 gallons and one circular (233 ft in circumference and 12 ft deep) containing 400,000 gallons. The tanks are seascaped, including coral reefs and even a shipwreck.

The largest salt water tank is that at Hanna-Barbera's Marineland of the Pacific located on the Palos Verdes Peninsula, Calif. It is 251½ ft in circumference and 22 ft deep, with a capacity of 640,000 gallons. The total capacity of the whole oceanarium is 2,500,000 gallons. Their killer whale "Orky" at 14,000 lb is the largest in captivity.

The earliest known collection of animals (not a public zoo) was that set up by Shulgi, a 3rd dynasty ruler of Ur in 2094–2047 BC at Puzurish in southeast Iraq.

Largest Aquarium

The world's largest aquarium is the $40 million Monterey Bay (Calif) Aquarium opened on Oct 20, 1984, with 83 tanks with a capacity of 716,-000 gallons. Exhibited are 5,500 specimens of 525 species of fauna and flora. The project was funded through a gift from David and Lucile Packard. The highest recorded attendances of any aquarium were 78,658 in a day on May 21, 1931 and 4,689,730 in the single year of 1931 at John G. Shedd Aquarium, 12th St and Lake Shore Drive, Chicago.

FIRST OCEANARIUM, Marineland of Florida, was opened in 1938 in St Augustine, and the leaping dolphins still thrill the crowds. Seven million gallons of sea water flow through the tanks every day.

Largest Park

The largest park is the Wood Buffalo National Park in Alberta, Canada (established 1922), which has an area of 11,172,000 acres (17,560 sq mi).

Largest Game Reserve

It has been estimated that throughout the world there are some 500 zoos with an estimated annual attendance of 330 million. The largest zoological preserve in the world is the Etosha Reserve, Namibia (South-West Africa), with an area which has grown since 1907 to 38,427 sq mi. (It is thus larger than Ireland.)

Oldest Zoo

The oldest known zoo is that at Schönbrunn, Vienna, Austria, built in 1752 by the Holy Roman Emperor Franz I for his wife Maria Theresa. The oldest privately owned zoo in the world is that of the Zoological Society of London, founded in 1826. Its collection is housed partly in Regent's Park, London (36 acres), and partly at Whipsnade Park, Bedfordshire (541 acres, opened 1931). At the stocktaking on Jan 1, 1986, it was found to house 9,797 specimens—2,486 mammals, 2,013 birds, 568 reptiles and amphibians, an estimated 1,430 fish, and an estimated total of 3,300 invertebrates. Locusts, bees and ants are excluded from these figures.

Chapter 3

The Natural World

1. NATURAL PHENOMENA

EARTHQUAKES

It is estimated that each year there are some 500,000 detectable seismic or micro-seismic disturbances of which 100,000 can be felt and 1,000 cause damage. The deepest recorded hypocenters are of 447 miles in Indonesia in 1933, 1934 and 1943. (Note: Seismologists record all earthquake dates with the year first, based *not* on local time but on Greenwich Mean Time.)

Kanamori Scale Magnitudes M_s	Gutenberg-Richter Scale Magnitude M_w	PROGRESSIVE LIST OF STRONGEST INSTRUMENTALLY RECORDED EARTHQUAKES	
8.8	8.6	Colombia coast	1906 Jan 31
(8.6)	8.6	Assam, India	1950 Aug 15
9.0	(8¼)	Kamchatka, USSR	1952 Nov 4
9.1	(8.3)	Andreanol, Aleutian Is., US	1957 Mar 9
9.5	(8.3)	Lebu, Chile	1960 May 22

Where $M_s = \frac{2}{3} (\log_{10} E - 11.8)$
and $M_w = \frac{2}{3} [\log_{10} (2E \times 10^4) - 10.7]$
Where E = energy released in dyne/cm

Worst Death Toll

The greatest loss of life occurred in the earthquake which rocked every city of the Near East and eastern Mediterranean *c.* July 1201. Contemporary accounts estimate the loss of life at 1.1 million. Less uncertain is the figure in the prolonged quake (*ti chen*) in the Shensi, Shansi and Honan provinces of China, of 1556 Feb 2 (New Style) (Jan 23 Old Style), when an estimated 830,000 people were killed. The highest death toll in modern times has been in the Tangshan earthquake (magnitude 8.2) in eastern China on 1976 July 27 (local time was 3:00 a.m. on July 28). A first figure published Jan 4, 1977 revealed 655,237 killed, later adjusted to 750,000. On Nov 22, 1979, the New China News Agency unaccountably reduced the death toll to 242,000. As late as Jan 1982, the site of the city was still a prohibited area. The greatest material damage was in the earthquake on the Kwanto plain, Japan, at 11:58 a.m. of 1923 Sept 1 (magnitude 8.2, epicenter in Latitude 35°15′N., Longitude 139°30′E.). In Sagami Bay, the sea bottom in one area sank 1,310 ft. The official total of persons killed and missing in this earthquake, called the *Shinsai* or Great 'Quake, and the resultant fires was 142,807. In Tokyo and Yokohama 575,000 dwellings were destroyed. The cost of the damage was estimated at $2,800 million. It has however been estimated that a 7.5-magnitude shock (G-R scale) 30 miles north of Los Angeles would result in damage estimated at $75 billion.

VOLCANOES

The total number of known active volcanoes is 850 of which many are submarine. The greatest concentration is in Indonesia, where 77 of its 167 volcanoes have erupted within historic times. The name "volcano" was first applied to the now dormant Vulcano Island in the Aeolian group in the Mediterranean, and that name derives from Vulcan, Roman god of destructive fire.

Highest Volcanoes

The highest extinct volcano in the world is Cerro Aconcagua (Stone Sentinel), 22,834 ft high, on the Argentine side of the Andes. It was first climbed on Jan 14, 1897 by Mathias Zurbriggen, and was the highest mountain climbed anywhere until June 12, 1907.

The highest dormant volcano is Ojos del Salado (22,588 ft). It has a small steaming crater below the summit at about 21,325 ft which makes it the highest active volcano as well. The volcano which has been regarded until now as the highest active is Volcán Antofalla (21,162 ft) in Argentina, though a more definite claim is made for Volcán Guayatiri or Guallatiri (19,918 ft), in Chile, which erupted in 1959, and was still smoking in 1985.

Longest Lava Flow

The longest lava flow, known as *pahoehoe* (twisted cord-like solidifications), is that from the eruption of Laki in southeast Iceland, which flowed 40½–43½ miles. The largest known prehistoric flow is the Roza basalt flow in North America, *c.* 15 million years ago, which had an unsurpassed length (300 miles), area (15,400 sq mi) and volume (300 cu mi).

Largest Crater

The world's largest *caldera* or volcano crater is that of Toba, north-central Sumatra, Indonesia, covering 685 sq mi.

Greatest Eruption

The total volume of matter discharged in the eruption of Tambora, a volcano on the island of Sumbawa, in Indonesia, Apr 5–7, 1815, has been estimated as 36.4 cu mi. The energy of this 1,395-mph eruption, which lowered the height of the island from 13,450 ft to 9,350 ft, was 8.4 × 10^{19} joules. The volcano thus lost 4,100 ft in height and a crater 7 mi in diameter was formed. This compares with a probable 15 cu mi ejected by Santorini and 4.3 cu mi ejected by Krakatoa. The internal pressure causing the Tambora eruption has been estimated at 46,500,000 lb per sq in.

The ejecta in the Taupo eruption in New Zealand c. AD 130 has been estimated at 33,000 million tons of pumice moving at one time at 400 mph. It flattened 6,180 sq mi (over 26 times the devastated area of Mt St Helens). Less than 20% of the 15.4 × 10^9 tons of pumice ejected in this most violent of all documented volcanic events fell within 125 miles of the vent.

LARGEST ACTIVE VOLCANO: On the big island of Hawaii, high up at 13,677 ft, is the peak of Mauna Loa, which erupted as recently as Apr 1984, and at all times its molten lava can be seen. (*Colorific*)

Largest Active Volcano

The world's largest active volcano is Mauna Loa (13,677 ft), Hawaii, which erupted in 1975 and in Apr 1984.

Largest Eruption in US

Mt St Helens, located in the Cascade Range in Wash State, about 50 miles northeast of Portland, Ore, had lain dormant for 123 years when it began to show signs of becoming active and violent in Mar 1980. By early May a bulge about 330 ft high was noticeable, and on May 18 a blast 500 times greater than the 20 kiloton atomic bomb that fell on Hiroshima, broke out the whole north side of the mountain. Lava flowed out at a speed of 250 mph.

Ash and steam caused the sun to be blotted out as far as 85 miles to the east in Yakima, Wash, causing havoc with breathing and tying up car, rail and air traffic in the whole area. The dust became a thick sludge that clogged sewers and chimneys, and did not wash away but stuck to each place it touched. Motorists were stopped in their tracks when ash-clogged air filters caused car engines to stall. (An eyewitness in Coeur D'Alene, Idaho, about 300 mi away, claims that town was also blacked out with an inch of ash.)

Over 100,000 acres of tall fir trees were defoliated and toppled. The eruption was estimated to have contained 96 billion cu ft of matter. It is costing $939 million and will take until 1995 to clean up all the devastation caused by the 1980 Mt St Helens eruption. Meanwhile, seismologists are keeping an eye on the lowered crater of the volcano, and noting that there was still some activity in the magma in 1985.

Greatest Explosion

The greatest explosion (possibly since Santoríni in the Aegean Sea *c.* 1470 BC) occurred *c.* 10:00 a.m. (local time), or 3:00 a.m. G.M.T., on Aug 27, 1883 with an eruption of Krakatoa, an island (then 18 sq mi) in the Sunda Strait between Sumatra and Java, in Indonesia. A total of 163 villages were wiped out, and 36,380 people killed by the wave it caused. Rocks were thrown 34 miles high, and dust fell 10 days later at a distance of 3,313 miles. The explosion was recorded 4 hours later on the island of Rodrigues, 2,968 miles away, as "the roar of heavy guns" and was heard over 1/13th part of the surface of the globe. This explosion has been estimated to have had about 26 times the power of the greatest H-bomb test detonation, but was still only a fifth of the size of the Santoríni cataclysm.

LARGEST ERUPTION IN US HISTORY: This was a forest of green fir trees before the eruption of Mt St Helens in 1980. (*AP Laserphoto*)

GEYSERS

Tallest Geyser

The Waimangu ("black water" in the Maori language) geyser, in New Zealand, erupted to a height in excess of 1,500 ft in 1904, but has not been active since it erupted violently at 6:20 a.m. Apr 1, 1917, killing 4 people.

Currently the world's tallest active geyser is the US National Park Service Steamboat Geyser, in Yellowstone National Park, Wyo, which erupted at intervals ranging from 5 days to 10 months between 1962 and 1969 to a height of 250–380 ft.

The *Geysir* ("gusher") near Mt Hekla in south-central Iceland, from which all others have been named, spurts, on occasion, to 180 ft, while the adjacent Strokkur, reactivated by drilling in 1963, spurts at 10–15 min intervals.

Greatest Geyser Discharge

The greatest measured water discharge from a geyser has been 990,000 gallons by the Giant Geyser in Yellowstone National Park, Wyo, which has been dormant since 1955.

---

2. STRUCTURE AND DIMENSIONS

The earth is not a true sphere, but flattened at the poles and hence an oblate spheroid. The polar diameter of the earth (7,899.806 miles) is 26.575 miles less than the equatorial diameter (7,926.381 miles). The earth has a pear-shaped asymmetry with the north polar radius being 148 ft longer than the south polar radius. There is also a slight ellipticity of the equator since its long axis (about Longitude 37° W.) is 522 ft greater than the short axis. The greatest departures from the reference ellipsoid are a protuberance of 240 ft in the area of Papua New Guinea, and a depression of 344 ft south of Sri Lanka (Ceylon) in the Indian Ocean.

The greatest circumference of the earth—at the equator—is calculated as 24,901.46 miles, compared with 24,859.73 miles at the meridian. The area of the surface is estimated to be 196,937,400 sq mi. The period of axial rotation, *i.e.* the true sidereal day, is 23 hours 56 min 4.0996 sec, mean time.

Earth's Structure

The mass of the earth is 6,585,600,000,000,000,000,000 tons and its density is 5.515 times that of water. The volume is an estimated 259,875,-300,000 cu mi. The earth picks up cosmic dust but estimates vary widely with 30,000 metric tons a day being the upper limit. Modern theory is that the earth has an outer shell or lithosphere 50 miles thick, then an outer and inner rock layer or mantle extending 1,745 miles deep, beneath which there is an iron-rich core of radius measuring 2,164 miles. If the iron-rich core theory is correct, iron would be the most abundant element in the earth. At the center of the core the estimated density is 13.09 g/cm^3; the temperature 4,000–4,500 °C and the pressure 23,600 tons f/sq in.

OCEANS

Largest Ocean

The area of the earth covered by the sea is estimated to be 139,670,000 sq mi, or 70.92% of the total surface. The mean depth of the hydrosphere was at one time estimated to be 12,450 ft, but recent surveys suggest a lower estimate of 11,660 ft. The total weight of the water is estimated as 1.45×10^{18} tons, or 0.022% of the earth's total weight. The volume of the oceans is estimated to be 308,400,000 cu mi, compared with 8,400,000 cu mi of fresh water.

The largest ocean is the Pacific. Excluding adjacent seas, it represents 45.8% of the world's oceans and is 64,186,300 sq mi in area. The average depth is 12,925 ft. From Guayaquil, Ecuador, on the east, to Bangkok, Thailand, on the west, the Pacific could be said to stretch 10,905 miles in the shortest straight navigable line.

Largest Sea

The largest of the seas (as opposed to oceans) is the South China Sea, with an area of 1,148,500 sq mi. The Malayan Sea comprising the waters between the Indian Ocean and the South Pacific, south of the Chinese mainland, covering 3,144,000 sq mi, is not now an entity accepted by the International Hydrographic Bureau.

Deepest Depths in the Ocean

The deepest part of the ocean was first pin-pointed in 1951 by the British Survey Ship *Challenger* in the Marianas Trench in the Pacific Ocean. The depth was measured by sounding and by echo-sounder and published as 5,960 fathoms (35,760 ft). Subsequent visits (1959–1980) to this same Challenger Deep have resulted in slightly deeper measurements, now refined to 5,968 fathoms (35,840 ft) or 6.79 miles made by the Japanese research vessel *Takuyo,* Feb 17–19, 1984 in Lat 11° 22′ 24″ N, Long 142° 35′ 30″ E. On Jan 23, 1960 the US Navy bathyscaphe *Trieste* descended to the bottom, which is 5,940 ft. A metal object, say a pound ball of steel, dropped into water above this trench would take nearly 64 min to fall to the sea bed 6.79 miles below, where hydrostatic pressure is over 18,000 lb per sq in.

Largest Gulf

The largest gulf in the world is the Gulf of Mexico, with an area of 580,000 sq mi and a shoreline of 3,100 miles from Cape Sable, Fla, to Cabo Catoche, Mexico.

Largest Bay

The largest bay measured by shoreline length is Hudson Bay in northern Canada with a shoreline of 7,623 miles and an area of 317,500 sq mi. The area of the Bay of Bengal however is bigger—839,000 sq mi.

Highest Sea-Mountain

The highest known submarine mountain or sea-mountain was one discovered in 1953 near the Tonga Trench between Samoa and New Zealand. It rises 28,500 ft from the sea bed, with its summit 1,200 ft below the surface.

Greatest Tides

The greatest tides in the world occur in the Bay of Fundy, which separates the peninsula of Nova Scotia from Maine and the Canadian province of New Brunswick. Burncoat Head in the Minas Basin, Nova Scotia, has the greatest mean spring range with 47.5 ft. A unique figure of 54½ ft was recorded at springs in 1953 at nearby Leaf Basin.

Tahiti experiences virtually no tide.

Extreme tides are due to lunar and solar gravitational forces affected by their perigee, perihelion, and conjunctions. Barometric and wind effects can superimpose an added "surge" element. Coastal and sea-floor configurations can accentuate these forces.

The normal interval between tides is 12 hours 25 min.

LONGEST FJORD IN LAND OF FJORDS: In Norway, the Sogne Fjord is only 3 mi wide at its widest, but it extends 113.7 mi inland from the sea, through spectacular highlands. The water is as much as 4,085 ft deep.

Longest Fjords

The longest "fjord" is the Nordvest Fjord arm of the Scoresby Sund in eastern Greenland, which extends inland 195 mi from the sea. The longest of Norwegian fjords is the Sogne Fjord, which extends 113.7 mi inland from Sygnefest to the head of the Lusterfjord arm at Skjolden. It averages barely 3 mi in width and has a deepest point of 4,085 ft. If measured from Huglo along the Bømlafjord to the head of the Sørfjord arm at Odda, the Hardangerfjorden can also be said to extend 113.7 mi. The longest Danish fjord is Limfjorden (100 mi long).

Greatest and Strongest Currents

The greatest current in the oceans of the world is the Antarctic Circumpolar Current or West Wind Drift Current, which was measured in 1969 in the Drake Passage between South America and Antarctica, to be flowing at a rate of 9,500 million cu ft per sec—nearly three times that of

NARROWEST STRAIT: The gap is only 45 yd wide between the Greek island of Euboea and the mainland.

the Gulf Stream. Its width ranges from 185 to 1,240 miles and has a proven surface flow rate of 4/10ths of a knot.

The world's strongest currents are the Nakwakto Rapids, Slingsby Channel, British Columbia, Canada (Lat. 51°05′N., Long. 127°30′W.) where the flow rate may reach 16.0 knots (18.4 mph).

Highest Waves

The highest officially recorded sea wave was measured by Lt Frederic Margraff, USN from the USS *Ramapo* proceeding from Manila, Philippines, to San Diego, Calif, on the night of Feb 6–7, 1933 during a 68-knot (78.3 mph) hurricane. The wave was computed to be 112 ft from trough to crest.

The highest instrumentally measured wave was one calculated to be exactly 86 ft high, recorded by the British ship *Weather Reporter* in the North Atlantic on Dec 30, 1972 in Lat. 59°N., Long. 19°W.

A landslip on July 9, 1958 caused a 100-mph wave to wash 1,720 ft high along the fjord-like Lituya Bay, Alaska.

Highest Seismic Wave

The highest recorded seismic sea wave, or *tsunami,* (often mistakenly called a "tidal wave") was one of an estimated 278 ft, which appeared off Ishigaki Island, Ryukyu Chain, Apr 24, 1971. It tossed an 850-ton block of coral more than 1.3 miles. *Tsunami* (a Japanese word meaning: *tsu,* overflowing; *nami,* a wave) have been observed to travel at 490 mph.

Evidence for a 1,000-ft ocean wave breaking on the southern shore of the island of Lanai, Hawaii, was reported on Dec 4, 1984. This occurred about 100,000 years ago, due to a meteorite, a volcanic eruption or a submarine landslide.

Icebergs

The largest iceberg on record was an Antarctic tabular iceberg of over 12,000 sq mi (208 miles long and 60 miles wide) sighted 150 miles west of Scott Island, in the South Pacific Ocean, by the USS *Glacier* Nov 12, 1956. This iceberg was larger than Belgium.

The 200-ft-thick Arctic ice island T.1 (140 sq mi), discovered in 1946, was tracked for 17 years.

The tallest iceberg measured was one of 550 ft reported off western Greenland by the USCG icebreaker *East Wind* in 1958.

Straits

The longest straits in the world are the Tatarskiy Proliv or Tartar Straits between Sakhalin Island and the USSR mainland, running 497 miles from the Sea of Japan to Sakhalinsky Zaliv. This distance is marginally longer than the Malacca Straits, which extend 485 miles.

The broadest named straits are the Davis Straits between Greenland and Baffin Island, which at one point narrow to 210 miles. The Drake Passage between the Diego Ramirez Islands, Chile, and the South Shetland Islands, is 710 miles across.

The narrowest navigable straits are those between the Aegean island of Euboea and the mainland of Greece. The gap is only 45 yd wide at Khalkis. The Seil Sound, Strathclyde, Scotland, narrows to a point only 20 ft wide where a bridge joins the island of Seil to the mainland and is thus said by the islanders to span the Atlantic.

LAND

There is satisfactory evidence that at one time the earth's land surface comprised a single primeval continent of 80 million sq mi, now termed Pangaea, and that this split about 190 million years ago, during the Jurassic period, into two super-continents, termed Laurasia (Eurasia, Greenland and North America) and Gondwanaland (comprising Africa, Arabia, India, South America, Oceania and Antarctica), named after Gondwana, India, which itself split 120 million years ago. The South Pole was apparently in the area of the Sahara as recently as the Ordovician period of *c*. 450 million years ago.

Rocks

The age of the earth is generally considered to be within the range 4,450 ± 50 million years, by analogy with directly measured ages of meteorites and of the moon. However, no rocks of this great age have yet been found on earth. Geological processes have presumably destroyed them.

The greatest reported age for any scientifically dated rock is 3800 ± 100 million years for granite gneiss rock found near Granite Falls in the Minnesota river valley, as measured by the lead-isotope and rubidium-uranium methods by the US Geological Survey and announced on Jan 26, 1975. These metamorphic samples compare with the Amîtsoq gneiss from Godthaab, Greenland unreservedly accepted to be between 3,700 and 3,750 million years. Zirconium silicate crystals from Mt Narrayer, Australia, were dated to 4,200 million years (1983).

The largest exposed isolated monolith is the 1,237-ft-high Mt Augustus (3,627 ft above sea level), discovered June 3, 1858 about 200 miles east of Carnarvon, Western Australia. It is an up-faulted monoclinal gritty conglomerate 5 miles long and 2 miles across and thus twice the size of the celebrated monolithic arkose Ayer's Rock (1,100 ft), 250 miles southwest of Alice Springs, in Northern Territory, Australia.

It was estimated in 1940 that La Gran Piedra, a volcanic plug in the Sierra Maestra, Cuba, weighs 68,718 tons.

Sheerest Wall

The 3,200-ft-wide northwest face of Half Dome, Yosemite, Calif, is 2,-200 ft high, but nowhere departs more than 7° from the vertical. It was first climbed (Class VI) in 5 days in July 1957 by Royal Robbins, Jerry Gallwas, and Mike Sherrick.

Largest and Smallest Continents

Of the earth's surface 41.25% or 81,200,000 sq mi is covered by continental masses and shelves of which only about two-thirds of 29.08% of the earth's surface (57,270,000 sq mi) is land above water, with a mean height of 2,480 ft above sea level. The Eurasian land mass is the largest, with an area (including islands) of 20,733,000 sq mi. The Afro-Eurasian land mass, separated artificially only by the Suez Canal covers an area of 32,233,000 sq mi or 56.2% of the earth's land mass.

The smallest is the Australian mainland, with an area of about 2,941,-526 sq mi, which, together with Tasmania, New Zealand, New Guinea and the Pacific Islands, is described as Oceania.

Land Remotest from the Sea

There is an as yet unpinpointed spot in the Dzoosotoyn Elisen (desert), in northern Xinjiang Uygur Zizhiqu (Sin Kiang), China's most northwesterly province, that is more than 1,500 miles from the open sea in any direction. The nearest large city to this point is Urumqi (Urumchi) to its south.

Largest Peninsula

The world's largest peninsula is Arabia, with an area of about 1,250,-000 sq mi.

Largest Islands

Discounting Australia, which is usually regarded as a continental land mass, the largest island is Greenland (renamed Kalaallit Nunaat, May 1, 1979), with an area of about 840,000 sq mi. There is some evidence that Greenland is in fact several islands overlaid by an ice-cap without which it would have an area of 650,000 sq mi. The northeast corner of S America is technically an island that might be 700,000 sq mi.

Remotest Islands

The remotest island in the world is Bouvet Øya (formerly Liverpool Island), discovered in the South Atlantic by J. B. C. Bouvet de Lozier Jan 1, 1739 and first landed on by Capt George Norris on Dec 16, 1825. Its position is 54°26'S., 3°24'E. This uninhabited Norwegian dependency is about 1,050 miles from the nearest land—the uninhabited Queen Maud Land coast of eastern Antarctica.

The largest island in a lake is Manitoulin Island (1,068 sq mi) in the Canadian (Ontario) section of Lake Huron. The island itself has a lake of 41.09 sq mi on it, called Manitou Lake, which is the world's largest lake within a lake, and in that lake are a number of islands.

LARGEST ISLAND
(above), formerly called
Greenland and colonized
by Denmark in 1782,
independent since 1979
and now named Kalaallit
Nunaat, contains few
towns as a plateau of ice
fills most of the huge
island. Along the east
coast is this Eskimo
settlement named
Angmagssalik. When
found by the Danish in
1884, the town had 416
Eskimos living like
people in the Stone Age.
(*Alex Hansen*)

SHEEREST WALL
(left): Cut by a glacier
in prehistoric time, Half
Dome in Calif's
Yosemite Valley is 2,200
ft high and no more
than 7° from vertical at
any point in its 3,200-ft
width. (*Bruce Coleman*)

The remotest inhabited island in the world is Tristan da Cunha, discovered in the South Atlantic by Tristão da Cunha, a Portuguese admiral, in Mar 1506. It has an area of 38 sq mi (habitable area 12 sq mi) and was annexed by the United Kingdom Aug 14, 1816. After evacuation in 1961 (due to volcanic activity), 198 islanders returned in Nov 1963. The nearest inhabited land is the island of St Helena, 1,320 miles to the northeast. The nearest continent, Africa, is 1,700 miles away.

Newest Island

The newest island is the lava islet of Fukuto Kuokanoba near Iwo Jima in the Pacific reported in Jan 1986. It measures 2,132 × 1,476 ft (1/10 of a sq mi) and is 40 ft above sea level.

Largest Atolls

The largest atoll is Kwajalein in the Marshall Islands, in the central Pacific. Its slender 176-mile-long coral reef encloses a lagoon of 1,100 sq mi.

The atoll with the largest land area is Christmas Atoll, in the Line Islands, in the central Pacific Ocean. It has an area of 248 sq mi. Its principal settlement, London, is only 2½ miles distant from Paris, its other settlement.

Greatest Archipelago

The greatest archipelago is the 3,500-mile-long crescent of over 13,000 islands that form Indonesia.

Highest Rock Pinnacle

The highest rock pinnacle is Ball's Pyramid near Lord Howe Island in the Pacific, which is 1,843 ft high, but has a base axis of only 220 yd. It was first scaled in 1965.

Longest Reef

The longest reef is the Great Barrier Reef off Queensland, northeastern Australia, which is 1,260 statute miles in length. Between 1959 and 1971 a large section between Cooktown and Townsville was destroyed by the proliferation of the Crown of Thorns starfish (*Acanthaster planci*).

Highest Mountains

An eastern Himalayan peak of 29,028 ft above sea level on the Tibet-Nepal border was first discovered to be the world's highest mountain in 1852. The 5½-mile-high peak was named Mt Everest after Sir George Everest (1790–1866). After a total loss of 11 lives since the first reconnaissance in 1921, Everest was finally conquered at 11:30 a.m. May 29, 1953, by Edmund Percival Hillary (b July 20, 1919, New Zealand), and the Sherpa, Tenzing Norgay (b Nepal 1914).

The mountain whose summit is farthest from the earth's center is the Andean peak of Chimborazo (20,702 ft), 98 miles south of the equator in Ecuador. Its summit is 7,057 ft further from the earth's center than the summit of Mt Everest. The highest mountain on the equator is Volcán Cayambe (18,996 ft), Ecuador, at Longitude 77° 58′ W. A mountaineer atop the summit would be moving at 1,038 mph relative to the earth's center due to the earth's rotation. If the mountaineer were just south of the summit, passing through a glacier at 16,000 ft, he would be on the only spot on earth where both latitude and temperature would be zero degrees.

HIGHEST MOUNTAIN: A team of Chinese scientists braves the intense cold and steep slopes of Mt Everest, 29,028 ft high.

The highest unclimbed mountain is now only the 31st highest—Zemu Gap Peak (23,320 ft) in the Sikkim Himalaya.

The world's tallest mountain measured from its submarine base (3,280 fathoms) in the Hawaiian Trough to peak is Mauna Kea (Mountain White) on the island of Hawaii, with a combined height of 33,476 ft, of which 13,796 ft are above sea level. Another mountain whose dimensions, but not height, exceed those of Mt Everest is the volcanic Hawaiian peak of Mauna Loa (Mountain Long) at 13,680 ft. The axes of its elliptical base, 16,322 ft below sea level, have been estimated at 74 mi and 53 mi. It should be noted that Cerro Aconcagua (22,834 ft) is more than 38,800 ft above the 16,000-ft-deep Pacific abyssal plain or 42,834 ft above the Peru-Chile Trench, which is 180 mi distant in the South Pacific.

Greatest Mountain Ranges

The greatest land mountain range is the Himalaya-Karakoram, which contains 96 of the world's 109 peaks of over 24,000 ft. The greatest of all mountain ranges is, however, the submarine Indian-East Pacific Oceans Cordillera, extending 19,200 miles from the Gulf of Aden to the Gulf of California by way of the seabed between Australia and Antarctica, with an average height of 8,000 ft above the base ocean depth. The longest mountain range above ground is the Andes of S America at about 5,000 mi.

Longest Lines of Sight

Alaska's Mt McKinley (20,320 ft) has been sighted from Mt Sanford (16,237 ft) 230 mi away. McKinley, so named in 1896, was called Denali (Great One) in the Athabascan language. Vatnajokull (6,952 ft) on the eastern coast of Iceland, has been seen by refracted light from the Faeroe Islands 340 mi distant across the Norwegian Sea.

Highest Halites

Along the northern shores of the Gulf of Mexico for 725 miles there exist 330 subterranean "mountains" of salt, some of which rise more than 60,000 ft from bedrock and appear as the low salt domes first discovered in 1862.

TALLEST SAND DUNES: In the Algerian section of the Saharan sand sea is this 1,410-ft-high mountain, with a "wave" length of nearly 3 mi. (*Robert Harding*)

Greatest Plateau

The most extensive high plateau is the Tibetan Plateau in Central Asia. The average altitude is 16,000 ft and the area is 77,000 sq mi.

Mount Rakaposhi (25,498 ft) rises 19,652 vertical ft from the Hunza Valley, Pakistan, with an overall gradient of 31° over a horizontal distance of 32,808 ft.

Sand Dunes

The highest measured sand dunes are those in the Saharan sand sea of Isaouane-n-Tifernine of east central Algeria at Lat. 26° 42′ N., Long. 6° 43′ E. They have a wave-length of nearly 3 miles and attain a height of 1,410 ft.

Deepest and Largest Depressions

The deepest depression so far discovered is the bed rock in the Bentley sub-glacial trench, Antarctica, at 8,326 ft below sea level.

The deepest exposed depression on land is the shore surrounding the Dead Sea, now 1,312 ft below sea level. The deepest point on the bed of this saltiest of all lakes is 2,388 ft below the Mediterranean. The deepest part of the bed of Lake Baykal in Siberia, USSR, is 4,872 ft below sea level.

The greatest submarine depression is a large area of the floor of the northwest Pacific which has an average depth of 15,000 ft.

The largest exposed depression in the world is the Caspian Sea basin in the Azerbaydzhani, Russian, Kazakh, and Turkmen republics of the USSR and northern Iran. It is more than 200,000 sq mi, of which 143,550 sq mi is lake area. The preponderant land area of the depression is the Prikaspiyskaya Nizmennost', lying around the northern third of the lake and stretching inland for a distance of up to 280 miles.

Longest and Shortest Rivers

The two longest rivers are the Amazon (*Amazonas*), flowing into the South Atlantic, and the Nile (*Bahr-el-Nil*) flowing into the Mediterranean. Which is the longer is more a matter of definition than of simple measurement.

Not until 1971 was the true source of the Amazon discovered by Loren McIntyre (US) in the snow-covered Andes of southern Peru. His expedition was sponsored by the Interamerican Geodetic Survey and the National Geographic Society. The Amazon begins with snowbound lakes and brooks that converge to form the Apurimac, a torrent in a deep canyon. The Apurimac joins other streams to become the Ene, the Tambo, then the Ucayali. From the confluence of the Ucayali and Maranon above Iquitos, Peru, the river is called Amazon for its final 2,300 miles as it flows eastward through Brazil into the Atlantic Ocean. Some of its tributaries—particularly the Rio Negro and the Rio Madeira—are themselves among the dozen largest rivers in the world. The Amazon has several mouths that widen toward the sea; thus the exact point of the river's end is uncertain. If the Para River estuary, the most distant mouth, is counted, the Amazon length is approximately 4,195 miles. Because of seasonal flooding and changes in channels, geographers tend to round off the length at 4,000 miles.

The first explorer to paddle the full length of the Amazon was Piotr Chmielinski (b 1953, Poland) who had been one of the expedition traversing the Colca Canyon (see page 139). Joe Kane (b 1953, San Francisco) walked 200 mi at the start and then joined in the paddling to Belem. Kayaks were used almost the whole way but a raft was needed over some rough rapids, where other members of the party joined in the paddling. The trip took 174 days, from Aug 29, 1985 to Feb 19, 1986, and was sponsored by Canoandes Expeditions, Inc (Wyoming).

The length of the Nile watercourse, as surveyed by M. Devrocy (Belgium) before the loss of a few miles of meanders due to the formation of Lake Nasser, behind the Aswan High Dam, was 4,145 miles. This course is the hydrologically acceptable one from the source in Burundi of the Luvironza branch of the Kagera feeder of the Victoria Nyanza *via* the White Nile (*Bahr-el-Jebel*) to the delta.

The world's shortest named river is the D River, Lincoln City, Ore, which connects Devil's Lake to the Pacific Ocean and is 440 ft long at low tide.

Largest Basin and Longest Tributaries

The largest river basin is that drained by the Amazon (4,007 miles). It covers about 2,720,000 sq mi, has about 15,000 tributaries and sub-tributaries, of which four are more than 1,000 miles long. This includes the longest of all tributaries, the Madeira, with a length of 2,100 miles, which is surpassed by only 14 rivers in the whole world.

The longest sub-tributary is the Pilcomayo (1,000 miles long) in South America. It is a tributary of the Paraguay River (1,500 miles long), which is itself a tributary of the Paraná (2,500 miles).

Greatest Flow

The greatest flow of any river is that of the Amazon, which discharges an average of 4,200,000 cu ft of water per sec into the Atlantic Ocean, rising to more than 7 million "cusecs" in full flood. The lower 900 miles of the Amazon average 50–60 ft and in some places reach 300 ft in depth.

DISCOVERER OF AMAZON SOURCE (above): Surveying the steep Andes mountain peak in Peru where the river begins with a tiny lake named for him, Loren McIntyre of Arlington, Va, enjoys the sunshine.

FIRST EXPLORERS (left) to travel the full length of the Amazon were Piotr Chmielinski and Joe Kane in kayaks. (© *Zbigniew Bzdak*)

WHERE THE BLACK WATERS MEET THE BROWN (below): The point in the Amazon near Manaos where the Rio Negro churns its black waters into the muddier waters of the main Amazon stream. The waters travel several miles downstream before merging.

The flow of the Amazon exceeds the flow of the next 8 largest rivers, is 60 times greater than that of the Nile, and its 8 trillion gallons a day would furnish 20 times the daily water need of the US for drinking, industry, farming and electric power.

Greatest River Bores

The bore on the Ch'ient'ang'kian (Hang-chou-fe) in eastern China is the most remarkable of the 60 in the world. At spring tides, the wave attains a height of up to 25 ft and a speed of 13-15 knots. It is heard advancing at a range of 14 miles.

The annual downstream flood wave on the Mekong River of Southeast Asia sometimes reaches a height of 46 ft. The greatest volume of any tidal bore is that of the Furo do Guajurú, a shallow channel that splits Ilha Caviana in the mouth of the Amazon.

Longest Estuary

The longest estuary is that of the often-frozen Ob', in the northern USSR, at 550 miles. It is up to 50 miles wide.

Largest Delta

The largest delta is that created by the Ganga (Ganges) and Brahmaputra in Bangladesh (formerly East Pakistan) and West Bengal, India. It covers an area of 30,000 sq mi.

Longest and Fastest-Moving Glaciers

It is estimated that 6,020,000 sq mi, or about 10.5% of the earth's land surface, is permanently glaciated. The longest glacier known is the Lambert Glacier, discovered by an Australian aircraft crew in Australian Antarctic Territory in 1956–57. It is up to 40 miles wide and, with its upper section known as the Mellor Glacier, it measures at least 250 miles in length. With the Fisher Glacier limb, the Lambert forms a continuous ice passage about 320 miles long. The longest Himalayan glacier is the Siachen (47 miles) in the Karakoram range, though the Hispar and Biafo combine to form an ice passage 76 miles long. The fastest-moving major glacier is the Quarayaq in Greenland which flows 65–80 ft per day.

Greatest Avalanches

The greatest avalanches, though rarely observed, occur in the Himalayas, but no estimate of their volume has been published. It was estimated that 120 million cu ft of snow fell in an avalanche in the Italian Alps in 1885. (See also *Disasters*.)

The 250-mph avalanche triggered by the Mt St Helens eruption in Wash May 18, 1979 was estimated to measure 96 billion cu ft.

Highest Waterfall

The highest waterfall (as opposed to a vaporized "Bridal Veil") is the Salto Angel (Angel Falls), in Venezuela, on a branch of the Carrao River, an upper tributary of the Caroní, with a total drop of 3,212 ft and the longest single drop 2,648 ft. It was rediscovered in 1935 by a US pilot named Jimmy Angel (d Dec 8, 1956). He later crashed nearby on Oct 9, 1937. The fall, known by the Indians as Cherun-Meru, was first reported by Ernesto Sanchez La Cruz in 1910.

Greatest Waterfall Flow

On the basis of the average annual flow, the greatest waterfalls are the

"LOST SEA": This 4½-acre underground lake in Tennessee was not discovered until 1905. It is 300 ft below the earth's surface, in Craighead Caverns.

HIGHEST WATERFALL: Angel Falls in Venezuela has this single drop of 2,648 ft, but the total fall is 3,212 ft (compared to 167 ft for the American Niagara Falls). Note the airplane passing in front of Angel Falls. There are other immensely high waterfalls in the area which are still unnamed. (*Ruth Robertson*)

Boyoma (formerly Stanley) Falls in Zaïre with 600,000 cusec (cu ft/sec). The Guaíra (Salto das Sete Quedas) on the Alto Paraná river between Brazil and Paraguay at times attained a peak flow rate of 1,750,000 cusec (cu ft/sec). The completion of the Itaipu dam in 1982 ended this claim to fame.

It has been calculated that, when some 5½ million years ago the Mediterranean basins began to be filled from the Atlantic through the Straits of Gibraltar, a waterfall was formed 26 times greater than the Guaíra and perhaps 2,625 ft high.

Widest Waterfalls

The widest waterfalls are Khône Falls (50–70 ft high) in Laos, with a width of 6.7 miles and a flood flow of 1,500,000 cu ft per sec.

The widest waterfall in the Americas is the spectacular Iguazú near the Argentina-Brazil-Paraguay intersect which is 2½ mi wide and 237 ft high, with a volume about twice that of Niagara (although this varies greatly—in 1975 it dried up for 4 days).

Largest Lakes

The largest inland sea or lake is the Kaspiskóye Móre (Caspian Sea) between southern USSR and Iran. It is 760 miles long and its total area is 139,000 sq mi. Of the total area, 55,280 sq mi (38.6%) are in Iran, where the lake is named the Darya-ye-Khazar. Its maximum depth is 3,-360 ft and its surface is 93 ft below sea level. Its estimated volume is 21,-500 cu mi of saline water. Its surface has varied between 105 ft below sea level (11th century) and 72 ft (early 19th century). The USSR government plans to reverse the flow of the upper Pechora River from flowing north to the Barents Sea by blasting a 70-mile-long canal with nuclear explosives into the south-flowing Kolva River so that via the Kama and Volga rivers the Caspian will be replenished.

The fresh-water lake with the greatest surface area is Lake Superior, one of the Great Lakes. The total area is about 31,800 sq mi, of which 20,700 sq mi are in the US (Minn, Wis and Mich) and 11,100 sq mi in Ontario, Canada. It is 600 ft above sea level. The fresh-water lake with the greatest volume is Baykal with an estimated volume of 5,520 cu mi.

Underground Lake

Reputedly the largest underground lake is the Lost Sea, which lies 300 ft underground in the Craighead Caverns, Sweetwater, Tenn. Discovered in 1905, it covers an area of 4½ acres.

Largest Lagoon

The largest is Lagoa dos Patos in southern Brazil. It is 158 mi long and extends over 4,110 sq mi.

Highest Lake

The highest steam-navigated lake is Lago Titicaca (maximum depth 1,214 ft), with an area of about 3,200 sq mi (1,850 sq mi in Peru, 1,350 sq mi in Bolivia), in South America. It is 100 miles long and is situated at 12,506 ft above sea level.

There is an unnamed glacial lake near Mt Everest at 19,300 ft. Tibet's largest lake, Nam Tso (772 sq mi), lies at an elevation of 15,060 ft.

Deepest Lake

The deepest lake is Ozero (Lake) Baykal in central Siberia, USSR. It is 385 miles long and between 20 and 46 miles wide. In 1957 the lake's Olkhon Crevice was measured to be 6,365 ft deep and hence 4,872 ft below sea level. In spite of its depth Baykal was in danger of pollution in the 1960's from the waste discharges of woodpulp mills on its shore.

Natural Bridge (Arch)

The longest natural bridge in the world is the Landscape Arch in the Arches National Park 25 miles north of Moab, Utah. This natural sandstone arch spans 291 ft and is set about 100 ft above the canyon floor. In one place erosion has narrowed its section to 6 ft.

Larger in mass, however, is the Rainbow Bridge, Utah, discovered on Aug 14, 1909, which has a span of 278 ft but is over 22 ft wide.

The highest natural arch is the sandstone arch 25 miles west-northwest of K'ashih, Sinkiang, China, estimated in 1947 to be nearly 1,000 ft tall, with a span of about 150 ft.

Longest and Largest Cave and Cavern

The most extensive cave system is under the Mammoth Cave National Park, Ky, first discovered in 1799. On Sept 9, 1972 an exploration group led by Dr John P. Wilcox completed a connection, pioneered by Mrs Patricia Crowther, on Aug 30, between the Flint Ridge Cave system and the Mammoth Cave system, so making a combined system with a total mapped passageway which is now over 330 mi.

The largest cave chamber is the Sarawak Chamber, Lobang Nasip Bagus, in the Gunung Mulu National Park, Sarawak, discovered and surveyed by the 1980 British-Malayasian Mulu Expedition. Its length is 2,300 ft; its average width is 980 ft and it is nowhere less than 230 ft high. It could garage 7,500 buses; Yankee Stadium would fit into one end.

DEEPEST CAVES BY COUNTRIES

These depths are subject to continuous revisions.
Depth in Ft

5,036	Réseau Gouffre Jean Bernard	France
4,495	Snieznaja Piezcziera	USSR
4,390	Puerta de Illamina	Spain
4,108	Sistema Huautla	Mexico
3,999	Schwersystem	Austria
3,964	Complesso Fighiera Corchia	Italy
3,304	Anou Ifflis	Algeria
3,018	Jama u Vjetrena brda	Yugoslavia
2,880	Holloch	Switzerland
2,520	Jaskinia Sniezna	Poland
2,464	Ghar Parau, Zagros	Iran

Tallest Stalagmite

The tallest known stalagmite is La Grande Stalagmite in the Aven Armand cave, Lozère, France, which has attained a height of 98 ft from the cave floor. It was found in Sept 1897.

Largest and Deepest Gorges

The largest land gorge is the Grand Canyon on the Colorado River in north-central Ariz. It extends from Marble Gorge to the Grand Wash Cliffs, over a distance of 217 miles, varies in width from 4 to 13 miles and is up to 5,300 ft deep.

The deepest land gorge is the Colca River Canyon in southern Peru, where the sides rise to a maximum of 14,339 ft on one side and about 10,607 ft on the other. It was first traversed by a Polish kayak team called CANOANDES from the Univ of Krakow, May 12–June 14, 1981. Known to the Indians and early Spanish settlers, the walls of the canyon contain the greatest agricultural terraces of all the Andes.

The submarine Labrador Basin Canyon is *c.* 2,150 miles long.

The deepest canyon in low relief territory is Hell's Canyon, dividing Oregon and Idaho. It plunges 7,900 ft from the Devil Mountain down to the Snake River.

A stretch of the Kali River in central Nepal flows 18,000 ft below its flanking summits of the Dhaulagiri and Annapurna groups.

The deepest submarine canyon yet discovered is one 25 miles south of Esperance, Western Australia, which is 5,000 ft deep and 20 miles wide.

DEEPEST GORGE: The Colca River Canyon in southern Peru is more than 2½ mi deep at its maximum. The river, which enters the Pacific after flowing down the Andes, was first traversed by this Polish expedition in 1981. (*Zbigniew Bzdak*)

Longest Stalactite

The longest known stalactite is a wall-supported column extending 195 ft from roof to floor in the Cueva de Nerja, near Málaga, Spain. Probably the longest free-hanging stalactite is one of 23 ft in the Poll, an Ionain cave in County Clare, Ireland.

The tallest cave column is probably the 128-ft high Flying Dragon Pillar in the Nine Dragons Cave (Daji Dong), Guizhou, China.

Largest Desert

Nearly an eighth of the world's land surface is arid with an annual rainfall of less than 9.8 in. The Sahara in North Africa is the largest in the world. At its greatest length, it is 3,200 miles from east to west. From north to south it is between 800 and 1,400 miles. The area covered by the desert is about 3,250,000 sq mi. The land level varies from 436 ft below sea level in the Qattara Depression, Egypt, to the mountain Emi Koussi (11,204 ft) in Chad. The diurnal temperature range in the western Sahara may be more than 80°F.

Largest Swamp

The largest swamp is the Gran Pantanal of Mato Grosso State, Brazil, which is 42,000 sq mi in area (half the size of Minnesota).

Sea Cliffs

The highest sea cliffs yet pinpointed anywhere in the world are those on the north coast of east Molokai, Hawaii, near Umilehi Point, which descend 3,300 ft to the sea at an average gradient of more than 55°.

---

3. WEATHER*

The meteorological records given here necessarily relate largely to the last 140 to 160 years, since data before that time are both sparse and often unreliable. Reliable registering thermometers were introduced as recently as c. 1820.

It is believed that 1.2 million years ago the world's air temperature averaged 95°F.

The longest continuous observations have been maintained at the Radcliffe Observatory, Oxford, England since 1815, though discontinuous records have enabled the Chinese to assert that 903 BC was a very bad winter.

Greatest Temperature Ranges

The highest *shade* temperature ever recorded was 136.4°F at Al' Aziziyah (El Azizia), Libya, on Sept 13, 1922.

The lowest *screen* temperature ever recorded was −128.6°F at Vostok (11,220 ft above sea level), Antarctica on July 22, 1983. A platinum thermometer was used. The coldest permanently inhabited place is the Si-

---

* For more specialized weather records, see "Weather Facts and Feats" (2nd edition), a Guinness Superlatives Book (Sterling).

berian village of Oymyakon (pop. 600) in the USSR, where the temperature reached −96°F in 1964.

The greatest temperature variation recorded in a day is 100°F (a fall from 44°F to −56°F) at Browning, Mont, Jan 23–24, 1916. The most freakish rise was 49°F in 2 min at Spearfish, SD, from −4°F at 7:30 a.m. to 45°F at 7:32 a.m. Jan 22, 1943.

The greatest recorded temperature ranges in the world are around the Siberian "cold pole" in the eastern USSR. Temperatures in Verkhoyansk (67°33′N, 133°23′E) have ranged 192°F from −94°F (unofficial) to 98°F.

Humidity and Discomfort

Human discomfort depends not merely on temperature but on the combination of temperature, humidity, radiation and wind speed. The US Weather Service uses a Temperature-Humidity Index, which equals two-fifths of the sum of the dry and wet bulb thermometer readings plus 15. A THI reading of 98.2 has been recorded twice in Death Valley, Calif—on July 27, 1966 (119°F, 31% humidity) and on Aug 12, 1970 (117°F, 37% humidity). A person driving at 45 mph in a car without a windshield in a temperature of −45°F would, by the chill factor, experience the equivalent of −125°F, which is within 3.5°F of the world record.

Most Equable Temperature

The location with the most equable recorded temperature over a short period is Garapan, on Saipan, in the Mariana Islands, Pacific Ocean. During the nine years 1927–35, inclusive, the lowest temperature recorded was 67.3°F Jan 30, 1934, and the highest was 88.5°F Sept 9, 1931, giving an extreme range of 21.2°F. Between 1911–66 the Brazilian offshore island of Fernando de Noronha had a minimum temperature of 65.5°F Nov 17, 1913, and a maximum of 89.6°F March 2, 1965, an extreme range of 24.1°F.

Upper Atmosphere

The lowest temperature ever recorded in the atmosphere is −225.4°F at an altitude of about 50 to 60 miles, during noctilucent cloud research above Kronogård, Sweden, July 27–Aug 7, 1963.

A jet stream moving at 408 mph at 154,200 ft (29.2 miles) was recorded by Skua rocket above South Uist, Outer Hebrides, Scotland, on Dec 13, 1967.

Thickest Ice

The greatest recorded thickness of ice on the earth's surface is 2.97 miles (15,670 ft) measured by radio echo soundings from a US Antarctic Research aircraft at 69°9′38″ S, 135°20′25″ E in Wilkes Land on Jan 4, 1975.

Waterspouts

The highest waterspout of which there is reliable record was one observed May 16, 1898, off Eden, NSW, Australia. A theodolite reading from the shore gave its height as 5,014 ft. It was about 10 ft in diameter. The Spithead waterspout off Ryde, Isle of Wight, England of Aug 21, 1878 was measured by sextant to be "about a mile" or 5,280 ft in height.

HAIL PILED HIGH: During a furious summer thunderstorm in Cheyenne, Wyo, Aug 2, 1985, a 3-ft cover of hailstones fell, along with 6 in of rain in 4 hours. "It was like someone opened a faucet overhead," said the mayor. Sudden floods followed that killed a dozen people.

LARGEST HAILSTONE: This 1.67-lb iced stone measured 17½ in in circumference. It fell in Coffeyville, Kans, in 1970.

HOTTEST STREAK: Death Valley, Calif, had 43 consecutive days of 120°F heat in 1917.

Lightning

The visible length of lightning strokes varies greatly. In mountainous regions, when clouds are very low, the flash may be less than 300 ft long. In flat country with very high clouds, a cloud-to-earth flash may measure 4 miles, though in the most extreme cases such flashes have been measured at 20 miles. The intensely bright central core of the lightning channel is extremely narrow. Some authorities suggest that its diameter is as little as half an inch. This core is surrounded by a "corona envelope" (glow discharge) which may be 10–20 ft wide.

The speed of a lightning discharge varies from 100 to 1,000 miles per sec for the downward leader track, and reaches up to 87,000 miles per sec (nearly half the speed of light) for the powerful return stroke.

Every few million strokes there is a giant discharge, in which the cloud-to-earth and the return lightning strokes flash from and to the top of the thunder clouds.

In these "positive giants" energy of up to 3,000 million joules (3×10^{16} ergs) has been recorded. The temperature reaches about 30,000 °C, which is more than five times greater than that of the surface of the sun.

Deepest Permafrost

The deepest recorded permafrost is more than 4,500 ft, reported from the upper reaches of the Viluy River, Siberia, USSR, in Feb 1982.

Most Intense Rainfall

Difficulties attend rainfall readings for very short periods but the figure of 1.50 in in 1 min at Barst, Guadeloupe, Nov 26, 1970, is regarded as the most intense recorded in modern times. The cloudburst of "near two foot in less than a quarter of half an hour" at Oxford, England, on the afternoon of May 31 (Old Style), 1682, is regarded as unacademically recorded.

Longest-Lasting Rainbow

A rainbow lasting for over 3 hours was reported from North Wales on Aug 14, 1979.

Hurricane Damage

The hurricane named Frederic in 1979 caused the most damage along the US coastline, according to the National Hurricane Center. $2.3 *billion* is estimated. The big hurricane, Alicia, in 1983 did $300 million less damage.

Cloud Extremes

The highest standard cloud form is cirrus, averaging 27,000 ft and above, but the rare nacreous or mother-of-pearl formation sometimes reaches nearly 80,000 ft. Cirrus cloud at 26,500 ft contains unfrozen but supercooled water at −31 °F. The lowest is stratus, below 3,500 ft. The cloud form with the greatest vertical range is cumulo-nimbus, which has been observed to reach a height of nearly 68,000 ft in the tropics.

Mirages

The largest mirage on record was that sighted in the Arctic at 83° N., 103° W. by Donald B. MacMillan in 1913. This type of mirage, known as the Fata Morgana, appeared as the same "hills, valleys, snow-capped peaks extending through at least 120 degrees of the horizon" that Peary had misidentified as Crocker Land 6 years earlier.

On July 17, 1939, a mirage of Snaefell Jokull glacier (4,715 ft) on Iceland was seen from the sea at a distance of 335–350 miles.

OTHER WEATHER RECORDS

Hottest Place (Annual mean): Dallol, Ethiopia, 94°*F, 1960–66.* In Death Valley, Calif, 120°F or more were recorded on 43 consecutive days, July 6–Aug 17, 1917. At Marble Bar, W Australia (maximums 121°F) maximum over 100°F for 160 consecutive days Oct 31, 1923–Apr 7, 1924.

Coldest Place (Extrapolated annual mean): Polus Nedostupnosti, Pole of Cold (78°S., 96°E.), Antarctica, −72°F (16°F lower than Pole). (Coldest measured mean): Plateau Station, Antarctica −70°F.

Greatest Rainfall (24 hours): 73.62 in, Cilaos, La Réunion, Indian Ocean, March 15–16, 1952. (Calendar month): 366.14 in, Cherrapunji, Meghalaya, India, July, 1861. (12 months): 1,041.78 in, Cherrapunji, Meghalaya, Aug 1, 1860–July 31, 1861.

Greatest Snowfall (24 hours): 76 in, Silver Lake, Colo, Apr 14–15, 1921. (12 months): 1,224.5 in, Paradise, Mt Rainier, Wash, Feb 19, 1971–Feb 18, 1972. (Single): 189 in, Mt Shasta Ski Bowl, Calif. (Greatest depth of snow on ground): 27.7 in at Helen Lake, Mt. Lassen, Calif Apr 1983.

Wettest Place (Annual mean): Tutunendo, Colombia, average 463.4 in.

Barometric Pressure (Highest): 1,083.8 mb (32 in), Agata, Siberia, USSR, (alt. 862 ft) Dec 31, 1968. (Lowest): 870 mb (25.69 in), 300 miles west of Guam in the Pacific Ocean on Oct 12, 1979 by the US Air Weather Service. The USS *Repose,* a hospital ship, recorded 856 mb (25.55 in) in the eye of a typhoon off Okinawa on Sept 16, 1945.

Maximum Sunshine (Year): 97% (over 4,300 hours), eastern Sahara. St Petersburg, Fla, had 768 consecutive days, Feb 9, 1967–March 17, 1969.

Minimum Sunshine: Nil at North Pole—for winter stretches of 186 days.

Thunder Days (Year): 322 days, Bogor (formerly Buitenzorg), Java, Indonesia (average, 1916–19). Between Lat 35° N and 35° S there are some 3,200 thunderstorms each 12 nighttime hours, some of which can be heard at a range of 18 miles.

Highest Surface Wind-speed: 231 mph, Mt Washington (6,288 ft), NH, Apr 12, 1934. 280 mph in a tornado at Wichita Falls, Tex, Apr 2, 1958.

Windiest Place: The Commonwealth Bay, George V Coast, Antarctica, where gales reach 200 mph.

Largest Hailstones: 1.67 lb (7½ in diameter, 17½ in circumference) Coffeyville, Kans, Sept 3, 1970. The *Canton Evening News* (Ohio) reported on Apr 14, 1981 that 5 were killed and 225 injured recently by a hailstorm with stones weighing up to 30 lb.

Driest Place (Annual mean): Less than 0.1 mm (thickness of a sheet of letter paper) on the Pacific Coast of Chile between Arica and Antofagasta.

Longest Drought: Desierto de Atacama, near Calama, Chile, almost rainless, although several times a century a squall may strike a small area of it.

Most Rainy Days (Year): Mt Waialeale (5,148 ft), Kauai, Hawaii, up to 350 days per year.

Longest Sea Level Fogs (Visibility less than 1,000 yd): Fogs persist for weeks on the Grand Banks, Newfoundland, Canada, and the average is more than 120 days per year.

Chapter 4

The Universe & Space

Light-Year

That distance traveled by light (speed 186,282.397 miles per sec, or 670,616,629.2 mph, *in vacuo*) in one tropical (or solar) year (365.24219878 mean solar days at Jan 0, 12 hours Ephemeris time in 1900 AD) and is 5,878,499,814,000 miles. The unit was first used in March 1888, and fixed at this constant in Oct 1983.

Magnitude

A measure of stellar brightness such that the light of a star of any magnitude bears a ratio of 2.511886 to that of a star of the next magnitude. Thus a fifth magnitude star is 2.511886 times as bright, while one of the first magnitude is exactly 100 (or 2.511886^5) times as bright, as a sixth magnitude star. In the case of such exceptionally bright bodies as Sirius, Venus, the moon (magnitude -12.71) or the sun (magnitude -26.8), the magnitude is expressed as a minus quantity.

Proper Motion

That component of a star's motion in space which, at right angles to the line of sight, constitutes an apparent change of position of the star in the celestial sphere.

The universe is the entirety of space, matter and antimatter. An appreciation of its magnitude is best grasped by working outward from the earth, through the solar system and our own Milky Way galaxy, once in each 237,000,000 years at a speed of 492,000 mph and has a velocity of 44,700 mph relative to stars in our immediate region and then on to the remotest extra-galactic nebulae and quasars.

Meteor Shower

Meteoroids are mostly of cometary or asteroidal origin. A meteor is the light phenomenon caused by entry of a meteoroid into earth's atmosphere. The greatest meteor "shower" on record occurred on the night of Nov 16–17, 1966, when the Leonid meteors (which recur every 33¼ years) were visible between western North America and eastern USSR. It was calculated that meteors passed over Arizona at a rate of 2,300 per min for a period of 20 min from 5 a.m. Nov 17, 1966.

Oldest and Largest Meteorites

The oldest dated meteorites are from the Allende Fall over Chihuahua, Mexico, Feb 8, 1969, dating back 4,610 million years.

It was reported in Aug 1978 that dust grains in the Murchison meteorite which fell in Australia in Sept 1969 predate the formation of the solar system 4,600 million years ago.

When a meteoroid penetrates to the earth's surface, the remnant, which could be either aerolite (stony) or siderite (metallic), is described as a meteorite. This occurs about 150 times per year over the whole land surface of the earth. Although the chances of being struck are deemed negligible, the most anxious time of day for meteorophobes is 3 p.m. In historic times, the only recorded person injured by a meteorite has been Mrs E. H. Hodges of Sylacauga, Alaska, on Nov 30, 1954, when a 9-lb stone went through her roof.

The largest known meteorite is one found in 1920 at Hoba West, near Grootfontein in southwest Africa. This is a block 9 ft long by 8 ft broad, weighing 132,000 lb.

The largest meteorite exhibited by any museum is the "Tent" meteorite, weighing 68,085 lb, found in 1897 near Cape York, on the west coast of Greenland, by the expedition of Commander (later Rear Admiral) Robert Edwin Peary (1856–1920). It was known to the Eskimos as the Abnighito and is now exhibited in the Hayden Planetarium in NYC.

The largest piece of stony meteorite recovered is a piece of 3,902 lb which was part of a shower that struck Jilin (formerly Kirin), China, March 8, 1976.

There was a mysterious explosion of 12½ megatons at Lat. 60° 55′ N., Long. 101° 57′ E., in the basin of the Podkamennaya Tunguska River, 40 miles north of Vanavar, in Siberia, USSR at 00 hrs 17 min 11 sec UT June 30, 1908. The cause was variously attributed to a meteorite (1927), a comet (1930), a nuclear explosion (1961) and to antimatter (1965). This devastated an area of about 1,500 sq mi, and the shock was felt more than 600 miles away.

The theory is now favored that this was the terminal flare of stony debris from a comet, possibly Encke's comet, at altitude of less than 20,000 ft. A similar event may have occurred over the Isle of Axeholm, Lincolnshire, Eng, a few thousand years before. A stony meteorite with a diameter of 6.2 miles striking the earth at 55,925 mph would generate an explosive energy equivalent to 100 million megatons. Such events should not be expected to recur more than once in 75 million years.

Largest Craters

It has been estimated that some 2,000 asteroid-earth collisions have occurred in the last 600 million years. A total of 96 collision sites or astroblemes have been recognized. A crater 150 miles across and a half mile deep has been postulated in Wilkes Land, Antarctica, since 1962. It would have been caused by a 14,560 million-ton meteorite striking at 44,000 mph. In Dec 1970 USSR scientists reported an astrobleme in the basin of the Popigai River with a 60-mile diameter and a maximum depth of 1,300 ft. There is a possible crater-like formation or astrobleme 275 miles in diameter on the eastern shore of Hudson Bay, where the Nastapoka Islands are just off the coast.

The largest proven crater is the Coon Butte or Barringer Crater, discovered in 1891 near Canyon Diablo, Winslow, northern Ariz. It is 4,150 ft in diameter and now about 575 ft deep, with a parapet rising 130–155 ft above the surrounding plain. It has been estimated that an iron-nickel mass with a diameter of 200–260 ft, and weighing about 2,240,000 tons, gouged this crater c. 25,000 BC.

Evidence was published in 1963 discounting a meteoric origin for the crypto-volcanic Vredefort Ring (diameter 26 miles) to the southwest of Johannesburg, South Africa, but this claim has now been reasserted.

The New Quebec (formerly the Chubb) "Crater," first sighted June 20, 1943, in northern Ungava, Canada, is 1,325 ft deep and measures 6.8 miles around its rim.

Fireball

The brightest fireball ever recorded photographically was one observed over Sumava, Czechoslovakia, Dec 4, 1974, by Dr Zdeněk Ceplecha, which had a momentary magnitude of −22, or 10,000 times brighter than a full moon.

Tektites

The largest tektite of which details have been published was one of 7.04 lb found in 1932 at Muong Nong, Saravane Province, Laos, and now in the Paris Museum.

Aurorae

Polar lights, known since 1560 as Aurora Borealis or Northern Lights in the northern hemisphere and since 1773 as Aurora Australis in the southern hemisphere, are caused by electrical solar discharges in the upper atmosphere and occur most frequently in high latitudes. Aurorae are visible at some time on *every* clear dark night in the polar areas within 20° latitude of the magnetic poles.

The extreme height of aurorae has been measured at 620 miles, while the lowest may descend to 45 miles.

Reliable figures exist only from 1952. Extreme cases of displays in very low latitudes were those reported at Cuzco, Peru (Aug 2, 1744); Honolulu, Hawaii (Sept 1, 1859); and, questionably, Singapore (Sept 25, 1909).

THE MOON

The earth's closest neighbor in space and only natural satellite is the moon, at a mean distance of 238,855 statute miles center-to-center or 233,812 miles surface-to-surface. In the present century the closest approach (smallest perigee) was 216,398 miles surface-to-surface or 221,441 miles center-to-center on Jan 4, 1912, and the farthest distance (largest apogee) was 247,675 miles surface-to-surface or 252,718 miles center-to-center on Mar 2, 1984.

The moon was only a few earth radii distant during the "Gerstenkorn period" 3,900 million years ago. It has a diameter of 2,159.3 miles and has a mass of 7.35×10^{19} metric tonnes with a mean density of 3.342. The average orbital speed is 2,287 mph.

The first direct hit on the moon was achieved at 2 min 24 sec after midnight (Moscow time) Sept 14, 1959, by the Soviet space probe *Lunik II* near the *Mare Serenitatis*. The first photographic images of the hidden side were collected by the USSR's *Lunik III* from 6:30 a.m. Oct 7, 1959, from a range of up to 43,750 miles, and transmitted to the earth from a distance of 292,000 miles. The first "soft" landing was made by the USSR's *Luna IX* in the area of the Ocean of Storms Feb 3, 1966.

Highest Moon Mountains

As there is no sea level on the moon, the heights of lunar mountains can be measured only in relation to an adopted reference sphere with a radius of 1,079.943 miles. Thus the greatest elevation attained on this basis by any of the 12 US astronauts has been 25,688 ft, on the Descartes Highlands, by Capt John Watts Young, USN, and Major Charles M. Duke, Jr, Apr 27, 1972.

Moon Samples

The age attributed to the oldest of the moon material brought back to earth by the *Apollo* program crews has been soil dated to 4,720 million years.

Temperature Extremes on the Moon

When the sun is overhead, the temperature on the lunar equator reaches 243 °F (31 °F above the boiling point of water). By sunset the temperature is 58 °F, but after nightfall it sinks to −261 °F.

Largest and Deepest Craters

Only 59% of the moon's surface is directly visible from the earth because it is in "captured rotation," *i.e.*, the period of rotation is equal to the period of orbit. The largest wholly visible crater is the walled plain Bailly, toward the moon's South Pole, which is 183 miles across, with walls rising to 14,000 ft. Partly on the averted side, the Orientale Basin measures more than 600 miles in diameter.

The deepest crater is the moon's Newton crater, with a floor estimated to be between 23,000 and 29,000 ft below its rim and 14,000 ft below the level of the plain outside. The brightest directly visible spot on the moon is *Aristarchus*.

CRATERS ON THE FAR SIDE OF THE MOON (left): Never seen on earth, the hidden side was first photographed by a Soviet space probe in 1959.

FAMOUS FOOTSTEP (below): The first step onto the moon left this print in the dust. Neil Armstrong, astronaut, had a quote prepared: "That's one small step for man, one giant leap for mankind." (*NASA*)

THE SUN

The earth's 66,620 mph orbit of 584,017,800 miles around the sun is elliptical; hence our distance from the sun varies. The orbital speed varies between 65,520 mph (minimum) and 67,750 mph. The average distance of the sun is 1.000000230 astronomical units or 92,955,829 miles. The closest approach (perihelion) is 91,402,000 miles, and the farthest departure (aphelion) is 94,510,000 miles.

Sun's Temperature and Dimensions

The sun has a central temperature of about 15,400,000K (K stands for the Kelvin absolute scale of temperatures), a core pressure of 1,650,000,-000 tons per sq in (25.4 PPa) and uses up nearly 4½ million tons of hydrogen per sec, thus providing a luminosity of 3×10^{27} candlepower, with an intensity of 1½ million candles per sq in. The sun has the stellar classification of a "yellow dwarf" and, although its density is only 1.407 times that of water, its mass is 332,946 times as much as that of the earth. It has a mean diameter of 865,370 miles. The sun with a mass of 1,958 × 10^{27} metric tonnes represents more than 99% of the total mass of the solar system, but will exhaust its energy in 10,000 million years.

Largest and Most Frequent Sunspots

To be visible to the *protected* naked eye, a sunspot must cover about one two-thousandth part of the sun's disc and thus have an area of about 500 million sq mi. The largest sunspot occurred in the sun's southern hemisphere on Apr 8, 1947. Its area was about 7,000 million sq mi, with an extreme longitude of 187,000 miles and an extreme latitude of 90,000 miles. Sunspots appear darker because they are more than 1,500 °C cooler than the rest of the sun's surface temperature of 5,525 °C. The largest observed solar prominence was one protruding 365,000 miles, photographed on Dec 19, 1973 during the third and final Skylab mission.

On Oct 1957 a smoothed sunspot count showed 263, the highest recorded index since records started in 1755 (*cf.* previous record of 239 in May 1778). In 1943 a sunspot lasted for 200 days from June to Dec.

Earliest Recorded Eclipses

The earliest extrapolated eclipses that have been identified are 1361 BC (lunar) and Oct 2136 BC (solar). For the Middle East only, lunar eclipses have been extrapolated to 3450 BC and solar eclipses to 4200 BC.

Longest Eclipse Duration

The maximum possible duration of an eclipse of the sun is 7 min 31 sec. The longest actually *measured* was June 20, 1955 (7 min 8 sec), seen from the Philippines. That of July 16, 2186 in the mid-Atlantic should last 7 min 29 sec. This will be the longest for 1,469 years. Durations can be extended by observers being airborne, as on June 30, 1973 when an eclipse was "extended" to 72 min for observers aboard a *Concorde* jet. An annular eclipse may last for 12 min 24 sec. The longest totality of any lunar eclipse is 104 min. This has occurred many times.

Most and Least Frequent Eclipses

The highest number of eclipses possible in a year is seven, as in 1935, when there were five solar and two lunar eclipses; or four solar and three lunar eclipses, as occurred in 1982. The lowest possible number in a year is two, both of which must be solar, as in 1944 and 1969.

Comets

The earliest records of comets date from the 7th century BC. The speeds of the estimated 2,000,000 comets vary from 700 mph in outer space to 1,250,000 mph when near the sun.

The brightest *periodical* comet, with a period of 75.81 years, is Halley's. Halley actually only *re*discovered in 1682 a comet that had been known for many centuries.

The successive appearances of Halley's Comet have been traced back to 467 BC. It was first depicted in the Nuremberg Chronicle of 684 AD. The first prediction of its return by Edmund Halley (1656–1742) proved true on Christmas Day, 1758, 16 years after his death.

The European satellite *Giotto* (launched July 2, 1985) penetrated to within 335 mi of the nucleus of Halley's Comet, Mar 13–14, 1986, to discover that it was 9.3 mi in length and velvet black in color.

Closest Comet Approach to Earth

On July 1, 1770 Lexell's Comet, traveling at a speed of 23.9 miles per sec (relative to the sun), came within 745,000 miles of the earth. However, the earth is believed to have passed through the tail of Halley's Comet, most recently on May 19, 1910.

Largest Comets

The tail of the Great Comet of 1843 trailed for 205 million miles. The bow shock of Holmes Comet of 1892 once measured 1½ million miles in diameter.

Shortest and Longest Comet Period

Of all the recorded periodic comets (these are members of the solar system), the one which most frequently returns is Encke's Comet, first identified in 1786. Its period of 1,206 days (3.3 years) is the shortest established. Not one of its 51 returns (to the end of 1977) has been missed by astronomers. Now increasingly faint, it is expected to "die" by Feb 1994. The most frequently observed comets are Schwassmann Wach mann I, Kopff and Oterma, which can be observed every year between Mars and Jupiter.

At the other extreme is Delavan's Comet of 1914, whose path has not been accurately determined. It is not expected to return for perhaps 24 million years.

PLANETS

The 9 planets (including the earth) are bodies within the solar system which revolve around the sun in definite orbits. The search for Planet X continues.

Largest, Fastest and Hottest Planets

Jupiter, with an equatorial diameter of 88,846 miles and a polar diam-

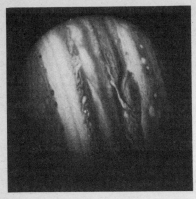

LARGEST PLANET: Jupiter, with an equatorial diameter of 88,846 miles and a volume 1,321.4 times that of the earth, is the largest planet in the solar system. Visible at the lower right is "Ganymede," the largest and heaviest satellite in the solar system. This photo was taken by "Voyager 1" on Jan 24, 1979, from more than 25 million miles away. (*NASA*)

eter of 83,082 miles, is the largest of the nine major planets, with a mass 317.83 times and a volume 1,321.4 times that of the earth. It also has the shortest period of rotation, with a "day" of only 9 hours 50 min 30.003 sec in its equatorial zone.

Mercury, which orbits the sun at an average distance of 35,983,100 miles, has a period of revolution of 87.9686 days, so giving the highest average speed in orbit of 107,030 mph.

A surface temperature of 864°F has been estimated from measurements made from Venus by the USSR probes *Venera* and US *Pioneer* Cytherean surface probes.

Smallest and Coldest Planets

The smallest and coldest planets, Pluto and its partner Charon (announced on June 22, 1978), have an estimated surface temperature of −360°F (100°F above absolute zero). Their mean distance from the sun is 3,674,488,000 miles and their period of revolution is 248.54 years. Pluto's diameter is about 1,860 miles and it has a mass about 1/470th that of the earth. Because of its orbital eccentricity, Pluto moved closer to the sun than Neptune between Jan 23, 1979 and March 15, 1999.

Nearest Planet to Earth

The fellow planet closest to the earth is Venus, which is, at times, about 25,700,000 miles inside the earth's orbit, compared with Mars' closest approach of 34,600,000 miles outside the earth's orbit. Mars, known since 1965 to be cratered, has temperatures ranging from 85°F to −190°F.

Venus has a canyon 4 mi deep and 250 mi long 1,000 mi south of Venusian equator.

Planet Features

By far the highest and most spectacular surface feature is Olympus Mons (formerly Nix Olympica) in the Tharsis region of Mars, with a diameter of 310–370 miles and a height of 75,450–95,150 ft above the surrounding plain.

Viewed from earth, by far the brightest of the five planets visible to the naked eye is Venus, with a maximum magnitude of −4.4. The faintest is

Pluto, with a magnitude of 15. Uranus at magnitude 5.5 is only marginally visible.

Earth is the densest planet with an average figure of 5.515 times that of water, while Saturn has an average density only about one-eighth of this value or 0.687 times that of water.

The most dramatic recorded conjunction (coming together) of the seven principal members of the solar system besides the earth (sun, moon, Mercury, Venus, Mars, Jupiter and Saturn) occurred on Feb 5, 1962, when 16° covered all seven during an eclipse. It is possible that the seven-fold conjunction of Sept 1186 spanned only 12°. The next notable conjunction will take place May 5, 2000.

Largest Asteroids

In the belt which lies between Mars and Jupiter, there are some 45,000 (3,226 numbered as of Jan 1986) minor planets or asteroids which are, for the most part, too small to yield to diameter measurement. The largest and first discovered (by G. Piazzi at Palermo, Sicily, Jan 1, 1801) of these is *Ceres*, with a diameter of 588 miles. The only one visible to the naked eye is asteroid 4 *Vesta* (diameter 318 miles), discovered March 29, 1807 by Dr Heinrich Wilhelm Olbers (1758–1840), a German amateur astronomer. The closest measured approach to the earth by an asteroid was 485,000 miles, in the case of *Hermes* on Oct 30, 1937 (asteroid now lost).

The most distant detected is 2060 *Chiron,* found between Saturn and Uranus Oct 18–19, 1977, by Charles Kowal from the Hale Observatory, Calif.

Largest and Smallest Satellites

The largest and heaviest satellite is *Ganymede* (Jupiter III) which is 2.017 times heavier than our moon and has a diameter of 3,270 miles.

The smallest satellite is *Leda* (Jupiter XIII) with a diameter of 9.3 miles. The Uranian satellite 1986 U7 found by *Voyager 2* is estimated to have a diameter of 9.3 mi also.

Most Satellites

Of the nine major planets, all but Venus and Mercury have known natural satellites. The planet with the most is Saturn with at least 17 satellites. The earth and Pluto are the only planets with a single satellite. The distance of the solar system's known satellites from their parent planets varies from the 5,827 miles of *Phobos* from the center of Mars to the 14,700,000 miles of Jupiter's outer satellite *Sinope* (Jupiter IX). The solar system has a total of at least 44 established satellites.

STARS

Largest and Most Massive Stars

The variable star ETA Carinae which is 9,100 light-years distant in the Carina Nebula of our own galaxy has a mass at least 200 times greater than our own sun. The object R136a in the Tarantula Nebula, an appendage of the Large Magellanic Cloud which was assessed to have a mass 2,100 times greater than our own sun is now known to be a small compact cluster of at least 8 bright stars each with a mass up to 100 times that of the sun. However, Betelgeux (top left star of Orion) has a diameter of 400 million miles, or about 500 times greater than the sun. In 1978 it was found to be surrounded not only by a dust "shell" but also an outer tenuous gas halo up to 5.3×10^{11} mi in diameter that is over 1,100 times the diameter of the star. The light from Betelgeux which reaches the earth today left the star in 1680 AD.

Smallest and Lightest Stars

A mass of 0.014 that of the sun is estimated for the very faint star RG 0058.8-2807 which was discovered by I. Neill Reid and Gerard Gilmore using the U.K. Schmidt telescope and was announced in Apr 1983. The white dwarf star L362-81 has an estimated diameter of 3,500 miles or only 0.0040 that of the sun.

Nearest Stars

Excepting the special case of our own sun, the nearest star is the very faint *Proxima Centauri,* discovered in 1915, which is 4.22 light-years (24,800,000,000,000) mi away. The nearest "star" visible to the naked eye is the southern hemisphere binary *Alpha Centauri,* or *Rigel Kentaurus* (4.35 light-years distant), with an apparent magnitude of -0.29. It was discovered by Nicolas L. da Lacaille (1713–62) in *c.* 1752. In 29,700 AD this binary will reach a minimum distance of 2.84 light-years and will appear as the second brightest "star" with an apparent mag. of -1.20.

Farthest Star

The solar system, with its sun's nine principal planets, 54 satellites, asteroids and comets was estimated in 1982 to be 28,000 light-years from the center of the lens-shaped Milky Way galaxy (diameter 70,000 light-years) so that the most distant stars in our galaxy are estimated to be 63,-000 light-years distant.

Brightest Star

Sirius A (*Alpha Canis Majoris*), also known as the Dog Star, is apparently the brightest star of the 5,776 stars visible in the heavens, with an apparent magnitude of -1.46. It is in the constellation *Canis Major* and is visible in the winter months of the northern hemisphere, being due south at midnight on the last day of the year. The Sirius system is 8.64 light-years distant and has a luminosity 26 times as much as that of the sun. It has a diameter of 1,450,000 miles and a mass of 4.26×10^{27} metric tons. The faint white dwarf companion star Sirius B has a diameter of only 6,000 miles but is 350,000 times heavier than the earth. Sirius will reach a maximum magnitude of -1.67 in *c.* 61,000 AD.

Most and Least Luminous Stars

If all the stars could be viewed at the same distance the most luminous would be ETA Carinae (see *Most Massive Star*) which now has a total luminosity 6,500,000 times greater than that of the sun, but at its peak brightness in 1843 was at least 10 times more luminous than this. The visually brightest star is the hypergiant Cygnus OB2 No. 12, which is 5,-900 light-years distant from our own galaxy and which has an absolute visual magnitude of -9.9 and is therefore visually <u>810,000 times brighter than our sun</u>. This brightness may be matched by the supergiant IV b 59 in the nearby galaxy Messier 101, but this depends on the distance adopted for this galaxy (estimates vary between 15,600,000 and 19,700,-000 light-years). The variable η Carinae in *c.* 1840 was perhaps visually 4 million times more luminous than the sun. The faintest star detected is the recently discovered RG 0058.8-2807 (see *Lightest Star*) which has a total luminosity only 0.00021 that of the sun and an absolute visual magnitude of 20.2, so that the visual brightness is less than one millionth that of the sun.

Constellations

The largest of the 89 constellations is *Hydra* (the Sea Serpent) which covers 1,302.844 sq degrees or 6.3% of the hemisphere and contains at least 68 stars visible to the naked eye (to 5.5 mag.). The constellation *Centaurus* (Centaur), ranking ninth in area, embraces, however, at least 94 such stars. The smallest constellation is *Crux Australis* (Southern Cross) with an area of 68.477 sq degrees compared with the 41,252.96 sq degrees of the whole sky.

Longest Name

The longest name for any star is *Shurnarkabtishashutu,* the Arabic for "under the southern horn of the bull."

Brightest Super-Nova

Super novae, or temporary "stars" which flare and then fade, occur perhaps five times in 1,000 years in our galaxy. The brightest "star" ever seen by historic man is believed to be the super-nova SN 1006 in Apr 1006 near *Beta Lupi* which flared for 2 years and attained a magnitude of −9 to −10. It is now believed to be the radio source G.327.6 + 14.5, nearly 3,000 light-years distant.

Stellar Planets

The first direct evidence of a planet-like companion was announced in Jan 1985 by D. McCarthy Jr, F. J. Law and R. G. Probst (US). It is an object in orbit 600 million miles from the very faint red dwarf star Van Biesbroeck 8 (VB8), 21 light-years distant in Ophiuchus.

Black Holes

This term for a star that has undergone complete gravitational collapse was first used by Prof John Archibald Wheeler at an Institute for Space Studies meeting in NYC on Dec 29, 1967.

The first tentative identification of a Black Hole was announced in Dec 1972 in the binary-star X-ray source Cygnus X-1. The best candidate is now LMC X-3 of 10 solar masses, 180,000 light-years distant, reported in Jan 1983. The critical size has been estimated to be as low as a diameter of 3.67 miles. In early 1978 supermassive Black Holes were suggested with a mass of 100 million suns—2×10^{35} metric tons. One at the center of the Seyfert galaxy, NGC 4151 in Canes Venatici, was estimated by Michael Preston (GB) in Oct 1983 to be of between 50–100 million solar masses.

THE UNIVERSE

Outside the Milky Way galaxy, which is part of the so-called Local Group of galaxies moving at a speed of 1,400,000 mph relative to the microwave background radiation in a direction offset 44° from the center of the Virgo cluster, there exist 10,000 million other galaxies.

The largest discrete object in the universe is a bent filament of galaxies in the constellations Pisces and Cetus, announced by Jack O. Burns and

David Batuski of the Univ of NM, Albuquerque, in May 1984 measuring 730 million light-years.

Farthest Visible Object

The most remote heavenly body visible to the naked eye is the Great Galaxy in *Andromeda* (Mag. 3.47) known as Messier 31. This is a rotating nebula of spiral form, its distance from the earth about 2,150,000 light-years, or about 12,600,000,000,000,000,000 miles, and it is moving toward us.

It is just possible, however, that, under ideal seeing conditions, Messier 33, the Spiral in Triangulum (Mag. 5.79), can be glimpsed by the naked eye of keen-sighted people at a distance of 2,360,000 light-years.

Quasars

An occultation of 3C-273, observed from Australia on Aug 5, 1962, enabled the existence of quasi-stellar radio sources ("quasars" or QSO's) to be announced by Maarten Schmidt (b Netherlands 1929). The red shift proved to be $z = 0.158$. Quasars have immensely high luminosity for bodies so distant and of such small diameter. In May 1983, it was announced that the quasar S50014+21 had a luminosity 1.1×10^{15} times greater than that of the sun. The first double quasar (0957 + 56) among the 1,500 known quasars was announced in May 1980.

Pulsars

The earliest observation of a pulsating radio source or "pulsar," CP 1919 (now PSR 1919 + 21), by Dr Jocelyn Bell Burnell was announced from the Mullard Radio Astronomy Observatory, Cambridgeshire, England, on Feb 24, 1968. It had been detected on Nov 28, 1967.

The fastest spinning is pulsar 1937 + 214 which is in the region of the minor constellation *Vulpecula* (the Fox), 16,000 light-years distant. It has a pulse period of 1.557806449 milli-sec and a spindown rate of 1.0511×10^{-19} sec/sec. However, the most accurate stellar clock is the second fastest pulsar, PSR 1953+29, which has a spindown rate of only 1×10^{-20} sec/sec.

Remotest Object

The interpretation of very large red shifts exhibited by quasars and the estimation of equivalent distances remain controversial. The record red shift of $z = 3.78$ for quasar PKS 2000 −330 has been interpreted as indicating proximity to "the observable horizon" of 16,300 million light-years or 96 + 21 zeros mi. It was announced in Aug 1985 that the most distant known galaxy, which is associated with the quasar PKS 1614+0.051 in Hercules, has a red shift of 3.218 (equal to a recession speed 89.4% of that of light). The 3K background radiation or primordial hiss discovered in 1965 by Arno Penzias and Robert Wilson of Bell Laboratories appears to be moving at a velocity of 99.9998% of the speed of light (*c*).

Age of the Universe

For the age of the universe a consistent value of 15 ± 3 eons or gigayears (an eon or gigayear being 1 billion years) is obtained from cosmochronology and nucleochronology. Based on the presently accepted Friedman models of the universe, with zero cosmological constant, then the equivalent Hubble ratio is about 60 km/sec Mpc, which compares to the most likely experimental value of 80 km s^{-1} Mpc^{-1}. In

1973 an *ex nihilo* creation was postulated by Edward P. Tryon (US). Modified versions of the Inflationary Model, originally introduced by Alan Guth (US) in 1981, now rival the "Big Bang" theory of creation.

ROCKETRY AND MISSILES

War rockets, propelled by a charcoal-saltpeter-sulphur gunpowder, were described by Tsen Kung Liang of China in 1042. These early rockets became known in Europe by 1258.

The first launching of a liquid-fueled rocket (patented July 14, 1914) was by Dr Robert Hutchings Goddard (1882–1945) (US) at Auburn, Mass, March 16, 1926, when his rocket reached an altitude of 41 ft and traveled a distance of 184 ft. The USSR's earliest rocket was the semi-liquid-fueled GIRD-IX tested Aug 17, 1933.

Longest Ranges

On March 16, 1962 Nikita Khrushchev, then Premier of the USSR, claimed in Moscow that the USSR possessed a "global rocket" with a range of about 19,000 miles (more than half the earth's circumference), capable of hitting any target in the world from either direction.

Most Powerful Rocket

It has been suggested that the USSR lunar booster which blew up at Tyuratam in the summer (July 3) of 1969 had a thrust of 10–14 million lb. There is some evidence of a launch of a USSR "G" class lunar booster, larger than Saturn V, May 11, 1973.

The most powerful rocket that has been publicized is the Saturn V, used for the Project Apollo and Skylab programs, on which development began in Jan 1962 at the John F. Kennedy Space Center, Merritt Island, Fla. The rocket is 363 ft 8 in tall, with a payload of over 82 tons in the case of *Skylab I*, and gulps 15 tons of propellant per sec for 2½ min. Stage I (S-IC) is 138 ft tall and powered by five Rocketdyne F-1 engines, using liquid oxygen (LOX) and kerosene, each delivering 1,514,000 lb thrust. Stage II (S-II) is powered by 5 LOX and liquid hydrogen Rocketdyne J-2 engines with a total thrust of 1,141,453 lb, while Stage III (designated S-IVB) is powered by a single 228,290-lb-thrust J-2 engine. The whole assembly generates 175,600,000 hp and weighs up to 7,600,000 lb when fully loaded, as in the case of *Apollo 17*. Saturn V was first launched Nov 9, 1967 from Cape Canaveral (then Kennedy), Fla.

Highest Velocity Space Vehicles

The first space vehicle to achieve the Third Cosmic velocity sufficient to break out of the solar system was *Pioneer 10*. The Atlas SLV-3C launcher with a modified Centaur D second stage and a Thiokol Te-364-4 third stage left the earth at an unprecedented 32,114 mph March 2, 1972. The highest recorded velocity of any space vehicle has been 149,125 mph by the US-German solar probe *Helios B* launched Jan 15, 1976.

Ion Rockets

Speeds of up to 100,000 mph are envisaged for rockets powered by an ion discharge. An ion thruster has been maintained for 9,715 hours (or 404 days 19 hours) at the Lewis Research Center in Cleveland, Ohio. Ion rockets were first used in flight by NASA's SERT I rocket, launched on July 20, 1964.

Closest Approach to the Sun by a Rocket

The research spacecraft *Helios B* approached within 27 million miles of the sun on Apr 16, 1976. It was carrying both US and West German instrumentation.

The first artificial satellite was successfully put into orbit at an altitude of 142/588 miles and a velocity of more than 17,750 mph from Tyuratam, a site located 170 miles east of the Aral Sea, on the night of Oct 4, 1957. This spherical satellite, *Sputnik* ("Fellow Traveler") 1, officially designated "Satellite 1957 Alpha 2," weighed 184.3 lb, with a diameter of 22.8 in, and its lifetime is believed to have been 92 days, ending on Jan 4, 1958. It was designed under the direction of Dr Sergey Pavlovich Korolyov (1907–66).

Earliest Successful Manned Satellites

The first successful manned space flight began at 9:07 a.m. (Moscow time), or 6:07 a.m. G.M.T., Apr 12, 1961. Flight Major (later Colonel) Yuriy Alekseyevich Gagarin (b March 9, 1934) completed a single orbit of the earth in 89.34 min in the USSR's space vehicle *Vostok* ("East") *1* (10,416 lb). The maximum speed was 17,560 mph and the maximum altitude 203.2 miles in a flight of 25,394.5 miles.

The explosion of the *Challenger S1L* space shuttle on Jan 28, 1986, the worst human disaster in space history, has caused NASA to delay further manned space exploration.

Manned Flight Altitude

The greatest altitude attained by man was when the crew of the ill-fated *Apollo XIII* was at apocynthion (*i.e.* their furthest point behind the moon) 158 miles above its surface and 248,665 miles above the earth's surface at 6:21 a.m. EST on Apr 15, 1970. The crew consisted of Capt James Arthur Lovell, Jr, USN (b Cleveland, Ohio, Mar 25, 1928); John L. Swigert, Jr (b Denver, Colo, Aug 30, 1931); and Fred Wallace Haise, Jr (b Biloxi, Miss, Nov 14, 1933).

The greatest altitude attained by a woman in flight is 174 mi by Svetlana Savitskaya (b 1948) of the USSR, second woman in space, during her flight in *Soyuz T7* launched on Aug 19, 1982. The record for a woman in an aircraft is 79,842 ft by Natalia Prokhanova (USSR) (b 1940) in an E-33 jet, May 22, 1965.

First Man-Made Object Leaves Solar System

The *Pioneer 10* spacecraft (see above) after covering 2,845 million miles in 11 years from launch date, left our known solar system of planets on June 13, 1983, by crossing the orbit of Neptune, the first object made by man to travel that far. In the next million years it will speed past the nearer stars, perhaps even find a 10th solar planet past Neptune and Uranus. If an alien body should encounter *Pioneer 10,* it will find a map on board giving earth's location in relation to 14 radio beacon stars and an engraving of two earthlings, one male, one female. *Pioneer 10* in 5 billion years, if not intercepted, may cross the rim of our galaxy. By that time, however, both sun and earth will no doubt be dead!

Astronauts

Earliest
Col Yuriy Gagarin
(b Mar 9, 1934) (USSR)
Vostok 1 Apr 12, 1961

First Woman
Lt-Col Valentina
Vladinirovna Tereshkova
(USSR) (48 orbits)
(b Mar 6 1937)
Vostok 6 June 16, 1963

First Space Walk
Lt-Col Aleksey A. Leonov
(b May 30, 1934) (USSR)
Voskhod 2 Mar 18, 1965

First Undisputed Fatality
Col Vladimir Komarov
(b Mar 16, 1927) (USSR)
Soyuz 1 Apr 23, 1967

First on Moon
Neil A. Armstrong
(b Aug 5, 1930) (US)
Apollo XI July 21, 1969

Longest on Moon
Capt Eugene A. Cernan (USN)
(b Mar 14, 1934) (US)
Dr Harrison H. Schmitt
(b July 3, 1935) (US)
74 hours 59½ min
Apollo 17 Dec 7–19, 1972

Youngest
Col Gherman S. Titov (USSR)
(25 yrs 329 days)
Vostok 2 Aug 6, 1961

Oldest
Karl G. Henize (US)
(58 years)
19th Space Shuttle July 29, 1985

First Untethered "Float" in Space
(wearing a Manned
Maneuvering Unit)
Man: Capt Bruce McCandless
(USN) (b 1938)
Challenger Feb 7, 1984

Woman: Dr Kathryn Sullivan
(b 1952) (US)
Challenger Oct 11, 1984

First Feminine Space Walk
Mme Svetlana
Savitskaya-Khatkovsky
Salyut 7 (USSR) July 25, 1984

Longest Manned Flight
236 days 22 hr 50 min
Dr. Oleg Y. Atkov, 35;
Leonid D. Kizim, 43; and
Vladimir A. Solovyev, 38
(USSR) 98.1 million miles
Soyuz T-10 Feb 8–Oct 20, 1984
Valeriy Ryumin (USSR)
3 flights aggregating 362 days

Most Journeys
Capt John Watts Young
(USN) (b 1930)
6 space flights to Dec 8, 1983
Total 34 days
19 hours 42 min 13 sec

The physical laws controlling the flight of artificial satellites were first propounded by Sir Isaac Newton (1642–1727) in his *Philosophiae Naturalis Principia Mathematica* ('Mathematical Principles of Natural Philosophy'), begun in March 1686 and first published in the summer of 1687.

First Repair in Space

The 98-ton US space shuttle, *Challenger,* was vaulted to an orbit 310 miles up, the highest a space shuttle has gone, to fetch and repair the disabled Solar Max satellite, Apr 6–13, 1984. The astronauts on board spent 7 hours 7 min in space walks, and after one unsuccessful grab, managed to latch onto the tumbling satellite with a long robot arm. It was then easy to bring it to rest in the *Challenger's* cargo bay, where two of the astronauts, Dr George D. Nelson and Dr James D. van Hoften used power tools designed for weightless conditions and replaced defective electronic units, and sent the satellite back into orbit. The repair maneuver cost about $48 million compared to $235 million to launch a new satellite. After accomplishing its mission in 7 days, the *Challenger* had to change landing plans because of bad weather at Cape Canaveral, Fla, and land visually instead at Edwards Air Force Base, Calif. This diversion added at least $200,000 to the cost of the mission as the space shuttle had to get back to its home base in Fla.

Telescope Satellite Launched into Space

An infrared telescope satellite was launched into space on Jan 25, 1983 to a height of 560 miles to follow a polar orbit and search for previously unseen stars, galaxies and other objects. The launch took place at Vandenberg Air Force Base, Calif. A McDonnell-Douglas Delta rocket propelled the $80 million satellite into orbit. The telescope is so sensitive it can, with its infrared radiation, detect a speck of dust a mile away.

Chapter 5

The Scientific World

ELEMENTS

All known matter in, on, and beyond the earth is made up of chemical elements. It is estimated that there are 10^{87} electrons in the known universe. The total of naturally-occurring elements so far detected is 94, comprising, at ordinary temperature, 2 liquids, 11 gases and 81 solids. The so-called "fourth state" of matter is plasma, when negatively charged electrons and positively charged ions are in flux.

Lightest and Heaviest Sub-Nuclear Particles

By Apr 1984, the existence of 30 "stable" particles, 53 meson resonance multiplets *and* 48 baryon resonance multiplets was accepted, representing the eventual discovery of 242 particles and an equal number of anti-particles. The heaviest "stable" particle fully accepted is the neutral weak gauge boson, the Z°, of mass 92.9 ± 1.6 GeV which was first detected in May 1983 by the UA1 Collaboration, CERN, Geneva, Switzerland using the 540 GeV Super Proton Synchrotron proton-antiproton beam collider. The heaviest particle known is the upsilon (4S) meson resonance of mass 10577 ± 1 meV and lifetime 3×10^{-23} sec, which consists of a bottom or beauty quark and its anti-quark, and which was first identified in Apr 1980 by two groups using the electron storage ring facilities at Cornell Univ, Ithaca, NY. Sub atomic concepts require that the masses of the graviton, photon, and neutrino should all be zero. Based on the sensitivities of various cosmological theories, upper limits for the masses of these particles are 7.6×10^{-67} g for the graviton; 3.0×10^{-53} g for the photon and 1.4×10^{-32} g for the neutrino (*cf.* 9.10953×10^{-28} g for the mass of an electron).

Newest Particles

It was announced in July 1984 that the UA1 Collaboration, CERN, Geneva, Switzerland had obtained tentative evidence for the existence of the sixth flavor of quark, the top or truth quark, of mass about 40 GeV. In Oct 1984 two groups using the Cornell Univ electron storage ring facilities identified two higher mass states of a combination of a bottom or beauty quark and its anti-quark, known as the upsilon (5S) and (6S) meson resonances of mass 10.86 GeV and 11.02 GeV and lifetimes 6×10^{-24} sec and 9×10^{-24} sec respectively.

The discovery in July 1984 by the Crystal Ball Collaboration, Hamburg, W Germany, of a particle of mass 8.32 GeV known as the "zeta," and which was associated with the existence of the important theoretical particle known as the Higgs boson, has not been confirmed.

Most and Least Stable Particles

Experiments in 1982 to 1984 have confirmed that the proton definitely has a lifetime in excess of 1×10^{30} years compared to theoretical predictions based on the "grand unified theory," which suggests that the lifetime may be less than 1×10^{34} years. The least stable or shortest-lived particles are the two baryon resonances N(2220) and N(2600), both 1.6×10^{-24} sec.

Most Absorbent Substance

The US Dept of Agriculture Research Service announced on Aug 18, 1974 that "H-span" or Super Slurper, composed of one half starch derivative and one fourth each of acrylamide and acrylic acid, can, when treated with iron, retain water 1,300 times its own weight.

Smelliest Substance

The most evil-smelling substance, of the 17,000 smells so far classified, must be a matter of opinion, but ethyl mercaptan (C_2H_5SH) and butyl seleno-mercaptan (C_4H_9SeH) are powerful claimants, each with a smell reminiscent of a combination of rotting cabbage, garlic, onions and sewer gas.

Most Expensive Perfume

The retail prices of the most expensive perfumes tend to be fixed at public relations rather than economic levels. The Chicago-based firm Jōvan marketed from Mar 1984 a cologne called Andron which contains a trace of the attractant pheromone androstenol which has a cost of $2,750 per oz.

Most Potent Poison

The rickettsial disease, Q-fever, can be instituted by a *single* organism but is only fatal in 1 in 1,000 cases. About 10 organisms of *Francisella tularenesis* (formerly known as *Pasteurella tularenesis*) can institute tularemia, variously called alkali disease, Francis disease or deerfly fever, and this is fatal in upwards of 10 cases in 1,000.

The most lethal man-made chemical is TCDD (2,3,7,8-tetrachlorodibenzo-p-dioxin) utilized in herbicides, discovered in 1872. It is said to be 150,000 times more deadly than cyanide.

Most Powerful Nerve Gas

VX, 300 times more toxic than phosgene ($COCl_2$) used in World War I, was developed at the Chemical Defence Experimental Establishment, Porton Down, Wiltshire, England in 1952. Patents applied for in 1962 and published in Feb 1974, showing it to be Ethyl S-2-diisopropylamimoethylphosphonothiolate. The lethal dosage is 10 mg-minute/m^3 airborne or 0.3 mg orally.

Most Powerful Drugs

The most powerful commonly available drug is d-Lysergic Acid Diethylamide tartrate (LSD-25, $C_{20}H_{25}N_3O$) first produced in 1938 for common cold research and as a hallucinogen by Dr Albert Hoffmann (Swiss) Apr 16–19, 1943.

The most potent analgesic drug is the morphine-like R33799, confirmed in 1978 to have almost 12,000 times the potency of morphine.

Interferon was reportedly available for $10 per millionth of a microgram.

Most Prescribed Drug

The top-selling prescription drug in the world is the anti-ulcer drug Tagamet marketed by Smithkline-Beckman of Philadelphia. The sales in 1981 were estimated at $800 million. The most prescribed drug in the United Kingdom is the tranquilizer Valium with over 1 million users.

Finest Powder

The ultimate in fine powder is solid helium, which was first postulated to be a monatomic powder as early as 1964.

SWEETEST SUBSTANCE: Seeds from katemfe, the plants that exude the sweetest known substance—much sweeter than sugar.

DRINK

Most Alcoholic Liquor

The strength of liquor is expressed by degrees proof. In the US, proof is double the actual percentage of alcohol (C_2H_5OH) by volume at 60°F in a liquor. Pure or absolute alcohol is thus 200 degrees proof. A "hangover" is avoided by the presence of toxic congenerics such as amyl alcohol ($C_5H_{11}OH$).

During independence (1918–40) the Estonian Liquor Monopoly marketed 196 proof potato alcohol. In 31 US states *Everclear* (190 proof or 95% alcohol) is marketed by the American Distilling Co, "primarily as a base for homemade cordials."

Liqueurs

The most expensive liqueur in France is *Eau de vie de pêche,* sold for 190 francs ($27.75) a bottle of 75 centiliters at Fauchon in Paris.

The most expensive bottle of spirits sold at auction was a magnum of *Grande Armée Fine Champagne Cognac* 1811 at Christie's of London on Nov 13, 1978, for £780 ($1,560). Grande Fine Champagne Cognac Biscuit du Boucher 1811 retails for 18,000 francs ($2,700) a bottle at Fauchon in Paris.

Most Expensive Wine

Record prices paid for single bottles *usually* arise when two or more self-promoters are seeking publicity. They bear little relation to the market value.

The highest price paid for any bottle has been £105,000 ($157,500) for a 1787 Chateau Lafite claret sold to Christopher Forbes (US) at Christie's London on Dec 5, 1985. The price was affected by the bottle having been initialed by Thomas Jefferson.

Oldest Vintage Wine

The oldest datable wine has been an amphora salvaged and drunk by Capt Jacques Cousteau from the wreck of a Greek trader sunk in the Mediterranean c. 230 BC. A wine jar recovered in Rome bears the label "Q. Lutatio C. Mario Cos," meaning that it was produced in the consulship of 102 BC. A bottle of 1748 Rudesheimer Rosewein was auctioned at Christie's of London, for £260 ($570) Dec 6, 1979.

Greatest Wine Auction and Tasting

The largest single sale of wine was conducted by Christie's of London, July 10–11, 1974 at Quaglino's Ballroom when 2,325 lots containing 432,000 bottles realized £962,190 (then $2,309,256).

The largest wine-tasting ever reported was that staged by the Wine Institute at St Francis Hotel, San Francisco, on July 17, 1980 with 125 pourers, 90 openers and a consumption of 3,000 bottles.

Strongest and Weakest Beer

The most alcoholic beer is Samichlaus Bier brewed by Brauerei Hürlimann of Zurich, Switzerland. It is 13.70% alcohol by volume at 20° C with an original gravity of 1117.8°. The strongest beer as measured by original gravity is the German EKU Kulminatur Urtyphell 28 with 1131.7° and 13.52% alcohol by volume at 20° C.

The weakest liquid ever marketed as beer was a sweet ersatz beer which was brewed in Germany by Sunner, Colne-Kalk, in 1918. It had an original gravity of 1000.96°, with less than 0.2% alcohol.

Largest and Smallest Bottles

The largest bottles normally used in the wine and spirit trade are the Jeroboam (equal to 4 bottles of champagne or, rarely, of brandy, and from 5 to 6½ bottles of claret, depending on whether the bottle was blown or molded) and the double magnum (equal, since c. 1934, to 4 bottles of claret or, more rarely, red burgundy). A complete set of champagne bottles would consist of the ¼ bottle, ½ bottle, bottle, magnum, Jeroboam, Rehoboam, Methuselah, Salmanazar, Balthazar and the Nebuchadnezzar, which has a capacity of 16 liters (33.8 pints), and is equivalent to 20 bottles.

In May 1958 a 5-ft-tall sherry bottle with a capacity of 20½ Imperial gallons (24.6 US gallons) was blown in Stoke-on-Trent, Staffordshire, England. This bottle, with the capacity of 131 normal bottles, was named an "Adelaide."

The smallest bottles of liquor now sold are White Horse bottles of Scotch whisky containing 1.3 milliliters (about 4/100ths of an ounce) for about 50 cents per bottle in "cases" of 12.

Largest Collections

The largest reported collection of unduplicated miniature bottles is one of 26,794 by Apr 1986 by David L. Maund of Eastleigh, England.

The largest collection of bottle caps is probably the collection of Helge

Friholm of Soborg, Denmark, which consists of 38,750 different undamaged caps from 145 countries as of Apr 24, 1986.

The largest reported collection of distilled spirits or liqueurs in any bar is 1,722 unduplicated labels collected by Ian Boasman at Bistro French, Preston, Lancashire, Eng, audited in May 1986. The greatest collection of whisky bottles is one of 3,100 unduplicated labels assembled by Sig Edward Giaccone at his Whiskyteca, Salo, Lake Garda, Italy.

Champagne Cork Flight

The longest distance for a champagne cork to fly from an untreated and unheated bottle 4 ft from level ground is 105 ft 9 in achieved by Peter Kirby at Idlewild Park, Reno, Nev, July 4, 1981.

PHOTOGRAPHY

Earliest Cameras

The earliest veiled reference to a photograph on glass taken in a camera was in a letter from Joseph Nicéphore Niepce (1765–1833), a French physician and scientist, dated July 19, 1822. It was a photograph of a copper engraving of Pope Pius VII taken at Gras, near Chalon-sur-Saône.

One of the earliest photographs taken was one of a diamond-paned window in Lacock Abbey, Wiltshire, England, taken in Aug 1835 by William Henry Fox Talbot (1800–1877), the inventor of the negative-positive process.

Largest and Smallest Cameras

The largest and most expensive industrial camera ever built is the 30¼-ton Rolls-Royce camera now owned by BPCC Graphics Ltd of Derby, England, completed in 1959. It measures 8 ft 10 in high, 8 ft 3 in wide and 46 ft long. The lens is a 63″ f/16 Cooke Apochromatic. It is still in full use.

Apart from cameras built for intra-cardiac surgery and espionage, the smallest camera that has been marketed is the circular Japanese "Petal" camera with a diameter of 1.14 in and a thickness of 0.65 in. It has a focal length of 0.47 in (12 mm).

Most Expensive Cameras

The most expensive complete range of camera equipment is that of Nikon of Tokyo, Japan who marketed a range of 25 cameras with 128 lenses and 523 accessories in 1985. The total cost of the range would exceed $185,000.

The highest auction price for an antique camera was £21,000 ($42,000) for a J. B. Dancer stereo camera patented in 1856 and sold at Christie's, London, on Oct 12, 1977.

Longest Negative

Using a 16-in Century Cirkut camera, Robert J. Paluzzi captured a 200-degree view of Las Vegas in a single shot on June 22, 1985. The resulting negative measured 9 ft by 16 in.

LONGEST NEGATIVE: Photographer Bob Paluzzi shows a contact print of his 200° super-wide landscape shot of the skyline of Las Vegas, Nev. With a 16-in camera, he took it all in a single shot.

Fastest Camera

A camera for fusion research built by the Rutherford-Appleton Laboratory at Essex Univ, Colchester, England and designed by Dr Tom Hall can register images at a rate of 3,000 million per sec.

First Aerial Photography

The earliest aerial photograph was taken in 1858 by Gaspard Félix Tournachon (1820–1910), *alias* Nadar, from a balloon near Villacoublay, on the outskirts of Paris, France.

TELESCOPES

Earliest Telescope

Although there is evidence that early Arabian scientists understood something of the magnifying power of lenses, the first known use of lenses to form a telescope has been attributed to Roger Bacon (c. 1214–92) in England. The prototype of modern refracting telescopes was completed by Johannes Lippershey for the Netherlands government on Oct 2, 1608.

Largest Reflector

The largest telescope is the alt-azimuth mounted, 236.2-inch telescope sited on Mt Semirodriki, near Zelenchukskaya in the Caucasus Mts, USSR, at an altitude of 6,830 ft. Work on the mirror, weighing 78 tons, was not completed until the summer of 1974. Regular observations were begun on Feb 7, 1976, after 16 years' work. The weight of the 138-ft-high assembly is 946 tons. Being the most powerful of all telescopes, its range, which includes the location of objects down to the 25th magnitude, represents the limits of the observable universe. Its light-gathering power

would enable it to detect the light from a candle at a distance of 15,000 miles.

Work started on Sept 15, 1985, on the $70 million Keck 393.7-in reflector comprising 36 independently controlled fitting hexagonal mirrors for Caltech and the Univ of California. It is sited on Mt Mauna Kea, Hawaii and due to be completed by 1989.

Note: The attachment of an electronic charge-coupled-device (CCD) increases the "light-grasp" of a telescope by a factor up to 100 fold. Thus a 200-in telescope achieves the light-gathering capacity of a 1,000-in telescope.

Largest Refractor

The largest refracting (*i.e.* magnification by lenses) telescope in the world is the 62-ft-long, 40-in telescope completed in 1897 at the Yerkes Observatory, Williams Bay, Wis, belonging to the University of Chicago. In 1900, a 49.2-in refractor 180 ft in length was built for the Paris Exposition, but its optical performance was too poor to justify attempts to use it.

Oldest and Highest Observatories

The oldest astronomical observatory building extant is the "Tower of the Winds" used by Andronichus of Cyrrhos in Athens, Greece, *c.* 70 BC.

The highest-altitude observatory in the world is the University of Denver's High Altitude Observatory at an altitude of 14,100 ft, opened in 1973, on Mt Evans, Colo. The principal instrument is a 24-in Ealing Beck reflecting telescope.

Largest Radio Telescope

The largest radio-telescope installation is the US National Science Foundation VLA (Very Large Array). It is Y-shaped with each arm 13 miles long with 27 mobile antennae (each 82 ft in diameter) on rails. It is 50 miles west of Socorro in the Plains of San Augustin, NM and was dedicated on Oct 10, 1980 at a cost of $78 million.

A computer-linked very long base-line array of 82-ft radio telescopes stretched over 2,600 miles on Lat 49.3 °N has been planned by the Canadian Astronomical Society.

VLA stands for Very Large Array. This installation near Socorro, NM, is the world's largest radio telescope. It has 27 mobile railed antennae and each arm is 13 miles long.

Space Telescope

The first space observatory was the Orbiting Solar observatory 0504 launched on Oct 18, 1967. The largest planned is a $1.2 billion NASA Space Telescope of 12 tons and 42 ft 7 in in overall length with a 94-in reflector scheduled to be placed in orbit at *c*. 300-mi altitude aboard a US Space Shuttle.

Largest Dish Telescopes

Radio waves of extraterrestrial origin were first detected by Karl Jansky of Bell Telephone Laboratories, Holmdel, NJ, using a 100-ft-long shortwave rotatable antenna in 1932. The largest trainable dish-type radio telescope is the 328-ft-diameter, 3,360-ton assembly at the Max Planck Institute for Radio Astronomy of Bonn in the Effelsberger Valley, W Germany; it became operative in May 1971. The cost of the installation, begun in Nov 1967, was DM36,920,000 ($14,760,000).

The world's largest dish-type radio telescope is the partially-steerable ionospheric assembly built over a natural bowl at Arecibo, Puerto Rico, completed in Nov 1963 at a cost of about $9 million. It has a diameter of 1,000 ft and the dish covers 18½ acres. Its sensitivity was raised by a factor of 1,000 and its range to the edge of the observable universe at some 15,000 million light-years by the fitting of new aluminum plates at a cost of $8,800,000. Rededication was on Nov 16, 1974.

The RATAN-600 radio telescope completed in the northern Caucasus, USSR, in 1976 has 895 metal mirror panels mounted in a circle 1,-890 ft across.

Solar Telescope

The world's largest solar telescope is the 480-ft-long McMath telescope at Kitt Peak National Observatory near Tucson, Ariz. It has a focal length of 300 ft and an 80-in heliostat mirror. It was completed in 1962 and produces an image measuring 33 in in diameter.

Planetaria

The ancestor of the planetarium is the rotatable Gottorp Globe, built by Andreas Busch in Denmark between 1654 and 1664 to the orders of Olearius, court mathematician to Duke Frederick III of Holstein. It is 34.6 ft in circumference, weighs 4 tons and is now preserved in Leningrad, USSR. The stars were painted on the inside.

The earliest optical installation was not until 1923 in the Deutsches Museum, Munich, by Zeiss of Jena, Germany.

The world's largest planetarium, with a diameter of 82½ ft, is in Moscow.

GEMS

Rarest and Commonest Minerals

The rarest mineral cannot be certainly established. The total known amount of scotlandite (PbSO$_3$) comprises only a few tens of milligrams. Though probably found in the 19th century in Leadhills, Strathclyde, Scotland this first naturally occurring yellowish sulphite was only certainly identified in 1978 by Dr R. S. W. Braithwaite. The world's commonest mineral is silicate of calcium, iron magnesium and manganese collectively known as olivine.

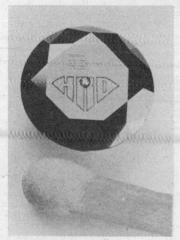

SMALLEST DIAMOND EVER CUT (left): This tiny 0.02-in gem cut in Antwerp into a "brilliant."

MOST EXPENSIVE GEM (right): Sold at auction for $4,580,000 in 1984, this Terestchenko blue diamond weighs 42.92 carats.

PRECIOUS STONE RECORDS

The carat was standardized at 205 mg (0.007054 oz) in 1877. The metric carat of 200 mg was introduced in 1914.

	Largest	Largest Cut Stone	Other Records
Diamond (pure crystallized carbon)	Diamond (pure crystallized carbon) 3,106 metric carats (over 1¼ lb)—*The Cullinan*, found by Mr Gray, Jan 25, 1905, in the Premier Mine, Pretoria, South Africa. The first synthetic diamonds were produced by Prof H. T. Hall at the General Electric Research Laboratories, on Dec 16, 1954. In Feb 1984 a Tass report from Leningrad, USSR, announced that the Institute of High Frequency Currents had produced an artificial diamond weighing 4½ lb.	530.2 metric carats. 74 facets. Cleaved from *The Cullinan* in 1908 in Amsterdam by Jak Asscher and polished by Henri Koe. Known as *The Star of Africa* No. 1 and now in the British Royal Sceptre. The *Cullinan II* is 317.40 carats. Third on the list of the 55 diamonds of more than 100 carats is the Great Mogul of 280 old carats lost in the sack of Delhi in 1739 and arguably the most valuable object ever lost. In Nov 1984 the Zale Corporation of NYC announced that it may be feasible to cut their pale yellow 890 carat uncut stone from Africa into a 550–600 carat cut stone.	Diamond is the hardest-known naturally occurring substance, with 5 times the indentation hardness of the next hardest mineral, corundum. The peak hardness on the Knoop scale is 8,400 compared with an average diamond of 7,000. The rarest color for diamond is blood red. The largest example is a flawless 5.05-carat stone found in 1927 in Lichtenberg, South Africa now in a private collection in the US. The diamond per carat record price of $113,000 was set by the 41.3-carat "Polar Star" bought in Geneva for $4.95 million Nov 21, 1980, by Mr Razeen Salih. The 42.92 carat Terestchenko blue diamond was auctioned at Christie's, Geneva, Switz, Nov 14, 1984 for $4,580,000. The largest blue diamond is the 45.85 carat Copenhagen Blue. The Argyle field of W Australia yielded 6.2 million carats in 1983 and 5.7 million in 1984, and is now the most prolific in the world.
Emerald (green beryl) [$Be_3Al_2(SiO_3)_6$]	86,136-carat natural beryl Gleim emerald. Found in Carnaiba, Brazil, Aug 1974. Carved by Richard Chan (Hong Kong). Appraised at $1,292,-000 in 1982.		An 18.35-carat ring was sold for $520,000 at Sotheby Parke Bernet, NYC, in Apr 1977.
Sapphire (corundum, any color but red) [Al_2O_3]	Sapphire (corundum, any color but red) [Al_2O_3] 2,302-carat stone found at Anakie, Queensland, Australia, in c. 1935, now a 1,318-carat head of President Abraham Lincoln (1809–65)	1,444-carat black star stone carved from a 2,097-carat stone in 1953–55 into a bust of Pres-Gen Dwight David Eisenhower (1890–1969).	*Note:* Both the sapphire busts are in the custody of the Kazanjian Foundation of Los Angeles. Auction record for a single stone was set by a step-cut sapphire of 66.03 carats at Sotheby's Zurich May 8, 1980, from the Rockefeller Collection at Sotheby's Zurich May 8, 1980.
Ruby (red corundum) [Al_2O_3]	Ruby (red corundum) [Al_2O_3] 8,500-carat semi-translucent to opaque natural ruby exhibited in Smithsonian, now cut in shape of Liberty Bell, 5½ in tall, exhibited in jeweler Kazan-	A gem-quality natural ruby of Burmese origin weighs 1,184 carats. The largest star ruby is the 650-carat Vidyaraj ruby in Bangalore, India.	Since 1955 rubies have been the world's most precious gem attaining a world record carat price of $100,639 at Christie's sale in Geneva in Nov 1979 in the case of a 4.12-carat caspian-shaped ruby. The ability to make corundum prisms for laser technology up to over 12 in in length seems to have little bearing on the market for natural

RECORDS FOR OTHER PRECIOUS MATERIALS

	Where Found	Notes on Present Location, etc.
Largest Pearl (Molluscan consecration) 14 lb 1 oz 9½ in long × 5½ in in diameter—*Pearl of Lao-tze*	At Palawan, Philippines, May 7, 1934 in shell of giant clam	The property of Wilburn Dowell Cobb, from 1936 until his death, valued at $4,080,000 in July 1971, sold on May 15, 1980 at auction in San Francisco by his estate for $200,000 to Peter Hoffmann, jeweler of Beverly Hills, Calif. In May 1982, an appraisal for the owners (Hoffmann and Victor Barbish) by the San Francisco Gem Laboratory suggested a value of $32,640,000.
Black Pearl 0.71 in diameter	Namarai Bay, Fiji Islands	Found by Yasuhiro on Jan 26, 1984.
Opal (SiO_2, NH_2O) 220 troy oz (yellow-orange)	Coober Pedy, South Australia	The Olympic australis (17,700 carats), found in Aug 1956, owned by Altmann & Cherny Pty Ltd is on public display in Melbourne and is valued at $1.8 million (US). An opal containing much "potch" (colorless material) named the Desert Flame was found at Andamooka, South Australia. The 34,215-carat mass first reported in Sept 1969 was broken up and auctioned off on Aug 29, 1978.
Rock Crystal (Quartz) (SiO_2) Ball: 106¾ lb 12% in in diameter, the *Warner* sphere	Burma (originally a 1,000-lb piece)	US National Museum, Washington, DC
Topaz $Al_2SiO_4(F,OH)_2$ "Brazilian Princess" 21,325 carats, 221 facets (light blue)	Light blue, from Brazil	Amer Museum of Natural History, NYC, from Dec 10, 1985. Valued at $1,066,350 or $50 per carat. Cut from a 75-lb crystal. World's largest faceted stone.
Amber (coniferous fossil resin) 33 lb 10 oz	Reputedly from Burma, acquired in 1860	Bought by John Charles Bowing (d 1893) for £300 in Canton, China. Natural History Museum, London, since 1940
Nephrite Jade $Ca_2(Mgte)_5(Si_8O_{11})_2(OH)_2$ Boulder of 143 tons (315,315 lb), 21,300 cu ft	Reported in China, Sept 17, 1978	Jadeite can be virtually any color except red or blue. The largest-known example is a block from Burma weighing 36.96 tons.
Marble (Metamorphosed $CaCO_3$) 100.8 tons (single slab)	Quarried at Yule, Colo	A piece of over 50 tons was dressed from this slab for the coping stone of the Tomb of the Unknown Soldier in Arlington National Cemetery, Va
Nuggets—Gold (Au) 7,560 oz (472½ lb) (reef gold) *Holtermann Nugget*	Beyers & Holtermann Star of Hope Gold Mining Co, Hill End, NSW, Australia Oct 19, 1872	The purest large nugget was the Holtermann nugget, found at Moliagul, Victoria, Australia, which yielded 220 lb of pure gold from a 630-lb slab of slate.
Silver (Ag) 2,750 lb troy	Sonora, Mexico	Appropriated by the Spanish Government before 1821

LARGEST FACETED STONE (below): The light blue topaz called the "Brazilian Princess," weighing 21,235 carats, has 221 facets and was cut from a 75-lb crystal. Now in NYC's American Museum of Natural History, it is valued at about $50 per carat—total $1,066,350.

LARGEST EMERALD (above): This 86,136-carat stone was found in Brazil in 1974. After carving it was worth $1,292,000.

HOPE DIAMOND (left): The second largest blue diamond, on exhibit in the Smithsonian Institution, Washington, DC, weighs 44.4 carats, but is reputed to carry a curse with it.

Hardest Gems

The hardest of all gems, and hardest known naturally occurring substance, is diamond, which is, chemically, pure carbon. Diamond has 5 times the indentation hardness of the next hardest mineral, corundum (Al_2O_3). Hardnesses are compared on Mohs' scale, on which talc is 1, a fingernail is 2½, window glass 5, topaz 8, corundum 9, and diamond 10.

Smallest Brilliant Cut Diamond

A diamond weighing 0.00063 of a carat, 0.02 in in size, is owned by Gebroedeus van den Wouwer of Antwerp, Belgium.

Largest Crystals

An 187-ton beryl ($Be_3Al_2Si_6O_{18}$) measuring 59 ft long and 11½ ft in diameter was recorded at Malakialina, Madagascar (formerly Malagasy Republic) in 1976.

A 520,000-carat (229-lb) aquamarine [Be_3AI_2 ($SiO_3)_6$] found near Marambaia, Brazil in 1910, yielded over 200,000 carats of gem-quality cut stones.

Densest Gem Mineral

The densest of all gem minerals is stibiotantalite [$(SbO)_2$ $(Ta,Nb)_2O_6$], a rare brownish-yellow mineral found in San Diego County, Calif with a density of 7.46 grams per cc. The alloy platiniridium has a density of more than 22.0.

Newest Gemstones

Tanzanite was discovered in Tanzania in 1969. It reached $1,200 per carat in 1977. The deep purple Royal Lavalite found in Hotazel, South Africa by Randy Polk of Phoenix, Ariz reached $1,300 per carat in 1982.

NUMERATION

In dealing with large numbers, scientists use the notation of 10 raised to various powers, to eliminate a profusion of zeros. Example: 19,160,-000,000,000 miles would be written 1.916×10^{13} miles. A very small number is treated similarly—for example, 0.0000154324 of a gram, would be written 1.54324×10^{-5} gram (g). Of the prefixes used before numbers the smallest is "tredo" from the Danish "tredyvo" for 30, indicating 10^{-30} of a unit. The highest is "dea" (Greek *deca,* ten) symbol D, indicating 10 groups of 3 zeros (10^{30}) or a nonillion.

Most Innumerate

The most innumerate people are the Nambiquara of northwest Matto Grosso of Brazil who lack any system of numbers. They do however have a verb which means "they are two alike."

Prime Numbers

A prime number is any positive integer (excluding 1) having no integral factors other than itself and unity, *e.g.* 2, 3, 5, 7, or 11. The lowest prime number is thus 2. The highest known prime number is $2^{216,091}-1$ discovered in Sept 1985 by analysts using a Cray X-MP/24 computer at Chevron Geosciences Co in Houston, Tex. It is the 30th known Marsenne prime, and contains 65,050 digits. The lowest non-prime or composite number (excluding 1) is 4.

Perfect Numbers

A number is said to be perfect if it is equal to the sum of its divisors other than itself, *e.g.* 1+2+4+7+14=28. The lowest perfect number is 6

(1+2+3). The highest known, and the 30th so far discovered, is $(2^{216,091}-1) \times 2^{216,090}$. It is a consequence of the highest known prime (see above).

Highest Numbers

The highest lexicographically accepted named number in the system of successive powers of ten is the centillion, first recorded in 1852. It is the hundredth power of a million, or one followed by 600 zeros. The highest named number outside the decimal notation is the Buddhist *asankhyeya,* which is equal to 10^{140}.

The number 10^{100} is designated a Googol, a term devised by Dr Edward Kasner of the US (d 1955). Ten raised to the power of a Googol is described as a Googolplex. Some conception of the magnitude of such numbers can be gained when it is said that the number of electrons in some models of the observable universe probably does not exceed 10^{87}.

The highest number ever used in a mathematical proof is a bounding value published in 1977 and known as Graham's number. It concerns bichromatic hypercubes and is inexpressible without the special "arrow" notation, devised by Knuth in 1976, extended to 64 layers. Mr Candelaria ("the only man infinity fears") of Loma Linda, Calif has devised a Large Number Denomination System concluding with a milli-decilli-fiveillionillion.

Most Accurate and Inaccurate Versions of "Pi"

The greatest number of decimal places to which *pi* (π) has been calculated is 16,777,216 by Yasumasu Kanada and Y. Tamura (Japan) July 24, 1985, after 30 hours on the main frame computer in Tokyo Univ. The published value to 2 million places, in what has been described as the world's most boring 800-page book, was 3.141592653589793 ... (omitting the next 1,999,975 places) ... 1457297909.

In 1897, the General Assembly of Indiana enacted in House Bill No. 246 that *pi* was *de jure* 4, for the most inaccurate version.

Longest and Shortest Time Measure

The longest measure of time is the *kalpa* in Hindu chronology. It is equivalent to 4,320 million years. In astronomy a cosmic year is the period of rotation of the sun around the center of the Milky Way galaxy, *i.e.* 225,000,000 years. In the Late Cretaceous Period of *c.* 85 million years ago, the earth rotated faster so resulting in 370.3 days per year, while in Cambrian times, some 600 million years ago, there is evidence that the year contained 425 days.

Owing to variations in the length of a day, which is estimated to be increasing irregularly at the average rate of about a millisecond per century, due to the moon's tidal drag, the second has been redefined. Instead of being 1/86,400th part of a mean solar day, it has since 1960 been reckoned as 1/31,556,925.9747th part of the solar (or tropical) year at 1900 AD, Jan 0 at 12 hours, Ephemeris time. In 1958 the second of Ephemeris time was computed to be equivalent to 9,192,631,770 ± 20 cycles of the radiation corresponding to the transition of a cesium 133 atom when unperturbed by exterior fields. The greatest diurnal change recorded has been 10 milliseconds on Aug 8, 1972, due to the most violent solar storm recorded in 370 years of observation.

The accuracy of the cesium beam frequency standard approaches 8 parts in 10^{14} compared to 2 parts in 10^{13} for the methane-stabilized helium-neon laser and 6 parts in 10^{13} for the hydrogen maser.

PHYSICAL EXTREMES (TERRESTRIAL)

Finest Balance

The most accurate balance is the Sartorius Model 4108, manufactured in Göttingen, W Germany, which can weigh objects of up to 0.5 grams (about .018 oz) to an accuracy of 0.01 µg or 0.00000001 g, which is equivalent to little more than one-sixtieth of the weight of the ink on a period dot (.).

Largest Bubble Chamber

The largest bubble chamber is the $7 million installation completed in Oct 1973, at Weston, Ill. It is 15 ft in diameter and contains 7,259 gallons of liquid hydrogen at a temperature of $-247\,°C$ ($-412.6\,°F$) with a superconducting magnet of 3 tesla.

Fastest Centrifuge

Ultra-centrifuges were invented by Theodor Svedberg (b Aug 30, 1884) (Sweden) in 1923.

The highest man-made rotary speed ever achieved and the fastest speed of any earth-bound object is 4,500 mph by a swirling tapered 6-in carbon fiber rod in a vacuum at Birmingham University, England, reported Jan 24, 1975.

Finest Cut

The $13 million Large Optics Diamond Turning Machine at the Lawrence Livermore National Laboratory, Calif was reported in June 1983 to be able to sever a human hair 3,000 times lengthwise.

Most Powerful Electric Current

The most powerful electric current generated is that from the Zeus capacitor at the Los Alamos Scientific Laboratory, NM. If fired simultaneously the 4,032 capacitors would produce for a few microseconds twice as much current as that generated elsewhere on earth.

Highest Measured Frequency

The highest *directly* measured frequency is a visible yellow-green light at 520.2068085 terahertz (a terahertz being a million million hertz or cycles per second) for the o-component of the 17-1 P(62) transition line of iodine 127. The highest measured frequency determined by precision metrology is a green light at 582.491703 terahertz for the b_{21} component of the R(15) 43-0 transition line of iodine 127. However with the decision on Oct 20, 1983 by the *Conférence Générale des Poids et Mesures* (CGPM) to exactly define the meter (m) in terms of the velocity of light (c) such that "the meter is the length of the path traveled by light in vacuum during a time interval of 1/299 792 458 of a second" then frequency (f) and wavelength (λ) are exactly interchangeable through the relationship $f\lambda = c$.

Hottest Flame

The hottest flame that can be produced is from carbon subnitride (C_4N_2) which at one atmosphere pressure is calculated to reach 5,261 K.

MOST POWERFUL LIGHT BEAM: This 2-mi-long Linear Accelerator at Stamford, Calif, produces a record light beam through a 4x½-in slit. (*Science Photo Library*)

Lowest Friction

The lowest coefficient of static and dynamic friction of any solid is 0.02, in the case of polytetrafluoroethylene ($[C_2F_4]_n$), called PTFE—equivalent to wet ice on wet ice. It was first manufactured in quantity by E. I. du Pont de Nemours & Co Inc in 1943, and is marketed as Teflon.

In the centrifuge at the University of Virginia a 30-lb rotor magnetically supported has been spun at 1,000 revolutions per sec in a vacuum of 10^{-6} mm of mercury pressure. It loses only one revolution per sec per day, thus spinning for years.

Smallest Hole

A hole of 40 Å (4×10^{-9} mm) was shown visually, using a JEM 100 C electron microscope and Quantel Electronics devices at the Dept of Metallurgy, Oxford, England, on Oct 28, 1979. To find such a hole is equivalent to finding a pinhead in a haystack measuring 1.2 miles × 1.2 miles.

An electron microscope beam on a sample of sodium beta-alumina at the Univ of Illinois in May 1983 bored a hole 2×10^{-9} m in diameter accidentally.

Most Powerful Laser Beams

The first illumination of another celestial body was achieved May 9, 1962, when a beam of light was successfully reflected from the moon by the use of a laser (light amplification by stimulated emission of radiation) attached to a 48-in telescope at MIT, Cambridge, Mass. The spot was estimated to be 4 miles in diameter on the moon. The device was propounded in 1958 by Dr Charles Hard Townes (b US 1915) of Bell Telephone Laboratories. Such a flash for 1/5,000th sec can bore a hole through a diamond by vaporization at 10,000 °C, produced by 2×10^{23} photons.

The "Shiva" laser was reported at the Lawrence Livermore Laboratory, Calif to be concentrating 2.6×10^{13} watts into a pinhead-sized target for 9.5×10^{-11} sec in a test on May 18, 1978.

Most Durable Light

The average bulb lasts for 750–1,000 hours. There is some evidence that a 5-watt carbide filament bulb made by the Shelby Electric Co and presented to Mr Bernell in the Fire Department, Livermore, Calif was first shedding light in 1901, and is still burning when lit.

Shortest Light Pulse

Charles Z. Shank and colleagues of the AT & T Laboratories in NJ achieved a light pulse of 8 femtoseconds (8×10^{-15} sec) announced in 1985. The pulse comprised only 4 or 5 wavelengths of visible light or 2.4 micrometers long.

Brightest Light

The brightest steady artificial light sources are laser beams, with an intensity exceeding the sun's 1,500,000 candles per sq in by a factor of well in excess of 1,000.

In May 1969 the USSR Academy of Sciences announced blast waves traveling through a luminous plasma of inert gases heated to 90,000 K. The flare-up for up to 3 microseconds shone at 50,000 times the brightness of the sun, viz. 75 billion candles per sq in. Of continuously burning sources, the most powerful is a 313-kW high pressure argon arc lamp of 1,200,000 candle power, completed by Vortek Industries, Inc of Vancouver, BC, Canada, in Mar 1984.

The synchrotron radiation from a 4 in × ½ in slit in the SPEAR high energy physics plant at the end of the 2-mile-long Stanford Linear Accelerator, Calif has been described as the world's most powerful light beam. (See photo, opposite page.)

The most powerful searchlight ever developed was one produced during the 1939–45 war by the General Electric Company Ltd at the Hirst Research Centre in Wembley, Greater London, England. It had a consumption of 600 kW and gave an arc luminance of 300,000 candles per sq in and a maximum beam intensity of 2,700 million candles from its parabolic mirror (diameter 10 ft).

Heaviest Magnet

The heaviest magnet is one measuring 196 ft in diameter, with a weight of 40,000 tons, for the 10 GeV synchrophasotron in the Joint Institute for Nuclear Research at Dubna, near Moscow.

Strongest and Weakest Magnetic Fields

The strongest continuous magnetic field strength achieved has been one of 33.6 teslas at the Tohoku Univ, Sendai, Japan, by Prof Yoshio Muto (b Aug 10, 1925) between 1:19 and 1:29 p.m. on May 29, 1985.

The weakest magnetic field ever measured is one of 8×10^{-15} tesla in the heavily shielded room at the Francis Bitter National Magnet Laboratory at MIT, Cambridge, Mass. It is used for research by Dr David Cohen into the very weak magnetic fields generated in the heart and brain.

Smallest Microphone

A microphone for a new technique of pressure measurement in fluid flow was developed in 1967 by Prof Ibrahim Kavrak of Bogazici Univ, Istanbul, Turkey. It has a frequency response of 10 Hz to 10 KHz and measures 0.06 × 0.03 in.

Most Powerful Microscopes

The most powerful microscope is the scanning tunneling microscope invented at the IBM Zurich, Switz, research laboratory in 1981. It has the magnifying ability of 100 million and is capable of resolving down to 1/100th the diameter of an atom (3×10^{-10}).

The lightest high power microscope in the world is the 1200 × McArthur Microscope made in Cambridge, England which weighs 9 oz.

Dr. Albert Crewe (b 1927, U.K.) of the University of Chicago is projecting a scanning electron microscope capable of seeing between atoms.

Loudest Noise

The loudest noise created in a laboratory is 210 decibels or 400,000 acoustic watts reported by NASA in Oct 1965. The noise came from a 48-ft steel and concrete test bed with 60-ft-deep foundations at Huntsville, Ala. Holes can be bored in solid material by this means and the audible range has been put at 100 mi.

Highest Note

The highest note yet attained is 60,000 megahertz (60 GHz) (60,000 million vibrations per sec), generated by a laser beam striking a sapphire crystal at MIT, Cambridge, Mass, in Sept 1964.

Most Powerful Particle Accelerator

The 6,562-ft diameter proton synchrotron at the Fermi National Accelerator Laboratory east of Batavia, Ill, is the highest-energy atom-smasher in the world. An energy of 500 billion (5×10^{11}) electron volts was attained on May 14, 1976. On Oct 13, 1985 a center of mass energy of 1.6 Tera electron volts (1.6×10^{12} electron volts) was achieved by colliding together beams of protons and anti-protons. This involves 1,000 superconducting magnets maintained at a temperature of −452°F by means of the world's largest helium liquefying plant, which produces 990 gallons per hour and began operating Apr 18, 1980.

The aim of CERN (*Conseil Européen pour la Recherche*) to collide beams of protons and antiprotons in their Super Proton Synchrotron (SPS) near Geneva, Switzerland, at 270 GeV × 2 = 540 GeV was achieved at 4:55 a.m. on July 10, 1981. This is the equivalent of striking a fixed target with protons at 150 TeV or 150,000 GeV.

The US Dept of Energy set up a study for a $5 billion Super Superconductivity Collider (SSC) 1995 with two 20 Te V proton and antiproton colliding beams on Aug 16 1983. If 8 tesla magnets were used the diameter would be 12.1 mi but with 3 tesla magnets this would be 32.5 mi.

Highest Pressures

The highest sustained laboratory pressures yet reported are of 1.72 megabars (12,300 tons force per sq in) achieved in the giant hydraulic diamond-faced press at the Carnegie Institution's Geophysical Laboratory in Washington, DC, reported in June 1978. This laboratory announced solid hydrogen achieved at 57 kilobars pressure on March 2, 1979. If created, metallic hydrogen is expected to be silvery white but soft, with a density of 1.1 g/cc. The pressure required for this transition is estimated by H. K. Mao and P. M. Bell to be 1 megabar at 25 °C. Using dynamic methods and impact speeds of up to 18,000 mph, momentary pressures of 75 million atmospheres (548,000 tons per sq in) were reported from the US in 1958.

Quietest Place

The "dead room," measuring 35 ft by 28 ft, in the Bell Telephone System Laboratory at Murray Hill, NJ is the most anechoic room in the world, eliminating 99.98% of reflected sound.

Sharpest Objects and Smallest Tubes

The sharpest objects yet made are glass micropipette tubes used in intracellular work on living cells. Techniques developed and applied by Prof Kenneth T. Brown and Dale G. Flaming of the Dept of Physiology, Univ of Calif, San Francisco, achieved by 1,977 beveled tips with an outer diameter of 0.02 μm and 0.01 μm inner diameter. The latter is smaller than the smallest known nickel tubing by a factor of 340 and is 6,500 times thinner than human hair.

Highest Temperatures

The highest man-made temperatures yet attained are those produced in the center of a thermonuclear fusion bomb, which are of the order of 300 million–400 million °C. Of controllable temperatures, the highest effective laboratory figure reported is 82 million degrees C at the Princeton (NJ) Plasma Physics Laboratory, in the fusion research PLT (Princeton Large Torus) in May 1980. A figure of 3,000 million °C was reportedly achieved in the USSR with Ogra injection-mirror equipment in c. 1962.

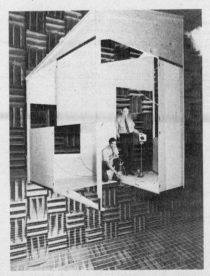

QUIETEST PLACE: An echoless test chamber at Bell Labs in Murray Hill, NJ, is used to study reverberation, the problem that sometimes occurs during telephone conference calls, when it sounds as if one of the speakers is talking into a barrel.

Lowest Temperatures

The lowest temperature reached is 3×10^{-8} Kelvin above absolute zero attained in a two-stage nuclear demagnetization cryostat at Espoo, Finland, by the team led by Prof Olli V. Lounasmaa (b 1930) and announced in June 1984. Absolute or thermodynamic temperatures are defined in terms of ratios rather than as differences reckoned from the unattainable absolute zero, which on the Kelvin scale is $-273.15\,°C$ or $-459.67\,°F$. Thus the lowest temperature ever attained is 1 in 9.1×10^9 of the melting point of ice ($0\,°C$ or $273.15K$ or $32\,°F$).

Tokyo University's Institute of Solid State Physics announced on Feb 15, 1983 that a team led by Prof. Kazuo Ono had attained a temperature within 0.00003 of a degree of absolute zero at which molecular motion ceases.

Smallest Thermometer

Dr. Frederich Sachs, a biophysicist at the State Univ of NY at Buffalo, has developed an ultramicrothermometer for measuring the temperature of single living cells. The tip is one micron in diameter, about 1/50th the diameter of a human hair.

Highest Vacuum

The highest or "hardest" vacuums obtained in scientific research are of the order of 10^{-14} torr, achieved at the IBM Thomas J. Watson Research Center, Yorktown Heights, NY in Oct 1976 in a cryogenic system with temperatures down to $-269\,°C$ ($-452\,°F$). This is equivalent to depopulating baseball-sized molecules from 1 yard apart to 50 miles apart.

Highest Velocity

The highest velocity at which any solid visible object has been projected is 335,000 mph in the case of a plastic disc at the Naval Research Laboratory, Wash DC, reported in Aug 1980.

Lowest Viscosity

The California Institute of Technology announced on Dec 1, 1957, that there was no measurable viscosity, *i.e.* perfect flow, in liquid helium II, which exists only at temperatures close to absolute zero ($-273.15\,°C$ or $-459.67\,°F$).

Highest Voltage

The highest potential difference ever obtained in a laboratory has been 32 ± 1.5 million volts by the National Electrostatics Corporation at Oak Ridge, Tenn, on May 17, 1979.

Chapter 6

The Arts & Entertainment

1. PAINTING*

Earliest Art

Evidence of Paleolithic art was first found in 1833 at Veyrier near Geneva, Switz, when Francois Mayor (1779–1854) found two harpoon-like objects decorated with geometric figures. The oldest known dated examples come from La Ferrassie, near Les Eyzies in the Périgord, France, in layers dated to *c.* 25,000 BC. Blocks of stone were found with engraved animals and female symbols; some of the blocks also had symbols painted in red ochre. Pieces of ochre with ground facets have been found at Lake Mungo, NSW, Australia, in a context *ante* 30,000 BC but there is no evidence whether these were used for body-painting or art.

Largest Paintings

Kimiko Hibino (b 1942) completed what is now the world's largest painting, showing over 800 species of the Animal Kingdom on a canvas 1.86 miles long and 7.2 ft wide (70,709 sq ft) on Oct 27, 1985. It was unveiled with the help of 3,000 volunteers along the bank of the Tamagawa River in Tokyo.

Panorama of the Mississippi, completed by John Banvard (1815–91) in 1846, showing the river scene for 1,200 miles in a strip probably 5,000 ft long and 12 ft wide, *was* the largest painting in the world, with an area of about 60,000 sq ft. The painting is believed to have been destroyed when the rolls of canvas, stored in a barn at Cold Spring Harbor, NY, caught fire shortly before Banvard's death May 16, 1891.

A painting of 32,400 sq ft with measurements of 120 ft × 270 ft was unveiled in Van Cortlandt Park in the Bronx, NYC on July 9, 1986. The artist, a New Yorker named Rey Hernandez (b. 1948), painted the entire vinyl canvas with oil based paint with the help of his wife, Diane, a Canadian artist. The painting was made in 18 sections and connected with rings on all sides as it was stretched out before a crowd of NYC officials as part of the salute to the Statue of Liberty.

---

* For further details on art, see *Art Facts and Feats,* A Guinness Superlatives Book (Sterling)

A painting, now only partially in existence, is *The Battle of Gettysburg*, completed in 1883, after 2½ years of work, by Paul Philippoteaux (France) and 16 assistants. The painting, 410 ft long, 70 ft high (28,700 sq ft), weighed 11,792 lb. It depicted the climax of the Battle of Gettysburg, in south-central Pa, July 3, 1863. In 1964, the painting was bought by Joe King of Winston-Salem, NC, after being stored by E. W. McConnell in a Chicago warehouse since 1933; due to deterioration, its height and area were trimmed down.

Jackson Bailey's *Life of Christ* exhibited by Religious Art Institute of America Inc. of Atlanta, Ga, comprises 50 panels 11 × 20 ft and was completed in 1968–70 with an area of 11,000 sq ft.

The largest "Old Master" is *Il Paradiso*, painted between 1587 and 1590 by Jacopo Robusti, *alias* Tintoretto (1518–94), and his son Domenico on Wall "E" of the Sala del Maggior Consiglio in the Palazzo Ducale (Doge's Palace) in Venice, Italy. The work is 72 ft 2 in long and 22 ft 11½ in high and contains some 350 human figures.

Most Valuable Painting

The "Mona Lisa" (*La Gioconda*) by Leonardo da Vinci (1452–1519) in the Louvre, Paris, was assessed for insurance purposes at the highest figure ever at $100 million for its move for exhibition in Washington, DC and NYC from Dec 14, 1962, to March 12, 1963. However, insurance was not concluded because the cost of the closest security precautions was less than that of the premiums. It was painted in *c.* 1503–07 and measures 30.5 × 20.9 in. It is believed to portray Mona (short for Madonna) Lisa Gherardini, the wife of Francesco del Giocondo of Florence, or Constanza d'Avalos, coincidentally nicknamed La Gioconda, mistress of Giuliano de Medici. Francis I, King of France, in 1517 bought the painting for his bathroom for 4,000 gold florins or 492 oz of gold now worth $330,000.

Highest Auction Prices

The highest price ever bid in a public auction for any painting was $10.4 million for *The Adoration of the Magi* by Andrea Mantegna (1431–1506), sold at Christie's London, on Apr 18, 1985 to the J. Paul Getty Museum at Malibu, Calif. Britain has to grant permission to allow its export to the US. In Dec 1985, it was strongly suggested that the painting may have been by the artist's son Francesco.

The highest price ever paid for a painting by a female artist is $1,100,-000, at Christie's, NYC on May 17, 1983, for *Reading Le Figaro* by Mary Cassatt (US) (1844–1926). She worked mainly from Paris.

Modern Painting

The record bid at auction for an Impressionist painting is $9,900,000 (including premium) for *Landscape with Rising Sun* by Vincent Van Gogh (1853–1890) from the estate of Mrs Florence J. Gould (d 1983) paid by an anonymous private collector at Sotheby Park Bernet, NYC, on Apr 25, 1985.

The auction record for an abstract painting is $2,156,000 for *Composition with Red, Blue and Yellow* by the Dutch modernist Piet Mondrian (1872–1944), sold to a private Japanese collector on June 26, 1983 at Christie's, London. Another of Mondrian's paintings was sold in 1982 for just over $1 million, a record price at the time.

HIGHEST-PRICED IMPRESSIONIST PAINTING: Sold at auction in Apr 1985, "Landscape with Rising Sun, St Remy" by Vincent van Gogh, the famous Dutch painter, brought $9,900,000 from a private collector at Sotheby Park Bernet, NYC.

MOST PROLIFIC LIVING PAINTER: Morris Katz (center) of NYC's Greenwich Village, who has produced more than 150,000 saleable paintings, presents one he finished in 2 min to the Guinness Museum in the Empire State Building. His painting of a skier in Oct 1985 took less time—only 43 sec.

Living Artist

The highest price paid at auction for a work by a living artist is $1,-819,596 for *Two Women* (22 × 28 in) by Willem de Kooning (b Apr 24, 1904), the Dutch-born American at Christie's, NYC on Nov 2, 1984.

The highest price paid for paintings in the lifetime of the artist is $1,-950,000 paid for the two canvases *Two Brothers* (1905) and *Seated Harlequin* (1922) by Pablo Diego José Francisco de Paula Juan Nepomuceno Crispin Crispiano de la Santisima Trinidad Ruiz y Picasso (1881–1973), born in Spain. This was paid by the Basle City government to the Staechelin Foundation to enable the Basle Museum of Art to retain the paintings after an offer of $2,560,000 had been received from the US in Dec 1967.

Most Prolific Painters

Picasso was the most prolific of all painters. During a career that lasted for 78 years, it has been estimated that he produced about 13,500 paintings or designs, 100,000 prints or engravings, 34,000 book illustrations, and 300 sculptures and ceramics plus drawings and tapestries. His lifetime work has been valued at $750,000,000. The Museum of Modern Art in NYC gave over its entire museum to a one-man show of Picasso's work, May–Sept 1980.

Morris Katz (b 1932) of Greenwich Village, NYC, is the most prolific painter of saleable works in the world. His total sold, as of Mar 5, 1986 was 153,629. Described now as a "realistic, impressionistic" modern artist, Katz appears regularly on cable TV on the "Instant Art Show." He paints with palette knife and crushed pads of toilet paper, and sells his paintings "cheap and often." He also set another record—painting a 16 × 25 canvas of a skier in 43 sec at the Limelight Nightclub, Chicago on Oct 16, 1985. He has demonstrated that he paints at the rate of 2.64 sq ft per min.

Miniature Portrait

The highest price ever paid for a portrait miniature is $172,500 by an anonymous buyer at a sale held by Sotheby's, London, Mar 24, 1980, for a miniature of Jane Broughton, age 21, painted on vellum by Nicholas Hilliard (1547–1619) in 1574. The painted surface measures 1.65 in in diameter.

Highest-Priced Drawing

The highest price ever paid for any drawing is £3,546,000 ($4,539,800) for a study of an apostle's head and hand for *The Transfiguration* in the Vatican by Raphael (Raffaello Santi 1483–1520) and sold for the 11th Duke of Devonshire (b 1920) at Christie's, London, July 3, 1984.

Most Repetitious Painter

Antonio Bin of Paris has painted the *Mona Lisa* on some 300 occasions. These copies sell for up to $1,500 each.

Youngest Exhibitor

Lewis Melville "Gino" Lyons (b Apr 30, 1962) painted his *Trees and Monkeys* on June 4, 1965, submitted it to the Royal Academy of Arts, England, on March 17, 1967, for its Annual Summer Exhibition, and it was exhibited on Apr 29, 1967.

Oldest and Largest Museums

The oldest museum in the world is the Ashmolean Museum in Oxford, England, built in 1679–83. Since 1924 it has housed an exhibition of scientific instruments.

The largest single museum is the American Museum of Natural History between 77th and 81st Sts on Central Park West, NYC. Founded in 1874, it comprises 19 interconnected buildings with 23 acres of floor space.

The largest complex of museums is Washington, D.C.'s Smithsonian Institution, comprising 13 museums with 5,600 employees. The most popular museum in numbers of visitors is the Smithsonian Air and Space Museum, which opened in July 1976. On one day in 1984 the doors had to be closed when 118,437 people crowded in. The total attendance at the Smithsonian is about 24 million per year.

Unusual Museums

If it were possible to select the most unusual museum, the OMSI—Oregon Museum of Science and Industry—located just a few miles from downtown Portland would be in the running, along with the "Pompidou" in Paris.

At OMSI, one is greeted in the lobby with a Gravitram which has tiny steel balls that jingle and jangle as they freely roll down a maze of tracks in an electronic kinetic sculpture.

Next you become a trickle of blood and walk through the atria of a heart that is 14 ft high and 22 ft long. When you have had your own heartbeat and blood pressure checked and displayed on a screen, you go to visit a transparent talking lady which describes each organ of the human body as it lights up.

Besides all this, you see the birth process exhibited, hear what deaf people hear, cuddle a baby chick as it is hatched, feel the skin of a boa constrictor, and watch bees making honey. In OMSI and its planetarium, the idea is to make you feel right at home and get answers to science questions.

The largest gallery showing modern art is located in Place Beaubourg, Paris, on the top floors of the Georges Pompidou National Center for Art and Culture. Named after the French president who first had the idea and who authorized the spending (some say foolishly) of many millions of francs, this museum is unusual on the outside. Looking more like an ocean liner or an ultramodern factory because of its escalator appendages, this art museum and library has changing exhibits on the lower floors, showing the latest in international art and design. Opened in 1977, it has a deluxe restaurant on its roof and a world record total of 183,000 sq ft of floor space.

Largest Galleries

The world's largest art gallery is the Winter Palace and the neighboring Hermitage in Leningrad, USSR. One has to walk 15 miles to visit each of the 322 galleries, which house nearly 3 million works of art and objects of archeological interest.

The most heavily endowed gallery is the J. Paul Getty Museum, Malibu, Calif, with $1,600,000,000 in Jan 1974 plus $90 million per year for acquisitions. It has 38 galleries.

OMSI (Oregon Museum of Science and Industry) in Portland has this enlarged heart (above) which pulsates as you walk through the giant display, 14 ft high and 22 ft long. (*Photo by Phillip Kerman*)

LARGEST MOSAIC (left): The four walls of the library of the University of Mexico tell the history of Mexico.

MUSEUMS today may not look like museums—this one (below) at first sight looks like a steamship. It is the modern art museum in Paris called "the Pompidou." Opened in 1977 in the midst of controversy, it also contains, besides its exhibit area, a library and a restaurant in its 183,000 sq ft of floor space. (*French Govt Tourist Office*)

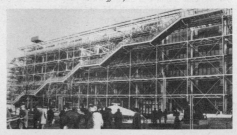

Finest Brush

The finest standard brush sold is the 000 in Series 7 by Winsor and Newton, known as the "triple goose." It is made of 150–200 Kolinsky sable hairs weighing 0.000529 oz.

Largest and Highest-Priced Poster

The largest recorded poster on paper was one measuring 32 ft × 168 ft 10 in for a total area of 22,292 sq ft, constructed by the students of Osaka Gakun Univ, Osaka, Japan, on Oct 7, 1984.

The students at Grimsley Senior High School, Greensboro, NC, made a still bigger poster of fabric measuring 43,938.54 sq ft (311 ft 4 in long, by 141 ft 10 in wide).

The record price is £62,000 ($93,000) for a poster advertising the 1902 Vienna Exhibition, designed by Koloman Maser (b Vienna, Mar 30, 1868, d Oct 18, 1918) sold at Christie's London on Apr 1, 1985.

Earliest Mural

The earliest known murals on man-made walls are the clay relief leopards at Catal Hüyük in southern Anatolia, Turkey, discovered by James Malaart at level VII in 1961 and dating from c. 6200 BC.

Largest Mural

The largest "mural" was unveiled in 44 colors on the 30-story Villa Regina condominium, Biscayne Bay, Miami, Fla, on Mar 14, 1984 covering 300,000 sq ft. The longest recorded continuous mural was one stretching 1509.8 ft on the wall surrounding the Aotea Centre construction site in Auckland, New Zealand, "painted" by over 3,000 members of the Auckland Star Jellybeans Club in 6 hours on Sept 8, 1985. It covered an area of 14,861 sq ft. *Future entries for this category will be assessed on overall area only.*

Stained Glass

The oldest stained glass in the world represents the Prophets in a window of the cathedral of Augsburg, Bavaria, Germany, dating from c. 1050.

The largest stained glass window is the complete mural of The Resurrection Mausoleum, Justice, Ill, measuring 22,381 sq ft, in 2,448 panels completed in 1971. The back-lit stained glass mural installed in 1979 in the atrium of the Ramada Hotel, Dubai, United Arab Emirates, is 135 ft high.

Largest Mosaic

The largest mosaic is on the walls of the central library of the Universidad Nacional Autónoma de México, Mexico City. There are four walls, the two largest measuring 12,949 sq ft each, representing the pre-Hispanic past.

2. SCULPTURES

Earliest Sculptures

The earliest known example of sculpture is a 2½-in-long figure of a horse carved from mammoth ivory dated to *c.* 28,000 BC, and found in the Vogelherd cave in W Germany. A piece of ox rib found in 1973 at Pech de l'Aze, Dordogne, France, in an early Middle Paleolithic layer of the Riss glaciation *c.* 105,000 BC appears to have several possibly intentionally engraved lines on one side. A churinga or curved ivory plaque rubbed with red ochre from the Middle Paleolithic Mousterian site at Tata, Hungary, has been dated to 100,000 BC by the thorium/uranium method.

Largest Sculptures

The largest sculptures are the mounted figures of Jefferson Davis (1808–89), Gen Robert Edward Lee (1807–70) and Gen Thomas Jonathan ("Stonewall") Jackson (1824–63), covering 1.33 acres on the face of Stone Mountain, near Atlanta, Ga. They are 90 ft high. Roy Faulkner was on the mountain face for 8 years 174 days with a thermo-jet torch, working with the sculptor Walker Kirtland Hancock and other helpers from Sept 12, 1963 to March 3, 1972.

The world's largest sculpture will probably not be completed for many years due to the death in 1982 of the sculptor who conceived the idea and spent 35 of his 74 years on the site at Thunderhead Mt in the southern Black Hills of South Dakota near Mt Rushmore. The sculptor, Korczak Ziolkowski, started blasting away at the first of 7 million tons of granite June 3, 1948. By 1982 he had the rough outline of the sculpture showing the Sioux Indian, Tashunca-Uitco, known as Chief Crazy Horse (*c.* 1849–77) mounted on his stallion carved and visible to passersby in the distance. Ziolkowski left enough funds (he had raised $4 million) so his wife and 10 children, along with the Crazy Horse Memorial Foundation, could continue the work. When and if completed the carving will measure 563 ft by 641 ft.

In 1984, another 200,000 tons of granite were blasted off the mountain face, bringing the total to 7.8 million tons.

Most Expensive Sculptures

The highest price ever paid for a sculpture is $3,900,000 paid by private treaty in London in early 1977 by the J. Paul Getty Museum, Malibu, Calif for the 4th-century BC bronze statue of a youth attributed to the school of Lysippus. It was found by fishermen on the seabed off Faro, Italy in 1963.

The highest price paid for the work of a living sculptor is $1,265,000 given at Sotheby Parke Bernet Galleries, NYC, May 21, 1982, for the 75-in-long elmwood *Reclining Figure* by Henry Moore (b Castleford, W Yorkshire, England, July 30, 1898).

Ground and Hill Figures

In the Nazca Desert south of Lima, Peru there are straight lines (one more than 7 miles long), geometric shapes and plants and animals drawn on the ground sometime between 100 BC and 700 AD for an uncertain but probably religious, astronomical or even economic purpose by a not pre-

LARGEST COMPLETED SCULPTURE (above): On Stone Mt, near Atlanta, Ga, these 90-ft-high figures of 3 Confederate heroes have been engraved with a thermo-jet torch. The project took more than 8½ years. Meanwhile near Mt Rushmore in S Dakota another sculptor died before finishing a still bigger sculpture—the "Crazy Horse Memorial" to the Sioux Indian chief.

MOST MASSIVE MOBILE (left): Alexander Calder's "White Cascade" can be seen in a bank in Philadelphia. (*Edw. J. Bonner*)

cisely identified civilization. They were first detected from the air *c.* 1928 and can only be recognized as artwork from the air.

In Aug 1968 a 330-ft-tall figure was found on a hill above Tarapacá, Chile.

Most Massive Mobile

The most massive mobile is *White Cascade* weighing more than 8 tons and measuring 100 ft from top to bottom installed on May 24–25, 1976 at the Federal Reserve Bank of Philadelphia. It was designed by Alexander Calder (1898–1976), whose first mobiles were exhibited in Paris in 1932, and whose *Big Crinkley* sold for a record $700,000 at Sotheby's NYC on May 10, 1984.

3. LANGUAGE AND LITERATURE

Earliest Language

The ability to speak is believed to be dependent upon physiological changes in the height of the larynx between *Homo erectus* and *Homo sapiens sapiens,* as developed *c* 45,000 BC.

The earliest written language discovered has been on Yangshao culture pottery from Paa-t'o, near Xi'an (Sian) in the Shanxi (Shensi) province of China found in 1962. This bears proto-characters for the numbers 5, 7 and 8 and has been dated to 5000–4000 BC.

The earliest dated pictographs are on clay tablets from Nippur, southern Iraq, from a level equivalent to Uruk V/VI and dated in 1979 to *c.* 3400 BC.

Tokens or tallies from Tepe Asiab and Ganji-I-Dareh Tepe in Iran have however been dated to 8500 BC.

Oldest Language

The written language with the longest continuous history is Chinese, extending over more than 6,000 years from the Yangshao culture. (*See above.*)

Oldest Words in English

It was first suggested in 1979 that languages ancestral to English and to Latvian (both Indo-European) split *c.* 3500 BC.

Shortly to be published research indicates that about 40 words of a pre-Indo-European substrate survive in English, including apple (apal), bad (bad), gold (gol), and tin (tin).

The earliest known piece of English writing (*c* 630 AD) is a fragment of Irish uncial script in an ecclesiastical history sold for $100,000 by the Folger Shakespeare Library, Wash, DC, to the British Rail Pension Fund at Sotheby's, London on June 25, 1985.

Commonest Language

Today's world total of languages and dialects still spoken is about 5,-000 of which some 845 come from India. The language spoken by more people than any other is Northern Chinese, or Mandarin, by an estimated 68% of the population, hence 695 million people in 1983. The so-called national language (*Běifanghuà*) is a standardized form of Northern Chinese (*Guóyǔ*) as spoken in the Peking area. This was alphabetized into *zhùyīn fùhào* of 37 letters in 1913. On Feb 11, 1938, the *Hanya-Pinyin-Fang'an* system, which is a phonetic pronunciation guide, was introduced.

The next most commonly spoken language and the most widespread is English, by an estimated 400 million in mid-1984. English is spoken by 10% or more of the population in 45 sovereign countries. In Great Britain and Ireland, there are 5 indigenous tongues known besides English: Cornish, Scots, Gaelic, Irish Gaelic, Welsh and Romany (gipsy).

Most Complex Language

The following extremes of complexity have been noted: Chippewa, the North American Indian language of Minnesota, has the most verb forms with up to 6,000; Tillamook, the North American Indian language of Oregon, has the most prefixes with 30; Tabassaran, a language in Daghestan, USSR, uses the most noun cases with 35; the Eskimo language uses 63 forms of the present tense and simple nouns have as many as 252 inflections.

In Chinese, the 40-volume *Chung-wen Ta Tz'u-tien* Dictionary lists 49,905 characters. *The Dictionary of Chinese Characters* (Sichuan and Huber) in 8 volumes will contain 20 million characters, when completed in 1989. The fourth tone of "i" has 84 meanings, varying as widely as "dress," "hiccough" and "licentious." The written language provides 92 different characters for "i⁴." The most complex written character in Chinese is that representing *xie* which has 64 strokes and means "talkative." The most complex in current use is *yu*, which consists of 32 strokes and means to urge or implore.

Largest Vocabulary

The English language contains about 490,000 words, plus another 300,000 technical terms, the most in any language, but it is doubtful if any individual uses more than 60,000. Those in Great Britain who have undergone a full 16 years of education use perhaps 5,000 words in speech and up to 10,000 words in written communications. The members of the International Society for Philosophical Enquiry (no admission for IQ's below 148) have an average vocabulary of 36,250 words.

Greatest Linguist

The most multilingual living person in the world is Georges Henri Schmidt (b Strasbourg, France, Dec 28, 1914), who served as Chief of the UN Terminology Section 1965–71. In the 1975 edition of *Who's Who in the United Nations* he listed "only" 19 languages because he was then unable to find the time to "revive" his former fluency in 12 others.

Powell Alexander Janulus (b 1939) has worked with 41 languages in the Provincial Court of British Columbia, Vancouver, Canada.

Oldest Alphabet

The oldest letter is "O," unchanged in shape since its adoption in the Phoenician alphabet *c.* 1300 BC. The newest letters added to the English alphabet are "j" and "v," which are of post-Shakespearean use, *c.* 1630. Formerly they were used only as variants of "i" and "u." There are now some 65 alphabets in use.

Longest Words

Lengthy concatenations and some compound or agglutinative words or nonce words are or have been written in the closed-up style of a single word.

The longest word ever to appear in literature occurs in *The Ecclesiazusae*, a comedy by Aristophanes (448–380 BC). In the Greek it is 170 letters long but transliterates into 182 letters in English, thus: lopadotemachoselachogaleokranioleipsanodrimhypotrimmatosilphioparaomelitokatakechymenokichlepikossyphophattoperisteralektryonoptekephalliokigklopeleiolagoiosiraiobaphetraganopterygon.

The term describes a fricassee of 17 sweet and sour ingredients, including mullet, brains, honey, vinegar, pickles, marrow (the vegetable) and ouzo (a Greek drink laced with anisette).

A compound word of 195 Sanskrit characters (which transliterates into 428 letters in the Roman alphabet) describing the region near Kanci, Tamil Nadu, India, appears in a 16th century work by Tirumalāmbā, queen of Vijayanagara.

The longest word in the Oxford English Dictionary is floccipaucinihilipilification (alternatively spelt in hyphenated form with "n" in seventh place), with 29 letters, meaning "the action of estimating as worthless," first used in 1741, and later by Sir Walter Scott (1771–1832). Webster's Third International Dictionary lists among its 450,000 entries pneumonoultramicroscopicsilicovolcanoconiosises (47 letters), the plural of a lung disease contracted by some miners.

The longest regularly formed English word is praetertranssubstantiationalistically (37 letters), used by Mark McShane in his novel *Untimely Ripped*, published in 1963. The medical term hepaticocholangiocholecystenterostomies (39 letters) refers to the surgical creations of new communications between gall bladders and hepatic ducts and between intestines and gall bladders. The longest in common use are disproportionableness and incomprehensibilities (21 letters). Interdenominationalism (22 letters) is found in Webster's and hence perhaps interdenominationalistically (28 letters) is permissible.

Most Meanings

The most overworked word in English is the word "set" which has 58 noun uses, 126 verbal uses and 10 as a participial adjective.

Most Synonyms

The condition of being inebriated has more synonyms than any other condition or object. Delacorte Press has published a selection of 1,224 from 2,241 compiled by Paul Dickson of Garrett Park, Md.

Most Succinct Word

The most challenging word for any lexicographer to define briefly is the Fuegian (southernmost Argentina and Chile) word *mamihlapinatapei* meaning "looking at each other hoping that either will offer to do something which both parties desire but are unwilling to do."

Longest Palindromic Words

The longest known palindromic word (same spelling backwards as forwards) is *saippuakivikauppias* (19 letters), the Finnish word for a dealer in lye. The longest in the English language is *redivider* (9 letters). The 9-letter word, *Malayalam*, is a proper noun given to the language of the Malayali people in Kerala, southern India, while *Kanakanak* near Dellingham, Alaska, is a 9-letter palindromic place name. The 9-letter word ROTAVATOR is a registered trademark belonging to Howard Machinery Ltd, of England. The contrived chemical term *detartrated* has 11 letters. In American English the word *releveler* is also a 9-letter palindrome, though in England it is spelled *releveller* and hence is not palindromic.

Commonest Words and Letters

In written English, the most frequently used words are in order: the, of, and, to, a, in, that, is, I, it, for *and* as. The most used in conversation is I. The commonest letter is "e" and the commonest initial letter is "T."

Worst Tongue-Twisters

The most difficult tongue-twister is deemed by Ken Parkin of Tees-

LONGEST PLACE NAME IN USE is this 57-letter Maori name for a hill in New Zealand. In 1959 the first letter in the third line was changed from "A" to "O".

side, England, to be "The sixth sick sheik's sixth sheep's sick"—especially when spoken quickly.

Longest Abbreviation

The 55-letter full name of Los Angeles (El Pueblo de Nuestra Señora la Reina de los Angeles de Porciuncula) is abbreviated to LA, or 3.63% of its length.

Longest Anagrams

The longest non-scientific English words which can form anagrams are the 18-letter transpositions "conservationalists" and "conversationalists." The longest scientific transposals are cholecystoduodenostomy/duodenocholecystostomy and hydropneumopericardium/pneumohydropericardium, each of 22 letters.

Largest Letters

The largest permanent letters in the world are the giant 600-ft letters spelling READYMIX on the ground in the Nullarbor near East Balladonia, W Australia. This was constructed in Dec 1971.

Smallest Letters

The 16 letters MOLECULAR DEVICES have been etched into a salt crystal by an electron beam so that the strokes are only 2 to 3 mm wide—the width of 20 hydrogen atoms. This was done by Michael Isaacson at Cornell University in Feb 1982.

Longest Place Names

The official name for Bangkok, capital of Thailand, is Krungthep Mahanakhon. The full name is, however: Krungthep Mahanakhon Bovorn Ratanakosin Mahintharayutthaya Mahadilok pop Noparatratchathani Burirom Udomratchanivetmahasathan Amornpiman Avatarnsathit Sakkathattiyavisnukarmprasit (167 letters) which, in the most scholarly transliteration, emerges with 175 letters.

The longest place name now in use is Taumatawhakatangihangakoauauotamatea (turipukakapikimaungahoronuku) pokaiwhenuakitanatahu, the unofficial 85-letter version of the name of a hill (1,002 ft above sea level) in the Southern Hawke's Bay district of North Island, New Zealand. This Maori name means "the hill whereon was played the flute of Tamatea, circumnavigator of lands, for his lady love." The official version has 57 letters (1 to 36 and 65 to 85).

Shortest Place Names

The shortest place names in the world are the French village of Y (population 143), so named since 1241, the Danish village Å on the island Fyn, the Norwegian village of Å (pronounced "Aw"), the Swedish place Å in Vikholandet, U in the Caroline Islands of the Pacific, and the Japanese town of Sosei which is alternatively called Aioi or O. There was once a 6 in West Virginia. Today in the US, there are 10 two-lettered place names, including 7 in Kentucky: Ed, Uz, Oz, Ep, and Or.

Most Spellings

The spelling of the Dutch town of Leeuwarden has been recorded in 225 versions since AD 1046.

Longest First Name

The longest name appearing on a birth certificate is that of Rhoshandiatellyneshiaunneveshenk Koyaanfsquatsiuty Williams born to Mr and Mrs James L. Williams in Beaumont, Tex, on Sept 12, 1984. On Oct 5, 1984, the father filed an amendment which expanded his daughter's first name to 1,019 letters and the middle name to 36 letters.

The longest Christian or given name on record is one of 622 letters given by Mr Scott Roaul Sör-Lökken of Missoula, Mont to his daughter Miss S. Ellen Georgianna Sör Lökken (b 1979). The "S" stands for a 598-letter name designed to throw a monkey wrench into the computers of federal bureaucracy. She is known as "Snow Owl" for short or "Oli" for shorter.

Most Christian Names

The great-great-grandson of Carlos III of Spain, Don Alfonso de Borbón y Borbón (1866–1934), had 94 Christian names, of which several were lengthened by hyphenation.

Shortest Personal Name

The commonest single-letter surname is O, prevalent in Korea, but with 52 examples in US phone books (1973–81) and 12 in Belgium. This name causes the most distress to those concerned with the prevention of cruelty to computers. Every other letter, except Q, has been traced in US phone books (used as a surname) by A. Ross Eckler. There are two one-letter Burmese names: E (calm), pronounced "aye," and U (egg), pronounced "oo." U used before the name means "uncle."

There exist among the 47,000,000 names on the Dept. of Health & Social Security index 6 examples of a one-lettered surname.

Commonest Family Names

The commonest family name in the world is the Chinese name Chang (Zhang) which is borne, according to estimates, by between 9.7% and 12.1% of the Chinese population, so indicating even on the lower estimate that there are at least some 104 million Changs—more than the entire population of all but 7 of the 170 other sovereign countries of the world.

The commonest surname in the English-speaking world is Smith. The most recent published count showed 659,050 nationally insured Smiths in Great Britain, of whom 10,102 are plain John Smith, and another 19,-502 are John plus one or more given-name Smiths. Including uninsured

DIARY DEVOTEE: (Left) George C. Edler looked like this in 1910 when he began keeping a diary, and now 76 years later (above) he is still at work on it each day in a nursing home in Bethesda, Md.

persons, there are over 800,000 Smiths in England and Wales alone. There are an estimated 2,382,500 Smiths in the US.

There are, however, estimated to be 1,600,000 persons in Britain with M', Mc or Mac (Gaelic "son of") as part of their surnames. The commonest of these is Macdonald which accounts for about 55,000 of the Scottish population.

Most Versions of a Family Name

Edward A. Nedelcov of Regina, Saskatchewan, Canada, has collected 990 versions of the spelling of his family name since Jan 1960. Mzilikazi of Zululand (b c. 1795) had his name chronicled in 325 spellings, according to research by Dr D. Kent Rasmussen.

Last Word

In the US, the determination to derive commercial or other benefit from being the last listing in the local telephone book has resulted in self-given names starting with up to 9 z's—the extreme example being Mr Zachary Zzzzzzzzzzra in the San Francisco book. Last in the book for North Hollywood, LA, however, is Mr B. Zzzzygot.

The last name in the 1985 London telephone book is the Zzzzzz Coffee Shop in Grays's Inn Road.

Oldest Printed Work

The oldest surviving printed work is a Korean scroll or *sutra,* printed from wooden blocks found in the foundations of the Pulguk Sa pagoda, Kyongju, South Korea, Oct 14, 1966. It has been dated no later than 704 AD. It was claimed in Nov 1973 that a 28-page book of Tang dynasty poems at Yonsei University, Korea, was printed from metal type c. 1160.

Oldest Mechanically Printed Book

It is generally accepted that the earliest mechanically printed full-length book was a "42-line" Gutenberg Bible, printed in Mainz, Germany, c. 1454 by Johann Henne zum Gensfleisch zur Laden, called "zu Gutenberg" (c. 1398–c. 1468). Work on watermarks published in 1967 indicates a copy of a surviving printed "Donatus" Latin grammar was made from paper made in c. 1450. The earliest exactly dated printed work is the Psalter completed Aug 14, 1457, by Johann Fust (c. 1400–1466) and Peter Schöffer (1425–1502), who had been Gutenberg's chief assistant. The earliest printing by William Caxton, though undated, would appear to be *The Recuyel of the Historyes of Troye* in Cologne in late 1473 to spring 1474.

Musical Manuscript

The highest price paid at auction for a musical manuscript was $595,-000 for Igor Stravinsky's *The Rite of Spring* on Nov 11, 1982 at Sotheby Parke Bernet, London, bought by Otto Haas for the Paul Sacher Collection, Basel, Switzerland.

Largest Publication

The largest publication in the world is the 1,112-volume set of *British Parliamentary Papers* of 1800–1900 published by the Irish University Press in 1968–1972. A complete set weighs 3.64 tons, cost $74,900 in mid-1985 and would take 6 years to read at 10 hours per day. The production and binding involved the death of 34,000 Indian goats and the use of $22,000 worth of gold ingots. The total print run was 500 sets, and the price per set in 1984 was $54,600.

Smallest Book

The smallest marketed bound printed book with cursive material is one printed on 22 gsm paper measuring 1 mm × 1 mm ($\frac{1}{25}$ × $\frac{1}{25}$ in), comprising the children's story "Old King Cole!" and published in 85 copies in Mar 1985 by The Gleniffer Press of Paisley, Scotland. The pages can only be turned (with care) by the use of a needle.

Largest and Longest Diaries

The diary of Edward Robb Ellis (b 1911) of NYC, begun in 1927, and continuing in its 58th year is estimated at more than 15 million words. It contains more than 32,000 pages in its 58 volumes.

George C. Edler (b 1889) has been keeping a diary since Jan 1, 1910, a total of 76 years to date, and is still continuing while confined to a nursing home in Bethesda, Md. The diaries are in bound book form— 76 volumes containing an estimated 2,859,000 words.

Longest Index

The Tenth Collective Index of *Chemical Abstracts,* completed in June 1983, contains 23,948,253 entries in 131,445 pages in 75 volumes, and weighs 380 lb.

Most Expensive Paged Work

The highest price paid for any book or any work of art was $11.9 million for the 226-leaf manuscript "The Gospel Book of Henry the Lion, Duke of Saxony" at Sotheby's London on Dec 6, 1983. The book, 13½ × 10 in, was illuminated by the monk Herimann in c. 1170 at Helmershansen Abbey with 41 full-page illustrations, and was bought by Hans Kraus of NYC for the Hermann Abs consortium.

The highest price ever paid for a printed book is $2,400,000 for one of the only 21 known complete copies of the Gutenberg Bible, printed in Mainz, (West) Germany, in c. 1454. It was bought from the Carl and Lily Pforzheimer Foundation by the University of Texas in a sale arranged by Quaritch of London in NYC, June 9, 1978.

The most expensive new book is *The Birds of America,* containing a full set of reproductions by John James Audubon (1785–1851) of ornithological prints, published by the Abbeville Press, NYC, to sell for $15,000.

Largest Dictionary

The largest English language dictionary is the 12-volume Royal quarto *The Oxford English Dictionary* of 15,487 pages published between 1884 and 1928 with a first supplement in 1933 and a further 4-volume supplement, edited by R. W. Burchfield. The final volume (Se-Z and the bibliography) was published in 1986. The work contains 414,825 word listings, 1,827,306 illustrative quotations and reputedly 227,779,589 letters and figures, 63.8 times more than the Bible. The greatest outside contributor has been Marghanita Laski with 175,000 quotations since 1958.

Deutsches Wörterbuch started by Jacob and Wilhelm Grimm in 1854 was completed in 34,519 pages and 33 volumes in 1971. Today's price is DM5,456.97 (now $2,000).

The New Grove Dictionary of Music and Musicians (edited by: Stanley Sadie, b 1930) published in 20 volumes by Macmillan's in Feb 1981 contains over 22 million words and 4,500 illustrations and is the largest specialist dictionary yet published.

Earliest and Largest Encyclopaediae

The earliest known encyclopaedia was compiled in Athens by Speusippus (*post* 408–*c.* 338 BC) in *c.* 370 BC. He was a nephew of Plato.

The largest encyclopaedia is *La Enciclopedia Universal Ilustrada Europeo-American* (J. Espasa & Sons, Madrid and Barcelona) totaling 105,000 pages in 104 volumes with 10 appendices and an annual supplement since 1935 comprising 165,200,000 words. The price is $2325.

Most Comprehensive Encyclopaedia

The most comprehensive English language encyclopaedia is the *Encyclopaedia Britannica,* first published in Edinburgh, Scotland, in Dec 1768–1771. A group of booksellers in the US acquired reprint rights in 1898 and complete ownership in 1899. In 1943, the *Britannica* was given to the University of Chicago. The current 30-volume 15th edition contains 33,141 pages and 43 million words from 4,277 contributors. It is now edited in Chicago and in London.

Oldest Bible

The oldest leather and papyrus Dead Sea Scrolls were discovered in Cave 4 near Qumran in 1952. They comprise fragments of Exodus and Samuel I dating to *c.* 225–200 BC.

The oldest known bible is the *Codex Vaticanus* written in Greek *ante* 350 AD and preserved in the Vatican Museum, Rome.

The earliest complete Bible *printed* in English was one edited by Miles Coverdale, Bishop of Exeter (*c.* 1488–1569), while living in Antwerp, and printed in 1535. William Tyndale's New Testament in English had, however, been printed in Cologne and in Worms, Germany in 1525 while John Wycliffe's first manuscript translation dates from 1382.

Maps

The oldest known map of any kind is a clay tablet depicting the Euphrates River flowing through northern Mesopotamia (Iraq), dated c. 3800 BC. The earliest printed map in the world is one of western China dated to 1115 AD.

The largest is a "Giant Relief Map of California," displayed in the Ferry Building, San Francisco, from 1924 to 1962, now in storage, which measures 450 × 18 ft and weighs 43 tons.

Highest-Priced Printed Document

A newly discovered copy of the Declaration of Independence, the 22nd copy known to exist, printed in 1776 by Samuel T. Freeman & Co, was auctioned to the Chapin Library, Williams College on Apr 22, 1983, at Christie's, NYC, for $412,500, setting a record for printed documents.

Highest-Priced Atlas

The highest price paid for an atlas is $700,000 for a Gerardus Mercator atlas of c. 1571 Europe sold at auction at Sotheby's, London, March 13, 1979.

Post Cards

The top-selling post card of all time was said to be a drawing by Donald McGill (1875–1962) with the caption: He: "Do you like Kipling?" She: "I don't know, you naughty boy, I've never kippled." It sold about 6 million. Between 1904 and his death, McGill sold more than 350 million cards to users and deltiologists (picture post card collectors).

Longest Novel

The longest important novel ever published is *Les hommes de bonne volonté* by Louis Henri Jean Farigoule (1885–1972), *alias* Jules Romains, of France, in 27 volumes in 1932–46. The English version, *Men of Good Will,* was published in 14 volumes in 1933–46 as a "novel-cycle." The 4,959-page edition published by Peter Davies Ltd has an estimated 2,070,000 words, excluding a 100-page index. The novel *Tokuga-Wa Ieyasu* by Sohachi Yamaoka has been serialized in Japanese daily newspapers since 1951. Now completed, it will require nearly 40 volumes in book form.

Most Prolific Writers

The champion of the goose-quill era was Józef Ignacy Kraszewski (1812–1887) of Poland, who produced more than 600 volumes of novels and historical works.

Until recently very high productivity had been attributed to Frank Richards, alias Charles Hamilton, (1875–1961) with up to 80,000 words a week in 1913 including the whole of the periodicals *Gem* (founded 1907) and *Magnet* (1908–40). In 1948 George Samways (b 1894) asserted that Hamilton used him and others as "ghost-writers."

Soho Tokutomi (1863–1957) wrote the history *Kinsei Nippon Kokuminshi* in 100 volumes of 42,468 total pages and 19,452,952 letters in 35 years.

The greatest number of novels by an English-language author is 904

The MOST PROLIFIC NOVELIST was Kathleen Lindsay (right) of South Africa who wrote 904 novels, using 2 other married names and 8 pen names, 2 of them masculine. (*Argus So. African Newspapers Ltd.*) Today's BEST-SELLING AUTHORESS is Barbara Cartland (above) with 390 million copies sold of her 390 light romances.

CRIME PAYS (left): Agatha Christie, the unrivaled "First Lady of Crime Writers" and author of the longest-running play, pauses between writing books which have sold 300 million copies in 103 languages. The photo was taken when she was in her prime. (*Popperfoto*)

by Kathleen Lindsay (Mrs Mary Faulkner) (1903–1973) of Somerset West, Cape Province, South Africa. She wrote under two other married names and 8 pen names, two of them masculine.

Baboorao Arnalkar (b June 9, 1907) of Maharashtra State, India, 1936-84 published 1,092 short mystery stories in book form and several non-fiction books.

After receiving a probable record 743 rejection slips, the British novelist John Creasey (1908–73), under his own name and 25 *noms de plume*, had 564 books totaling more than 40 million words published from 1932 to his death on June 9, 1973.

The writer with the longest series of books is Margaret Farrar, whose crossword puzzle books first published Apr 10, 1924 reached a total of 133 by the time of her death in June 1984.

Top-Selling Authors

Currently the top-selling authoress is Barbara Cartland with global sales of over 400 million copies for 418 titles in 17 languages. In 1986 she published 26 titles.

The all-time sales estimate of books by Erle Stanley Gardner (1889–1970) (US) to Jan 1, 1986, is 319,034,707 copies in 37 languages. The top-selling woman crime writer has been Dame Agatha Christie (*née* Agatha Mary Clarissa Miller), later Lady Mallowan (formerly Mrs Archibald Christie) (1890–1976). Her 87 crime novels have sold an estimated 300 million copies in 103 languages. *Sleeping Murder* was published posthumously in 1977.

It was announced on March 13, 1953, that 672,058,000 copies of the works of Marshal Josef Vissarionovich Dzhugashvili, also known as Stalin (1879–1953), had been sold or distributed in 101 languages.

Best Sellers

Excluding versions of the Bible, the world's all-time best selling copyright book is the *Guinness Book of World Records* first published from London in Sept 1955 by the Guinness Brewery to settle arguments in Britain's pubs and edited by Norris Dewar McWhirter (b Aug 12, 1925) and his twin Alan Ross McWhirter (killed Nov 27, 1975). Its cumulative sale in 25 languages to mid-1986 is in excess of 51 million copies.

It is believed that the 1879 edition of *The McGuffey Reader*, compiled by Henry Vail and published for school distribution in the US by Van Antwerp Bragg and Co, sold 60 million copies in the pre-copyright era.

The novel with the highest sales has been *Valley of the Dolls* (first published March 1966) by Jacqueline Susann (Mrs Irving Mansfield) (1921–74) with a world-wide total of 27,465,000 to May 1, 1985. In the first 6 months Bantam sold 6.8 million.

The longest duration on the *New York Times* best sellers' list (founded 1935) is "A Light in the Attic" by Shelby Silverstein (b 1932) which on Jan 10, 1985 had its 112th week on the lists.

Dell Publishing's author, Danielle Steel, during the years since Dec 1981 (225 consecutive weeks) has had at least one book of hers on a major best-seller list and in each of the 5 years has had 3 of her books on the *NY Times* lists in stretches ranging from one week to 17 weeks.

Greatest Advance

The greatest advance royalty paid for any book is $5,000,000 paid for an unpublished work titled *Whirlwind* by James Clavell at an auction in

NYC won by William Morrow & Co and its affiliated company, Avon Books, both of NYC.

Slowest Seller

. The accolade for the world's slowest-selling book (known in publishing as slooow-sellers) probably belongs to David Wilkins' Translation of the New Testament from Coptic into Latin, published by Oxford University Press in 1716 with 500 copies. Selling an average of one each 139 days, it remained in print for 191 years.

Oldest Authoress

The oldest authoress was Mrs Alice Pollock (*née* Wykeham-Martin) (1868–1971) of Haslemere, Surrey, England, whose book *Portrait of My Victorian Youth* (Johnson Publications) was published in March 1971 when she was aged 102 years 8 months.

Youngest Authoress

The youngest recorded commercially published author is Dorothy Straight (b May 25, 1958) of Washington, DC, who wrote *How the World Began* in 1962, aged 4. It was published in Aug 1964 by Pantheon Books.

Most Rejections

The greatest recorded number of publishers' rejections for a manuscript is 223 (by Mar 1986) for the 130,000-word manuscript *World Government Crusade* written in 1966 by Gilbert Young (b 1906) of Bath, Eng. The record for rejections before publication (and wide acclaim) is 69 from 55 publishers in the case of Prof. Steven Goldberg's *The Inevitability of Patriarchy*.

Worst Possible Writing

In a contest in May 1984, judged by professors of English at San Jose State University (Calif), the winning sentence, written by Steve Garman, city manager of Pensacola, Fla, reads: "The lovely woman-child Kaa was mercilessly chained to the cruel post of the warrior-chief Beast, with his barbarian tribe now attacking wood at her nubile feet, when the strong clear voice of the poetic and heroic Handsomas roared, 'Flick your Bic, crisp that chick, and you'll feel my steel through your last meal.'"

This "wonderfully terrible" sentence had anticlimax, wordiness, misplaced modifiers, overblown triteness, and parody, all aspects of bad writing the judges were looking for. First prize: a word processor.

More than 4,000 entries were received; Garman, the winner, submitted four different entries.

Highest-Paid Writer

In 1958, a Mrs Deborah Schneider of Minneapolis wrote 25 words to complete a sentence in a competition for the best blurb for Plymouth cars. She won from about 1,400,000 entrants the prize of $500 every month for life. On normal life expectations she would collect $12,000 per word. (By 1984, it had passed $6,000 per word.) No known anthology includes Mrs Schneider's deathless prose.

Longest Biography

The longest biography in publishing history is that of Sir Winston Churchill by his son Randolph (4,832 pages) and Martin Gilbert (13,830 pages) to date comprising some 8,214,000 words.

Georges Simenon (b Feb 13, 1903, Liege, Belgium) wrote 22 autobiographical books from 1972 to date.

Oldest Publishing House

Cambridge University Press has a continuous history of printing and publishing since 1584. The University received Royal Letters Patent to print and sell all manner of books on July 20, 1534.

Fastest and Slowest Publishing

The fastest time in which a book has been published is less than 24 hours by Corgi Books (Eng) from receipt of final manuscript to finished copies, in the case of John Lisners' *The House of Horrors,* a 223-page paperback on the mass murderer in North London, Dennis Nilsen sentenced to life imprisonment at 4:23 pm on Nov 4, 1983. (Also see *Crime,* chapter 10.)

The slowest was the German dictionary *Deutsche Worterbuch,* begun by the brothers Grimm in 1854 and finished in 1971.

Slowest proofreading record goes to Oxford Univ Press who sent out proofs of *Constable's Presentment to the Dugdale Society* in Dec 1949 and received them back 35 years later, in Dec 1984.

Highest Printings

The world's most widely distributed book is the Bible, which has been translated into 286 languages and portions of it into a further 1,522 languages. This compares with 222 languages for *Lenin.* It has been estimated that between 1815 and 1975 some 2,500,000,000 copies were printed of which 1,500,000,000 were handled by Bible Societies.

It has been reported that 800 million copies of the red-covered booklet *Quotations from the Works of Mao Tse-tung* were sold or distributed between June 1966, when possession became virtually mandatory in China, and Sept 1971, when their promoter, Marshal Lin Piao, died in an air crash.

The total disposal through non-commercial channels by Jehovah's Witnesses of *The Truth That Leads to Eternal Life,* published by the Watchtower Bible and Tract Society of Brooklyn, NYC (1968), reached 105,250,000 in 115 languages by May 1, 1984.

Most Misprints

The Times of London holds the record for 97 misprints in 5½ column inches on page 19 of its Aug 22, 1978 issue. The passage concerned "Pop" (Pope) Paul VI.

Largest Printers

The largest printers in the world are R. R. Donnelley & Co of Chicago. The company, founded in 1864, has plants in 15 main centers, and has turned out $1,814,000,000 worth of work per year. More than 133,-000 tons of inks and 1,645,000 tons of paper and board are consumed every year.

The largest printer under one roof is the US Government Printing Office in Washington, DC, founded in 1860. The Superintendent of Documents sold in 1984 almost $60 million worth of US governmental publications every year and has had as many as 20,000 (now 17,200) titles in print.

Longest-Lived Comic Strip

The most durable newspaper comic strip has been the Katzenjammer Kids (Hans and Fritz) created by Rudolph Dirks, first published in the *New York Journal* on Dec 12, 1897, and carried on by his son.

The earliest strip was *The Yellow Kid* which first appeared in the *New York Journal* on Oct 18, 1896. The most widely syndicated is "Peanuts"® by Charles Schulz, which is syndicated by United Feature Syndicate in 26 languages in 2,012 newspapers in 56 countries with an estimated circulation of 78½ million daily. It began in Oct 1950.

Most Widely Syndicated Columnist

The most widely syndicated columnist is Ann Landers (Mrs Jules Lederer) (b July 14, 1918) whose words now appear after 30 years in 1,000 newspapers with an estimated readership of 85 million.

Ranan R. Lurie (b May 26, 1932) is the most widely syndicated political cartoonist in the world. His work is published in 51 countries in 400 newspapers with a circulation of 62 million copies.

Most Expensive Autographs

The highest price ever for a single letter is $110,000 ($100,000 to the seller plus $10,000 commission to the auction gallery) paid on Oct 18, 1979 at the Hamilton Galleries, NYC, for a tiny note—actually a receipt—signed by Button Gwinnett (1732–77) of Georgia, one of the lesser known signers of the Declaration of Independence.

HIGHEST PRINT RUN: Surpassing all writers was Mao Tse-Tung, whose "Quotations" was distributed or sold in a quantity estimated at 800 million copies. Possession of a copy was virtually mandatory for each Chinese adult between 1966 and 1971.

The highest price for the autograph of a living person was $12,500 paid at the Hamilton Galleries on Jan 22, 1981, for a letter from President Ronald Reagan praising Frank Sinatra.

A record $4,675 was paid at a Hamilton sale on Aug 12, 1982 by Barry D Hoffman for the signed portrait of Al Capone (1899–1947).

Most Expensive Expense Account

An expense account by Paul Revere, dated Jan 3, 1774 and signed by John Hancock, was auctioned for $70,000 at Sotheby Parke Bernet, NYC, April 26, 1978.

Most Valuable Autographs

Only one example of the signature of Christopher Marlowe (1565–93) is known. It is in the Kent County Archives, England, on a will of 1583. It is estimated that a seventh Shakespearean signature would realize at least $1.5 million at auction.

Most Autographs

Dong Kingman, well-known Chinese-American watercolor artist, signed personally 10,000 each of 12 of his lithographed paintings (making 120,000 in all) in Hong Kong in 12 days of continuous sitting, May 8–19, 1980, for Rocky Aoki's Benihana Collection.

Bond Signing

The greatest feat of autographing was performed by Arne Aaaser of Den Norske Creditbank, Oslo, Norway. He signed 20,000 bonds in 16 hours 2 min 50 sec, March 4–5, 1982.

Poets Laureate

The youngest Poet Laureate was Laurence Eusden (1688–1730), who at the age of 30 years 3 months on Dec 24, 1718, was appointed. The greatest age at which a poet has succeeded is 73 in the case of William Wordsworth (1770–1850) on Apr 6, 1843. The longest-lived Laureate was John Masefield, who died on May 12, 1967, aged 88 years 345 days. The longest which any poet has worn the laurel is 41 years 322 days, in the case of Alfred (later the 1st Lord) Tennyson (1809–92), who was appointed Nov 19, 1850, and died in office Oct 6, 1892.

Most Successful Poem

If by Joseph Rudyard Kipling (1865–1936), first published in 1910, has been translated into 27 languages and according to Kipling was "anthologized to weariness."

Christmas Cards

The greatest number of personal Christmas cards sent out is believed to be 62,824 by Werner Erhard of San Francisco, founder of est, in Dec 1975.

Letters to the Editor

The *Upper Dauphin Sentinel,* Pa, published a letter of 25,513 words over 8 issues from Aug to Nov 1979, written by John Sultzbaugh of nearby Lykens, Pa.

The shortest literary correspondence on record was that between Victor Marie Hugo (1802–85) and his publisher, Hurst and Blackett, in 1862. The author was on holiday and anxious to know how his new novel *Les Misérables* was selling. He wrote "?". The reply was "!".

Longest Letter

The longest personal letter based on word count is one of 1,402,344 words, mailed by Alan Foreman of Erith, Kent, Eng, to his wife Janet on Jan 25, 1984.

Largest Libraries

The largest library is the Library of Congress (founded Apr 24, 1800), on Capitol Hill, Washington, DC. By 1986, it contained 90 million items, including 20 million books and pamphlets. With the James Madison Memorial Building, which was dedicated in Apr 1980, the buildings contain 64.6 acres of floor space and 532 miles of book shelves.

The largest non-statutory library is the New York Public Library (founded 1895) on Fifth Avenue, NYC, with a floor area of 525,276 sq ft and 88 miles of shelving. Including 81 branch libraries, its collection embraces 11,949,333 volumes, 14,466,478 manuscripts, and 363,679 maps.

Overdue Books

The most overdue book taken out by a known borrower was a book on febrile diseases (London, 1805, by Dr J. Currie) checked out in 1823 from the University of Cincinnati Medical Library and reported returned Dec 7, 1968, by the borrower's great-grandson Richard Dodd. The fine was calculated as $2,264, but waived.

Most Personal Mail

The highest confirmed count of letters received by any private citizen in a year is 900,000 letters by baseball star Henry Aaron, reported by the US Postal Department in June 1974, the year that he surpassed Babe Ruth's career home run record. About a third of them were letters of hate.

Oldest Newspapers

A copy has survived of a news pamphlet published in Cologne, Germany in 1470.

The oldest existing newspaper in the world is the Swedish official journal *Post och Inrikes Tidningar*, founded in 1645. It is published by the Royal Swedish Academy of Letters.

Most Newspapers

The US had 1,692 English-language daily newspapers on May 1, 1985. They had a combined net paid circulation of 62 million copies per day. The peak year for US newspapers was 1910 when there were 2,202. The leading newspaper readers in the world are the people of Sweden, where 580 newspapers were sold per each 1,000 persons in 1985.

Largest and Smallest Newspaper Issue

The most massive single issue of a newspaper was *The New York Times* of Sunday, Oct 17, 1965. It comprised 15 sections with a total of 946 pages, including about 1,200,000 lines of advertising. Each copy weighed 7½ lb and sold for 50 cents locally.

The largest page size ever used has been 51 in × 35 in for *The Con-*

stellation, printed in 1859 by George Roberts as part of the Fourth of July celebrations in NYC.

The smallest original page size has been 3 × 3¾ in of the *Daily Banner* (25 cents per month) of Roseberg, Ore, issues of which, dated Feb 1 and 2, 1876, survive.

Highest Newspaper Circulation

The first newspaper to achieve a circulation of 1 million was *Le Petit Journal,* Paris, which reached this figure in 1886 when selling at 5 centimes.

The highest circulation for any newspaper is that for the *Yomiuri Shimbun* (founded 1874) of Japan which attained a figure of 14,134,187 on Apr 1, 1986. This has been achieved by totaling the figures for editions published in various centers with a morning circulation of 9,167,300 and an evening circulation of 4,966,887. It has a staff of 3,060 and 436 bureaus.

Trud, the Soviet trade union daily, is printed in 53 cities in 15.4 million copies of which only 70,000 are bought at newsstands.

HIGHEST CIRCULATION: "Parade," the Sunday newspaper color supplement which is distributed with 268 newspapers, has a total circulation of 29,800,000 weekly and has the highest advertising rates per page. The "Parade" covers feature stars such as Shirley MacLaine and Bryant Gumbel.

Largest Circulation Periodicals

The largest circulation of any weekly periodical is that of *TV Guide*, which, in 1974, became the first magazine in history to sell a billion copies in a year. The weekly average for July to Dec 1985 was 16,898,-697.

In its 39 basic international editions the *Reader's Digest* (established Feb 1922) circulates 28,000,000 copies monthly, in 15 languages, including a US edition of 16,250,000 copies guaranteed.

Parade, the syndicated Sunday newspaper color magazine supplement, is distributed with 268 newspapers every Sunday. The current circulation (1985) is 29,800,000.

Most Durable Advertiser

The Jos Neel Co, a clothing store in Macon, Ga (founded 1880) has run an ad in the *Macon Telegraph* every day in the upper left hand corner of page 2 since Feb 22, 1889 or 35,405 times to Feb 1986.

Advertising Rates

The highest price ever for a single page of advertising is $332,800 for a four-color back cover of *Parade* in 1985 (circulation see above). The record for a four-color inside page is $284,360 in *Parade* (in Jan 1985). The advertising revenue from the Nov 1982 US edition of *Reader's Digest* was a peak $14,716,551.

The highest expenditure ever incurred on a single advertisement in a periodical is $3,200,000 by Gulf and Western Industries for insertions in the Feb 5, 1979 *Time* magazine (US and selected overseas editions).

The world's highest newspaper advertising rate is 37,350,000 yen ($155,000) for a full page in the morning edition and 30,825,000 yen ($128,000) for the evening edition of the *Yomiuri Shimbun* of Tokyo (Apr 1984), at the rate of 240 yen to the dollar (now in decline).

Crossword Puzzles

The earliest known crossword was a 9 × 9 Double Diamond published in *St. Nicholas* magazine for children for Sept 1875 in NYC. However, a 25-letter acrostic of Roman provenance was discovered on a wall in Cirencester, England in 1868.

The largest published crossword has been one compiled by Robert Trucot of Québec, Canada. It comprised 82,951 squares, 12,489 clues across and 13,125 down and covered 38.28 sq ft

---

4. MUSIC*

Earliest Instruments

Whistles and flutes made from perforated phalange bones have been found at Upper Paleolithic sites of the Aurignacian Period (*c.* 25,-000–22,000 BC), *e.g.* at Istallóskö, Hungary, and in Molodova, USSR.

---

* *Guinness Book of Music* (Sterling) can be referred to for a more detailed treatment of musical facts and records.

LARGEST ORGAN: The 6-tiered keyboard for the 30,067 pipes in the John Wanamaker store's organ in Philadelphia, the biggest organ functioning today.

Pianos

The earliest pianoforte in existence is one built in Florence, Italy, in 1720, by Bartolommeo Cristofori (1655–1731) of Padua, and now preserved in the Metropolitan Museum of Art, NY.

The grandest grand piano built was one weighing 1⅓ tons and measuring 11 ft 8 in long, made by Chas. H. Challen & Son Ltd of London in 1935. The longest bass string measured 9 ft 11 in and the tensile stress on the 726-lb frame was 33.6 tons.

The highest price ever paid for a piano is $390,000 for a Steinway grand of c. 1888 sold at Sotheby Parke Bernet, NYC on March 26, 1980 for the Martin Beck Theatre and bought by a non-pianist.

Organs

The largest and loudest musical instrument ever constructed and now only partly functional is the Auditorium Organ in Atlantic City, NJ. Completed in 1930, this heroic instrument has two consoles (one with seven manuals and another movable one with five), 1,477 stop controls and 33,112 pipes ranging in tone from 3/16 in to the 64-ft tone. It had the volume of 25 brass bands, with a range of 7 octaves. It also had the loudest organ stop, operated by a pressure of 100 in of water (3½ lb sq in) which created a pure trumpet note of ear-splitting volume, more than six times the volume of the loudest locomotive whistles.

The largest fully functional organ today is the six-manual 30,067-pipe Grand Court Organ in the John Wanamaker main store in Philadelphia, installed in 1911 and enlarged before 1930. It has a 64-ft tone *gravissima* pipe.

The largest church organ is in Passau Cathedral, Germany. It was completed in 1928 by D. F. Steinmeyer & Co. It has 16,000 pipes and five manuals.

The most powerful electronic organ is the 5,000-watt Royal V. Rogers organ, designed by Virgil Fox with 465 speakers, installed by Orient Shoji Co in Chuo-Ku, Tokyo, Japan in June 1983.

The chapel organ at the US Military Academy at West Point, NY, has, since 1911, been expanded from 2,406 to 18,200 pipes.

Double Bass Viol

The largest double bass ever constructed was 14 ft tall, built in 1924 in Ironia, NJ by Arthur K. Ferris, allegedly on orders from the Archangel Gabriel. It weighed 1,300 lb with a sound box 8 ft across, and had leathern strings totaling 104 ft. Its low notes could be felt rather than heard.

Most Valuable Cello

The highest price paid at auction for a violoncello is $290,000 at Sotheby's, London on Nov 8, 1978 for a Stradivarius made in Cremona, Italy in 1710.

Most Durable Musicians

Elise Maude Stanley Hall (1877–1976) gave piano recitals for 90 years, giving her final concert in Rustenburg, Transvaal, S Africa aged 97. Charles Bridgeman (1779–1873) of All Saints Parish Church Hertford, Eng, who was appointed organist in 1792, was still playing 81 years later in 1873. Norwegian pianist Reidar Thommesen (b June 7, 1889) played over 30 hours a week in theatre cafés when he was in his 90's.

Most Valuable Violin

At an auction for the Lady Blunt Stradivarius violin of 1721, the asking price was £820,000 ($1,148,000) at Sotheby's London on Nov 14, 1985, but bids failed to reach that level.

The highest price ever *paid* at auction for a violin or any musical instrument is £396,000 ($495,000) for La Cathédrale Stradivari dated 1707 at Sotheby's London on Nov 22, 1984. Some 700 of the 1,116 violins by Stradivarius (1644–1737) have survived. His Alarol violin was confirmed by Jacques Francais to have been sold in 1981 by private treaty by W. E. Hill Co (Eng) for $1.2 million to a Singaporean.

Most Durable Fiddlers

Rolland S. Tapley retired as a violinist from the Boston Symphony Orchestra after playing for a reputedly unrivaled 58 years from Feb 1920 to Aug 27, 1978. Otto E. Funk, 62, walked 4,165 miles from NYC to San Francisco, playing his Hopf violin every step of the way westward. He arrived June 16, 1929, after 183 days on the road.

Largest and Most Expensive Guitars

The largest and presumably also the loudest playable guitar is one 14 ft 3¼ in tall and 309 lb, built by Joe Kovacic of Lado Musical, Inc., Scarborough, Ont, Canada.

The most expensive standard-sized guitar is the German chittara battente, built by Jacob Stadler (dated 1624), which sold for £10,500 ($25,-200) at Christie's, London, June 12, 1974.

Largest Harp

What is probably the world's largest true playable harp was built in 1982 in Santa Fe, N Mex. Standing 13 ft 4 in high and measuring 7½ ft in width and 48 in in depth, it is built to scale 2½ times as large as a concert harp. The work of Wave Roark Barron with Kristin Novaswan and Lee Barron, it has an enclosed sound box, a harmonic curve, 41 stainless steel aircraft cable strings, brushed steel revolving base, hand molded redwood trunk seat for two, and can be plucked by hand or played by wind. Sale price: $15,000.

Largest Brass Instrument

The largest recorded brass instrument is a tuba standing 7½ ft tall, with 39 ft of tubing and a bell 3 ft 4 in across. This contrabass tuba was constructed for a world tour by the band of John Philip Sousa (1854–1932), the "march king," *c.* 1896–98, and is still in use. This instrument is now owned by a circus promoter in South Africa.

Longest Alphorn

The longest alphorn measuring 78 ft 9½ in long and weighing 183 lbs was made of spruce wood by Swiss-born Peter Wutherich, 65, of Boise, Idaho, and exhibited first on Apr 16, 1984, for CBS-TV News. It took 600 hours of labor over a year and a half. Sound takes 70.6 milliseconds to emerge from the bowl after entry into the mouthpiece.

Largest Drum

The largest drum ever constructed was one 12 ft in diameter weighing 600 lb for the Boston World Peace Jubilee of 1872.

Easiest and Most Difficult Instruments

The American Music Conference announced in Sept 1977 that the easiest instrument is the ukelele and the most difficult are the French horn and the oboe. The latter has been described as "the ill woodwind that no one blows good."

Highest and Lowest Notes

The extremes of orchestral instruments (excluding the organ) range between a handbell tuned to g′′′′′ or 6,272 cycles per sec, and the sub-

BIGGEST PLAYABLE TRUE HARP: It stands 13 ft 4 in tall and is built to scale 2½ times as large as a concert harp. It can be played by wind. (*Dr. Steve Lustbader*)

LARGEST MARCHING BAND: 4,524 in all (3,182 musicians and 1,342 majorettes, etc.) from 52 high school bands in the Los Angeles area played and marched together at the Dodgers Stadium prior to the baseball game on Apr 15, 1985. Danny Kaye was the director. (*LA Dodgers*)

contrabass clarinet, which can reach C,, or 16.4 cycles per sec. The highest note on a standard pianoforte is C''''', 4,186 cycles per sec, which is also the violinist's limit. In 1873, a sub double bassoon able to reach B,,,# or 14.6 cycles per sec was constructed, but no surviving specimen is known. The extremes for the organ are g''''''' (the sixth G above middle C) (12,544 cycles per sec) and C,,, (8.12 cycles per sec) obtainable from ¾-in and 64-ft pipes, respectively.

Stringed Instruments

The largest moveable stringed instrument ever constructed was a pantaleon with 270 strings stretched over 50 sq ft, used by George Noel in 1767.

The greatest number of musicians required to operate a single instrument was the 6 needed to play the gigantic orchestrion, known as the Appolonican, built in 1816 and played until 1840.

Marching Bands

The largest marching band was assembled by the Los Angeles Dodgers at Dodger Stadium on Apr 15, 1985. It consisted of 3,182 musicians and 1,342 majorettes, flag bearers, drill team members and directors for a total of 4,524 students from 52 high schools in the area. They played 3 tunes as well as the National Anthem under the directorship of Danny Kaye.

The longest recorded musical march by a marching band is one of 37.9 miles from Lillehammer to Hamar, Norway, in 15 hours when, on May 10, 1980, 26 of 35 members of the Trondheim Brass Band survived the playing of 135 marches.

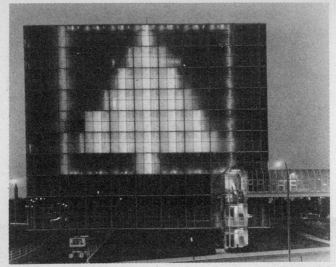

LARGEST SOUND-LIGHT DISPLAY: "Oxylights"® is a 125x95-ft synthesizer overlooking Niagara Falls from the NY side, built by Occidental Chemical Corp, with sound by Moog Electronics. It forms an exterior glass-paneled wall for Occidental's award-winning 9-story office building. The display was unveiled on Nov 23, 1985, and ran for 44 evenings as the centerpiece of the annual Festival of Lights.

Largest Choir

Excluding "sing-alongs" by stadium crowds, the largest choir is one of 60,000 which sang in unison as a finale of a choral contest among 160,-000 participants in Breslau, Germany on Aug 2, 1937.

Largest Orchestras

The most massive orchestra ever assembled was one of 20,100 at the Ullevaal Stadium, Oslo, June 28, 1964, made up of Norges Musikkorps Forbund bands from all over Norway.

On June 17, 1872, Johann Strauss the Younger (1825–99) conducted an orchestra of 987 instruments supported by a choir of 20,000, at the World Peace Jubilee in Boston, Mass. There were 400 first violinists.

Greatest Classical Concert Attendance

The greatest attendance at any classical concert was an estimated 800,-000 at a free open-air concert by the NY Philharmonic on the Great Lawn of Central Park, NYC, on July 5, 1986, as part of the Statue of Liberty Weekend. A record number of police—22,000—kept order and "fostered a friendly mood" for the entire weekend in Manhattan.

Pop Concert Attendance

Estimating the size of audiences at open-air events where no one pays admission is often left to police departments, newspaper and television

BIGGEST CROWD ever to witness a sound-light display (below) saw laser-beam pictures flashed on buildings' screens in downtown Houston, Tex. An estimated 3,100,000 people came to enjoy the show— searchlights prying the clouds, as well as music composed for the occasion by Jean-Michel Jarré of France (left).

reporters, city officials, concert promoters and the featured players' publicity agents. Although the crowds are enormous in Central Park, NYC, on the Washington Mall and elsewhere, estimates vary widely and there is no way to check accuracy.

The best claims are: 400,000 at an Elton John concert in Central Park on Sept 13, 1980; 500,000 (?) at a Simon and Garfunkel reunion concert also in Central Park a year later. Diana Ross is said to have drawn 800,-000 to her Central Park concert that was rained out on July 21, 1983.

A claim of 600,000 was made for a rock festival ("Summer Jam") at Watkins Glen, NY July 29, 1973. Of those attending, only 150,000 actually paid for admission. There were 12 "sound towers."

Some 175,000 in the Maracaña Stadium, Rio de Janeiro, Brazil paid to hear Frank Sinatra (b 1915) sing on Jan 26, 1980.

Largest Sound & Light Displays

The Occidental Chemical Corp introduced its "Oxylights," the world's largest sound/music synthesizer on Nov 25, 1985 in Niagara Falls, NY. It used the 125 × 95 ft wall of a building to display in lights, snowflakes, bells, Christmas trees, and cloudbursts of color, created by sound.

With French composer Jean-Michel Jarré (b Aug 24, 1948) providing the original score for his live performance, with searchlights prying into clouds above Houston, Tex, and laser pictures being flashed on skyscraper screens, some 1,300,000 are estimated by the police to have come to see the free *son et lumiere* show on Apr 5, 1986. It also caused the biggest traffic jam in Houston history.

Most Prolific Composers

The most prolific composer of all time was probably Georg Philipp Telemann (1681–1767) of Germany. He composed 12 complete sets of services (one cantata every Sunday) for a year, 78 services for special occasions, 40 operas, 600 to 700 orchestral suites, 44 Passions, plus concertos and chamber music.

The most prolific symphonist was Johann Melchior Molter (*c.* 1695–1765) of Germany, who wrote 165. Joseph Haydn (1732–1809) of Austria wrote 104 numbered symphonies, some of which are regularly played today.

Most Rapid Composer

Among classical composers the most rapid was Wolfgang Amadeus Mozart (1756–91) of Austria, who wrote *c.* 1,000 operas, operettas, symphonies, violin sonatas, divertimenti, serenades, motets, concertos for piano and many other instruments, string quartets, other chamber music, masses and litanies, of which only 70 were published before he died, aged 35. His opera *The Clemency of Titus* (1791) was written in 18 days and three symphonic masterpieces, *Symphony No. 39 in E flat major, Symphony No. 40 in G minor* and the *"Jupiter" Symphony No. 41 in C major,* were reputedly written in the space of 42 days in 1788. His overture to *Don Giovanni* was written in full score at one sitting in Prague in 1787 and finished on the day of its opening performance.

Longest Symphony

The longest of all single classical symphonies is the orchestral *Symphony No. 3 in D minor* by Gustav Mahler (1860–1911) of Austria. This work, composed in 1896, requires a contralto, a women's and a boys' choir, in addition to a full orchestra. A full performance requires 1 hour 40 min, of which the first movement alone takes between 30 and 36 min.

The *Symphony No. 2* (the Gothic, now renumbered as *No. 1*), composed in 1919–22 by Havergal Brian (1876–1972) was played by over 800 performers (4 brass bands) in the Victoria Hall, Hanley, Staffordshire, England on May 21, 1978, conducted by Trevor Stokes. A recent broadcast required 1 hour 45½ min. Brian wrote an even vaster work based on Shelley's *Prometheus Unbound* lasting 4 hours 11 min but the full score has been missing since 1961.

The symphony *Victory at Sea* written by Richard Rodgers and arranged by Robert Russell Bennett for NBC-TV in 1952 lasted 13 hours.

Longest Piano Compositions

The longest continuous non-repetitious piece for piano ever specifically composed for the piano has been "The Well-Tuned Piano" by La Monte Young first presented by the Dia Art Foundation at the Concert Hall, Harrison St, NYC on Feb 28, 1980. The piece lasted 4 hours 12 min 10 sec.

Symphonic Variations, composed by Kaikhosru Shapurji Sorabji (b

PAID ATTENDANCE was 175,000 at the concert Frank Sinatra (left) gave in Rio de Janeiro, Brazil, in 1980. PAYMENT of $2 million was earned in one 26-week season of piano concerts by Wladziu Valentino Liberace (right).

1892) into 500 pages of close manuscript in 3 volumes in the 1930's, would last for 6 hours at the prescribed tempo.

Greatest Span

The pianist Sergei Vassilievitch Rachmaninov (1873–1943) had a span of 12 white notes and could play a left-hand chord of C, E flat, G, C, G.

Highest-Paid Pianist

The highest-paid classical concert pianist was Ignace Jan Paderewski (1860–1941), Prime Minister of Poland (1919–21), who accumulated a fortune estimated at $5 million of which $500,000 was earned in a single season in 1922–23. The *nouveau riche* wife of a US industrialist once required him to play in her house behind a curtain.

Wladziu Valentino Liberace (b May 16, 1917 West Allis, Wis) has earned more than $2 million per 26-week season with a peak of $138,000 for a single night's performance at Madison Square Garden, NYC, in 1954.

Between 1937 and 1976, Artur Rubinstein (1887–1982) commanded 70 percent of the gross takings at his concerts.

Highest-Paid Singers

Of great fortunes earned by singers, the highest on record are those of Enrico Caruso (1873–1921), the Italian tenor, whose estate was about $9 million, and the Italian-Spanish coloratura soprano Amelita Galli-Curci (1889–1963), who received about $3 million. In 1850, up to $653 was paid for a single seat at the concerts given in the US by Johanna ("Jenny") Maria Lind (1820–87), later Mrs Otto Goldschmidt, the "Swedish Nightingale." She had a range of nearly three octaves, of which the middle register is still regarded as unrivaled.

The tenor "Count" John Francis McCormack (1884–1945) of Ireland gave 10 concerts to capacity audiences in a single season in Carnegie Hall, NYC.

David Bowie drew a fee of $1.5 million for a single show at the US Festival in Glen Helen Regional Park, San Bernardino County, Calif on May 26, 1983. The 4-man Van Halen rock singing group attracted a matching fee.

Surpassing the $81 million grossed by Michael Jackson's "Victory Tour" July–Dec 1984, is the tour which Bruce Springsteen made beginning in Apr 1984 that grossed an estimated $117 million. It ended with 4 nights in the LA Coliseum (capacity 85,000) when $5,800,000 was grossed.

Longest and Shortest Operas

The longest of commonly performed operas is *Die Meistersinger von Nürnberg* by Wilhelm Richard Wagner (1813–83) of Germany. A normal uncut performance of this opera as performed by the Sadler's Wells company between Aug 24 and Sept 19, 1968 entailed 5 hours 15 min of music. *The Heretics* by Gabriel von Wayditch, a Hungarian-American, is orchestrated for 110 pieces and lasts 8½ hours.

The shortest published was *Deliverance of Theseus* by Darius Milhaud (b Sept 4, 1892) first performed in 1928, which lasts for 7 min 27 sec.

Longest Aria

The longest single aria, in the sense of an operatic solo, is Brünnhilde's immolation scene in Wagner's *Götterdämmerung*. A well-known recording has been precisely timed at 14 min 46 sec.

Longest Operatic Encore

The longest listed in the *Concise Oxford Dictionary of Opera* was of the entire opera of Cimarosa's called *Il Matrimonio Segreto* at its premiere in 1792. This was at the command of Austro-Hungarian Emperor Leopold II (1790–92).

It was reported on July 5, 1983 that Placido Domingo received 83 curtain calls and was applauded for 1 hour 30 min after singing the lead in Puccini's *La Boheme* at the State Opera House in Vienna, Austria.

Opera Houses

The largest is the Metropolitan Opera House, Lincoln Center, NYC, completed in Sept 1966, at a cost of $45,700,000. It has a capacity of 3,-800 seats in an auditorium 451 ft deep. The stage is 234 ft in width and 146 ft deep. The tallest opera house is one housed in a 42-story building on Wacker Drive in Chicago.

The Teatro della Scala (La Scala) in Milan, Italy, shares with the Bolshoi Theatre in Moscow, the distinction of having the greatest number of tiers. Each has 6 with the topmost being nicknamed the *Galiorka* by Russians.

Youngest and Oldest Opera Singers

The youngest opera singer in the world has been Jeanette Gloria (Ginetta) La Bianca, (b Buffalo, NY May 12, 1934) who made her official debut as Rosina in *The Barber of Seville* at the Teatro dell'Opera, Rome, May 8, 1950, aged 15 years 361 days, but who appeared as Gilda in *Rigoletto* at Velletri, Italy, 45 days earlier. Miss La Bianca was taught by Lucia Carlino and managed by Angelo Carlino.

The tenor Giovanni Martinelli sang Emperor Altoum in *Turandot* in Seattle, Wash Feb 4, 1967, when aged 81.

Danshi Toyotake (b Aug 1, 1891) has been singing *Gidayu* for 86 years.

Oldest Bell

The oldest bell is the tintinnabulum found in the Babylonian Palace of Nimrod in 1849 by Mr (later Sir) Austen Henry Layard (1817–94). It dates from *c*. 1100 BC. The oldest known tower bell is one in Pisa, Italy dated MCVI (1106).

Largest Carillon

The largest carillon (minimum of 23 bells) is the Laura Spelman Rockefeller Memorial carillon in Riverside Church, NYC. It has 74 bells weighing 112 tons. The bourdon, giving the note lower C, weighs 40,926 lb. This 20.5-ton bell, cast in England, with a diameter of 10 ft 2 in, is the largest *tuned* bell.

Heaviest Bell

The heaviest bell is the Tsar Kolokol, cast on Nov 25, 1735 in Moscow. It weighs 210 tons, measures 19 ft 4¼ in in diameter, is 19 ft 3 in high, and its greatest thickness is 24 in. The bell is cracked, and a fragment, weighing about 12 tons, is broken from it. The bell has stood, unrung, on a platform in the Kremlin, in Moscow, since 1836.

The heaviest bell in use is the Mingun bell, weighing 101.4 tons, in Mandalay, Burma, which is struck by a teak boom from the outside. It has a diameter of 16 ft 8½ in at the lip.

The heaviest swinging bell in the world is the Petersglocke in the

HEAVIEST BELL: On the Kremlin terrace rests this Tsar Kolokol bell, weighing 216 tons, with a 12-ton fragment (opposite side) broken from it. It has been there since 1836.

southwest tower of Cologne Cathedral, Germany, cast in 1923, with a diameter of 11 ft 1¾ in, weighing 28.4 tons.

Oldest Songs

The oldest known song is the *shaduf* chant, which has been sung since time immemorial by irrigation workers on the man-powered pivoted-rod bucket raisers of the Nile water mills (or *saqiyas*) in Egypt. The oldest known harmonized music performed today is the English song *Sumer is icumen in* which dates from *c.* 1240.

Top Songs of All Time

The most frequently sung songs in English are *Happy Birthday to You* (based on the original *Good Morning to All*, by Mildred and Patty S. Hill of New York, published in 1935 and in copyright until 2010); *For He's a Jolly Good Fellow* (originally the French *Malbrouk*), known at least as early as 1781, and *Auld Lang Syne* (originally the Strathspey *I fee'd a Lad at Michaelmas*), some words of which were written by Robert Burns (1759–96). *Happy Birthday* was sung in space by the Apollo IX astronauts March 8, 1969.

Top Selling Sheet Music

Sales of three non-copyright pieces are known to have exceeded 20 million copies, namely *The Old Folks at Home* by Stephen Foster (1855), *Listen to the Mocking Bird* (1855) and *The Blue Danube* (1867). Of copyright material, the two top-sellers are *Let Me Call You Sweetheart* (1910, by Whitson and Friedman) and *Till We Meet Again* (1918, by Egan and Whiting), each with some 6 million by 1967. Other huge sellers have been *St Louis Blues, Stardust* and *Tea for Two*.

Most Successful Song Writer

In terms of sales of single records, the most successful of all song writers has been Paul McCartney, formerly of the Beatles and the Wings. Between 1962 and Jan 1, 1978 he wrote jointly or solo 43 songs which sold one million or more records.

National Anthems

The oldest national anthem is the *Kimigayo* of Japan, in which the words date from the 9th century. The anthem of Greece constitutes the first four verses of the Solomos poem, which has 158 verses. The shortest anthems are those of Japan, Jordan and San Marino, each with only four lines. Of the 23 wordless national anthems, the oldest is that of Spain, dating from 1770.

Longest Rendering of an Anthem

"God Save the King" was played non-stop 16 or 17 times by a German military band on the platform of Rathenau Railway Station, Brandenburg, on the morning of Feb 9, 1909. The reason was that King Edward VII was struggling inside the train to get into his German Field-Marshal uniform before he could emerge.

Longest and Shortest Hymns

The longest hymn is *Hora novissima tempora pessima sunt; vigilemus* by Bernard of Cluny (12th century), which runs to 2,966 lines. In English the longest is *The Sands of Time Are Sinking* by Mrs Anne Ross Cousin, *née* Cundell (1824–1906), which is in full 152 lines, though only 32 lines in the Methodist Hymn Book. The shortest hymn is the single verse in Long Metre *Be Present at Our Table, Lord,* anonymous but attributed to "J. Leland."

Most Prolific Hymnists

Mrs Frances Jane Van Alstyne, *née* Crosby (US) (1820–1915), wrote more than 8,500 hymns although she had been blinded at the age of 6 weeks. She is reputed to have knocked off one hymn in 15 minutes. Charles Wesley (1707–88) wrote about 6,000 hymns. In the seventh (1950) edition of *Hymns Ancient and Modern* the works of John Mason Neale (1818–66) appear 56 times.

---

5. THEATRE

Theatre as we know it has its origins in Greek drama performed in honor of a god, usually Dionysus. The earliest amphitheatres date from the 5th century BC. The largest of all known is one at Megalopolis in central Greece, where the auditorium reached a height of 75 ft and had a capacity of 17,000. The first stone-built theatre in Rome (erected in 55 BC) could accommodate 40,000 spectators.

Oldest Theatre

The oldest indoor theatre is the Teatro Olimpico in Vicenza, Italy. Designed in the Roman style by Andrea di Pietro, *alias* Palladio (1508–80), it was begun three months before his death and finished in 1582 by his pupil Vincenzo Scamozzi (1552–1616). It is preserved today in its original form.

Largest and Smallest Theatres

The largest building used for theatre is the National People's Congress Building (*Ren min da hui tang*) on the west side of Tian An Men Square, Peking, China. It was completed in 1959 and covers an area of 12.9 acres. The theatre seats 10,000 and is only occasionally used as such, as in 1964 for the play "The East Is Red."

The highest capacity purpose-built theatre is the Perth Entertainment Centre in Western Australia, completed at a cost in Australian dollars of $8.3 million in Nov 1976, with a capacity of 8,003 seats. The stage area is 12,000 sq ft.

The smallest regularly operated professional theatre is the Piccolo in Juliusstrasse, Hamburg, W Germany. It was founded in 1970 and has a maximum capacity of 30 seats.

Largest Stage

The largest stage is in the Ziegfeld Room, Reno, Nev with a 176-ft passerelle, 3 main elevators capable of lifting 1,200 show girls, two 62½-ft-circumference turntables and 800 spotlights.

Largest Amphitheatre

The largest amphitheatre ever built is the Flavian amphitheatre or Colosseum of Rome, Italy, completed in 80 AD. Covering 5 acres and with a capacity of 87,000, it has a maximum length of 612 ft and maximum width of 515 ft.

LONGEST RUN: For the finale of performance no. 3,389 of "A Chorus Line" on Sept 29, 1983 which broke the record for a Broadway show, 332 players who had appeared during the run in all roles were invited and appeared on stage. In mid-1986, the play was still running, and 23 million people had seen it on stage. (*Photo © 1983 Martha Swope, Courtesy of Merle Debuskey & Associates*)

Longest Runs

The longest continuous run of any show is of *The Mousetrap* by Agatha Christie (Lady Mallowan) (1890–1976). This thriller opened at the Ambassadors Theatre (capacity 453), London, Nov 25, 1952 and moved after 8,862 performances "down the road" to St Martin's Theatre, London, March 25, 1974. The 30th Anniversary performance on Nov 25, 1982 was the 12,481st.

The Vicksburg Theatre Guild of Vicksburg, Miss, have been playing the melodrama *Gold in the Hills* by J. Frank Davis discontinuously but every season since 1936.

The greatest number of performances of any theatrical presentation is 46,250 (to May 6, 1986) in the case of *The Golden Horseshoe Revue*—a show staged at Disneyland Park, Anaheim, Calif. The show was started on July 16, 1955 and has been seen by 16 million people. The three main performers nowadays, Dick Hardwick (formerly it was Wally Boag), Fulton Burley, and Betty Taylor, play as many as five houses a day in a routine lasting 45 min.

The long-run record for a "Broadway" show of any type was set on Sept 29, 1983, when *A Chorus Line* had its 3,389th performance at the Shubert Theatre. It is estimated that 23 million people saw it during the 4,484 performances to May 15, 1986 since it opened on July 25, 1975.

The Broadway record for the longest run of a drama (rather than a musical) is 3,224 performances (including benefits, etc.) by *Life With Father,* written by Howard Lindsay and Russel Crouse. The play opened at the Empire Theatre on Nov 8, 1939, and closed July 12, 1947, at the Alvin Theatre.

The longest-running musical is the off-Broadway show *The Fantasticks* by Tom Jones and Harvey Schmidt which reached its 10,864th per-

MOST SUCCESSFUL THEATRE OWNER: Jules Field has had his Sullivan St Playhouse in NYC rented for the same play, "The Fantasticks" for more than 26 years. On June 8, 1986, the play, for which Field is the associate producer, gave its 10,864th performance.

formance on June 8, 1986, after 26 years. *The Fantasticks* was scheduled to close on that date, but the closing announcement stirred up so much new demand for tickets, that the musical play has had to stay open indefinitely. The show has set a record by playing all these years in the same theatre, the Sullivan Street Playhouse, Greenwich Village, NYC, owned by Jules Field.

One-Man Shows

The longest run of one-man shows is 849 by Victor Borge (b Copenhagen Jan 3, 1909) in his *Comedy in Music* from Oct 2, 1953, to Jan 21, 1956, at the Golden Theater, NYC.

The world aggregate record for one-man shows is 1,700 performances of *Brief Lives* by Roy Dotrice (b Guernsey, England, May 26, 1923) including 400 straight at the Mayfair Theatre, London, ending July 20, 1974. He was on stage for more than 2½ hours per performance of this 17th century monologue, and required 3 hours for makeup and 1 hour for removal, thus aggregating 40 weeks in the chair as well.

Most Durable Leading Actors

In Japan, Kanmi Fujiyama (b 1929) played the lead role in 10,288 performances by the comedy company Sochiku Shikigeki from Nov 1966 to June 1983.

Dame Anna Neagle (1904–86) played the lead in *Charlie Girl* at the Adelphi Theatre, London, England, for 2,062 of 2,202 performances between Dec 15, 1965 and March 27, 1971. She played the same rôle a further 327 times in 327 performances in Australasia.

Marian Seldes did not miss a single performance in Ira Levin's longrunning Broadway hit *Deathtrap* from the show's opening on Feb 26, 1978, to its close on June 27, 1982. She portrayed the character Myra Bruhl in 1,793 consecutive performances.

Youngest Broadway Producer

Margo Feiden (Margo Eden) (b NY, Dec 2, 1944) produced the musical *Peter Pan*, which opened Apr 3, 1961, when she was 16 years 5 months old. She wrote *Out Brief Candle,* which opened Aug 18, 1962, and is now a leading art dealer.

Longest Play

The longest recorded theatrical production has been "The Acting Life" staged in the Tom Mann Theatre, Sydney, Australia on Mar 17–18, 1984 with a cast of 10. The production required 19½ hours (21 hours with intermissions).

Most Ardent Theatregoer

Dr H. Howard Hughes (b 1902) of Fort Worth, Tex, professor emeritus ar Texas Wesleyan University, attended 5,512 shows in the period 1956–1983.

Edward Sutro (1900–78) in England saw 3,000 first-night productions from 1916 to 1956, and possibly more than 5,000 in his 60 years of theatre-going.

Shakespeare

The longest play is *Hamlet,* with 4,042 lines and 29,551 words, 1,242 words longer than *Richard III.* Of Shakespeare's 1,277 speaking parts, the longest is the title role in *Hamlet* with 11,610 words.

Wrestling Shows

The wrestler who has received most for a single bout has been Kanii Antonio Inoki of Japan on Jun 26, 1976. He received $2 million for the wrestler vs. boxer bout against Muhammad Ali in the Budokan Arena, Tokyo, Japan which ended in a "draw."

Lou Thesz has won 7 of the world's many "world" titles. "Fabulous" Moolah won major US women's alliance titles over the longest span starting in 1956.

The heaviest ever wrestler has been William J. Cobb of Macon, Ga. (b 1926), who was billed in 1962 as the 802-lb "Happy" Humphrey. Ed "Strangler" Lewis (1890–1966) *né* Robert H. Friedrich, fought 6,200 bouts in 44 years losing only 33 matches. He won world titles in 1921, 1922, 1928 and 1931–32.

Shortest Criticism

The shortest dramatic criticism in theatrical history was that attributed to Wolcott Gibbs (1902–58), writing about the farce *Wham!* He wrote the single word "Ouch!"

Versatility in Show Business Awards

The only 3 performers to have won Oscar, Emmy, Tony and Grammy awards have been Helen Hayes (b 1900) 1932–1976; Richard Rodgers (1902–1979), composer of musicals; and Rita Moreno (b 1931) 1961–1977.

Barbra Streisand (b Apr 24, 1942 in Brooklyn, NYC) received Oscar, Grammy and Emmy awards in addition to a special "Star of the Decade" Tony award.

Highest-Paid Entertainers

The highest-paid entertainer, Dolly Parton, earns $400,000 for a live concert. Johnny Carson's fee for the non-televised Sears Roebuck Centenary in Oct 1984 was set at $1 million.

HIGHEST PAY FOR A PERFORMANCE (left): Singer Dolly Parton earned $400,000 for a single concert. (*Pictorial Press*)

LONGEST OFF-STAGE CHORUS LINE (below): 516 dancers lined up around the musicians at the Minneapolis Metrodome on Sept 16, 1985 for the 25th anniversary of the Vikings football team. (*Beth Obermeyer*)

MAN OF 3,350 DISGUISES: Jan Leighton is the "great imitator." Here you see him as 1. Benjamin Franklin. 2. Sigmund Freud. 3. Thomas Jefferson. 4. William Shakespeare. 5. Albert Einstein. 6. General Douglas MacArthur. 7. Napoleon. 8. Jan Leighton as himself.

Ice Shows

Holiday on Ice Productions Inc, founded by Morris Chalfen in 1945, stages the world's most costly live entertainment with up to seven productions playing simultaneously in several of 75 countries drawing 20 million spectators paying $40 million in a year. The total number of skaters and other personnel exceeds 900.

Longest Chorus Line

The longest chorus line in theatre history was up to 120 in some of the early *Ziegfeld Follies*. In the finale of *A Chorus Line* on the night of Sept 29, 1983, when it broke the record as the longest-running Broadway show ever, 332 top-hatted "strutters" appeared on the stage. The Rockettes at Radio City Music Hall, NYC, regularly have 36 precision-timed dancers.

Off-stage the longest chorus line was 516, performing on the field of the Metrodome in Minneapolis for the 25th anniversary of the Minnesota Vikings football team on Sept 16, 1985. The event was under the direction of Beth Obermeyer.

Shortest Runs

The shortest run on record was that of *The Intimate Revue* at the Duchess Theatre, London, March 11, 1930. Anything which could go wrong did. With scene changes taking up to 20 minutes apiece, the management scrapped seven scenes to get the finale on before midnight. The run was described as "half a performance."

A number of Broadway productions open and close the same night. There were 11 such "turkeys" in the 1978–79 season.

The largest loss incurred was probably the estimated $4 million lost on *A Doll's Life*, Sept 23–26, 1982.

Most Rôles

The greatest recorded number of theatrical, film and television rôles is 3,330 from 1951 to Apr 24, 1986 by Jan Leighton (US). (*See above.*)

Fashion Shows

The most prolific producer and most durable commentator of fashion shows is Adalene Ross of San Francisco, with over 4,702 in both categories to mid-1986.

---

6. RADIO BROADCASTING

The earliest description of a radio transmission system was written by Dr Mahlon Loomis (b Fulton County, NY, July 21, 1826, d 1886) on July 21, 1864, and demonstrated between two kites more than 14 mi apart at Bear's Den, Loudoun County, Va, in Oct 1866. He received US Patent No. 129971, entitled Improvement in Telegraphing, on July 20, 1872.

Earliest Patent

The first patent for a system of communication by means of electromagnetic waves, numbered No. 12039, was granted June 2, 1896, to the Italian-Irish Marchese, Guglielmo Marconi (1874–1937). A public demonstration of wireless transmission of speech was given in the town square of Murray, Ky, in 1892 by Nathan B. Stubblefield. He died, destitute, March 28, 1928. The first permanent wireless installation was at The Needles on the Isle of Wight, Hampshire, England, by Marconi's Wireless Telegraph Co, Ltd, in Nov 1896.

Earliest Broadcast

The first advertised broadcast was made on Dec 24, 1906, by Canadian-born Prof Reginald Aubrey Fessenden (1868–1932) from the 420-ft mast of the National Electric Signaling Company at Brant Rock, Mass. The transmission included Handel's *Largo*. Fessenden had achieved the broadcast of speech as early as Nov 1900, but this was highly distorted.

Transatlantic Transmissions

The earliest transatlantic wireless signals (the letter S in Morse Code) were received by Marconi, George Stephen Kemp and Percy Paget from a 10-kilowatt station at Poldhu, Cornwall, England, at Signal Hill, St John's, Newfoundland, Canada, at 12:30 p.m. Dec 12, 1901. Human speech was first heard across the Atlantic in Nov 1915, when a transmission from the US Navy station at Arlington, Va, was received by US radio-telephone engineers up on the Eiffel Tower, Paris.

Earliest Radio-Microphone

The first radio-microphone, which was in essence also the first "bug," was devised by Reg Moores (GB) in 1947, and first used on 76 MHz in the ice show *Aladdin* at Brighton Sports Stadium, England, in Sept 1949.

Smallest Set

The Toshiba AM-FM RP=1070 with built-in loudspeaker measures 3.5 × 2.1 × 0.05 in, and with battery weighs 2½ oz.

Most Radio Stations

The country with the greatest number of radio broadcasting stations is the US. As of Apr 1985, there were 9,512 stations licensed by the FCC.

Highest Radio Listener Response

The highest recorded response to a radio show occurred Nov 27, 1974, when on a 5-hour talk show on WCAU, Philadelphia, Howard Sheldon, the astrologist, registered a total of 388,299 calls on the "Bill Corsair Show."

The longest running solo feature in Great Britain today is *Letter from America* by (Alfred) Alistair Cooke, Hon KBE (b Salford, Eng, Nov 20, 1908), first broadcast on Mar 24, 1946.

Most Heard Broadcaster

Larry King has broadcast on network for 27½ hours a week since Jan 30, 1978 from Wash DC on Mutual Broadcasting Systems to all 50 states (now on 272 stations).

Longest on the air at one time was David Santamaria Maggiolo of the Dominican Republic who made a continuous broadcast of 500 hours, 20 min, Nov 18–Dec 8, 1985.

Topmost Prize on Radio

Mary Buchanan, 15, on WKRQ, Cincinnati, won a prize of $25,000 a year for 40 years ($1 million) on Nov 21, 1980.

Most Assiduous Radio Ham

Richard C. Spenceley (d July 30, 1982) of KV4AA at St. Thomas, US Virgin Islands built his contacts (QSO's) to a record level of 48,100 in 365 days in 1978.

7. TELEVISION

The invention of television, the instantaneous viewing of distant objects by electrical transmissions, was not an act but a process of successive and interdependent discoveries. The first commercial cathode ray tube was introduced in 1897 by Karl Ferdinand Braun (1850–1918), but was not linked to "electric vision" until 1907 by Boris Rosing of Russia in St Petersburg (now Leningrad). A. A. Campbell Swinton (GB 1863–1930) published the fundamentals of television transmission June 18, 1908 in a brief letter to *Nature* entitled "Distant Electric Vision." The earliest public demonstration of television was given on Jan 27, 1926, by John Logie Baird (1888–1946) of Scotland, using a development of the mechanical scanning system suggested by Paul Gottlieb Nipkov (1860–1940) on Jan 6, 1884. He had achieved the transmission of a Maltese Cross over 10 ft in Hastings, East Sussex, England, in Feb 1924, and the first facial image (of William Taynton, 15) on Oct 30, 1925. Taynton had to be bribed with 2 shillings sixpence. A patent application for the Iconoscope had been filed Dec 29, 1923, by Dr Vladimir Kosma Zworykin (born in Russia 1889, became a US citizen in 1924, d 1982). It was not issued until Dec 20, 1938.

Kenjiro Takayanagi (b Jan 20, 1899) succeeded in transmitting a 40-line electronic picture on Dec 25, 1926 with a Braun cathode-ray tube and a Nipkow disc at Hamamatsu Technical College, Japan. Baird launched his first television "service" via a BBC transmitter on Sept 30, 1929 and marketed the first sets, The Baird Televisions, in May 1930. Public transmissions on 30 lines were made from Aug 22, 1932 until Sept 11, 1935.

Video Tape Recording

Alexander M. Poniatoff first demonstrated video tape recording, known as Ampex (his initials plus "ex" for excellence) in 1956.

INVENTOR OF RADIO: Guglielmo Marconi first patented a radio on June 2, 1896, and he received the first wireless signal from across the Atlantic in 1901.

The earliest demonstration of a home video recorder was on June 24, 1963, at the BBC News Studio at Alexandra Palace, London, of the Telcan developed by Norman Rutherford and Michael Turner of the Nottingham Electronic Valve Co.

In 1985, some 674 million tapes were rented from more than 23,000 video rental stores in the US, compared with 26 million tapes in 1980, according to Tim Baskerville, the publisher of Video Marketing Newsletter in LA.

Earliest Service

The first high-definition (*i.e.* 405 lines) television broadcasting service was opened from Alexandra Palace, London, Nov 2, 1936, when there were about 100 sets in the UK. A television station in Berlin, Germany, began low-definition (180 line) transmission March 22, 1935. The transmitter burned out in Aug 1935.

Greatest TV Audience

It has been estimated that one-third of the world's population (1.6 billion people) watched the "Live Aid" telethon concerts on July 13–14, 1985 to raise funds for Ethiopia, including stations hooked up by a record 12 satellites. This was the most successful appeal ever made on TV.

The greatest estimated number of viewers worldwide for a pre-scheduled event is 2,500 million for the live and recorded transmissions of the XXIIIrd Olympic Games in LA July 27-Aug 13, 1984. ABC-TV aired 187½ hours on 56 cameras.

The serial which attracted the highest viewership was the final first-run episode of M*A*S*H on Feb 28, 1983, on CBS-TV which drew an estimated total audience of 125 million people in the US, with a 60.3 rating and a 77% share of the viewing audience.

Television Viewing

The Jan 1986 projection for US households with TV sets is 86.5 million, with 38 million having cable TV. The number of homes with color sets reached 77,700,000 (89.8%) by Jan 1986.

In 1986, there were an estimated 500 million homes with TV sets in the world, of which 86.5 million were in the US, with 8,250 TV stations worldwide, of which 1,149 were in the US.

The National Coalition on TV Violence published an estimate in June 1985 that by his 16th birthday the *average* US child will have seen 50,000 TV murders or attempted murders and 200,000 acts of violence. Between ages 2 and 11, the average viewing time is 27.3 hours per week.

Iceland has a TV-free day on Thursday to reduce disruption of family life. Otherwise transmissions are normally limited to between 8 and 11 p.m. July 1982 was declared a TV-free month. Upper Volta had only one set for each 1,000 inhabitants by 1974.

Transatlantic Transmission

The earliest transatlantic satellite transmission was achieved at 1 a.m. July 11, 1962, *via* the active satellite *Telstar I* from Andover, Me, to

HIGHEST PAY for a single taping of TV was $2 million to singer Kenny Rogers in Feb 1983 by HBO.

Pleumeur Bodou, France. The picture was of Frederick R. Kappell, Chairman of the American Telephone and Telegraph Company, which owned the satellite. The first "live" broadcast was made July 23, 1962, and the first woman to appear was the *haute couturière* Ginette Spanier, directrice of Balmain, Paris, the next day.

On Feb 9, 1928 the image of J. L. Baird (see above) and of a Mrs Howe was transmitted from Station 2 KZ at Coulsdon, Surrey, Eng to Station 2 CVJ, Hartsdale, NY.

Largest TV Prize

On July 24, 1975, WABC-TV, NYC transmitted the first televised Grand Tier draw of the State Lottery in which the winner took the grand prize of $1 million.

Highest Definition

A TV system with a 1,125-line definition was demonstrated by NHK (Nippon Hoso Kyokai) built by Hitachi and Sony at Brighton, Sussex, Eng on Sept 19, 1982.

Largest Contracts

The highest rate for any TV contract ever signed was one for $7 million for 7 hours of transmission with NBC by Marie Osmond, announced on Mar 9, 1981. This includes talent and production costs.

John William Carson (b Oct 23, 1925) host of *The Tonight Show,* has a contract reportedly calling for annual payment of $5 million for the one-hour show he hosts 4 times weekly.

Currently, television's highest-paid performer is Tom Selleck, who earns $220,000 per episode for *Magnum, P.I.,* which falls short of the record set by Carroll O'Connor, star of *Archie Bunker's Place,* who contracted for payments of $275,000 for each of the 1982–83 season's 22 half-hour episodes.

Singer Kenny Rogers was reported in Feb 1983 to have been paid $2 million for a single taping of a concert for HBO (Home Box Office) TV Channel.

The highest-paid current affairs or news performer is Dan Rather of CBS who reportedly signed an $8 million contract for 5 years from 1982.

Peter Falk (b Sept 16, 1927), the disarmingly persistent detective, Columbo, was paid from $300,000 to $350,000 per single episode for his series of 6, so totaling $1,950,000 in 1976.

Commercial Payments

In 1977, James Coburn of Beverly Hills, Calif was reputedly paid $500,000 for uttering two words on a series of Schlitz beer commercials. The words "Schlitz Light" were thus priced at a quarter of a million dollars per syllable.

The highest fee paid for a 30-second commercial is $1.5 million paid by Japanese TV in Dec 1985 to Boy George for promoting gin.

Faye Dunaway was reported in May 1979 to have been paid $900,000 for uttering 6 words for a Japanese department store TV commercial.

Most Expensive Production

The Winds of War, a 7-part Paramount World War II saga, aired by ABC in 1983 cost $42 million over 14 months of shooting. Its final episode had a rating of 41 and a 56% share (of the sets turned on).

Longest Program

The longest pre-scheduled telecast on record was one of 163 hours 18 min by GTV 9 of Melbourne, Australia, covering the Apollo XI moon mission July 19–26, 1969.

The longest continuous TV transmission under a single director was 25 hours exactly, by host Deb Williams, producer Tom McLaughlin, and director Rick Ray in Portland, Ore, over Rogers Cable TV. At the end, Miss Williams was carried off the set on a stretcher and placed in a waiting ambulance.

Most Durable TV Shows and Performances

The most durable show is NBC's *Meet the Press,* first transmitted Nov 6, 1947 and weekly since Sept 12, 1948. It was originated by Lawrence E. Spivak, who until 1975 appeared weekly as either moderator or panel member.

Joe Franklin started in 1951 on ABC-TV NY with his show and in 1965 switched to WOR-TV. He hosted his 21,700th broadcast on June 1, 1986 after a total of 35 consecutive years.

Over a period of 40 years, Hugh Downs appeared on camera on network television 9,915½ hours to July 31, 1985.

Greatest Sale

The greatest number of episodes of any TV program ever sold was 1,144 episodes of *Coronation Street* to CBKST, Saskatoon, Saskatchewan, Canada, by Granada Television, May 31, 1971. This constituted 20 days 15 hours 44 min of continuous viewing. A further 728 episodes (Jan 1974–Jan 1981) were sold to CBC (Canadian Broadcasting Company) in 1982.

Highest TV Advertising Rates

ABC announced that its rate for advertising on the 1985 Super Bowl broadcast was $550,000 per half minute.

Largest and Smallest Sets

The largest is the Sony Jumbo Tron color TV screen at the Tsukuba

International Exposition '85 near Tokyo, in Mar 1985, which measured 80 ft × 150 ft.

The Seiko TV-Wrist Watch launched on Dec 23, 1982 in Japan has a 1.2 in screen and weighs only 2.8 oz. Together with the receiver unit and the headphone set the entire black-and-white system, costing 108,000 yen (then $463), weighs only 11.3 oz. The smallest single-piece TV set is the Casio-Keisanki TV-10 weighing 11.9 oz with a 2.7 in screen launched in Tokyo in July 1983.

The smallest color TV set is the liquid crystal display (LCD) Japanese Epson launched in 1985 with dimensions of 3 × 6¾ × 1⅛ in, weighing, with batteries and its 52,800 crystals, only 16 oz.

Most Prolific Producer

The most prolific TV producer is Aaron Spelling (b 1928) (of "Dynasty" fame) who, in the 29 years from 1956 to mid-1985, produced more than 1,580 episodes totaling 2,037 hours of air time as well as 199½ hours of movies and 3 feature films. The total hours equals 12.1 million feet of film, which, if projected 24 hours a day, would take over 3 months to screen.

Most Prolific Scriptwriter

The most prolific television writer is the Rt. Hon. Lord Willis (b Jan 13, 1918), known as Ted Willis, who in the period 1949–86 has created 32 series, 29 stage plays, and 33 feature films. He had 24 plays produced. His total output since 1942 can be estimated at 18,250,000 words.

MOST PROLIFIC PRODUCER: Aaron Spelling, producer of "Dynasty," "Dallas," and many other TV shows, has put on 1,580 TV episodes since 1956. To view all of his produced work would take a full 93.4 days. (*Rex Features*)

8. MOTION PICTURES*

The earliest motion pictures ever taken were by Louis Aimé Augustin Le Prince (1842?–90). He reportedly achieved dim moving outlines on a white-washed wall at the Institute for the Deaf, Washington Heights, NYC, as early as 1885. The earliest surviving film is from his camera patented in Britain taken in early Oct 1888 of the garden of his father-in-law Joseph Whitley in Rounday, Leeds, W Yorkshire, at 10 to 12 frames per sec.

The first commercial presentation of motion pictures was at Holland Bros Kinetoscope Parlor at 1155 Broadway, NYC, on Apr 14, 1894. Viewers could see 5 films for 25 cents or 10 for 50 cents from a double row of Kinetoscopes developed by William Kennedy Laurie Dickson (1860–1935), assistant to Thomas Alva Edison (1847–1931).

The earliest publicly presented film on a screen was *La Sortie des Ouvriers de l'Usine Lumière* probably shot in Aug or Sept 1894 in Lyon, France. It was exhibited at 44 Rue de Rennes, Paris, on Mar 22, 1895, by the Lumière brothers, Auguste Marie Louis Nicholas (1862–1954) and Louis Jean (1864–1948).

Earliest Sound Movie ("Talkie")

The earliest sound-on-film motion picture was achieved by Eugene Augustin Lauste (b Paris, Jan 17, 1857) who patented his process Aug 11, 1906 and produced a workable system using a string galvanometer in 1910 at Benedict Road, Stockwell, London.

The earliest public presentation of sound on film was by the Tri-ergon process at the Alhambra cinema, Berlin, Germany on Sept 17, 1922.

Dr Lee de Forest (1873–1961) was responsible for the screening in the US of the first sound picture before a paying audience at the Rialto Theatre, NYC, Apr 15, 1923. The first all-talking picture was Warner Bros' *Lights of New York,* shown at the Strand Theatre, NYC, July 6, 1928.

Movie Theatres

The earliest structure designed and exclusively used for exhibiting projected films is believed to be one erected at the Atlanta Show, Ga, in Oct 1895 to exhibit C. F. Jenkins' phantoscope.

The largest is the Radio City Music Hall, NYC, opened on Dec 27, 1932, with 5,945 seats (now 5,882). The Roxy, opened in NYC on Mar 11, 1927, had 6,214 seats (later 5,869) but was closed Mar 29, 1960. Cineplex, opened at the Toronto Eaton Centre, Canada, on Apr 19, 1979, has 18 separate theatres with an aggregate capacity of 1,700. The largest drive-in cinema is Loew's Open Air at Lynn, Mass, with a capacity for 5,000 cars.

Biggest Screen

The permanently installed cinema screen with the largest area is one 92 ft 9 in × 70 ft 6 in, installed in the Keong Emas Imax Theatre, Taman Mini Park, Jakarta, Indonesia, opened Apr 20, 1984. It was made by Harkness Screens Ltd of Hertfordshire, England.

---

* For more records and greater details on this subject, see *Guinness Film Facts and Feats,* by Patrick Robertson (1980, Sterling).

BIGGEST MOVIE SCREEN: The Imax Theatre (left) in Taman Mini Park, Jakarta, Indonesia, which opened in Mar 1984, boasts a screen (right) which is 92 ft 9 in × 70 ft 6 in.

A temporary screen 297 × 33 ft (9,801 sq ft) was used at the 1937 Paris Exposition. A TV screen 80 × 150 ft (12,000 sq ft) was set up at the Tsukuba International Exposition in Tokyo in Mar 1985.

Most and Least Expensive Films

The highest ever budgeted film has been *Star Trek* which received its world premiere in Washington, DC on Dec 6, 1979. Paramount stated that the cost of this space epic directed by Robert Wise and produced by Gene Roddenberry, was $46 million. A figure of $60 million has been attributed to *Superman II* but never substantiated.

The least expensive film was Cecil Hepworth's highly successful release of *Rescued by Rover* in 1905 in England which cost $37.40.

Film Rights

The highest price ever paid for film rights is $9,500,000 announced on Jan 20, 1978 by Columbia for *Annie*, the Broadway musical by Charles Strouse, based on the comic strip *Little Orphan Annie*.

Highest Box Office Gross

The box office gross championship for films is highly vulnerable to inflated ticket prices. Calculations based on the 1983 value of the dollar show that *Gone With the Wind* with Clark Gable (1901–1960) and Vivien Leigh (1913–1967) released in 1939 is unsurpassed at $312 million.

The highest numerical (as opposed to value) dollar champion is Steven Spielberg's *ET: The Extra Terrestrial,* released on June 11, 1982, and which by Jan 2, 1983 had grossed $322 million. On May 29, 1983 *The Return of the Jedi* (20th Century Fox) grossed $8,440,105 for a single day record, and a record $6,219,929 for its opening day on May 25, 1985.

Film Rentals

Variety, the trade publication that is highly respected for its accuracy, lists *E.T.* as tops for rentals through Dec 31, 1985, with *Ghostbusters, Indiana Jones* and *Beverly Hills Cop* the three 1984 issues, and no 1985 films, joining the top 10 of all time.

WORLD'S MOST BEAUTIFUL WOMAN? Hollywood gave this appellation to Greta Garbo, but who would have believed it when she appeared in 1921 as a 16-year-old in this film (left) in her native Sweden. By 1927, after she had become a big star, she liked to be serenaded by a 3-piece female group with a violin, cello, and vocalist—"to get in the mood."

HIGHEST PAID STUNT MAN (right): Dar Robinson received $100,000 for a jump from 1,100 ft up with his parachute not opening until 300 ft from the ground. (*Photo by David A Boehm*)

HIGHEST BOX OFFICE GROSS (left): "E.T. The Extra Terrestrial" set the record with $322 million. The little charmer is seen here with his producer Stephen Spielberg. (*Courtesy Universal Pictures and Mr Spielberg*)

Movie-Going

The Chinese Ministry of Culture reported in Sept 1984 that there were 27,000 million cinema attendances in 1983—or nearly 27 per person per year. The Soviet Union claims to have most movie theatres in the world, with 163,400 in 1974, but this includes buildings merely equipped with even 16-mm projectors. The US has 16,965 actual movie theatres (1979).

San Marino has more seats for watching films per total population than any other country, with one cinema for each 1,512 inhabitants. The least number are in Saudi Arabia (population 8.4 million) which has no movie theatres.

Longest Films

The longest film ever premiered was the 48-hour-long *The Longest Most Meaningless Movie in the World* in 1970. It was British-made and later cut to 90 min.

The longest movie series, the Japanese *Tora-San* series, consisted of 32 feature films by Aug 1983.

Highest Earnings by an Actor

The highest rate of pay in cinema history was $12 million paid to Sylvester Stallone (b NYC, July 6, 1946) for *Rocky IV*, besides the as yet uncomputed share of the box office receipts. This may well be exceeded by his salary plus profit share for *Rambo,* which Hollywood sources predict will be $20 million.

The highest paid actress in 1985 was Meryl Streep (b Summit, NJ, 1949) with $3 million for her role in *Out of Africa.*

Stuntman Earnings

Dar Robinson was paid $100,000 for the 1,100-ft-high leap he made from the CN Tower in Toronto in Nov 1979 for *High Point.* His parachute opened at only 300 ft above the ground.

Largest Studios

The largest complex of film studios is that of Universal Studios at Universal City, Los Angeles. The back lot contains 561 buildings with 34 sound stages.

Most Films Seen

Albert E. Van Schmus (b 1921) saw 16,945 films in 32 years (1949–1982) as a rater for Motion Picture Association of America Inc.

Sal Piro of Greenwich Village, NYC, has seen the *Rocky Horror* movie 873 times during the 11 years it has been showing.

Most Prolific Director

Allan Dwan (1895–1981), the Canadian-born pioneer, directed, from 1909 to the early 1960's, more than 400 films.

Most Portrayed Character

The character most frequently recurring on the screen is Sherlock Holmes, created by Sir Arthur Conan Doyle (1859–1930). Sixty-seven actors portrayed Holmes in 186 films between 1900 and 1984.

Largest Loss

It was reported on Nov 20, 1980 that United Artists had withdrawn its

MOST VERSATILE ACTOR: Although Robert Duvall has appeared in 33 movies in major roles, hardly anyone recognizes him on the screen or on the street. Perhaps that is because he always looks different and plays different roles each time. Take a look: In (1) at the left he is the "consigliere" to the Coreleone family in "The Godfather—Part II" (1974). In (2) he plays Dr. Watson in "the 7 Per Cent Solution" (1976). (3) "True Confessions" and (4) "Tender Mercies," the 1983 movie for which he won an Oscar for "best actor."

4-hour-long *Heaven's Gate* because its total cost including distribution and studio overheads had reached $57,000,000.

Most Violent Movie

A study on the portrayal of violence showed the worst film on record was *Red Dawn,* released in the US in 1984, with acts of violence occurring at the rate of 134 per hour or 2.23 per min.

Most Versatile Performer

Robert Duvall who has appeared in 33 films in the last 20 years including some major hits (and has also appeared on Broadway) was called most versatile by the *New York Times.* He won his first Oscar for "best actor" in 1984.

Competing with him for the title is Robert De Niro, who has been a street kid, psycho, soldier, ball player, mobster, musician, boxer and buffoon in movies.

Most Oscars

Walter (Walt) Elias Disney (1901–66) won more "Oscars"—the awards of the Academy of Motion Picture Arts and Sciences, instituted on May 16, 1929, for 1927–28—than any other person. The physical count comprises 20 statuettes and 12 other plaques and certificates, including posthumous awards.

The only performer to win four Oscars for her starring rôles has been Katharine Hepburn (b Hartford, Conn, Nov 9, 1909), in *Morning Glory* (1933), *Guess Who's Coming to Dinner* (1967), *The Lion in Winter* (1968) and *On Golden Pond* (1981). She was nominated 12 times.

Only 4 actors have won 2 Oscars in starring roles—Fredric March in 1932, 1946; Spencer Tracy in 1937, 1938; Gary Cooper in 1941, 1952; and Marlon Brando in 1954, 1972.

Edith Head (d. 1981) won 8 individual awards for costume design.

The youngest person ever to win an Oscar was Shirley Temple (b Apr 23, 1928) with her 1934 honorary award at age 5, and the oldest is George Burns (b Jan 20, 1896) at age 80 for *The Sunshine Boys*.

The film with most awards has been *Ben Hur* (1959) with 11. The film with the highest number of nominations was *All About Eve* (1950) with 14. It won 6.

Oscars are said to have been named after Oscar Pierce of Texas. When the figurines were first delivered to the executive offices of the Academy of Motion Picture Arts and Sciences, the Executive Secretary exclaimed, "Why, they look just like my Uncle Oscar." And the name stuck.

9. RECORDED SOUND

The phonograph was first *conceived* by Charles Cros (1842–88), a French poet and scientist who described his idea in sealed papers deposited in the French Academy of Sciences Apr 30, 1877. The first practical device was realized by Thomas Alva Edison (1847–1931), who gained his first patent Feb 19, 1878 for a wax cylinder machine constructed by his mechanic, John Kruesi. It was first demonstrated on Dec 7, 1877, and patented on Feb 19, 1878. The horizontal disc was introduced by Emile Berliner (1851–1929).

Earliest Recordings

The earliest birthdate of anyone whose voice is recorded is Alfred, first Baron Tennyson (b Aug 6, 1809). The earliest born singer was Peter Schram, the Danish baritone of whom a cylinder was made in the role of Don Giovanni on his 70th birthday, Sept 5, 1889.

Oldest Records

The oldest records in the BBC library are white wax cylinders dating from 1888. The earliest commercial disc recording was manufactured in 1895. The BBC library, the world's largest, contains over 1 million records, including 5,250 with no known matrix.

The earliest jazz record made was *Indiana* and *The Dark Town Strutters Ball*, recorded for the Columbia label in NYC on or about Jan 30, 1917 by the Original Dixieland Jazz Band, led by Dominick (Nick) James La Rocca (1889–1961). This was released May 31, 1917. The first jazz record to be released was the ODJB's *Livery Stable Blues* (recorded Feb 24), backed by *The Dixie Jass Band One-Step* (recorded Feb 26), released by Victor on March 7, 1917.

Smallest Record

The smallest functional record is one 1⅜ in in diameter of "God Save the King" of which 250 were made by HMV Record Co in 1924.

SMALLEST RECORD RECORD: Only 1⅜ in in diameter, this is functional—one of 250 made in Britain in 1924, by the HMV Record Co, recording "God Save the King."

Tape Recordings

Magnetic recording was invented by Valdemar Poulsen (1869–1942) of Denmark with his steel wire Telegraphone in 1898 (US Patent No. 661619). Fritz Pfleumer (German patent 500900) introduced tape in 1928. Plastic tapes were devised by BASF of Germany in 1932–35, but were not marketed until 1950 by Recording Associates of NYC. In Apr 1983, Olympic Optical Industry Co of Japan marketed a microcassette recorder 4.2 in × 2 in × 0.55 in weighing 4.4 oz.

Most Successful Solo Recording Artists

On June 9, 1960 the Hollywood Chamber of Commerce presented Harry Lillis (*alias* Bing) Crosby, Jr (1904–77) with a platinum disc to commemorate the alleged sale of 200 million from 2,600 singles and 125 albums he had recorded. On Sept 15, 1970 he received a second platinum disc when Decca Records claimed a sale of 300,650,000 discs. No independently audited figures of his global lifetime sales from his royalty reports have ever been published, and experts regard figures so high as this, before the industry became highly developed, as exaggerated.

No independently audited figures have ever been published for Elvis Aaron Presley (b Tupelo, Miss, 1935–77). In view of Presley's worldwide tally of over 170 major hits on singles and over 80 top-selling albums from 1956 and continuing after his death, it may be assumed that it was he who succeeded Crosby as the top-selling solo artist of his time.

CBS Records reported in Aug 1983 that sales of albums by Julio Iglesias (b 1943) in 6 languages had surpassed the 100 million mark.

Most Successful Group

The singers with the greatest sales of any group have been The Beatles. This group from Liverpool, England, comprised George Harrison (b Feb 25, 1943), John Ono (formerly John Winston) Lennon (b Oct 9, 1940; d Dec 8, 1980), James Paul McCartney (b June 18, 1942) and Richard Starkey, *alias* Ringo Starr (b July 7, 1940). The all-time Beatles sales

RECORD SETTERS: (Above) Leading in record sales by groups are still The Beatles whose discs sold 100 million singles and 100 million albums to the end of 1978, and are still selling although the group has split up. In the solo singers race, Bing Crosby (300 million records sold) was succeeded by Elvis Presley (right) who had major hits with 170 singles and 80 albums.

by May 1985 have been estimated by EMI at over 1,000 million discs and tapes.

All 4 ex-Beatles sold many million further records as solo artists. Since their break-up in 1970, it is estimated that the most successful group in the world is the Swedish foursome ABBA (Agnetha Faltskog, Bjorn Ulvaeus, Benny Andersson and Anni-Frid Lyngstad) with a total of 215 million discs and tapes by May 1985.

Earliest Golden Disc

The earliest recorded piece eventually to aggregate a total sale of a million copies were performances by Enrico Caruso (b Naples, Italy, 1873, d 1921) of the aria *Vesti la giubba* (*On with the Motley*) from the opera *I Pagliacci* by Ruggiero Leoncavallo (1858–1919), the earliest version of which was recorded on Nov 12, 1902.

The first single recording to surpass the million mark was Alma Gluck's rendition of *Carry Me Back to Old Virginny* on the Red Seal Victor label on a 12-in single-faced (later backed) record (No. 74420).

The first actual golden disc was one sprayed by RCA Victor for presentation to Alton "Glenn" Miller (1904–44) for his *Chattanooga Choo Choo* on Feb 10, 1942.

Most Golden Discs

The only *audited* measure of gold, platinum and multiplatinum singles and albums within the US is certification by the Recording Industry Association of America introduced Mar 14, 1958. Out of the 2,582 RIAA awards made to Jan 1, 1985, The Beatles with 47 (plus one with Billy Preston) have most for a group. Paul McCartney has an additional 27 awards outside the group, and with Wings (including one with Stevie Wonder and one with Michael Jackson).

The most awards to an individual is 51 to Elvis Presley, spanning 1958 to Jan 1, 1986. Globally, however, Presley's total of million-selling singles has been authoritatively put at "approaching 80."

Biggest Sellers

The greatest seller of any record to date is *White Christmas* by Irving Berlin (b Israel Bailin, at Tyumen, Russia, May 11, 1888), with 30 million for the Crosby single (recorded May 29, 1942) and more than 100 million in other versions.

The highest claim for any "pop" record is an unaudited 25 million for *Rock Around the Clock,* copyrighted in 1953 by the late Max Freedman and James E. Myers, under the name of Jimmy De Knight, and recorded Apr 12, 1954 by Bill Haley and the Comets.

With all the profits of the enterprise (£35.3 million or $52 million) going to the Ethiopian Famine Relief Fund the centerpiece, the single record *Do They Know It's Christmas?,* written and produced by Bob Geldof and Madge Ure (UK) and played by an all-star ensemble of British musicians under the name Band Aid, sold 3.6 million copies on discs and cassettes by May 1986 in the UK and 7½ million more worldwide.

In the US simultaneously on July 13–14, 1985 for Ethiopian aid, the recorded song was *We Are The World* and sales of this record and ancillary items amounted to an estimated $20 million.

The best selling album of all time is *Thriller* by Michael Joseph Jackson (b Gary, Ind, Aug 29, 1958) with global sales in excess of 38.5 million copies to Aug 1, 1985.

Michael Jackson was signed for the largest sum ever paid for an individual endorsement (estimated at $50 million) by Pepsi-Cola on May 6, 1986.

The first classical long-player to sell a million was a performance featuring the pianist Harvey Lavan (Van) Cliburn, Jr (b Kilgore, Tex, July 12, 1934) of the *Piano Concerto No. 1* by Pyotr Ilyich Tchaikovsky (1840–93) of Russia. This recording was made in 1958 and sales reached 1 million by 1961, 2 million by 1965 and about 2,500,000 by Jan 1970.

Most-Recorded Songs

Three songs have each been recorded over 1,000 times—*Yesterday* by Paul McCartney and John Lennon, with 1,600 versions between 1965 and Jan 1, 1986; *Tie a Yellow Ribbon Round the Old Oak Tree,* written by Irwin Levine and L. Russell Brown, with more than 1,200 versions recorded from 1973 to Apr 1985; and *My Way,* music by Jacques Revaux and the late Claude Francois, with English lyrics by Paul Anka (b Ottawa, Canada, July 30, 1941).

Best-Seller Chart Records

Singles record charts were first published by *Billboard* on July 20, 1940, when the No. 1 record was *I'll Never Smile Again* by Tommy Dorsey (b Nov 19, 1905, d Nov 26, 1956). Three discs have stayed at the top for a record 13 consecutive weeks—*Frenesi* by Artie Shaw from Dec 1940; *I've Heard that Song Before* by Harry James from Feb 1943; and *Goodnight Irene* by Gordon Jenkins and the Weavers from Aug 1950. *Tainted Love* by Soft Cell stayed on the chart for 43 consecutive weeks from Jan 1982. The Beatles have had the most No. 1 records (21) and Elvis Presley has had the most hit singles on the *Billboard Hot* 100—149 from 1956 to May 1986.

Billboard first published an album chart on March 15, 1945, when the No. 1 record was *King Cole Trio* featuring Nat "King" Cole (b March 17, 1919, d Feb 15, 1965). *South Pacific* was No. 1 for 69 weeks (non-consecutive) from May 1949. *Dark Side of the Moon* by Pink Floyd enjoyed its 621st week on the charts in May 1985 (over 17 million sold). The Beatles had the most No. 1 recordings (15) and Presley the most hit albums (93 from 1956 to May 1986).

Most Recordings

Miss Lata Mangeshkar (b 1928) has reportedly recorded between 1948 and 1984 not less than 30,000 solo, duet and chorus-backed songs in 20 Indian languages. She frequently has 5 sessions in a day and has "backed" 2,000 films.

Phonographic Identification

Dr Arthur B. Lintgen (b 1932) of Rydal, Pa, has unique and proven ability to identify the music on phonograph records purely by visual inspection without hearing a note.

Loudest Pop Group

The amplification for *The Who* concert at Charlton Athletic Football Ground, London, England, May 31, 1976, provided by a Tasco PA system, had a total power of 76,000 watts from eighty 800 W Crown DC 300 A amplifiers and twenty 600 W Phase Linear 200's. The readings at 50 m (164 ft) from the front of the sound system were 120 decibels.

Sound engineer Rob Cowlyn with Duran Duran claimed that the audience's level of anticipatory screaming in Australia in Nov 1983 exceeded 120 dB *before* the group came on stage.

The claim by the US group Manowar, a heavy metal rock band, to have reached a reading of 160 dB in Oct 1984 is unsupportable.

Exposure to high noise levels is known to cause PSH—Permanent Shift of Hearing or partial to total instant deafness.

Grammy Awards

The record number of Grammy awards in a year is 8 by Michael Jackson in 1984. The all-time record is 25 since 1958 by the orchestral conductor Sir Georg Solti (GB) (b Budapest, Hungary, Oct 21, 1912).

Chapter 7

The World's Structures

EARLIEST STRUCTURES

The earliest known human structure is a rough circle of loosely piled lava blocks found in 1960 on the lowest cultural level at the Lower Paleolithic site at Olduvai Gorge in Tanzania, revealed by Dr Mary Leakey in Jan 1960. The structure was associated with artifacts and bones on a work-floor, dating to *circa* 1,700,000 BC.

The earliest evidence of *buildings* yet discovered is that of 21 huts with hearths or pebble-lined pits and delimited by stake holes, found in Oct 1965 at the Terra Amata site in Nice, France, thought to belong to the Acheulián culture of 120,000 years ago. Excavation carried out between June 28 and July 5, 1966 revealed one hut with palisaded walls having axes of 49 and 20 ft.

The oldest free-standing structures, described in 1647, are now believed to be the megalithic temples at Mgarr and Skorba in Malta and Ggantija in Gozo, dating from *c.* 3250 BC.

The remains of a stone tower 20 ft high built into the walls of Jericho have been excavated, and dated to 5000 BC, the foundation of the walls to as early as 8350 BC.

1. BUILDINGS FOR WORKING

Largest Industrial Building

The largest industrial plant in the world is the Nizhniy Tagil Railroad Car and Tank Plant, USSR, which has 204.3 acres of floor space. It has an annual capacity to produce 2,500 T-72 tanks.

Largest Commercial Buildings

The greatest ground area covered by any building under one roof is the auction building of the cooperative VBA (Verenigde Bloemenveilingen Aalsmeer), which measures 848.7 yd × 598 yd with a floor surface of 84.82 acres. A new extension will increase this to 91.05 acres. The first section of this site of the world's largest flower auction at Aalsmeer, Netherlands, was completed in Feb 1972.

The building with the largest cubic capacity is the Boeing Company's

LARGEST FLOOR: The Dutch flower market at Aalsmeer now has almost 85 acres under one roof, but needs an extension to cover up to 91 acres more, because at this auction place 7 million blooms are sold every day.

TALLEST OFFICE BUILDING: The Sears Tower dominates the Chicago skyline with its 110 stories, 16,000 windows, and height of 1,454 ft (1,559 ft counting TV towers). In gross area, however, the Sears Tower contains only 4,400,000 sq ft compared to the World Trade Center's total of 8,740,000 sq ft.

main assembly plant at Everett, Wash, completed in 1968. The building, constructed for the manufacture of Boeing 747 jet airliners, has a maximum height of 115 ft and has a capacity of 200 million cu ft.

Largest Scientific Building

The most capacious scientific building is the Vehicle Assembly Building (VAB) at Complex 39, the selected site for the final assembly and launching of the Apollo moon spacecraft on the Saturn V rocket, at the John F. Kennedy Space Center (KSC) on Merritt Island near Cape Canaveral, Fla. It is a steel-framed building measuring 716 ft in length, 518 ft in width and 525 ft in height. The building contains four bays, each with its own door 460 ft high. Construction began in Apr 1963 by the Ursum Consortium. Its floor area is 343,500 sq ft (7.87 acres) and its capacity is 129,482,000 cu ft. The building was "topped out" on Apr 14, 1965 at a cost of $108,700,000.

Largest Administrative Building

The largest ground area covered by any office building is that of the Pentagon, in Arlington, Va. Built to house the US Defense Department's offices, it was completed Jan 15, 1943 and cost about $83 million. Each of the outermost sides of the Pentagon is 921 ft long and the perimeter of the building is about 1,500 yd. The 5 stories of the building enclose a floor area of 6½ million sq ft. During the day 29,000 people work in the building. The telephone system of the building has more than 44,000 telephones connected by 160,000 miles of cable and its 220 staff members handle 280,000 calls a day. Two restaurants, 6 cafeterias and 10 snack bars and a staff of 675 form the catering department of the building. The corridors measure 17 miles in length and there are 7,748 windows to be cleaned.

Largest Office Buildings

The largest office buildings with the largest rentable space are the twin towers comprising the World Trade Center in NYC, with a total of 4,-370,000 sq ft (100.32 acres) in each. The taller tower (Tower Two) is 1,-362 ft 3¼ in high. The tip of the TV antenna on Tower One is 1,710 ft above street level.

Tallest Buildings

The *tallest* office building is the Sears Tower, the national headquarters of Sears Roebuck & Co on Wacker Drive, Chicago, with 110 stories, rising to 1,454 ft and completed in 1974. Its *gross* area is 4,400,000 sq ft (101.0 acres). It was "topped out" on May 4, 1973, surpassing the World Trade Center in New York in height, at 2:35 p.m. Mar 6, 1973 with the first steel column reaching to the 104th story. The addition of two TV antennae brought the total height to 1,559 ft. The building's population is 16,700, served by 103 elevators and 18 escalators. It has 16,000 windows.

Tentative plans for a 169-story 2,300-ft-tall building, projected to cost $1,250 million, for the Chicago Loop, were published on Oct 27, 1981. Plans for a 150-story, 1,670-ft-tall tower, on the upper West Side of NYC, entitled Television City, were unveiled by Donald Trump on Nov 15, 1985.

Largest Construction Project

The Madinat Al-Jubail Al-Sinaiyah project in Saudi Arabia

(1976–1996) covering 230,412.8 acres is the largest in history. The work force on the city and industrial port complex is increasing to a peak of 33,187 from the mid-1982 figure of 17,200. The total earth-moving and dredging volume will reach 0.82 of a cubic mile.

Largest Garages and Parking Lots

The largest car park is the West Edmonton Mall in Edmonton, Alberta, Canada, which has covered garaging for 20,000 vehicles, and overflow facilities for 10,000 more cars.

The largest private garage is one of 2 stories built outside Bombay, India, for the private collection of 176 cars owned by Prandal Bhogilal (b 1939).

The largest multistoried garage is the KMB Overhaul Centre operated by the Kowloon Motors Bus Co Ltd, Hong Kong. Built for double-decker buses, its 4 floors occupy more than 11.6 acres.

Sewage Works

The largest single full treatment sewage works is the West-Southwest Treatment Plant, opened in 1940 on a site of 501 acres in Chicago. It serves an area containing 2,940,000 people. It treated an average of 835,-000,000 gal of wastes per day in 1973. The capacity of its sedimentation and aeration tanks is 1.6 million cu yd.

Largest Hangars

The largest hangar is Hangar 375 ("Big Texas") at Kelly Air Force Base, San Antonio. The high bay area measures 2000 × 300 × 90 ft, with 4 doors each 250 ft wide and 60 ft high, weighing 657 tons. It is surrounded by a 44-acre concrete apron.

Delta Air Lines' jet base, on a 140-acre site at Hartsfield International Airport, Atlanta, Ga has 36 acres under its roof.

Air-Supported Structure

The largest air-supported roof is the roof of the 80,600-capacity octagonal Pontiac Silverdome Stadium, Mich measuring 522 ft wide and 722 ft long. Air pressure of 5 lb per sq in supports the 10-acre translucent fiberglass roofing. The structural engineers were Geiger-Berger Associates of NYC. It caved in during a snowstorm and gale in 1984 and the damage cost was estimated at $5 million, according to *The Detroit News*. The largest standard-size air hall was a temporary military structure in Lima, Ohio, which was 860 ft long, 140 ft wide and 65 ft high made by Irvin Industries of Stamford, Conn.

Wooden Buildings

The oldest extant wooden buildings are those comprising the Pagoda, Chumanar Gate, and the Temple of Horyu (Horyu-ji), at Nara, Japan, built between 670 and 715 AD. The nearby Daibutsuden, built in 1704–11, once measured 285.4 ft long, 167.3 ft wide and 153.3 ft tall. The present dimensions are 188 ft × 165.3 ft × 159.4 ft.

The largest all-wood buildings are the two US Navy airship hangars built in 1942–43 at Tillamook, Ore. Now worth $6 million, they are used by the Louisiana-Pacific Corp as a sawmill. They measure 1,000 ft long, 170 ft high at the crown and 296 ft wide at the base.

Tallest Chimneys and Cooling Towers

The tallest chimney is the $5½ million International Nickel Company's stack, 1,245 ft 8 in tall, at Copper Cliff, Sudbury, Ontario, Canada, completed in 1970. It was built by Canadian Kellogg Ltd in 60 days, and the diameter tapers from 116.4 ft at the base to 51.8 ft at the top. It weighs 42,998 tons and became operational in 1971.

The world's most massive chimney rises 1,148 ft at Puentes, Spain, built by the M. W. Kellogg Co. It contains 20,600 cu yd of concrete and 2,900,000 lb of steel and has an internal volume of 6,700,000 cu ft.

The largest cooling tower is adjacent to the nuclear power plant at Uentrop, W Germany, completed in 1976, which is 590 ft tall.

Grain Elevator

The largest single-unit grain elevator is that operated by the C-G-F Grain Company at Wichita, Kans. Consisting of a triple row of storage tanks, 123 on each side of the central loading tower or "head house," the unit is 2,717 ft long and 100 ft wide. Each tank is 120 ft high, with an inside diameter of 30 ft, giving a total storage capacity of 20 million bushels of wheat. The largest collection of elevators is at Thunder Bay, Ontario, Canada, on Lake Superior, with a total capacity of 103.9 million bushels.

Largest Embassy

The largest embassy is the USSR embassy on Bei Xiao Jie, Peking, China, in the northeastern corner of the walled city. The whole 45-acre area of the old Orthodox Church mission (established 1728), now known as the *Bei guan,* was handed over to the USSR in 1949.

Largest Filling Station

"Little America," west of Cheyenne, Wyo, at the junction of Interstate Routes 80 and 25 claims to be the world's biggest gas station with 52 diesel and gas pumps—none self-service. The highest in the world is at Leh, Ladakh, India at 12,001 ft operated by Indiaoil.

OLDEST WOODEN BUILDING: The Pagoda at Nara, ancient capital of Japan, was built about 715 AD, and celebrated its 1,271st birthday in 1986. (*Robert Harding*)

2. BUILDINGS FOR LIVING

Castles and Forts

Fortifications existed in all the great early civilizations, including that of ancient Egypt from 3000 BC. Fortified castles in the more accepted sense only existed much later. The oldest in the world is that at Gomdan, Yemen, which originally had 20 stories and dates from before 100 AD.

The largest inhabited castle is the British Royal residence of Windsor Castle, Berkshire. It is primarily of 12th-century construction and is in the form of a waisted parallelogram, 1,890 ft × 540 ft. The total area of Dover Castle (England), however, covers 34 acres with a width of 1,100 ft and a curtain wall of 1,800 ft, or, if underground works are taken in, 2,300 ft.

The largest ancient castle is Hradcany Castle, Prague, Czechoslovakia, built in the 9th century. It is a very oblong, irregular polygon with an axis of 1,870 ft and an average traverse diameter of 420 ft, with a surface area of 18 acres.

The walls of Ur (now Muquyyar), destroyed in 2000 BC, were 88½ ft in thickness.

Largest Palaces

The largest palace is the Imperial Palace (*Gu gong*) in the center of Peking (*Beijing*, northern capital), China, which covers a rectangle 1,050 yd × 820 yd, an area of 177.9 acres. The outline survives from the construction of the third Ming emperor Yung-lo of 1402–24, but due to constant rearrangements most of the intramural buildings are 18th century. These consist of 5 halls and 17 palaces of which the last occupied by the last Empress was the Palace of Accumulated Elegance (*Chu xia gong*) until 1924.

The Palace of Versailles, 14 mi southwest of Paris, has a facade with 375 windows, 634 yd in length. The building, completed in 1682 for Louis XIV, required over 30,000 workmen.

Brunei, a former British protectorate on the island of Borneo, newly independent (1984), completed in Jan 1984 the largest residential palace currently in use. Built for the Sultan, it reportedly cost $422 million, has its own mosque and heliport, 1,788 rooms, a garage for the Sultan's 110 cars and space for 800 vehicles in all, and 2 mi of air conditioning. The whole of Brunei has only 500 mi of roads.

The world's largest moats are those which surround the Imperial Palace in Peking. From plans drawn by French sources they appear to measure 54 yd wide and have a total length of 3,600 yd. The city's moats total 23½ miles in all.

Tallest Residential Buildings

The tallest block of apartments is Lake Point Towers of 70 stories, 645 ft high in Chicago.

The newly constructed condominium Metropolitan Tower on W 57 St, NYC, overlooking Central Park, is higher—716 ft in all—but is not entirely devoted to apartments. Just 45 of its 78 stories are residential and the lower floors are sold to commercial enterprises. Builder-developer is the Harry Maclowe Real Estate Co.

TALLEST APARTMENT HOUSE: From the 78th floor of the new Metropolitan Tower, 57th St. NYC, the tenant gets this view, with Fifth Ave on the right and Central Park West on the left.

NARROWEST HOUSE (left): 58 inches is the width of this home in Portsmouth, Eng. (*Gary Lee Crossley*)

INSIDE THE WORLD'S GRANDEST RESIDENCE (below): The Palm Garden of Biltmore House, Asheville, NC. (*Biltmore Estate*)

Largest Hotels

The Hilton Hotel in Las Vegas (built 1974–81) with 3,174 bedrooms claims to be the largest hotel, although it has fewer bedrooms than the Hotel Rossiya in Moscow with 3,200 bedrooms. The Hilton also has 12 international restaurants, 125,000 sq ft of convention space and a 10-acre rooftop recreation deck and a stage show dining hall. Over 3,600 are employed.

This compares with the 12-story Hotel Rossiya in Moscow, with 3,200 rooms providing accommodation for 6,000 guests, opened in 1967. It would thus require more than 8½ years to spend one night in each room. In addition, there is a 21-story "Presidential" tower in the central courtyard. The hotel employs about 3,000 people and has 93 elevators. The ballroom is reputed to be the world's largest. Muscovites are not permitted as residents while foreigners are charged 16 times more than the very low rate charged to officials of the USSR. The Izmailovo Hotel complex, opened July 1980 for the XXIInd Olympic Games in Moscow, was designed to accommodate 9,500 people.

Tallest Hotels

The tallest new hotel, measured from the street level of its main entrance to the top, is the 741.9-ft-tall 73-story Westin Stamford Hotel in Raffles City, Singapore, "topped out" in Mar 1985. The $235 million hotel is operated by Westin Hotel Co. Their Detroit Plaza Hotel in Detroit (almost a duplicate of their Peachtree Center Plaza Hotel in Atlanta, Ga) is slightly taller. This hotel, opened in early 1977, is 748 ft tall starting from its lower street level, when measured from its back entrance to the top.

Most Expensive Homes

The most expensive private house ever built is the Hearst Ranch at San Simeon, Calif. It was built 1922–39 for William Randolph Hearst (1863–1951), at a total cost of more than $30 million. It has more than 100 rooms, a 104-ft-long heated swimming pool, an 83-ft-long assembly hall and a garage for 25 limousines. The house would require 60 servants to maintain it.

The residence of the late king of Saudi Arabia in London, Kenstead Hall, with the adjoining property, was put on the market in Aug 1982 for £16 million (then $27 million).

Largest House

The largest private house in the world is 250-room Biltmore House in Asheville, NC. It is owned by George and William Cecil, grandsons of George Washington Vanderbilt II (1862–1914). The house was built between 1890 and 1895 on an estate of 119,000 acres, at a cost of $4,100,000, and is now valued at $55 million with 12,000 acres.

Most Expensive Hotel Suite

The costliest hotel accommodation was, before the hotel closed on Jan 31, 1985, the Royale Suite of the Hotel Nova-Park Elysées in Paris which rented for 35,000 francs (1982 = c. $5,500) per day. On three complete floors, it consisted of 8 rooms with 7 bathrooms, 3 terraces, and a conference room! It had a private telex machine plus 6 telephone lines. Designed for political figures (Jimmy Carter was one of the first occupants), the windows in the suite were made of bullet-proof glass and an anti-bugging device added to the security. There was a back door and a private elevator direct to the garage for fast escapes.

Largest Lobby

The world's largest hotel lobby is that of The Grand Hotel Taipei, Taiwan, completed on Oct 10, 1973. It measures 154 × 114 ft and is 31½ ft high.

Smallest Residence

The British naval veteran Alexander Wortley (1900–80) lived his last 20 years in a green painted box in the garden of David Moreau in Langley Park, Buckinghamshire, England. It measured 5 × 4 × 3 ft with an extension for his feet—"small enough to keep women out." He paid no rent or taxes and did not believe in insurance, pensions or governments.

Spas

The largest spa measured by number of available hotel rooms is Vichy, Allier, France, with 14,000 rooms. Spas are named after the watering place called Spa in the Liège province of Belgium where hydropathy was developed from 1626. The highest French spa is Barèges, Hautes-Pyrénées, at 4,068 ft above sea level.

---

3. BUILDINGS FOR ENTERTAINMENT

Largest Circus

The largest permanent circus is Circus Circus, Las Vegas, Nev, opened Oct 18, 1968 at a cost of $15 million. It covers an area of 129,000 sq ft capped by a 90-ft-high tent-shaped flexiglass roof. (Circus Stunt records are in Chapter 11.)

The largest traveling circus is the Circus Vargas in the US which can accommodate 5,000 people under its Big Top.

Largest Casino

The largest casino in the world is the Resorts International Casino, Atlantic City, NJ, with a monthly record play of $29.3 million in July, 1983. The Casino comprises 60,000 sq ft containing 127 gaming tables and 1,640 slot machines. Attendances total over 35,000 daily at peak weekends.

Night Clubs

The oldest night club (*boîte de nuit*) was "Le Bal des Anglais" at 6 Rue des Anglais, Paris 5, France. Founded in 1843, it closed *c.* 1960.

The largest night club in the world is Gilley's Club (formerly Shelly's) built in 1955 and extended in 1971 on Spencer Highway, Houston, Tex. It has a seating capacity of 6,000 under one roof covering 4 acres.

In the more classical sense the largest night club is "The Mikado" in the Akasaka district of Tokyo, Japan, with a seating capacity of 2,000. It is "manned" by 1,250 hostesses. Binoculars are essential to an appreciation of the floor show.

The lowest night club is the "Minus 206" in Tiberias, Israel, on the shores of the Sea of Galilee. It is 676 ft below sea level. An alternative

HIGHEST RESTAURANT: At Chacaltaya, high in the Bolivian Andes, 17,519 ft up, is this ski resort eatery. (*South American Pictures*)

LARGEST STADIUM of any type: Strahov Stadium in Prague, Czechoslovakia, has space for 240,000 spectators. The field is big enough for up to 40,000 gymnasts, the largest aggregation of aerobics practitioners.

candidate is "Outer Limits," opposite the Cow Palace, San Francisco, which was raided for the 151st time on Aug 1, 1971. It has been called both "The Most Busted Joint" and "The Slowest to Get the Message."

Restaurants

The earliest restaurant was opened in 1725 in Calle de Cuchilleras 17, Madrid. The painter Goya was a dishwasher there in 1765 when he was 19. The Paris restaurant now serving most "covers" per day is La Cupole, with 2,000. The highest restaurant in the world is at the Chacaltaya ski resort, Bolivia at 17,519 ft.

Largest Harem

The world's most capacious harem is the Winter Harem of the Grand Seraglio at Topkapi, Istanbul, Turkey completed in 1589 with 400 rooms. By the time of the deposing of Abdul Hamid II in 1909 the number of *carge* (those who serve) had dwindled from 1,200 to 370 odalisques with 127 eunuchs.

Largest Stadiums

The largest stadium is the open Strahov Stadium in Praha (Prague), Czechoslovakia. It was completed in 1934 and can easily accommodate 240,000 spectators for mass displays of up to 40,000 Sokol gymnasts or aerobic devotees.

The largest football (soccer) stadium is the Maracaña Municipal Stadium in Rio de Janeiro, Brazil, which has a normal capacity of 205,000, of whom 155,000 may be seated. A crowd of 199,854 was accommodated for the World Cup final between Brazil and Uruguay on July 16, 1950. A dry moat, 7 ft wide and over 5 ft deep, protects players from spectators and *vice versa*.

The largest covered stadium in the world is the Azteca Stadium, Mexico City, opened in 1968, which has a capacity of 107,000, of whom nearly all are under cover.

The largest retractable roof is being constructed to cover the 60,000-capacity Toronto Blue Jays new stadium near the CN Tower for completion by Aug 1988. The diameter will be 679 ft.

Largest One-Piece Roof

The transparent acrylic glass "tent" roof over the Munich Olympic Stadium, W Germany, measures 914,940 sq ft in area. It rests on a steel net supported by masts. The roof of longest span is the 680-ft diameter of the Louisiana Superdome. The major axis of the elliptical Texas Stadium, Irving, Tex, completed in 1971 is, however, 787 ft 4 in.

Largest Indoor Arena

The largest indoor stadium is the 13-acre $173-million 273-ft-tall Superdome in New Orleans, La, completed in May 1975. Its maximum seating capacity for conventions is 97,365 or 76,791 for football. Box suites rent for $35,000, excluding the price of admission. A gondola with six 312-in TV screens produces instant replay.

Largest Amusement Park

The largest amusement resort is Disney World on 28,000 acres of Orange and Osceola Counties, 20 miles southwest of Orlando in central Florida. It was opened on Oct 1, 1971. This $400 million investment attracted 10,700,000 visitors in its first year, and well above 20 million each year 1981–85, for a total of 200 million.

The $900 million Epcot Center (Experimental Prototype Community of Tomorrow) next to Disney World near Orlando was opened in Oct 1982. Peak days see 120,000 at Epcot and Magic Kingdom, the two parks in Orlando.

The most attended resort in the world is Disneyland, Anaheim, Calif (opened 1955) where the total number of visitors reached 250 million on Aug 24, 1985. The greatest attendance on one day was 82,516 on Aug 16, 1969.

Largest Carousel

The *Columbia,* located in Marriott's Great America in Santa Clara, Calif, is a gilded double-decker carousel 100 ft or 10 stories high from base to pinnacle, and 27½ ft in circumference. It can carry 115 passengers. On board are 103 carousel animals (including on the lower level 36 "jumping" horses, 6 standing horses, a 50-year-old horse, a camel, giraffe, lion, tiger, dragon, deer, sea horse, 2 ostriches, pigs, cats and rabbits) and 2 chariots. On the upper level are 45 more "jumping" horses and another chariot. This merry-go-round runs at a speed of 7 revolutions per min. Construction cost was $1.9 million

Fairs

The earliest major international fair was the Great Exhibition of 1851 in the Crystal Palace, Hyde Park, London, which in 141 days attracted 6,039,195 admissions.

The largest International Fair site was that for the St Louis-Louisiana Purchase Exposition, which covered 1,271.76 acres. It also staged the 1904 Olympic Games and drew an attendance of 19,694,855.

The record attendance for any fair was 64,218,770 for Expo '70 held on an 815-acre site at Osaka, Japan, from March to Sept 13, 1970. It made a profit of 19,439,402,017 yen (over $45 million).

Ferris Wheel

The original Ferris Wheel, named after its constructor, George W. Ferris (1859–96), was erected in 1893 at the Midway, Chicago, at a cost of $385,000. The wheel was 250 ft in diameter, 790 ft in circumference, weighed 1,198 tons, and carried 36 cars each seating 60 people, making a total of 2,160 passengers. The structure was removed in 1904 to St Louis, and was eventually sold as scrap for $1,800.

In 1897, a Ferris Wheel with a diameter of 300 ft was erected for the Earl's Court Exhibition, London. It had 10 1st-class and 30 2nd-class cars.

The largest wheels now operating are "Giant Peter" at Himeji Central Park, Himeji City, Hyogo, and one at the city of Tsukuba, both in Japan, and with a height of 278 ft 10 in. The latter has 46 cars with capacity for 384 riders.

Longest Slide

The longest slide in the world is the Bromley Alpine Slide on Route 11 in Peru, Vt. This has a length of 4,600 ft (0.87 mile) and a vertical drop of 820 ft.

Largest Pleasure Beach

The largest pleasure beach is Virginia Beach, Va. It has 28 miles of

LONGEST ROLLER COASTER (above): With a "stimulating" drop pf 141 ft, "The Beast" at King's Island, near Cincinnati, O, runs at a top speed of 64.77 mph over 7,400 ft of track, including 800 ft of tunnel and a 540° banked double turn. (*Rick Norton, King's Island*)

LARGEST CAROUSEL (left): Of the 120 carousels left in the US (at one time there were 2,000) the tallest is the "Columbia" at Marriott's Great America, Santa Clara, Calif. This double-decker gilded merry-go-round designed by R. Duell & Associates is 100 feet high and can carry 115 passengers.

beach front on the Atlantic and 10 miles of estuary frontage. The area which embraces 255 sq mi, contains 134 hotels and motels.

Pleasure Piers

The longest pleasure pier is Southend Pier at Southend-on-Sea in Essex, England. It is 1.34 miles in length, and was first opened in Aug 1889, with final extensions made in 1929. In 1949–50, the pier had 5,750,-000 visitors. The resort with most piers is Atlantic City, NJ, with 6 existing pre-World War II and 5 currently.

Roller Coasters

The maximum speeds claimed for roller coasters have in the past been exaggerated for commercial reasons. The twin-track, triple-helix American Eagle at Marriott's Great America, Gurnee, Ill, opened on May 23, 1981, has a vertical drop of 147.4 ft on which a speed of 66.31 mph is reportedly reached. The longest roller coaster in the world is *The Beast* at King's Island near Cincinnati, Ohio. Scientific tests at the base of its 141-ft-high drop returned a speed of 64.77 mph on Apr 5, 1980. The total track length of 7,400 ft incorporates 800 ft of tunnels and a 540-degree banked double turn.

The tallest is the 246-ft-high *Moonsault Scramble* at Fujikyu Highland Park, Japan, opened June 24, 1983. Its speed is 65.2 mph.

Bars

The largest beer-selling establishment is the Mathäser, Bayerstrasse 5, Munich, W Germany, where the daily sale reaches 100,000 pints. It was established in 1829, was demolished in World War II, rebuilt by 1955, and now seats 5,500 people. Consumption at the Dube beer halls in the Bantu township of Soweto, Johannesburg, South Africa, may, however, be higher on some Saturdays when the average of 7,160 gallons (57,280 pints) is far exceeded.

The longest permanent bar is the 340-ft-long bar in Lulu's Roadhouse, Kitchener, Ontario, Canada opened on Apr 3, 1984. The famous Working Men's Club bar at Mildura, Victoria, Australia has a counter 290 ft in length, served by 27 pumps. Temporary bars have been erected of greater length.

The bar at Erickson's on Burnside Street, Portland, Ore in its heyday (1883–1920) ran continuously around and across the main saloon, measuring 684 ft. The chief bouncer, Edward "Spider" Johnson, had a chief assistant named "Jumbo" Reilly who weighed 320 pounds and was said to resemble "an ill-natured orangutan." Beer was 5 cents for 16 fluid ounces.

Ballroom

The largest dance floor, 256 ft long, is one used for championships at Earl's Court Exhibition Hall, Kensington, London.

---

4. TOWERS AND MASTS

Tallest Structure

The tallest structure is the guyed Warszawa Radio mast at Konstantynow 60 miles northwest of Warsaw, Poland, which is 2,120 ft 8 in tall, or more than four-tenths of a mile. The mast was completed July 18, 1974 and put into operation July 22, 1974. Work began on the tubular steel construction, with its 15 steel guy ropes, in 1970. It was designed by Jan Polak and weighs 615 tons. The mast is so high that anyone falling off the top would reach terminal velocity, and hence cease to be accelerating, before hitting the ground. It recaptured for Europe a record held in the US since the Chrysler Building surpassed the Eiffel Tower in 1929.

Tallest Tower

The tallest self-supporting tower (as opposed to a guyed mast) is the $44 million CN Tower in Metro Centre, Toronto, Canada. It rises to 1,-822 ft 1 in. Excavation began Feb 12, 1973, for the 145,000-ton structure of reinforced, lost-tensioned concrete, and it was "topped out" Apr 2, 1975. A 416-seat restaurant revolves in the 7-floor Sky Pod at 1,140 ft, from which the visibility extends to hills 74½ miles distant. Lightning strikes the top about 200 times (in 30 storms) each year.

The tallest tower built before the era of television masts is the Tour Eiffel (Eiffel Tower), in Paris, designed by Alexandre Gustave Eiffel (1832–1923) for the Paris Exhibition and completed on March 31, 1889. It was 985 ft 11 in tall, now extended by a TV antenna to 1,052 ft 4 in, and weighs 8,091 tons. The maximum sway in high winds is 5 in. The whole iron edifice, which has 1,792 steps, took 2 years, 2 months, and 2 days to build and cost 7,799,401 francs 31 centimes.

---

5. BRIDGES

Oldest

Arch construction was understood by the Sumerians as early as 3200 BC and a reference exists to a Nile bridge in 2650 BC. The oldest surviving datable bridge is the slab stone single arch bridge over the River Meles in Smyrna (now Izmir), Turkey, which dates from c. 850 BC.

Longest Suspension Bridge

The longest bridge span is the main span of the Humber Estuary Bridge in England, at 4,626 ft. Work began on July 27, 1972. The towers are 533 ft 1⅝ in tall from datum and are 1⅜ inches out of parallel, to allow for the curvature of the earth. Including the Hessle and Barton side spans, the bridge stretches 1.37 miles. The bridge was structurally completed on July 18, 1980 at a cost of £91 million (about $185 million) and was opened by HM the Queen on July 17, 1981. Tolls ranging from £1 for cars to £7.50 for heavy vehicles, operative from May 4, 1981, are the highest in Britain.

The Mackinac Straits Bridge between Mackinaw City and St Ignace, Mich is the longest suspension bridge measured between anchorages (1.58 miles) and has an overall length, including viaducts of the bridge proper measured between abutment faces, of 3.63 miles. It was opened in Nov 1957 (dedicated June 28, 1958) at a cost of $100 million and has a main span of 3,800 ft.

The double-deck road-railroad Akashi-Kaikyo suspension bridge linking Honshu and Shikoku, Japan, is planned to be completed in 1988. The main span will be 5,840 ft in length with an overall suspended length with side spans totaling 11,680 ft. Work began in Oct 1978, and the eventual cost is expected to exceed 1 trillion yen ($4,500 million).

Plans for a bridge over the Messina Straits to link Sicily to the Italian mainland are dependent upon the budget of the European Common Market (EEC). One preliminary study calls for towers 1,000 ft tall, a span of more than 2 mi, and a cost of about $3,000 million.

Longest Cantilever Bridge

The Québec Bridge (Pont de Québec) over the St Lawrence River in Canada has the longest cantilever span—1,800 ft between the piers and 3,239 ft overall. It carries a railroad track and two roadways. Begun in 1899, it was finally opened to traffic Dec 3, 1917, at a cost of Can. $22,-500,000 and 87 lives.

LONGEST COVERED BRIDGE. The Trans-Canada Highway goes over this 1899 bridge at Hartland, New Brunswick. According to custom, you should cross your fingers, hold your breath and make a wish as you drive through. If you can hold your breath all the way across, your wish will be granted. (*Robert Harding*)

NARROWEST DRAWBRIDGE: To let sailboats with tall masts go through, the Somerset Bridge in Bermuda has an 18-in-wide wooden flap in the center.

Longest Steel Arch Bridge

The longest steel arch bridge is the New River Gorge Bridge near Fayetteville, W Va, completed in 1977, with a span of 1,700 ft.

Widest and Narrowest Bridges

The widest long-span bridge is the 1,650-ft-long Sydney Harbour Bridge, Australia, which is 160 ft wide. It carries 2 electric overhead railroad tracks, 8 lanes of roadway and a cycleway and footway. It was officially opened March 19, 1932.

The Crawford Street Bridge in Providence, RI, has a width of 1,147 ft.

The Somerset drawbridge in Bermuda has in the center an 18-in-wide wooden flap that opens to allow the masts of sailboats to pass through.

Covered Bridge

The longest covered bridge is that at Hartland, New Brunswick, Canada, measuring 1,282 ft overall, completed in 1899.

Railroad Bridges

The longest railroad bridge in the world is the Huey P. Long Bridge, Metairie, La, with a railroad section 22,996 ft (4.35 miles) long. It was completed Dec 16, 1935, with a longest span of 790 ft.

The Yangtse River Bridge completed in 1968 in Nanking, China, is the longest combined highway and railroad bridge. The rail deck is 4.20 miles and the road deck an additional 2.85 miles.

Floating Bridge

The longest floating bridge is the Second Lake Washington Bridge in Seattle, Wash. Its total length is 12,596 ft and its floating section measures 7,518 ft (1.42 miles). It was built at a cost of $15 million, and completed in Aug 1963.

Busiest Bridge

The world's busiest bridge is the Howrah Bridge across the River Hooghly in Calcutta, India. In addition to 57,000 vehicles a day it carries an incalculable number of pedestrians across its 1,500-ft-long 72-ft-wide span.

Highest Bridges

The highest bridge is the suspension bridge over the Royal Gorge of the Arkansas River in Colorado. It is 1,053 ft above the water level. It has a main span of 880 ft and was constructed in 6 months, ending on Dec 6, 1929. The highest railroad bridge in the world is at Fades, outside Clermont-Ferrand, France. It was built 1901–09 with a span of 472 ft and is 435 ft above the River Sioule. The highest road bridge is at an altitude of 18,380 ft near Khardungla, Ladakh, India, built by the Indian army in Aug 1982. Called the Bailey Bridge, it is only 98.4 ft long.

Longest Bridging

The world's longest bridging is the Second Lake Pontchartrain Causeway, opened March 23, 1969, joining Lewisburg and Metairie, La. Its length is 126,055 ft (23.87 miles). It cost $29,900,000 and is 228 ft longer than the adjoining First Causeway completed in 1956.

The longest railroad viaduct in the world is the rock-filled Great Salt Lake railroad trestle, carrying the Southern Pacific Railroad 11.85 miles across the Great Salt Lake, Utah. It was opened as a pile and trestle bridge March 8, 1904, and converted to rock fill in 1955–1960.

The longest stone arch bridging in the world is the 3,810-ft-long Rockville Bridge north of Harrisburg, Pa with 48 spans containing 219,-520 tons of stone and completed in 1901.

Largest Aqueducts

The greatest of ancient aqueducts was the Aqueduct of Carthage in Tunisia, which ran 87.6 miles from the springs of Zaghouan to Djebel Djougar. It was built by the Romans during the reign of Publius Aelius Hadrianus (117–138 AD). By 1895, 344 arches still survived. Its original capacity has been calculated at 8,400,000 gallons per day. The triple-tiered aqueduct Pont du Gard, built in 19 AD near Nimes, France, is 160 ft high. The tallest of the 14 arches of the Aguas Livres Aqueduct, built in Lisbon, Portugal, in 1784, is 213 ft 3 in.

The longest aqueduct, in the modern sense of a water conduit as opposed to an irrigation canal, is the California State Water Project aqueduct, completed in 1974 to a length of 826 miles, of which 385 miles is canalized.

LONGEST AND HIGHEST AQUEDUCTS: The Romans were famous for the building of aqueducts as their cities were dependent on a steady supply of water. In Carthage (now Tunisia) the Romans built an aqueduct 87.6 miles long. The triple-tiered aqueduct Port du Gard near Nimes, France (right), built in 19 AD, is the highest in the ancient world—160 ft high.

6. CANALS

Relics of the oldest canals in the world, dated by archeologists to c. 4000 BC, were discovered near Mandali, Iraq, early in 1968.

Longest Canals

The longest canalized system is the Volga-Baltic Canal opened in Apr 1965. It runs 1,850 miles from Astrakhan up the Volga, via Kuybyshev, Gorkiy and Lake Ladoga, to Leningrad, USSR. The longest canal of the ancient world was the Grand Canal of China from Peking to Hangchou. It was begun in 540 BC and not completed until 1327 AD by which time it extended for 1,107 miles. The estimated work force c. 600 AD reached 5 million on the Pien section. By 1950 the silt had piled up to the point that

LONGEST SHIP CANAL: A satellite view from space of the 100-mi-long Suez Canal looking south near the point where it enters the Red Sea. Egypt is to the right and Saudi Arabia to the distant left. (*Daily Telegraph*)

it was, in no place, more than 6 ft deep. It is now, however, opened up and plied by ships of up to 2,240 tons.

The Beloye More (White Sea) Baltic Canal from Belomorsk to Povenets in the USSR is 141 miles long with 19 locks. It was completed with the use of forced labor in 1933 and cannot accommodate ships of more than 16 ft in draught.

The longest big ship canal is the Suez Canal, linking the Red and Mediterranean Seas, opened Nov 16, 1869, but inoperative from June 1967 to June 1975. The canal was planned by the French diplomat Ferdinand de Lesseps (1805–1894) and work began Apr 25, 1859. It is 100.6 miles in length from Port Said lighthouse to Suez Roads, 197 ft wide. The work force was 8,213 men and 368 camels. The USS *Shreveport* transited southbound Aug 15–16, 1984 in a record 7 hours 45 min. A vessel with a beam of 159.7 ft and a length of 1081.5 ft, the SS *British Progress*, a VLCC (Very Large Crude Carrier), was the largest vessel to transit the Suez. (The Panama Canal width is more than 50 ft narrower.)

Busiest Canal

The busiest big ship canal is the Panama, first transited on Aug 15, 1914. In 1974, there were a record 14,304 ocean-going transits. The largest liner to transit is *Queen Elizabeth 2* (66,851 gross tons) in Jan 1980, for a toll of $89,154.62. The ships with the greatest beam to transit have been the 4 US battleships of the *Iowa* class with beams of 108 ft 2 in. The lowest toll was 36 cents for the swimmer Richard Halliburton in 1928. The fastest transit was 2 hours 41 min by the US Navy hydrofoil *Pegasus* on June 20, 1979.

Seaway

The longest artificial seaway is the St Lawrence Seaway (189 miles long) along the NY State-Ontario border from Montreal to Lake Ontario, which enables ships up to 728 ft long and 26.2 ft draught some of which are of 29,000 tons, to sail 2,342 miles from the North Atlantic, up the St Lawrence Estuary and across the Great Lakes to Duluth, Minn, on Lake Superior (602 ft above sea level). The project cost $470 million and was opened Apr 25, 1959.

Irrigation Canal

The longest irrigation canal is the Karakumskiy Kanal, stretching 528 miles from Haun-Khan to Ashkhabad, Turkmenistan, USSR. In Sept 1971 the navigable length was reported to have reached 280 miles. The length of the $925 million project will eventually reach 930 miles.

Largest and Deepest Locks

The largest single lock is the sea lock at Zeebrugge, Belgium, measuring 1640 × 187 × 75.4 ft giving a volume of 857,066 cu yd. The Berendrecht Lock, Antwerp, Belgium, planned for completion in 1986 will have the same length but a width of 223 ft and a depth of 70.5 ft giving a volume of 956,000 cu yd.

The deepest lock is the John Day Dam lock on the Columbia River, Ore and Wash, completed in 1963. It can raise or lower barges 113 ft and is served by a 1,100-ton gate.

The highest lock elevator overcomes a head of 225 ft at Ronquières on the Charleroi-Brussels Canal in Belgium. Two 236-wheeled caissons, each able to carry 1,512 tons, take 22 min to cover the 4,698-ft-long ramp.

Largest Canal Cut

The Gaillard Cut (known as the "Ditch") on the Panama Canal is 270 ft deep between Gold Hill and Contractor's Hill with a bottom width of 500 ft. In one day in 1911 as many as 333 dirt trains each carrying 400 tons left this site. The total amount of earth excavated for the whole Panama Canal was 666,194,450 sq yd to Oct 1, 1979. This total will be raised by the further widening of the Gaillard Cut.

---

7. DAMS

The earliest known dams were those uncovered by the British School of Archeology in Jerusalem in 1974 at Jawa in Jordan. These stone-faced earth dams are dated to c. 3200 BC.

Most Massive Dam

Measured by volume, the largest dam is the 98-ft-high New Cornelia Tailings earthfill dam on the Ten Mile Wash, Ariz with a volume of 274,015,735 cu yd, completed in 1973 to a length of 6.74 miles.

The Chapetón dam in Argentina is planned to have a volume of 387,-400,000 cu yd.

Highest Dam

The highest dam will be the Rogunsky earthfill dam in the USSR which will have a final height of 1,098 ft across the Vakhsh River, Tadjikistan, with a crest length of only 2,165 ft. Building since 1973, completion date is still unconfirmed. Meanwhile, the tallest is the 984-ft-high Narek dam in the USSR.

Largest Concrete Dam

The largest concrete dam, and the largest concrete structure, is Grand Coulee Dam on the Columbia River, Wash. Work on the dam was begun in 1933, it began working on Mar 22, 1941 and was completed in 1942 at a cost of $56 million. It has a crest length of 4,173 ft and is 550 ft high. It contains 10,585,000 cu yd of concrete and weighs about 19,285,000 tons. The hydroelectric power plant (now being extended) will have a capacity of 9,780,000 kW.

Longest River Dam and Sea Dam

The longest river dam is the 44.7-mi-long 134.5-ft-high Yacyreta-Apipe dam completed in 1983 across the Paraná on the Paraguay–Argentina border.

In the early 17th century, an impounding dam of moderate height was built in Lake Hungtze, Kiangsu, China, to a reputed length of 62 miles.

The longest sea dam is the Afsluitdijk stretching 20.195 miles across the mouth of the Zuider Zee in two sections of 1.553 miles (mainland of North Holland to the Isle of Wieringen) and 18.641 miles (Wieringen to Friesland). It has a sea-level width of 293 ft and a height of 24 ft 7 in.

Strongest Structure

The world's strongest structure will be the 793-ft-high Sayano-Shusenskaya dam on the Yenisey River, USSR. Under construction, it is designed to bear a load of 20,160,000 tons from a fully filled reservoir of 41,000 million cu yd capacity.

Largest Reservoirs and Man-Made Lake

The most voluminous man-made reservoir is the Kahkovskaya Reservoir, USSR, with a volume of 147,550,000 acre-ft.

The largest artificial lake measured by surface area is Lake Volta, Ghana, formed by the Akosombo dam, completed in 1965. By 1969, the lake had filled an area of 3,275 sq mi with a shoreline 4,500 miles in length.

The completion in 1954 of the Owen Falls Dam near Jinja, Uganda, across the northern exit of the White Nile River from the lake Victoria Nyanza, marginally raised the level of that *natural* lake by adding 166 million acre-ft, and technically turned it into a reservoir with a surface area of 17,169,920 acres (26,828 sq mi).

The $4 billion Tacurai Dam will, by 1985, convert the Tocantins River in Brazil into an 1,180-mile long chain of lakes.

Largest Polder

The largest of the five great polders in the old Zuider Zee, The Netherlands, will be the 149,000-acre (232.8-sq-mi) Markerwaard. Work on the 66-mi-long surrounding dike was begun in 1957. The water area remaining after the erection of the 1927–32 dam (20 mi in length) is called IJssel Meer, which will have a final area of 487.5 sq mi.

Largest Levees

The most massive levees ever carried out are the Mississippi levees begun in 1717 and vastly augmented by the US Government after the disastrous floods of 1927. These extend for 1,732 miles along the main river from Cape Girardeau, Mo, to the Gulf of Mexico and comprise more than 1,000 million cu yd of earthworks. Levees on the tributaries comprise an additional 2,000 miles. The 650-mile segment from Pine Bluff, Ark, to Venice, La, is continuous.

---

8. TUNNELS

Longest Tunnel

The longest tunnel of any kind is the NYC-W Delaware water supply tunnel begun in 1937 and completed in 1944. It has a diameter of 13 ft 6 in and runs for 105 miles from the Roundout Reservoir in the Catskill Mountains into the Hillview Reservoir, on the border line of NYC and Yonkers.

Bridge-Tunnel

The longest bridge-tunnel system is the Chesapeake Bay Bridge-Tunnel, extending 17.65 miles from Virginia's eastern shore to Virginia Beach, Va. It cost $200 million, took 42 months to complete, and opened on Apr 15, 1964. The longest bridged section is Trestle C (4.56 miles long) and the longest tunnel is the Thimble Shoal Channel Tunnel (1.09 miles).

Railroad Tunnel

The longest main-line rail tunnel is the 13-mile-1,397-yd Oshimizu Tunnel (Daishimizu) on the Tokyo-Niigata Joetsu line in central Honshu, Japan, under the Tanigawa Mt, which was holed through on Jan 25, 1979. The cost of the whole project has reached $6,300 million.

Road Tunnel

The longest road tunnel is the 10.14-mile-long two-lane St Gotthard Road Tunnel from Goschenen to Airolo, Switzerland, opened to traffic on Sept 5, 1980. Nineteen lives were lost during the construction, which cost almost $400 million since 1969.

The largest-diameter road tunnel was blasted through Yerba Buena Island in San Francisco Bay. It is 76 ft wide, 58 ft high and 540 ft long. More than 35 million vehicles cross on its two decks every year.

Sub-Aqueous Tunnel

The longest sub-aqueous railroad tunnel is the Seikan Rail Tunnel (33.46 miles), 787 ft beneath sea level and 328 ft below the sea bed of the Tsugaru Strait between Tappi Saki, Honshu, and Fukushima, Hokkaido, Japan. Tests started on the sub-aqueous section of 14½ mi in 1964, construction began in June 1972, the tunnel was holed through on Jan 27, 1973 (after a loss of 34 lives) and in Mar 1985 the tunneling was finished after 20 years 10 months. The cost was about $3,750,000,000.

Subway Tunnel

The longest continuous vehicular tunnel is the Moscow Metro underground railroad line from Belyaevo to Medvedkovo. It runs 19.07 mi and was completed in 1978–79.

An experiment at MIT on Apr 25, 1985 in which Thomas Stockebrand, using a working model of a supersonic subway tunnel, demonstrating before world leaders in the field, pneumatically pulled a table tennis ball through 950 ft of small-diameter pipe at 1,040 mph. This was intended to prove that a railway system could be built to operate at velocities greater than the speed of sound.

Irrigation, Hydroelectric and Sewerage Tunnels

The longest irrigation tunnel is the 51.5-mile-long Orange-Fish Rivers Tunnel, South Africa, begun in 1967, at an estimated cost of $150 million. The boring was completed in Apr 1973. The lining to a minimum thickness of 9 in will give a completed diameter of 17 ft 6 in.

The Majes project in Peru involves 60.9 miles of tunnels for hydroelectric and water supply purposes. The dam is at 13,780 ft altitude.

The Chicago TARP (Tunnels and Reservoir Plan) involves 120 miles of sewerage tunneling.

Canal Tunnel

The longest canal tunnel is that on the Rove Canal between the port of Marseilles, France and the Rhône River, built in 1912–27. It is 4.53 mi long, 72 ft wide and 50 ft high, involving 2¼ million cu yd of excavation.

LONGEST IRRIGATION TUNNEL: Measuring from this point, the mouth of the Orange-Fish Rivers Tunnel in S Africa, the length is 51½ mi. Begun in 1967, the boring was completed in 1973. (*South African Embassy*)

Tunneling

The longest unsupported example of a machine-bored tunnel is the Three Rivers Water Tunnel driven 30,769 linear ft with a 10.5-ft-diameter for the City of Atlanta, Ga from Apr 1980 to Feb 1982. S & M Constructors Inc of Cleveland, Ohio, achieved 179 ft in a day through the granite, schist and gneiss.

Wind Tunnels

The largest wind tunnel is a low-speed tunnel with a closed test section measuring 40 × 80 ft, built in 1944, at Ames Research Center, Moffett Field, Calif. The tunnel encloses 900 tons of air and cost approximately $7 million. The maximum volume of air that can be moved is 60 million cu ft per min. On July 30, 1974, NASA announced an intention to increase it in size to 80 × 120 ft for 345-mph speeds with a 135,000 hp system.

The most powerful is the 216,000-hp installation at the Arnold Engineering Test Center at Tullahoma, Tenn, opened in Sept 1956. The highest Mach number attained with air is Mach 27 at the plant of the Boeing Company, Seattle, Wash. For periods of microseconds, shock Mach numbers of the order of 30 (22,830 mph) have been attained in impulse tubes at Cornell University, Ithaca, NY.

---

9. SPECIALIZED STRUCTURES

Advertising Signs

The largest neon advertising sign measures 210 × 55 ft, built for Marlboro cigarettes at Kowloon, Hong Kong, in May 1986. It contains 35,000 ft of neon tubing and weighs 126½ tons.

Broadway's largest billboard has been 11,426 sq ft in area—equivalent to 107 ft × 107 ft. Broadway's largest working sign in Times Square, NYC, in 1966, showed two 42½-ft-tall "bottles" of Haig Scotch Whisky and an 80-ft-long "bottle" of Gordon's Gin being "poured" into a frosted glass.

The largest sign advertising an American city is the 370-ft-wide HOLLYWOOD sign in the hills above Los Angeles, placed by the Hollywood Chamber of Commerce. The letters (30 × 45 ft) are crumbling, and to obtain funds for their restoration, Hugh Hefner, publisher of *Playboy*, held a party in the spring of 1979, the proceeds of which amounted to $45,000.

The most conspicuous sign ever erected was the electric Citroën sign on the Eiffel Tower, Paris. It was switched on on July 4, 1925 and could be seen 24 miles away. It was in six colors with 250,000 lamps and 56 miles of electric cables. The letter "N" which terminated the name "Citroën" between the second and third levels measured 68 ft 5 in in height. The whole apparatus was taken down after 11 years in 1936.

An interior-lit fascia advertising sign in Clearwater, Fla, completed by Adco Sign Corp in Apr 1983 measures 1,168 ft 6½ in in length.

The most massive animated sign today is reputed to be outside the Circus Circus Hotel, Reno, Nev, named Topsy the Clown. It is 127 ft tall and weighs 44.8 tons with 1.4 miles of neon tubing. The clown's smile measures 14 ft across.

LARGEST LIVING ADVERTISING SIGN: An aerial view of the 8,259 pine trees in Bendix Woods Nature Center, New Carlisle, Ind, that spell out the name of the factory. The trees were planted as seedlings in 1936 and now stand 60 ft tall.

The highest advertising signs are the four Bank of Montreal logos atop the 72-story 935-ft-tall First Canadian Place Building in Toronto. Each sign, built by Claude Neon Industries Ltd measures 20 ft × 22 ft, and was lifted into place by helicopter.

Longest Breakwater

The longest breakwater protects the port of Galveston, Texas. The granite South Breakwater is 6.74 miles long.

Cemetery

The world's largest cemetery is one in Leningrad, USSR, which contains over 500,000 of the 1,300,000 victims of the German army's siege of 1941–42.

The world's largest crematorium is at the Nikolo-Arkhangelskoye Cemetery, East Moscow, completed in March 1972. It has 7 twin furnaces and several Halls of Farewell for atheists.

Tallest Columns

The tallest columns (as opposed to obelisks) are the 36 fluted pillars of Vermont marble in the colonnade of the Education Building, Albany, NY. Each one measures 90 ft tall and 6½ ft in base diameter.

The tallest load-bearing stone columns are those measuring 69 ft in the Hall of Columns of the Temple of Amun at Karnak, opposite Thebes on the Nile, the ancient capital of Upper Egypt. They were built in the 19th dynasty in the reign of Rameses II in *c.* 1270 BC.

Largest Dome

The world's largest dome is the Louisiana Superdome in New Orleans. It has an outside diameter of 680 ft. (For more details, see *Largest Indoor Arena.*) The largest dome of ancient architecture is that of the Pantheon, built in Rome in 112 AD, with a diameter of 142½ ft.

Doors

The largest doors are the 4 in the Vehicle Assembly Building near Cape Canaveral, Fla with a height of 460 ft. (See *Largest Scientific Building*.)

The world's heaviest door is that leading to the laser target room at Lawrence Livermore National Laboratory, Calif. It weighs 360 tons, is up to 8 ft thick and was installed by Overly.

Largest Drydock

The largest drydock is Okopo No 1 at Choje Island in S Korea, with a maximum shipbuilding capacity of 1,200,000 tons deadweight. It measures 1,722.4 ft long × 430 ft wide, and was completed in 1979.

Longest and Highest Fences

The longest fence is the dingo-proof fence enclosing the main sheep areas of Australia. The wire fence is 6 ft high, goes 1 ft underground, and stretches for 3,437 miles, more than the distance from Seattle to NY. The Queensland State Government discontinued full maintenance in 1982, but 310 mi is now being repaired.

The tallest fences are security screens 03.6 ft high built by Harrop-Allin of Pretoria to keep out Soviet RP67 rocket missiles from fuel depots and refineries in South Africa.

Tallest Flagpole

The tallest flagpole ever erected was outside the Oregon Building at the 1915 Panama-Pacific International Exposition in San Francisco. Trimmed from a Douglas fir, it stood 299 ft 7 in in height.

The tallest unsupported flagpole is the 282-ft-4-in tall steel pole weighing 120,000 lb, erected on Aug 22, 1985 at the Canadian Expo '86 in Vancouver, Brit Columbia. It supports a gigantic hockey stick 205 ft long.

Tallest Fountain

The tallest fountain is at Fountain Hills, Ariz built at a cost of $1½ million for McCulloch Properties Inc. At full pressure of 375 lb/sq in and at a rate of 7,000 gallons/min, the 560-ft column of water weighs more than 8 tons. The nozzle speed achieved by the three 600 hp pumps is 146.7 mph.

Longest Jetty

The longest deep-water jetty is the Quai Hermann du Pasquier at Le Havre, France with a length of 5,000 ft. Part of an enclosed basin, it has a constant depth of water of 32 ft on both sides.

Largest Kitchen

The largest kitchen ever set up has been the Indian Government field kitchen set up in Apr 1973 at Ahmadnagar, Maharashtra, in the famine area. The kitchen daily provided 1.2 million subsistence meals.

Tallest Lampposts

The tallest lighting columns ever erected are four 208 ft 4 in high made in France and installed by a British company at Sultan Qaboos Sports Complex, Muscat, Oman.

Lighthouses

The $23 million 328-ft-tall rock lighthouse built in 1983–85 24.8 mi southwest of L'Ile d'Ouessant, Brittany, France, is visible at 40 nautical mi. With reflective clouds at optimal altitude the loom is detectable in Isles of Scilly 105 mi distant.

The lights with the greatest visible range are those 1,092 ft above the ground on the Empire State Building, NYC. Each of the four-arc mercury bulbs has a rated candlepower of 450 million, visible 80 miles away on the ground and 300 miles away from aircraft. They were switched on on March 31, 1956.

The tallest lighthouse is the steel tower 348 ft tall near Yamashita Park in Yokohama, Japan. It has a power of 600,000 candles and a visibility range of 20 miles.

Largest Maze

The largest maze is Il Labirinto at Villa Pisani, Stra, Italy with 4 mi of paths. Napoleon was "lost" in it in 1807. The oldest dateable representation of a labyrinth is that on a clay tablet from Pylos, Greece, from c. 1200 BC.

The largest hedge maze is at Longleat, Wiltshire, Eng with 1.69 mi of paths flanked by 16,180 yew trees. It was opened on June 6, 1978 and measures 381 × 187 ft.

Tallest Monolith

The tallest menhir (upright rough stone found in nature) is the 425-ton Grand Menhir Brisé, now in 4 pieces, which originally stood 69 ft high at Locmariaquer, Brittany, France.

Tallest Monuments

The tallest monument is the stainless steel Gateway to the West Arch in St Louis, completed Oct 28, 1965, to commemorate the westward expansion after the Louisiana Purchase of 1803. It is a sweeping arch, spanning 630 ft and rising to a height of 630 ft, which cost $29 million. It was designed in 1947 by Eero Saarinen (d 1961).

The tallest monumental column commemorates the battle of San Jacinto (Apr 21, 1836), on the bank of the San Jacinto River near Houston, Tex. General Sam Houston (1793–1863) and his force of 743 Texan troops killed 630 Mexicans (out of a total force of 1,600) and captured 700 others, with the loss of 9 men killed and 30 wounded. Constructed in 1936–39, at a cost of $1½ million, the tapering column is 570 ft tall, 47 ft square at the base, and 30 ft square at the observation tower, which is surmounted by a star weighing 220 tons. It is built of concrete, faced with buff limestone, and weighs 35,150 tons.

Largest Prehistoric Monuments

The largest megalithic prehistoric monuments are the 28½-acre earthworks and stone circles of Avebury, Wiltshire, England rediscovered in 1646. The earliest calibrated date in the area of this neolithic site is c. 4200 BC. The whole work is 1,200 ft in diameter with a 40-ft ditch around the perimeter and required an estimated 15 million man-hours of work. The largest trilithons exist at Stonehenge, to the south of Salisbury Plain, Wiltshire, with single sarsen blocks weighing over 50 tons and requiring over 550 men to drag them up a 9° gradient. The earliest stage in the construction of the ditch has been dated to 2800 BC. Whether Stone-

LARGEST MAZE: Made of high stands of 16,180 yew trees, this maze at the Longleat Stately Home, Eng, has 1.69 mi of paths. An added attraction at the estate is the lions. (*Longleat Estate*)

henge was a lunar calendar, a temple, or an eclipse-predictor is still debated.

Naturist Resorts

The oldest naturist resort (the term "nudist camp" is deplored by naturists) is Der Freilichtpark, Klingberg, W Germany, established in 1903. The largest is the Beau Valley Country Club, Warmbaths, South Africa, extending over 988 acres with up to 20,000 visitors a year. However, 100,000 people visit the smaller Centre Helio-Marin at Cap d'Agde, southern France, which covers 222 acres.

Obelisks

The longest an obelisk has remained *in situ* is that still at Heliopolis, near Cairo, Egypt, erected by Senusret I *c.* 1750 BC.

The largest standing obelisk (of Tuthmosis III's day) was 118.1 ft tall when brought from Aswan, Egypt, by Emperor Constantine in 357 AD. It was repositioned in the Piazza San Giovanni in Laterane, Rome, on Aug 3, 1588. It now stands 107.6 ft tall and weighs 502.3 tons.

A heavier but unfinished and not standing obelisk remains at Aswan, probably commissioned by Queen Hatshepsut *c.* 1490 BC. It is 136.8 ft in length and weighs 1289.5 tons.

Longest Pier

The longest pier is the Dammam Pier, Saudi Arabia, on the Persian Gulf with an overall length of 6.79 miles. The work was begun in July 1948 and completed March 15, 1950. The area was subsequently developed into the King Abdul Aziz Port with 39 deep-water berths.

Largest and Oldest Pyramids

The largest pyramid, and the largest monument ever constructed, is the Quetzalcóatl at Cholula de Rivadabia, 63 miles southeast of Mexico City. It is 177 ft tall and its base covers an area of nearly 45 acres. Its total volume has been estimated at 4.3 million cu yd, compared with 3,360,000 cu yd for the Pyramid of Cheops. The pyramid-building era here was between the 2nd and 6th centuries AD.

The oldest known pyramid is the Djoser step pyramid at Saqqâra, Egypt, constructed by Imhotep to a height of 204 ft, originally with a Tura limestone casing, c. 2650 BC. The largest known single block came from the Third Pyramid of Mycerinus and weighs 319.2 tons. The oldest New World pyramid is that on the island of La Venta in southeastern Mexico built by the Olmec people c. 800 BC. It is 100 ft tall with a base dimension of 420 ft.

Most Massive Scaffolding

The 152-ft-high Statue of Liberty on a 150-ft-high pedestal in NY Harbor, a gift from France in 1886, in going through a period of renovation (1984–86), had scaffolding surrounding it that is the largest freestanding scaffolding in the world. Designed and installed by Universal Builders Supply Inc. of Mount Vernon, NY, the structure consists of over 6,000 aluminum components, weighs 160,000 lb, and is proportioned to withstand hurricane wind gusts of 100 mph. The 420-ft-long access ramp, together with the internal and external scaffolds, was constructed by an average of 22 very proud workers, battling winter conditions. The crane, from the top of its 315-ft corner tower, lowered Miss Liberty's rusting flame and torch to the ground on July 4, 1984.

Largest Scarecrow

The largest scarecrow, named Peuntjo, was built by the "de Binkel" youth club in Creil, The Netherlands, on June 29, 1985. It was 41.9 ft tall with a spread of 35.7 ft.

Largest Snow Construction

The largest snow construction was the Ice Palace built in Jan 1986 in St. Paul, Minn during its Winter Carnival. Designed and built by Ellerbe Associates, Inc., it used 30,000 blocks of ice and stood 120 ft high, the height of a 12–15 story building.

The largest snowman was 32 ft tall, built in Feb 1986 at the Schaumburg (Ill) Snow Festival. Some of the 100 tons of snow had to be trucked in from Mich.

Longest Stairs

The longest is the service staircase for the Niesenbahn funicular which rises to 7,759 ft near Spiez, Switzerland. It has 11,674 steps and a banister. The T'ai Chan temple stairs of 6,600 stone-cut steps in the Shantung Mts, China, ascend 4,700 ft in 5 miles.

The longest spiral staircase is one 1,103 ft deep with 1,520 steps, in-

ICE PALACE (left): The largest snow construction is this 30,000-ice-block, 120-ft-high twin tower in St Paul, Minn made for the 1986 Winter Carnival.

LARGEST SNOWMAN (above): Some of the 100 tons of snow needed to build this 32-ft-tall Snow King at the Schaumburg (Ill) Snow Festival in Jan 1986 had to be imported from across the border in Mich. (*Daily and Sunday Herald, Ill.*)

STATUE OF DISTINCTION (left): A rare photo of perhaps the world's shortest-lived statue. Erected in Hungary in honor of the Swedish diplomat, Raoul Wallenberg, who saved 90,000 Jews from extermination by the Nazis, the statue was destroyed 10 days after the Soviets occupied Hungary in 1956.

BIGGEST SCAFFOLDING (above): For the workers to repair the statue of Miss Liberty in NY Harbor 1984–86, this massive scaffolding, 315 ft high to the top of the torch, had to be built. (*Fred R. Tannery*)

TALLEST OBELISK (left), as seen through the world's tallest columns at the Temple of Karnak, Luxor, Egypt. It took 1,700 years to build. (*David Cadisch*)

stalled in the Mapco-White County Coal Mine, Carmi, Ill, by Systems Control Inc in 1981.

Tallest Statue

The tallest full-figure statue is that of the "Motherland," an enormous prestressed concrete female figure on Mamayev Hill, outside Volgograd, USSR, designed in 1967 by Yevgenyi Vuchetich, to commemorate victory in the Battle of Stalingrad (1942–43). The statue from its base to the tip of a sword clenched in her right hand measures 270 ft.

The Indian Rope Trick statue by Calle Örnemark near Jonkoping, Sweden, measures 337 ft from the feet of the *fakir* to the top of the rope 9.8 in in diameter. Its total weight is 159 tons.

Largest Tomb

The largest tomb is that of Emperor Nintoku (d *c.* 428 AD) south of Osaka, Japan. It measures 1,594 ft long × 1,000 ft wide × 150 ft high.

Tallest Totem Pole

The tallest totem pole is 173 ft tall raised on June 6, 1973 at Alert Bay, British Columbia, Canada. It tells the story of the Kwakiutl and took 76 man-weeks to carve.

Largest Tent

The largest tent ever erected was one covering an area of 188,368 sq ft (4.32 acres) put up by the firm of Deuter from Augsburg, W Germany, for the 1958 "Welcome Expo" in Brussels, Belgium.

Longest Wall

The Great Wall of China, completed during the Ch'in dynasty, reign of Shih Huang-ti (246–210 BC), has a main-line length of 2,150 miles with a further 1,780 miles of branches and spurs, with a height of from 15 to 39 ft and up to 32 ft thick. It runs from Shanhaikuan, on the Gulf of Pohai, to Yümên-kuan and Yang-kuan and was kept in repair up to the 16th century. Some 32 miles of the Wall have been destroyed since 1966. Part of the Wall was blown up to make way for a dam in July 1979. On Mar 6, 1985 a report from China stated that a 5-year-long survey proved that the total length had been 6,200 mi.

Water Tower

The tallest is in Union, NJ, built in 1965 to a height of 210 ft, with a capacity of 250,000 gal.

Waterwheel

The largest waterwheel is the Mohammadieh Noria wheel at Hama in Syria, with a diameter of 131 ft. It dates from Roman times.

Largest Windows

The largest sheet of glass ever manufactured was one of 538.2 sq ft, or 65 ft 7 in × 8 ft 2½ in, exhibited by the Saint Gobain Company in France at the *Journées Internationales de Miroiterie* in March 1958. The largest single windows are those in the Palace of Industry and Technology at Rondpoint de la Défense, Paris, with an extreme width of 715.2 ft and a maximum height of 164 ft.

Wine Casks

The largest wooden wine cask is the Heidelberg Tun completed in 1751 in the cellar of the Friedrichsbau Heidelberg, W Germany. Its capacity is 1,855 hectolitres (48,985 US gallons).

The oldest is in use since 1715 at Hugelet Fils (founded 1639) Riquewihr, Haut-Rhin, France by the most recent of the 12 generations of the family.

Wine Cellar

The largest wine cellars are at Paarl, those of the Ko-operative Wijnbouwers Vereeniging (K.W.V.), near Capetown, in the center of the wine district of South Africa. They cover an area of 25 acres and have a capacity of 36 million gallons.

The Cienega Winery of the Almaden Vineyards in Hollister, Calif covers 4 acres and can house 37,300 oak barrels containing 1.83 million gallons of wine.

Ziggurat (Stage or Temple Tower)

The largest surviving ziggurat (from the verb *zaqaru*, Babylonian, to build high) is the Ziggurat of Ur (now Muquyyar, Iraq) with a base 200 ft × 150 ft built to at least 3 stories of which only the first and part of the second now survive to a height of 60 ft. It has been dated between *c.* 2113 BC and *c.* 2096 BC.

The largest ziggurat ever built was by the Elamite King Untash *c.* 1250 BC, known as the Ziggurat of Choga Zanbil, 18.6 mi from Haft Tepe, Iran. The outer base was 344 ft and the fifth "box" 91.8 ft nearly 164 ft above.

Largest Hotel Move

The 3-story brick Hotel Fairmount (built 1906) in San Antonio, Tex, which weighed 3,200,000 lb, was moved on 36 dollies with pneumatic tires over city streets approximately 5 blocks, over a bridge, which had to be reinforced. The move by Emmert Industrial of Portland, Ore, took 4 days in all, Mar 30–Apr 2, 1985, and cost $650,000. The final site of the historic hotel, which will be restored at a cost of about $4 million, is about 3 blocks south of the landmark, The Alamo.

Largest Building Demolished by Explosives

The largest was the 21-story Traymore Hotel, Atlantic City, NJ on May 26, 1972. The 600-room hotel had a cubic capacity of 6,495,500 cu ft. Controlled Demolition Inc of Towson, Md did the job.

The tallest chimney ever demolished by explosives was the Matla Power Station chimney, Kriel, South Africa, on July 19, 1981. It stood 902 ft high and was brought down by Dykon, Inc. of Tulsa, Okla for the Electrical Supply Commission of Johannesburg, S Africa.

The greatest recorded simultaneous smokestack demolition was when 18 were felled at the London Brick Company Coronation Works at Bedfordshire, England, on Nov 30, 1980 when Mrs Wyn Witherall fired the 100 lb of explosives laid by T. W. Robinson & Co.

LARGEST WATERWHEEL: Built in Roman times, the wheel in northern Syria on the River Orontes is 131 ft in diameter. (*Robert Harding*)

LARGEST BUILDING MOVE: The Fairmount Hotel in San Antonio, Tex, a 79-year-old structure weighing 3,200,000 lb, 45 ft high, was moved by Emmert Industrial Corp of Portland, Ore, 5 blocks down the street and across a bridge to its new location, Mar 30–Apr 2, 1985.

MINES

Earliest (*World*)[1]	41,250 BC ± 1600	Haematite (red iron ore)	Hhohho district, Swaziland
Deepest (*World*)[1]	12,391 ft	Gold, Western Deep Levels (temp 131 °F 55 °C)	Carletonville, South Africa
Copper (*deepest, open cast*)	2,590 ft	Bingham Canyon (began 1904) diameter 2.3 miles	Utah
Copper (*largest underground*)	356 miles tunnels	San Manuel Mine, Magma Copper Co	Arizona
Lead (*largest*)	>10 percent of world output	Viburnum Trend	Southeast Missouri
Gold Mining Area (*largest*)	>51 percent of world output	38 mines of the Witwatersrand Discovery in 1886	South Africa
Gold Mine (*largest, world*)[2]	12,100 acres	East Rand Proprietary Mines Ltd	Boksburg, Transvaal, South Africa
Gold Mine (*richest*)	49.4 million fine oz	Crown Mines (all-time yield)	Transvaal, South Africa
Iron Mine (*largest*)	22,400 million tons rich ore	Lebedinsky (45–65% ore)	Kursk region, USSR
Platinum (*largest*)	1,000,000 oz per annum	Rustenberg Group, Impala plant	Springs, South Africa
Tungsten Mine (*largest*)	2,205 tons per day	Union Carbide Mount Morgan mine	near Bishop, Calif
Uranium (*largest*)	5,000 tons of uranium oxide	Rio Tinto Zinc open cast pit	Rössing, Namibia (SW Africa)
Spoil Dump (*largest, world*)	275 million cu yd	New Cornelia Tailings	Ten Mile Wash, Arizona
Quarry (*largest, world*)	2.81 sq mi. 2,540 ft deep. 3,700 million tons	Bingham Canyon Copper Mine	near Salt Lake City, U
Open Cast Coal Mine (*largest*)	1,130 ft deep. 8 sq mi area	Fortuna-Garsdorf (lignite) (began 1955)	near Bergheim, W Germ

[1] Sinking began in June 1957. Scheduled to reach 12,730 ft by 1992 with 14,000 ft or 2.65 mi regarded as the limit. No 3 vertical ventilation shaft is the world's deepest shaft at 9,675 ft. This mine requires 145,600 tons of air per day and refrigeration which uses all the energy it would take to make 37,000 tons of ice. An underground shift comprises 11,500 men. The deepest exploratory coal mining shaft is one reaching 6,700 ft near Thorez in the Ukrainian Donbas field, USSR, in Aug 1983.

[2] The world's most productive gold mine may be Muruntau, Kyzyl Kum, Uzbekistan, USSR. According to one western estimate it produces 88 tons of gold in a year. It has been estimated that South Africa has produced in 96 years (1886–1982) 36,400 tons or more than 31 percent of all gold mined since 3900 BC.

10. BORINGS AND MINES

Man's deepest penetration into the earth's crust is a geological exploratory drilling in the Kola peninsula, USSR, begun in 1970. On Dec 28, 1983, 39,370 ft or 7.45 mi was reached. Progress has understandably greatly slowed to 1,640 ft per year as the eventual target of 49,212 ft, in 1989-90 is neared. The drill bit is mounted on a turbine driven by a mud pump. The temperature at 6.83 mi was already 392° F.

The W German government announced that an 8.75-mi deep hole will be drilled into the earth's crust by 1995 at an estimated cost of $150 million. The super hole will be drilled starting in 1988, either in the Black Forest or northeastern Bavaria.

The deepest recorded drilling into the sea bed is by the *Glomar Challenger* of the US Deep Sea Drilling Project to 5,709 ft off northwestern Spain in 1976. The deepest site is now 23,077 ft below the surface on the western wall of the Marianas Trench in May 1978.

Largest Gas Deposits

The largest gas deposit in the world is at Urengoi, USSR, with an eventual production of 200,000 million cu meters per year through 6 pipelines, from proved reserves of 7 million cu meters. The trillionth cu meter was produced on Apr 23, 1986.

Largest Gas Tank

The largest gas holder or tank is that at Fontaine l'Eveque, Belgium, where disused mines have been adapted to store up to 17,650 million cu ft of gas at ordinary pressure. Probably the largest conventional gas tank is that at Wien-Semmering, Vienna, Austria, completed in 1968, with a height of 274 ft 8 in and a capacity of 10.59 million cu ft.

Oil Fields

The largest oil field is the Ghawar Field, Saudi Arabia, developed by ARAMCO, which measures 150 miles by 22 miles.

Greatest Gusher

The greatest ever recorded blew at Alborz No 5 well near Qum, Iran on Aug 26, 1956. The uncontrolled oil gushed to a height of 170 ft at 120,000 barrels per day. It was closed after 90 days work by B. Mostofi and Myron Kinley of Texas.

The Lake View No. 1 gusher in Calif on Mar 15, 1910 may have yielded 125,000 barrels in its first 24 hours.

Greatest Flare

The greatest gas fire ever burnt was at Gassi Touil in the Algerian Sahara from noon on Nov 13, 1961 to 9:30 a.m. on Apr 28, 1962. The pillar of flame rose 450 ft and the smoke 600 ft. It was eventually extinguished by Paul Neal ("Red") Adair (b 1932), of Houston, Tex, using 550 lb of dynamite. His fee was understood to be about $1 million.

Wells

The deepest water well is the Stensvad Water Well 11-W1 7,320 ft deep, drilled by the Great Northern Drilling Co Inc in Rosebud County, Mont in Oct-Nov 1961.

The Thermal Power Co geothermal steam well begun in Sonoma County, Calif in 1955 is now down to 9,029 ft.

Greatest Oil Spill

The worst oil spill in history was 260,000 tons of oil from the supertankers *Atlantic Empress* and *Aegean Captain* when they collided off Tobago on July 19, 1979.

The slick from the Mexican marine blow-out beneath the drilling rig *Ixtoc I* in the Bay of Campeche, Gulf of Mexico on June 3, 1979 reached 400 miles by Aug 5, 1979. It eventually was capped on Mar 24, 1980, after a loss of 3 million barrels.

Oil Platforms

The world's most massive oil platform is the *Stratfjord B* Concrete Gravity-base platform built at Stavanger, Norway, and operated by Mobil Exploration Norway Inc until Dec 31, 1986. Tow-out to its permanent field began on Aug 1, 1981, and it was the heaviest object ever moved—899,360 tons ballasted weight. She was towed by 8 tugs with a combined power of 115,000 hp. The height of the concrete structure is 670 ft and the overall height 890 ft. It thus weighs almost three times the weight of each of the towers of the World Trade Center (324,800 tons).

The tallest production platform is the 1,132-ft-tall Shell Cognac platform built in 1976 and placed outside the Mississippi River (La) delta.

MOST MASSIVE OIL PLATFORM: Weighing almost 3 times that of each of the twin towers of the World Trade Center (NYC), namely 324,800 tons, this oil platform off Stavanger, Norway, with its ballast making it 899,360 tons, was the heaviest object ever moved when it was towed into place in 1981. (*Statoil*)

Chapter 8

The Mechanical World

1. SHIPS

Aborigines are thought to have been able to cross the Torres Strait from New Guinea to Australia, then at least 43¼ miles across, as early as 40,000 BC. They are believed to have used double canoes. An 18-in paddle found at Star Carr, North Yorkshire, England, has been dated to c. 7600 BC.

The earliest surviving "vessel" is a pinewood dugout found in Pesse, Netherlands, now in the Provincial Museum, Assen, dated to c. 6315 BC ± 275.

The oldest surviving boat is the 142-ft-long 40-ton Nile boat (Royal Ship of Cheops) buried near the Great Pyramid of Khufu, Egypt, c. 2515 BC, and now reassembled.

The oldest shipwreck ever found is one of a Cycladic trading vessel located off the islet of Dhokos, near the Greek island of Hydra, reported in May 1975 and dated to 2450 BC ± 250.

Earliest Power Vessels

Propulsion by steam engine was first achieved when in 1783 the Marquis Jouffroy d'Abbans ascended a reach of the Saône River near Lyons, France in the 180-ton paddle steamer *Pyroscaphe*.

The tug *Charlotte Dundas* was the first successful power-driven vessel. She was a stern paddle-wheel steamer built for the Forth and Clyde Canal, Scotland, in 1801–02 by William Symington (1763–1831), using a double-acting condensing engine constructed by James Watt (1736–1819).

The screw propeller was invented and patented by the Kent, England, farmer Sir Francis Pettit Smith (1808–71) in 1836.

Oldest Vessels Afloat

The oldest active steam ship is the *Skibladner*, which has plied Lake Mjøsa, Norway, since 1856. Originally built in Motala, Sweden, she has had two major refittings.

The oldest mechanically propelled boat of certain date is the 48-ton Bristol steam-driven dredger or drag-boat *Bertha* of 50 ft, designed by I. K. Brunel (1806–59) in 1844 and afloat at the Exeter Maritime Museum, Devon, England.

G. H. Pattinson's 40-ft steam launch *Dolly,* raised after 67 years from

Ullswater, England in 1962, and now on Lake Windermere, also probably dates from the 1840's.

Sailing Ships

The oldest square-rigged sailing vessel is the restored SV *Ciudad de Inca,* built near Barcelona, Spain in 1858. She is 125 ft overall with a gross weight of 127 tons. She was restored in 1981–82 for operation by the China Clipper Society of Maidstone, Kent.

The largest sailing vessel ever built was the *France II* (5,806 gross tons), launched at Bordeaux in 1911. The *France II* was a steel-hulled, 5-masted barque (square-rigged on 4 masts and fore and aft rigged on the aftermost mast). Her hull measured 418 ft overall. Although principally designed as a sailing vessel with a stump topgallant rig, she was also fitted with two steam engines. She was wrecked in 1922.

The only 7-masted sailing vessel ever built was the 375.6-ft-long *Thomas W. Lawson* (5,218 gross tons), built at Quincy, Mass in 1902. She was lost in the English Channel on Dec 15, 1907.

The largest sailing vessel in service is the 342-ft 4-masted barque *Kruzenshtern* built in *c.* 1933 and used by USSR marine schools of Kaliningrad and Murmansk.

Largest Junks

The largest junk on record was the seagoing *Cheng Ho,* flagship of Admiral Cheng Ho's 62 treasure ships, of *c.* 1420, with a displacement of 3,100 tons and a length variously estimated up to 538 ft and believed to have had 9 masts.

A river junk 361 ft long, with treadmill-operated paddle wheels, was recorded in 1161 AD. A floating fortress 600 ft square, built by Wang Chun on the Yangtze, took part in the Chin-Wu river war, *c.* 280 AD. Present-day junks do not, even in the case of the Chiangsu traders, exceed 170 ft in length.

Earliest Turbine

The first turbine ship was the *Turbinia,* built in 1894, at Wallsend-on-Tyne, England, to the design of Charles Algernon Parsons (1854–1931). The *Turbinia* was 100 ft long and of 44½ tons displacement with machinery consisting of three steam turbines totaling about 2,000 shaft hp. At her first public demonstration in 1897 she reached a speed of 34.5 knots (39.7 mph).

Largest Human-Powered Ships

The largest human-powered ship was the giant Tessarakonteres 3-banked catamaran galley with 4,000 rowers built for Ptolemy IV *c.* 210 BC in Alexandria, Egypt. It measured 420 ft with up to 8 men to an oar of 38 cubits (57 ft) in length.

The longest canoe is the 117-ft-long, 20-ton Kauri wood Maori war canoe *Nga Toki Matawhaorua,* built with adzes at Kerikeri Inlet, New Zealand in 1940 to hold a crew of 70 or more. The "Snake Boat" *Nadubhagom,* 135 ft long from Kerala, southern India has a crew of 109 rowers and 9 "encouragers."

Longest Day's Run Under Sail

The longest day's run calculated for any commercial vessel was one of 462 nautical miles (532.0 statute miles) by the clipper ship *Champion of the Seas* (2,722 registered tons) of the Liverpool Black Ball Line running

MOST DANGEROUS NUCLEAR SUBMARINE: This USSR Typhoon class sub is one of 3 of the largest known. Secretly built at a covered shipyard, this 33,000-ton sub carrying 20 SS NX 20 missiles, each with 7 independently targeted warheads, was caught on the surface by a British photographer. With its power, it alone can obliterate any country within 5,000 mi of it.

before a northwesterly gale in the south Indian Ocean under the command of Capt. Alex Newlands in 1864. The elapsed time between the fixes was 23 hours 17 min giving an average of 19.97 knots.

Largest Wooden Ships

The heaviest wooden ship ever built was the *Richelieu*, 333 ft 8 in long and of 9,558 tons, launched in Toulon, France, on Dec 3, 1873. The longest modern wooden ship ever built was the New York-built *Rochambeau* (1867–72), formerly *Dunderberg*. She measured 377 ft 4 in overall. It should be noted that the biblical length of Noah's Ark was 300 cubits or, at 18 in to a cubit, 450 ft (but see *Largest Junks*).

Fastest Atlantic Crossing

The fastest Atlantic crossing was made by the *United States* (then 51,988, later 38,216, gross tons), former flagship of the United States Lines. On her maiden voyage between July 3 and 7, 1952, from NYC to Le Havre, France and Southampton, England she averaged 35.59 knots, or 40.98 mph, for 3 days 10 hours 40 min (6:36 P.M. GMT July 3, to 5:16 A.M. July 7) on a route of 2,949 nautical miles from the Ambrose Light Vessel, NJ to the Bishop Rock Light, Isles of Scilly, Cornwall, England. During this run, July 6–7, 1952, she steamed the greatest distance ever covered by any ship in a day's run (24 hours)—868 nautical miles, hence averaging 36.17 knots (41.65 mph). The maximum speed attained from her 240,000 shaft hp engines was 38.32 knots (44.12 mph) in trials June 9–10, 1952.

Fastest Pacific Crossing

The fastest crossing of the Pacific Ocean (4,840 nautical miles) was 6 days 1 hour 27 min by the containership *Sea-Land Commerce* (50,315 tons) from Yokohama, Japan to Long Beach, Calif, June 30–July 6, 1973, at an average speed of 33.27 knots (38.31 mph).

Largest Sails

Sails are known to have been used for marine propulsion since 3500 BC. The largest spars ever carried were those in the British Royal Navy battleship *Temeraire,* completed at Chatham, Kent, on Aug 31,

1877. She was broken up in 1921. The fore and main yards measured 115 ft in length. The foresail contained 5,100 sq ft of canvas, weighing 2 tons, and the total sail area was 25,000 sq ft. H M Battleship *Sultan* was ship-rigged when completed at Chatham, Kent, Eng, on Oct 10, 1871 and carried 34,100 sq ft of sails plus 15,300 sq ft of stunsails. She was not finally broken up until 1946.

Largest Passenger Liner

The original *Queen Elizabeth,* no longer afloat, was the heaviest ship ever built with 83,673 gross tons originally (later 82,998), but a length of 1,031 ft, some 4 ft shorter than the *Norway.* Her last passenger voyage ended on Nov 15, 1968. In 1970 she was removed to Hong Kong to serve as a floating marine university and renamed *Seawise University.* On Jan 9, 1972 she was set on fire by 3 simultaneous outbreaks. The gutted hull was cut up and removed by 1978. (*Seawise* was a pun on the new owner's initials— C. Y. Tung (1911–1982).)

The largest liner afloat and longest liner ever built is the *Norway* of 70,202.19 gross tons and 1,035 ft 7½ in in length. She was built as the *France* in 1961 and renamed after purchase in June 1979 by Knut Kloster of Norway. Her second maiden voyage was from Southampton on May 7, 1980.

The *Queen Elizabeth II,* of 67,140 gross tons with an overall length of 963 ft, set a "turn-around" record of 5 hours 47 min in NYC on Nov 21, 1983. Her 96-day 1986 world cruise cost $146,895 per person in the penthouse suite.

Largest Battleships

The largest battleship now is the USS *New Jersey,* with a full-load displacement of 65,000 tons and an overall length of 887 ft 7 in, exactly 4 in longer than its sister ships, the *Iowa,* the *Missouri,* and the *Wisconsin,* which at the time of commissioning in 1943–44 all displaced 45,000 tons. She was on active service last (with her nine 16-inch guns, capable of firing projectiles of 2,700 lb a distance of 23 mi) off the Lebanon coast, Dec 14, 1983–Feb 26, 1984. The USS *Iowa* was reactivated in May 1984 at a cost of $405 million.

The Japanese battleships *Yamato* (completed on Dec 16, 1941 and sunk southwest of Kyushu by US planes on Apr 7, 1945) and *Musashi* (sunk in the Philippine Sea by 11 bombs and 16 torpedoes on Oct 24, 1944) were the largest battleships ever commissioned, each with a full-load displacement of 72,809 tons. With overall length of 863 ft, a beam of 127 ft and a full-load draught of 35½ ft, they mounted nine 18.1-in guns in three triple turrets. Each gun weighed 162 tons and was 75 ft in length, firing a 3,200-lb projectile.

Longest, Fastest and Deepest Submarines

The largest submarines are of the USSR Typhoon class code-named Oscar. The launch of the first at the secret covered shipyard at Severodvinsk on the White Sea was announced by NATO on Sept 23, 1980. It is believed to have a dived displacement of 33,000 tons, and measure 557.6 ft overall and be armed with 20 SS NX 20 missiles with a 5,000-nautical-mile range, each with 7 warheads. By 1987, two others being built in Leningrad will also be operational, each deploying 140 warheads.

The Russian Alfa-Class nuclear-powered submarines have a reported maximum speed of 42 knots (about 48 mph). With use of titanium steel they are believed to be able to dive to 2,500 ft. A US spy satellite over Leningrad's naval yard on June 8, 1983 showed they were being lengthened and are now 260.1 ft long.

The two US Navy vessels able to descend 12,000 ft are the 3-man *Trieste II* (DSV 1) of 303 tons, recommissioned in Nov 1973, and the DSV 2 (deep submergence vessel) USS *Alvin*. The *Trieste II* was reconstructed from the record-breaking bathyscaphe *Trieste*, but without the Krupp-built sphere, which enabled it to descend to 35,820 ft.

Largest Aircraft Carriers

The warships with the largest full-load displacement in the world are the Nimitz class US Navy aircraft carriers USS *Theodore Roosevelt, Dwight D. Eisenhower, Carl Vinson* at 91,487 tons. They are 1,092 ft in length overall and have a speed well in excess of 30 knots with their nuclear-powered 260,000 shaft hp geared steam turbines. They have to be refueled after about 900,000 miles steaming. Their complement is 6,300. The total cost of the *Abraham Lincoln*, laid down at Newport News, in Dec 1984, will exceed $3¼ billion, excluding the 90-plus aircraft carried. The USS *Enterprise* is, however, 1,102 ft long and thus still the longest warship ever built.

Most Landings

The greatest number of plane landings on an aircraft carrier in one day was 602 achieved by Marine Air Group 6 of the US Pacific Fleet Air Force aboard the USS *Matanikou* on May 25, 1945 between 8 A.M. and 5 P.M.

Fastest Destroyer

The highest speed attained by a destroyer was 45.25 knots (51.84 mph) by the 3,120-ton French destroyer *Le Terrible* in 1935. She was built in Blainville and powered by four Yarrow small-tube boilers and two Rateau geared turbines giving 100,000 shaft hp. She was removed from the active list in 1957.

Largest Hydrofoil

The largest naval hydrofoil is the 212-ft-long *Plainview* (347 tons full load), launched by Lockheed Shipbuilding and Construction Company at Seattle, Wash June 28, 1965. She has a service speed of 50 knots (57 mph).

Three 165-ton Supramar PTS 150 Mk. III hydrofoils, carrying 250 passengers at 40 knots, ply the Malmö-Copenhagen crossing between Sweden and Denmark. They were built by Westermoen Hydrofoil Ltd of Mandal, Norway.

A 500-ton wing ground effect vehicle capable of carrying 900 tons has been reported in the USSR.

Containerships

Shipborne containerization began in 1955 when the tanker *Ideal X* was converted by Malcolm McLean (US). She carried containers only on deck.

The largest containerships are the 12 built by US Lines in Korea in 1984–85. They are capable of carrying 4,482 TEU (20 ft equivalent units = 20 ft containers).

Largest Barges

Four RoRo (roll-on roll-off) barges, of the *El Rey* class of 16,700 tons and 580-ft length each, built by FMC Corp of Portland, Ore and operated by the Crowley Maritime Corp of San Francisco are currently the largest. They carry up to 376 trailer trucks each with tri-level loading, between Florida and Puerto Rico.

Largest Tanker

The largest tanker and ship of any kind is the 624,038 ton-deadweight *Seawise Giant* converted for C. Y. Tung in 1979. (The name is a pun on the owner's initials.) She is 1,504 ft long with a beam of 225 ft 11 in, has a draught of 80 ft 9 in. She was converted by Nippon Kokan in 1980 by adding a 265-ft-8-in midship section.

Largest Cargo Vessel

The largest vessel capable of carrying dry cargo is the Liberian ore/oil carrier *World Gala* of 282,460 dwt with a length of 1,109 ft and beam of 179 ft, completed in 1973. A 365,000-dwt ore carrier is being built in Korea for the Norwegian owner Sig Bergesen Dy, and is due for delivery in Oct 1986.

Largest Whale Factory

The largest whale factory ship is the USSR's *Sovietskaya Ukraina* (32,034 gross tons), with a summer deadweight of 51,520 tons completed in Oct 1959. She is 714 ft 6 in in length and 84 ft 7 in in the beam.

Most Powerful Tug

The most powerful tug is Smit Singapore commissioned in Apr 1984 by Smit Tak International, of 22,000 hp and 189 tons bollard pull at full power. She is 246.7 ft long and 51.5 ft wide.

Largest Car Ferry

The largest car and passenger ferry is the 37,800-gross-ton M/S *Olympia* which entered service across the Baltic Sea between Helsinki and Stockholm on Apr 28, 1986. Built in Abo, Finland for the Viking Line, she is 581 ft long, 95 ft in the beam and can carry 2,500 passengers and 600 cars.

Largest Propeller

The largest ship propeller is the triple-bladed screw of 36 ft 1 in diameter made by Kawasaki Heavy Industries Ltd on Mar 17, 1982 for the 208,000-ton bulk-ore tanker *Hoei Maru*.

Most Powerful Dredger

The most powerful dredger is the 468.4-ft-long *Prins der Nederlanden* of 10,586 grt. Using two suction tubes, she can dredge 22,400 tons of sand from a depth of 115 ft in less than one hour.

LARGEST TANKER (above): The "Seawise Giant," more than ¼ mi long, was converted in 1980 for the Japanese owner, C. Y. Tung.

LARGEST SHIP'S PROPELLER (right): It now propels the 208,000-ton bulk-ore Japanese tanker, "Hoei Maru." It is 36 ft 1 in in diameter.

Most Powerful Icebreaker

A 61,000-ton nuclear-powered barge-carrying merchantman designed for work along the USSR's Arctic coast was completed in early 1982 and is known to be designed to break ice.

The longest purpose-built icebreaker is the 25,000-ton 460-ft-long *Rossiya*, powered by 75,000 hp nuclear engines built in Leningrad and completed in 1985. A new Can-$500 million, 100,000 hp, 636-ft-long icebreaker of the Polar Class 8 was ordered by the Canadian government in Oct 1985.

The largest *converted* icebreaker has been the 1,007-ft-long SS *Manhattan* (43,000 shp), which was converted by the Humble Oil Co. into a 150,000-ton icebreaker with an armored prow 69 ft 2 in long. She made a double voyage through the North-West Passage in Arctic Canada from Aug 24 to Nov 12, 1969. The North-West Passage was first navigated by Roald Amundsen (Norway) in the sealing sloop *Gjöa* on July 11, 1906.

Most Expensive Yacht

The refit of the $25 million 470-ft-long Saudi Arabian royal yacht *Abdul Aziz*, built in Denmark, was completed on June 22, 1984 at Vospers Yard, Southampton, Eng at a cost of $11.25 million.

Fastest Building of a Ship

The fastest-ever building time for a major ship was 4 days 15 hours in the case of the 10,920-ton displacement *Robert E. Peary* at Kaiser's Yard, Portland, Ore, from Nov 8 (keel laid) to launch on Nov 12, 1942. She was operational on Nov 15 and was No 440 of the fleet of 2,742 11.6-knot Liberty Ships built in 18 US shipyards from Sept 27, 1941.

Largest River Boat

The largest inland river boat is the 378-ft-long SS *Admiral* now undergoing a 6-year $26.7 million renovation at St Louis, Mo as a Mississippi floating "entertainment center."

Largest Collision

The closest approach to an irresistible force striking an immovable object occurred on Dec 16, 1977, 22 miles off the coast of southern Africa, when the tanker *Venoil* (330,954 dwt) struck her sister ship *Venpet* (330,869 dwt).

Survival after Shipwreck

The longest recorded survival alone on a raft is 133 days (4½ months) by Second Steward Poon Lim (b Hong Kong) of the UK Merchant Navy, whose ship, the SS *Ben Lomond*, was torpedoed in the Atlantic 565 miles west of St Paul's Rocks at Lat 00° 30′ N and Long 38° 45′ W at 11:45 A.M. on Nov 23, 1942. He was picked up by a Brazilian fishing boat off Salinópolis, Brazil, Apr 5, 1943, and was able to walk ashore. In July 1943 he was awarded the British Empire Medal, and now lives in NYC.

Maurice and Maralyn Bailey survived 118⅓ days in an inflatable dinghy 4½ ft in diameter in the northeast Pacific from March 4 to June 30, 1973.

Largest Wreck

Energy Determination is the largest ship ever wrecked. Weighing 312,186 dwt this VLCC (Very Large Crude Carrier) blew up and broke in two in the Straits of Hormuz on Dec 12, 1979. Her full value was $58 million. The largest wreck removal was carried out in 1979 by Smit Tak International, who removed the remains of the 139,900-ton French tanker *Betelgeuse* from Bantry Bay, Ireland, within 20 months.

Deepest Anchorage

The deepest anchorage ever achieved is one of 24,600 ft in the mid-Atlantic Romanche Trench by Capt Jacques-Yves Cousteau's research vessel *Calypso*, with a 5½-mile-long nylon cable, on July 29, 1956.

Earliest Launching

On Apr 8, 1986, the type-22 frigate HMS *Coventry* was launched from the Swan Hunter yard, Tyneside, Eng, at 3:45 A.M. on a cold, wet and windy morning. Fearing that an industrial dispute might delay the launching, it had been moved ahead by 12 hours.

Shortest Tow

On Aug 17, 1982, near Abidjan on the Ivory Coast, Capt B. Nicholson in command of the 8,000-hp MV Dee Service successfully towed a locking pin to secure the tanker *Philips Enterprise* to a floating pump station a total distance of 4 in.

Hovercraft (Skirted Air-Cushion Vehicle)

The ACV (air-cushion vehicle) was first made a practical proposition by Sir Christopher Sydney Cockerell (b June 4, 1910), a British engineer who had the idea in 1954, published his Ripplecraft report 1/55 on Oct 25, 1955, and patented it on Dec 12, 1955. The earliest patent relating to air-cushion craft was applied for in 1877 by John I. Thornycroft (1843–1928) of Chiswick, London and the Finn, Toivo Kaario, developed the idea in 1935.

The first flight by a hovercraft was by the 4½-ton Saunders Roe SR-N1 at Cowes, Isle of Wight, on May 30, 1959. With a 1,500-lb-thrust Viper turbojet engine, this craft reached 68 knots in June 1961.

The first hovercraft public service was run across the Dee Estuary by the 60-knot 24-passenger Vickers-Armstrong VA-3 between July and Sept 1962.

The longest hovercraft journey was one of 5,000 mi through 8 West African countries between Oct 15, 1969 and Jan 3, 1970 by the British Trans-African Hovercraft Expedition.

The largest civil hovercraft is the 342-ton British built SRN 4 MK III with a capacity of 418 passengers and 60 cars. It is 185 ft in length, powered by 4 Siddeley Marine Proteus engines which give a maximum speed in excess of the permitted cross-Channel operating speed of 65 knots.

FASTEST WARSHIP is this hovercraft, the USN SES-100B, a 78-ft 112-ton test vehicle that sped 103.9 mph on Chesapeake Bay in 1980.

The fastest warship is the 78-ft 112-ton US Navy test vehicle SES-100B. She attained a record 91.9 knots (103.9 mph) on Jan 25, 1980 on the Chesapeake Bay Test Range, Md.

The 3,000-ton US Navy Large Surface Effect Ship (LSES) was built by Bell Aerospace under contract from the Department of Defense in 1977–81.

The greatest altitude a hovercraft is operating at is on Lago Titicaca, Peru, where since 1975 an HM2 Hoverferry has been hovering 12,506 ft above sea level.

2. ROAD VEHICLES*

CARS

Most Cars

For 1984 it was estimated that the US, with 168,607,000 vehicles, passed 37.9 percent of the total world stock of 411,113,000.

Earliest Automobiles

The earliest car of which there is record is a 2-ft-long steam-powered model, constructed by Ferdinand Verbiest (d 1687), a Belgian Jesuit priest, which he described in his *Astronomia Europaea*. His 1668 model was possibly inspired either by Giovanni Branca's description of a steam turbine published in 1629, or by writings on "fire carts" during the Chu dynasty (*c.* 800 BC).

The earliest full-scale automobile was the first of two military steam tractors completed at the Paris Arsenal in 1769 by Nicolas-Joseph Cugnot (1725–1804). This vehicle reached about 2¼ mph. His second, larger tractor, completed in 1771, today survives in the *Conservatoire national des arts et métiers* in Paris.

The first passenger-carrying automobile was a steam-powered road vehicle carrying 8 passengers built by Richard Trevithick (1771–1833). It first ran on Dec 24, 1801 in Cornwall, Eng.

The Swiss Isaac de Rivaz (d 1828) built a carriage powered by his "explosion engine" in 1805.

The first practical internal-combustion-engined vehicle was built by a Londoner, Samuel Brown (patented Apr 25, 1826) whose 4-hp 2-cylinder atmospheric-gas 88-liter engined carriage climbed Shooters Hill, Blackheath, Kent, England in May 1826.

Earliest Gasoline-Driven Cars

The first successful gasoline-driven car, the Motorwagen, built by Karl-Friedrich Benz (1844–1929) of Karlsruhe, ran at Mannheim, Germany in late 1885. It was a 560-lb 3-wheeler reaching 8–10 mph. Its sin-

---

* Automotive records in greater detail may be found in *Car Facts and Feats*, one of the Guinness Family of Books (Sterling).

gle-cylinder 4-stroke chain-drive engine (bore 91.4 mm, stroke 160 mm) delivered 0.85 hp at 200 rpm. It was patented on Jan 29, 1886. Its first 1-km road test was reported in the local newspaper of June 4, 1886, under the news heading "Miscellaneous." Two were built in 1885 of which one has been preserved in "running order" at the Deutsches Museum, Munich.

Earliest Registrations

The world's first plates were probably introduced by the Parisian police in France in 1893. The first American plates were in 1901 in NY. Registration plates were introduced in Britain in 1903. The original A1 plate was secured by the 2nd Earl Russell (1865–1931) for his 12-hp Napier. This plate, willed to Trevor Laker of Leicester, was sold in Aug 1959, for £2,500 (then $7,000) in aid of charity. License plate No 3 was reported sold at a Hong Kong government auction for US $131,600 in Jan 1984.

Fastest Diesel-Engined Car

The diesel-engined prototype 230-hp 3-liter Mercedes C 111/3 attained 203.3 mph in tests on the Nardo Circuit, Italy, Oct 5–15, 1978, and in Apr 1978 averaged 195.390 mph for 12 hours, so covering a world record 2,399.76 mi.

Fastest Road Cars

Various detuned track cars have been licensed for road use but are not purchasable production models. Manufacturers of very fast and very expensive models understandably limit speed tests to stipulated engine revs. The fastest current manufacturer's *claim* (as opposed to independent road-tests) for production road cars is "in excess of 200 mph terminal velocity" for the Vector W2A custom-order car from Vector Cars, Venice, Calif. The claimed speed at 7,000 rpm by the 1984 Ferrari 308 GTO is 189.5 mph. Aston Martin announced on Mar 1, 1985 the production of 50 Vantage-Zagatos with 432 bph engines and a speed of 186.4 mph costing $108,000. The Vantage was first seen in public at the Geneva show in Mar 1986, with the first prototype running a month later. The highest ever *tested* speed is 179.9 mph for the Lamborghini Countach LP 500 S in Mar 1984. The car was kept out of the "red sector," *i.e.* at below 7,000 rpm.

The highest road tested acceleration reported is 0–60 mph in 4.1 sec for an MG Metro 6R4 International Rally Car in 1986.

Largest Cars

Of cars produced for private road use, the largest has been the Bugatti "Royale" Type 41, known as the "Golden Bugatti," of which only 6 (not 7) were made at Molsheim, France by the Italian, Ettore Bugatti, and all survive. First built in 1927, this car has an 8-cylinder engine of 12.7 liter capacity, and measures over 22 ft in length. The hood is over 7 ft long.

Of custom-built cars the longest is a 16-wheeled 60-ft-long Cadillac called "The American Dream" (see photo and caption above).

Most Expensive Special Cars

The most expensive car to build was the Presidential 1969 Lincoln Continental Executive delivered to the US Secret Service on Oct 14, 1968. It has an overall length of 21 ft 6.3 in with a 13-ft-4-in wheelbase and, with the addition of 2 tons of armor plate, weighs 12,000 lb. The

FASTEST CARS

Category	mph	Car	Driver	Place	Date
Jet-Engined (official)	633.468	Thrust 2	Richard Noble (GB)	Black Rock Desert, Nevada	Oct 4, 1983
Rocket-Engined (official)	622.287	Blue Flame	Gary Gabelich	Bonneville, Utah	Oct 23, 1970
Wheel-Driven (turbine)	429.311	Bluebird	Donald Campbell (UK)	Lake Eyre, Australia	July 17, 1964
Wheel-Driven (multi-engine)	418.504	Goldenrod	Robert Summers	Bonneville, Utah	Nov 12, 1965
Wheel-Driven (single-engine)	357.391	Herda-Knapp-Milodon	Bob Herda	Bonneville, Utah	Nov 2, 1967
Rocket-Engined (unofficial)*	739.666	Budweiser Rocket	Stan Barrett	Edwards Air Force Base, California	Dec 17, 1979

* This published speed of Mach 1.0106 is *not* officially sanctioned by the USAF whose Digital Instrumented Radar was not calibrated or certified. The radar information was *not* generated by the vehicle directly but by an operator aiming the dish by means of a TV screen. To claim a speed to 6 significant figures appears quite unsustainable.

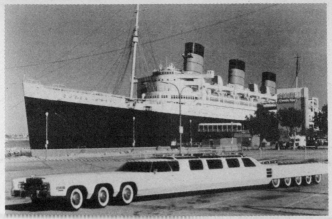

EXHIBIT LIMOUSINE: This 60-ft-long, 20,000-lb car, called "The American Dream," has 16 wheels, 2 Cadillac front-wheel-drive engines, a swimming pool, a hot tub, a water bed, a helicopter landing pad, a crystal chandelier and living quarters including 3 color TV's, one giant screen, a microwave oven, video cassette recorder, 10-speaker stereo, 10 telephones in all, mirrored ceiling, cocktail table and hardwood flooring. The car has 8 steerable axles, one engine mounted up front which drives 3 of them and a second engine in the rear driving the other 5. The limo requires 2 drivers communicating by radio through headsets, and is operated like a hook-and-ladder fire engine in going around corners. While it is not allowed on normal streets, it is operable, but is mostly used for automotive shows and movies. In this picture, it is on the dock at Long Beach, Calif, alongside the Hotel Queen Mary. It is owned by Jay Ohrberg of Hollywood, Calif, and is for sale at $2 million. Fifty people can crowd into it at one time.

cost for research, development and manufacture was estimated at $500,000, but it is rented for a mere $5,000 per annum. Even if all four tires were to be shot out it can travel at 50 mph on inner rubber-edged steel discs.

Carriage House Motor Cars Ltd of NYC in March 1978 completed 4 years' work on converting a 1973 Rolls-Royce, including lengthening it by 30 in. The price tag was $500,000.

Most Expensive Standard Cars

The most expensive British standard car is the Rolls-Royce 8-cylinder 6,750 cc Silver Spur limousine quoted in 1986 at £159,467 (incl tax) ($239,200). More expensive are custom-built models.

Jack Barclay Ltd of Berkeley Square, London, quotes £350,000 ($525,000) for an armor-plated Rolls-Royce Phantom VI (incl tax).

The unrivaled collector of Rolls-Royces was Bhagwan Shri Rajneesh (b 1931), the Indian mystic of Rajneeshpuram, Oregon. His disciples bestowed 93 of these upon him before his deportation in Nov 1985.

HIGHEST-PRICED USED CAR: This 19-ft-long yellow Rolls-Royce Phantom V touring limousine of 1965, once owned by The Beatles, was sold at auction at Sotheby Parke Bernet, NYC, for $2,299,000 on June 29, 1985. The purchaser was Jim Pattison, Canadian businessman, who exhibits it at his museums.

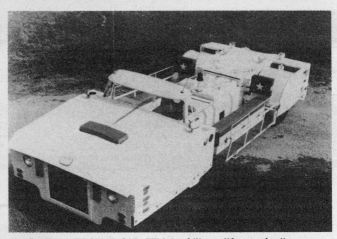

MULTI-DIRECTIONAL CAR: With its ability to lift up and roll sideways, this 11-wheeled vehicle, called "Futuristic," gets out of tight parking spaces with ease. When the car's side wheels drop, the body is lifted hydraulically onto them. Then the Ford V-8 gasoline-fed motor rolls the car to the side as fast as 20 mph. Built over a period of 20 years by John Patricia of Sussex, NJ, the car is only 21½ ft long and 7½ ft wide, but can carry 14 people.

Most Expensive Used Cars

The greatest price paid for a used car is $2,299,000 for the 19-ft-long yellow Rolls-Royce once owned by The Beatles. It was sold at a Sotheby's auction of rock-and-roll memorabilia in NYC on June 29, 1985 to James Pattison, chairman of the Expo '86 World's Fair in Vancouver, BC, Canada, and owner of the Ripley chain of museums. Mr. Pattison plans to use the car for promotional purposes. Purchased by John Lennon in 1966, the car was painted in a psychedelic floral motif created by a gypsy mystic and later donated for charity fund-raising to the Cooper-Hewitt Museum, an arm of the Smithsonian.

The greatest collection of vintage cars is the William F. Harrah Collection of 1,700, estimated to be worth more than $4 million, in Reno, Nev. Mr Harrah was still looking for a Chalmers-Detroit 1909 Tourabout, an Owen car of 1910–12, and a Nevada Truck of 1915 when he died.

Most Inexpensive

The cheapest car of all time was the 1922 Red Bug Buckboard, built by Briggs and Stratton Co of Milwaukee, Wis listed at $150–$125. It had a 62-in wheel base and weighed 245 lb. The early models of the King Midget cars were sold in kit form for self-assembly for as little as $100 as late as 1948.

Longest in Production

The longest any car has been in mass production is 47 years (1938 to date), including wartime interruptions, in the case of the Volkswagen "Beetle" series, originally designed by Ferdinand Porsche. The 20 millionth car came off the final production line in Mexico on May 15, 1981 and 20,630,000 had been built by Jan 1986. Residual production continues in South America.

Largest Engines

The most powerful piston-engine car is "Quad A1." It was designed and built in 1964 by Jim Lytle and was first shown in May 1965 at the Los Angeles Sports Arena. The car features 4 Allison V–12 aircraft engines with a total of 6,840 cu in (112,087 cc) displacement and 12,000 hp. The car has 4-wheel drive, 8 wheels and tires, and dual 6-disc clutch assemblies. The wheelbase is 160 in. It weighs 5,860 lb and has 96 spark plugs and 96 exhaust pipes.

The largest car ever used was the "White Triplex," sponsored by J. H. White of Philadelphia. Completed early in 1928, after 2 years' work, the car weighed about 4½ tons and was powered by three Liberty V12 aircraft engines with a total capacity of 81,188 cc developing 1,500 bhp at 2,000 rpm. It was used to break the world speed record, but crashed at Daytona, Fla on March 13, 1929.

Currently, the most powerful car on the road is the 6-wheeled Jameson-Merlin powered by a 27,000-cc 1,760-hp Rolls-Royce V12 Merlin aero-engine, governed down to a maximum speed of 185 mph. It has a range of 300 miles with tanks of 72-gallon capacity. The vehicle weighs 2.96 tons overall.

Largest Production-Car Engine

The highest engine capacity of a production car was 13½ liters (824 cu in), in the case of the Pierce-Arrow 6-66 Raceabout of 1912–18, the

Peerless 6-60 of 1912–14 and the Fageol of 1918. The most powerful current production car is the Lamborghini Countach 5000 Squattroval-vole with a 5,167-cc V12 engine developing 455 bph.

Most Durable Car

The highest recorded mileage for a car was 1,184,880 authenticated miles by Aug 1978 for a 1957 Mercedes 180D owned by Robert O'Reilly of Olympia, Wash. Its subsequent fate is unknown.

R. L. Bender of Madison, Wis claimed 1,020,000 mi for his car in Dec 1983. Bender's car reached 1,021,041 mi on June 9, 1984. He has been driving it since 1958.

Gasoline Consumption

On July 9, 1985 the Mechanical Engineering Department of King's College, London won the Shell-*Motor* magazine prize at Silverstone, Northants, Eng with 4,010 mi per gallon.

Longest Fuel Range

The greatest distance driven without refueling on a tank full of fuel (19.41 gals) is 1,150.3 mi by an Audi 100 turbo-diesel driven by Stuart Bladon with his son Bruce (navigator) and Bob Proctor (RAC observer) across Eng from Land's End to John O'Groats and back to West Falkirk in 22 hours 28 min in July 1984. The average speed was 51.17 mph giving 59.27 mpg.

Using cottonseed oil as fuel and an adapted 4-cyl diesel engine, Alan Buck and Sheila Stoll of Carmel, Calif, drove 6,500 mi in 5 days 9 hours in a van carrying 250 gal of fuel (using 224) from Monterey, Calif to NYC and back *non-stop* (with dual controls) in Aug 1982, averaging 50 mph and 29 mpg (cost 5¢/mi).

Go-Karting

The highest mileage recorded in 24 hours on a closed twisting circuit was 1,018 laps of a mile each for a 4-man team (Owen Nimmo, Gary Ruddock, Jim Timmins, and Danny Upshaw) on Sept 4–5, 1983 at Erbsville Kartway, Waterloo, Ont, Canada. The kart was 5 hp 140 cc Honda-engined.

Two-Wheel Driving

The longest recorded distance for driving on 2 wheels is 129.9 mi in an Opel Kadett by Michael Signoret at the Paul Ricard circuit in Provence, France, on Mar 14, 1985.

Round-the-World Driving

The fastest circumnavigation embracing more than an equator's length of driving (24,901.47 road miles) is one in 74 days 1 hour 11 min by Garry Sowerby (driver) and Ken Langley (navigator) of Canada from Sept 6 to Nov 19, 1980 in a Volvo 245 westward from Toronto through 4 continents and 23 countries. The distance covered was 26,738 miles.

The folk-singers Manfred Müller and Paul-Ernst Luhrs drove around the world covering 78 countries and 174,000 mi between Mar 30, 1964 and Apr 23, 1984. They started and finished in Bremerhaven, W Germany.

The first traverse of the world's greatest land mass (Afro-Eurasia) was achieved by Richard Pape, who, driving south, left the North Cape of Norway in an Austin A90 on July 28 and arrived in Cape Town, S

LONGEST ON TWO WHEELS After Kenneth Eriksson of Åppelbo, Sweden, drove this Opel Kadett on only 2 wheels for 12½ miles, his feat was surpassed by Michael Signoret in Provence, France, who drove his Opel Kadett on 2 wheels for 129.9 miles.

Africa, on Oct 22, 1955 with the milometer recording 17,500 mi after 86 days. The speed record for the same route was set by Ken Langley and Garry Sowerby of Canada driving north in 28 days 13 hours 10 min for 12,531 mi Apr 4–May 2, 1984.

Solar-Powered Vehicle

The highest speed attained under IHPVA (International Human Powered Vehicle Association) rules by a solely solar-powered vehicle is 24.74 mph at Bellflower, Calif, on July 1, 1984 by *Sunrunner,* designed by Joel Davidson and Greg Johanson of Photovoltaic Power Systems.

Battery-Powered Vehicle

John Owen and Roy Harvey traveled 919 mi from John O'Groats, Eng, to Land's End in a Sinclair C5 in 103 hours 15 min from Apr 30 to May 4, 1985. David Turner and Tim Pickard of Turners of Boscastle Ltd, Cornwall, Eng, traveled 875 mi from Land's End to John O'Groats in 63 hours in a Freight Rover Leyland Sherpa powered by a Lucas electric motor on Dec 21–23, 1985.

Rocket-Powered Ice Sled

The highest speed recorded is 247.93 mph by *Oxygen* driven by Sammy Miller (b Apr 15, 1945) on Lake George, NY, on Feb 15, 1981.

Steam Cars

On Aug 19, 1985 Robert E. Barber broke the 79-year-old steam-car record, driving no. 744, *Steamin' Demon,* at 145.607 mph on the Bonneville Salt Flats, Utah. It was built by the Barber-Nichols Engineering Co.

Longest Skid Marks

The longest recorded skid marks on a public road were 950 ft long, left by a Jaguar car involved in an accident on the M.1 near Luton, Bedfordshire, England June 30, 1960. Evidence given in the High Court case *Hurlock v. Inglis and others* indicated a speed "in excess of 100 mph" before the application of the brakes.

The skid marks made by the jet-powered *Spirit of America,* driven by Craig Breedlove, after the car went out of control at Bonneville Salt Flats, Utah Oct 15, 1964, were nearly 6 miles long.

Driving in Reverse

Charles Creighton (1908–70) and James Hargis of Maplewood, Mo drove their Ford Model A 1929 roadster in reverse from NYC to Los Angeles (3,340 miles), July 26–Aug 13, 1930 *without* stopping the engine once. They arrived back in NY on Sept 5, again in reverse, thus completing 7,180 miles in 42 days.

Creighton was a mechanic and Hargis an interior decorator. Their motto was "Seeing America Backward" and this motto was inscribed on the car. They almost failed to start. When leaving NYC a taxicab ran into them, smashing a fender and bending the running board. Nevertheless the pair refused to stop for repairs. They had attached the headlights to the rear of the car, and drove at speeds varying from 8 to 10 mph. On the open road they locked the gear shift in reverse so it would not pop out.

The highest average speed attained in any non-stop reverse drive exceeding 500 miles was achieved by Gerald Hoagland, who drove a 1969 Chevrolet Impala 501 miles non-stop in 17 hours 38 min at Chemung Speed Drome, NY July 9–10, 1976 to average 28.41 mph.

Brian "Cub" Keene and James "Wilbur" Wright drove their Chevrolet Blazer 9,031 mi in 37 days (Aug 1–Sept 6, 1984) through 16 US states and Canada. Though it was prominently named "Stuck in Reverse," law enforcement in Okla refused to believe it and insisted they drive in reverse reverse, i.e. forwards, out of the state.

Longest Tow

The longest tow on record was one of 4,759 miles from Halifax, Nova Scotia to Canada's Pacific coast, when Frank J. Elliott and George A. Scott of Amherst, Nova Scotia persuaded 168 passing motorists in 89

BUILT TO DRIVE BACKWARDS: This 1929 Ford Model A roadster may look funny with its headlights in the rear, but it carried its owners, Charles Creighton and James Hargis 7,180 miles from NYC to LA and back entirely in reverse gear in just 42 days.

days to tow their Model T Ford (in fact, engine-less) to win a $1,000 bet on Oct 15, 1927.

Taxis

The largest taxi fleet is that in Mexico City, with 60,000 "normal" taxis, plus minibuses (*pesaros*) (communal "fixed route" taxis) and *settas* (airport taxis) in mid-1984.

The longest fare on record is one of 7,533 miles through 10 countries from Marble Arch, London, England, from Sept 19 to Oct 18, 1981. The trip was sponsored for charity and the driver was Stephen Tillyer.

Francis Edward Kenyon (b 1904) was continuously licensed as a cab driver in Manchester, Eng, for 57 years 36 days, 1924–1981.

Largest Vehicles and Windshield Wipers

The most massive vehicle ever constructed is the Marion 8-caterpillar crawler used for conveying *Saturn V* rockets to their launching pads at the John F. Kennedy Space Center, Cape Canaveral, Fla. It measures 131 ft 4 in by 114 ft and two of them built at the same time cost $12,300,000. The loaded train weight is 9,000 tons. Its windshield wipers with 42-in blades are the world's largest.

The most massive automotive land vehicle is "Big Muskie," the 10,700-ton mechanical shovel built by Bucyrus-Erie for the Musk mine. It is 487 ft long, 151 ft wide and 222 ft high with a grab capacity of 325 tons.

The longest vehicle ever built is the Arctic Snow Train now owned by the world-famous wire-walker Steve McPeak (see Chapter 11). This 54-wheeled 572-ft-long vehicle was built by R G Le Tourneau, Inc of Longview, Tex for the US Army. Its gross train weight is 400 tons with a top speed of 20 mph and it was driven by a crew of 6 when used as an "Overland Train" for the military. McPeak repaired it and every punctured tire lone-handed in often sub-zero temperatures in Alaska. It generates 4,680 shp and has a capacity of 7,826 gallons.

Buses

The first municipal motor bus service was inaugurated on Apr 12, 1903, between the Eastbourne railway station and Meads, East Sussex, in England. A steam-powered bus named *Royal Patent* ran between Gloucester and Cheltenham, England, for 4 months in 1831.

The longest regularly scheduled bus route is by "Across Australia Coach Lines," which inaugurated a regularly scheduled service between Perth and Brisbane on Apr 9, 1980. The route is 3,389 miles and takes 75 hours 55 min.

The longest buses are the 12-ton, 76-ft-long articulated buses, with 121 passenger seats and room for an additional 66 "strap-hangers," built by the Wayne Corp of Richmond, Ind for use in the Middle East.

The largest bus fleet consists of 6,580 single-deck buses in Rio de Janeiro, Brazil in 1983.

Largest Ambulance

The largest ambulances are the 59-ft-0½-in-long articulated Alligator Jumbulances Mark VI, VII and VIII, operated by The Across Trust to convey the sick and handicapped on holidays and pilgrimages from Britain to Continental Europe. They are built by Van Hool of Belgium with Fiat engines, cost £176,000 ($316,800) and convey 44 patients and staff.

Largest Dump Truck

The largest dump truck is the Terex Titan 33-19 manufactured by the Terex Division of the General Motors Corp. It has a loaded weight of 604.7 tons and a capacity of 350 tons. When unloading, its height is 56 ft. The 16-cylinder engine delivers 3,300 hp and the fuel tank holds 1,560 gallons. It went into service in Nov 1974.

Largest Tires

The largest tires are manufactured in Topeka, Kans by the Goodyear Co for giant dump trucks. They are 11 ft 6 in in diameter, weigh 12,500 lb and cost $75,000. A tire 17 ft in diameter is believed to be the practical upper limit.

Largest Load

On July 14–15, 1984, John Brown Engineers & Contractors BV (Eng) moved the Conoco Kotter Field production deck with a roll-out weight of 4,193 tons for the Continental Netherlands Oil Company of Leidsenhage, Netherlands.

Largest and Most Powerful Tractor

The largest tractor is the $459,000 22-ton US Dept of Agriculture Wide Tractive Frame Vehicle completed by Ag West of Sacramento, Calif in June 1982. It measures 33 ft between its wheels which are designed to run on permanent paths, and weighs 24.1 tons.

The sport of tractor-pulling was put on a national US championship basis in 1967 at Bowling Green, Ohio where the winner was "The Purple Monster" built and driven by Roger E. Varns. Today there are 12 classes ranging up to "12,200 lb unlimited."

Largest Earth Mover

The largest earth mover is the 110.2-ton T-800 built at the Lenin Tractor Works in Chelyabinsk, USSR, announced in Sept 1984.

Most Powerful Fire Engine

The most powerful fire appliance is the 860-hp 8-wheel Oshkosh fire truck used for aircraft fires. It can discharge 49,920 gallons of foam through 2 turrets in just 150 sec. It weighs 66 tons.

The fastest is the Jaguar XJ12 "Chubb Firefighter," which in Nov 1982 attained a speed of 130.57 mph in servicing the *Thrust 2* land speed record trials.

Most Powerful Wrecker

The most powerful wrecker is the Vance Corp 28-ton 30-ft-long Monster No. 2 stationed at Hammond, Ind. It can lift in excess of 179 tons on its short boom.

Lawn Mowers

The widest gang mower on record is the 5.6-ton 60-ft-wide 27-unit Big Green Machine, used by the sod farmer Jay Edgar Frick of Monroe, Ohio. It mows an acre in 60 sec.

Amphibious Vehicle Circumnavigation

The only circumnavigation of the world by an amphibious vehicle was achieved by Ben Carlin (Australia) (d Mar 7, 1981) in an amphibious

LONGEST LOAD: This 275-ft-long high-pressure steel gas storage vessel weighing 261 tons was transported to a new location in London on July 10, 1985. The overall train length was 325 ft.

LARGEST TRACTOR: This 33-ft-wide giant is so large that it has its own catwalk between wheels that run on permanent tracks.

MOST MASSIVE LAND VEHICLE: "Big Muskie" is a shovel so big (grab capacity 325 tons) that it can gobble up a full-sized bulldozer in its bucket comfortably. (*Alan Russell*)

jeep "Half-Safe." He completed the last leg of the Atlantic crossing (the English Channel) on Aug 24, 1951. He arrived back in Montreal, Canada on May 8, 1958 having completed a circumnavigation of 39,000 miles over land and 9,600 miles by sea and river. He was accompanied on the transatlantic stage by his ex-wife Elinore (US) and on the long transpacific stage (Tokyo to Anchorage) by Broye Lafayette De Mente (b Mo, 1928).

Longest Motor Trip

The longest continuous trailer tour was one of 143,716 miles by Harry B. Coleman and Peggy Larson in a Volkswagen Camper from Aug 20, 1976 to Apr 20, 1978 through 113 countries. Saburo Ouchi (b Feb 7, 1942) of Tokyo, Japan, drove 167,770 miles in 91 countries from Dec 2, 1969 to Feb 10, 1978.

Snowmobiles

Richard and Raymond Moore and Loren Matthews drove their snowmobile 5,876 mi from Fairbanks, Alaska to Fenton, Mich, in 39 days from Feb 3–Mar 13, 1980.

The record speed for a snowmobile is 148.6 mph, set by Tom Earhart (US) in a Budweiser-Polaris snowmobile designed and owned by Bob Gaudreau, at Lake Mille Lacs, Minn, on Feb 25, 1982.

COACHES

The Spies Traveling Co of Denmark on May 7, 1986 organized the longest procession of horse-drawn carriages ever. They transported 750 people on 70 carriages through the woods around Copenhagen to celebrate the coming of spring. The cavalcade extended for some 3,020 ft "nose to tail."

MOTORCYCLES

Earliest

The earliest internal-combustion-engined motorized bicycle was a wooden-framed machine built during Oct-Nov 1885 by Gottlieb Daimler (1834–1900) of Germany at Bad Cannstatt and first ridden by Wilhelm Maybach (1846–1929). It had a top speed of 12 mph and developed one-half of one hp from its single-cylinder 264-cc 4-stroke engine at 700 rpm. Known as the "Einspur," it was lost in a fire in 1903. The earliest factory which made motorcycles in quantity was opened in 1894 by Heinrich and Wilhelm Hildebrand and Alois Wolfmüller at Munich, Germany. In its first 2 years this factory produced over 1,000 machines, each having a water-cooled 1,488-cc twin-cylinder 4-stroke engine developing about 2.5 bhp at 600 rpm—the highest capacity motorcycle engine ever put into production.

Fastest Track Motorcycle

There is no satisfactory answer to the identity of the fastest track machine, other than to say that the current Kawasaki, Suzuki and Yamaha machines have all been geared to attain speeds marginally in excess of 186 mph under race conditions.

Most Expensive Motorcycle

A 1912 Henderson Model A was auctioned for $18,000 in June 1980 in the US.

Fastest Road Motorcycle

The 115-bhp Japanese Honda V65 Magna with a liquid-cooled, in-line V4, 16-valve DoHC engine of 1,098-cc capacity has a design speed of 173 mph.

Duration

The longest time a solo motorcycle has been kept in non-stop motion is 500 hours by Owen Fitzgerald, Richard Kennett and Don Mitchell who covered 8,432 miles in Western Australia July 10–31, 1977.

BICYCLES AND UNICYCLES

The first design for a machine propelled by cranks and pedals, with connecting rods, has been attributed to Leonardo da Vinci (1452–1519) or one of his pupils, dated c. 1493. The earliest such design actually built was in 1839–40 by Kirkpatrick Macmillan (1810–78) of Dumfries, Scotland. It is now in the Science Museum, London.

Smallest Bicycle

The world's smallest wheeled *rideable* bicycle is one with 1½-in wheels made of US silver dollars, with a wheelbase of 2¾ in, a seat 7 in from the floor and pedals of ¾ in, built and ridden by Charly Charles in his act at Circus Circus Hotels in Reno and Las Vegas, Nev. Prof Thomas L. Harrington of the Univ of Nevada, Reno, figures that in the 14 years Charly has been riding his miniature bikes on the stage he has traversed 3,343 mi.

With slightly smaller wheels (1.37-in), weighing 24.6 oz, a bicycle with more leg room was built and ridden by Jacques Puyoou of Pau, France in 1983. He has also built a tandem bike 14.1-in long to accommodate Mme Puyoou.

Largest Bicycle

A classic Ordinary bicycle with a 65¼-in front wheel and an 18-inch back wheel was constructed by the Coventry Machinists Co in 1881. It is now owned by Paul Foulkes-Halbard of Crowborough, Sussex, Eng.

A bicycle with an 8-ft-2½-in front wheel with pedal extenders was built in 1878 for circus demonstrations.

Longest Bicycle

The longest true tandem bicycle ever built (*i.e.* without a third stabilizing wheel) is one of 66 ft 11 in for 35 riders built by the Pedalstompers Westmalle of Belgium. They rode c. 195 ft in practice on Apr 20, 1979. The machine weighs 2,425 lb.

Fastest Cycle Riding

The speed records for human-powered vehicles are 61.94 mph (single rider) by John Seibert at La Garita, Colo, Oct 27, 1980, and 62.92 mph (multiple riders) by Dave Grylls and Leigh Barczewski at the Ontario Speedway, Calif, May 4, 1980. (Also see Chapter 12—*Cycling*.)

Unicycles

The tallest unicycle ever mastered is one 101 ft 9 in tall ridden by Steve McPeak (with a safety wire or mechanic suspended to an overhead crane) for a distance of 376 ft in Las Vegas Oct 19, 1980. The freestyle riding of ever taller unicycles (that is, without any safety harness) must inevitably lead to serious injury or fatality.

TINIEST BICYCLE (above): Charly Charles of Las Vegas holds the bike with silver dollars as wheels which he built and rides. (*Las Vegas News Bureau*)

DOUBLE-DECKER TANDEM BIKE (right): From the ground to the upper story handlebars is 11.1 ft. Built by Kesaichiro Tagawa of Osaka, Japan, this two-seater is 16.4 ft long.

3. RAILROADS*

Earliest

Wagons running on wooden rails were used for mining as early as 1550 at Leberthal, Alsace, near the French-German border, and at the Broseley Colliery, Shropshire, England in Oct 1605. Richard Trevithick (1771–1833) built his first steam locomotive for the 3-ft-gauge iron plateway at Coalbrookdale, Shropshire, in 1803, but there is no evidence that it ran. The first known to have *run* was his second locomotive, which drew wagons with men riding on them in a demonstration run at Penydarren, Wales, on Feb 22, 1804, but it broke the plate rails.

The first permanent public railway to use steam traction was the Stockton & Darlington, from its opening on Sept 27, 1825. The 7.84-ton *Locomotion* could pull 53.7 tons at a speed of 15 mph. It was designed and driven by George Stephenson (1781–1848).

The first regular steam passenger service was inaugurated over a one-mile section on the 6¼-mi Canterbury & Whitstable Railway in Kent, Eng, May 3, 1830, hauled by the engine *Invicta*.

The first practical electric railway was Werner von Siemens' oval meter-gauge demonstration track about 328 yd long at the Berlin Trades Exhibition on May 31, 1879.

Fastest Rail Speed

> The highest speed attained by a railed vehicle is 6,121 mph or Mach 8 by an unmanned rocket sled over the 9½-mile-long rail track at White Sands Missile Range, NM on Oct 5, 1982.

The world's fastest rail speed with passengers is 321.2 mph by the Maglev (magnetic levitation) ML-500 test train over the 4.3 mi JNR experimental track at Miyazaki, Japan in Dec 1979.

The highest speed recorded on any national rail system is 236 mph by the French SNCF high-speed train TGV-PSE on trial near Tonnerre Feb 26, 1981. The TGV (Train à Grande Vitesse), inaugurated in 1981, two years later reduced its scheduled time for the Paris–Lyon run of 264 miles from 2 hours 14 min to 2 hours exactly, so averaging 132 mph. The peak speed attained was 168 mph.

Fastest Steam Locomotives

The highest speed ever ratified (over 440 yd) for a steam locomotive was 125 mph by the LNER 4-6-2 No. 4468 *Mallard* (later numbered 60022), which hauled seven coaches weighing 268.8 tons gross, down Stoke Bank, near Essendine, between Grantham and Peterborough, England, on July 3, 1938. Driver Joseph Duddington was at the controls with Fireman Thomas Bray. The engine suffered some damage. On June

---

* See also *The Guinness Rail Factbook* (Sterling). A progressive table of railroad speed records since 1829 appears also in the 1977 edition of the *Guinness Book of World Records*, page 309.

12, 1905, a speed of 127.06 mph was claimed for the "Pennsylvania Special" near Elida, Ohio, but has never been accepted by leading experts.

Most Powerful Locomotive

The most powerful steam locomotive, measured by tractive effort, was No. 700, a triple-articulated or triplex 2–8–8–8–4–6-cylinder engine which the Baldwin Locomotive Co built in 1916 for the Virginian Railroad. It had a tractive force of 166,300 lb working compound and 199,560 lb working simple.

Probably the heaviest train ever hauled by a single engine was one of 17,100 tons made up of 250 freight cars stretching 1.6 miles by the *Matt H. Shay* (No. 5014), a 2–8–8–8–2 engine which ran on the Erie Railroad from May 1914 until 1929.

Greatest Load

The heaviest single pieces of freight ever conveyed by rail are limited by the capacity of the rolling stock. The world's strongest and only rail carrier, with a capacity of 889.7 tons, is the 370.4-ton, 36-axle, 301-ft-10-in-long "Schnabel," built for a US railway by Krupp, W Germany in Mar 1981.

The heaviest load ever moved on rails was the Church of the Virgin Mary built in 1548 at Most, Czechoslovakia, weighing nearly 12,000 tons, moved in Oct-Nov 1975 because it was in the way of mining for coal deposits. It was moved 800 yd at 0.0013 mph over a period of 4 weeks at a cost of $15,300,000.

Most Traveling

Using Amtrak's "All Aboard America" $299 ticket, valid for a month,

Loose Cabooses

With railroads going out of business, cabooses are being scrapped. When 19 cabooses were being offered on bid by the Reading Railroad, Milton and Lois Denlinger of Strasburg, Pa put in a bid and the cars "showed up in the middle of a blizzard with no place to put them but in our back yard." Since then, wanting to preserve the quaint little red cars, the "best of yesteryear," the Denlingers have added 19 more cabooses of every variety for the largest private collection without a doubt. They added sleeping quarters to some of them and also have 500 toy cabooses.

James J. Brady of Wilmington, O, traveled through 442 (out of 498) stations over 21,485 unduplicated mi of track (out of 23,000) Feb 11–Mar 11, 1984.

The record number of countries traveled through entirely by train in 24 hours is 10 by W. M. Elbers and R. G. Scholten, Sept 9–10, 1985. They started in Yugoslavia, traveling via Austria, Italy, Liechtenstein, Switzerland, France, Luxembourg, Belgium, and the Netherlands, arriving in W Germany 22 hours 47 min later.

John E. Ballenger of Dunedin, Fla has logged 76,485 mi of unduplicated rail routes in North and South America in his lifetime.

Handpumped Railcars

The fastest time set in the now annual races at Port Moody, BC, Canada, over 300 meters (985 ft) by a 5-man team (1 pusher, 4 pumpers) is 33.54 sec on June 27, 1982.

Waiting Rooms

The largest waiting rooms are the four in Peking Station, Chang'an Boulevard, Peking, China, opened in Sept 1959, with a total standing capacity of 14,000.

Largest, Highest and Oldest Stations

The biggest railroad station is Grand Central Terminal, NYC, built 1903–13. It covers 48 acres on 2 levels with 41 tracks on the upper level and 26 on the lower. On average, more than 550 trains and 180,000 people per day use it, with a peak of 252,288 on July 3, 1947.

The highest station is Condor, Bolivia, at 15,705 ft on the meter-gauge Rio Mulato-to-Potosí line.

The oldest station in the world is Liverpool Road Station, Manchester, England, first used in 1830. It is now part of a museum.

Steepest Grade

The steepest standard gauge gradient by adhesion is 1:11 between Chedde and Servoz on the meter gauge electric SNCF Chamonix line, France.

Highest Track

The highest standard gauge (4 ft 8½ in) track is on the Peruvian State Railways at La Cima, on the Morococha Branch at 15,806 ft above sea level. The highest point on the main line is 15,688 ft in the Galera tunnel.

Widest and Narrowest Gauges

The widest gauge in standard use is 5 ft 6 in. This width is used in Spain, Portugal, India, Pakistan, Bangladesh, Sri Lanka, Argentina and Chile. In 1885, there was a lumber railway in Oregon with a gauge of 8 ft.

The narrowest gauge on which public services are operated is 10¼ in on the Wells Harbour (0.7 mi) and the Wells-Walsingham Railways (4 mi) in Norfolk, England.

Longest Line

The longest run is one of 5,864¼ miles on the Trans-Siberian Line between Moscow and Nakhodka in the Soviet Far East. There are 97 stops on the journey, which takes 8 days 4 hours 25 min. The 1,927.5-mi Baykal-Amur Magistral (BAM) northern line, begun with forced labor in 1938, was restarted in 1974 and put into service on Oct 27, 1984. It will cut 310 miles off the route around the southern end of Lake Baykal. A total of 10,000 million cu ft of earth was removed and 1,987 bridges built in this $10 billion project.

Longest Straight Length

The longest straight is on the Commonwealth Railways Trans-Australian line over the Nullarbor Plain from Mile 496 between Nurina and Loongana, Western Australia, to Mile 793 between Ooldea and Watson, South Australia, 297 miles dead straight although not level.

Longest Platform

The longest railroad platform is the Khargpur platform in West Bengal, India, which measures 2,733 ft in length. The State Street Center subway platform in "The Loop" in Chicago measures 3,500 ft in length.

Subways

The earliest (first section opened Jan 10, 1863) and one of the most extensive underground railway or rapid transit systems of the 67 in the world is that of the London Underground, with 251 miles of route, of which 82 miles is bored tunnel and 20 miles is "cut and cover." This whole system is operated by a staff of 11,000 serving 272 stations. The 453 trains comprising 3,875 cars carried 672 million passengers in 1984.

The subway with most stations is operated by the NYC Transit Authority (first section opened on Oct 27, 1904) with a total of 231.73 route miles of track and a record 1,096,006,529 passengers in 1979. The stations are close set and total 458. The record for traveling the whole sys-

BUSIEST RAIL SYSTEM: The Japanese National Railways (which includes the Tokyo subway) carries 18.8 million people daily. Their crack train is the Shingansen express train shown here passing Mt. Fuji.

tem was 21 hours 8½ min by Mayer Wiesen and Charles Emerson, Oct 8, 1973.

The busiest subway system is that in Greater Moscow with as many as 6½ million passengers per day. At mid-1985, it had 123 stations and 123 mi of track.

Longest Freight Train

The longest and heaviest freight train on record was one about 4 miles in length consisting of 500 coal cars with three 3600 hp diesels pulling and three more in the middle, on the Iaeger, West Virginia, to Portsmouth, Ohio stretch of 157 miles on the Norfolk and Western Railway on Nov 15, 1967. The total weight was nearly 47,250 tons.

Busiest Rail System

The most crowded rail system is the Japanese National Railways, which in 1985 carried 18,860,000 passengers daily. Professional pushers are employed to squeeze in passengers before the doors can be closed. Among articles reported lost in the crush in 1984 were 522,704 umbrellas, 309,446 clothing items, 228,925 books and stationery items, 193,289 accessories and 185,390 purses.

Longest Tramway Journey

The longest tramway journey now possible is from Krefeld St Tönis to Witten Annen Nord, W Germany. With luck at the 8 interconnections the 65.5-mile trip can be achieved in 5½ hours. By late 1977 there were still some 315 tramway systems surviving, of which the longest is that of Leningrad, USSR, with 2,500 cars on 53 routes.

Oldest Trams

The oldest trams in revenue service in the world are Motor Cars 1 and 2 of the Manx (Isle of Man) Electric Railway, dating from 1893.

Model Railways

The non-stop duration record for a model train (locomotive plus 6 coaches) is 864 hours 30 min from June 1 to July 7, 1978, covering 678 miles, organized by Roy Catton at "Pastimes" Toy Store, Mexborough, S. Yorkshire, England.

The longest recorded run by a model *steam* locomotive is 144 miles in 27 hours 18 min by the 7¼-in gauge "Winifred" built in 1974 by Wilf Grove at Thames Ditton, Surrey, England on Sept 8–9, 1979. "Winifred" works on 80 lb/sq-in pressure and is coal-fired with a 2⅛-in bore cylinder and a 3⅛-in stroke.

The most miniature model railway ever built is one of 1:1000 scale by Jean Damery (b 1923) of Paris. The engine ran on a 4½-volt battery and measures ⁵⁄₁₆ in overall.

---

4. AIRCRAFT*

Note: The use of the Mach scale for aircraft speeds was introduced by Prof Ackeret of Zurich, Switzerland. The Mach number is the ratio of the velocity of a moving body to the local velocity of sound. This was first employed by Dr Ernst Mach (1838–1916) of Austria in 1887. Thus Mach 1.0 equals 760.98 mph at sea level at 15 ° C (59 °F) and is assumed, for convenience, to fall to a constant 659.78 mph in the stratosphere, *i.e.* above 11,000 m (36,089 ft).

Earliest Flights

The first controlled and sustained power-driven flight occurred near Kill Devil Hill, Kitty Hawk, NC at 10:35 A.M. on Dec 17, 1903, when Orville Wright (1871–1948) flew the 12-hp chain-driven *Flyer I* for a distance of 120 ft, at an airspeed of 30 mph, a ground speed of 6.8 mph and an altitude of 8–12 ft for about 12 sec, watched by his brother Wilbur (1867–1912), 4 men and a boy. Both brothers, from Dayton, Ohio, were bachelors because, as Orville put it, they had not the means to "support a wife as well as an airplane." The *Flyer* is now in the National Air and Space Museum of the Smithsonian Institution, Washington, DC.

The first hop by a man-carrying airplane entirely under its own power was made when Clément Ader (1841–1925) of France flew in his *Eole* for about 164 ft at Armainvilliers, France, on Oct 9, 1890. It was powered by a lightweight steam engine of his own design which developed about 20 hp (15 kW).

The earliest "rational design" for a flying machine (according to the British Royal Aeronautical Society) was published by Emanuel Swedenborg (1688–1772) in Sweden in 1717.

Transatlantic Flights

The first crossing of the North Atlantic by air was made by Lt-Cdr (later Rear Admiral) Albert C. Read (1887–1967) and his crew (Stone, Hinton, Rodd, Rhoads and Breese) in an 84-knot Curtiss flying boat NC-4 of the US Navy from Trepassy Harbour, Newfoundland, Canada *via* the Azores, to Lisbon, Portugal, May 16 to 27, 1919. The whole flight of 4,717 miles originating from Rockaway Air Station, Long Island, NY,

---

* For more detail and more records see *Guinness Book of Aircraft Facts and Feats* (Sterling).

on May 8, required 53 hours 58 min terminating at Plymouth, England on May 31. The Newfoundland-Azores leg (1,200 miles) took 15 hours 18 min at 81.7 knots.

The first non-stop transatlantic flight was achieved 18 days later, from 4:13 P.M. GMT on June 14, 1919 from Lester's Field, St John's, Newfoundland, 1,960 miles to Derrygimla bog near Clifden, Co Galway, Ireland, at 8:40 A.M. GMT June 15, when the pilot Capt John William Alcock (1892–1919), and Lt Arthur Whitten Brown (1886–1948) flew across in a Vickers *Vimy,* powered by two 360-hp Rolls-Royce *Eagle VIII* engines.

The first round-trip, non-stop transatlantic flight took place on Aug 6, 1945, when 2 USAAF bombers flew non-stop from Hunter Air Force Base, Georgia, to simulated targets in southern Europe and return. The 10,000-mi flight took 25 hours 23 min, and involved 4 mid-air refuelings, 2 in complete darkness.

FIRST TO FLY (left): Were it not for these men, the Wright brothers, Wilbur and Orville, air flight might not have been possible. Here they are on the way to making their historic flight dressed in stiff collars and ties. The take-off in 1903 came after a ground speed of 6.8 mph was reached. The plane flew for 12 sec at a height of 8–12 ft. (*Air & Space Museum, Washington*)

AMERICAN PACESETTER (below): The first person to fly solo across the Atlantic, Charles A. Lindbergh became an instant hero. He did it in a tiny plane "The Spirit of St. Louis" in 1927 in a 33½-hour ordeal and won

The 79th man to complete a transatlantic trip but the first to fly alone was Capt (later Col and Brig Gen) Charles A. Lindbergh (1902–74), who took off in his 220-hp Ryan monoplane *Spirit of St Louis* at 12:52 P.M. GMT on May 20, 1927 from Roosevelt Field, Long Island, NY. He landed at 10:21 P.M. GMT on May 21, 1927 at Le Bourget airfield, Paris, France. His flight of 3,610 miles lasted 33 hours 29½ min and he won a prize of $25,000.

The record for the most transatlantic flights is held by TWA Capt Charles M. Schimpf who logged a total of 2,880 Atlantic crossings, at the rate of 6.4 per month, between Mar 1948 and his retirement in Sept 1984.

The transatlantic flight speed record is 1 hour 54 min 56.4 sec by Maj James V. Sullivan, 37, and Maj Noel F. Widdifield, 33, flying a Lockheed SR-71A eastwards on Sept 1, 1974. The average speed, slowed by refueling by a KC-135 tanker aircraft, for the NY-London stage of 3,461.53 miles was 1,806.963 mph. The solo record (Gander to Gatwick) is 8 hours 47 min 32 sec by Capt John J. A. Smith in a Rockwell 685 on March 12, 1978.

Transpacific Flight

The first non-stop Pacific flight was by Maj Clyde Pangborn and Hugh Herndon in the Bellanca cabin plane *Miss Veedol* from Sabishiro Beach, Japan, 4,558 miles to Wenatchee, Wash in 41 hours 13 min on Oct 3–5, 1931. (For earliest crossing see 1924 flight below.)

The longest non-stop flight was one of 7,950 statute mi from Melbourne, Aust to LA by Pan Am Clipper flight 816 on July 2, 1984 when the scheduled stop in Sydney was cancelled because of a strike. The pilot was Capt David Riggs and the flight took 13 hours 59 min.

Circumnavigational Flights

A strict circumnavigation of the earth requires passing through two antipodal points and is thus a minimum distance of 24,859.75 miles. (The FAI permits flights which exceed the length of the Tropic of Cancer or Capricorn, namely 22,858.754 miles, to be called round-the-world.)

The earliest such flight (26,345 miles) was made by two US Army Douglas DWC amphibians in 57 "hops." The *Chicago* was piloted by Lt Lowell H. Smith and Lt Leslie P. Arnold and the *New Orleans* was piloted by Lt Erik H. Nelson and Lt John Harding. The planes took off from Seattle, Wash on Apr 6, 1924 and landed back there on Sept 28, 1924.

The earliest solo claim was by Wiley Hardemann Post (1898–1935) (US) in the Lockheed Vega *Winnie Mae*, starting and finishing at Floyd Bennett Field, NYC July 15–22, 1933, in 10 "hops." His distance of 15,596 miles with a flying time of 115 hours 36 min was, however, at too high a latitude to qualify.

The first non-stop round-the-world flight was completed on Mar 2, 1949, by the USAF's Boeing B-50 Superfortress *Lucky Lady II,* piloted by Capt James Gallagher from Carswell AFB, Tex in 94 hours 1 min. The aircraft was refueled 4 times on its 23,452-mile flight.

The fastest flight has been a non-stop easterly flight of 45 hours 19 min by 3 USAF B-52's led by Maj-Gen Archie J. Old, Jr. They covered 24,325 miles on Jan 16–18, 1957, finishing at March AFB, Riverside, Calif having averaged 525 mph with 4 in-flight refuelings by KC-97 aerial tankers.

The smallest aircraft to complete a circumnavigation is a 20-ft-11-in single-engined 180-hp Thorp T-18, built in his garage by its pilot Donald

SUPERSONIC SPEEDSTERS: 4 Concordes flying in formation. These planes, with as many as 128 passengers, cruise at up to Mach 2.2 (1,450 mph). (*British Airways*)

P. Taylor of Sage, Calif. His 26,190-mile flight in 37 stages took 176 flying hours, ending in Oshkosh, Wis on Sept 30, 1976.

Jet-Engine Flight

Proposals for jet propulsion date back to 1909, by Capt Marconnet of France and Henri Coanda (1886–1972) of Rumania, and to the turbojet proposals of Maxime Guillaume in 1921. The earliest tested run was that of the British Power Jets Ltd's experimental WU (Whittle Unit) on Apr 12, 1937, invented by Flying Officer (now Air Commodore Sir) Frank Whittle (b Coventry, June 1, 1907), who had applied for a patent on jet propulsion in 1930.

The first flight by an airplane powered by a turbojet engine was made by the Heinkel He 178, piloted by Flugkapitän Erich Warsitz, at Marienehe, Germany Aug 27, 1939. It was powered by a Heinkel He S3b engine (834-lb as installed with long tailpipe) designed by Dr Hans von Ohain and first tested in Aug 1937.

Circum-Polar Flight

The first circum-polar flight was flown solo by Capt Elgen M. Long, 44, in a Piper Navajo, Nov 5 to Dec 3, 1971. He covered 38,896 miles in 215 flying hours. The cabin temperature sank to −40°F over Antarctica.

Supersonic Flight

The first supersonic flight was achieved Oct 14, 1947 by Capt (later Brig-Gen) Charles ("Chuck") Elwood Yeager, USAF retired (b Feb 13, 1923), over Edwards Air Force Base, Muroc, Calif in a US Bell XS-1 rocket plane (*Glamorous Glennis*), with Mach 1.015 (670 mph) at an altitude of 42,000 ft. In Feb 1986, Yeager was still breaking records. He flew from Burbank, Calif to LaGuardia Airport, NYC, in 5 hours, 23 min in a Piper-Cheyenne 400-LS, a record for a business turboprop plane of less than 13,000 lb.

The first woman to fly faster than the speed of sound was Jacqueline Cochran (US), who on May 18, 1953, flew a North American F-86 Sabre at 652 mph.

Closest Prediction

In 1955 Mrs Helen Thomas of Cambridge, Mass predicted what air travel would be like in 1985 and came closest to being 100% accurate in a TWA contest. She forecast, with amazing accuracy, that commercial airliners would have ranges of 5,000 miles, cruise at about 700 mph, carry about 300 people and be powered by "bypass jets." For her to spend a weekend in Hawaii, Australia, Rome or in Cairo would be no problem, she predicted. TWA stored the contest entries in a vault for 30 years until 1985 when the $50,000 prize was awarded to Mrs Thomas. The judges for TWA included Charles "Pete" Conrad, Jr., famous astronaut, as well as TWA officials.

Heaviest and Smallest Planes

The highest recorded gross takeoff weight of any aircraft has been 425 tons in the case of a Boeing 747-200B jumbo jet during certification tests of its Pratt & Whitney JT9D-7Q engines on May 23, 1979.

A Boeing 747 (Capt Eric Moody) became the "world's heaviest glider" when all 4 engines stopped at 37,000 ft up, due to volcanic ash from Mt Galunggung, Indonesia on June 24, 1982 on Flight BA 009 with 263 aboard. The crew got the engines restarted after 13 min and landed the plane at Jakarta.

The $40 million Piasecki Helistat, comprising a framework of light-alloy and composite materials to mount 4 Sikorsky SH-34J helicopters and the envelope of a Goodyear ZPG-2 patrol airship, was exhibited on Jan 26, 1984 at Lakehurst, NJ. Designed for use by the US Forest Service and designated Model 94-37J Logger, it has an overall length of 343 ft and is intended to carry a payload of 24 tons.

Three planes vie for the record as the world's smallest. The "Sky Baby" designed by Ray Stits of Riverside, Calif and first flown by the co-builder Robert H. Starr of Tempe, Ariz, May 26, 1952, weighs 452 lb empty, is 9 ft 10 in long, with wing span of 7 ft 2 in, and has top air speed of 185 mph. Another record smallest plane was designed and built by Starr and first flown by him in Ariz on Jan 28, 1984. Called the "Bumble Bee," it weighs more (756 lb) but is shorter, 9 ft 4 in long, with a wing span of 6 ft 6 in, and a top air speed of 180 mph. Both planes use Continental C-85 engines. A third plane with the smallest wing span (6 ft 3 in) and lightest in weight (252 lb empty) is the "Baby Bird" built by Donald R. Stits. It is longer (11 ft), is powered by a 55-hp 2-cylinder Hirth engine, and was first flown by Harold Nember on Aug 4, 1984 at a top speed of 110 mph at Camarillo, Calif.

The smallest jet is the 280-mph *Silver Bullet* built by Bob Bishop with a 17-ft wing span and weighing 432 lb.

Ultralight Plane

On Aug 3, 1985, Anthony A. Cafaro (b Nov 30, 1951) flew a ULA single-seater *Gypsy Skycycle*, having a maximum weight of 245 lb, a maximum speed of 65 mph, and a capacity of 5 gal for 7 hours 31 min at Dart Field, Detroit, Mich. Nine fuel pickups were completed during the flight.

Solar-Powered Flight

The solar-powered *Solar Challenger*, designed by a team led by Dr Paul MacCready, was flown for the first time entirely under solar power on Nov 20, 1980. On July 7, 1981, piloted by Steve Ptacek (US), the *Solar Challenger* became the first aircraft of this category to achieve a crossing of the English Channel. Taking off from Pontois-Cormeilles, Paris, the 163-mi journey to Manston, Kent, Eng, was completed in 5 hr 23 min at a maximum altitude of 11,000 ft. The aircraft has a wing span of 47 ft.

Largest and Fastest Airliners

The highest capacity jet airliner is the Boeing 747 jumbo jet, first flown on Feb 9, 1969. It has a capacity of from 385 to more than 500 passengers with a maximum speed of 602 mph. Its wing span is 195.7 ft and its length, 231.8 ft. It entered service on Jan 22, 1970. The Boeing 747–300 with a lengthened upper deck, which allows an extra 37 passengers, entered service in Mar 1983.

The greatest passenger load on a commercial airliner was 674 people—306 adults, 328 children and 40 babies—from the cyclone-devastated Darwin to Sydney, Australia on Dec 29, 1974.

The supersonic BAC/Aerospatiale *Concorde,* first flown on March 2, 1969, with a capacity of 128 passengers, cruises at up to Mach 2.2 (1,450 mph). It flew at Mach 1.05 on Oct 10, 1969, exceeded Mach 2 for the first time on Nov 4, 1970, and became the first supersonic airliner used for passenger service on Jan 21, 1976, when Air France and British Airways opened service simultaneously between, respectively, Paris-Rio de Janeiro and London—Bahrain. Services between London-NY and Paris-NY began Nov 22, 1977. The NY-London record time is 2 hours 56 min 35 sec set Jan 1, 1983.

Heaviest and Fastest Bombers

The heaviest bomber is the 8-jet swept-wing Boeing B-52H *Stratofortress,* which has a maximum takeoff weight of 488,000 lb. It has a wing span of 185 ft and is 157 ft 6¾ in in length, with a speed of over 650 mph. The B-52 can carry 12 SRAM thermonuclear short-range attack missiles or 24 750-lb bombs under its wings and 8 more SRAMs or 84 500-lb bombs in the fuselage.

The fastest operational bombers are the French Dassault Mirage IV, which can fly at Mach 2.2 (1,450 mph) at 36,000 ft; the General Dynamics FB-111A, with a maximum speed of Mach 2.5; and the Soviet swing-wing Tupolev Tu-26 known as "Backfire," which has an estimated over-target speed of Mach 2.0 to 2.5 and a combat radius of 3,570 miles.

Highest Air Speed

The official air speed record is 2,193.167 mph by Capt Eldon W. Joersz and Maj George T. Morgan, Jr, in a Lockheed SR-71A near Beale Air Force Base, Calif on July 28, 1976 over a 10–15-mi course.

The fastest fixed-wing craft was a North American Aviation X-15A-2, which flew for the first time (after modification from X-15A) on June 25, 1964, powered by a liquid oxygen and ammonia rocket propulsion system. Ablative materials on the airframe enabled a temperature of 3,000°F to be withstood. The landing speed was 210 knots (242 mph) momentarily. The highest speed attained was 4,520 mph (Mach 6.72) when piloted by Maj William J. Knight, USAF (b 1930) on Oct 3, 1967. An earlier version piloted by Joseph A. Walker (1920–66) reached 354,-200 ft (67.08 miles) over Edwards Air Force Base, Calif on Aug 22, 1963. The program was suspended after the final flight of Oct 24, 1968.

The US NASA Rockwell International Space Shuttle Orbiter *Columbia* was launched from the Kennedy Space Center, Cape Canaveral, Fla, commanded by Commander John W. Young USN and piloted by Robert L. Crippen on Apr 12, 1981 after the expenditure of $9,900 million since 1972. *Columbia* broke all records for space by a fixed-wing craft with 16,600 mph at main engine cut-off. After re-entry from 400,000 ft, experiencing temperatures of 3,920°F, she glided home weighing 108 tons with the highest ever landing speed of 216 mph on Rogers Dry Lake, Calif on Apr 14, 1981. Under a new FAI category P for aero-spacecraft, the *Columbia* is holder of the current absolute world record for duration of 8 days 00 hr 4 min 45 sec, with 2 astronauts, but *Challenger* (launched June 18, 1983) has since set a duration record of 6 days 2 hr 23 min 59 sec with 5 astronauts including Sally K. Ride, the first female space shuttle astronaut, and on a previous mission it set a new record altitude of 206.36 miles.

Columbia also holds the current absolute world record for the greatest mass lifted to altitude, a figure of 235,634 lb.

Fastest Jet

The fastest jet aircraft is the USAF Lockheed SR-71 reconnaissance aircraft which first flew on Dec 22, 1964 and attained a speed of 2,193.167 mph July 28, 1976 (official record). It is reportedly capable of attaining an altitude ceiling of close to 100,000 ft. The SR-71 has a wing span of 55.6 ft, a length of 107.4 ft and weighs 170,000 lb at takeoff. Its reported range is 2,982 miles at Mach 3 at 78,750 ft. At least 30 are believed to have been built.

The fastest combat aircraft in service is the USSR Mikoyan MIG-25 fighter (code name "Foxbat"). The reconnaissance "Foxbat-B" has been tracked by radar at about Mach 3.2 (2,110 mph). When armed with 4 large underwing air-to-air missiles known to NATO as "Acrid," the fighter "Foxbat-A" is limited to Mach 2.8 (1,845 mph). The single-seat "Foxbat-A" spans 45 ft 9 in, is 78 ft 2 in long, and has a maximum take-off weight of 82,500 lb.

Fastest Piston-Engined Aircraft

The fastest speed at which a piston-engined plane has ever been measured was for a cut-down privately owned Hawker *Sea Fury* which attained 520 mph in level flight over Texas in Aug 1966, piloted by Mike Carroll (k 1969) of Los Angeles.

The FAI accredited record for a piston-engined aircraft is 517.055 mph over Mojave, Calif by Frank Taylor (US) in a modified North American P-51D *Mustang* powered by a 3,000-hp Packard Merlin, over a 15–25 km course, on July 30, 1983.

Fastest Biplane

The fastest recorded biplane was the Italian Fiat C. R. 42B, with a 1,010-hp Daimler-Benz DB601 A engine, which attained 323 mph in 1941. Only one was built.

Most Capacious Aircraft

The Aero Spacelines Guppy-201 has a cargo hold with a usable volume of 39,000 cu ft and a maximum takeoff weight of 85 tons. Wing span is 156.2 ft, length 143.8 ft and overall height 48.5 ft.

The Soviet Antonov AN-124 *Ruslan* has a cargo hold with a usable volume of 35,800 cu ft and a maximum takeoff weight of 446.4 tons. It is powered by 4 Lotarev D-18T turbofans, giving a cruising speed of up to 528 mph at 39,370 ft and a range of 2,796 mi.

LARGEST WING SPAN: This mammoth wooden flying boat, the "Spruce Goose," is being moved to a land location as it can't fly (never would, except for one 1,000-yd flight in 1947). The men standing on the wing (319 ft 11 in across) give you an idea of its size. Howard Hughes had it built; it has been at anchor in Long Beach (Calif) Harbor from 1947 to 1980, when it was sold to entrepreneur Jack Wrather who made it into a walk-through museum next to the "Queen Mary," a dockside museum too. In the boat watching the maneuver along with hundreds on shore is (then) Governor Jerry Brown. (*Dean Moon*)

LARGEST CAPACITY: The "Guppy" holds a cargo of 39,000 cu ft. (*Aero Spacelines*)

Largest Wing Span

The "Spruce Goose," the wooden flying boat with the world's largest wing span—319 ft 11 in—but which could not fly for more than a thousand yards, was moved by giant cranes in 1982 6 mi across the harbor in Long Beach (Calif) to rest in a 700-ft-diameter dome to become a walk-through museum. Alongside is the *Queen Mary* which from 1936 to 1940 was the world's largest ocean liner. Now at Pier J in Long Beach, one can within a few hours and a few yards examine both record holders.

The transferral of the "Spruce Goose" (nickname of the Hercules) from water to land was witnessed by several hundred people including Calif Governor Edmund G. (Jerry) Brown, Jr (see boat in left hand corner of photo). The tremendous size of the aircraft, which is 218 ft 8 in long, is emphasized by the tiny size of the men seen standing on the wing.

The move was a brilliant engineering feat by Goldcoast Corp aided by the US Navy barge crane YD-171 on Feb 22, 1982.

The "Spruce Goose" was piloted on its test run by the man who had it built, Howard R. Hughes (1905–76), who later became the fabulous multimillionaire recluse. On Nov 2, 1947, he revved up the 8 propeller-driven engines and taxied the 213-ton craft across the water and up to a height of 70 ft. For 1,000 yards, it stayed up and then it set down into the harbor and never flew again. Hughes had spent $40 million on it.

Fastest Propeller-Driven Aircraft

The Soviet Tu-114 turboprop transport is the fastest propeller-driven airplane. It recorded a speed of 545.076 mph carrying heavy payloads over measured circuits. It is developed from the Tupolev Tu-95 bomber, known in the West as the "Bear," and has four 14,795-hp engines. The turboprop-powered Republic XF-84H prototype US Navy fighter which flew on July 22, 1955 had a top design speed of 670 mph, but was abandoned.

Largest Aircraft Propeller

The largest aircraft propeller ever used was the 22-ft-7½-in diameter Garuda propeller, fitted to the Linke-Hofmann R II built in Wroclaw, Poland, which flew in 1919. It was driven by four 260-hp Mercedes engines and turned at only 545 rpm.

Flight Duration

The flight duration record is 64 days, 22 hours, 19 min and 5 sec, set by Robert Timm and John Cook in a Cessna 172 "Hacienda." They took off from McCarran Airfield, Las Vegas, Nev just before 3:53 P.M. local time on Dec 4, 1958 and landed at the same airfield just before 2:12 P.M. on Feb 7, 1959. They covered a distance equivalent to 6 times around the world with continued refueling without landing.

The record for duration without refueling is 84 hours 32 min, set by Walter E. Lees and Frederic A. Brossy in a Bellanca monoplane with a 225-hp Packard Diesel engine, at Jacksonville, Fla, May 25–28, 1931.

The longest non-stop flight without refueling was a 12,519-mile flight from Okinawa to Madrid, Spain, by a USAF B-52H in 1962.

The longest solo non-stop flight without refueling was 73 hours 21 min 36 sec by Jerry D. Mullens in a Class C-1 Phoenix Dec 5–8, 1981 over a closed circuit between Okla City and Jacksonville, Fla. He covered a total distance of 10,007.1 mi.

Youngest and Oldest Pilots

The youngest age at which anyone has ever qualified as a military pilot is 15 years 5 months in the case of Sgt Thomas Dobney (b May 6, 1926) of the British Royal Air Force. He had lied about his age (14 years) on induction.

The wholly untutored James A. Stoodley, aged 14 years 5 months, took his 13-year-old brother John on a 29-min joy ride in an unattended Piper Cub trainer aircraft at Ludgershall, Wiltshire, England in Dec 1942.

The youngest solo pilot has been Cody A. Locke in a Cessna 150 aircraft near Mexicali, Mexico on Feb 24, 1983, when aged 9 years 316 days.

The oldest pilot is Ed McCarty (b Sept 18, 1885) of Kimberly, Idaho who in 1979 was flying his rebuilt 30-year-old Ercoupe at the age of 94. Glenn E. Messer of Birmingham, Ala has been flying "steady" since May 13, 1911.

Greatest Altitude

The official altitude record by an aircraft taking off from the ground under its own power is 123,524 ft (23.39 miles) by Aleksandr Fedotov (USSR) in a Mikoyan E-266M (MIG-25) aircraft, powered by two 30,865-lb thrust turbojet engines on Aug 31, 1977.

Most Flying Hours

Max Conrad (1903–79) (US) logged 52,929 hours 40 min of flight time, a total of more than 6 years airborne, between 1928 and mid-1974. He completed 150 transatlantic crossings in light aircraft.

The record supersonic passenger is Fred Finn who made 604 Concorde crossings by June 1986.

Most Takeoffs and Landings from Airports

Al Yates and Bob Phoenix of Texas made 193 takeoffs and daylight landings at unduplicated airfields in 14 hours 57 min in a Piper Seminole on June 15, 1979.

Longest and Shortest Scheduled Flights

The longest scheduled non-stop flight is the weekly Pan-Am Sydney-San Francisco non-stop Flight 816 (13 hours 25 min) in a Boeing 747 SP (Special Performance) opened in Dec 1976 over 7,475 statute miles. The

YOUNGEST PILOT: Cody Locke, not yet 10 years old, flew a Cessna solo in Mexico in 1983.

longest delivery flight by a commercial jet is 8,936 nautical miles or 10,290 statute miles from Seattle, Wash to Cape Town, South Africa by South African Airway's Boeing 747 SP *Matroosberg*. She made the 17-hour-22½-min flight loaded with 196.5 tons of pre-cooled fuel March 23–29, 1976.

The shortest scheduled flight is made by Loganair between the Orkney Islands (Scotland) of Westray and Papa Westray, which has been flown with twin-engined 10-seat Britten-Norman Islander transports since Sept 1967. Though scheduled for 2 minutes, in favorable wind conditions it has been accomplished in 58 sec by Capt Andrew D. Alsop.

Gary W. Rovetto of Island Air on Mar 21, 1980 flew on the scheduled flight from Center Island to Decatur Island, Wash in 41 sec.

Air Safety

Experiments at Langley Air Force Base in Virginia include hurling dead chickens at airplanes traveling 700 mph to see how jets can avoid hitting birds that cause accidents. The "chicken gun" is a converted 20-ft cannon that shoots 4-lb chickens at engines, windshields and landing gear.

Largest Airports

The largest airport is the $2,625 million King Khalid International Airport outside Riyadh, Saudi Arabia, covering an area of 86 sq mi, opened on Nov 14, 1983. It has the world's largest control tower 243 ft in height.

The Hajj Terminal at the $2,940 million King Abdul-Aziz airport near Jeddah is the world's largest roofed structure covering 370 acres.

The present 6 runways and 5 terminal buildings of the Dallas/Fort Worth Airport, Tex are planned to be extended to 9 runways and 13 terminals with 260 gates with an ultimate capacity for 150 million passengers annually.

The largest airport terminal is Hartsfield Atlanta International Airport opened Sept 21, 1980, with floor space covering 50.50 acres. It has 138 gates handling nearly 50 million passengers annually but has a capacity for 75 million.

Highest and Lowest Airports

The highest airport in the world is La Sa (Lhasa) Airport in Tibet at 14,315 ft. The highest landing ever made by a fixed-wing plane was at 19,947 ft on Dhaulagiri, Himalaya, by a Pilatus Porter, named *Yeti*, supplying the 1960 Swiss Expedition. The lowest landing field is El Lisan on the east shore of the Dead Sea, 1,180 ft below sea level, but during World War II BOAC short C-class flying boats operated from the surface of the Dead Sea 1,292 ft below sea level. The lowest international airport is Schiphol, at Amsterdam, Holland at 13 ft below sea level. Although not an international airport, the one nearby at Rotterdam at 15 ft below sea level is lower.

Busiest Airport

The busiest airport is the Chicago O'Hare International Airport, with a total of 746,376 movements and 49,954,362 passengers in 1985. This

LARGEST HELICOPTER: Weighing 115 tons, the Soviet's Mil Mi-12
V-12 helicopter, known as "Homer," has a rotor span of 219 ft 10 in and
a length of 121 ft 4½ in. (*K. J. A. Brookes*)

represents a takeoff or landing every 42.25 sec around the clock.
Heathrow Airport outside London handles more *international* traffic
than any other.

The busiest landing area ever has been Bien Hoa Air Base, South
Vietnam, which handled more than one million takeoffs and landings in
1970. The largest "helipad" was An Khe, South Vietnam.

Airport Distance to City Centers

The airport farthest from the city center it allegedly serves is Vira-
copos, Brazil, which is 60 miles from São Paulo. The Gibraltar airport is
880 yd from the center.

Fastest Helicopters

The official world speed record for a pure helicopter is 228.9 mph set
by Gourguen Karapetyan in a Mil A-10 on a 15–25 km course near Moscow, on Sept 21, 1978.

Longest Runway

The longest runway is 7 miles in length (of which 15,000 ft is con-
creted) at Edwards Air Force Base on the bed of Rogers Dry Lake at
Muroc, Calif. The whole test center airfield extends over 65 sq mi. In an
emergency, an auxiliary 12-mile strip is available along the bed of the
Dry Lake.

The longest civil airport runway is one of 16,076 ft (3.04 miles) at
Pierre van Ryneveld Airport, Upington, South Africa, constructed in 5
months, Aug 1975–Jan 1976.

A paved runway 20,500 ft long (3.88 mi) appears on maps of Jordan at
Abu Husayn.

The most southerly major runway is at Mt Pleasant, E Falkland Island
at Lat 51° 50′S, measuring 2.42 mi, which took 16 months to build and
was completed in May 1985.

Round the World by Helicopter

H. Ross Perot, 23, and Jay Coburn, both of Dallas, Tex, made the first helicopter circumnavigation of the globe in "Spirit of Texas" Sept 1–30, 1982. The first solo round-the-world flight in a helicopter was completed by Dick Smith (Australia) on July 22, 1983. Flown from and to the Bell Helicopter facility at Fort Worth, Tex, in a Bell Model 206L Long Ranger III, his unhurried flight began on Aug 5, 1982 and covered a distance of 35,258 miles.

Largest, Strongest and Smallest Helicopters

The largest helicopter is the Soviet Mil Mi-12 ("Homer"), also known as the V-12. It is powered by four 6,500-hp turboshaft engines, and has a span of 219 ft 10 in over its rotor tips with a fuselage length of 121 ft 4½ in and weighs 115.7 tons.

On Feb 3, 1982, at Podmoscovno in the Soviet Union, a Mil Mi-26 heavy-lift helicopter, crewed by G. V. Alfeurov and L. A. Indeev (co-pilot), lifted a total mass of 125,153.8 lb to a height of 6,560 ft.

Highest Helicopters

The altitude record for helicopters is 40,820 ft by an Aerospatiale SA 315 B *Lama* over France on June 21, 1972. The highest recorded landing has been at 23,000 ft, below the southeast face of Everest, in a rescue sortie in May 1971. The World Trade Center Helipad is 1,385 ft above street level in NYC, on the South Tower.

Autogyros

The autogyro or gyroplane, a rotorcraft with an unpowered rotor turned by the airflow in flight, preceded the practical helicopter with engine-driven rotor. Juan de la Cierva (Spain) made the first successful autogyro flight with his model C.4 (commercially named an *Autogiro*) at Getafe, Spain, on Jan 9, 1923.

Wing Cdr Kenneth H. Wallis (GB) holds the straight-line distance record of 543.27 miles, set in his WA-116F autogyro on Sept 28, 1975 non-stop from Lydd, England to Wick, Scotland. Wallis flew his WA-116, with 72-hp McCulloch engine, to a record speed of 111.2 mph over a 1.86-mi straight course on May 12, 1969. On July 20, 1982, he established a new autogyro altitude record of 18,516 ft in his WA-121/Mc. This, the smallest and lightest Wallis autogyro to date, is powered by a 100-hp Wallis/McCulloch engine.

Flying Boats

The fastest flying boat ever built has been the Martin XP6M-1 Seamaster, the US Navy 4-jet-engined minelayer, flown in 1955–59 with a top speed of 646 mph. In Sept 1946, the Martin JRM-2 Mars flying boat set a payload record of 68,327 lb.

The official flying-boat speed record is 566.69 mph, set by Nikolai Andrievsky and a crew of 2 in a Soviet Beriev M-10, powered by 2 AL-7 turbojets, over a 10–15 mile course on Aug 7, 1961. The M-10 holds all 12 records listed for jet-powered flying boats, including an altitude of 49,088 ft set by Georgiy Buryanov and crew over the Sea of Azov Sept 9, 1961.

Ballooning

I. William Deiches (b 1934) of Brentwood, Essex, Eng, has adduced that the "mace-head" of the Scorpion King *c.* 3100 BC found at Hierakonpolis, Egypt is in reality a depiction of a paneled hot-air balloon of papyrus construction.

The earliest recorded ascent was by a model hot-air balloon invented by Father Bartolomeu de Gusmão (*né* Lourenço) (b Santos, Brazil, 1685), which was flown indoors at the Casa da India, Terreiro do Paço, Portugal on Aug 8, 1709.

The record distance (great-circle distance between takeoff and first landing point) traveled by a balloon is 5,208.68 miles by the Raven experimental helium-filled balloon *Double Eagle V,* with a capacity 399,053 cu ft, Nov 9–12, 1981, from Nagashima, Japan, to Covello, Calif. The crew for this first manned balloon crossing of the Pacific Ocean was Ben L. Abruzzo, Rocky Aoki, Ron Clark and Larry M. Newman.

Ex-USAF Col Joe Kittinger (also see Parachuting) became the first man to complete a solo transatlantic crossing by balloon. Accomplished in the 10,593 cu ft helium-filled balloon *Rosie O'Grady* between Sept 14–18, 1984, Kittinger lifted off from Caribou, Maine, and completed a distance of approximately 3,543 miles before landing at Montenotte, northern Italy in 86 hr. The first balloon crossing of the North Atlantic had been made during Aug 12–17, 1978 in the gas balloon *Double Eagle II* crewed by Ben L. Abruzzo, Maxie L. Anderson and Larry M. Newman.

The first crossing of the US was by the helium-filled balloon *Super Chicken III* (pilots Fred Gorell and John Shoecraft) from Costa Mesa, Calif, 2,515 mi to Blackbeard's Island, Ga Oct 9–12, 1981.

The world's distance record for hot-air balloons is 717.52 miles, set by French balloonists Michel Arnould and Hélène Dorigny, Nov 25–26, 1981, in the Cameron Type A-530 *Semiramis,* from Ballina, County Mayo, Eire, to St Christophe-en-Boucherie, France. This flight has also been homologated by the FAI as a new world duration record for hot-air balloons of 29 hours 5 min 48 sec, and in addition the *Semiramis* is now the largest hot-air balloon ever built, with a volume of 530,000 cu ft.

The FAI endurance and distance record for a gas and hot-air balloon is 96 hours 24 min and 2,074.817 miles by *Zanussi* crewed by Donald Allan Cameron (GB) and Major Christopher Davey which failed by only 103 miles to achieve the first balloon crossing of the Atlantic on July 30, 1978.

Highest Manned and Unmanned Balloons

The highest altitude attained by an unmanned balloon was 170,000 ft, by a Winzen Research balloon of 47,800,000 cu ft, launched at Chico, Calif, in Oct 1972.

The official record for a manned balloon is 113,740 ft by Cdr Malcolm D. Ross, USNR, and the late Lt-Cdr Victor E. Prother, USN, in an ascent from the deck of USS *Antietam* on May 4, 1961 over the Gulf of Mexico.

The altitude record for a hot-air balloon was set by Julian Nott (GB), who, on Oct 31, 1980, attained an altitude, which has been ratified by the FAI, of 55,137 ft, taking off from Longmont, near Denver, Colo, in the Cameron-built ICI balloon *Innovation*. The record altitude in an open basket is 53,000 ft by Chauncey Dunn (US) on Aug 1, 1979. He wore a pressure suit.

Largest Balloon

The largest balloon built is one with an inflatable volume of 70 million cu ft, by Winzen Research Inc, Minnesota.

Human-Powered Flight

The distance record for human-powered flight was set June 12, 1979 by Dr Paul MacCready's man-powered 70-lb aircraft *Gossamer Albatross* with a 96-ft wing span, piloted and pedaled by 136-lb Bryan Allen. The *Albatross* took off from Folkestone, England and landed at Cap Gris-Nez, France 2 hours 49 min later, a flight spanning 22.26 miles, winning the £100,000 (then $200,000) prize offered by Henry Kremer for the first man-powered crossing of the English Channel.

The 70-lb *Gossamer Condor* (96-ft wing span) designed by Dr Paul MacCready flew the figure-of-8 course between pylons 880 yd apart, powered by Bryan Allen at Shafter Airport, Calif on Aug 23, 1977 to win the £50,000 (then $85,000) Kremer prize. The flight lasted 7 min 27.5 sec.

Airships

The earliest flight of an airship was by Henri Giffard from Paris in his steam-powered coal-gas 88,300-cu ft 144-ft-long rigid airship Sept 24, 1852.

The largest non-rigid airships ever constructed were the US Navy ZPG 3-Ws. Four were built with a capacity of 1,516,300 cu ft, were 403.4 ft long and 85.1 ft in diameter, with a crew of 21. The first one flew on July 21, 1958, but crashed into the sea in June 1960.

The largest rigid airship (except for her sister ship, the *Hindenburg*, which was 5.6 ft longer) was the 236-ton German *Graf Zeppelin II* (LZ130), with a length of 803.8 ft and a capacity of 7,062,100 cu ft. She made her maiden flight on Sept 14, 1938 and in May and August 1939 made radar spying missions in British air space. She was dismantled in April 1940.

The most people ever carried in an airship were 207 in the US Navy *Akron* in 1931. The transatlantic record is 117 by the German *Hindenburg* in 1937.

The FAI accredited distance record for airships is 3,967.1 miles, set by the German *Graf Zeppelin*, captained by Dr Hugo Eckener between Oct 29 and Nov 1, 1928. The German Zeppelin L59 flew from Yambol, Bulgaria to south of Khartoum, Sudan and returned Nov 21–25, 1917 to cover a minimum of 4,500 mi.

The longest recorded flight by a non-rigid airship (without refueling) is 264 hours 12 min by a US Navy Goodyear-built ZPG-2 class ship (Cdr J. R. Hunt, USN) from the S Weymouth, Mass Naval Air Station March 4, 1957 and landing back at Key West, Fla March 15 after having flown 9,448 miles.

The world altitude, duration and distance records, of 10,365 ft, 1 hr 26 min 52 sec, and 23.03 miles, respectively, are held by the Cameron D-38 *hot-air* airship flown at Cunderdin, W. Australia on Aug 27, 1982 by R. W. Taaffe (Australia).

Model Aircraft

The record for altitude is 26,929 ft by Maynard L. Hill (US) on Sept 6, 1970, using a radio-controlled model, who on July 4, 1983 set a closed-circuit distance record of 1,231 mi. The free-flight speed record is 213.70 mph by V. Goukoune and V. Myakinin (both USSR) with a radio-controlled model at Klementyeva, USSR, on Sept 21, 1971. The record duration flight is one of 32 hours 7 min 40 sec by Eduard Svoboda (Czechoslovakia) flying a radio-controlled glider Aug 23–24, 1980. An indoor model with a rubber motor, designed by J. Richmond (US), set a duration record of 52 min 14 sec on Aug 31, 1979.

The smallest model aircraft to fly is one weighing 0.004 oz powered by attaching a horsefly and designed by the insectonaut Don Emmick of Seattle, Wash on July 24, 1979. One flew for 5 min at Kirkland, Wash.

Paper Airplane

The flight duration record for a paper aircraft over level ground is 16.89 sec by Ken Blackburn in the Reynolds Coliseum at NC State Univ, Raleigh, on Nov 29, 1983. A paper plane was witnessed in Aug 1933 to have flown 1¼ miles after a throw by "Chick" C. O. Reinhart from a 10th-story office window at 60 Beaver Street, NYC across the East River. It was helped by a hot updraft from a coffee-roasting plant.

The indoor record with a 12-ft ceiling is 1 min 33 sec set in the Fuji TV studios, Tokyo, Japan on Sept 21, 1980. An indoor distance record of 193 ft was set by Tony Felch of La Crosse, Wis at the LaCrosse Center on May 21, 1985.

---

5. POWER PRODUCERS

Earliest and Largest Windmills

The earliest recorded windmills are those used for grinding corn in Iran (Persia) in the 7th century AD. The oldest Dutch mill is the tower-mill at Zeddam, Gelderland, built c. 1450.

The largest Dutch windmill is the Dijkpolder, in Maasland, built in 1718. The sails measure 95¾ ft from tip to tip. The tallest windmill in The Netherlands is De Walvisch, in Schiedam, built to a height of 108 ft in 1794.

The most powerful wind generator is the 3,000-kW 492-ft-tall turbine, built by Grosse Wind energie-Anlage, which was set up in 1982 on the Friesian coast of W Germany. A $10.5-million 3,000-kW aero generator with 196-ft-10-in blades on Burgar Hill, Evie, Orkney Islands, is planned for completion by Taylor Woodrow in 1986. It should yield 9 million kW/hours per year.

The largest conventional windmill is the £11.2 million GEC MOD-5A installation on the north shore of Oahu, Hawaii, which will produce 7,300 kW when the wind reaches 32 mph with 400-ft rotors. Installation started in Mar 1984.

Atomic Power

The first atomic pile was built in an abandoned squash court at the University of Chicago. It "went critical" at 3:25 P.M. on Dec 2, 1942. The largest atomic power station is the one in Fukushima, Japan, having 9 reactors giving 7,747 MW.

The largest single nuclear reactor is the 1,450-MW (net) reactor at the Ignalina station, Lithuania, USSR, put on full power in Jan 1984. The largest under construction is the CHOOZ-B1 reactor in France which is scheduled for operation in 1991 and will have a net capacity of 1,457 MW.

Tokamak-7, the prototype thermonuclear reactor was declared in January 1982 by USSR academician Velikhov to be operating "reliably

NEW GIANT POWER STATION: The Itaipu plant on the Brazil-Paraguay border began generating a record 12,600,000 KW from 18 turbines in 1984.

SOLAR ONE: What looks like a field of mirrors is actually a field of mirrors. To create a solar power plant that yields 10 million watts, 1,818 mirrors had to be strategically placed to reflect the Calif sun. Total cost: $141 million. (*Franklin Berger*)

for months on end." The world's largest experimental station is the Joint European Torus at Culham, Oxfordshire, Eng, built in 1979–84.

Largest Power Plant

Currently, the most powerful installed power station is the Grand Coulee, Wash, with 9.7 million kilowatt hours (ultimately 10,080 MW), which began operating in 1942.

The $11-billion Itaipu project on the Paraná River on the Brazil-Paraguay border began generating power formally on Oct 25, 1984 and will by 1988–89 attain 12,600,000 KW from 18 turbines. Construction began in 1975 with a force reaching 28,000 workers.

A 20,000-MW power station project on the Tunguska River, USSR, was announced in Feb 1982.

The largest coal-fired power complex at Ekibastuz, Kazakhstan, USSR, began generating in May 1982.

Solar Power Plant

The largest solar furnace is the $141-million 10-MW "Solar I," 12 miles southeast of Barstow, Calif, first tested in Apr 1982. It comprises 1,818 mirrors in concentric circles focused on a boiler atop a 255-ft high tower. Sunlight from 222 heliostats is concentrated on a target 114 ft up in the power tower.

The $30-million thermal solar energy system at Pakerland Packing Co, Green Bay, Wis, completed in Jan 1984, comprises 9,750 4×8 ft collectors covering 7.16 acres. It will yield up to 8,000 million BTU's a month.

Largest Generator

Generators in the 2,000,000 kW (or 2,000 MW) range are now in the planning stages both in the UK and the US. The largest operational turbo-generator is 1,450 MW being installed at the Ignalina Atomic Power Station in Lithuania and is now in operation. (See p. 234.)

Biggest Blackout

The greatest power failure in history struck 7 northeastern US states and Ontario, Canada, Nov 9–10, 1965. About 30 million people in 80,000 sq mi were plunged into darkness. Two people were killed. In NYC the power failed at 5:27 P.M. on Nov 9, and was not fully restored for 13½ hours. The total losses resulting from another NYC power failure, on July 13, 1977, which lasted for 52 min, but as long as 25 hours in some areas, have been estimated at $1 billion, including losses due to looting.

Tidal Power Station

The first major tidal power station is the *Usine marèmotrice de la Rance,* officially opened on Nov 26, 1966 at the Rance estuary in the Golfe de St Malo, Brittany, France. Built in 5 years, at a cost of $75,600,000, it has a net annual output of 544 million kW/h. The 880-yd barrage contains 24 turbo-alternators.

A $46 million pilot Annapolis River project for the Bay of Fundy, Nova Scotia, Canada, was begun in 1981.

The $1,000 million Passamaquoddy project for the Bay of Fundy, Maine and New Brunswick remains a project.

Biggest Boiler

The largest boilers ever designed are those ordered in the US from the

Babcock & Wilcox Co with a capacity of 1,330 MW, so involving the evaporation of 9,330,000 lb of steam per hour.

Longest-Lasting Battery

The zinc foil and sulfur dry pile batteries made by Watlin and Hill of London in 1840 have powered ceaseless tintinnabulation inside a bell jar at the Clarendon Laboratory, Oxford since 1840.

Largest Turbines

The largest hydraulic turbines are those rated at 815,000 kW (equivalent to 1.1 million hp), 32 ft in diameter, with a 449-ton runner and a 350-ton shaft, installed by Allis-Chalmers at the Grand Coulee "Third Powerplant" in Wash.

The largest reversible pump-turbine is that made by Allis-Chalmers for the Bath County Project, Va. It has a maximum rating of 457 MW as a turbine and maximum operating head of 1,289 ft. The impeller/runner diameter is 20 ft 9 in with a synchronous speed of 257.1 rpm.

---

6. ENGINEERING

The earliest machinery still in use is the *dâlu*—a water-raising instrument known to have been in use in the Sumerian civilization which originated *c.* 3500 BC in Lower Iraq—even earlier than the *Saqiyas* of the Nile.

Largest Blast Furnace

The largest blast furnace is one with an inner volume of 179,040 cu ft and a 48-ft 6½-in diameter hearth at the Oita Works, Kyushu, Japan, completed in Oct 1976, with an annual capacity of 4,905,600 tons.

Highest Cable Cars

The highest and longest aerial ropeway is the Teleférico Mérida (Mérida téléphérique) in Venezuela, from Mérida City (5,379 ft) to the summit of Pico Espejo (15,629 ft), a rise of 10,250 ft. The ropeway is in four sections, involving 3 car changes in the 8-mile ascent in one hour. The fourth span is 10,070 ft in length. The two cars work on the pendulum system—the carrier rope is locked and the cars are hauled by means of three pull ropes powered by a 230-hp motor. They have a maximum capacity of 45 persons and travel at 32 ft per sec (21.8 mph).

The longest single-span ropeway is the 13,500-ft-long span from the Coachella Valley to Mt San Jacinto (10,821 ft), Calif opened Sept 12, 1963.

Largest Cat Cracker

The largest catalytic cracker is the Exxon Co's Bayway Refinery plant at Linden, NJ with a fresh feed rate of 5,040,000 gallons per day.

Longest Conveyor Belt

The longest single-flight conveyor belt is one of 18 miles in W Australia by Cable Belt Ltd of England.

The longest multi-flight conveyor is one of 62 miles between the phosphate mine near Bucraa and the Atlantic port of El Aaiun, Morocco, built by Krupp and completed in 1972. It has 11 flights of between 5.6 and 6.8 miles in length and was driven at 10.06 mph, but has been closed down due to Polisario Front guerrilla activity.

The longest conveyor belt is the Compagnie Minière de l'Ogooué installation built in 1959–62 at the Moanda manganese mine in Gabon which extends 47.2 miles. It has 858 towers and 2,800 buckets with 96.3 miles of wire rope running over 6,000 idler pulleys.

Most Powerful Cranes

The most powerful cranes are those aboard the semi-submersible vessel *Balder* operated by Heerema Marine Contractors, Switzerland. It has one 3,000 and one 2,000 ton capacity crane which, working in tandem, can raise a 5,000 ton piece. Its capacity has now been raised to close to 6,600 tons.

Brown & Root (US) announced the building of a 150,000-ton crane-ship with lifting capacity of more than 7,000 tons in Dec 1983.

The 92.3-ft-wide Rahco (R. A. Hanson Disc Ltd.) gantry crane at the Grand Coulee Dam Third Powerplant was tested to lift a load of 2,500 tons in 1975. It successfully lowered a 3,944,000-lb generator rotor with an accuracy of 1/32 in.

The tallest mobile crane is the 890-ton Rosenkranz K10001 with a lifting capacity of 1,100 tons and a combined boom and jib height of 663 ft. It is carried on 10 trucks, each limited to 75 ft 8 in and an axle weight of 130 tons. It can lift 33.6 tons to a height of 525 ft.

Dragline Excavators

The Ural Engineering Works at Ordzhonikidze, USSR, completed in March 1962, has a dragline known as the ES-25(100) with a boom of 328 ft and a bucket with a capacity of 31.5 cu yd. The largest walking dragline (and also the largest automotive land vehicle) is "Big Muskie," the Bucyrus-Erie 4,250W with an all-up weight of 13,440 tons and a bucket capacity of 220 cu yd on a 310-ft boom. This, the largest mobile land machine, is now operating on the Central Ohio Coal Co's Muskingum site in Ohio.

HIGHEST CABLE ROPEWAY: The Teleférico Mérida in Venezuela is also the longest. It rises 5,379 ft to the summit of Pico Espejo at 15,629 ft above sea level. The cable car ride takes an hour. (*South American Pictures*)

LARGEST FORK LIFT: Manufactured by Kalmar LMV of Sweden, this monster is shown lifting a load of 80 metric tonnes. (*J. Barnes*)

Fastest Passenger Elevators

Graham Coates (UK) established an involuntary duration record when trapped in an elevator for 62 hours in Brighton, Eng, May 24–26, 1986.

The fastest domestic passenger elevators are the express elevators to the 60th floor of the 787.4-ft-tall "Sunshine 60" building, Ikebukuro, Tokyo, Japan, completed Apr 5, 1978. They were built by Mitsubishi Corp and operate at a speed of 2,000 ft per min, or 22.72 mph.

Much higher speeds are achieved in the winding cages of mine shafts. A hoisting shaft 6,800 ft deep, owned by Western Deep Levels Ltd in South Africa, winds at speeds of up to 40.9 mph (3,595 ft per min). Descending at a speed of even 10 mph causes "otisitis" (popping of the ears).

First and Longest Escalators

The name "escalator" was registered in the US on May 28, 1900, but the earliest "Inclined Elevator" was installed by Jesse W. Reno on the pier at Coney Island, NYC in 1896.

The longest escalators on the Leningrad Underground, USSR, at Lenin Square, have 729 steps and a vertical rise of 195 ft 9½ in.

The longest "moving sidewalks" are those installed in 1970 in the Neue Messe Centre, Düsseldorf, W Germany, which measure 738 ft between comb plates.

Largest Excavator

The largest excavator is the 14,325-ton bucket wheel excavator being assembled at the open-cast lignite mine of Hambach, W Germany with a

MOVING STAIRWAY TO THE STARS: (Left) In 4 stages outdoors at Ocean Park, Hong Kong, this escalator has an overall length of 745 ft, rising 377 ft from bottom to top. (Below) The luxurious covered stairs can carry 4,000 passengers in either direction at the same time, making it the longest and largest escalator ride ever built.

rating of 260,000 cu yd per 20-hour working day. It is 690 ft in length and 269 ft tall. The wheel is 222 ft in circumference with 6.5-cu-yd buckets.

Largest Forging

The largest forging on record is a generator shaft 55 ft long weighing 450,600 lb forged by Bethlehem Steel in Oct 1973 for Japan.

Largest Fork-Lift Truck

Kalmar LMV of Sweden manufactured in 1985 10 counter-balanced fork-lift trucks capable of lifting loads up to 88.4 tons at a load center of 90.5 in. They were built to handle the large diameter pipeline in the Libyan "Great Man-Made River Project."

Largest Lathe

The largest lathe is the 126-ft long 458.6-ton giant lathe built by Waldrich Siegen of Germany in 1973 for the South African Electricity Supply Commission at Rosherville. It has a capacity for 330-ton work pieces and a swing-over bed 16 ft 5 in in diameter.

Greatest Lifting Operation

The heaviest lifting operation in engineering history was of the 41,000-ton roof of the Velodrome in Montreal, Canada, in 1975. It was raised some 4 in by jacks to strike its centering.

Largest Nuts

The largest nuts ever made weigh 11,713.5 lb each and have an outside diameter of 52 in and a 25-in thread. Known as "Pilgrim Nuts," they are manufactured by Doncasters Moorside Ltd of Oldham, England, for use on the columns of a large forging press.

Largest Oil Tanks

The largest oil tanks ever constructed are the five Aramco 1½ million-barrel capacity storage tanks at Ju'aymah, Saudi Arabia. The tanks are 72 ft tall with a diameter of 386 ft and were completed Mar 1980.

Longest Pipelines

The longest crude oil pipeline is the Interprovincial Pipe Line Co's installation from Edmonton, Alberta, Canada, to Buffalo, NY, a distance of 1,775 miles. Along the length of the pipe 13 pumping stations maintain a flow of 8,280,000 gallons of oil per day.

The eventual length of the Trans-Siberian Pipeline will be 2,319 miles, running from Tuimazy through Omsk and Novosibirsk to Irkutsk. The first 30-mile section was opened in July 1957.

The world's most expensive pipeline is the Alaska pipeline running 798 miles from Prudhoe Bay to Valdez. By completion of the first phase in 1977 it had cost at least $6,000 million. The pipe is 48 in in diameter and will eventually carry up to 2 million barrels of crude oil per day.

The longest submarine pipeline is that of 264 miles for natural gas from the Union Oil Platform to Rayong, Thailand, opened on Sept 12, 1981.

The longest natural gas pipeline is the Trans-Canada Pipeline which by 1974 had 5,654 miles of pipe up to 42 in in diameter. The Tyumen-Chelyabinsk-Moscow-Brandenburg gasline stretches 2,690 miles.

The longest water pipeline runs a distance of 350 miles to the Kalgoorlie gold fields from near Perth, W Australia. Engineered in 1903, the system has since been extended five-fold by branches.

The large caliber Urengoi-Uzhgovod line to W Europe begun in Nov 1982 stretched 2,765 mi when completed on July 25, 1983. It has a capacity of 42,000 million cu yd per year.

Largest Press

The two most powerful production machines are forging presses in the US. The Loewy closed-die forging press, in a plant leased from the US Air Force by the Wyman-Gordon Co at North Grafton, Mass weighs 10,600 tons and stands 114 ft 2 in high, of which 66 ft is sunk below the operating floor. It has a rated capacity of 50,000 tons, and went into operation in Oct 1955. The other similar press is at the Aluminum Company of America in Cleveland.

There has been a report of a press in the USSR with a capacity of 83,025 tons at Novo Kramatorsk. The Bêché and Grohs counterblow forging hammer, manufactured in W Germany, is rated at 66,000 tons.

Fastest Printer or Typesetting Machine

The fastest printer is the Radiation Inc electrosensitive system at the Lawrence Radiation Laboratory, Livermore, Calif. High speed recording of up to 30,000 lines per min each containing 120 alphanumeric characters is attained by controlling electronic pulses through chemically impregnated recording paper which is rapidly moving under closely spaced fixed styli. It can thus print the wordage of the whole Bible (773,692 words) in 65 sec—3,333 times as fast as the world's fastest human typist.

Largest Radar Installations

The largest of the three installations in the US Ballistic Missile Early Warning System (BMEWS) is the one near Thule, Greenland 931 miles from the North Pole, completed in 1960 at a cost of $500 million. Its sister stations are at Cape Clear, Alaska, completed in July 1961, and a $115 million installation at Fylingdales Moor, North Yorkshire, England completed in June 1963. The largest scientific radar installation is the 21-acre ground array at Jicamarca, Peru.

Largest Transformer

The largest single-phase transformers are rated at 1,500,000 kV of which 8 are in service with the American Electric Power Service Corporation. Of these, 5 step down from 765 to 345 kV.

Longest and Highest Transmission Lines

The longest span between pylons of any power line is that across the Sogne Fjord, Norway, between Rabnaberg and Fatlaberg. Erected in 1955 by the Whitecross Co Ltd of Warrington, England as part of the high-tension power cable from Refsdal power station at Vik, it has a span of 16,040 ft and a weight of 13 tons. In 1967, two further high-tensile steel/aluminum lines 16,006 ft long, and weighing 37 tons, manufactured by Whitecross and British Insulated Callender's Cables Ltd, were erected here.

The highest power lines are those across the Straits of Messina, with towers of 675 ft (Sicily side) and 735 ft (Calabria) and 11,900 ft apart.

The highest voltages now carried are 1,330,000 volts on the DC Pacific Inter-tie in the US for a distance of 1,224 miles. The Ekibastuz DC transmission lines in Kazakhstan, USSR, are planned to be 1,490 miles long with a 1,500,000-volt capacity.

Largest Valve

The largest valve is the 32-ft diameter 190-ton butterfly valve designed by Boving & Co Ltd of London for use at the Arnold Air Force Base engine test facility in Tennessee.

Longest and Strongest Wire Rope

The longest wire ropes are the 4 made at British Ropes Ltd, Wallsend, Tyneside, England, each measuring 14.9 miles. The ropes are 35 mm in diameter, weigh 120 tons each and were ordered for use in the construction of the 2,000 MW cross-Channel power cable.

The thickest ever made are spliced crane strops 11¼ in thick, made of 2,392 individual wires in March 1979 by British Ropes at Willington Quay, Tyneside, England, designed to lift loads of 3,000 tons.

The heaviest wire ropes (4 in number) are each of 130 metric tons, made for the twin-shaft system of Western Deep Levels Gold Mine, S Africa.

TIMEPIECES

Oldest Clocks

The earliest mechanical clock, that is, one with an escapement, was completed in China in 725 AD by I Hsing and Liang Ling-tsan.

The oldest surviving working clock is the faceless clock dating from 1386, or possibly earlier, at Salisbury Cathedral, Wiltshire, England, which was restored in 1956 having struck the hours for 498 years and ticked more than 500 million times. Earlier dates, ranging back to *c.* 1335, have been attributed to the weight-driven clock in Wells Cathedral, Somerset, England, but only the iron frame is original. A model of Giovanni de Dondi's heptagonal astronomical clock of 1348–64 was completed in 1962.

Largest Clock

The most massive clock is the Astronomical Clock in the Cathedral of St Pierre, Beauvais, France, constructed between 1865 and 1868. It contains 90,000 parts and measures 40 ft high, 20 ft wide and 9 ft deep. The Su Sung clock, built in China at K'aifeng in 1088–92, had a 22-ton bronze armillary sphere for 1⅔ tons of water. It was removed to Peking in 1126 and was last known to be working in its 40-ft-high tower in 1136.

The largest clockface is in the floral clock at Tokachigaoka Park, Otofuke, Hokkaido, Japan, completed on Aug 1, 1982 with a diameter of 59 ft 0.⅝-in.

Public Clocks

The largest four-faced clock is that on the building of the Allen-Bradley Co of Milwaukee, Wis. Each face has a diameter of 40 ft 3½ in with a minute hand 20 ft in overall length.

The largest single-faced clock is the octagonal Colgate clock on the Hudson River shore in Jersey City, NJ, which has a 50-ft diameter and a minute hand 27 ft 3 in in length.

The tallest four-faced clock is on the Williamsburgh Savings Bank, Brooklyn, NYC. It is 430 ft above street level.

Most Accurate Time Measurer

The most accurate time-keeping devices are the twin atomic hydrogen masers installed in 1964 in the US Naval Research Laboratory, Washington, DC. They are based on the frequency of the hydrogen atom's transition period of 1,420,450,751,694 cycles per sec. This enables an accuracy to within one sec in 1,700,000 years.

Most Accurate Clock

The most accurate and complicated clockwork is the Olsen clock, installed in the Copenhagen Town Hall, Denmark. The clock, which has

LARGEST CLOCK: The single-faced Colgate clock on the Hudson river shoreline in Jersey City, NJ, has a 50-ft diameter and a minute hand 27 ft 3 in long. (*Colgate-Palmolive Co.*)

LARGEST CLOCK FACE: This floral clock in Hokkaido, Japan has a face of more than 59 ft in diameter.

more than 14,000 units, took 10 years to make and the mechanism of the clock functions in 570,000 different ways. The celestial pole motion of the clock will take 25,753 years to complete a full circle, the slowest moving designed mechanism in the world. The clock is accurate to 0.5 sec in 300 years—50 times more accurate than the previous record.

Most Expensive Clock

The Thomas Tompion (1639–1713) English-made bracket clock, which sold at auction at Christie's, London, for £110,000 on June 2, 1980, was bought by the British Museum in a private sale for £500,000 (approx. $750,000) on July 15, 1982.

Longest Pendulum

The longest pendulum is 73 ft 9¾ in on the water-mill clock installed by Hattori Tokeiten Co. in the Shinjuku NS Building, Tokyo, Japan, in 1983.

Computers

A geared calculator dated c. 80 BC was found in the sea near Antikythera Island off northwest Crete in April 1900.

The earliest programmable electronic computer was the 1,500-valve Colossus. It was run in Dec 1943 at Bletchley Park, England, to break the German coding machine Enigma. It arose from a concept published in 1936 by Dr Alan Mathison Turing (1912–54). It was declassified on Oct 25, 1975.

The first stored-program computer was the Manchester University Mark I which incorporated the Williams storage cathode ray tube (pat. Dec 11, 1946). It ran its first program written by Prof Tom Kilburn (b 1921) for 52 min on June 21, 1948.

Computers were greatly advanced by the invention of the point-contact transistor by John Bardeen and Walter Brattain in July 1948, and the junction transistor by R. L. Wallace, Morgan Sparks and Dr William Shockley in early 1951.

The concept of the integrated circuit, which has enabled micro-miniaturization, was first published on May 7, 1952 by Geoffrey W. A. Dummer (b 1909) in Wash DC. The Microcomputer was achieved in 1969–73 by M. E. Hoff Jr of Intel Corporation with the production of the microprocessor silicon chip "4004."

The computer planned to be the world's biggest by a factor of 40 is the $50 million NASF (Numerical Aerodynamic Simulation Facility) at NASA's Ames Research Center, Palo Alto, Calif. The tenders from CDC and Burroughs called for a capacity of 12.8 gigaflops (12,800 million complex calculations per sec).

Most Powerful and Fastest Computer

The world's most powerful and fastest computer is the liquid-cooled Cray-2, named after Seymour R. Cray of Cray Research, Inc., Minneapolis. Its memory has a capacity of 256 million 64-bit words, resulting in a capacity of 32 million bytes of main memory. It attains speeds of 250 million floating point operations per sec. The cost of a mid-range system was quoted in Oct 1985 at $17 million.

Smallest Word Processor

The world's smallest word processor, the Easi-Text 1350, was introduced by Minimicro of Huntington, Eng, in Apr 1986. It is based on the

Sharp PC-1350 computer which measures 7.2 × 2.8 × 0.6 in and the entire system including an A4 size Epson P-80 printer fits into an executive briefcase.

Megabits

The megabit barrier was broken in Feb 1984, with the manufacture of a 1024K bit integrated circuit, the size of a drawing pin head and as thin as a human hair, by 4 Japanese companies, Hitachi, NEC, NTT Atsugi Electrical Communications and Toshiba. Toshiba announced that manufacture of an 80 picosecond LSI (large scale integration) chip of gallium arsenide would start in 1985–86.

IBM had announced the first 512K bit 120 nanosecond dynamic access memory chip ⅜ in square from Essex Junction, Vt, on Sept 15, 1983.

Oldest Watch

The oldest watch (portable clockwork timekeeper) is one made of iron by Peter Henlein in Nürnberg, Bavaria, Germany, c. 1504. The earliest wristwatches were those of Jacquet-Droz and Leschot of Geneva, Switzerland, dating from 1790.

Longest Watch

A facsimile Swatch watch was made for demonstration and draped from the roof of the Comme Bank building, Frankfurt, W Germany in Dec 1985. It was 469 ft long, weighed 14.3 tons, and had a face 54 ft in diameter including the case.

Smallest and Thinnest Watch

The smallest watches are produced by Jaeger Le Coultre of Switzerland. Equipped with a 15-jeweled movement, they measure just over ½ in in length and 3/16th in in width. The movement, with its case, weighs under ¼ oz.

The thinnest wristwatch is the Swiss Concord Delirium IV which measures 0.039 in (0.98 mm) in thickness and retailed for $16,000 in June 1980 with an 18-carat gold bracelet.

Most Expensive Watches

Excluding watches with jeweled cases, the most expensive standard men's pocket watch is the Swiss *Grande Complication* by Audemars-Piguet, which retailed for $100,000 in Jan 1985.

The *Kallista* watch with 130 carats of precious stones by Vacheron et Constantin of Geneva, Switzerland was valued in Apr 1981 at $5 million.

The record price for an antique watch is $1,005,375 paid at Christie's, Geneva, Switzerland on May 13, 1986 by a European collector for a gold-enameled and diamond-set pocket watch with a movement from c. 1650, by the Parisian maker Jehan Cremfdorff. At the same auction, $153,750 was paid for a 1955 Patek Philippe wristwatch, one of only three. It includes a perpetual calendar and records the phases of the moon.

Largest Sundial

The largest sundial is one with a 28-ft-4-in gnomon (column) and a vertical height of 17 ft 1 in, dedicated on Oct 10, 1913 in San Francisco.

Chapter 9

The Business World

In this chapter, the pound sterling has been converted, unless otherwise noted, at an average exchange rate of £1 = $2.20 for 1979, $2.30 for 1980, $1.80 for 1981, $1.56 for 1982, $1.50 for 1983, $1.40 for 1984 and early 1985, $1.50 for late 1985 and 1986, and at the prevailing exchange rates for earlier years.

1. COMMERCE

Greatest Assets

The business with the greatest amount in physical assets has been the Bell System, which comprised the American Telephone and Telegraph Company, and its subsidiaries. The Bell System's total assets on the consolidated balance sheet at the time of its divestiture and breakup into 8 companies on Dec 31, 1983 reached $149,529 million. The plant included more than 142 million telephones. The number of employees was 1,036,000. The company's market value of $47,989 million was held among 3,055,000 shareholders. A total of 20,109 shareholders had attended the Annual Meeting in Apr 1961, thereby setting a world record.

Currently the largest assets of any corporation are $69,160 million by the Exxon Corporation, the world's largest oil company, on Jan 1, 1986. It has 146,000 employees. The first company to have assets in excess of $1 billion was the United States Steel Corporation with $1,400 million at the time of its creation by merger in 1917.

Greatest Sales

The first company to surpass $1 billion in annual sales was the US Steel Corporation in 1917. Now there are 570 corporations with sales exceeding $1 billion including 272 from the US. The *Fortune 500 List* of Apr 1986 is headed by General Motors Corp of Detroit with $96,371,700,000 for 1985.

Greatest Profit and Loss

The greatest net profit made by any corporation in 12 months is $7,647 million by American Telephone and Telegraph Co, Oct 1, 1981–Sept 30, 1982.

The greatest loss ever recorded is also by AT&T, which lost $4,900 million in the fourth quarter of 1983 immediately after the breakup of the monopoly, when losses had to be taken on a one-time basis.

The Argentine government-owned Petroleum Company (YPF) is reported to have lost $4,643,995,000 in 1983.

Greatest Bankruptcy

William G. Stern (b Hungary, 1936), of Golders Green, north London, England, a US citizen since 1957, who set up Welstar Group Holding Co in the London property market in 1971, was declared bankrupt for $229,480,345 in Feb 1979. This figure rose to $314,875,000 by Feb 1983. He was discharged for $600,000, suspended for 2½ years on Mar 28, 1983.

Esal Commodities declared it was in debt for a record £170 million ($238 million) in London on Jan 18, 1985. In connection with this, Rajendra Sethia (b 1950) was arrested in New Delhi, India, on Mar 2, 1985, on charges including criminal conspiracy and forgery and was declared bankrupt as well by the High Court in London. His personal debts were estimated at £140 million ($196 million).

Largest Employer

The world's largest employer is Indian Railways with 1,600,000 staff in 1984.

Largest Write-Off

The largest reduction of assets in the history of private enterprise was the $800 million write-off of Tristar aircraft development costs by Lockheed announced Nov 23, 1974.

Largest Jury Award

A Texas jury on Dec 10, 1985 awarded the Pennzoil Company of Texas $11.12 billion in a suit against Texaco, headquartered in White Plains, NY, for improperly enticing the Getty Oil Co to back out of a merger with Texaco in 1984.

Greatest Barter Deal

The biggest barter in trading history was 36 million barrels of oil valued at $10,800,000,000 given by the Royal Saudi Airline for 10 Boeing 747 airliners in July 1984.

Largest Take-Overs

The largest corporate take-over agreement in commercial history is by Chevron (formerly Standard Oil Co of California) which on June 15, 1984 bought Gulf Oil Corp for $13,231,253,000. The fees of the financial intermediaries were estimated by *Fortune* to be $63.9 million.

The greatest auction in the corporate world was the purchase of Hughes Aircraft Co by General Motors Corp for $5,000 million on June 5, 1985.

Accountants

The largest firm of accountants worldwide is Arthur Andersen & Co, with 1985 revenues of $1,574 million, of which $1,182 million was in the US.

Advertising Agency

The largest advertising agency is Saatchi & Saatchi/Compton Ltd of London, following their acquisition of the US agency, Ted Bates Worldwide, announced on May 12, 1986. *Advertising Age* lists the new group's billings at about $7,500 million.

Biggest Advertiser

The biggest advertiser is Sears Roebuck and Co with $975.3 million spent in 1985, excluding its catalogue.

Aerospace Company

The largest in the field is United Technologies of Hartford, Conn, with 1984 sales of $16,331,757,000 and assets of $9,904 million. The work force numbers 205,000.

Cessna Aircraft Co of Wichita, Kans had total sales of $718.1 million in 1985. The company holds the record for producing 176,300 aircraft since Clyde Cessna's first was built in 1911.

Largest Airlines

The largest airline is the USSR State airline "Aeroflot," so named since 1932. This was instituted on Feb 9, 1923, with the title of Civil Air Fleet of the Council of Ministers of the USSR, abbreviated to "Dobrolet." It operates 1,300 aircraft over about 560,000 miles of routes, employs 500,000 people and carried 106 million passengers to 97 countries in 1981. Most luggage is "self-handled," and smoking is allowed only after 4 hours flying.

The commercial airline carrying the greatest number of passengers was United Airlines, based in Chicago, which carried 38,113,000 passengers in 1985, down from 41,273,000 in 1984. The line has 357 planes operating, and more than 55,000 employees.

Aluminum Producer

The largest producer of primary aluminum is Alcan Aluminium Ltd of Montreal, Canada with its affiliated companies. It had an output of 2,445,345 tons in 1985.

Art Auctioneering

The largest and oldest firm of art auctioneers is the Sotheby Parke Bernet Group of London and New York, founded in 1744. The turnover in 1984–85 was $678.7 million. The highest total for any house sale auction was theirs on May 18–27, 1977, at the 6th Earl of Rosebery's home at Mentmore, Buckinghamshire, England, which reached £6,389,933 ($10,900,000). The government had turned down an offer of £2 million.

The highest total sale of fine art is $39,286,500 on May 14, 1985. This sale of Impressionist and modern paintings saw 11 works selling for over $1 million each at the NYC galleries of Sotheby's.

Bookstores

The bookshop with the most titles and the longest shelving (30 miles of it) is W. & G. Foyle Ltd of London. First established in 1904 in a small shop in Islington, the company is now at 119–125 Charing Cross Road. On one site, the area is 75,825 sq ft.

The most capacious individual bookstore measured by square footage is Barnes & Noble Bookstore on Fifth Avenue at 18th Street, NYC, with 154,250 sq ft and 12.87 miles of shelving.

Breweries

The largest single brewing organization is Anheuser-Busch, Inc based

FIRST 5 & 10: Frank W. Woolworth
got a big start in this shop in Lancaster, Pa.

in St Louis, with 11 breweries in the US. In 1985 the company sold 68,000,000 US barrels, the greatest annual volume ever produced by a brewing company. The company's St Louis plant covers 100 acres and after completion of current modernization will have an annual capacity in excess of 13,000,000 US barrels.

The largest brewery on a single site is Adolph Coors Co of Golden, Colo, where 14,738,000 barrels were sold in 1985.

Car Manufacturer

In 1980, Japan with 11,043,000 vehicles overtook the US as the world's No. 1 motor car manufacturer.

The largest car manufacturer and largest manufacturing company in the world is General Motors Corp of Detroit. During the year 1985, worldwide sales totaled $96,371,700,000. Its assets on Dec 31, 1985, were valued at $63,832,800,000, and there were 811,000 employees.

The largest single automobile plant is the Volkswagenwerk, Wolfsburg, W Germany, with 58,000 employees and a capacity of 4,056 vehicles daily. The surface area of the factory buildings is 371 acres and that of the whole plant, with 43.5 miles of rail sidings, is 4,892 acres.

Chain Store

F. W. Woolworth, which celebrated its centenary year in 1979, now operates the largest chain—5,822 stores worldwide. Frank W. Woolworth, with an idea that he could sell merchandise for a nickel, rented a counter in an already existent Watertown, NY, general store in 1878. Then he opened his first "Five Cent Store" in Utica, NY on Feb 22, 1879. This failed after 6 months. Next he opened a "Five Cent Store" in Lancaster, Pa, which soon became a "5-&-10¢ Store." This succeeded. The 1985 income from continuing operations was $177 million.

Chocolate Factory

The largest chocolate and confectionary factory is that built by Hershey Foods Corp of Hershey, Pa in 1903–05. It now has 2 million sq ft of floor space.

Computer Company

The largest computer firm is International Business Machines Corp (IBM) which had assets in Dec 1985 of $52,634 million and gross income of $50,056 million. In 1979 it made the largest borrowing in corporate history with $1 billion. Its worldwide employees numbered 394,930. There are about 792,506 shareholders.

Largest Department Store

The largest single store is R. H. Macy & Co Inc at Broadway and 34th St, NYC. It has a floor space of 2,151,000 sq ft, and 12,000 employees who handle 400,000 items. The sales of the company and its subsidiaries in 1984–85 were $4,368,386,000. Mr. Rowland Hussey Macy's sales on his first day at his fancy goods store on 6th Avenue, Oct 27, 1858, were recorded as $11.06.

The department store with the fastest moving merchandise is the Marks & Spencer store at Marble Arch, London, where £1,600 ($2,400) worth of goods per sq ft of selling space per year is believed to be an understatement.

Distillery

The largest distilling company is The Seagram Company Ltd of Canada. Its sales in the year ending Jan 31, 1986 totaled $2,970,669,000. The group employs about 14,300 people, including about 5,000 in the U.S.

Fishery

With a single throw of the net, 120 million fish were caught by the Norwegian boat M/S *Flomann* in the Barents Sea, Aug 28, 1983. The catch weighed 2,724 tons.

General Merchandise at Retail

The largest general merchandising retailer is Sears Roebuck and Co of Chicago (founded by Richard Warren Sears in the North Redwood railroad station in Minnesota in 1886). Worldwide revenues, including its consumer and financial subsidiaries, were $40,715 million in the year ending Dec 31, 1985. It had 799 retail stores and 2,361 catalogue merchants. The corporation's total assets were valued at $66,417 million.

Grocery Store Chain

The largest grocery chain is Safeway Stores Inc of Oakland, Calif with sales in 1985 amounting to $19,650,542,000 and assets of $2,026,481,000, on Dec 28, 1985 with 2,365 stores and 164,385 employees.

Hotels

The top revenue-earning hotel business is Holiday Inns hotel system with 1985 revenues of $5,900 million from 1,688 hotels (317,628 rooms) in 53 countries at Dec 31, 1985. The business was founded by Charles Kemmons Wilson with his first inn on Summer Avenue in Memphis, Tenn in 1952.

Insurance

The largest life insurance policy ever written was one for $44 million for a Calgary land developer, Victor T. Uy, in Feb 1982 by Transamerica Occidental Life Insurance Co of California. The salesman was local manager Lorenzo F. Reyes.

Linda Mullendore, wife of a murdered Oklahoma rancher, received some $18 million as of Nov 14, 1970, the largest pay-out on a single life. Her husband had paid $300,000 in premiums in 1969.

Insurance Companies and Losses

The company with the highest volume of insurance in force is the Prudential Insurance Company of America of Newark, NJ with $580.9 billion at Dec 31, 1985, which is more than 2½ times the National Debt figure of the United Kingdom. Consolidated assets are $115.7 billion.

The largest single association is the Blue Cross, the medical insurance organization, with a membership of about 77,496,584 on Sept 30, 1985. Benefits paid out in 1985 totaled $37,862 million.

The largest marine insurance loss was $82 million for the self-propelled semi-submersible drilling platform Ocean Ranger (14,914 tons gross) built for Ocean Drilling & Exploration Co of New Orleans in 1976. On Feb 15, 1982 she was lost with 84 lives in the Hibernia Field, off Newfoundland.

The largest sum claimed for consequential losses is $1,700 million against owning, operating and building corporations, and Claude Phillips, resulting from the 66-million-gallon oil spill from M. T. *Amoco Cadiz* on the Brittany coast on Mar 16, 1978.

Mineral Water

The largest mineral water firm is Source Perrier, near Nimes, France

LARGEST INSURANCE CLAIM: Like a beached whale, the oil tanker "Amoco Cadiz" went down off France in 1978. Oil, 66 million gallons of it, spilled on the Brittany coast, and the claim for consequential losses was filed for $1.7 billion against the owners, operators and shipbuilders. (*Colorific*)

with an annual production of more than 2.3 billion bottles, of which 1.3 billion now come from Perrier and Contrexeville. The French drink about 60 liters (63½ qts) of mineral water per person per year.

Oil Refinery

The world's largest refinery has been the Amerada Hess refinery at St Croix, Virgin Islands, with an annual capacity of 30,900,000 tons.

Paper Company

The largest company in paper, fiber and wood products is Georgia-Pacific of Atlanta, with 1985 sales of $6,716 million, and 40,000 workers.

Pharmaceutical Company

The largest company marketing pharmaceuticals and health care products, Johnson & Johnson of New Brunswick, NJ, had 1985 sales of $6,421,300,000.

Photographic Store

The photographic store with the largest selling area is Jessop of Leicester Ltd's Photo Centre, Hinckley Road, Leicester, England which opened in June 1979 with an area of 27,000 sq ft.

Public Relations

The largest public relations firm is Burton-Marsteller of NYC, a unit of Young & Rubicam, whose net fee income for 1985 was $104,667,000. Hill & Knowlton Inc have most offices worldwide with 56, including one in Beijing, China.

Publishing

The publishing company generating most net revenue is Time Inc of NYC, with $3,404 million in 1985. The largest educational book publishing concern in the world is the Book Division of McGraw-Hill Inc of NYC, with sales of $460,222,000 in 1985, with 1,300 new books and educational products.

Restaurants

The largest restaurant chain is McDonald's Corp in Oakbrook, Ill, founded Apr 15, 1955, in Des Plaines, a suburb of Chicago, by Ray A. Kroc (1903–84), BH (Bachelor of Hamburgerology). By Dec 31, 1985, the number of restaurants licensed and owned in 41 countries and territories reached 8,901 with an aggregate output of 55 billion 100% beef hamburgers. Sales systemwide in 1985 surpassed $11 billion.

Shipbuilding

In 1985, there were 18,156,526 gross tons of ships, excluding sailing ships, barges, and vessels of less than 100 gross tons, completed throughout the world. The figures for Rumania and the People's Republic of China are incomplete. Japan completed 9,502,831 gross tons (52.34% of the world's total).

The leading shipbuilding firm in 1985 was Hyundai of S Korea which completed 44 vessels of 1,385,607 gross tons.

Shipping Line

The largest shipping owners and operators are the Exxon Corporation, whose fleets of owned/managed and chartered tankers in 1985 totaled a daily average of 12,700,000 deadweight tons.

Shopping Centers

The largest shopping center is the $900 million W Edmonton Mall, Alberta, Canada, first opened on Sept 15, 1981 and completed 4 years later. It covers 5 million sq ft on 110 acres, encompasses 828 stores and services, as well as 6 major department stores. Parking is provided for 30,000 vehicles for more than 500,000 shoppers per week.

The world's first shopping center was Roland Park Shopping Center in Baltimore, Md, built in 1896.

The world's largest wholesale merchandise market is the Dallas Market Center, located on Stemmons Freeway, Dallas, Tex, with nearly 9.3 million sq ft in 8 buildings. The complex covers 150 acres with some 3,400 permanent showrooms displaying merchandise of more than 26,000 manufacturers. The center attracts 600,000 buyers each year to its 38 annual markets and trade shows.

Soft Drink Producer

The world's most popular soft drink is Coca-Cola with over 301 million sold per day by early 1985 in more than 155 countries. "Coke" was invented by Dr John S. Pemberton of Atlanta, Ga in 1886, the company was formed in 1892, and its famous bottle was patented in 1915. The secret "7X" formula was unchanged until 1985 when Coca-Cola had 21.7% of the $28 billion market to Pepsico's 18.8%.

Pepsico's overall 1985 sales of $8.47 billion were $340 million higher than Coca-Cola's in 1985.

Steel Company

The largest producer of steel has been Nippon Steel of Tokyo, which produced 31,487,400 tons of steel and steel products in 1985. The Fukuyama Works of Nippon Kokan has a capacity of more than 17 million tons per annum. Its work force is 76,000.

Sugar Mill

The highest recorded output for any sugar mill was set in 1966–67 by Ingenio de San Cristobal y Anexas, S.A. of Veracruz, Mexico, with 273,310 tons refined from 3,181,897 tons of cane ground.

The largest cane sugar plant is the California & Hawaii Sugar Co plant founded in 1906 at Crockett, Calif with an output of 8 million lb per day.

Tobacco Company

The largest tobacco company is the group of subsidiaries and affiliates of B.A.T. Industries (British-American Tobacco Co Ltd, founded in London in 1902). They operate 116 tobacco factories in 52 countries. Consolidated turnover in 1985 was $19,044 million and total assets were $13,260 million Dec 31, 1985. The Group's sales in 1985 topped 567,000 million cigarettes.

The largest cigarette plant is the $300 million Philip Morris plant at Richmond, Va, which opened in Oct 1974. It employs 5,500 people producing 530 million cigarettes a day.

Toy Store

The biggest toy store is Hamley's of Regent Street Ltd, founded in

London in 1760 in the Holborn area, and moved to Regent Street in 1901. It has selling space of 45,000 sq ft on 6 floors with over 300 employees during the Christmas season. It was taken over by Debenhams on May 12, 1976.

Undertaker (or Mortician)

The world's largest undertaking business is the SCI (Service Corporation International) with 279 funeral homes and 40 flower shops and limousine fleets with associated cemeteries. Their annual revenue in the most recession-proof of industries was $208,536,000 in the year ending Apr 30, 1983.

FINANCE

The oldest Stock Exchange of the 138 listed in the world is said to be that in Amsterdam, The Netherlands, founded in 1602. The stock exchange in Antwerp, Belgium, claims to have been established in 1531.

Largest Investment House

The largest securities company and once the world's largest partnership (124 partners before becoming a corporation in 1959), is Merrill Lynch, Pierce, Fenner & Smith, Inc of NYC (founded Jan 6, 1914). Its parent, Merrill Lynch & Co, has assets of $51.6 billion, 45,000 employees, 1,116 offices around the world, and 4.9 million customer accounts.

Highest Value Stock

The highest price quoted for a share of F. Hoffmann-La Roche of Basel, Switzerland, was 101,000 Swiss Fr (then $38,486) on Apr 23, 1976.

Highest Face Value of a Share

American Express Co, through Lehman Bros, underwriter, offered preferred stock at $500,000 per share on Aug 28, 1984.

Largest Reverse Stock Split

On June 7, 1982, Madison National Life Insurance Co of Middleton, Wis split its stock selling over-the-counter 20,000 to 1, specifically reducing authorized shares from 1,500,000 to 75 shares total.

Largest New Issue

The largest security offering in history was one of $1,375 million in American Telephone and Telegraph Co stock in a rights offer on 27,500,000 shares of convertible preferred stock on June 2, 1971.

Greatest Personal Loss and Gain

The highest recorded personal paper losses on stock values have been those of Ray A. Kroc, chairman of McDonald's Corp with $64,901,718 on July 8, 1974 and Edwin H. Land, president of Polaroid Corp with $59,397,355 May 28–29, 1974, when Polaroid stock closed $12.12 down at 43¼ on that day.

An investor who paid $375 in the morning of Dec 10, 1985 for an option on Pennzoil could have cashed it at the end of the same day for $10,250, for the fastest gain in history. The stock jumped from 19¾ to 83 that day.

New York Stock Exchange (NYSE) Records

The highest index figure on the Dow Jones average (instituted Oct 1896) of selected industrial stocks during a day's trading was 1,909.03 on July 2, 1986.

The record for a day's trading is 236,565,110 shares on Aug 3, 1984. The old record trading volume in a day on the NYSE of 16,410,030 shares on Oct 29, 1929, the "Black Tuesday" of the famous "crash," was not surpassed until the first 20-million-share day (20,410,000) was achieved on Apr 10, 1968, when the ticker tape fell 47 minutes behind.

The Dow Jones industrial average, which had hit a low of 381.71 on Sept 3, 1929, plunged 30.57 points on Oct 29, 1929, on its way to the Depression's lowest point of 41.22 on July 8, 1932. The largest decline in one day was 61.87 points on July 7, 1986.

The greatest paper loss in NYSE listed securities in a year was $209,957 million in 1974.

The record-setting daily increase of 28.40 on Oct 30, 1929, was most recently bettered on Nov 3, 1982, when the Dow Jones index increased 43.41 points.

The largest stock trade was a block of 48,788,800 shares of Navistar Intl Corp at $10 a share on Apr 10, 1986.

The value of stocks listed on the NYSE reached an all-time high $2,204,114,975,745 on Mar 31, 1986.

The greatest market value of a listed corporation was $32 billion for IBM at the end of 1985.

Largest Bank

The International Bank for Reconstruction and Development (founded Dec 27, 1945), the "World Bank" (a UN specialized agency) at 1818 H Street NW, Wash, DC, has an authorized share capital of $75 billion. There were 146 members with a subscribed capital of $58,000 million on June 30, 1985. The International Monetary Fund in Wash, DC, had 149 members with total quotas of SDR89,305.1 million ($1,000,861.2 million) as of Apr 1986.

The USSR State Bank was claimed by Tass to be the world's largest on Jan 15, 1983 incorporating "nearly 4,500 banking institutions within its single system." No asset figures were disclosed.

The commercial bank with the greatest assets is Citicorp of NYC with $173,597 million at Dec 31, 1985. The Barclays Bank group had some 5,300 branches and offices in over 75 countries in Dec 1985. The bank with the most branches is the State Bank of India which has 10,836 branches on Jan 1, 1986.

Bank Building

The tallest bank building is the Bank of Montreal's First Bank Tower, Toronto, Canada which has 72 stories and stands 935 ft high. The largest bank vault, measuring 350 × 100 × 8 ft and weighing 879 tons, is in the Chase Manhattan Building, NYC, completed in May 1961. Its six doors weigh up to 40 tons apiece but each can be closed by the pressure of a forefinger.

Bank Bail Out

On July 26, 1984 the Federal Deposit Insurance Corp bought $4.5 billion in bad loans from the Continental Illinois National Bank of Chicago for $3.5 billion and also "gave" $1 billion cash in return for preferred stock.

LAND

The world's largest landowner is the United States Government, with a holding of 732 million acres (1,143,800 sq mi), which is more than the area of the 8th largest country, Argentina, and 12.8 times larger than the UK. The world's largest private landowner is reputed to be International Paper Co, with 9 million acres.

Land Values

Currently the most expensive land is in the Ginza district of Tokyo, where the site of the Crown nightclub was bought on Oct 28, 1985 for $18,300 per sq ft.

The price for a grave site with excellent *Fung Shui* in Hong Kong may cost US $33,800 for a 4 × 10 ft plot. The China Square Inch Land Ltd at a charity auction on Dec 2, 1977 sold 1 sq cm (0.155 sq in) of land at Sha Tau Kok for HK $2,000 (the equivalent of US $17,405,833,737 per acre).

Greatest Urban Land Sale

The 3 square blocks of land under Rockefeller Center, NYC, were sold by Columbia Univ to Rockefeller Center for $400 million in Mar 1985.

Highest and Lowest Rent

The highest rentals in the world for prime sites, according to *World Rental Levels* by Richard Ellis of London are in Manhattan, NYC ($63 per sq ft) and London ($48), but, with service charges and taxes added, London's rates reach $82 per sq ft.

> The rent for a 3-room apartment in the Fuggerei in Augsburg, W Germany, since it was built by Jacob Fugger in 1519, has been 1 Rhine guilder (now DM 1.72 or less than $1) per month. Fugger was the extremely wealthy philanthropist who pioneered social welfare.

Greatest Land Auction

The greatest auction ever was that at Anchorage, Alaska, on Sept 11, 1969, for 179 tracts of 450,858 acres of the oil-bearing North Slope, Alaska. An all-time record bid of $72,277,133 for a 2,560-acre lease was made by the Amerada Hess Corporation-Getty Oil consortium. The bid indicated a price of $28,233 per acre.

---

2. MANUFACTURED ARTICLES

Antique

The largest antique ever sold has been the London Bridge in March 1968. The sale was made by Ivan F. Luckin of the Court of Common Council of the Corporation of London to the McCulloch Oil Corp of Los Angeles for $2,460,000. Over 10,000 tons of facade stonework were reassembled at a cost of $6.9 million at Lake Havasu City, Ariz, and "re-dedicated" Oct 10, 1971.

Auction

The highest amount ever paid at auction for a work of art was $11.9 million for a 12th-century illuminated manuscript "The Gospels of Henry the Lion" at Sotheby's, London Dec 6, 1983. (See page 196.)

Bathtub

A bathtub made entirely of gold, with an appraised value of $5 million, was reported in Lagos, Nigeria in Jan 1984. Owned by a former high-ranking official of the ousted government, it was taken into his vacation home in England. The underwriters called to insure the house agreed to insure everything but the tub, and suggested it best be left in a bank.

Beds

The bed made in 1984 for Stephen King's "Cat's Eye" movie set a new record—40 ft 9 in long, 20 ft 9 in wide, with headboard 21 ft 1½ in high, and footboard 15 ft 8¼ in high. The pillows measured 12 ft by 8 ft.

The heaviest bed is a waterbed 9 ft 7 in wide and 9 ft 10 in long, owned by Milan Vacek of Canyon Country, Calif, since 1977. The thermostatically heated water alone weighs 4,205 lb.

Blankets

The largest blanket ever made measured 68 × 100 ft and weighed 600 lb. It was knitted in 20,160 6-in squares in 10 months (Oct 1977–July 1978) by the English *Woman's Weekly* readers for Action Research for The Crippled Child.

Candle

A candle 80 ft high and 8½ ft in diameter was exhibited at the 1897 Stockholm Exhibition by the firm of Lindahls. The overall height was 127 ft.

Carpets and Rugs

A 52,225-sq-ft 28-ton red carpet was laid along the Avenue of the Americas from Radio City Music Hall to the NY Hilton Feb 13, 1982, by the Allied Corp for the "Night of 100 Stars" show in NYC.

The most magnificent carpet ever made was the Spring carpet of Khusraw made for the audience hall of the Sassanian palace at Ctesiphon, Iraq. It was about 7,000 sq ft of silk and gold thread, encrusted with emeralds. It was cut up as booty by military looters in 635 AD and from the known realization value of the pieces must have had an original value of some $2,400 million.

The Bikaner Woollen Mills, India announced in Mar 1985 that they had achieved 2,600 knots per sq in.

The most finely woven old carpet known is one with more than 2,193 knots per sq in from a fragment of an Imperial Mughal prayer carpet of the 17th century, now in the Altman collections in the Metropolitan Museum of Art, NYC.

Chair

The world's largest chair is the 2,000-lb, 33-ft-1-in-high, 19-ft-7-in-wide chair constructed by Anniston Steel & Plumbing Co, Inc for Miller's Office Furniture in Anniston, Ala, and completed in May 1981.

Chandeliers

The largest chandeliers were a set of 10 built for the palace of the Sultan of Brunei in 1983.

Cigars

The largest cigar ever made measures 16 ft 8½ in, weighs 577 lb 9 oz, and contains 3,330 tobacco leaves wrapped around a core of cardboard. It took Tinus Vinke and Jan Weijmer 243 hours to make and is now in the Tobacco Museum in Kampen, The Netherlands.

The largest marketed cigar in the world is the 14-in Valdez Emperado by San Andres Cigars.

Joseph Hruby of Lyndhurst, Ohio, has the largest known collection of cigar bands with 170,146 different examples, dating from *c.* 1895.

The most expensive standard cigar, the 11½-in-long Don Miguel "Cervantes," retails at $23.25.

Cigarettes

The heaviest smokers in the world are the people of the US where about 640 billion cigarettes (an average of 3,750 per adult) were consumed at a cost of some $21.2 billion in 1981. The people of China, however, were estimated to consume 725 billion in 1977.

The world's most popular cigarette is "Marlboro," a filter cigarette made by Philip Morris, which sold 268 billion units in 1985.

The longest cigarettes ever marketed were "Head Plays," each 11 in long and sold in packets of 5 in the US in about 1930, to save tax. The shortest were "Lilliput" cigarettes, each 1¼ in long and ⅛ in in diameter, made in Great Britain in 1956.

The world's largest collection of cigarettes is that of Robert E. Kaufman, MD, of NYC. In Apr 1986, he had 7,945 different brands of cigarettes with 43 kinds of tips made in 172 countries. The oldest brand represented is "Lone Jack," made in the US *c.* 1885. Both the longest and shortest (see above) are represented.

Cigarette Cards

The earliest known tobacco card is "Vanity Fair" dated 1876 issued by Wm S. Kimball & Co of Rochester, NY. The largest known collection is that of Edward Wharton-Tigar (b 1913) of London with a collection of more than 1 million cigarette and trade cards in about 45,000 sets.

Cigarette Lighter

The most expensive table cigarette lighter is the 18-carat gold Dunhill Lighthouse lighter, in the shape of a lighthouse, set on an island base of amethyst. It weighs 35.28 lb and the base weighs 112 lb. The windows of the lighthouse are amethyst. Priced at $56,000 it was offered in 1985 at Alfred Dunhill, London.

Credit Card Collection

The largest collection of valid credit cards, as of Mar 16, 1986, is one of 1,189, all different, by Walter Cavanagh (b 1943) of Santa Clara, Calif (known as "Mr Plastic Fantastic"). The cost of acquisition was nil, and he keeps them in the world's longest wallet, 250 ft long, weighing 35 lb.

Curtains

The largest functional curtain is one 550 ft long × 65 ft high in the Brabazon hangar at British Aerospace Filton, Bristol, used to enclose aircraft in the paint-spraying bay. It is electrically drawn.

The largest curtain ever built was the bright orange-red 4½-ton 185-ft-high curtain suspended 1,350 ft above and across the Rifle Gap, Grand Hogback, Colo, by the Bulgarian-born sculptor Christo (*né* Javacheff), 36, on Aug 10, 1971. It blew apart in a 50-mph gust of wind 27 hours later. The total cost of displaying this work of art was $750,000.

Christo, because he thought 11 tiny uninhabited man-made pine-stubbled islands in Biscayne Bay between Miami and Miami Beach, Fla, needed shiny pink surfaces "to translate the rich colors of the sky to the water," managed to drape the islands with skirts of woven plastic—6½ million sq ft in all—on May 7, 1983. Air travelers said the islands looked like giant pink water lilies extending 200 feet out from the shores, and "made nearby buildings look like toys." *"Surrounded Islands"* was Christo's name for the project.

Dolls

The most outsize girl doll ever paraded was made by the Belgian student body KSA on May 15, 1983 in Ostend. It measured 167 ft 6 in overall. The most massive boy doll built was one 62 ft 4 in high by the Fermain Youth Club, Macclesfield, Eng, on Nov 5, 1983.

A rag doll 38.8 ft long and properly proportioned was made at Linvilla Orchards, Media, Pa in Sept 1983.

Dress

The EVA suits for extra-vehicular activity worn by space shuttle crews from 1982 had a unit cost of $2.3 million.

The dress with the highest price tag ever exhibited was one designed by Serge Lepage, and exhibited in the Schiaparelli spring/summer collection in Paris on Jan 23, 1977. Called "The Birth of Venus" and studded with 512 diamonds, it carried a record price tag of 7.5 million francs (then $1.5 million).

Emperor Field Marshal Jean-Bédel Bokassa's coronation robe, with a 39-ft-long train, was encrusted with 785,000 pearls and 1,220,000 crystal beads by Guiselin of Paris for $144,500 for use at Bangui, Central African Empire in Dec 1977.

A platinum bikini valued at $9,500 was made by Mappin and Webb Jewelers, London. It was worn by Miss United Kingdom in the 1977 Miss World beauty pageant.

Fabrics

The most expensive of all cloths is Shatoosh (or Shatusa), a brown-gray wool from the throat hair of Indian goats. It is more expensive than vicuña and was sold by Neiman-Marcus of Dallas at $1,000 per yard, but supplies have now dried up.

The oldest surviving fabric discovered from Level VI A at Çatal Hüyük, Turkey, has been radio-carbon dated to 5900 BC.

Fuji Keori Ltd of Osaka, Japan, manufactured vicuña cloth at $3,235 per meter in July 1983.

BISCAYNE BAY with man-made skirts. Christo, the artist who likes to wrap everything, draped 11 islands off Miami shores in 1983. They looked like this from the air. © *Christo 1980–83.*

The most expensive fabric obtainable is an evening-wear fabric 37½ in wide, hand embroidered, sequinned and pearl-beaded in a series of designs on pure silk grounds. One design has as many as 29,900 tiny sequins and pearls per sq yd, and is designed by Alan Hershman of London; it costs $975 per meter.

Fireworks

The largest firework ever produced was *Universe I* exploded for the Lake Toya Festival, Hokkaido, Japan on Aug 28, 1983. The 928-lb shell was 42.5 in in diameter and burst to a diameter of 2,830 ft, with a 5-color display.

The longest firework, a "waterfall," was produced for the Yonago-Gaina Festival in Tottori, Japan and ignited at 8:50 P.M. on Aug 4, 1985. It was 4,920 ft long.

Flags

The oldest known flag is one dating to *c.* 3000 BC, found in 1972 at Khablis, Iran. Made of metal, it measures 9 × 9 in, and depicts an eagle, lions and goddesses.

The largest flag made, "The Great American Flag," was first displayed in Evansville, Ind on Mar 22, 1980 (in 1981, in front of the Washington Monument in Washington, DC and on Flag Day 1983 on the Ellipse south of the White House). It weighs 7.7 tons and measures 411 × 210 ft. The project is the brainchild of Len Silverfine, who has donated it to the White House.

The largest flag *flown* from a flagstaff is a Brazilian national flag measuring 229 ft 3 in × 328 ft 1 in in the capital, Brasília. The study of flags is known as vexillology.

Floats

The largest float is the 150-ft-long, 22-ft-wide "Agree" Float, bearing 51 All-American Homecoming Queens, used at the Orange Bowl parade, Miami, Fla, Dec 29, 1977.

Furniture

The largest item of furniture is the wooden bench in Green Park, Obiharo, Hokkaido, Japan, which seats 1,282 people and measures 1,321 ft 4 in long. It was completed by a team of 770 on July 19, 1981. (Also see *Sofa.*)

Glass

The most priceless example of the art of glass-making is usually regarded as the Portland Vase which dates from late in the 1st century BC or 1st century AD. It was made in Italy and was in the possession of the Barberini family in Rome from at least 1642. It was eventually bought by the Duchess of Portland in 1792, but smashed while in the British Museum on Feb 7, 1845.

The thinnest glass made is 0.0003 in thick for liquid crystal display (LCD) watches by Corning Glass Works of NYC.

Gold Plate

The gold coffin of the 14th century BC Pharaoh Tutankhamen discovered by Howard Carter on Feb 16, 1923 in the Valley of the Kings, western Thebes, Egypt weighs 243 lb. It is on exhibit in the Cairo Museum.

LARGEST PARADE OF FLAGS: 13,000 American flags (3 x 5 ft each) were unfurled in Honolulu, Hawaii, on July 4, 1985 by NSA (Nichiren Shoshu Soka Gakkai of America). It was part of the "Aloha—We Love America and the World" celebration.

Jig-Saw Puzzles

The largest jig-saw puzzle ever made was one 76 ft × 48 ft with 14,000 small, irregular-shaped interlocking pieces in a design called "Rose-Petal Place," sponsored by Hallmark Cards, Inc, outside Macy's NYC Herald Square store on Aug 19, 1984.

Fujisankei Communications Group of Japan commissioned Yanoman Co to produce a puzzle 10.63 × 19.29 ft with 61,752 pieces. Each piece was sold for charity.

Custom-made Stave puzzles made by Steve Richardson of Vermont, of 2,300, pieces, cost $3,700 in Jan 1983.

Keys

Harley O. (Rowdy) Yates of Tahoe, Calif, has collected 33,394 different keys from 50 companies in 51 years.

Knife

The penknife with the greatest number of blades is the Year Knife made by the cutlers Joseph Rodgers & Sons Ltd, of Sheffield, England, whose trademark was granted in 1682. The knife was built in 1822 with 1,822 blades, and was designed to match the year of the Christian era until 2000 AD, but had to halt at 1,973 because there was no more space for blades.

Matchbox Labels

Collectors of labels are phillumenists. The oldest match label of accepted provenance is that of Samuel Jones c. 1830. The finest collection of trademark labels (excluding any bar or other advertising labels) is some 280,000 pieces collected by Robert Jones of Indianapolis.

Matchstick Structure

Emmanuel George Venetucci (b Mar 26, 1925) of Palos Park, Ill, took 12 years (30,000 working hours) between 1950 and 1962 to make a

CARPET OF KEYS:
Rowdy Yates spreads out his full collection of 33,394 different keys he has garnered during the past 51 years

matchstick replica of the Milan (Italy) Cathedral. It is 15 ft long, 8 ft wide and rises 10 ft from the floor to the top of the dome. Made of wooden and cardboard matches and toothpicks, it contains 1 million pieces total.

Miniature Tools

For a hobby and to prove that a 4-finger hand crippled from baby-hood is not a handicap, Paul V. Buchanan (b 1922) of Murray, Ky, makes miniature tools by filing them from brass scraps. In 40 years of work, he has completed more than 100 pieces.

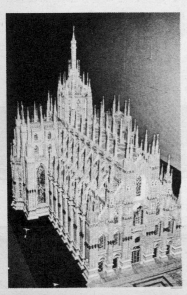

MATCHSTICK CATHEDRAL (left): Emmanuel George Venetucci of the Chicago area spent 12 years making this replica of Milan Cathedral with 1 million matchsticks and toothpicks.

MINIATURE TOOLS (below) made by filing brass scrap. Paul Buchanan, with one crippled 4-finger hand, created these and 100 pieces like them over a period of 40 years.

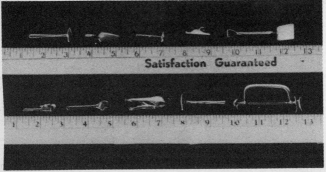

Satisfaction Guaranteed

Needles

The earliest needles were made of bone. The largest recorded needle is one 6 ft 1 in long made by George Davies of Thomas Somerfield, Eng, for stitching on mattress buttons lengthways. One is preserved in the National Needle Museum, Forge Mill, Redditch, Eng.

Nylon

The lowest denier nylon yarn ever produced is the 6 denier used for stockings exhibited at the Nylon Fair in London in Feb 1956. The sheerest stockings normally available are 9 denier. An indication of the thinness is that a hair from the average human head is about 50 denier.

Pens

The most expensive writing pens were 18-carat pairs of pens (one fiber-tipped and one ballpoint) capped by diamonds of 3.88 carats sold by Alfred Dunhill Ltd, London, for £9,943 ($17,900) the pair.

The most expensive fountain pen was the Mont Blanc 18-carat gold and platinum nibbed Meisterstück made by Dunhill's in Hamburg, W Germany, which retailed in Jan 1983 for $4,250.

Pipe

A very large meerschaum pipe with a bowl fashioned into a portrayal of Antony and Cleopatra had been priced at $15,000 by Racine and Laramie of San Diego, Calif, in Feb 1982.

Pistol

In Dec 1983 it was reported that Mr Ray Bily (US) owned an initialled gold pistol made for Hitler which was valued for insurance purposes at $375,000.

Post Cards

Deltiology is claimed to be the third largest collecting hobby next only to stamps and coins. Austria issued the first cards in 1869 followed by Britain in 1872.

The highest price paid for a post card was $4,400 for one of 5 known Mucha Waverly Cycle post cards. It was sold by Susan Brown Nicholson of Lisle, Ill, in Sept 1984.

Quilts

The world's largest quilt, designed by A. Platteau, was made by the people of Kortrijk-Rollegem, Belgium. It comprises 16,240 squares measuring 69.6 × 99.5 ft. On Aug 28, 1982 it was hoisted by two cranes.

Ropes

The largest rope ever made was a coir fiber launching rope with a circumference of 47 in made in 1858 for the British liner *Great Eastern* by John and Edwin Wright. It consisted of four strands, each of 3,780 yarns.

The longest fiber rope ever made without a splice was one of 10,000 fathoms (11.36 miles) of 6½-in circumference manila by Frost Brothers (now British Ropes Ltd) in London in 1874.

Salt and Pepper Shakers

The largest collection consists of 12,746 sets, stored in two buildings in

SALT AND PEPPER SETS: Mrs. Ruth Rasmussen has collected 12,746 pairs. They more than fill this closet.

Traer, Iowa. It belongs to Mrs. Ruth Rasmussen, who has been collecting since 1946.

Shoes

Emperor Bokassa of the Central African Empire (now Republic) commissioned pearl-studded shoes from the House of Berluti, Paris for his self-coronation in Dec 1977 at a cost of $85,000.

The most expensive sports shoes obtainable are the mink-lined golf shoes with 18-carat gold embellishments and ruby-tipped gold spikes by Stylo Matchmakers International Ltd of Northampton, England, which retail for $12,000 per pair.

The most valuable evening shoes are the pair produced by Reinhard Seufert of Stuttgart, W Germany. He values one shoe at $26,000. The shoes are made of gold leather, with rhinestone screws, and adorned with an emerald (on one shoe only, the higher-valued one) brooch, jeweled initial of the wearer, and high heels encrusted also with stones. They are rented for a "pompous shoe effect" for stage and TV.

James Smith, founder of James Southall & Co of Norwich, England, introduced sized shoes in 1792.

The largest shoes ever sold, excluding those made for cases of elephantiasis, are a pair of size 42 built for the giant Harley Davidson of Avon Park, Fla. The largest shoes normally available are size 14.

For advertising and display purposes facsimiles of shoes and boots weighing up to 1½ tons have been constructed.

Silver

The largest single pieces of silver are the pair of water jugs of 10,408 troy oz (867.3 troy lb) made in 1902 for the Maharajah of Jaipur (1861–1922). They are 5 ft 3 in tall with a circumference of 8 ft 1½ in and have a capacity of 1,800 Imperial gallons (2,162 US gallons). They are now in the City Palace, Jaipur. The silversmith was Gorind Narain.

Sofa

The longest standard sofa manufactured for market is the King Talmage Sofa, 12 ft 2 in in length made by the Talmageville Furniture Manufacturers, Calif. Barton Grange Hotel, near Preston, Lancashire, Eng bought a 14-ft-long pink leather settee for £3,250 ($3,900) on Oct 4, 1984.

Table

A buffet table 3,304 ft 10 in long was set up for the 400th anniversary of Hudiksvall, Sweden, June 19, 1982. Some 4,000 people including HM The King of Sweden were seated.

Tablecloth

The world's largest tablecloth is one 219 yd long × 2 yd wide double damask, made by John S. Brown & Sons Ltd of Belfast, N Ireland, and shipped to a royal palace in the Middle East. There was also an order for matching napkins for 450 places.

Tapestries

The earliest known examples of tapestry-woven linen are three pieces from the tomb of Thutmose IV, the Egyptian pharaoh, dating from 1483 to 1411 BC.

The largest single piece of tapestry ever woven is "Christ in His Majesty," measuring 72 ft by 39 ft, designed by Graham Vivian Sutherland (1903–80) for an altar hanging in Coventry Cathedral, Eng. It cost £10,500 ($29,400), weighs 680 lb and was delivered from Pinton Frères of Felletin, France, on Mar 1, 1962.

LARGEST SILVER: One of the pair of water jugs which are the largest single pieces of silver ever made. They accompanied the Maharajah of Jaipur to the coronation of King Edward VII of GB in 1902 so he did not have to rely on water from the Thames River. (*Maharajah Sawai Man Singh II Museum Trust*)

Time Capsule

The largest time capsule is the Tropico Time Tunnel measuring 10,000 cu ft in a cave in Rosamond, Calif, sealed by the Kern Antelope Historical Society on Nov 20, 1966, and intended for opening in the year 2866.

Typewriters

The first patent for a typewriter was by Henry Mill in 1714, but the earliest known working machine was made by Pellegrine Turri (Italy) in 1808.

Vase

The largest vase on record is one 8 ft high, weighing 650 lb, thrown by Sebastiano Maglio at Haeger Potteries of Dundee, Ill (founded 1872) during Aug 1976.

The Chinese ceramic authority, Chingwah Lee of San Francisco, was reported in Aug 1978 to have appraised a unique 39-in K'ang Hsi 4-sided vase, then in a bank vault in Phoenix, Ariz, at $60 million.

Wallet

The most expensive wallet ever made is a platinum-cornered, diamond-studded crocodile creation by Louis Quatorze of Paris and Mikimoto of Tokyo selling at £56,000 ($72,000) in Sept 1984.

Wreaths

The most expensive wreath on record was that presented to Sri Chinmoy in NYC, on July 11, 1983 by Ashrita Furman and Pahar Meltzer. It was handled by the Garland of Divinity's Love Florist, contained 10,000 flowers, and cost $3,500.

Zipper

The largest zip-fastener is 2,074 ft long, with 119,007 nylon teeth. It seals the covers of aquatic cables by RIRI, Mendrisio, Switzerland.

ANTIQUE SALES AT AUCTION

ART NOUVEAU. The highest auction price for any piece of *art nouveau* is $360,000 for a spider-web leaded glass mosaic and bronze table lamp by L. C. Tiffany at Christie's, NYC on Apr 8, 1980.

BED. A 1930 black lacquer king-size bed made by Jean Durand was auctioned at Christie's, NYC on Oct 2, 1983 for $75,000.

BLANKET. The most expensive blanket was a Navajo Churro handspun serape of *c.* 1852 sold for $115,500 (including premium) at Sotheby's, NYC on Oct 22, 1983.

CARPET. In 1946 the Metropolitan Museum of Art, NYC privately paid $1 million for the 26.5 × 13.6 ft Anhalt Medallion carpet made in Tabriz or Kashan, Persia *c.* 1590. The highest price ever paid at auction for a carpet is £231,000 ($360,000) for a 17th century "Polonaise" silk and metal thread carpet at Sotheby's, London on Oct 13, 1982.

CERAMICS. The Greek urn painted by Euphronios and thrown by Euxitheos in *c.* 530 was brought by private treaty by the Metropolitan Museum of Art, NYC, for $1.3 million in Aug 1972.

CHAIR. The highest price ever paid for a single chair is $275,000 on

Oct 23,1982 at Sotheby's, NYC, for the Chippendale side chair attributed to Thomas Affleck of Philadelphia, and made in *c.* 1770.

CIGARETTE CARD. The most valuable card is one of the 6 known baseball series cards of Honus Wagner, who was a non-smoker, which was sold in New York in Dec 1981 for $25,000.

DOLLS. The highest price paid at auction for a doll is $33,880 for a dimple-cheeked "character doll" from Kammer & Reinhart (1909) at Sotheby's, London, May 20, 1984.

FURNITURE. The most expensive piece of furniture ever auctioned has been a mahogany and ebony collector's chest of drawers believed to have been made for Marie Antoinette by G. Benneman. It was anonymously bought at Ader Picard Tajan, Monaco, on Nov 11, 1984 for £1,300,000 ($1,820,000).

GLASS. The record is £520,000 ($1,040,000) plus premium for a Roman glass cage-cup of *c.* 300 AD measuring 7 in in diameter and 4 in in height, sold at Sotheby's, London, on June 4, 1979 to Robin Symes. It was the highest price paid for any antiquity.

GOLD PLATE. The highest price for any gold artifact is £950,400 ($1,425,600) for a 22-carat font made by Paul Storr to the design of Humphrey Repton in 1797. It was sold by Lady Anne Cavendish-Bentinck and bought by Armitage of London at Christie's on July 11, 1985.

GUN. The highest price ever paid for a single gun is £125,000 ($312,500) given by the London dealers, F. Partridge, for a French flintlock fowling piece made for Louis XIII, King of France, *c.* 1615 and attributed to Pierre le Bourgeoys (d 1627) of Lisieux, France. This piece, now in the Metropolitan Museum of Art, NYC, was included in the collection of the late William Goodwin Renwick (US) sold by Sotheby's, London, Nov 21, 1972. (Also see Pistol.)

HAT. The highest price ever paid for a hat is $66,000 by the Alaska State Museum at a NYC auction in Nov 1981 for a Tlingit Kiksadi ceremonial frog helmet from *c.* 1600.

HIGHEST-PRICED GOLD ARTIFACT: $1,425,600 was the record price paid at auction at Christie's, London in 1985 for this 13½ × 13½-in christening font. This amounts to $6,421 per oz.

ICON. The record auction price for an icon is $150,000 paid at Christie's, NYC on Apr 17, 1980 for *The Last Judgement* (from the George R. Hann collection, Pittsburgh, Pa) made in Novgorod in the 16th century.

JADE. The highest price ever paid for an item in jade is $396,000 (including premium) at Sotheby's, NYC on Dec 6, 1983 for a mottled brownish-yellow belt-hook and pendant mask of the Warring States Period of Chinese history.

JEWELS. The highest auction price paid for any jewels is $4,237,500 approximately (with the buyer's premium, over $4.6 million) for two pear-shaped diamond drop earrings of 58.6 and 61 carats at Sotheby's, Geneva, Switzerland, Nov 14, 1980. Neither the buyer nor seller was disclosed.

MIRRORS. Twin Chippendale mirrors were sold for £280,000 ($420,000) to Roy Miles, a London dealer, at Christie's, London, on Apr 10, 1986.

MUSICAL BOX. The highest price paid for a musical box is £19,000 ($22,800) (not including premium) for a Swiss-made box made for the special envoy to the Shah of Persia in 1901. Sold at Sotheby's, London, on Jan 23, 1985.

PAPERWEIGHT. The highest price ever paid for a glass paperweight is $143,000 (including premium) at Sotheby's, NYC on Dec 2, 1983 for a blue glass weight made at Pantin, Paris *post* 1850.

PISTOL. The highest price paid at auction for a pistol is £110,000 ($253,000) at Christie's, London on July 8, 1980 for a Sadeler wheel-lock holster pistol from Munich dated *c.* 1600.

PLAYING CARDS. The highest price paid for a deck of playing cards is $143,352 (including premium) by the Metropolitan Museum of Art, NYC, at Sotheby's, London on Dec 6, 1983.

PORCELAIN AND POTTERY. The highest auction price for any ceramic or any Chinese work of art is £720,000 ($1,296,000) (not including premium) for a blue and white Ming vase of 1426–35 bought by Hirano of Japan at Sotheby's, London, in Dec 1981.

POT LID. The highest price paid for a pot lid is $5,940 for a seaweed-patterned "Spanish Lady" lid sold at Phillips, London, on May 19, 1982.

SILVER. The highest price ever paid for silver is £612,500 ($1,163,750) for the pair of Duke of Kingston tureens made in 1735 by Meissonnier and sold by Christie's, Geneva on Nov 8, 1977. The 100-piece Paul de Lamerie service made for the seventh Earl of Thanet c. 1745 was sold by Lord Hothfield at Sotheby's, London on Nov 22, 1984 for £825,000 ($1,031,250), more English pounds, but fewer US dollars.

SNUFF BOX. The highest price ever paid for a snuff box is Sw. Fr. 1,540,000 (then $678,643) in a sale at Christie's, Geneva on May 11, 1982 for a gold snuff box dating from 1760–65 and once owned by Frederick the Great of Prussia. It was purchased by S. J. Phillips, the London dealers, for stock.

SPOONS. A Wiener Werkstätte spoon by Josef Hoffmann, Austria c. 1905, was sold at Sotheby's, London for £17,600 ($26,400) on Apr 28, 1983. A set of 13 Henry VIII Apostle spoons owned by Lord Astor of Hever were sold for £120,000 ($216,000) on June 24, 1981 at Christie's, London.

STAINED GLASS. The largest price paid at auction for any work in stained glass was $110,000 paid at Christie's, NYC on May 26, 1983, for a Frank Lloyd Wright door with a tree-of-life design. It had been made for a house in Buffalo c. 1903.

STUFFED BIRD. The highest price ever paid for a stuffed bird is £9,000 (then $32,400). This was given on Mar 4, 1971 at Sotheby's, London, by the Iceland Natural History Museum for a specimen of the Great Auk (*Alca impennis*) in summer plumage, which was taken in Iceland c. 1821; this particular specimen stood 22½ in high.

SWORD. The highest price recorded for a sword is $145,000 paid for the gold sword of honor presented by the Continental Congress of 1779 to Gen Marie Joseph Paul Lafayette, sold at Sotheby Parke Bernet, NYC, on Nov 20, 1976.

TABLE. A Philadelphia tea table was auctioned at Christie's, NYC, on Jan 25, 1986 for $1,045,000, the highest price ever paid for a piece of American furniture.

TAPESTRY. The highest price paid for a tapestry is £550,000 ($1,155,000) for a Swiss medieval tapestry frieze in two parts dated

---

Eric deWilde, a Hollywood, Fla schoolboy, found a bag of diamonds on a railroad track in Mar 1983, partly crushed by train wheels. At Christie's NYC, on June 20–21, 1984, the found jewels were auctioned off for $350,000. The highest single item was a man's 5.9 carat diamond ring that brought $27,000. DeWilde received all the proceeds from his discovery which came about when he was searching with a flashlight for his missing bicycle.

1468–76 at Sotheby's, Geneva, Switzerland, Apr 10, 1981, by the Basle Historische Museum.

THIMBLE. The record auction price for a thimble is £8,000 ($18,400) paid by the London dealer Winifred Williams at Christie's, London on Dec 3, 1979 for a Meissen dentil-shaped porcelain piece of c. 1740.

TOY. The auction record for a toy is £25,500 ($35,700) for a model train set of Stephenson's *Rocket* made by Marklin of Germany in tin plate in 1909 sold at Sotheby's, London on May 29, 1984.

TYPEWRITER. The highest price paid for an antique machine is £3,000 ($6,450) for an 1886 Daw and Tait machine auctioned at Sotheby's, London on Dec 12, 1980.

WALKING STICK. The highest auction price for a walking stick has been $24,200 at Sotheby Parke Bernet, NYC in 1983 for an octagonal whale ivory nobbed stick decorated by scrimshanders in 1845.

---

3. AGRICULTURE

Origins

It has been estimated that only 21% of the world's land surface is cultivable and that only 7.6% is actually under cultivation. Evidence adduced in 1971 from Nok Nok Tha and Spirit Cave, Thailand tends to confirm plant cultivation and animal domestication was part of the culture c. 11,000 BC. Goats were herded on Mt Carmel, Palestine (now Israel) as early as 16,000 BC, and were domesticated at Asiab, Iran by c. 8050 BC. Dogs were domesticated at Star Carr, Yorkshire, Eng by c. 7700 BC. The earliest definite date for sheep is c. 7200 BC at Argissa-Magula, Thessaly, Greece, and for pig and cattle c. 7000 BC at the same site. The earliest date certain for horse is c. 4350 BC from Dereivka, Ukraine, USSR.

Ancient trackings sighted by a US space shuttle in 1982 indicate perhaps an even earlier domestication of draft animals.

Farms

The largest farms are collective farms in the USSR. These have been reduced in number from 235,500 in 1940 to only 18,000 in 1980, and have been increased in size so that units of over 60,000 acres are not uncommon.

The pioneer farm of Laucidio Coelho near Campo Grande, Mato Grosso, Brazil, c. 1901 was 3,358 sq mi (2,150,000 acres) with 250,000 head of cattle at the time of his death in 1975.

Largest Chicken Ranch

The largest chicken ranch is the Croton Egg Farm, Croton, Ohio, which has 4.8 million hens laying some 3.7 million eggs daily.

Largest Turkey Farm

The largest turkey farm is that of Bernard Matthews Ltd, centered at Great Witchingham, Norfolk, England, with 2,500 workers tending 7,900,000 turkeys.

Largest Cattle Station

The largest cattle station is the Anna Creek station of 11,626.8 sq mi, S

TURKEY-GUTTING CHAMP: Mrs Madge Colenso of Surrey, Eng, shows the way she handled the cleaver in gutting a record 94 turkeys in an hour. (*Farmers Weekly*)

Australia, owned by the Kidman family. (It is thus 23% the size of Eng.) The biggest component is Strangway at 5,449 sq mi. Until 1915 the Victoria River Downs Station, Northern Territory, was over three times larger, with an area of 22,400,000 acres (35,000 sq mi).

Largest Sheep Station

The largest sheep station is Commonwealth Hill, in the northwest of South Australia. It grazes between 60,000 and 70,000 sheep, about 700 cattle and 54,000 <u>uninvited</u> kangaroos, in an area of 4,080 sq mi. The largest sheep move on record occurred when 27 horsemen moved a mob of 43,000 sheep 40 miles from Barcaldine to Beaconsfield Station, Queensland, Australia, in 1886.

Largest Community Garden

The largest recorded community garden project is that operated by the City Beautiful Council, and the Benjamin Wegerzyn Garden Center in Dayton, Ohio. It comprises 1,173 allotments, each of 812¼ sq ft.

Largest Piggery

The largest piggery is at the Sljeme pig unit in Yugoslavia, which is able to process 300,000 pigs in a year. Even bigger units may exist in Rumania, but details are lacking.

Mushroom Farm

The largest mushroom farm is Butler County Mushroom Farm Inc, founded in 1937 in a disused limestone mine near West Winfield, Pa. It has over 1,000 employees working underground, in a maze of galleries 110 miles long, producing about 48,000 lb of mushrooms per year.

Multiple Births (Livestock)

A cow named "Lyubik" gave birth to 7 calves at Mogilev, USSR, it was reported on Apr 25, 1964. Five live and one dead calf were recorded from a Friesian at Te Puke, New Zealand, July 27, 1980, but none survived. A case of 5 live calves at one birth was reported in 1928 by T. G. Yarwood of Manchester, England. The lifetime prolificacy record is 30 by a cross-breed cow owned by G. Page of Wilmington, England. She died in Nov 1957, aged 32. A cross-Hereford calved in 1916 produced her 30th calf in May 1955, and died in May 1956, aged 40. She was owned by A. J. Thomas of Dyfed, Wales. A Danish black and white bull named "Soender Jylland's Jens" left 220,000 surviving progeny by artificial insemination when put to sleep aged 11 in Copenhagen in Sept 1978.

The highest recorded number of piglets in one litter is 36 of which only one was lost at the age of one month and 35 survived to adulthood. A 3-year-old sow named "Old Faithful" on the farm of Lloyd Hofmeyer, south of Sanborn, Iowa, farrowed a litter Apr 17–20, 1965. It was her 4th litter, and she weighed 1,000 lb just before giving birth.

A case of 8 lambs at a birth was reported by D. T. Jones of Priory Farm, Gwent, Wales, in June 1956, and by Ken Towse of Buckton, Eng, in Mar 1981 but none lived. A case of a sheep living to 26 years was recorded in flock book records by H. Poole, Wexford, Ireland. Many cases of sextuplet lambs have been reported.

Egg-Laying

The highest authenticated rate of egg-laying is by a white leghorn chicken hen, # 2988 at the College of Agriculture, Univ of Missouri, with 371 eggs in 364 days in an official test, conducted by Prof Harold V. Biellier, ending on Aug 29, 1979.

The heaviest egg *reported* is one of 16 oz with double yolk and double shell, laid by a white leghorn at Vineland, NJ, Feb 25, 1956. The largest *recorded* was one of "nearly 12 oz" for a 5-yolked egg 12¼ in around the long axis and 9 in around the shorter axis laid by a Black Minorca at Mr Stafford's Damsteads Farm, Mellor, Lancashire, England in 1896.

The highest claim for the number of yolks in a chicken's egg is 9 reported by Mrs Diane Hainsworth of Hainsworth Poultry Farms, Mt Morris, NY, in July 1971 and also from a hen in Kirghizia, USSR in Aug 1977.

The white goose "Speckle" owned by Donny Brandenberg of Goshen, Ohio, on May 3, 1977 laid a 24-oz egg measuring 13½ × 9½ in in circumference.

An Aylesbury duck laid 457 eggs in 463 days including an unbroken run of 375 in 375 days before dying on Feb 7, 1986. The duck belonged to Annette and Angela Butler of Princes Risborough, Bucks, Eng.

Crop Yields

A yield of 352.64 bushels of corn (15½% moisture) from an acre, using De Kalb XL-54, was achieved by Roy Lynn, Jr near Kalamazoo, Mich, Sept 30, 1977.

The highest recorded yield for sugar beet is 62.4 tons per acre by Andy Christensen and Jon Giannini in the Salinas Valley, California.

The greatest number of US barrels of potatoes picked in a 9½ hr day is 235 by Walter Sirois (b 1917) of Caribou, Maine, on Sept 30, 1950.

Milk Yields

The highest recorded world lifetime yield of cows' milk is 465,224 lb by the cow named #289, a Holstein Friesian (b Sept 6, 1964) (d May 1, 1984), owned by Manuel Maciel & Son, Hanford, Calif.

The greatest recorded yield for one lactation (365 days) is 55,661 lb by the Holstein "Beecher Arlinda Ellen" owned by Mr and Mrs Harold L. Beecher of Rochester, Ind in 1975. The highest reported milk yield in a day is 241 lb by "Urbe Blanca" in Cuba on or about Jan 23, 1982.

The record for hand milking was set by Andy Faust at Collinsville, Okla, in 1937 when he achieved 120 gallons in 12 hr.

The highest recorded milk yield for any goat is 7,714 lb in 365 days by "Osory Snow-Goose" owned by Mr and Mrs G. Jameson of Leppington, NSW, Australia in 1977. A 15-year-old goat owned by Mrs Nanbui Meghani of Bhuj, Gujarat, India, was reported in Nov 1984 to have lactated continuously for 12 years.

Butter Fat Yield

The world record lifetime yield is 16,370 lb by the US Holstein "Breezewood Patsy Bar Pontiac" in 3,979 days. Her lactation record for 365 days of 2,230 lb was reported on Oct 8, 1976.

Cheese

The most active cheese-eaters are the people of France, with an annual average in 1983 of 43.6 lb per person. The biggest producer is the US with a factory production of 4,773,500,000 lb in 1980.

The largest cheese ever made was a cheddar of 34,591 lb, made in 43 hours, Jan 20–22, 1964, for the Wisconsin Cheese Foundation by Steve Siudzinski of Langes Corners, Wis, for exhibition at the NY World's Fair. It was transported in a specially designed 45-ft-long refrigerated tractor trailer "Cheese-Mobile."

Heaviest Cattle, Pigs and Sheep

Of heavyweight cattle the heaviest on record was a Holstein-Durham cross named "Mount Katahdin" exhibited by A. S. Rand of Maine, 1906–10 and frequently weighed at an even 5,000 lb. He was 6 ft 2 in at the shoulder with a 13 ft girth and died in a barn fire c. 1923.

The highest recorded birthweight for a calf is 225 lb from a British Friesian cow at Rockhouse Farm, Swansea, Wales, in 1961.

The heaviest hog recorded was the Poland-China hog "Big Bill" of 2,552 lb measuring 9 ft long with a belly on the ground, owned by Burford Butler of Jackson, Tenn, and chloroformed in 1933. Raised by W. J. Chappall, he was mounted and displayed in Weakely County, Tenn until 1946.

The highest recorded birthweight for a lamb is 38 lb at Clearwater, Sedgwick County, Kansas, in 1975, but neither this lamb nor the ewe survived.

Sheep Shearing

The highest recorded speed for sheep shearing in a working day was that of John Fagan, who machine-sheared 804 lambs (average 89.3 per hour) in 9 hours at Hantoru Rd, Pio Pio, New Zealand, on Dec 8, 1980. The hand-shearing (solo blade) record for a 9-hour day is 353 lambs by Peter Casserly of Christchurch, New Zealand, Feb 13, 1976.

In a shearing marathon, 4 men machine-sheared 2,519 sheep in 24 hours at Stewarts Trust, Waikia, Southland, New Zealand, on Feb 11, 1982.

Mr Lavor Taylor (b Feb 27, 1896) of Ephraim, Utah claims to have sheared 515,000 sheep to May 1984.

Chicken Plucking

The record time for plucking chickens clean was set in the 1976 championship contest at Masaryktown, Fla, Oct 9, when a team of 4 women (Doreena Cary, Diane Grieb, Kathy Roads and Dorothy McCarthy) plucked 12 birds naked in 32.9 sec.

Leaving a single feather produces the cry "Fowl!"

Ernest Hausen (1877–1955) of Fort Atkinson, Wisc, died undefeated after 33 years as a champion. On Jan 19, 1939 he was timed for one chicken at 4.4 sec, and reportedly twice did 3.5 sec a few years later.

Turkey Plucking

Vincent Pilkington of Cootehill, County Cavan, Ireland, killed and plucked 100 turkeys in 7 hours 32 min on Dec 15, 1978. His record for a single turkey is 1 min 30 sec on RTE Television in Dublin on Nov 17, 1980.

Joe Glaub (US) killed 7,300 turkeys in a "working" day on May 23, 1983. Mrs Madge Colenso gutted 94 turkeys in 60 min at Rivington Farm, Burstow, Surrey, Eng, on Dec 20, 1984.

Largest Hop Field

The largest hop field is one of 1,836 acres near Toppenish, Wash, owned by John I. Haas, Inc, the world's largest hop growers, with hop farms in Calif, Ida, Ore and Wash with a total area of 3,560 acres.

Largest Vineyard

The largest vineyard extends over the Mediterranean façade between the Rhone and the Pyrenees in the départements (provinces) of Aude, Hérault, Gard and Pyrénées-Orientales. It has an area of 2,075,685 acres of which 52.3% is *monoculture viticole.*

Largest Rice Farm

The largest contiguous wild rice (*Zizania aquatica*) farm is Clearwater Rice Inc at Clearbrook, Minn with 2,000 acres. In 1982 it yielded 306,132 lb.

Largest Wheat Field

The largest single fenced field sown with wheat was one of 35,000 acres, sown in 1951 near Lethbridge, Alberta, Canada.

LIVESTOCK SALES RECORDS

Note: Some exceptionally high livestock auction sales are believed to result from collusion.

Bull

The highest price ever paid for a bull is $2,500,000 for the beefalo (a ⅜ bison, ⅜ charolais, ¼ Hereford) "Joe's Pride" sold by D. C. Basolo of Burlingame, Calif to the Beefalo Cattle Co of Canada, of Calgary, Alberta, on Sept 9, 1974.

Cow

The highest price ever paid for a cow is $1,025,000 for the Holstein "Allendairy Glamorous Ivy" by Albert Cormier of Georgetown, Ont, Canada, at the Doeberiener dispersal sale at Jamestown, Pa, on Nov 20, 1982.

Sheep

The highest price ever paid for a ram is $A79,000 (about $73,500) by the Gnowangerup Animal Breeding Centre, Western Australia for a Merino ram from the Colinsvale Stud, Mount Bryan, South Australia, at the Royal Adelaide Show on Sept 10, 1981.

The highest price ever paid for wool is $A187 per kg greasy ($62 per lb) for a bale of Saxon Merino fleece from the Launceston, Tasmania sales on Feb 28, 1986. It was sold by Jim McEwan of Trefusis to Fujii Keori Ltd of Osaka, Japan. This Japanese firm has been top bidder since 1972.

Pig

The highest price ever paid for a pig is $56,000 for a cross-bred harrow named "Bud," owned by Jeffrey Roemisch of Hermleigh, Tex, and bought by E. A. "Bud" Olson and Phil Bonzio on Mar 5, 1985.

Horse

The highest price for a draught horse is $47,500 paid for the 7-year-old Belgian stallion "Farceur" by E. G. Good at Cedar Falls, Iowa Oct 16, 1917.

$56,000 PIG: "Bud," a cross-bred barrow, although not the heaviest hog, sold for that much at auction in Tex in Mar 1985.

Chapter 10

The Human World

1. POLITICAL AND SOCIAL

The land area of the earth is estimated at about 57,267,400 sq mi (including inland waters), or 29.08% of the world's surface area.

Largest Political Division

The British Commonwealth of Nations, a free association of 49 sovereign independent states and 27 non-sovereign states and dependencies, covers an area of 13,095,000 sq mi with a population which in 1980 surpassed 1,000 million.

COUNTRIES

The world comprises 170 sovereign countries and 59 separately administered non-sovereign territories, making 229. The United Nations still list the *de jure* territories of East Timor (now incorporated into Indonesia), Western Sahara (now in Morocco) and the uninhabited Canton and Enderbury Islands (now disputed between the US and Kiribati) but do not list the three Baltic States of Estonia, Latvia and Lithuania though their forcible incorporation into the USSR in 1940 has never been internationally recognized. Neither do they list the *de facto* territories of Taiwan, Mayotte or Spanish North Africa, the 4 Antarctic Territories or the Australian Territory of Coral Sea Islands and Heard and McDonald Islands.

Largest Country

The country with the greatest area is the Union of Soviet Socialist Republics (the Soviet Union), comprising 15 Union (constituent) Republics with a total area of 8,648,500 sq mi, or 15% of the world's total land area, and a total coastline (including islands) of 66,090 miles. The country measures 5,580 miles from east to west and 2,790 miles from north to south. Its population mid-1984 was estimated at 275.5 million.

Smallest Country

The smallest independent country is the State of the Vatican City, which was made an enclave within the city of Rome, Feb 11, 1929. The enclave has an area of 108.7 acres (0.17 sq mi).

The maritime sovereign country with the shortest coastline is Monaco with 3.49 miles excluding piers and breakwaters.

The world's smallest republic is Nauru, less than 1 degree south of the equator in the Western Pacific. It became independent on Jan 31, 1968, has an area of 5,263 acres (8.2 sq mi) and a population of 7,000 (latest estimate, mid-1984).

The smallest colony in the world is Gibraltar (since 1969, the City of Gibraltar), with an area of 2½ sq mi. However, Pitcairn Island, the only inhabited (58 people at Dec 31, 1985) island of a group of 4 (total area 18½ sq mi), has an area of 1½ sq mi, or 960 acres.

The official residence, since 1834, of the Grand Master of the Order of the Knights of Malta, totaling 3 acres and comprising the Villa del Priorato di Malta on the lowest of Rome's seven hills (the 151-ft Aventine), retains certain diplomatic privileges as does 68 Via Condotti. The order has accredited representatives to foreign governments. Hence, it is sometimes cited as the smallest "state" in the world.

Flattest and Most Elevated Countries

The country with the lowest highest point is the Republic of the Maldives, which attains 8 ft above sea level. The country with the highest lowest point is Lesotho, a kingdom surrounded by the Republic of South Africa. The egress of the Senqu (Orange) riverbed is 4,530 ft above sea level.

Frontiers

The country with the most land frontiers is China, with 13—Mongolia, USSR, N Korea, Hong Kong, Macau, Vietnam, Laos, Burma, India, Bhutan, Nepal, Pakistan, and Afghanistan. These extend for 14,900 mi. France, if all her *Départements d'outre-mer* are included, may, if her territorial waters are extended, have 20 frontiers.

The longest *continuous* frontier is between Canada and the US, which (including the Great Lakes boundaries) extends for 3,987 miles (excluding 1,538 miles with Alaska).

The frontier which is crossed most frequently is that between the US and Mexico. It extends for 1,933 miles and has more than 120 million crossings every year. The Sino-Soviet frontier, broken by the Sino-Mongolian border, extends for 4,500 miles with no reported figures of crossings.

The "frontier" of the Holy See (Vatican City) in Rome measures 2.53 miles. The land frontier between Gibraltar and Spain at La Linea, closed in June 1969 and reopened at midnight, Feb 4–5, 1985, measures 1,672 yd. Zambia, Zimbabwe, Botswana and Namibia (South West Africa) almost merge.

Populations

The daily increase in the world's population is 215,850, or 149.9 per minute. For past, present and future estimates, see table.

Most Populous Country

The largest population of any country is that of China, which in *pinyin* is written Zhongguo (central land). The census of July 1982 was 1,008,175,288 (excluding Taiwan, Hong Kong and Macao). The rate of natural increase in the People's Republic of China is now estimated to be 38,700 a day or 14.1 million per year. The mid-year 1986 estimate would then be close to 1,065 million. The census required 5,100,000 enumerators to work for 10 days. India is set to overtake China during the next century.

WORLD POPULATION—PROGRESSIVE ESTIMATES

Date	Millions	Date	Millions
10000 BC	c. 5	1960	3,049
1 AD	c. 200	1970	3,704
1000	c. 275	1975	4,033
1250	375	1980	4,432
1500	420	1981	4,508
1650	550–600	1982	4,586
1700	615	1983	4,465
1750	720	1984	4,763
1800	900	1985	4,845
1900	1,625	1986	4,925
1920	1,862	2000	6,100
1930	2,070	2025	8,200
1940	2,295	2100	10,500
1950	2,513		

NOTE: The UN publication "State of World Population, 1984" forecast that the world population will not stabilize until 2095 at c. 10,500 million but will reach 6,100 million by Dec 31, 2000.

The all-time peak annual increase of 2.0% c. 1958–1962 had declined to 1.73% by 1975–1980. By 1990 this should decline to 1.5%. This, however, produces an annual increment of 80 million to even higher figures in the 1990s. The French demographer Biraben has calculated that 60,000 million people died between 40,000 BC and 1980 AD. This indicates that there have thus been some 65,000 million specimens of *Homo sapiens sapiens* who ever lived.

Least Populous State

The independent state with the smallest population is the Vatican City or the Holy See (see *Smallest Country*), with 728 inhabitants in mid-1978, and a zero birth rate.

Most Sparsely Populated Territory

Antarctica became permanently occupied by relays of scientists as of Oct 1956. The population varies seasonally and reaches 2,000 at times.

The least populated territory, apart from Antarctica, is Kalaallit Nunaat (formerly Greenland), with a population of 52,000 (estimate of mid-1983) in an area of 840,000 sq mi, giving a density of one person to every 16.15 sq mi. Some 84.3% of the island comprises an ice cap.

Most Impenetrable Boundary

The 858-mile-long "Iron Curtain," dividing the Federal Republican (West) and the Democratic Republican (East) parts of Germany, utilizes 2,230,000 land mines and 50,000 miles of barbed wire, in addition to many watchtowers containing detection devices. The last of 55,000 SM-70 scatter guns was removed on Nov 30, 1984. The whole 270-yd-wide strip occupies 133 sq mi of E German territory and costs an estimated $7 billion to build and maintain. It reduced the westward flow from more than 200,000 in 1961 to a trickle of 30 (including 8 guards in 1985). The death toll has been 184 since 1962. Construction of the second wall began in E Berlin in Mar 1984.

Most Densely Populated Places

The most densely populated territory is the Portuguese province of Macau (or Macao), on the southern coast of China. It has an estimated population of 343,000 (mid-1984) in an area of 6.2 sq mi, giving a density of 55,300 per sq mi.

The Principality of Monaco, on the south coast of France, has a population of 27,000 (estimated mid-1984) in an area of 473 acres, giving a density of 38,179 per sq mi. Recent marine filling-in increased the acreage by some 20%.

Singapore has 2,558,000 (end 1984) people in an inhabited area of 73 sq mi, with a density of 34,479 per sq mi.

Of countries over 1,000 sq mi, the most densely populated is Bangladesh with a population of 96,730,000 (mid-1984 estimate) living in 55,126 sq mi at a density of 1,754 per sq mi.

The Indonesian island of Java (with an area of 48,763 sq mi) had a population of 94,693,000 (1981 estimate), giving a density of 1,941 per sq mi.

Of territories with an area of more than 400 sq mi, Hong Kong (405 sq mi) contains 5,579,000 people (estimated Mar 1985), giving the territory a density of 13,775 per sq mi. Hong Kong is now the most populous of all colonies. The name "Hong Kong" is the transcription of the local pronunciation of the Peking dialect version of Xiang gang (a port for incense). The 1976 by-census showed that the West area of the urban district of Mong Kok on the Kowloon Peninsula had a density of 652,910 people per sq mi. In 1959, at the peak of the housing crisis in Hong Kong, it was reported that in one house designed for 12 people the number of occupants was 459, including 104 in one room and 4 living on the roof.

CITIES

Most Populous City

The most populous "urban agglomeration" in the world is the Tokyo-Yokohama Metropolitan Area, of 1,081 sq mi, containing an estimated 29,002,000 people in 1981. The municipal population of Tokyo in 1985 was 11,903,900. The population of the metropolitan area of Greater Mexico City in 1981 was published as 16,248,500 with the city proper at 8,389,800 (1954 est).

Oldest City

The oldest known walled town is Jericho (Ariha), about 5 miles north of the Dead Sea. Radio-carbon dating on specimens from the lowest levels reached by archeologists indicate habitation there by perhaps 3,000 people as early as 7800 BC. The settlement of Dolni Vestonice, Czechoslovakia has been dated to the Gravettian culture c. 27,000 BC. The oldest capital city in the world is Dimashq (Damascus), capital of Syria. It has been continuously inhabited since c. 2500 BC.

Elevations of Cities, Capitals and Dwellings

The highest capital city, before the domination of Tibet by China, was Lhasa, at an elevation of 12,087 ft above sea level.

HIGHEST CAPITAL CITY: La Paz, the administrative capital of Bolivia, is 11,916 ft up in the Andes, and its airport is 1,469 ft still higher up. The highest lake in the world, Titicaca, is only 30 mi away. (*Tony Morrison*)

La Paz, the administrative and *de facto* capital of Bolivia, stands at an altitude of 11,916 ft above sea level. Its El Alto airport is at 13,385 ft. The city was founded in 1548 by Capt Alonso de Mendoza on the site of an Indian village named Chuquiapu. It was originally called Ciudad de Nuestra Señora de La Paz (City of Our Lady of Peace), but in 1825 was renamed La Paz de Ayacucho, its present official name. Sucre, the legal capital of Bolivia, stands at 9,301 ft above sea level.

The new town of Wenchuan, founded in 1955 on the Chinghai-Tibet road, north of the Tangla Range, is the highest at 16,732 ft above sea level.

The settlement of Ein Bokek, which has a synagogue on the shores of the Dead Sea, is the lowest town in the world at 1,299 ft below sea level.

The northernmost capital is Reykjavik, Iceland, at 64° 08′ N. Its population was estimated to be 80,000 (1985).

Largest Town in Area

The largest town in area is Mount Isa, Queensland, Australia. The area administered by the City Council is 15,822 sq mi.

Most Remote Town from Sea

The town most remote from the sea is Urumqi (formerly Tihwa, Sinkiang), capital of the Uighur Autonomous Region of China, at a distance of about 1,400 miles from the nearest coastline. Its population was estimated to be 320,000 in 1974.

Emigration

More people emigrate from Mexico than from any other country. An estimated 000,000 emigrated illegally into the US in 1976 alone.

Immigration

The country which regularly receives the most legal immigrants is the US. It has been estimated that in the period 1820–1984, the US received 51,950,349 *official* immigrants. One immigrant in every 24 in the US is, however, an *illegal* immigrant. Another 700,000 were added in 1980.

Birth Rate

The highest estimated by the UN is 54.6 per 1,000 for Kenya in 1980. The rate for the whole world was 27.5 per 1,000 in 1982. A world-wide survey published in July 1981 showed only Nepal (48.9) with a still rising birth rate. Excluding Vatican City, where the rate is negligible, the lowest recorded rate is 9.5 for the Federal Republic of (W) Germany for 1984. The fastest falling is in Thailand where the 3.3 average number of children per family has fallen to 1.8 in 10 years.

Death Rate

The rate for the whole world was 10.7 per 1,000 in 1982. The highest of the latest available recorded death rates is 40 deaths per 1,000 of the population in Kampuchea (Cambodia) (1975–80). The lowest of the latest available recorded rates is 3 deaths per 1,000 in Tonga in 1853.

Natural Increase

The rate of natural increase for the whole world is estimated to be 27.5 − 10.7 = 16.8 per 1,000 in 1982, compared with a peak 22 per 1,000 in 1965. The highest of the latest available recorded rates is 40.4 (54.6 − 14.2) in Kenya in 1980.

The lowest rate of natural increase in any major independent country is W Germany with a negative figure of − 1.8 per 1,000 for 1984 (9.5 births and 11.3 deaths).

Sex Ratio

There were estimated to be 1,006.7 men in the world for every 1,000 women (1981). The country with the largest recorded shortage of males is the USSR, with 1,145.9 females to every 1,000 males (1981 census). The country with the largest recorded woman shortage is Pakistan, with 906 to every 1,000 males in 1981. The figures are, however, probably under-enumerated due to *purdah,* a policy that keeps women from appearing in public.

Marriage Ages

The country with the lowest average age for marriage is India, with 20.0 years for males and 14.5 for females. At the other extreme is Ireland, with 26.8 for males and 24.7 for females. In the People's Republic of China, the *recommended* age for marriage for men has been 28 and for women 25.

Divorces

The country with the most divorces is the US with a total of 1,155,000 in 1984—a rate of 46.49% of the then current annual total of marriages. The all time high was reached in 1981—1,213,000 or 49.75%.

Infant Mortality

Based on deaths before one year of age, the lowest of the latest available recorded rates is 6.2 deaths per 1,000 live births in Finland and Iceland in 1982. The world rate in 1978 was 91 per 1,000 live births.

The highest recorded infant mortality rate reported has been 195 to 300 per 1,000 live births for Burma in 1952, and 259 for Zaïre in 1950.

In Ethiopia the infant mortality rate was unofficially estimated to be nearly 550 per 1,000 live births in 1969. Many Third World countries have ceased to make returns.

Life Expectation

World expectation of life is rising from 47.4 years (1950–55) to 64.5 years (1995–2000). There is evidence that life expectation in Britain in the 5th century AD was 33 years for males and 27 years for females. In the decade 1890–1900 the expectation of life among the population of India was 23.7 years.

Based on the latest available data, the highest recorded expectation of life at age 12 months is 74.54 years for males in Japan and 80.18 years for females in Japan (1985).

The lowest recorded expectation of life at birth is 27 years for both sexes in the Vallée du Niger area of Mali in 1957 (sample survey, 1957–58). The figure for males in Gabon was 25 years in 1960–61, but 45 for females.

STANDARDS OF LIVING

Housing

For comparison, a dwelling unit is defined as a structurally separated room or rooms occupied by private households of one or more persons and having separate access or a common passageway to the street. The country with the greatest recorded number of private dwelling units was India, which had 100,251,000 occupied in 1972.

The average new house in the US in 1984 cost $100,000.

Hospitals

The largest hospital is the Pilgrim State Hospital, a mental hospital at

West Brentwood, LI, NY, with 3,618 beds. It formerly contained 14,200 beds.

The busiest maternity hospital in the world was the Mama Yemo Hospital in Kinshasa, Zaïre, with 41,930 deliveries in 1976. The record "birthquake" occurred on one day in May 1976 with 175 babies born. It had 599 beds.

The largest psychiatric institute is at UCLA.

The longest stay in a hospital occurred when Martha Nelson was admitted to the Columbus State Institute for the Feeble-Minded in Ohio in 1875, and stayed until she died in Jan 1975, aged 103 years 6 months, in the Orient State Institution, Ohio, spending more than 99 years in institutions.

Physicians

The country with the most physicians is the USSR, with 831,300, or one to every 307 persons. China had an estimated 1.4 million paramedical personnel known as "barefoot doctors" by 1981.

Nine children (4 sons and 5 daughters) of Dr Antonio B Vicencio of Los Angeles qualified as physicians, 1964–82. Henry Lewis Lutterloh and Elizabeth Grantham of Chatham County, NC, were the grandparents of 19 medical doctors. From 1850 to 1962 they practiced a total of 704 man-years.

Psychiatrists and Psychologists

The country with the most psychiatrists is the US. The registered membership of the American Psychiatric Association (inst. 1894) was 27,000 in 1984. The membership of the American Psychological Association (inst. 1892) was 66,000 in 1985.

Dentists

The country with the most dentists is the US, where 145,000 were registered members of the American Dental Association in 1985.

GOVERNMENT

Oldest Ruling House

The Emperor of Japan, Hirohito (b Apr 29, 1901), is the 124th in line from the first Emperor, Jimmu Tenno or Zinmu, whose reign was traditionally from 660 to 581 BC, but probably from c. 40 to c. 10 BC. He has been Emperor since Dec 25, 1926, and is currently the world's longest reigning monarch.

Longest Reigns

The longest recorded reign of any monarch is that of Pepi (Phiops) II, a Sixth Dynasty Pharaoh of ancient Egypt. His reign began in c. 2281 BC when he was aged 6, and is believed to have lasted c. 94 years.

Minhti, king of Arakan (Burma), is reputed to have reigned for 95 years between 1279 and 1374.

Musoma Kanijo, chief of the Nzega district of western Tanganyika (now part of Tanzania), reputedly reigned for more than 98 years from 1864, when aged 8, until his death on Feb 2, 1963.

The longest reign of any European monarch was that of Afonso I Henriques of Portugal. He ascended the throne first as a count and then as king on Apr 30, 1112 and died on Dec 6, 1185 after a reign of 73 years 220 days.

Shortest Reign

The Crown Prince Luis Filipe of Portugal was mortally wounded at the time that his father was killed by a bullet, which severed his carotid artery, in the streets of Lisbon on Feb 1, 1908. He was thus technically King of Portugal (Dom Luis III) for about 20 minutes.

Youngest King and Queen

Forty-six of the world's 170 sovereign states are not republics. They are led by 1 Emperor, 14 Kings, 3 Queens (one, Elizabeth II, as head of 16 other Commonwealth countries), 4 princely rulers, 1 Sultan, 3 Emirs, a Pope, a Sheikh, a Ruler and one elected monarch.

The youngest king is King Mswati III of Swaziland, who was crowned on Apr 25, 1986, age 18. He was the 67th son of King Subhusa II. The youngest queen is Margrethe II of Denmark (b Apr 16, 1940).

British Royalty

The longest reign was that of Queen Victoria (reigned 1837–1901), 63 years 216 days. She lived 81 years 243 days. King George III (reigned 1760–1820) was the longest reigning king, 59 years 96 days.

The shortest reign was 13 days, July 6–19, 1553, by Jane (Lady Jane Grey) who was beheaded soon after at the age of 17. She is known as the "9-day Queen" because she delayed her acceptance of the allegiance of the Lords of the Council until July 9 and wasn't actually proclaimed queen until July 10, 1553.

The king with the most legitimate children was Edward I (reigned 1272–1307), known as Longshanks, who had 18. King Henry I (b 1068–d 1135), in addition to having 1 (possibly 2) legitimate son(s) and a daughter, had at least 20 bastard children (9 sons, 11 daughters) and possibly 22 by 6 mistresses. Queen Anne (b 1665–d 1714) had 17 pregnancies, but produced only 5 live births.

The most married ruler was Henry VIII (reigned 1509–47) who married 6 times.

For the period Oct 30, 1683 to Feb 6, 1685, there were 7 English monarchs living simultaneously. George II had just been born, Charles II was still alive, as were James II, William and Mary, Anne, George I, and also Richard Cromwell, who had been Head of State 1658–59, and who lived under the alias John Clarke until 1712.

Highest-Paid Legislators

The most highly paid of all the world's legislators are US Senators, who from Jan 1, 1985 receive $72,600 in salary, plus honoraria of $20,940. In addition, up to $1,021,167 per year is allowed for office help, with a salary limit of $50,000 for any one staff member per year (limited to 16). Besides, Senators are authorized up to $143,000 per year, depending on the state, for an Official Office Expense Account from which are paid official travel expenses, telegrams, long-distance telephone calls, air-mail postage, stationery, subscriptions to newspapers, and office expenses in the home state. When abroad they have access to "counterpart funds." They also are entitled to very low charges for filming, speech and radio transcriptions, and beauty treatments (females only).

A retiring President electing to also take his Congressional pension (if any) would enjoy a combined pension of $103,500 per annum.

Largest Legislature

The largest legislative assembly is the National People's Congress of the People's Republic of China. The Congress which convened in 1978 had 3,497 members.

Longest UN Speech

The longest speech made in the UN was one of 4 hours 29 min by the president of Cuba, Fidel Castro Ruiz (b Aug 13, 1927) on Sept 26, 1960.

Filibusters

The longest continuous speech in the history of the US Senate was that of Senator Wayne Morse of Oregon, Apr 24–25, 1953, when he spoke on the Tidelands Oil Bill for 22 hours 26 min without resuming his seat. Senator Strom Thurmond, Democrat (SC), spoke against the Civil Rights Bill for 24 hours 19 min, Aug 28–29, 1957, interrupted only briefly by the swearing-in of a new Senator.

The record for a filibuster in any legislature is 43 hours by Texas State Senator Bill Meier from Euless, who spoke against nondisclosure of industrial accidents in May 1977.

Oldest Treaty

The world's oldest treaty is the Anglo-Portuguese Treaty of Alliance signed in London over 600 years ago on June 16, 1373. The text was confirmed "with my usual flourish" by John de Banketre, Clerk.

Constitutions

The world's oldest constitution is that of the US ratified by the necessary Ninth State (New Hampshire) on June 21, 1788 and declared to be in effect on Mar 4, 1789. The only countries without one-document constitutions are Israel, Libya, New Zealand, Oman, and the United Kingdom.

First Female Elected Head of State

President Vigdís Finnbogadóttir (b 1930) of Iceland became the first democratically elected female head of state on June 30, 1980 and took office on Aug 1, 1980.

First State to Allow Female Vote

Wyoming, while still a territory in 1869, allowed women suffrage.

Longest Term of Office

The longest serving current prime minister is Lee Kuan Yew (b Sept 16, 1923) of Singapore who started his 28th year in office on June 5, 1986.

Andrei Andrevich Gromyko (b July 6, 1909) Minister of Foreign Affairs of the USSR from Feb 15, 1957, having been Deputy Foreign Minister from 1946, until he was elected President of the USSR on July 1, 1985.

As minister for non-ferrous metallurgy in the USSR, Pyotr Lomako (b 1904) has served since 1940, and is still in place June 1986, having served on the Central Committee of the CPSU since 1952.

The longest span as a legislator was 83 years by József Madarász (1814–1915). He first attended the Hungarian Parliament in 1832–6 as *oblegatus absentium* (*i.e.* on behalf of an absent deputy). He was a full member in 1848–50 and from 1861 until his death on Jan 31, 1915.

LARGEST ELECTION: 379 million people voted in 1984 in India at 480,000 polling places, choosing from among 5,301 candidates. (*Rex Feature*)

Most Coups

Statisticians contend that Bolivia, since it became a sovereign country in 1825, has had 190 *coups d'état.* The most recent occurred on June 30, 1984, when President Herman Siles Zuazo, 70, was kidnapped from his official residence by 60 armed men.

Largest Elections

The largest elections were those beginning on Dec 24, 1984 for the 542-seat Indian *Lok Sabha* (House of the People) in which 379 million eligible voters chose from among 5,301 candidates at 480,000 polling places manned by a 2½ million staff.

The most candidates for one office were 301 to represent Belguum City in the State Assembly in Karnataka, India, on Mar 5, 1985.

Closest Elections

The ultimate in close general elections occurred in Zanzibar (now part of Tanzania) on Jan 18, 1961, when the Afro-Shirazi Party won by a single seat, after the seat of Chake-Chake on Pemba Island had been gained by a single vote.

The narrowest recorded percentage win in an election would seem to be for the office of Southern District highway commissioner in Mississippi on Aug 7, 1979. Robert E. Joiner was declared winner over W. H. Pyron with 133,587 votes to 133,582. The loser got more than 49.9999% of the votes.

Most One-Sided Elections

North Korea recorded a 100% turn-out of electors and a 100% vote for the Workers' Party of Korea in the general election of Oct 8, 1962.

The next closest approach was in Albania on Nov 14, 1982 when a single voter spoiled national unanimity for the official (and only) Communist candidates, who thus obtained only 99.99993 percent of the poll in a 100 percent turn-out of 1,627,968.

The highest personal majority won by any politician has been 424,545 votes from a total electorate of 625,179 achieved by Ram Bilas Paswan, the Janata candidate for Hajipur in Bihar, India, in Mar 1977.

In the Liberian presidential election of 1927 President Charles D. B. King (1875–1961) was returned with a majority over his opponent, Mr Thomas J. R. Faulkner of the People's Party, officially announced as 234,000. President King thus claimed a "majority" more than 15½ times greater than the entire electorate.

Communist Parties

The largest national Communist party outside the USSR (which had 19 million members in 1986) and Communist states has been the Partito Comunista Italiano (Italian Communist Party), with a membership of 2,300,000 in 1946. The total fell to 1,600,000 by 1986. The membership in mainland China was estimated to be 39 million in 1986.

Voting Ages

The eligibility extremes for voting are 15 years of age in the Philippines and 25 years in Andorra.

---

2. MILITARY AND DEFENSE

WAR

Longest War

The longest of history's countless wars was the "Hundred Years' War" between England and France, which lasted from 1338 to 1453 (115 years), although it may be said that the nine Crusades from the First (1096–1104) to the Ninth (1270–91), extending over 195 years, comprised a single Holy War.

The Swiss Jean Jacques Babel estimated that since *c.* 3500 BC there have only been 292 years without recorded warfare.

Shortest War

The shortest war on record was that between the UK and Zanzibar (now part of Tanzania) from 9:02 to 9:40 A.M. on Aug 27, 1896. The UK battle fleet under Rear-Adm Harry Holdsworth Rawson (1843–1910) delivered an ultimatum to the self-appointed Sultan Sa'id Khalid to evacuate his palace and surrender. This was not forthcoming until after 38 min of bombardment. Admiral Rawson received the Brilliant Star of Zanzibar (first class) from the new Sultan Hamud ibn Muhammad. It was proposed at one time that elements of the local populace should be compelled to defray the cost of the ammunition used.

Most Destructive War

In the Paraguayan war of 1864–70 against Brazil, Argentina and Uruguay, Paraguay's population was reduced from 1,400,000 to 220,000, of whom only 30,000 were adult males.

Largest Armed Forces

Numerically, the largest regular armed force is that of the USSR with 5,300,000 (1985). China's People's Liberation Army of 3.9 million will lose 1 million by 1987. Her reserves number 10.75 million and her paramilitary forces of armed and unarmed militias are estimated by the International Institute of Strategic Studies at some 12 million. The US military manpower is 2,151,568 (1985).

Largest Navies

The largest navy in terms of manpower is the US Navy, with 568,780 sailors and 196,240 Marines in mid-1984. The active strength in 1985 included 4 nuclear-powered with 10 other aircraft carriers, 2 battleships, 95 nuclear attack submarines and 4 diesel attack submarines, 29 cruisers, 68 destroyers, 101 frigates, and 61 amphibious warfare ships.

The USSR Navy has a larger submarine fleet of 371 vessels (121 nuclear, 250 diesel). It has 6 aircraft carriers, 39 cruisers and 47 nuclear-armed and 22 gun destroyers.

Oldest Army

The oldest army is the 83-strong Swiss Guard in the Vatican City, with a regular foundation dating back to Jan 21, 1506. Its origins, however, extend back before 1400.

Largest Army

Numerically, the world's largest army is that of the People's Republic of China, with a total strength of some 2,975,000 in mid-1985. The total size of the USSR's army in mid-1985 was estimated by The International Institute of Strategic Studies at 1,995,000 men.

Tallest and Youngest Soldiers

The tallest soldier of all time was Väinö Myllyrinne (1909–63) who was inducted into the Finnish Army when he was 7 ft 3 in and later grew to 8 ft 3 in. The youngest, Marshal Duke of Caxias (b Aug 25, 1803–d May 7, 1880) entered an infantry regiment of the Brazilian army at the age of 5 in 1808, and became a military hero and statesman.

Largest Air Force

The greatest air force of all time was the US Army Air Corps (now called the US Air Force), which had 79,908 aircraft in July 1944, and 2,411,294 personnel in March 1944. The US Air Force, including strategic air forces, had 603,900 personnel and 4,000 combat aircraft in mid-1985. The USSR Air Force is undergoing massive reorganization, but best estimates indicate 465,000 men in mid-1984. It had 5,950 combat aircraft and 2,300 armed helicopters. In addition, the USSR's Offensive Strategic Rocket Forces had about 325,000 operational personnel in mid-1983.

Longest Marches

The longest march in military history was the famous Long March by the Chinese Communists in 1934–5. In 368 days, of which 268 days were days of movement, from Oct to Oct, their force of 90,000 covered 6,000 miles from Kiangsi to Yenan in Shensi via Yünnan. They crossed 18 mountain ranges and six major rivers and lost all but 22,000 of their force in continual rear-guard actions against Nationalist Kuo-min-tang (KMT) forces.

The record road march (11 men with 40 lb packs) over a marathon (26 miles 385 yds) was 6 hours 26 min 23.22 sec by Company D, 1st Battalion, US Army Intelligence School, Fort Devens, Mass. on June 30, 1983.

Earliest Tanks

The first tank was "No. 1 Lincoln," modified to become "Little Willie," built by William Foster & Co Ltd of Lincoln, England. It first ran on Sept 8, 1915. Tanks were first taken into action by the Heavy Section Machine Gun Corps, which later became the Royal Tank Corps, at the battle of Flers-Courcelette, France on Sept 15, 1916. The Mark I Male, which was armed with a pair of 6-lb guns and 4 machine-guns, weighed 31.4 tons and was driven by a motor developing 105 hp, which gave it a maximum road speed of 3 to 4 mph.

Heaviest and Fastest Tanks

The heaviest tank ever constructed was the German Panzer Kampfwagen Maus II, which weighed 212 tons. By 1945 it had reached only the experimental stage and was not proceeded with.

The heaviest operational tank used by any army was the 91.3-ton 13-man French Char de Rupture 2C bis of 1923. It carried a 155-mm howitzer and had two 250-hp engines giving a maximum speed of 8 mph. The most heavily armed tank since 1972 has been the Soviet T-72 with a 125-mm high velocity gun.

The world's fastest tank is the British Scorpion AFV which can reach 50 mph, with 75% payload.

Earliest Guns

Although it cannot be accepted as proved, the best opinion is that the earliest guns were constructed in North Africa, possibly by Arabs, *c.* 1250. The earliest representation of an English gun is contained in an illustrated manuscript dated 1326 at Oxford. The earliest anti-aircraft gun was an artillery piece on a high-angle mounting used in the Franco-Prussian War of 1870 by the Prussians against French balloons.

Largest Guns

The two most massive guns ever constructed were used by the Germans in the siege of Sevastapol on the Eastern Front in World War II. They were of a caliber of 800 mm (31.5 in) with barrels 94 ft 8½ in long, and named *Dora* and *Gustav*. Their remains were discovered, one near Metzenhof, Bavaria in Aug 1945 and the other in the Soviet zone of Germany. They were built by Krupp as railway guns, carried on 24 cars, two of which had 40 wheels each. The whole assembly of the gun was 141 ft long and weighed 1,482 tons, requiring a crew of 1,500 men. The range for a 9¼-ton projectile was 29 miles.

Greatest Range

The greatest range ever attained by a gun is by the HARP (High Altitude Research Project) consisting of two 16-in/50-caliber barrels in tandem, 119.4 ft long and weighing 165 tons, at Yuma, Ariz. On Nov 19, 1966, a 185-lb projectile was fired to an altitude of 111.8 miles (590,550 ft). The static V3 underground firing tubes built by the Germans in 50° shafts at Mimoyecques, near Calais, France to bombard London were never operative, due to RAF bombing.

The famous long-range gun which shelled Paris in World War I in March 1918 was the *Kaiser Wilhelm Geschütz,* with a caliber of 220 mm

GUN WITH GREATEST RANGE: The HARP can shoot two 16-in/50-caliber barrels, one after the other, each 119.4 ft long and 165 tons in weight. A 185-lb projectile was fired to a height of 590,550 ft in a test in Ariz in 1966.

(8.66 in), a designed range of 79.5 miles and an achieved range of 76 miles. The "Big Berthas" were mortars of 420-mm (16.53-in) caliber with a range of less than 9 miles.

Largest Catapults

The largest military catapults, or onagers, could throw a missile weighing 60 lb a distance of 500 yd.

Largest Cannon

The highest caliber cannon ever constructed is the *Tsar Puchka* (King of Cannons), now housed in the Kremlin, Moscow. It was built in the 16th century with a bore of 920 mm (36.2 in) and a barrel 10 ft 5 in long. It weighs 44 tons.

The Turks fired up to seven shots per day from a bombard 26 ft long, with an internal caliber of 42 in, against the walls of Constantinople (now Istanbul) Apr 12-May 29, 1453. It was dragged by 60 oxen and 200 men and fired a stone cannonball of 1,200 lb.

Mortars

The largest mortars ever constructed were Mallets mortar (Woolwich Arsenal, London, 1857), and the "Little David" of World War II, made in the US. Each had a caliber of 920 mm (36¼ in), but neither was ever used in action.

The heaviest mortar used was the tracked German 600-mm (23.6-in) siege piece known as "Karl" used against Stalingrad.

Bombs

The heaviest conventional bomb ever used operationally was the British Royal Air Force's "Grand Slam," weighing 22,000 lb and measuring

25 ft 5 in long, dropped on Bielefeld railway viaduct, Germany, March 14, 1945. In 1949, the US Air Force tested a bomb weighing 42,000 lb at Muroc Dry Lake, Calif.

The heaviest known nuclear bomb has been the 9,900-ton (explosive power) bomb carried by US B-52 bombers. These bombs (12 ft 0½ in in length) were phased out by Jan 1984.

Atomic Bombs

The two atom bombs dropped on Japan by the US in 1945 each had an explosive power equivalent to that of 12,500 tons (12.5 kilotons) of trinitrotoluene, called TNT. The one dropped 1,670 ft above Hiroshima, code-named "Little Boy," was 10 ft long and weighed 9,000 lb.

The most powerful thermonuclear device so far tested is one with a power equivalent to 57 million tons of TNT, or 57 megatons, detonated by the USSR in the Novaya Zemlya area at 8:33 A.M. GMT on Oct 30, 1961. The shock wave was detected to have circled the world three times, taking 36 hours 27 min for the first circuit. Some estimates put the power of this device at between 62 and 90 megatons. The largest US H-bomb tested was the 18–22 megaton "Bravo" at Bikini Atoll, Marshall Islands, Mar 1, 1954. On Aug 9, 1961, Nikita Khrushchev, then the Chairman of the Council of Ministers of the USSR, declared that the Soviet Union was capable of constructing a 100-megaton bomb, and announced the possession of one in East Berlin, Germany, on Jan 16, 1963. Such a device could make a crater in rock 355 ft deep and 1.8 miles wide and a fireball of 46,000 ft, or 8.7 miles, in diameter.

Atom bomb theory began with Albert Einstein's publication of the $E = mc^2$ formula in *Annalen der Physik* in Leipzig on May 14, 1907. It became practical with the mesothorium experiments of Otto Hahn (1879–1968), Fritz Strassman (b 1902) and Lise Meitner (1878–1968) on Dec 17, 1938. Work started in the USSR on atomic bombs in June 1942, although the first chain reaction was not achieved until Dec 1945, by Dr Igor Vasilyevich Kurchatov (1903–60).

The concept of a thermonuclear fusion bomb was that of Edward Teller (b 1908) in 1942. Development was ordered by President Truman on Jan 30, 1950 and code-named "Super." The bomb only became practical as a result of a calculation by the Polish-born American, Stanislaw Ulam (1909–84).

Largest Nuclear Weapons

The most powerful ICBMs are the USSR's SS-18s (Model 5) believed to be armed with ten 750-kiloton MIRVs (multiple independently-targetable re-entry vehicles). Models 1 and 3 have a single 20-megaton warhead. The US Minuteman III has 3 MIRVs each of 335 kiloton force.

No official estimate has been published of the potential power of the device known as Doomsday, but this far surpasses any tested weapon. If it were practicable to construct, it is speculated that a 50,000-megaton cobalt-salted device could wipe out the entire human race except people who were deep underground and who did not emerge for at least five years.

Nuclear Delivery Vehicles

As of Jan 1, 1985, the USSR deployed 2,547 strategic nuclear delivery vehicles or 297 above SALT II contractual ceiling. The US on the same date deployed 1,814 vehicles or 436 below the 2,250 SALT II limit. The comparative number of warheads has been estimated at USSR—9,900 and US—10,174.

> ### "Star Wars"
> The first reported successful "high frontier" interception test in outer space by the US Strategic Defense Initiative occurred over the Pacific on June 10, 1984.

Largest "Conventional" Explosion

The largest use of conventional explosive was for the demolition of the fortifications and U-Boat pens at Helgoland on April 18, 1947. A net charge of 4,253 tons was detonated by Commissioned Gunner E. C. Jellis of the Royal Navy team headed by Lt F. T. Woosnam aboard *HMS Lasso* lying 9 miles out to sea.

Most Bombed Country

The most heavily bombed country has been Laos. It has been estimated that between May 1964 and Feb 26, 1973 some 2½ million tons of bombs of all kinds were dropped along the North to South Ho Chi Minh Trail supply route to South Vietnam.

---

3. JUDICIAL

LEGISLATION AND LITIGATION

Longest Trial

The longest trial in criminal history was *People of the State of California* vs *Angelo Buono, Jr.* involving 10 charges of the Hillside murders of young women from Oct 18, 1977 to Feb 1978. The jury trial took 345 trial days over 2 years 2 days (Nov 16, 1981–Nov 18, 1983) with a 57,079-page transcript, 400 witnesses and 2,000 exhibits. Judge Ronald M. George imposed nine sentences of life without parole on Jan 9, 1984.

Best-Attended Trial

The greatest attendance at any trial was at that of Major Jesús Sosa Blanco, aged 51, for an alleged 108 murders. At one point in the 12½-hour trial (5:30 P.M. to 6 A.M., Jan 22–23, 1959), 17,000 people were present in the Havana Sports Palace, Cuba. Blanco was executed on Feb 18, 1959.

Largest Award Won Without Attorney

Dr Mark Feldman, a podiatric surgeon of Lauderhill, Fla, became the first litigant in person (without the services of an attorney) to secure 7 figures ($1 million) before a jury in compensatory and punitive damages in Sept 1980. The case concerned conspiracy and fraud alleged against 6 other doctors.

Highest Bail

The highest bail ever ordered was $1 billion each for two suspected illicit drug dealers in Suffolk County, Long Island, NY. Judge Louis L. Ohlig of the District Court was the judge, who said, "They're not going to be handled with kid gloves any more." The suspects were alleged to be part of a ring that smuggled $24 million of cocaine per month into the US.

Abul Hassen Ebtehaj, later Chairman of the Iranian Bank in Teheran, was granted bail in 1977 in excess of $50 million.

Breach of Contract

The greatest damages ever awarded for a breach of contract were £610,392 ($1,709,000), awarded July 16, 1930, to the Bank of Portugal against the printers Waterlow & Sons Ltd of London, arising from their unauthorized printing of 580,000 five-hundred escudo notes in 1925. This award was upheld in the House of Lords on Apr 28, 1932. One of the perpetrators, Arthur Virgilio Alves Reis, served 16 years (1930–46) in jail.

Greatest Personal Injury Damages

The greatest personal injury damages ever awarded were to an unnamed boy born during a complicated 45-min birth at the US Army's Letterman General Hospital in 1979. If the child, which had "total cerebral palsy," lives out his expected years, the potential US government payment could amount to $70 million. The first payment was received on Sept 30, 1983.

On Nov 24, 1983 a jury in Corpus Christi, Tex awarded punitive damages of $106 million against Ford Motor Co for alleged design faults in the Ford Mustang II in which Bevary Durrill, 20, died in 1974. An appeal is pending.

The largest sum given for invasion of privacy was $40 million awarded to author-actress Jackie Collins by a Federal jury of 6 women on June 16, 1983 in NYC for use of nude photos published in 1980 by the magazine *Adelina* incorrectly identified as being of her.

The largest single cash payment settlement for a single person has been $6,800,000 to John Coates, 42, a lawyer from Austin, Tex against Remington Arms Co Inc *et al,* on Oct 2, 1978. The case concerned severe injury from a defectively made hunting rifle.

The highest damages ever quantified have been $14,387,674 following the crash of a private aircraft at South Lake Tahoe, Calif, on Feb 21, 1967, to the sole survivor Ray Rosendin, 45, by the Santa Clara Superior Court on March 8, 1972. Rosendin was awarded *inter alia* $1,069,374 for the loss of both legs and disabling arm injuries and $1,213,129 for the loss of his wife. Punitive damages against Avco-Lycoming Corp, which allegedly violated Federal regulations when it rebuilt the aircraft engine owned by Rosendin Corp, were originally set at $10½ million but were overturned on appeal.

Defamation Suits

A sum of $16.8 million was awarded to Dr John J. Wild, 58, at the Hennepin District Court of Minnesota on Nov 30, 1972, against the Minnesota Foundation and others for defamation, bad-faith termination of a contract, and interference with professional business relationships, plus $10.8 million in punitive damages. The Supreme Court of Minnesota reduced the award to $1.5 million on Jan 10, 1975, but allowed Dr. Wild the option of a new trial. There was a no-disclosure clause in the settlement.

The $39.6 million awarded in Columbus, O on Mar 1, 1980, to Robert Guccione, publisher of *Penthouse*, for defamation against Larry Flynt, publisher of *Hustler*, was reduced by Judge Craig Wright to $4 million on Apr 17, 1980. The hearing ended in May 1982 with *Penthouse* being cleared of libel.

A $640-million libel suit was brought by the Calif resort La Costa against *Penthouse* and its publisher in Mar 1975. In May 1982 a jury found for the magazine. In July their verdict was set aside by a Calif judge, who was then removed from the case. Costs exceed $10 million to date.

Greatest Compensation for Wrongful Imprisonment

Isadore Zimmerman (1917–83) of NY spent 24 years in prison before his conviction for murdering a cop was overturned because of new evidence. On his release at age 66 he was awarded $1 million, which is equivalent to $42,000 for each year he spent in prison. But, after legal fees and expenses, he ended up with only 60 percent of the million. Zimmerman decided not to appeal the award, and died a little more than a year later.

The largest award previously was made on Aug 12, 1975, to William De Palma (b 1938) of Whittier, Calif, who obtained a $750,000 settlement for 16 months' wrongful imprisonment in McNeil Island Federal Prison, Wash. He had been given a 15-year sentence for armed robbery in Buena Park, Calif, on forged fingerprint evidence in 1968.

Alimony

The highest alimony awarded by a court has been $2,261,000 against George Storer Sr, 74, in favor of his third wife Dorothy, 73, in Miami, Fla, on Oct 29, 1974. Mr Storer, a broadcasting executive, was also ordered to pay his ex-wife's attorney $200,000 in fees.

Belgian-born Sheika Dena Al-Fassi, 23, filed the highest ever alimony claim of $3 billion against her former husband Sheik Mohammed Al-Fassi, 28, of the Saudi Arabia royal family, in LA, Calif, in Feb 1982. Explaining the size of the settlement claim, Lawyer Marvin Mitchelson alluded to the Sheik's wealth which included 14 homes in Florida alone and numerous private aircraft. When in 1983 she was awarded $81 million she declared herself "very very happy" if she was able to collect.

Patent Case

The greatest settlement ever made in a patent-infringement suit was $55.8 million in Pfizer, Inc vs International Rectifier Corp and Rochelle Laboratories over the antibiotic dioxycycline on July 5, 1983.

Greatest Lien

The greatest lien ever imposed by a court is 40 billion lire ($64,800,000) on Apr 9, 1974 in Milan, upon Vittorio and Ida Riva for back taxes allegedly due on a chain of cotton mills around Turin, Italy inherited by their brother Felice (who left for Beirut) in 1960.

Heaviest Fine

It was reported in Jan 1979 that Carlo Ponti, husband of Sophia

HEAVIEST FINE: The Italian courts announced in 1979 that Sophia Loren's husband, Carlo Ponti, was to be fined the equivalent of $26.4 million for unpaid taxes.

Loren, was to be fined the equivalent of $26.4 million by the Italian courts in connection with claims for taxes alleged to be due but unpaid.

Longest Lease

The longest lease on record is for 10 million years for a plot for a sewage tank adjoining Columb Barracks, Ireland, signed on Dec 3, 1888.

Most Literal Legal Interpretation

Eugene Schneider of Carteret, NJ, cut his $80,000 home in half with a chain saw in July 1976 after his wife sued him for divorce, thus fulfilling in his eyes the equal division of property required by NJ law. Encouraged by this case, Virgil M. Everhart of Central City, Ky, 57, chopped and sawed away at his house with TV cameras turning on Jan 20, 1983, until he was stopped by a judge who criticized his "cute trick" and made an alimony award to his wife instead.

Shortest and Longest Wills

The shortest valid will in the world is "Vse zene," the Czech for "All to wife," written and dated Jan 19, 1967, by Herr Karl Tausch of Langen, Hesse, Germany. The shortest will contested but subsequently admitted to probate in English law was the case of *Thorne v. Dickens* in 1906. It consisted of the three words "All for Mother" in which "mother" was not his mother but his wife.

The longest will on record was that of Mrs Frederica Evelyn Stilwell Cook (US), proved on Nov 2, 1925 at Somerset House, London. It consisted of four bound volumes containing 95,940 words.

Youngest Judges

No collated records on the ages of judicial appointments exist. However, David Elmer Ward had to await the legal age of 21 before taking office after nomination in 1932 as Judge of the County Court at Fort Myers, Fla.

Most Successful Criminal Lawyer

Sir Lionel Luckhoo, senior partner of Luckhoo and Luckhoo, of Georgetown, Guyana, succeeded in getting his 245th successive murder charge acquittal by Jan 1, 1985.

Multimillionaire Melvin M Belli (b July 30, 1907) took display ads in the press on his 77th birthday to celebrate his "unparalleled 50-year career in law defending the injured and the poor."

Largest Law Firm

Baker & McKenzie, founded in Chicago in 1949, is the largest law firm with 815 lawyers in 35 offices in 25 different countries.

CRIME AND PUNISHMENT

Mass Killing

The best estimate of the number of Jewish victims of the Holocaust or the genocidal "Final Solution" ordered by Adolf Hitler (1889–1945) in Apr 1941 and continued into May 1945 is 5.8 million.

During the regime of Mao Tse-tung (1949–65), 26,300,000 Chinese were said by the USSR to have been killed by government forces. The estimate by the US Senate Judiciary Committee is 32.25 to 61.7 million.

Saving of Life

The greatest number of people saved from extinction by one man is an estimated 90,000 Jews in Budapest, Hungary, from July 1944 to Jan 1945 by the Swedish diplomat Raoul Wallenberg (b Aug 4, 1912). After escaping an assassination attempt by the Nazis, he was imprisoned without trial by the Soviet Union. On Feb 6, 1957 Mr Gromyko said Prisoner "Walenberg" had died in a cell in Lubyanka jail, Moscow, July 16, 1947. Sighting reports within the Gulag system have persisted for 40 years after his disappearance. He was made an Honorary Citizen of the US on Oct 5, 1981 and, in Mar 1984, there was agitation in Hungary to restore his removed statue to St. Stephan's Park, in Budapest.

Terrorist Outrages

The greatest civilian death toll from a terrorist bomb was 329 killed when an Air India Boeing 747 was destroyed by a bomb over the North Atlantic while approaching Shannon, Ireland on June 23, 1985.

Largest Criminal Organization

The largest syndicate of organized crime is the Mafia (derived from an Arabic expression connoting beauty, excellence allied with bravery) or La Cosa Nostra ("our thing") which is said to have infiltrated the executive, judiciary and legislative branches of the US Government.

It consists of some 3,000 to 5,000 individuals in 25 "families" federated under "The Commission." Their purported turnover in vice, gambling, protection rackets, tobacco, bootlegging, hijacking, narcotics, loan-sharking, prostitution and some legitimate business was estimated in a *US News & World Report* of Dec 1982 at $200 billion per year.

The biggest Mafia killing was Sept 11–13, 1931, when the topmost man, Salvatore Maranzano, *Il Capo di Tutti Capi,* and 40 allies were liquidated.

The Mafia is said to have got its start in the US in New Orleans in 1869. The greatest breaches of the vow of silence were by Joseph Valachi who "sang like a canary" in 1963 and by Tommaso Buschetta, 56, in 1984.

Murder Rates

The country with the highest recorded murder rate is Brazil with 104 registered homicides per 100,000 of the population in 1983, or 370 per day.

A total of 592 deaths was attributed to one Colombian bandit leader, Teófilo ("Sparks") Rojas, aged 27, between 1948 and his death in an ambush near Armenia on Jan 22, 1963. Some sources attribute 3,500 slayings to him, 1945–62.

The highest homicide rates recorded in NYC have been 58 in a week in July 1972, and 13 in a day in Aug 1972. In 1973, the total for Detroit (population then 1,500,000) was 751. The Chicago Crime Commission in Mar 1983 published a list of 1,081 unsolved gang slayings since 1919.

The country with the lowest officially recorded rate in the world is the Maldives (islands in the Indian Ocean, pop. 100,833 in 1966) with a nil rate among its nationals since its independence in July 1965. In the Indian state of Sikkim, in the Himalayas, murder is practically unknown, while in the Hunza area of Kashmir, in the Karakoram, only one definite case by a Hunzarwal has been recorded since 1900.

Suicide

The estimated daily rate of suicides throughout the world surpassed 1,000 in 1965. The country with the highest recorded suicide rate is Hungary, with 42.6 per 100,000 of the population in 1977. The country with the lowest recorded rate is Jordan, with a single case in 1970 and hence a rate of 0.04 per 100,000.

The final total number of victims of the mass cyanide poisoning of the Peoples Temple cult near Port Kaituma, Guyana, Nov 18, 1978 was 913. The leader was the paranoid "Rev" Jim Jones of San Francisco, who had deposited millions of dollars overseas.

The volcanic crater of Mt Mihara on an island in Sagami Bay, south of Yokohama, Japan was the scene of more than 1,000 suicides in 1933–36.

Mass Poisonings

On May 1, 1981, the first victim of the Spanish cooking-oil scandal fell ill. On June 12 it was discovered that his cause of death was the use of "denatured" industrial colza from rape seed. By May 1984 the toll was over 350 dead with thousands maimed. The manufacturers Ramon and Elias Ferrero await trial in Carabanchel Jail, Madrid.

Largest Hangings

The most people hanged from one gallows were 38 Sioux Indians by William J. Duly outside Mankato, Minn, for the murder of unarmed citizens on Dec 26, 1862.

The Nazi Feldkommandant simultaneously hanged 50 Greek resistance men as a reprisal in Athens on July 22, 1944.

Longest Prison Sentences

A 10,000-year sentence was imposed on Dudley Wayne Kyzer (Deuel Wilhelm Davies), 40, on Dec 4, 1981, in Tuscaloosa, Ala, for a triple murder (including his mother-in-law) in 1976. A sentence of 384,912 years was *demanded* at the prosecution of Gabriel March Grandos, 22, at

Palma de Mallorca, Spain, March 11, 1972, for failing to deliver 42,768 letters, a sentence of 9 years per letter.

Juan Corona, a Mexican-American, was sentenced on Feb 5, 1973, at Fairfield, Calif, to 25 consecutive life terms for murdering 25 migrant farm workers he had hired, killed and buried in 1970–71 near Feather River, Yuba City, Calif. His 20th century record was surpassed in 1974 by Dean Corll (27 victims) of Houston, Tex, and in 1980 by John Wayne Gacy (33 victims).

Longest Time Served

Paul Geidel (b Apr 21, 1894) was convicted of 2nd degree murder on Sept 5, 1911 as a 17-year-old porter in a NYC hotel. He was released from the Fishkill Correctional Facility, Beacon, NY, aged 85, on May 7, 1980, having served 68 years 8 months 2 days—the longest recorded term in US history. He had first refused parole in 1974.

Greatest Mass Arrest

The greatest mass arrest reported in a democratic country was of more than 13,000 people in an antiwar demonstration designed to block rush-hour traffic in Wash, DC, May 3–5, 1971.

Most Secure Prison

After it became a maximum security Federal prison in 1934, no convict was known to have lived to tell of a successful escape from the prison on Alcatraz Island in San Francisco Bay. A total of 23 men attempted it, but 12 were recaptured, 5 shot dead, one drowned and 5 presumed drowned. On Dec 16, 1962, three months before the prison was closed, one man reached the mainland alive, only to be recaptured on the spot. John Chase was imprisoned for a record 26 years on Alcatraz.

Most Expensive Prison

Spandau Prison, Berlin, built 100 years ago for 600 prisoners, is now used solely for the person widely and officially purported to be the Nazi war criminal Rudolf Hess (b Apr 26, 1894). The cost of maintenance has been estimated at $415,000 per year for the staff of 105.

Longest Prison Escape

The longest recorded escape by a prisoner who was eventually recaptured was that of Leonard T. Fristoe, 77, who escaped from Nevada State Prison, on Dec 15, 1923, and was turned in by his son on Nov 15, 1969, at Compton, Calif. He had 46 years of freedom under the name Claude R. Willis. He had killed two sheriff's deputies in 1920.

Greatest Jail Break

In Feb 1979, US Army Col Arthur "Bull" Simons (ret) led a band of 14 to break into Gasre prison, Teheran, Iran, to rescue two fellow Americans. Some 11,000 other prisoners took advantage of this and the Islamic revolution in what became history's largest jail break.

In July 1971, Raoul Sendic and 105 other Tupamaro guerrillas escaped from a Uruguayan prison through a tunnel 298 ft long.

Theft

The government of the Philippines announced on Apr 23, 1986 that it had succeeded in identifying $860.8 million that had been "salted away" by former president Ferdinand Edralin Marcos (b Sept 11, 1917) and his wife Imelda. The total stolen, it was asserted, since Nov 1965, was believed to be between $5 and $10 billion.

Robbery

The greatest robbery on record was that of the Reichsbank following Germany's collapse in Apr/May 1945. The Pentagon described the event first published in the *Guinness Book* in 1957 as "an unverified allegation." *Nazi Gold,* a book by Ian Sayer and Douglas Botting published in 1984, revealed full details and estimated the total haul at current values as £2,500 million ($3 billion).

The greatest amount lost in a small robbery was on Nov 26, 1983 when £26,369,778 ($36,000,000) worth of gold and platinum in the form of 6,800 bars, together with diamonds and travelers checks, in 76 boxes were removed by 6 masked men from a warehouse vault of Brinks Mat Ltd at Heathrow, England. Michael McAvoy, 32, of East Dulwich, and Brian Robinson, 41, of Lewisham, were each sentenced to 25 years at the Old Bailey on Dec 3, 1984.

An equal amount (est. $36 million) was lost in a haul from 352 safe deposit boxes in Banca Nazionale del Lavoro, Italy, during June 29–July 2, 1984.

Art Theft

The greatest recorded robbery by market valuation was the removal of 19 paintings, valued at $19,200,000, taken from Russborough House, Blessington, Ireland, the home of Sir Alfred and Lady Beit, by 4 men and a woman, Apr 26, 1974. They included the $6.9 million Vermeer *Lady Writing a Letter with her Maid.* The paintings were recovered May 4, 1974, near Glandore, Ireland. Dr Rose Bridgit Dugdale (b 1941) was subsequently convicted.

THEFT: When Imelda Marcos left her 3,000 pairs of shoes in the Philippines palace, she and her husband were accused of "salting away" between $5 and $10 billion out of government funds. (*AP Wirephoto*)

It is arguable that the value of the *Mona Lisa* at the time of its theft from the Louvre on Aug 21, 1911, was greater than this figure. It was recovered in Italy in 1913 when Vincenzo Perruggia was charged with its theft.

On Sept 1, 1964, antiquities reputedly worth $23 million were recovered from 3 warehouses near the Pyramids in Egypt.

In a theft from the National Anthropology and History Institute, Mexico City, on Dec 25, 1985, some 140 "priceless" gold, jade and obsidian artifacts were taken.

Bank Robbery

During the extreme civil disorder prior to Jan 22, 1976, in Beirut, Lebanon, a guerrilla force blasted the vaults of the British Bank of the Middle East in Bab Idriss and cleared out safe deposit boxes with contents valued by former Finance Minister Lucien Dahadah at $50 million, and by another source at an "absolute minimum" of $20 million.

Jewel Robbery

The greatest recorded theft of jewels was from the bedroom of the "well-guarded" villa of Prince Abdel Aziz Ben Ahmed Al-Thani near Cannes, France, July 24, 1980, valued at $16 million.

Train Robbery

The greatest recorded train robbery occurred between 3:03 A.M. and 3:27 A.M. on Aug 8, 1963, when a General Post Office mail train from Glasgow, Scotland was ambushed at Sears Crossing and robbed at Bridego Bridge near Mentmore, Buckinghamshire, England. The gang escaped with about 120 mailbags containing £2,631,784 ($6,053,103) worth of bank notes being taken to London for pulping. Only £343,448 ($961,654) was recovered.

Maritime Fraud

A cargo of 198,000 tons of Kuwaiti crude oil on the supertanker *Salem* at Durban was sold without title to the South African government in Dec 1979. The ship mysteriously sank off Senegal on Jan 17, 1980 leaving the government to pay $305 million to Shell International who owned the shipment.

Greatest Kidnapping Ransom

Historically, the greatest ransom paid was that for their chief, Atahualpa, by the Incas to the Spanish conquistador Francisco Pizarro, in 1532–33 at Cajamarca, Peru, which included a hall full of gold and silver, worth in modern money some $170 million.

The greatest ransom ever extorted is $60 million for the release of two businessmen, the brothers Jorge Born, 40, and Juan Born, 39, of Argentina, paid to the left-wing urban guerrilla group Montoneros in Buenos Aires, June 20, 1975.

The youngest person ever kidnapped has been Carolyn Wharton, who was born at 12:46 P.M., March 19, 1955, in the Baptist Hospital, Beaumont, Tex, and kidnapped by a woman disguised as a nurse at 1:15 P.M., when the baby was aged 29 min.

Greatest Hijack Ransom

The highest amount ever paid to aircraft hijackers has been $6 million by the Japanese government in the case of a JAL DC-8 held at Dacca airport, Bangladesh on Oct 2, 1977 with 38 hostages. Six convicted criminals were also exchanged. The Bangladesh government had refused to sanction any retaliatory action.

Customs Fraud

The Amway Corp pleaded guilty to defrauding the Canadian government out of more than $25 million (US) through customs violations, 1965–80.

Greatest Currency Forgery

The greatest recorded forgery was the German Third Reich government's forging operation, code name "Bernhard," engineered by S.S. *Sturmbannführer* Alfred Naujocks in 1940–41. It involved £150 million (now about $300 million) worth of Bank of England £5 notes.

Biggest Bank Fraud

The largest amount of money named in a defalcation case has been a gross 222 million Swiss francs ($75,900,000) at the Lugano, Switzerland, branch of Lloyd's Bank International Ltd Sept 2, 1974. Mark Colombo was arrested pending charges including falsification of foreign currency accounts and suppression of evidence.

Computer Fraud

Between 1964 and 1973, some 64,000 fake insurance policies were created on the computer of the Equity Funding Corporation involving $2,000 million.

Stanley Mark Rifkin (b 1946) was arrested in Carlsbad, Calif by the FBI on Nov 6, 1978, charged with defrauding a Los Angeles bank of $10.2 million by manipulation of a computer system. In June 1980 he was sentenced to 8 years.

Welfare Swindle

The greatest welfare swindle yet worked was that of the gypsy Anthony Moreno, on the French Social Security in Marseilles. By forging birth certificates and school registration forms, he invented 197 fictitious families and 3,000 children on which he claimed benefits from 1960 to mid-1968. Moreno, nicknamed "El Chorro" (the fountain), was later reported free of extradition worries and living in luxury in his native Spain having absquatulated with an estimated $6,440,000.

Largest Narcotics Haul

The greatest drug haul ever achieved was 13.5 tons of cocaine with a street value of $1,200 million taken in the Caqueta jungle province of Colombia on Mar 10, 1984 in 10 processing plants protected by the armed wing of the Colombian Communist Party FARC (Fuerzas Armadas Revolucionarias Columbias). The US ambassador estimated that the haul was equal to one quarter of the annual consumption of cocaine in the US.

In Oct 1983, it was estimated that the narcotics crime in the US was running at $80,000 million per annum with cocaine dealers turning a profit of $35,000 million and illegal domestic "green collar" marijuana growers netting $13,900 million.

The bulkiest marijuana haul was 3,192 tons of Colombian marijuana in the 14-month-long "Operation Tiburon" concluded by the DEA with the arrest of 495 people and the seizure of 95 vessels, announced on Feb 5, 1982.

---

4. ECONOMIC

MONETARY AND FINANCE

Largest Check

The greatest amount paid by a single check in the history of banking was equivalent to $2,046,700,000, handed over by Daniel P. Moynihan, then the US Ambassador to India, in New Delhi, Feb 18, 1974. An internal US Treasury check for $4,176,969,623.57 was drawn on June 30, 1954.

Smallest Check

Dean Moon of Santa Fe Springs, Calif, was due one cent from a miscalculation on a UPS shipment and the transportation company delivered a check for the full amount.

A check of similar amount, sent by Robert W. Alvord of Wash, DC, in payment for a shortage claim was duly accepted and deposited by Wells Fargo Credit Corp.

Still another 1¢ check was issued by the Citizens National Bank & Trust Co of Baytown, Tex, for the Houston Light & Power Co to reimburse Arvin E. Bandy, but he never cashed it.

Largest Budget

The greatest annual expenditure budgeted by any country is $979,900 million by the US Government (federal expenditure) for the fiscal year 1986. The highest-ever revenue was $771,100 million for the same fiscal year.

In the US, the greatest surplus was $8,419,469,844 in 1947–48, and the greatest budgeted deficit was the $212,300 million for the fiscal year ending Sept 30, 1985.

Foreign Aid

The total net foreign aid given by the US Government between July 1, 1945, and Jan 1, 1985, was $243,481 million.

The country which received most US aid in 1985 was Israel with $3,750 million. US foreign aid began with $50,000 to Venezuela for earthquake relief in 1812.

Highest Tax Rates

The country with the most confiscatory taxation is Norway where in Jan 1974 the Labor Party and Socialist Alliance abolished the 80% top limit. Some 2,000 citizens were then listed in the *Lignings Boka* as paying more than 100% of their taxable income. The shipping magnate Hilmer Reksten was assessed at 491%.

Highest Tax Demand

The highest recorded personal tax demand is one for $336 million for 70% of the estate of Howard Hughes.

Least Taxed People

The lowest income tax is paid by the citizens of Bahrain, Kuwait, Brunei and Qatar, where the rate, regardless of income, is zero.

Poorest Country

The lowest annual income per person in any country is $80 in 1982 for Chad.

National Wealth Per Capita

The richest nation, measured by average income per capita of population, is Nauru (pop. 8,000 in 1983), with $21,400 in 1983. The US, which had taken the lead in 1910, was 6th behind Nauru and United Arab Emirates (1), Brunei (2), Qatar (3), Kuwait (4) and Switzerland (5).

It has been estimated that the value of all physical assets in the US in Jan 1983 was $12.5 trillion or $53,800 per head.

National Debt

The largest national debt is that of the US, where the gross Federal public debt surpassed the trillion dollar mark in 1981. By May 1986, it had reached $2,112 million.

Foreign Debt

The country most heavily in overseas debt is Brazil with $103 billion by mid-1985. The highest per capita is that of Chile with $17,000 million for a population of 11.5 million in mid-1983 or $1,478 per person.

Gross National Product

The country with the largest GNP is the US, reaching $3 trillion in 1981. By Dec 31, 1985, it was running at $3,988.5 billion.

Gold Reserves

The country with the greatest monetary gold reserve is the US, whose Treasury had 266.66 million fine oz of the world's 950 million fine oz on hand in Mar 1986. Valued at $315 per fine oz, these amounts translate to $82,780 million and $300,000 million, respectively. The US Bullion Depository at Fort Knox, 30 miles southwest of Louisville, Ky, has been the principal depository of US gold since 1936. Gold is stored in 446,000 standard mint bars of 400 troy oz (439 oz avoirdupois), measuring 7 × 3⅝ × 1⅝ in.

Worst Inflation

The world's worst inflation occurred in Hungary in June 1946, when the 1931 gold pengö was valued at 130 quintillion (1.3×10^{20}) paper pengös. Notes were issued for "Egymillard" billion (1 followed by 21 zeros or 10^{21}) pengös on June 3 and withdrawn on July 11, 1946. Notes for 1 sextillion or 10^{27} pengös were issued for tax payments only.

In Germany, on Nov 6, 1923, the circulation of Reichsbank marks reached 400,338,326,350,700,000,000, a level of inflation 755,700 million times the 1913 levels.

The country with the current highest annual rate of inflation was Bolivia with 8,000+%. It peaked in Oct 1985 with 24,000%, or an annual rate of 23,503% for Sept 1984–Sept 1985.

MOST VALUABLE: In Canadian dollars, this 37½-in diameter souvenir gold coin when minted in early 1986 was worth $1,547,290.35 (US $1,102,106.70). Made of 14K gold ¾-in thick, it was the centerpiece of the exhibit at Expo '86 Vancouver, protected at all times by a guard. Weight was exactly 364.52 lb. (*Philippe Martin-Morice*)

Currency

Paper money is an invention of the Chinese, first tried in 910 AD and prevalent by 970 AD. The world's earliest bank notes (*banco-sedlar*) were issued in Stockholm, Sweden, in July 1661. The oldest surviving bank note is one for 5 dalers dated Dec 6, 1662.

The largest paper money ever issued was the one kwan note of the Chinese Ming dynasty issue of 1368–99, which measured 9 × 13 in and was printed on mulberry-bark paper. Three of them were sold at auction for a total of $1,000 in London on Oct 7, 1983. The smallest note ever issued by a bank was the 10 bani note of the Ministry of Finance of Rumania, issued in 1917. It measured (printed area) 1.09 × 1.49 in.

Of German *notgeld* (emergency notes) the smallest were the 1-3 pfennig of Passau (1920–21) measuring 0.70 × 0.72 in. A 200-billion-mark note of the 1920's was auctioned in London Oct 7, 1983 for $255.

Highest and Lowest Denomination Currency

The highest denomination notes in circulation are US Federal Reserve

COINS

Oldest	*c.* 670 BC: electrum staters of King Gyges of Lydia, Turkey[1]
Earliest Dated	MCCXXXIIII (1234): Bishop of Roskilde coins, Denmark (6 known)
Heaviest	43 lb 7¼ oz: Swedish 10 daler copper plate, 1644. See Million Dollar Gold Piece (below)
Lightest and Smallest	0.002 g or 14,000 to the oz: Nepalese silver ¼ Jawa, *c.* 1740
Most Expensive	Agrigentum decadrachm sold by private treaty to Nelson Bunker Hunt for $900,000, Oct 1980
Rarest	Many "singletons" known: for example, only 700 Axumite coins are known, of which only one was made of bronze and gold of Kaleb I *c.* 500 AD

[1] Chinese uninscribed "spade" money of the Chou dynasty has been dated to *c.* 770 BC

Bank notes for $10,000. They bear the head of Salmon Portland Chase (1808–73), Secretary of the Treasury during Civil War days. None have been printed since July 1944 and the US Treasury announced in 1969 that no further notes higher than $100 would be issued. Only 348 of the $10,000 bills remain in circulation.

The lowest denomination legal tender bank note is the 1 sen (or 1/100th of a rupiah) Indonesian note. Its exchange value in mid-1984 was 1,000 to the US penny.

Greatest Coin Collection

The highest price paid for a coin collection has been $7,300,000 by Steven C. Markoff of A-Mark Coin Co Inc of Beverly Hills, Calif, for a hoard of 407,000 US silver dollars from the La Vere Redfield estate in a courtroom auction in Reno, Nev on Jan 27, 1976.

Million Dollar Gold Piece

The largest souvenir coin was one single piece issued on Mar 21, 1986 for the World Exposition '86 in Vancouver, BC, Canada—a $1 million gold piece, 37½ in in diameter, ¾ in thick, weighing 365 lb avoirdupois (5,337 troy oz) in 14-carat gold. The gold was borrowed from Leach & Garner Co., and the coin was minted by them.

World's Biggest Win at Gambling

The world's biggest gambling win is $20 million in a NY State lottery on July 26, 1984, by Venero Pagano of the Bronx, NYC, a retired carpenter. He receives $952,380 per year (less tax) for 20 years.

World's Biggest Loss

An unnamed Italian industrialist was reported to have lost $1,920,000 in five hours at roulette in Monte Carlo, Monaco, on March 6, 1974. A

Saudi Arabian prince was reported to have lost more than $1 million in a single session at the Metro Club, Las Vegas, Nev, in Dec 1974.

Largest Slot Machine

The world's biggest slot machine (or one-armed bandit) is Super Bertha (555 cu ft) installed by Si Redd at the Four Queens Casino, Las Vegas, Nev, in Sept 1973. Once in every 25 billion plays it may yield $1 million for a $10 investment.

Biggest Slot-Machine Win

The biggest beating handed to a "one-armed bandit" was an alleged $2,478,716.15 by Rocco Dinubilo from Fresno, Calif at Harrah's Tahoe Casino, Nev, on Dec 31, 1983. It is doubtful that the money was ever paid.

Largest Treasure Troves

The greatest discovery of treasure is the estimated $2 billion of gold coins and platinum ingots from the sunken Tsarist battleship *Admiral Nakhimov* of 8,524 tons 200 ft down off the Japanese island of Tsushima. She was sunk during the Russo-Japanese War, May 27, 1905.

The largest hoard ever found was one of about 80,000 aurei in Brescello near Modena, Italy, in 1814 believed to have been deposited *c.* 37 BC. The numerically largest hoard ever found was the Brussels hoard of 1908 containing *c.* 150,000 coins. A hoard of 56,000 Roman coins was found at Cunetio near Marlborough, Wiltshire, Eng on Oct 15, 1978.

A figure of $2 billion of bullion has also been ascribed to the *San Jose* which sank in 700–1,200 ft of water off Colombia in 1708. Diving began in Aug 1984.

On July 20, 1985, two sons of Mel Fisher found the main cargo of the Spanish *Nuestra Senhora de Atocha* sunk off Key West, Florida in 1622. The value of the cargo already recovered was $80 million, but is now expected to attain close to $400 million mainly in silver bars.

Largest Mint

The largest mint is the US Mint built in 1965–69 on Independence Mall, Philadelphia, covering 500,000 sq ft (11½ acres) with an annual capacity on a 3-shift 7-day-a-week production of 8,000 million coins. A single stamping machine can produce coins at a rate of 10,000 per hour.

Largest Coin Display

A 10-mi-5-ft-7-in-long line of 662,353 quarters was laid edge-to-edge by 100 volunteers in Atlanta working on Mar 16, 1985 for the National Kidney Foundation of Georgia under the sponsorship of WFOX radio and the Women of Georgia Power. It was the longest and also the most valuable amassed collection, worth $165,788.25.

Most Massive Coins

The holed stone discs used for money on the Yap Islands are the most massive coins ever known. Yap, a 38.7-sq-mile group of islands in the western Pacific is part of the US Trust Territory. The stone discs vary in size from "small change" of less than 9 in diameter to cartwheel-size stones 12 ft across. Even a medium-sized stone coin is valuable enough to be traded for an 18-ft canoe or one wife!

The limestone blocks, which came centuries ago from the Palau Islands 300 miles away, were transported by Yap islanders in small boats, and the danger involved increased the value of the stones. Once they reached Yap, the stones had to be rounded without breaking and a hole drilled through the center so they could be strung and carried on poles. This process might have taken 2 years to complete with the crude implements available.

Copper, cast in the form of a cross, is still used to purchase brides among the peoples of isolated northern Rhodesia (now Zimbabwe). Stones are not the only unusual items that have been used as coins. Teas cast into bricks were used for 900 years or more as currency in China, Tibet and other Asian countries. They were stamped with the value and name of the issuing bank. North American Indians made "wampum" (money) out of strings of beads to trade with colonists and among themselves. The Chinese also made spade-shaped coins of bronze, and round copper coins with square center holes which they called "cash."

LABOR

Trade Unions

The largest union is Solidarność (Solidarity) in Poland, founded in Nov 1980, which by Oct 1981 was reported to have 8 million members. The union with the longest name is probably the International Association of Marble, Slate and Stone Polishers, Rubbers and Sawyers, Tile and Marble Setters' Helpers and Marble Mosaic and Terrazzo Workers' Helpers (Wash DC).

Labor Disputes

A labor dispute concerning monotony of diet and working conditions was recorded in 1153 BC in Thebes, Egypt. The earliest recorded strike was one by an orchestra leader from Greece named Aristos in Rome *c.* 309 BC. The cause was meal breaks.

The longest recorded strike ended on Jan 4, 1961, after 33 years. It concerned the employment of barbers' assistants in Copenhagen, Denmark. The longest recorded major strike was one at the plumbing fixtures factory of the Kohler Co in Sheboygan, Wis between Apr 1954 and Oct 1962. The strike is alleged to have cost the United Automobile Workers union about $12 million to sustain.

Working Careers

The longest working life has been 98 years by Mr Izumi of Japan (see page 15) who started work goading draft animals at a sugar mill at Isen, Tokanushima, Japan in 1872. He became a sugar cane farmer and retired in 1970, aged 105. He died in 1986, aged 120.

Susan O'Hagan (1802–1909) was in domestic service with 3 generations of the Hall family of Lisburn, near Belfast, Northern Ireland, for 97 years from the age of 10 to light duties at 107.

The longest recorded industrial career in one job was that of Miss Polly Gadsby who started at the age of 9 and worked 86 years wrapping elastic for the same company in Leicester, England until she died in 1932 at the age of 95.

Highest and Lowest Unemployment

The highest recorded percentage unemployment was in Great Britain on Jan 23, 1933, when the total of unemployed persons on the Employment Exchange registers was 2,903,065, representing 22.8% of the insured working population.

In Switzerland in Dec 1973 (population 6,600,000), the total number of unemployed was said to be 81.

Lowest Wages

Probably the lowest wage paid in industry is $2.65 per day paid in Haiti, according to the *NY Times.*

FOOD AND DRINK

Calories

Of all countries in the world, based on the latest available data, Belgium and Luxembourg have the largest available total of calories per person. The net supply averaged 3,645 per day in 1974. The lowest *reported* figure is 1,728 calories per day in Upper Volta (now Burkina Faso) in 1974. The highest calorific value of any foodstuff is that of pure animal fat, with 930 calories per 100 grams (3.5 oz). Pure alcohol provides 710 calories per 100 grams.

(Per capita per day)

Protein Australia and New Zealand 3.79 oz (1969)	**Tea**[2] Ireland—0.36 oz (1977)
Cereals[1] Egypt—21.95 oz (1966–67)	**Coffee**[3] Finland—1.28 oz (1980)
Sugars Bulgaria—6.26 oz (1977)	**Water** US—1,600 gal (1984)
Meat US—10.89 oz (1977)	**Beer** W Germany—0.708 pints (1981)
Sweets Britain—1.20 oz (1979)	**Wine** France—0.44 pints (1980)
Liquor Poland—0.026 pints (1978)	

[1] Figures for 1977 from China suggest a possible consumption (including rice) of 31.3 oz.
[2] The most expensive tea is "Oolong Peach Blossom." In June 1983 it retailed for $27.83 per lb in London. Tea-bags were invented by Thomas Sullivan of New York in 1904.
[3] The most expensive coffee is Jamaican Blue Mountain which retails for up to $24 per lb in the US.

Prohibition

The longest-lasting imposition of prohibition against consumption of alcoholic beverages has been 26 years in Iceland (1908–34). Other prohibitions have been in Russia, later the USSR (1914–24), and the US (1920–33). The Faroe Islands have had a public (as opposed to private licensed) prohibition since 1918.

Most Expensive Food

The most expensively priced food (as opposed to spice) is First Choice Black Perigord truffles which retail at $13.20 per 0.44 oz can.

However, in Jan 1985 in the Hafr El-Baten market, Riyadh, Saudi Arabia local truffles sold for SR 5000 for 3 kg, equivalent to $60 per 0.44 oz.

Spices

Prices for wild ginseng (root of *Panax quinquefolius*), from the Chan Pak Mt area of China, thought to have aphrodisiacal quality, were reported in Nov 1977 to be as high as $23,000 per oz in Hong Kong. Total shipments from Jilin province do not exceed 141 oz per year. The leading medical journal in the US has likened its effects to "corticosteroid poisoning."

The world's rarest and most prized condiment is Cà Cuong, a secretion recovered in minute amounts from beetles in northern Vietnam. Owing to war conditions, the price rose to $100 per ounce before supplies virtually ceased in 1975.

The hottest of all spices is claimed to be Siling labuyo from the Philippines. The chili pepper or Capsicum known as Tepin from southwestern US comes in pods ⅛ in in diameter. A single dried gram will produce detectable "heat" in 68.3 lb of bland sauce.

Candy

The top-selling candies are Life Savers, with 29,651,840,000 rolls sold between 1913 and June 30, 1980. A tunnel formed by the holes in the middle placed end to end would stretch to the moon and back three times. Thomas Syta of Van Nuys, Calif made one last 7 hours 10 min (with hole intact) on Jan 15, 1983.

Largest Banquets

It was estimated that 30,000 attended an outdoor military feast at Radewitz, Poland, on June 25, 1730, thrown by King August II (1709–33).

The greatest number of people served indoors at a single sitting was 18,000 municipal leaders at the Palais de l'Industrie, Paris, on Aug 18, 1889.

At the wedding of cousins Menachem Teitelbaum, 18, and Brucha Sima Melsels, 18, conducted by their grandfather Grand Rabbi Moses at Uniondale, LI, NY on Dec 5, 1984 the attendance of the Satmar sect of Hasidic Jews was estimated at 17,000 to 20,000. Meal Mart of Brooklyn, a kosher caterer, provided the food, including 2 tons of gefilte fish.

The menu for the main 5½-hour banquet at the Imperial Iranian 2,500th anniversary gathering at Persepolis in Oct 1971 (see *Party Giving* in Chapter 11), was probably the most expensive ever compiled. It comprised quail eggs stuffed with Iranian caviar, a mousse of crayfish tails in Nantua sauce, stuffed rack of roast lamb, with a main course of roast peacock stuffed with *foie gras,* fig rings, and raspberry sweet champagne sherbet. Wines included *Château Lafite Rothschild* 1945 at $100 per bottle from the cellars of Maxim's, Paris.

Biggest Barbecues

The most monumental barbecue has been one for 15,000 people who consumed 46,386 barbecued chicken halves at Iolani School, Honolulu, Hawaii on Jan 31, 1981. Ernie Morgado prepared the chickens.

At the 1982 holding of the annual Fancy Farm Picnic, Kentucky (est. 1880) on August 6 the consumption of mutton, pork and chicken meat reached 15,000 lb. The cook was Harold Carrico.

At the Sertoma Club Barbecue, New Port Richey, Fla, 21,112 lb of beef were consumed Mar 7–9, 1986.

Largest Breads

The longest loaf ever baked was a rosca de Reyes 2,132 ft 2½ in in length and 1.25 tons in weight at the Exelaris Hyatt Regency Hotel, Acapulco, Mexico on Jan 6, 1985. If a consumer of the rosca (twisted loaf) finds the embedded bread doll he has to throw the next rosca party.

The largest pan loaf baked was one of 224 lb measuring 5 ft 6¾ in × 2 ft 3½ in × 2 ft 11¾ in at San Lameer Complex, Natal, S Africa on May 26, 1984.

Largest Cakes

The largest cake ever created was a 90,000-lb 8,800-sq-ft "Duncan Hines" cake that used 31,026 boxes of a yellow cake mix, 20,000 layers of 3 lb each, topped with 30,000 lb of vanilla icing. It took 24 hours to assemble under the direction of Chef Franz Eichenauer after 32 hours of baking in Austin, Tex on Feb 20, 1986 to celebrate the 150th anniversary of the founding of Texas. To cut the cake at the City Coliseum, Prince Charles of Great Britain was on hand. The cake was big enough to feed 300,000 people.

The tallest recorded free-standing cake was one of 71 tiers, 45 ft 5 in high completed by the management and staff of the Hyatt Central Plaza Banquet Hotel, Bangkok, Thailand, on Sept 12, 1985.

Gingerbread House

Using 650 gingerbread "bricks" and 195 "shingles," plus 1,030 lb of icing, and 100 lb of dark chocolate to line the inside, a 17-ft-high gingerbread house was built in the Sheraton Central Park Hotel, Arlington, Tex for Christmas 1985. Almost 3 yds wide, the project took 7 days (over 200 hours overtime) to build. The main door was purposely constructed so small that only little kids and elves could enter.

Cookies

The best-selling cookie is Nabisco's Oreo, which sold 6 billion individual cookies in 1982, and 100 billion in all since its introduction in 1912. About $1 out of every $10 spent on cookies in grocery stores is spent on Oreos. In celebration of Oreo's 75th anniversary on June 5, 1986, a milk and cookies party was held in NYC, when 10,000 cookies (and 8,500 oz of milk) were served to 3,800 celebrants.

Largest Chocolate

The heaviest chocolate Easter egg ever made was one weighing 7,561 lb 13½ oz, measuring 10 ft high, made by Siegfried Berndt at "Macopa" Patisserie, Leicester, England, and completed on Apr 7, 1982. An egg 17 ft 9⅜ in tall weighing 5,121 lb was exhibited by Patisserie Eueen Lauwers at Schelle, Belgium on Mar 19, 1983.

The largest chocolate "model" was one measuring 32 ft 9½ in × 16 ft 4.6 in × 28.7 in high for the 1992 Olympic Center in Barcelona, Spain, by the Gremi Provincial de Pastigeria Confiteria School in Nov 1985.

LARGEST LOLLIPOP (left): It couldn't fit on the scale, so this 2,052½-lb heart-shaped candy on a stick made by the Hyatt Regency Memphis (Tenn) Hotel, had to be broken up to be eaten.

LARGEST BREAD (right): This loaf weighed 224 lb and measured 5 ft 6¾ in × 2 ft 3½ in × 2 ft 11¾ in when baked in Natal, S Africa on May 26, 1984.

LARGEST CAKE (below): 90,000 lb and 8,800 sq ft in size, this cake, baked for 32 hours in 1986 in Austin for the 150th birthday of Texas, was big enough to feed 300,000 people. Prince Charles (GB) was there to cut it.

LARGEST GINGERBREAD HOUSE (above): With an entrance too small for adults to enter, this house (except for the floor) is all food. (*Sheraton Arlington, Tex*)

TALLEST WEDDING CAKE (right): 71 tiers (45 ft 5 in) high, this pyramid of a cake rises high above the third floor in the atrium of the Hyatt Central Plaza Hotel in Bangkok, Thailand. The cake was made by the hotel's staff.

Largest Hamburger

The largest hamburger on record was one of 5,005 lb 13.8 oz made on Oct 13, 1985 by Spur Steak Ranches (Pty) Ltd at Anchor Bay, Cape Town, S Africa. The burger had a diameter of 23 ft 3½ in and was cut into over 15,750 portions after grilling.

Largest Lollipop

A lollipop weighing 2,052½ lb, made at the Hyatt Regency Memphis (Tenn) Hotel on Feb 20, 1986, was so big it could not fit on one scale and had to be broken into 11 pieces. Although created for display purposes, this huge heart-shaped candy on a stick (720 lb of sugar and 1,452 lb of corn syrup) was eaten by the hotel's employees.

Longest Noodles

The longest continuous cooked noodle (939 ft 11 in) was made in Louisville, Colo, by 4 families who joined recipes and noodles for 8 hours on Sept 1, 1985, built a special 20 × 5-ft cooker, and used 230 lb of charcoal, along with 50 lb of flour and 36 eggs.

Mark Pi at his China Gate Restaurant in Columbus, O, set a record by making 2,048 noodle strips in 34.5 sec on Feb 12, 1982, each strip exceeding 5 ft in length.

Largest Omelet

The largest omelet was one made of 45,000 eggs in a pan 10 × 43 ft, cooked by the Kinsman's Mothers' March of British Columbia, Canada, at Hotel Meridien, Vancouver, on Jan 27, 1986.

Largest Pancake

A pancake of 20-ft diameter, 4 in thick, weighing 2,107 lb, containing 900 lb of pancake mix, 1,600 lb of maple syrup, 15 blocks of butter, and 100 gal of milk, was built in Highgate, Franklin County, Vt, on Aug 18, 1984, under the auspices of Jim Hilton of St Albans, Vt. The pancake was flipped over on its charcoal-fired pan by a helicopter and crane, during its 6 hours on the fire.

Longest Pastry

The longest pastry in the world is the "record" pastry 1,607 ft 2 in in length made by the Gothenburg Patissiers Association of Sweden (organizer Sven Gustavsson) at the Liseberg Amusement Park on June 15, 1983.

Largest Paella

The largest paella ever made was one with a diameter of 32 ft 9 in and a depth of 1 ft 5½ in built in the Plaza de Catalunya, Cornella de Llobregat, Barcelona, Spain on June 24, 1984 for 15,000 people. It included 1,650 lb of meat and 660 lb of pimientos.

Largest Pies

The largest apple pie ever baked was that by a TV Chef, Glynn Christian, in a 40 ft × 23 ft dish at Hewitts Farm, Chelsfield, Kent, England on Aug 25–27, 1982. Over 600 bushels of apples were included in the pie which weighed 30,115 lb.

The largest cherry pie weighed 7 tons and contained 4,950 lb of cherries. It measured 14 ft 4 in in diameter, 24 in in depth and was baked on

LONGEST NOODLE: Built over a charcoal fire in Louisville, Colo, by 4 families, the longest continuous noodle turned out to be 939 ft 11 in long.

LARGEST PANCAKE: A helicopter and crane were needed to flip this 20-ft-diameter pancake that weighed about one ton, cooked over a charcoal fire for 6 hours in Highgate, Vt, on Aug 18, 1984.

the grounds of the Medusa Cement Corporation, Charlevoix, Mich, May 15, 1976, as part of the town's Bicentennial celebration.

The largest meat pie ever baked weighed 12,880 lb, measuring 18 × 6 ft 18 in deep, the eighth in the series of Denby Dale, W Yorkshire (Eng) pies, to mark four royal births, baked on Sept 5, 1964. The first was in 1788 to celebrate King George III's return to sanity, but the fourth (Queen Victoria's Jubilee, 1887) went a bit "off" and had to be buried in quicklime.

The largest mince pie was one of 2,260 lb, measuring 20 × 5 ft, baked at Ashby-de-la-Zouch, Leicestershire, England, Oct 15, 1932.

At Pecanland Mall in Monroe, La, on July 22, 1985, volunteers baked a pecan pie 12 ft in diameter, 3½ in deep, with ingredients that weighed 2,350 lb. The pan weighed an additional 1,300 lb. Kerosene blown heaters were used beneath the pie pan for baking.

Largest Pizza

The largest pizza ever baked was one measuring 86 ft 7 in in diameter, hence 5,895 sq ft in area, completed by Marco Cagnazzo at Norwood Hypermarket, Johannesburg, S Africa on Mar 31, 1984.

Largest Potato Chip

Charles Chip Inc of Moundville, Pa, produced chips 4 × 7 in from outsize potatoes in Feb 1977.

Largest Popsicle®

The largest iced lollipop on a stick was one of 5,750 lb, constructed for the Westside Assembly of God Church, Davenport, Iowa, Sept 7, 1975.

Mashed Potatoes

A single serving of mashed potatoes weighing 18,260 lb was prepared from instant mashed potato flakes and water in a ready-mix concrete truck and poured into a platform 16 ft by 16 ft (256 sq ft) in Grand Forks, N Dakota before a Potato Bowl football game on Sept 4, 1982. (*No further claims in this category will be considered.*)

Largest Salad

A 28-ton salad made by 30 people on Apr 16, 1983, in a circular swimming pool in Belle Glade, Fla, had to be seasoned with 112 gallons of dressing. The 4-ft-deep salad included 36,000 heads of lettuce (4 varieties) and Chinese cabbage, 300 lb of carrots, 400 lb of red radishes, 120 lb of white radishes, 250 lb of celery, and 180 lb of tomatoes, but no onions. It was served at the 1983 Black Gold Jubilee with catfish on Saturday and at a barbecue on Sunday.

Largest Salami

The largest salami on record is one 29 ft 2¾ in long with a circumference of 28 in, weighing 734.13 lb, cooked by Don Smallgoods for Australian Safeway Stores at Broadmeadow, Vic, on Apr 23, 1982.

Longest Sausage

The longest sausage ever made (pork) was in one continuous linked chain stretching 46,760 ft (8.856 mi) and placed on Sept 23, 1983 on 16 stainless steel racks of the maker, M&M Meat Shops of Kitchener, Ont, Canada. Total weight was 17,484 lb.

MOST TREMENDOUS SALAD: A swimming pool was needed for 30 people in Belle Glade, Fla, to toss this 28-ton, 36,000-heads-of-lettuce salad. The 4-ft-deep salad contained all the usual ingredients, except onions.

MOST GIGANTIC ICE CREAM SUNDAE: More than 6,000 lb bigger than the previous record, this ice cream sundae weighing 33,616¾ lb was "constructed" by the Knudsen Corp (LA) and Smucker's (Ohio and LA). It took 50 people over 7 hours to build it, while dry ice kept it from melting.

Strawberry Bowl

A "bowl" of 513 lb of strawberries was filled at Battle, E Sussex, Eng, on July 4, 1985.

Longest Banana Split

The longest banana split ever made was one 4 mi in length made by the Zeta Beta Tau fraternity of Bowling Green State Univ, Ohio, on Aug 25, 1985.

Largest Sundae

The most gigantic ice cream sundae, weighing 33,616.75 lb, was constructed July 28, 1985 by the Knudsen Corp of LA and Smucker's of Ohio at the Disneyland Hotel in Anaheim, Calif. The 10-ft-tall, 30-million-calorie sundae included 26,020 lb of ice cream, 7,521.75 lb of topping, and 75 lb of whipped cream. The topping included 2,287 lb of chocolate fudge, 1,706 lb of butterscotch, 1,732 lb of caramel, as well as strawberry, pineapple and cherry syrup. Fork lifts and ladders were used to stack the ice cream blocks.

Largest Dish

The largest single dish is roasted camel, prepared occasionally for Bedouin wedding feasts. Cooked eggs are stuffed in fish, the fish stuffed in cooked chicken, the chickens stuffed into a roasted sheep carcass and the sheep stuffed into a whole camel.

ENERGY

To express the various forms of available energy (coal, liquid fuels and water power, etc., but omitting vegetable fuels and peat), it is the practice to convert them all into terms of coal.

The highest consumption is in the US with an average of 29,131 lb per annum per person. With only 5.3% of the world's population, the US consumes 28.6% of the world's gasoline and 32.9% of the world's electric power. For comparison, 14,035 lb was the UK average per person in 1979. The lowest recorded average for 1974 was 28.6 lb per person in Rwanda.

MASS COMMUNICATIONS
AND TRANSPORTATION

Merchant Shipping

The world total of merchant shipping (excluding vessels of less than 100 tons gross, sailing vessels and barges) was 76,395 vessels of 416,268,534 tons gross on July 1, 1985. The largest merchant fleet as of mid-1985 was under the flag of Liberia with 1,808 ships of 58,179,717 tons gross.

Largest and Busiest Ports

Physically, the largest port is the Port of NY and NJ. The port has a navigable waterfront of 755 miles (460 miles in NY State and 295 miles in NJ) stretching over 92 sq mi. A total of 261 general cargo berths and 130 other piers gives a total berthing capacity of 391 ships at one time. The total warehousing floor space is 18,400,000 sq ft (422.4 acres).

The world's busiest port and largest artificial harbor is the Rotterdam-Europoort in the Netherlands, which covers 38 sq mi with 76 mi of quays. It handled 31,457 seagoing vessels carrying a total of 251 million metric tons of seagoing cargo, and about 182,000 barges, in 1985. It is able to handle 310 seagoing vessels simultaneously, of up to 318,000 metric tons and 72 ft draught.

Airlines

The country with the busiest airlines system is the US, where 277,182,916,000 revenue passenger miles were flown on the larger US certified air carriers in domestic operations in 1985. This was equivalent to an annual trip of 1,168 miles for every inhabitant of the US.

Railroads

The country with the greatest length of railroad is the US, with 184,235 miles of track on Jan 1, 1985.

Roads and Traffic

The country with the greatest length of road is the US (50 states), with 3,891,781 mi of graded roads on Jan 1, 1985.

The highest traffic volume of any point is at East Los Angeles, where there is an interchange of the Santa Ana, Pomona, Golden State, Hollywood, San Bernardino and Santa Monica Freeways with a 24-hour average on weekdays of 458,060 vehicles in 1983—over 318 per min. The most heavily traveled stretch of road is between 43rd and 47th Sts on the Dan Ryan Expressway in Chicago, with an average daily volume of 254,700 vehicles.

The place with the highest traffic density is Hong Kong. By Jan 1, 1984, there were 302,118 motor vehicles on 778.9 mi of serviceable roads giving a density of 4.53 yd per vehicle.

For busiest bridge, see page 258.

Widest, Narrowest and Shortest Streets

The widest street is the Monumental Axis, running for 1½ miles from the Municipal Plaza to the Plaza of the Three Powers in Brasília, the capital of Brazil. The 6-lane boulevard was opened in Apr 1960 and is 273.4 yd wide.

The Bay Bridge Toll Plaza has 23 lanes (17 westbound) serving San Francisco and Oakland.

The world's narrowest street is in the village of Ripatransone in the Marche region of Italy. It is called Vico della Virilità (Virility Alley) and is 16.9 in wide.

The title of "The Shortest Street in the World" has been claimed since 1907 by McKinley St in Bellefontaine, Ohio, which is built of vitrified brick and measures 30 ft in length. This title has been disputed by Bacup, Lancashire, Eng where "Elgin Street" by the old market measures 17 ft 0 in, but is not "carriageable."

Steepest and Crookedest Streets

The steepest streets are Filbert St, Russian Hill and 22nd St, Dolores

WIDEST STREET: Brasilia, the capital of Brazil, built in 1960, has streets laid out with room to spare. The widest is the Monumental Axis, which has 6 lanes, 3 going in one direction and 200 yards away 3 parallel lanes going in the opposite direction. In between are official buildings, parks and loops leading to crossroads as seen here. (*Duncan Rabin/Daily Telegraph*)

Heights, San Francisco, with gradients of 31.5% or a rise of 1 ft for every 3.17 ft.

A claim has been made for Baldwin Street, Dunedin, New Zealand, which has been surveyed to have a rise of 1 ft every 1,266 ft.

Lombard Street in San Francisco between Hyde and Leavenworth has 8 consecutive 90-degree turns of 20-ft radius as it descends steeply one way.

Earliest Parking Meters

The earliest parking meters ever installed were those put in the business district of Oklahoma City, Okla, on July 19, 1935. They were the invention of Carl C. Magee (US).

Earliest Traffic Lights

Semaphore-type traffic *signals* were set up in Parliament Square, London in 1868, with red and green gas lamps for night use. The first electric traffic lights were installed on Aug 5, 1914 in Cleveland, O, at Euclid Ave and 105th St. Besides having red and green lights on cross arms 15 ft above the ground, there was a buzzer to call pedestrians' attention to each change.

Highest Trail

The highest trail is an 8-mile stretch of the Kang-ti-suu between Khaleb and Hsin-chi-fu, Tibet, which in two places exceeds 20,000 ft. The highest motor road is one 733.2 miles long between Tibet and southwestern Sinkiang, completed in Oct 1957, which includes passes of an altitude up to 18,480 ft above sea level.

CROOKEDEST STREET: San Francisco has plenty of steep hills, but none is as crooked and steep as Lombard. It has 8 consecutive 90-degree turns of 20-ft radius on the way down. Yes, it's one-way.

Europe's highest pass (excluding the Caucasian passes) is the Col de Restefond (9,193 ft) completed in 1962 with 21 hairpins between Jausiers and Saint Etienne-de-Tinée, France. It is usually closed between early Oct and early June. The highest motor road in Europe is the Pico de Veleta in the Sierra Nevada, southern Spain. The shadeless climb of 22.4 miles brings the motorist to 11,384 ft above sea level and became, on completion of the road on the southern side of the peak in summer 1974, arguably Europe's highest "pass."

Longest Highways and Street

The longest motorable road is the Pan-American Highway which stretches from northwest Alaska to Santiago, Chile, thence goes eastward to Buenos Aires, Argentina and terminates in Brasilia, Brazil. There remains a gap of 250 miles, known as the Tapon del Darién in Panama, and the Atrato Swamp in Colombia.

The longest Interstate Highway in the US is Route 90 which goes 2,909.52 mi from Boston to Seattle.

Lowest Road

The lowest road is that along the Israeli shores of the Dead Sea, 1,290 ft below sea level. The lowest pass is the Rock Reel Pass in Everglades National Park, Fla, which is 3 ft above sea level.

Biggest Square

The Tien An Men (Gate of Heavenly Peace) Square in Peking, described as the navel of China, extends over 98 acres.

Traffic Jam

The longest traffic jam ever reported was that of Feb 16, 1980 which stretched northward from Lyon, France 109.3 miles towards Paris.

Inland Waterways

The country with the greatest length of inland waterways is Finland. The total length of navigable lakes and rivers is about 31,000 miles.

Drivers' Licenses

Regular drivers' licenses are issuable as young as 15 and without a driver education course only in Hawaii and Mississippi. Thirteen US states issue restricted juvenile licenses at 14.

The easiest test for a driver's license is given in Egypt, where the ability to drive 6 meters (19.7 ft) forward and 6 meters in reverse has been deemed sufficient. In 1979 it was reported that accurate reversing between 2 rubber traffic cones had been added, but this soon led to the substitution of white lines when too many cones were destroyed.

Worst Driver

It was reported that a 75-year-old *male* driver received 10 traffic tickets, drove on the wrong side of the road four times, committed four hit-and-run offenses and caused six accidents, all within 20 minutes, in McKinney, Tex, on Oct 15, 1966.

Competing with him for this title is John Hogg who, at age 28, in the Edinburgh, Scotland High Court on Nov 27, 1975, received 5¾ years in jail and his 3rd, 4th and 5th life bans for drunken driving in a stolen car without having a driver's license. For his previous 40 offenses he had been banned for 71½ years from driving.

POSTAGE STAMPS

EARLIEST	Put on sale in London May 1, 1840	1 penny Black of Great Britain, Queen Victoria, 68,158,080 printed. Available for pre-payment of postage
HIGHEST PRICE (TENDER)	$1 million	5 cent Blue Alexandria US cover, Nov 25, 1846 by Georg Normann *via* David Feldman of Geneva on May 9, 1981.
HIGHEST PRICE (AUCTION)	$850,000 $935,000 (with buyer's premium)	British Guiana 1¢ black on magenta provisional postmarked '4 Ap., 1856' by Irwin R. Weinberg syndicate to anonymous collector at Waldorf-Astoria, NYC Apr 5, 1980.
HIGHEST PRICE (ERROR)	$864,386	First issue (1894) of German state of Baden, 9 Kreuzer, printed in error on blue-green paper intended for 6 Kreuzer, instead of dull rose. Only 3 examples known. One sold at auction for $864,386 on Mar 16, 1985 in Wiesbaden, W Germany.
LARGEST PHILATELIC PURCHASE	$11,000,000	Marc Haas collection of 3,000 US postal and pre-postal covers to 1869 by Stanley Gibbons International Ltd of London in Aug 1979.
LARGEST (SPECIAL PURPOSE)	9¾ × 2¾ in	Express Delivery of China, 1913.
LARGEST (STANDARD POSTAGE)	6.3 × 4.33 in	Marshall Islands 75 cents issued Oct 30, 1979.
SMALLEST	0.31 × 0.37 in	10 cent and 1 peso Colombian State of Bolivar, 1863–66.
HIGHEST DENOMINATION	£100 (then $500)	Red and black, George V, of Kenya, 1925–27.
LOWEST DENOMINATION	3,000 pengö of Hungary	Issued 1946 when 150 million million pengö = 1p 1.6×10^{-14} = 1 US penny.
RAREST	Unique examples include	British Guiana (now Guyana) 1 cent black on magenta of 1856 (see above); Swedish 3 skilling banco yellow color error of 1855. Gold Coast provisional of 1885 and US postmaster stamps from Boscawen, New Hampshire, and Lockport, NY.

Most Durable Driver

The Goodyear Tire and Rubber Co test driver Weldon C. Kocich drove 3,031,577 mi from Feb 5, 1953 to July 20, 1984, so averaging 96,345 mi per year.

Oldest Driver

Roy M. Rawlins (b July 10, 1870) of Stockton, Calif was warned for driving at 95 mph in a 55-mph zone in June 1974. On Aug 25, 1974, he was awarded a Calif State license valid until 1978, but he died on July 9, 1975, one day short of his 105th birthday. Mrs Maude Tull of Inglewood, Calif, who began driving after her husband's death, when she was aged 91, was issued a renewal of her license on Feb 5, 1976, then aged 104.

Walter Herbert Weake of England drove for 75 years without ever having an accident. He began driving in 1894 and drove daily until his death, at age 91, in 1969.

Most Failures on Learner's Test

The record for persistence in taking and failing a test for a driver's license is held by Mrs Miriam Hargrave (b Apr 3, 1908) of Wakefield, Yorkshire, England, who failed her 39th driving test in 8 years on Apr 29, 1970, when she "crashed" through a set of red lights. She finally passed her 40th driving test on Aug 3, 1970. She spent $720 on 212 driving lessons and could no longer afford to buy a car. In 1978, she was reported to dislike right-hand turns.

Mrs Fannie Turner (b 1903) of Little Rock, Ark, passed her *written* test for a driver's license on her 104th attempt in Oct 1978.

Telephones

There were approximately 285,723,398 telephones in the world on Jan 1, 1984, it was estimated by the American Telephone and Telegraph Co. The country with the greatest number was the US with 114,349,000 (about the same number as in all of Europe), equivalent to 483 for every 1,000 people.

The greatest total of calls made in any country is in the US, with 434,569 million in 1984 (1,837 calls per person).

The city with most telephones is NYC, which had 5,808,145 (821 per 1,000 people) as of Jan 1, 1985. In 1983, Washington, DC, reached the record of 1,730 telephones per 1,000 people.

Largest Switchboard

The world's biggest switchboard is that in the Pentagon, Wash, DC, with 25,000 lines and an annual phone bill of $8.7 million.

Smallest Telephone

A push-button phone measuring 2¼ in wide × 4¾ in long × ¾ in maximum to ⅜ in minimum thickness built by Gary Friedman, an electronic engineering student at Cal State Northridge, Calif is allegedly the world's smallest workable phone. It is designed to be used as a lineman's handset.

Longest Telephone Cable

The longest submarine telephone cable is the Commonwealth Pacific Cable (COMPAC), which runs for 9,340 mi from Sydney, Australia *via* Norfolk Island, Fiji, and Hawaii to Port Alberni, Canada. It cost about

$98 million and was inaugurated on Dec 2, 1963. The final splice was made on Mar 24, 1984.

Postal Services

The country with the largest mail is the US, whose people posted 140.1 billion letters and packages in 1985. The US Postal Service then employed 744,490 people with the world's largest vehicle fleet—200,811 cars and trucks.

The US also takes first place in the average number of letters which each person mails during one year. The figure was 589 in 1985.

---

5. EDUCATION

Universities

The Sumerians had scribal schools soon after 3500 BC. The oldest existing educational institution is the University of Karueein, founded in 859 AD in Fez, Morocco. The University of Bologna (Italy) was founded in 1088.

The university with the greatest enrollment in the world is the State University of New York, which had 156,175 students enrolled in 1984–85. Its oldest college, at Potsdam, NY, was founded in 1816.

Bids for building the $3.4-billion University of Riyadh, Saudi Arabia, were accepted in June 1978. The University will house 15,000 families and have its own mass transportation system.

The largest existing university building is the M. V. Lomonosov State University on the Lenin Hills, south of Moscow. It stands 787.4 ft tall, has 32 stories and 40,000 rooms. It was constructed in 1949–53.

The most northerly university is Inupiat University of the Arctic at Barrow, Alaska on Lat 71°16′N. Eskimo subjects are featured in the curriculum.

Youngest Professors

The youngest at which anybody has been elected to a chair (full professorship) in a university is 19, in the case of Colin MacLaurin (1698–1746), who was admitted to Marischal College, Aberdeen, Scotland as Professor of Mathematics on Sept 30, 1717. In 1725 he was made Professor of Mathematics at Edinburgh University on the recommendation of Sir Isaac Newton, who was a professor at Cambridge, aged 26.

In July 1967, Dr Harvey Martin Friedman, PhD (b Sept 23, 1948) was appointed Assistant Professor of Mathematics at Stanford University, Calif, on Sept 1, 1967, just 3 weeks before his 19th birthday.

Most Durable Professors

Dr Joel Hildebrand (1881–1983), Professor Emeritus of Physical Chemistry at the University of California, Berkeley, first became an Assistant Professor in 1913, and 68 years later, in 1981 published his 275th research paper.

Youngest Undergraduates

The most extreme recorded case of undergraduate juvenility was that of William Thomson (1824–1907), later Lord Kelvin, who entered Glasgow University aged 10 years 4 months in Oct 1834, and matriculated on Nov 14, 1834.

Ruth Lawrence (b 1971) of Huddersfield, W Yorkshire, Eng, was accepted for entrance to Oxford at the age of 12, and graduated two years later (July 4, 1985) with a first class degree, top of 191 entrants.

Jay Luo of Garden City, Mich (b Apr 4, 1970) graduated from Boise State Univ, Idaho, with a BS degree in math *cum laude* on May 16, 1982, at the age of 12 years 42 days.

Youngest Doctorate

Carl Witte of Lochau, Germany was made a doctor of philosophy when age 12 on Apr 13, 1814, at the Univ of Giessen, Germany.

The youngest to receive a Doctor of Medicine degree is Avi Ben-Abraham (b Nov 18, 1957, Kfar-Saba, Israel) who graduated with his M D *summa cum laude* on Mar 4, 1976 from the Univ of Perugia, Italy, at the age of 18 years 3 months. He had started to read and write at the age of 2.

Most Graduates in Immediate Family

Mr & Mrs Albert Kunz of Bloomington, Ind, saw all their 8 sons and 5 daughters graduate from Indiana Univ between 1932 and 1956.

Largest School

South Point High School, Calcutta, India, had an enrollment of 12,350 regular students in 1983–84.

Most Expensive College

The annual cost of keeping a pupil at Le Rosey, Gstaad, Switzerland in 1983-84 was reputed to be $20,000.

The most expensive US college is Bennington with annual tuition only for 1985–86 at $12,780, the highest among 3,200 colleges surveyed.

YOUNGEST MD: At age 18 years 3 months, Avi Ben-Abraham received his Doctor of Medicine degree from the Univ of Perugia, Italy.

Highest Endowment

The greatest single gift in the history of higher education has been $125 million to Louisiana State Univ by C. B. Pennington in 1983.

Most Schools Attended

The documented record for the greatest number of schools attended by a pupil is 265 by Wilma Williams, now Mrs R. J. Horton, from 1933 to 1943 when her parents were in show business in the US.

Lectures and Speakers

Bob Jones of Wellington, New Zealand, in 1980, addressed a seminar of 1,048 people in Auckland on property. He received $US 140,000 (NZ $200,000) equal to $11,666 per hour. In March 1981, it was reported that both Johnny Carson and Bob Hope commanded fees of $40,000 an appearance.

---

6. RELIGIONS

Oldest Religious Custom

Human burial, which has religious connotations, has been known from c. 60,000 BC among *Homo sapiens neanderthalensis* in the Shanidar cave, N Iraq. The earliest named prophet was Zoroaster (Zarathushtra) dated to c. 1600 BC. He has 250,000 followers today.

Largest Religious Membership

Religious statistics are necessarily only approximate. The test of adherence to a religion varies widely in rigor, while many individuals, particularly in the East, belong to two or more religions.

Christianity is the leading religion, with some 1.07 billion adherents in 1985. The Vatican statistics office reported that in 1983 there were 825,592,000 Roman Catholics. The largest non-Christian religion is Islam (Muslim) with about 560 million followers.

Largest Clergy

The largest religious organization is the Roman Catholic Church, with 152 cardinals, 716 archbishops, 3,076 bishops, 406,376 priests and 935,221 nuns in 1985. There are about 420,000 churches.

World Jewry

The total of world Jewry was estimated to number 16,000,000 in 1985. The highest concentration was in the US, with 7,300,000 of whom 2 million are in the NY area. The total in Israel is 3,255,000. The total in Tokyo is only 400.

The Judaic way of life was formulated as early as 2000 BC.

Earliest Shrine

A sculpted stone face, half primate/half feline, discovered by Dr Leslie Freeman of the Univ of Chicago in the El Juyo cave shrine, northern Spain, is the oldest known religious shrine and is dated to c. 12,000 BC. The oldest surviving Christian church is Qal'at es Salihiye in eastern Syria, dating from 232 AD.

Largest Temple

The largest religious building ever constructed is Angkor Wat (City Temple), enclosing 402 acres, in Cambodia (now Kampuchea). It was built to the God Vishnu by the Khmer King Suryavarman II in the period 1113–50. Its curtain wall measures 1,400 × 1,400 yd and its population, before it was abandoned in 1432, was at times 80,000. The whole complex of 72 major monuments, begun *c.* 900 AD, extends over 15 × 5 miles.

The largest Buddhist temple is Borobudur, near Jogjakarta, Indonesia, built in the 8th century. It is 103 ft tall and 403 ft square.

The largest Mormon temple is in Salt Lake City, Utah, completed in Apr 1983, with a floor area of 253,015 sq ft.

Largest Synagogue

The largest synagogue is the Temple Emanu-El on Fifth Ave at 65th St, NYC. The temple, completed in Sept 1929, has a frontage of 150 ft on Fifth Ave and 253 ft on 65th St. The sanctuary proper can accommodate 2,500 people, and the adjoining Beth-El Chapel seats 350. When all the facilities are in use, more than 6,000 people can be accommodated.

Largest Mosque

The largest mosque ever built was the now ruined al-Malawiya mosque of al-Mutawakil in Samarra, Iraq, built in 842 852 AD and measuring 401,408 sq ft (9.21 acres) with dimensions of 784 × 512 ft.

The world's largest mosque in use is the Umayyad Mosque in Damascus, Syria, built on a 2,000-year-old religious site measuring 515 × 318 ft, thus covering an area of 3.76 acres.

The largest mosque will be the Merdeka Mosque in Djakarta, Indonesia, which was begun in 1962. The cupola will be 147.6 ft in diameter and the capacity in excess of 50,000 people.

Largest Church

The largest church is the basilica of St Peter, built between 1492 and 1612 in Vatican City, Rome. Its length, measured from the apse, is 611 ft 4 in. Its area is 162,990 sq ft. The inner diameter of the famous dome is 137 ft 9 in and its center is 390 ft 5 in high. The external height is 457 ft 9 in.

The elliptical Basilique de St Pie X at Lourdes, France, completed in 1957 at a cost of $5,600,000, has a capacity of 20,000 under its giant span arches and a length of 656 ft.

The crypt of the underground Civil War Memorial Church in the Guadarrama Mountains, 28 miles from Madrid, Spain, is 853 ft in length. It took 21 years (1937–58) to build, at a reported cost of $392 million and is surmounted by a cross 492 ft tall.

Smallest Church

The smallest church is the Union Church at Wiscasset, Maine, with a floor area of 7 ft × 4½ ft.

Largest and Smallest Cathedrals

The largest is the cathedral church of the Episcopalian Diocese of NY, St John the Divine, with a floor area of 121,000 sq ft and a volume of 16,822,000 cu ft. The cornerstone was laid on Dec 27, 1892, and work on the Gothic building was stopped in 1941, then restarted in earnest in July

1979. In NY it is referred to as "Saint John the Unfinished." The nave is the longest in the world, 601 ft in length, with a vaulting 124 ft in height.

The cathedral covering the largest area is that of Santa María de la Sede in Seville, Spain. It was built in Spanish Gothic style between 1402 and 1519 and is 414 ft long, 271 ft wide and 100 ft high to the vault of the nave.

The smallest church in the world designated as a cathedral is that of the Christ Catholic Church, Highlandville, Mo. Consecrated in July 1983 it measures 14 × 17 ft and has seating for 18 people.

Tallest Spires

The tallest *cathedral* spire is on the Protestant Cathedral of Ulm in Germany. The building is early Gothic and was begun in 1377. The tower, in the center of the west façade, was not finally completed until 1890 and is 528 ft high.

The tallest *church* spire is that of the Chicago Temple of the First Methodist Church on Clark St, Chicago. The building consists of a 22-story skyscraper (erected in 1924) surmounted by a parsonage at 330 ft, a "Sky Chapel" at 400 ft and a steeple cross at 568 ft above street level.

Minarets and Pagodas

The tallest minarets are the four of 344 ft 5 in being built for a new mosque in Shah Alam, Selangor, Malaysia. The tallest free-standing stone tower is the Qutb Minar, south of New Delhi, India, built in 1194 to a height of 238 ft.

The tallest pagoda is the Phra Pathom Chedi at Nakhon Pathom, Thailand, which was built for King Mongkut in 1853–70. It rises to 377 ft.

The oldest pagoda in China is Sung-Yo Ssu in Honan, built with 15 12-sided stories in 523 AD, though the 326-ft-tall Shwedagon Pagoda, Rangoon, Burma is built on the site of a 27-ft-tall pagoda dating to 585 BC.

Most Valuable Sacred Object

The sacred object of the highest intrinsic value is the 15th-century gold Buddha in the Temple of Three Friends in Bangkok, Thailand. It is 10 ft tall and weighs an estimated 6 tons. At the current value of $325 per fine ounce, its value has been calculated at $62.4 million for the gold alone. The gold under the plaster exterior was only found in 1954.

Biggest Demonstrations

A figure of 2,700,000 was published from China for the demonstration against the USSR in Shanghai Apr 3–4, 1969, following border clashes, and one of 10 million for the May Day celebrations of 1963 in Peking.

Largest Crowd

The greatest recorded number of human beings assembled with a common purpose was an estimated 12,700,000 at the Hindu feast of Kumbh-Mela, which was held at the confluence of the Yamuna (formerly called the Jumna), the Ganges and the invisible "Sarasvati" at Allahabad, Uttar Pradesh, India, on Jan 19, 1977. The holiest time during this holiest day since 1833 was during the planetary alignment between 9:28 and 9:40 A.M., during which only 200,000 achieved immersion to wash away the sins of a lifetime.

Popes, Cardinals and Bishops

LONGEST PAPAL REIGN: Pius IX, Giovanni Maria Mastai-Ferretti (1848–1878), 31 years 236 days

SHORTEST PAPAL REIGN: Stephan II (752), 2 days

LONGEST-LIVED POPE: St Agatho (d 681), ?106 years; Leo XIII, Gioacchino Pecci (1810–1903), 93 years 140 days

YOUNGEST ELECTED POPE: Benedict IX—Theophylact (c. 1020–1056) in 1032, at 11 or 12 years—3 terms as Pope

LAST MARRIED POPE (before celibacy rule): Adrian II (867–872)

LAST POPE WITH CHILDREN: Alexander VI—Rodrigo Borgia (1431–1503), father of six; elected 1492

SLOWEST ELECTION: Gregory X—Teobaldi Visconti, 31 months, Feb 1269—Sept 1, 1271

FASTEST ELECTION: Julius II, on first ballot, Oct 21, 1503

LAST NON-CARDINAL POPE: Urban VI—Bartolomeo Prignano (1318–89), Archbishop of Bari, Apr 8, 1378

SLOWEST CANONIZATION: St Leo III, over span of 857 years (816–1673)

OLDEST CARDINAL: Georgio da Costa (b Portugal, 1406, d Rome Sept 18, 1508), aged 102 years

OLDEST LIVING CARDINAL: Pietro Parente (b Feb 16, 1891), had 93rd birthday 1984

YOUNGEST CARDINAL: Luis Antonio de Bourbon (b July 25, 1727) elected Dec 19, 1735, aged 8 years 137 days

YOUNGEST LIVING CARDINAL: Alfonso Lopez Trujillo of Colombia (b Nov 18, 1935) appointed when aged 47 years 76 days

LONGEST-SERVING CARDINAL: Cardinal Duke of York, grandson of James VII of Scotland and II of England (1747–1807), 60 years 10 days

LONGEST-SERVING BISHOP: Bishop Louis François de la Baume de Suze (1603–90) 76 years 273 days from Dec 6, 1613

Non-Italian Popes

The current Pope John Paul II, elected Oct 16, 1978 (b Karol Wojtyla, May 18, 1920, at Wadowice, near Krakow, Poland) is the first non-Italian Pope since 1522.

Saints

There are 1,848 "registered" saints (including 60 St Johns), of whom 628 are Italians, 576 French and 271 from the British Isles. The first US-born saint is Mother Elizabeth Ann Bayley Seton (1774–1821) who was canonized Sept 14, 1975. The total includes 76 Popes.

The shortest interval that has elapsed between the death of a saint and his canonization was in the case of St Anthony of Padua, Italy, who died on June 13, 1231 and was canonized 352 days later on May 30, 1232.

The other extreme is represented by Pope St Leo III who died on June 12, 816, and was made a saint in 1673—857 years later.

Largest Funeral

The funeral of C. N. Annadurai (d Feb 3, 1969) Madras (India) Chief Minister was, according to some press reports, attended by 15 million. The longest funeral was probably that of Vice Admiral Viscount Nelson on Jan 9, 1806. Ticket holders were seated in St Paul's Cathedral, London by 8:30 A.M. Many were unable to leave until after 9 P.M.

The queue at the grave of the *chansonier* and guitarist Vladimir Visotsky (d July 28, 1980) stretched 6.2 mi.

WORST ACCIDENTS & DISASTERS IN THE WORLD

	Deaths		
Pandemic	75,000,000	Eurasia: The Black Death (bubonic, pneumonic and septicaemic plague)	1347–51
Genocide	c. 35,000,000	Mongol extermination of Chinese peasantry	1311–40
Influenza	21,640,000	Worldwide: Influenza	Apr–Nov 1918
Famine	c. 20,000,000[1]	Northern China (revealed May 1981)	1969–71
Earthquake	1,100,000	Near East and E. Mediterranean	c. July 1201
Circular Storm	1,000,000[2]	Ganges Delta isles, Bangladesh	Nov 12–13, 1970
Flood	900,000	Yellow (Hwang-ho) River, China	Oct 1877
Landslide	180,000	Kansu Province, China	Dec 16, 1920
Atomic Bomb	141,000	Hiroshima, Japan	Aug 6, 1945
Conventional Bombing	c. 140,000[3]	Tokyo, Japan	Mar 10, 1945
Volcanic Eruption	92,000	Tambora Sumbawa, Indonesia	Apr 5–7, 1815
Avalanche (mud)	c. 23,000	Nevado Del Ruiz, Colombia	Nov 13, 1985
Avalanche (ice and debris)	c. 18,000[4]	Yungay, Huascáran Mt, Peru	May 31, 1970
Marine (single ship)	c. 7,700	*Wilhelm Gustloff* (25,484 tons) torpedoed off Danzig by USSR submarine S-13	Jan 30, 1945
Dam Burst	c. 5,000	Manchu River Dam, Morvi, Gujarat, India	Aug 11, 1979
Panic	c. 4,000[5]	Chungking, China (air raid shelter)	c. June 8, 1941
Smog	2,850	London (Eng) fog	Dec 5–13, 1951
Industrial (Chemical)	2,500[11]	Bhopal, India at Union Carbide plant (plus c.200,000 injured)	Dec 2–3, 1984

(continued)

	Deaths		
Tunneling (Silicosis)	c. 2,500	Hawk's Nest hydro-electric tunnel, W Va	1931–35
Explosion	1,963[6]	Halifax, Nova Scotia, Canada	Dec 6, 1917
Fire (single building)	1,670[7]	The Theatre, Canton, China	May 1845
Mining	1,572[8]	Honkeiko Colliery, China (coal dust explosion)	Apr 26, 1942
Riot	c. 1,200	NYC (anticonscription riots)	July 13–16, 1863
Road	c. 1,100[9]	Gasoline tanker explosion inside Salang Tunnel, Afghanistan	Nov 2 or 3, 1982
Mass Suicide	913	People's Temple Cult by cyanide, Jonestown, Guyana	Nov 18, 1978
Crocodiles (disputed)	c. 900	Japanese soldiers, Ramree Island, Burma	Feb 19–20, 1945
Fireworks Show[13]	>800	Dauphine's wedding, Seine, Paris	May 16, 1770

Notes. 1.—In 1770 the great Indian famine carried away a proportion of the population estimated as high as one third, hence a figure of tens of millions. The figure for Bengal alone was probably about 10 million. The loss in the Northern China famine, Feb 1877–Sept 1878, was 9.5 million.

2.—The figure published in 1972 for the Bangladeshi disaster was from Dr Afzal, Principal Scientific Officer of the Atomic Energy Authority Centre, Dacca. One report asserted that less than half of the population of the 4 islands of Bhola, Charjabbar, Hatia and Ramagati (1961 Census 1.4 million) survived. The most damaging hurricane reported was Hurricane Frederic in 1979 with an estimated loss of $2,300 billion.

3.—The number of civilians killed by the bombing of Germany has been put variously as 593,000 and "over 635,000." Total Japanese fatalities in World War II were 600,000 (conventional) and 220,000 (nuclear).

4.—This avalanche occurred when an earthquake broke off the north peak of Huascarán, Peru's highest mountain, 22,205 ft high. It scooped up more ice and snow from the glacier below, then dirt and boulders, in all about 100 million tons, which fell upon Yungay. The earthquake killed about 60,000 people in all. A total of 10,000 Austrian and Italian troops is reported to have been lost in the Dolomite valley of Northern Italy on Dec 13, 1916 in more than 100 avalanches. The total is probably exaggerated though bodies were still being found in 1952. 4,000 killed, Santa Valley, below Huascarán, Peru, Jan 10, 1962.

5.—It was estimated that some 5,000 people were trampled to death in the stampede for free beer at the coronation celebration of Czar Nicholas II in Moscow in May 1896.

6.—Some sources maintain that the final death toll was over 3,000 on Dec 6–7.

7.—>200,000 killed in the sack of Moscow, freed by Tartars, May 1571. The worst-ever hotel fire killed 162 at the Hotel Daeyungak, Seoul, South Korea, Dec 25, 1971. The worst circus fire killed 323 at the Gran Circus Norte-Americano, Niteroi, Brazil, on Dec 17, 1961.

8.—The worst gold mining disaster in South Africa was 152 killed due to flooding in the Witwatersrand Gold Mining Co gold mine in 1909.

(continued)

	Deaths		
Railroad	>800	Bagmati River, Bihar State, India	June 6, 1981
Tornado	689	South Central States, US (3 hours)	March 18, 1925
Aircraft (Civil)	583	KLM-Pan Am Boeing 747 ground crash, Tenerife, Canary Islands (Single plane: Japan Airlines 747 in central Japan, 520 killed Aug 12, 1985.)	March 27, 1977
Man-Eating Animal	436	Champawat district, India, tigress shot by Col Jim Corbett	1907
Terrorism	329	Bomb aboard Air India Boeing 747, crashed into Atlantic south of Ireland. Sikh extremists suspected.	June 23, 1985
Bacteriological and Chemical	c. 300	Novosibirsk B&CW plant, USSR	Apr-May 1979
Hail	246	Moradabad, Uttar Pradesh, India	Apr 20, 1888
Truck Bomb	243	US Marine Barracks, Beirut, Lebanon	Oct 23, 1983
Submarine	130	*Le Surcouf* rammed in Caribbean	Feb 18, 1942
Offshore Oil Plant	123	Alexander L. Kielland "Hotel," North Sea	March 27, 1980
Helicopter	54	Israeli military "Sea Stallion," West Bank	May 10, 1977
Ski Lift (Cablecar)	42	Cavalese resort, Northern Italy	March 9, 1976
Mountaineering	40[10]	USSR expedition on Mt Everest	Dec 1952
Nuclear Reactor	31[12]	Chernobyl No 4, Ukraine, USSR	Apr 25, 1986
Elevator	23	Vaal Reefs Gold Mine lift fell 1.2 miles	May 27, 1980
Lightning	21	Hut in Chinamasa Kraal near Umtali, Rhodesia (single bolt)	Dec 23, 1975

Deaths

Yacht Racing	19	28th Fastnet Race 23 boats sank or abandoned in Force 11 gale	Aug 13–15, 1979
Space	7	US Space Shuttle *Challenger*	Jan 28, 1986
Nuclear Waste Accident	high but undisclosed	Venting of plutonium wastes, Kyshtym, USSR	*c.* Dec 1957

9.—Some estimates ran as high as 2,700 victims from monoxide asphyxiation when Soviet military sealed off both ends of a 1.7-mi long tunnel.

10.—According to Polish sources, not confirmed by the USSR. On Mt Fuji, Japan 23 died in a blizzard and avalanche on March 20, 1972.

11.—Explosion followed leak of fumes. Final death toll obscured by litigation. Published estimates of the 11,000 killed at the BASF chemical plant explosion at Oppau, W Germany, on Sept 21, 1921, were exaggerated. The best estimate is 561 killed.

12.—Total deaths from cancer will not become apparent for many years, but are certain to constitute the worst ever for such disaster.

13.—Panic following the fireworks show caused a crush of people at the narrow exit doors. The deaths were not directly due to fireworks.

Chapter 11

Human Achievements

1. ENDURANCE AND ENDEAVOR

TRAVEL AND EXPLORATION

Lunar Conquest

Neil Alden Armstrong (b Wapakoneta, Ohio, of Scottish-Irish-German ancestry, Aug 5, 1930), command pilot of the *Apollo XI* mission, became the first man to set foot on the moon on the Sea of Tranquillity at 02:56 and 15 sec A.M. GMT on July 21, 1969. He was followed out of the Lunar Module *Eagle* by Col Edwin Eugene Aldrin, Jr (b Glen Ridge, NJ, of Swedish, Dutch and British ancestry, Jan 20, 1930), while the Command Module named *Columbia* piloted by Lt-Col Michael Collins (b Rome, Italy, of Irish and pre-Revolutionary American ancestry, Oct 31, 1930) orbited above.

Eagle landed at 20:17 and 42 sec GMT July 20 and blasted off at 17:54 GMT on July 21, after a stay of 21 hours 36 min. The *Apollo XI* had blasted off from Cape Kennedy, Fla at 13:32 GMT July 16 and was a culmination of the US space program, which, at its peak, employed 376,600 people and attained in the year 1966–67 a peak budget of $5,900 million.

There is evidence that Pavel Belgayev was the cosmonaut selected by the USSR for a manned lunar flight in *Zond 7* on Dec 9, 1968 (219 days before the *Apollo XI* flight), but no launch took place.

Speed in Space

The fastest speed at which humans have traveled is 24,791 mph when the Command Module of *Apollo X* carrying Col (now Brig-Gen) Thomas Patten Stafford, USAF (b Weatherford, Okla, Sept 17, 1930), Cdr (now Capt) Eugene Andrew Cernan and Cdr (now Capt) John Watts Young, USN (b San Francisco, Sept 24, 1930) reached their maximum speed on their trans-earth return flight at an altitude of 400,000 ft on May 26, 1969.

The highest speed ever attained by a woman is 17,470 mph by Valentina Vladimirovna Tereshkova-Nikolayev during her 48-orbit flight in *Vostok VI* June 16–19, 1963.

The highest speed ever achieved by a woman aircraft pilot is 1,669.89 mph by Svetlana Savitskaya (USSR), reported on June 2, 1975.

Speed on Land

The highest speed ever claimed on land is an unofficial 739.666 mph or Mach 1.0106 in a one-way run by Stan Barrett (US) in the *Budweiser Rocket*, a rocket-engined 3-wheeled car at Edwards Air Force Base, Calif on Dec 17, 1979 (but see also p. 290).

The *official* one-mile land speed record is 633.468 mph set by Richard Noble (b 1946) on Oct 4, 1983 over the Black Rock Desert, Nev, in his 17,000 thrust Rolls-Royce Avon 302 jet-powered *Thrust 2*, designed by John Ackroyd.

The highest land speed recorded by a woman is 524.016 mph by Mrs Kitty O'Neil Hambleton (US), in the 48,000-hp rocket-powered 3-wheeled S.M.1 *Motivator* over the Alvard Desert, Ore, on Dec 6, 1976. Her official 2-way record was 512.710 mph and she probably touched 600 mph momentarily.

Speed on Water

The highest speed ever achieved on water is an estimated 300 knots (345 mph) by Kenneth Peter Warby (b May 9, 1939) on the Blowering Dam Lake, NSW, Australia Nov 20, 1977, in his unlimited hydroplane *Spirit of Australia*. The official world water speed record is 319.627 mph, set Oct 8, 1978, by Warby on the Blowering Dam Lake.

The record for propeller driven craft is 215.33 mph by Eddie Hill in his supercharged hydroplane, the *Texan*, on Lake Irvine, Calif, June 5, 1983. On a one-way run, the *Climax* reached a speed of 205.19 mph.

The fastest woman on water is Mary Rife (US), who has driven a drag boat, *Proud Mary*, at more than 190 mph.

Most Traveled Man

The most traveled living American is Parke G. Thompson of Akron, Ohio, whose blanket coverage of the nations and territories of the world lacks only Pitcairn Is, the 4 Antarctic territories and Fernando de Noronha. In 1986, he managed to visit N Korea, which had previously been "impenetrable." He has visited every state of the US including 78 of the 87 metropolitan areas and 86 of the 100 biggest major cities; all but 2 of the Canadian provinces and their capitals; all of the states of Australia and their capitals; 14 of the Russian Soviet republics and their capitals and Siberia; 5 major cities in India; the major cities of China; 5 states of Malaysia; 7 of the United Arab Emirates, and even the most remote island in the world, Tristan da Cunha. His grand total is 301 countries and geographical areas out of 308.

The most traveled child is George Chauncey Clouse (b Dec 6, 1979) of Indiana who had been to 114 countries before his sixth birthday.

The man who had more mileage in visiting more countries than anyone in his time was Jesse Hart Rosdail (1914–77) of Elmhurst, Ill, a 5th grade teacher. Of all the separately administered countries and territories listed in the *UN Population Report*, he had visited all excepting only N Korea and French Antarctic Territories. He estimated his mileage to visit 215 countries at 1,626,605 statute miles.

Fred Jurgen Specovius (b 1942) (W Germany) and Georgio Ricalto (b 1934) (Italy) have both visited all 170 sovereign countries. Specovius has also visited all the non-sovereign territories except 6 (3 more than Ricalto).

The most traveled man in the horseback era was probably the Methodist preacher Francis Asbury (b Birmingham, Eng), who traveled 264,000 mi in N America from 1771 to 1815, preaching 16,000 sermons.

MOST TRAVELED MAN: In back of Parke G. Thompson is the former palace of the Dalai Lama of Tibet, in Lhasa, the "forbidden city." Lhasa lost its title as the highest capital in the world at 12,087 ft (to La Paz, Bolivia) when Tibet was dominated by China and Lhasa was no longer the capital. Thompson has been to all the nooks and crannies of the globe, except Pitcairn Is and the 4 Antarctic territories. He has even penetrated N Korea.

Longest Airstrip Ticket

The longest recorded was one 39 ft 4½ in issued for $4,500 to M. Bruno Levnen of Brussels, Belgium in Dec 1985 for a trip of 53,203 mi on 80 airlines involving 109 stopovers.

Fastest Round-the-World Trip

The fastest time for a round-the-world journey on scheduled flights for a circumnavigation is 44 hours 6 min by David J. Springbett, 41, of Taplow, England from Los Angeles eastward via London, Bahrain, Singapore, Bangkok, Manila, Tokyo and Honolulu Jan 8–10, 1980 over a 23,068-mile route.

The F.A.I. accepts any flight, taking off and landing at the same point, which is as long as the Tropic of Cancer (22,858.754 miles) as a circumnavigational flight.

Round-the-World N-S

The first to go via both poles, a British expedition of two, Sir Ranulph Twisleton-Wykeham Fiennes and Charles Burton (GB), made the journey of 35,000 mi in just under 3 years. They crossed the Antarctic in open snowmobiles and were the first to cross the 9,000-ft-high Scott Glacier.

North Pole Conquests

The claims of both of the two US Arctic explorers, Dr Frederick Albert Cook (1865–1940) and Rear Adm Robert Edwin Peary, USN (1856–1920), in reaching the North Pole are subject to positive proof.

The earliest indisputable attainment of the North Pole over the sea ice was at 3 P.M. (CST) on Apr 19, 1968, by Ralph Plaisted (US) and three companions after a 42-day trek in four snowmobiles. Their arrival was independently verified 18 hours later by a US Air Force weather aircraft. The sea bed is 13,410 ft below the North Pole.

Naomi Uemara (b 1941), the Japanese explorer and mountaineer, became the first person to reach the North Pole in a solo trek across the Arctic ice cap at 04:45 GMT May 1, 1978. He had traveled 450 miles, setting out on March 7 from Cape Edward, Ellesmere Island, in northern Canada. He averaged nearly 8 miles per day with his sled "Aurora" drawn by 17 huskies.

The first woman to set foot on the North Pole was Mrs Fran Phipps, wife of the Canadian bush pilot Weldy Phipps, Apr 5, 1971. Galina Aleksandrovna Lastovskaya (b 1941) and Lilia Vladislavovna Minina (b 1959) were crew members of the USSR atomic icebreaker *Arktika* which reached the Pole on Aug 17, 1977.

The Soviet scientist Dr Pavel A. Gordienko and 3 companions were arguably the first ever to stand on the exact point Lat 90° 00′N (± 300 meters) on Apr 23, 1948.

Arctic Crossing

The first crossing of the Arctic Sea ice was achieved by the British Trans-Arctic Expedition which left Point Barrow, Alaska, Feb 21, 1968, and arrived at the Seven Island Archipelago northeast of Spitzbergen 464 days later on May 29, 1969, after a haul of 2,920 statute miles and a drift of 700 miles, compared with a straight-line distance of 1,662 miles. The team was Wally Herbert (leader), 34, Maj Ken Hedges, 34, Allan Gill, 38, Dr Roy Koerner, 36 (glaciologist), and 40 huskies. This was the longest sustained (sled) journey ever made on polar pack ice and the first undisputed conquest of the North Pole by sled. Temperatures sank to −47° F during the trek.

(Also see *Polar Circumnavigation*)

South Pole Conquests

The first men to cross the Antarctic circle (Lat 66° 30′ S) were the 193-crew of the *Resolution* (462 tons) under Capt James Cook (1728–79), the English navigator, and *Adventure* (336 tons) under Lt T. Furneaux, at 39° E, Jan 17, 1773.

The first person known to have sighted the Antarctic ice shelf was Capt. F. F. Bellinghausen (Russian) (1778–1852) on Jan 27, 1820 from the vessels *Vostock* and *Mirnyi*. The first person known to have sighted the mainland of the continent was Capt William Smith (1790–1847) and Master Edward Bransfield, of the British Royal Navy, in the brig *Williams*. They saw the peaks of Trinity Land 3 days later on Jan 30, 1820.

The South Pole (altitude 9,186 ft on ice and 336 ft bed rock) was first reached at 11 A.M. Dec 16, 1911, by a Norwegian party, led by Capt Roald Engebreth Gravning Amundsen (1872–1928), after a 53-day march with dog sleds from the Bay of Whales, to which he had penetrated in the *Fram*. Subsequent calculations showed that Olav Olavson Bjaaland (the last survivor, dying in June 1961, aged 88) and Helmer Hanssen probably passed within 400–600 meters of the exact pole. The other two party members were Sverre H. Hassell and Oskar Wisting.

The first woman to set foot on Antarctica was Mrs Karoline Mikkelsen on Feb 20, 1935. No woman stood on the South Pole until Nov 11, 1969, when Lois Jones, Eileen McSavenay, Jean Pearson, Terry Lee Tickhill (all US), Kay Lindsay (Australia) and Pam Young (New Zealand) arrived by air.

Antarctic Crossing

The first surface crossing of the Antarctic continent was completed at 1:47 P.M. March 2, 1958, after a 2,158-mile trek lasting 99 days from Nov 24, 1957, from Shackleton Base to Scott Base via the Pole. The crossing party of 12 was led by Dr (now Sir) Vivian Ernest Fuchs (b Feb 11, 1908).

The 2,600-mile trans-Antarctic leg of the 1980-82 Trans Globe Expedition was achieved in 66 days on Jan 11, 1981 having passed through the South Pole on Dec 23, 1980. The 3-man party on snowmobiles comprised Sir Ranulph Fiennes (b 1944), Oliver Shepard and Charles Burton.

Polar Circumnavigation

Sir Ranulph Fiennes and Charles Burton of the British Trans-Globe Expedition traveled south from Greenwich, Eng (Sept 2, 1979), via the South Pole (Dec 17, 1980) and the North Pole (Apr 11, 1982), and back to Greenwich arriving after a 35,000 mile trek on Aug 29, 1982.

The only Arctic crossing achieved in a single season was that by Fiennes and Burton from Alert via the North Pole to the Greenland Sea in open snowmobiles.

First on Both North and South Poles

Dr. Albert P. Crary, a member of the party that made the first airplane landing at the North Pole on May 3, 1952, subsequently became Chief Scientist of the US Antarctic Research Program and led a scientific oversnow tractor traverse from McMurdo Sound on the coast to the South Pole, arriving at the South Pole on Feb 12, 1961. Crary thereby became the first person ever to have set foot at both North and South Poles, pre-empting David Porter by 18 years.

Longest Sled Journeys

The longest totally self-supporting sled journey was one of 1,080 mi across Greenland (W–E) June 18–Sept 5, 1934 by a British team led by Capt Martin Lindsay, with 49 dogs. A Ross Sea party of 10 in the Antarctic sledged over 2,000 mi in 300 days from May 6, 1975 during which time 3 died.

Greatest Ocean Descent

The record ocean descent was achieved in the Challenger Deep of the Marianas Trench, 250 miles southwest of Guam, when the Swiss-built US Navy bathyscaphe *Trieste,* manned by Dr Jacques Piccard (b 1914) and Lt Donald Walsh, USN, reached the ocean bed 35,820 ft (6.78 miles) down, at 1:10 P.M. Jan 23, 1960. The pressure of the water was 16,883 lb per sq in (1,215.6 tons per sq ft), and the temperature 37.4° F. The descent required 4 hours 48 min and the ascent 3 hours 17 min.

Deep Diving Records

The record depth for the extremely dangerous activity of breath-held diving is 344 ft by Jacques Mayol (France) off Elba, Italy in Dec 1983 for men and 147½ ft by Giuliana Treleani (Italy) off Cuba in Sept 1967 for women. Mayol descended on a sled in 104 sec and ascended in 90 sec.

The record dive with SCUBA (self-contained underwater breathing apparatus) is 437 ft by John J. Gruener and R. Neal Watson (US) off Freeport, Grand Bahama, on Oct 14, 1968.

The record dive utilizing gas mixtures (nitrogen, oxygen and helium) is a simulated dive of 2,250 ft in a dry chamber by Stephen Porter, Len Whitlock and Erik Kramer at the Duke University Medical Center, Durham, NC, Feb 3, 1981 in a 43-day trial in an 8-ft sphere.

Patrick Raude and 5 Comex divers left and returned to the bell *Petrel* at 1,643 ft off Cavalaire, France, in 1982.

Deepest Underwater Escapes

The deepest underwater rescue achieved was of the *Pisces III* in which Roger R. Chapman, 28, and Roger Mallinson, 35, were trapped for 76 hours when it sank to 1,575 ft, 150 miles southeast of Cork, Ireland, Aug 29, 1973. It was hauled to the surface by the cable ship *John Cabot* after preliminary work by *Pisces V, Pisces II* and the remote control recovery vessel US CURV, on Sept 1, 1973.

The greatest depth of an actual escape without any equipment has been from 225 ft by Richard A. Slater from the rammed submersible *Nekton Beta* off Catalina Island, Calif on Sept 28, 1970.

Deepest Salvage

The greatest depth at which salvage has been achieved is 16,500 ft by the bathyscaphe *Trieste II* (Lt Cdr Mel Bartels, USN) to attach cables to an "electronics package" on the sea bed 400 miles north of Hawaii, May 20, 1972.

Project Jennifer by USS *Glomar Explorer* in June–July 1974, to recover a Golfclass USSR submarine 750 miles northwest of Hawaii cost $550 million but was not successful.

The deepest salvage by robot was the recovery in July 1985 from the ocean floor off Ireland at 6,700 ft of 2 "black boxes" containing the flight recorders from the crashed Air-India 747 plane. The robot submarine "Scarab I" worked with a hydrophone and a side-scan radar "fish" towed by a surface ship.

Salvage by Divers

The deepest salvage operation ever achieved with divers was on the wreck of HM Cruiser *Edinburgh* sunk on May 2, 1942, in the Barents Sea off northern Norway inside the Arctic Circle in 803 ft of water. Twelve divers dived on the wreck in pairs using a bell from the *Stephaniturm* (1,423 tons) over 32 days under the direction of former RN officer and project director Michael Stewart from Sept 17 to Oct 7, 1981. The 431 gold ingots were divided; $26.3 million to the USSR, $13.15 million to GB and some $32.4 million to the salvage contractors, Jessop Marine Recoveries Ltd (10%) and Wharton Williams Ltd (90%). John Rossier, 28, was the first to touch the gold. The longest decompression time was 7 days 10 hours 27 min. The $71.85 million is an all-time record, but 34 bars worth $6 million were believed unrecovered.

MARRIAGE AND DIVORCE

Longest Marriages

The longest recorded marriage is one of 86 years between Sir Temulji Bhicaji Nariman and Lady Nariman from 1853 to 1940 resulting from a cousin marriage when both were five. Sir Temulji (b Sept 3, 1848) died, aged 91 years 11 months, in Aug 1940 in Bombay.

An 86th wedding anniversary was achieved by Lazarus Rowe of Greenland, NH, and Molly Webber, both born in 1725, married at 18, and died in 1829.

The only reliable instance of an 83rd anniversary celebrated by a couple marrying at normal ages is that between the late Edd (105) and Margaret (99) Hollen (US) who celebrated their 83rd anniversary on May 7, 1972. They were married in Kentucky on May 7, 1889.

Longest Engagement

The longest engagement on record is one of 67 years between Octavio Guillen, 82, and Adriana Martinez, 82. They finally took the plunge in June 1969, in Mexico City.

Most Marriages

The greatest number of marriages accumulated in the monogamous world is 27 by the former Baptist minister of religion Mr Glynn de Moss "Scotty" Wolfe (US) (b 1908), who first married in 1927. His latest wife is 15-year-old Daisy Delgado (b Dec 29, 1970), a Filipino from Liloan, Cebu. His oldest wife was 38 at the time of marriage. He says he has had 41 children but had only 25 mothers-in-law as he remarried two of his former wives.

Mrs Beverly Nina Avery, then aged 48, a barmaid from Los Angeles, set a monogamous world record in Oct 1957 by obtaining her 16th divorce, this one from Gabriel Avery, her 14th husband. She alleged outside the court that 5 of the 14 had broken her nose.

The most often-marrying millionaire, Thomas F. Manville (1894–1967), contracted his 13th marriage to his 11th wife, Christine Erdlen Popa (1940–71) aged 20, in NYC on Jan 11, 1960, when he was 65. His shortest marriage (to his 7th wife) effectively lasted only 7½ hours. His fortune of $20 million came from asbestos, which he unfortunately could not take with him.

Giovanni Vigliotto (b Fred Jipp, NYC, Apr 3, 1936 or b Nikolai Peruskov, Siracusa, Sicily, Apr 3, 1929) was arrested in Panama City, Fla, on Dec 30, 1981, for a record 104 bigamous marriages in more than 27 US states and 14 other countries between 1949 and 1981. Four victims were aboard one ship in 1968. He said he specialized in "larceny by deception." Convicted on Mar 28, 1983, in Phoenix, Ariz, he was sentenced to a maximum of 34 years in prison (28 for fraud, 6 for bigamy) and fined $336,000.

Oldest Bridegroom

The oldest recorded bridegroom has been Harry Stevens, 103, who married Thelma Lucas, 84, at the Caravilla (Wis) Retirement Home on Dec 3, 1984.

Mass Wedding Ceremony

The largest mass wedding ceremony was one of 5,837 couples from 83 countries officiated over by the controversial Sun Myung Moon (b 1920) of the Holy Spirit Association for the Unification of World Christianity in Seoul, S Korea, on Oct 14, 1982.

Most Expensive Wedding

The wedding of Mohammed, son of Shaik Zayid ibn Sa'id al-Makhtum, to Princess Salama in Abu Dhabi in May 1981 lasted 7 days and

CHILLY WEDDING: With penguins as witnesses, Bruno
(photographer) married Heather (actress) in an ice cave in Antarctica on
international territory at midnight. They stood on 3 ft of packed snow,
15 ft underground, with the thermometer at 32°.

cost an estimated $33 million including a purpose-built stadium for
20,000.

The most expensive private wedding is reputed to be that of Maria
Niarchos, 20, to Alix Chevassus, 36, at her father's estate in Normandy,
France on June 16, 1979. Guests consumed an estimated 12,000 bottles
of champagne and red wine; the supply of caviar outweighed the demand in four football-field-sized tents. The cost is conservatively estimated at $500,000.

Wedding in Ice Cave

"When you're in love you're always warm," said 99 year old Bruno J
Zehnder, photographer, as he was married to actress Heather May
standing on 3 ft of snow in an ice cave, 32 degrees cold, 15 ft underground in Antarctica on international territory at midnight on January
17, 1985. Zehnder had proposed to his bride while on an icebreaker from
Argentina headed for Antarctica. She had permission from the Argentine president to accompany him and to take along her black silk dress
with a 20-ft white train for the wedding. A flock of Adelie penguins (in
black-and-white) witnessed the wedding.

Most Married Couple

Jack V. and Edna Moran of Seattle, Wash have married each other 40
times since the original and only really necessary occasion on July 27,
1937 in Seaside, Ore. Subsequent ceremonies have included those at
Banff, Canada (1952), Cairo, Egypt (1966) and Westminster Abbey,
London (1975).

Oldest Divorce

Ida Stern, 91, and her husband Simon Stern, 97, of Milwaukee, Wis, were divorced on Feb 2, 1984, in the circuit court of Milwaukee.

Golden Anniversaries

Despite the advent of the computer, records on golden (or 50th) wedding anniversaries remain largely uncollated. Unusual cases reported include that of Mrs Agnes Mary Amy Mynott (b May 25, 1887) who attended the golden anniversary of her daughter Mrs Violet Bangs of St Albans in Dec 20, 1980, some 23 years after her own. Triplets Lucille (Mrs Vogel), Marie (Mrs McNamara) and Alma (Mrs Prom) Pufpaff all celebrated their golden anniversaries on Apr 12, 1982, having all married in Cleveland, Minn, in 1932.

The Munn family (John, May and Carroll) of Greenville, Ohio, set a record of more than 200 years of marriage when two brothers and a sister celebrated wedding anniversaries of 65 years, 66 years and 69 years in 1984.

MARINE RECORDS

Three pages of charts of Marine Records—circumnavigation of the world, transatlantic and transpacific—appear in the 1983 Guinness Book of World Records. Only new records since then are carried in this section.

A non-stop circumnavigation is entirely self-maintained; no water supplies, equipment or replacements of any sort may be taken aboard en route.

Earliest Circumnavigation by Motorboat

David Scott Cowper (GB) drove his 42-ft motorboat, the *Mabel E. Holland*, around the world alone from Plymouth, Eng, through the Panama Canal and back to Plymouth in 170 days 2 hours 15 min (average 165.7 mi/day) in 1984.

Fastest Atlantic Crossing

Patrick Moran (France) with a crew of 3 in *Jet Services II*, a 60-ft sloop-catamaran, crossed from Sandy Hook, NJ, to Land's End, Eng, in 8 days 16 hours 36 min (375.16 mi/day) in 1984.

New small boat records were set going both W–E and E–W. Starting from Allerton, Mass, in his 8-ft-11-in *God's Tear* on Oct 30, 1982, Wayne Dickinson (US) sailed for 142 days, reaching NW Eire on Mar 22, 1983. Starting from Las Palmas, Canary Islands, on Dec 25, 1982, Eric Peters (GB) in his 5-ft-10½-in barrel floated 46 days, reaching Guadeloupe in the West Indies on Feb 8, 1983.

The first single-handed row Trans-Pacific E–W was by Peter Bird, 36 (GB) in his *Hele-on-Britannia* 32 ft long, from San Francisco Aug 23, 1982 to Great Barrier Reef, Australia June 14, 1983—294 days. Distance estimated at 9,000 miles.

Sailing Blind

Hank Dekker, 42, in his 25-ft sloop, *Dark Star*, became the first blind man to sail alone from San Francisco to Honolulu in Aug 1983. He used

Braille charts, a Braille compass, a talking clock, and a navigational system that reads the position aloud. A former race car driver, Dekker lost his sight in 1972.

Fastest Circumnavigation, Solo, Nonstop

Dodge Morgan (US) in the 60-ft-long Bermudan sloop, *American Promise,* sailed W–E via Cape Horn from Bermuda on Nov 12, 1985 and traversed 25,671 mi in 150 days 1 hour 6 min at the rate of 171.1 mi/day, returning to Bermuda Apr 11, 1986.

This voyage was faster but less in mileage than the one achieved by Alain Colas (France) in the 70-ft-long trimaran *Manureva* (ex *Pen Duick IV*) who went 30,067 mi in 169 days 4 hours 11 min in 1974 at a speed of 177.7 mi/day.

OCEAN-GOING CHINESE JUNK: "Intrepid Dragon II," built in Hong Kong, 80 ft long, owned by Glasfur E. Rathburn, sailed from Hong Kong and crossed the Atlantic twice, rounding Africa and navigating the Panama Canal.

STUNTS AND MISCELLANEOUS ENDEAVORS

Accordion Playing. Tom Luxton of Oldbury, W Midlands, England, played 84 hours continuously in Aug 1982.

Apple Peeling. The longest single unbroken apple peel on record is 172 ft 4 in peeled by Kathy Wafler, 17, of Wolcott, NY, in 11 hours 30 min at the Long Ridge Mall, Rochester, NY, Oct 16, 1976. The apple weighed 20 oz.

Apple Picking. The greatest recorded performance is 365½ US bushels picked in 8 hours by George Adrian, 32, of Indianapolis, on Sept 23, 1980.

Baby Carriage Pushing. The greatest distance covered in 24 hours in pushing a perambulator is 345.25 miles by Runner's Factory of Los Gatos, Calif with an all-star team of 57 California runners June 23–24, 1979. A 10-man team of British Royal Marines from Lympstone, Devon, Eng, with an adult "baby" covered 252.65 mi in 24 hours, Mar 31–Apr 1, 1984.

Balancing on One Foot. The longest recorded duration for balancing on one foot is 34 hours by Shri N. Ravi in Sathy Amangalam City, Tamil Nadu, India, Apr 17–18, 1982. The disengaged foot may not be rested on the standing foot nor may any sticks be used for support or balance, but 5-minute rest breaks are allowed after each hour.

Balloon Flights. The longest reported toy balloon flight is one of 10,000 miles approximately from Dobbs Ferry, NY to Wagga Wagga, Australia. The helium-filled balloon was released by 11-year-old Justin Fiore on Apr 19, 1982 along with others at the Springhurst Elementary School. Justin had a stamped, self-addressed envelope attached to his. R. D. Spraggou found it in the scrub on his sheep station in partially deflated but not punctured condition on May 25, 1982.

Balloon Release. The largest ever mass balloon release was one of 1,121,448 helium balloons (after deducting 88,152 balloons that failed) at Skyfest's Salute to Walt Disney, Disneyland, Anaheim, Calif on Dec 5, 1985. The release was directed by Balloonart by Treb, Inc. of LA.

Ball Punching. The duration record is 146 hours 20 min by Pat McEnteggart of Shallon, Julianstown, Ireland, Feb 27–Mar 5, 1981.

Band, One-Man. The greatest number of instruments played in a single rendition is 314 in 1 min 23.07 sec by Rory Blackwell in Devon, Eng, on May 27, 1985.

Rory Blackwell, aided by his left-footed perpendicular percussion-pounder and his right-footed horizontal 4-pronged differential beater, played 24 (4 melody, 20 percussion) instruments in TV South West Studios, Plymouth, Eng, on May 2, 1985.

Dave Sheriff of Rugby, England, played his one-man band of 12 instruments (at least 3 instruments played simultaneously) for 100 hours, 20 min, Mar 24–28, 1986 at Coventry, Eng.

Milton J. (Buddy) Thornton, a blind musician of Abilene, Tex, played 12 instruments simultaneously for 3 min on television on May 17, 1984. The instruments were snare drum, bass drum, tomtom, guitar, bass gui-

MORE THAN A MILLION BALLOONS (above): Exactly 1,121,448 helium balloons were released at one time on Dec 5, 1985, at Disneyland by the City of Anaheim, Calif, beating the previous record of a mere 384,800 set in Japan in 1984. The simultaneous release of the stacks of balloons was directed by Treb Heining of Balloonart by Treb.

ONE-MAN BAND (right): Rory Blackwell (Eng) can play 314 different instruments in 1 min 23.07 sec, and 24 instruments simultaneously in a single tune.

tar, tambourine, cowbells, cymbal, high-hat cymbal, block, maracas and harmonica.

Band Marathons. The longest recorded "blow-in" is 100 hours 2 min by the Du Val Senior High School band, Lanham, Md, directed by Louis Scarci, May 13–17, 1977.

Band, Pop. The playing duration record for a 4-man pop group is 147 hours by The Decorators, Jan 8–14, 1986 at Boxhill-on-Sea, Eng.

BATHTUB RACING
(above): The annual race with motorized tubs across the rough straits from Nanaimo to Vancouver, BC, Canada, covers a 36-mi course.

MOST ON A BICYCLE
(left): Sixteen members of the Mito-Itomi Unicycle Club of Mito Ibaragi, Japan, piled onto this bike in a record-setting stunt.

BELLS ARE RINGING
(below): This group of 12 rang their handbells for 56 hours 3 min continuously in Sheffield, Eng, in July 1985, breaking their own record of 3 years previous. (*Dave Muscroft*)

Barrel Jumping (on ice skates). The official distance record is 29 ft 5 in over 18 barrels by Yvon Jolin at Terrebonne, Quebec, Canada, in 1981. The feminine record is 20 ft 4½ in over 11 barrels by Janet Hainstock in Mich on Mar 15, 1980.

Bathtub Racing. The record for the annual international 36-mile Nanaimo-to-Vancouver, British Columbia, bathtub race is 1 hour 29 min 40 sec by Gary Deathbridge, 25 (Australia) July 30, 1978. Tubs are limited to 75 in and 6-hp motors. The greatest distance for paddling a hand-propelled bathtub in 24 hours is 90.5 mi by 13 members of the Aldington (Kent, Eng) Social Club May 28–29, 1983.

The longest reported bathtub push was 564.7 miles from Cleveland, O to NYC's Empire State Building by 6 members of Tau Kappa Epsilon fraternity of Cleveland State University in 66 hours 5 min from Sept 8–18, 1983. The bathtub was on bicycle-type wheels and average speed was 9 mph.

Baton Twirling. Victor Cerda, Sol Lozano, Harry Little III (leader) and Manuel Rodriguez, twirled batons for 122½ hours, June 24–29, 1984, in El Sereno, Calif.

Beard of Bees. The ultimate beard of bees was achieved by Max Beck of Arcola, Pa, with 70,000 bees weighing 20 lb, reported in Oct 1985.

Bed of Nails. The duration record for non-stop lying on a bed of nails (sharp 6-in nails 2 in apart) is 274 hours 2 min by Inge Widar Svingen, ending on TV's "Good Morning, Norway" program on Nov 3, 1984. Much longer durations are claimed by uninvigilated *fakirs*—the most extreme case being *Silki* who claimed 111 days in São Paulo, Brazil, ending on Aug 24, 1969.

Note that the category of "Iron Maiden" (lying between 2 beds of nails with added weight on top) has been retired with the ultimate record being set at 1,642½ lb endured by Komar (Vernon E. Craig) of Wooster, Ohio at Old Chicago Towne March 6, 1977. No further claims for publication will be entertained or published.

Bed Pushing. The longest recorded push of a normally stationary object is 3,233 miles 1,150 yd in the case of a wheeled hospital bed by a team of 9, all employees of Bruntsfield Bedding Centre, Edinburgh, Scotland June 21–July 26, 1979.

Bell Ringing. The longest recorded handbell ringing recital has been one of 56 hours 3 min by the 12 Handbell Ringers of Ecclesfield School, Sheffield, England, July 21–23, 1985.

Bicycle Stunts. On Apr 2, 1984, at Mito Ibaragi, Japan, 16 members of the Mito-Itomi Unicycle Club rode on a single bicycle a distance of 164 ft.

The longest duration standing upright on the back wheel only of a bicycle is 1 hour 16 min 54 sec by Craig Strong (GB) at Edmonton, North London, on Jan 7, 1983.

Rudi Jan Jozef De Greef (b Dec 28, 1955) stayed stationary without support for 10 hours at Meensel-Kiezegem, Belgium, Nov 19, 1982. David Steed of Tucson, Ariz, former recordholder at 9½ hours, later is said to have stayed for 24 hours.

Billiard Table Jumping. Joe Darby (1861–1937) cleared a 12-ft billiard table lengthwise, taking off from a running start, using only a 4-in-high solid wooden block, at Wolverhampton, England, Feb 5, 1892.

Boomerang Throwing. The earliest mention of a word similar to "boomerang" is "wo-mur-rang" in Collins' *Account N.S. Wales Vocabulary,* published in 1798. The earliest certain Australian account of a returning boomerang (term established in 1827) was in 1831 by Major (later Sir) Thomas Mitchell. Curved throwing sticks for hunting wild fowl were found in the tomb of Tutankhamen, dating from the mid-14th century BC.

World championships and codified rules were not established until 1970. The Boomerang Association of Australia's championship record for distance reached before the boomerang returns is 364.1 ft (diameter) by Bob Burwell in Nov 1981 at Albury. The longest under US rules for out-and-return is 375 ft by Peter Ruhf at Randwick, Sydney, Australia, June 28, 1982. The longest flight duration (with self-catch) is 28.9 sec by Bob Burwell at Albury, NSW, Aust, on Apr 7, 1984. The greatest number of consecutive two-handed catches on record is 653 by Bob Croll (Victoria, Aust) on Apr 7, 1984, the same occasion.

Brick Carrying. The record for carrying a brick (8 lb 15 oz) in a nominated ungloved hand with the arm extended in an uncradled downward pincer grip is 45 miles by David and Kym Barger of Lamar, Mo on May 21, 1977.

The feminine record of 22½ miles was set by Wendy Morris of Walsall, Eng, on Apr 28, 1986.

Brick Throwing. The greatest reported distance for throwing a standard 5-lb building brick is 146 ft 1 in by Geoffrey Capes at Braybrook School, Cambridgeshire, England, on July 19, 1978.

Bubble Gum Blowing. The largest bubble blown measured 22 in in diameter, created by Mrs Susan Montgomery Williams of Fresno, Calif, in her home Apr 19, 1985, while a *National Enquirer* photographer watched. He also measured with a "gumputer" calipers on a horizontal rather than a vertical basis, to eliminate any elongation due to gravity.

CPR (Cardio-Pulmonary Resuscitation). The longest time that a team of 2 continuously performed CPR (15 compressions alternating with 2 breaths) is 53 hours by Robert Stanbary and Wyatt Pace of Bloomington, Ill, Sept 27–29, 1985, at St Joseph's Hospital Medical Center in Bloomington.

Camping Out. The silent Indian *fakir* Mastram Bapu "contented father" has remained on the same spot by the roadside in the village of Chitra for 22 years, 1960–82.

Canal Jumping. In the sport of Fierljeppen at Winsam, Friesland, The Netherlands, the record is 61 ft 0¾ in across the water with a 40-ft aluminum pole set by Aarth de Wit in Aug 1983.

Card Throwing. Kevin St Onge threw a standard playing card 185 ft 1 in on the Henry Ford Community College campus, Dearborn, Mich, June 12, 1979.

Carriage Driving. The only man to drive 48 horses in a single hitch is Dick Sparrow of Zearing, Iowa, 1972–77. The lead horses were 135 ft away.

Catapulting. The greatest recorded distance for a catapult shot is 1,362 ft by James F. Pfotenhauer, using a patented 16½-ft "Monarch IV Su-

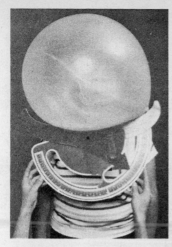

BIGGEST BUBBLE BLOWN (left): Susan Montgomery Williams of Fresno, Calif, looks like a creature from outer space as she blows a record 22-in-diameter bubble, while it is being measured by a "gumputer."

CHAMPAGNE FOUNTAIN (below): To launch a new brand of Calif wine, the promoters built this 44-story 24.7-ft-high pyramid of 10,404 glasses and successfully poured the champagne down without toppling the mountain.

BIGGEST FLYING RING AUDIENCE (below): Wini McKay swung high over a crowd of 85,000 people at the Los Angeles Coliseum in 1980.

Stunts and Miscellaneous Endeavors ▪ 441

pershot" and a 53-caliber lead shot on Ski Hill, Escanaba, Mich, on Sept 10, 1977.

Champagne Fountain. The tallest successfully filled column of champagne glasses is one 44 stories (24.7 ft) high, filled from the top and using 10,404 long-stemmed glasses, achieved by Pascal Leclerc at the Biltmore Hotel, LA, on June 18, 1984.

CIRCUS RECORDS

A table of historic circus records from 1859 to date was published in the 1985 Edition on p. 434. New records set since 1975 are below:

Flying Trapeze. Downward circles or "Muscle grinding"—1,350 by Sarah Denu (age 14) (US) Madison, Wis, May 21, 1983. Single heel hang on swinging bar, Angela Revelle (Angelique), Australia, 1977.

Highest Aerial Act. Ian Ashpole (b Jan 15, 1956) of Ross-on-Wye, Eng, performed a trapeze act suspended from a hot-air balloon 16,420 ft up over Cambridgeshire and Suffolk counties, Eng, on May 16, 1986.

Triple Twisting Double Somersault. Tom Robin Edelston to catcher John Zimmerman, Circus World, Fla, Jan 20, 1981.

Full Twisting Triple and the Quadruple Somersault. Vasquez Troupe, Miguel Vasquez to catcher Juan Vasquez at Ringling Bros, Amphitheatre, Chicago, in Nov 1981. On Sept 20, 1984, Miguel performed a triple somersault in a layout position (no turn) to catcher Juan at the Sports Arena in LA.

Triple Back Somersault with 1½ Twists. Terry Cavaretta Lemus (now Mrs St Jules) at Circus Circus, Las Vegas, Nev, in 1969.

Teeter Board. Six-man high perch pyramid, Emilia Ivanova (Bulgaria) of the Kehaiovi Troupe at Inglewood, Calif, July 21, 1976.

Trampoline. Septuple twisting back somersault to bed and quintuple twisting back somersault to shoulders by Marco Canestrelli to Belmonte Canestrelli at Madison Square Garden, NYC, on Jan 5 and Mar 28, 1979. Richard Tison (France) performed a triple twisting triple back somersault for television near Berchtesgaden, W Germany on June 30, 1981.

Flexible Pole. Double full twisting somersault to a 2-in-diameter pole by Roberto Tabak (aged 11) of the Robertos troupe in Sarasota, Fla, in 1977. Triple full twisting somersault by Corina Colonelu Mosoiann (age 13) at Madison Sq Garden, NYC, on Apr 17, 1984.

Human Pyramid (or Tuckle). Twelve (3 high) supported by a single understander. Weight 1,700 lb by Tahar Douis of the Hassani Troupe at BBC TV Studio, on Dec 17, 1979. Nine high by top-mounter Josep-Joan Martinez Lozano, 10, of the Colla Vella dels Xiquets 39 ft tall on Oct 25, 1981 in Valls, Spain.

Clapping. The duration record for continuous clapping (sustaining an average 160 claps per min audible at 120 yd) is 54 hours by V. Jeyaraman of Tamil Nadu, India, Dec 13–15, 1985.

Coin Balancing. The tallest column of coins ever stacked on the edge of a coin is 205 Canadian 25-cent pieces on top of a Canadian Olympic Commemorative which was freestanding vertically on the base of a coin flat on the surface by Bruce McConachy (b 1963) of W Vancouver, British Columbia, for Fuji TV, Tokyo, Feb 24, 1985.

Alex Chervinsky (b Feb 22, 1908) of Lock Haven, Pa, achieved a pyramid of 390 coins on his 77th birthday.

Coin Snatching. The greatest number of British 10-pence coins (slightly larger than the US 25-cent piece) caught clean from being flipped from the back of a forearm into the same palm is 85 by Andrew Gleed at the *Guinness World of Records,* London, on May 29, 1986.

Crawling. The longest continuous voluntary crawl (progression with one or the other knee in unbroken contact with the ground) on record is 27 mi by Chris Lock at Bristol, Eng, Aug 18–19, 1984.

The Baptist lay preacher Hans Mullikin, 39, arrived at the White House in Washington, DC on Nov 23, 1978, having crawled all but 8 of the 1,600 miles from Marshall, Tex.

Over a space of 15 months ending Mar 9, 1985, Jagdish Chander, 32, crawled 870 mi in India, to propitiate his favorite Hindu goddess Mata.

Crochet. Mrs Barbara Jean Sonntag (b 1938) of Craig, Colo, crocheted 330 shells plus 5 stitches (equivalent to 4,412 stitches) in 30 min, at a rate of 147 stitches per min, on Jan 13, 1981. She also set a record for a crochet chain on Oct 31, 1981 when she finished a strand 34.9 mi long. Mrs Sybille Anthony bettered all marathons of this kind in a 120-hour crochet marathon at Toombul Shoppingtown, Queensland, Australia, Oct 3–7, 1977.

Cucumber Slicing. Norman Johnson of the Blackpool College of Art and Technology, England sliced 12 in of a 1½-in-diameter cucumber at 22 slices to the inch (total 244 slices) in 13.4 sec on Apr 3, 1983 in Cologne, W Germany.

Dancing. Marathon dancing must be distinguished from dancing mania, which is a pathological condition. The worst outbreak of dancing mania was at Aachen, Germany in July 1374, when hordes of men and women broke into a frenzied dance in the streets which lasted for hours till injury or complete exhaustion ensued.

The most severe marathon dance (staged as a public spectacle in the US) was one by Mike Ritof and Edith Boudreaux, who logged 5,148 hours 28½ min to win $2,000 at Chicago's Merry Garden Ballroom, Belmont and Sheffield, Ill, from Aug 29, 1930, to Apr 1, 1931. Rest periods were progressively cut from 20 to 10 to 5 to nil minutes per hour with 10-in steps and a maximum of 15 sec for closure of eyes.

Largest Dance. A crowd estimated at 25,000 by the local newspapers attended a "Moonlight Serenade" outdoor evening of dancing to the music of the Glenn Miller orchestra in Buffalo, NY, on July 20, 1984 on a 450-ft-long dance floor around the M&T Bank Building.

Dancing, Ballet. The greatest number of spins called for in classical ballet choreography is the 32 in Swan Lake by Tschaikovsky. Miss Rowena Jackson (later Chatfield) (b 1925, Invercargill, New Zealand) achieved 121 such turns at her class in Melbourne, Australia, in 1940.

Dancing, Ballroom. The individual continuous record is 120 hours 30 min by Alain Dumas June 28–July 3, 1983 at the Disco-Shop, Granby, Quebec, Canada. 9 girls worked shifts as his partner.

The most successful professional ballroom dancing champions have been Bill Irvine and Bobbie Irvine of London who won 13 world titles, 1960–72.

The oldest competitive ballroom dancer is Albert J. Sylvester (b Nov 24, 1889) of Corsham, Wiltshire, England, who on Apr 26, 1977, won the topmost amateur Alex Moore award for a 10-dance test with his partner, Paula Smith, in Bath, England. By 1981 he had won nearly 50 medals and trophies since he began dancing in 1964.

Dancing, Belly and Charleston. The longest recorded example of a belly dance was one of 106 hours by Eileen Foucher at Rush Green Hospital, Romford, Eng, July 30–Aug 3, 1984. The Charleston duration record is 110 hours 58 min by Sabra Starr of Lansdowne, Pa, Jan 15–20, 1979.

Dancing, Conga. The longest recorded conga line was a "snake" of 8,659 people belonging to the Camping and Caravanning Club of GB and Ireland, SE Region, on Sept 4, 1982.

Dancing, Disco (including Jive, Twist and Go-Go). The duration record for non-stop jiving is 97 hours 42 min by Richard Rimmer (with a relay of partners) of Surrey, England, Nov 11–16, 1979. Under the strict rules of the European Rock n' Roll Association the duration pair record is 22 hours by Mirco and Manuela Catalano at the Olympia Shopping Centre, Munich, W Germany Feb 6–7, 1981.

The longest recorded disco dancing marathon is one of 371 hours by John Sharples of Preston, England, Jan 18–Feb 3, 1982.

Dancing, Flamenco. The fastest flamenco dancer ever measured is Solero de Jerez, aged 17, who, in Brisbane, Australia in Sept 1967, in an electrifying routine attained 16 heel taps per sec or 960 per min.

Dancing, High Kicking. The record for high kicks (heel to ear level) is 10,376 in 6 hours 5 min 55 sec by Alagarajah Srikandarjah (Sri Lanka) at Aubigny, France, on July 22, 1984.

Tara Hobbs, 13, set a speed record of 95 kicks in 1 min on BBC-TV on Sept 2, 1984.

Veronica Evans (GB) set a speed record of 50 kicks in 25 sec in Manchester, Eng, on Dec 24, 1931.

Dancing, Limbo. The lowest height for a flaming bar under which a limbo dancer has passed is 6⅛ in off the floor at Port of Spain Pavilion, Toronto, on June 24, 1973, by Marlene Raymond, 15. Strictly no part of the body other than the sole or side of the foot should touch the ground, though brushing the shoulder blade does not in practice usually result in disqualification.

The record on roller skates is 5¼ in by Sandra Siviour on Mar 30, 1985, and by Tracey O'Callaghan on June 2, 1984, both at Bexley, Aust, to equal the mark set by Denise Culp of Rock Hill, SC, on Jan 22, 1984.

Dancing, Square. An estimated total of 20,000 dancers took part in the National Square Dance Convention in Louisville, Ky on June 26, 1983.

Dancing, Tap. The fastest *rate* ever measured for a tap dancer is 1,440 taps per min (24 per sec) by Roy Castle on the BBC-TV *Record Breakers* program on Jan 14, 1973. Roy achieved 1 million taps in 23 hours, 44 min at the "Guinness World of Records," London, Oct 31–Nov 1, 1985.

The greatest assemblage of tap dancers ever in a single routine is 3,565 in a group organized by Macy's NYC, who danced in 34th St on Sept 8, 1985.

The longest distance tap-danced non-stop is 5.4 mi by a group of 11, led by Rosie Radiator of San Francisco, who tap-danced from Union Square around the city to Ghirardelli Square, on Aug 26, 1984.

Dance Band. The most protracted session is one of 321 hours (13 days 9 hours) by the Black Brothers of Bonn, W Germany ending on Feb 2, 1968. Never less than a quartet were in action during the marathon.

Debating. The longest Parliamentary-style debate in the US took place at Vassar College, Poughkeepsie, NY, between 2 teams of 2, who debated continuously (except for authorized rest breaks of 5 min after each hour) for 100 hours 6 min, Jan 24–28, 1986. The subject debated was "The government that governs least governs best." Rules set by the American Parliamentary Debate Association were followed. The Vassar Debate Society participating members were: Daniel Blum '88 and Evan Brenner '88 (pro) and Scott Cooper '87 and Anne Louise Gibbins '89 (con) with Scott Kirkpatrick '88 as moderator.

With 175 formal speakers the Oxford Union Society, Eng, debated for 193 hours, 49 min May 21–29, 1986.

Diving, Highest Shallow. Henri La Mothe (b 1904) set a record by diving 28 ft into 12⅜ inches of water in a child's wading pool on Apr 7, 1979 in Northridge, Calif for a Guinness TV program. He struck the water chest first at a speed of 28.4 mph.

LOWEST LIMBO: Marlene Raymond, 15, slithered under a flaming bar 6⅛ in off the floor without letting any part of her anatomy except her feet touch the floor.

Diving, High. The highest regularly performed head-first dives are those of professional divers from La Quebrada ("the break in the rocks") at Acapulco, Mexico, a height of 87½ ft. The leader of the 27 divers in the Club de Clavadistas is Raul Garcia (b 1928) with more than 35,000 dives. The first feminine accomplishment was by Mrs Barbara Winters (b Nov 12, 1953), née Mayer, on Dec 7, 1976. The base rocks are 21 ft out from the takeoff, necessitating a leap 27 ft out. The water is only 12 ft deep.

The world record high dive is 174 ft 8 in by Randal Dickison (US) at

DOMINO TOPPLING: Two Americans, John Wickham and Erez Klein, in Japan, toppled 255,389 dominoes which took 5 weeks to set up and 53 min to tumble. (*National Hemophilia Foundation*)

DEVOTED DRUMMER: For more than 1,009 hours Laurent Rebboah, 20, sat in San Jose, Calif, and wore his drumsticks "into a pile of toothpicks," playing on his drums and cymbals in late 1983.

Ocean Park, Hong Kong, on Apr 6, 1985. The women's record is 120 ft by Lucy Wardle (US) at the same exhibition.

On May 8, 1885, Sarah Ann Henley, aged 24, jumped from the Clifton Suspension Bridge across the Avon, England. Her 250-ft fall was slightly cushioned by her voluminous dress and petticoat acting as a parachute. She landed, bruised and bedraggled, in the mud on the Gloucestershire bank and was carried to a hospital by four policemen.

On Feb 11, 1968, Jeffrey Kramer, 24, leaped off the George Washington Bridge 250 ft above the Hudson, River, NYC and survived. Of the 696 (to Jan 1, 1980) identified people who have made 240-ft suicide dives from the Golden Gate Bridge, San Francisco since 1937 only 12 survived, and the only one who managed to swim ashore unaided was Todd Sherratt, 17.

Col Harry A. Froboess (Switzerland) jumped 360 ft into the Bodensee from the airship *Graf Hindenburg* June 22, 1936.

The greatest height reported for a dive into an air bag is 326 ft by the stuntman Dan Koko from the top of Vegas World Hotel and Casino into a 20 × 40 × 14 ft target on Aug 13, 1984. His impact speed was 88 mph. The women's record is held by Kitty O'Neil who dived 180 ft from a helicopter over Northridge, Calif onto an air cushion 30 × 60 ft on Sept 9, 1979.

Domino Toppling. The greatest number of dominoes set up single-handed and toppled in a row is 281,581 out of 320,236 set up by Klaus Friedrich, 22, of Weilheim, in Fuerth, W Germany on Jan 27, 1984. They fell in 12 min 57.3 sec, having taken 31 days (10 hours daily) to set up.

The record for a team of two setting up is the tumble of 255,389 dominoes in 53 min Aug 24, 1980, at Hakone, Japan. John Wickham and Erez Klein (both US), under the sponsorship of the National Hemophilia Foundation (US), spent 5 weeks setting up the colored dominoes which were toppled not only in long multiple rows, but also in concentric circles and geometric patterns, setting off rockets, releasing eggs that rolled into hot frying pans, and going up ramps. The event appeared on Japanese TV and can be seen on tape at the Guinness Museums.

Drumming. The duration drumming record is 1,009 hours, 6 min, 20 sec (more than 42 days), set by Laurent Rebboah, 20, of Cupertino, Calif, at the Aloha Roller Palace in San Jose, Calif, Sept 22–Nov 3, 1983. He used 11 cymbals, one drumhead, and an uncounted number of drumsticks which he wore "into a pile of toothpicks" in the record-setting marathon. Cozy Powell, rock star, played 400 separate drums in 58 sec on the *Record Breakers* TV show on BBC London, Nov 5, 1985.

Ducks and Drakes. (Stone-Skipping). In Sonoma County, Calif, in the first tournament held on the Russian River, a record of 29 skips (14 plinkers and 15 pitty-pats) was set by Arthur Ring, 69, on Aug 4, 1984. Forty skips are alleged to be possible with 2-in-wide artificial discs with centered dimples.

Egg Hunt. The greatest egg hunt on record involved about 72,000 hard boiled hen eggs, about 40,000 candy eggs, and more than 10,000 participants, spread out over the property of the Garrison family in Homer, Ga, on Easter Sunday, 1985. This was the 26th egg hunt under the same auspices.

Egg Shelling. Two kitchen hands, Harold Witcomb and Gerald Harding, shelled 1,050 dozen eggs in a 7¼-hour shift at Bowyers, Trowbridge, Wiltshire, England Apr 23, 1971. Both are blind.

Egg and Spoon Racing. Chris Riggio of San Francisco completed a 28½-mile fresh egg and dessert spoon marathon in 4 hours 34 min Oct 7, 1979.

Egg Throwing. The longest authenticated distance for throwing a fresh hen's egg without breaking is 317 ft 10 in by Risto Antikainen to Jyrki Korhonen at Siilinjarvi, Finland, on Sept 6, 1982.

Escapology. The most renowned of all escape artists has been Ehrich Weiss, *alias* Harry Houdini (1874–1926), who pioneered underwater escapes from locked, roped and weighted containers while handcuffed and shackled with irons.

One of the major manufacturers of straitjackets acknowledges that an escapologist "skilled in the art of bone and muscle manipulation" could escape from a standard jacket in seconds. There are, however, methods by which such circumvention can itself be circumvented. Nick Janson of Benfleet, Essex, Eng, has demonstrated his ability to escape from handcuffs locked on him by more than 1,000 different police officers.

Fashion Show. The longest distance covered by girl models is 71.1 miles Sept 19–21, 1983 by Roberta Brown and Lorraine McCourt at Parke's Hotel, Dublin, Ireland. The male model Eddie Warke covered a further 11.9 miles on the catwalk. The compère throughout was Marty Whelan of Radio 2.

Feminine Beauty. Female pulchritude, being qualitative rather than quantitative, does not lend itself to records. It has been suggested that if the face of Helen of Troy (*c.* 1200 BC) was capable of launching 1,000 ships, then a unit of beauty sufficient to launch one ship should be called a millihelen.

The earliest international beauty contest was staged by P.T. Barnum (US), in June 1855. The earliest Miss America contest was staged at Atlantic City, NJ in 1921, and was won by a thin blue-eyed blonde with a 30-in bust, Margaret Gorman.

The annual Miss World contest begun in London in July 1951 and the annual Miss Universe contest, inaugurated in Long Beach, Calif, in 1952 are the world's largest. In the latter, the greatest number of countries represented has been 80 in 1983 at St Louis. The most successful country has been the US, with winners in 6 contests. All of the contestants have to spend 3 weeks training for the presentation on TV for the night the winner is decided. The city where the contest is held is reported to have to pay $800,000 for the privilege.

In the Miss World contest, the UK is the only nation to produce 5 winners. The maximum number of contestants was 72 in 1983.

Ferris Wheel Riding. The endurance record for big wheel riding is 37 days by Rena Clark and Jeff Block at Frontier Village Amusement Park, San Jose, Calif July 1–Aug 7, 1978.

Flute Marathon. The longest recorded time is 50 hours 44 min by flautist Ken Munson, 46, of Las Vegas, Nev, on Dec 30–31, 1984. Munson previously held the record at 43 hours from 1975–77.

Flying Disc. See *Throwing Games,* in Chapter 12.

Gladiatorial Combat. Emperor Trajan of Rome (98–117 AD) staged a display involving 4,941 pairs of gladiators over 117 days. Publius Ostorius, a freedman, survived 51 combats in Pompeii.

Gold Panning. The fastest time recorded for "panning" 8 planted gold nuggets with a 10-in-diameter pan is 9.23 sec by Bob Box of Ahwahnee, Calif in the 23rd World Gold Panning Championship at Knott's Berry Farm, Buena Park, Calif Mar 5–6, 1983. Box beat 86 contestants. The record for women was set at the same time by Susan Bryeans of Fullerton, Calif at 10.03 sec.

Golf Ball Balancing. Lang Martin of Charlotte, NC succeeded on Feb 9, 1980 in balancing 7 new golf balls vertically without using any adhesive, beating his own record of 6 in 1977.

Grape Catching. The longest distance for catching a grape in the mouth that has been thrown from a site on the same ground level is 319 ft 8 in by Arden Chapman of Pioneer, La, July 18, 1980. The Northeast Louisiana Univ football field was used for the event. Jerry "Pete" Mercer, the thrower, stood in one end zone and on the 20th attempt, Chapman caught the grape on the track at the opposite end of the field. A slight cross wind was blowing.

The greatest height from which a grape was dropped and caught in the mouth was 660 ft 2.79 in from a Tokyo (Japan) building on Mar 1, 1986. The catcher, Paul Tavilla of Arlington, Mass, a produce merchant, surpassed his own record. "At 80 mph it hurts," he is quoted as saying.

Grave Digging. It is recorded that Johann Heinrich Karl Thieme, sexton of Aldenburg, Germany dug 23,311 graves during a 50-year career. In 1826, his understudy dug *his* grave.

Guitar Playing. The longest recorded solo guitar-playing marathon is one of 264 hours by Ron Woodley of Raymore, Mo, June 19–30, 1984, in his home town.

Hairdressing. Avi Cohen of Ben Bashi Hair Salon, Brooklyn, NY, cut, styled and blow-dried hair continuously for 400 hours June 16–July 2, 1986.

Hair Splitting. The greatest reported achievement in hair splitting has been that of the former champion cyclist and craftsman Alfred West (1901–85) who succeeded in splitting a human hair 17 times into 18 parts on 8 occasions.

Handshaking. A world record for handshaking was set by President Theodore Roosevelt (1858–1919), when he shook hands with 8,513 people at a New Year's Day White House Presentation in Wash, DC, on Jan 1, 1907.

Gary Craig of Hartford, Conn, a radio personality, claims to have shaken 15,000 hands in 6 hours 25 min at the Eastern States Exposition in Springfield, Mass on Sept 25, 1982, setting what he called a "blistering pace."

Generally outside public life this record has become meaningless because aspirants either shake hands with anyone passing by or else shake the same hands repetitively.

Hand-to-Hand Balancing. The longest horizontal dive achieved in any hand-to-hand balancing act is 22 ft by Harry Berry (top mounter) and Nelson Soule (understander) of the Bell-Thazer Brothers from Kentucky, who played at state fairs and in vaudeville 1908–17. Berry used a 10-ft tower and trampoline for impetus.

Hitchhiking. The title of world champion hitchhiker is claimed by Bill Heid of Allen Park, Mich, who from 1964 to 1985 obtained free rides of 305,870 mi. He doesn't believe in using a thumbing technique; just approaches cars at stoplights.

Stephen Burns of Melbourne, Australia, hitchhiked around all 48 coterminous US states in 26 days 6 hours in an 11,438-mi trip in 56 vehicles, Sept 8–Oct 4, 1984.

Hoop Rolling. In 1968 it was reported that Zolilio Diaz (Spain) had rolled a hoop 600 miles from Mieres to Madrid and back in 18 days.

Hopscotch. The longest recorded hopscotch marathon is one of 101 hours 15 min by Mark Harrison and Tony Lunn at the Studio Night Club, Leicester, Eng, Sept 30–Oct 4, 1985.

House of Cards. The greatest number of stories achieved in building free-standing houses of standard playing cards without creasing the cards or using any adhesives is 68 by John Sain, 15, a high school sophomore. His 12-ft-10-in tower, completed Aug 3, 1983, using 15,714 cards, was built in modern skyscraper form at the Univ of Notre Dame engineering school where his father is a teacher.

Hula-Hooping. The highest claim for sustaining gyrating hoops between shoulders and hips is 81 by William K. Chico Johnson (b July 8, 1939) on BBC in London, Sept 19, 1983. Three complete gyrations are mandatory. The women's record is 65 by Melody Howe (US) on BBC-TV in Mar 1985. The longest recorded marathon for a single hoop is 72 hours by Kym Coberly in Denton, Tex, Oct 17–20, 1984.

Human Cannonball. The record distance for firing a human from a cannon is 175 ft in the case of Emanuel Zacchini, son of the pioneer Hugo Zacchini, in the Ringling Bros and Barnum & Bailey Circus, in 1940. His muzzle velocity was estimated at 54 mph. On his retirement the management was fortunate in finding that his daughter, Florinda, was of the same caliber.

An experiment on Yorkshire TV in England on Aug 17, 1978, showed that when Sue Evans, 17, was fired from a cannon, she was ⅜ in shorter in height on landing.

In the Halifax explosion of Dec 6, 1917 (see *Worst Accidents*), A. B. William Becker (d 1969) was blown some 1,600 yd and found, still breathing but deaf, in a tree.

Human Chair (Unsupported Circle). The highest number recorded of people who have demonstrated the physical paradox of all being seated without a chair is an unsupported circle of 10,323 employees of the Nissan Motor Co at Komazawa Stadium, Tokyo, Japan, Oct 23, 1982.

Human Fly. The longest climb achieved on the vertical face of a building occurred on May 25, 1981, when Daniel Goodwin ("Spider Man"), 25, of Kennebunkport, Maine, climbed up the face of the Sears Tower, Chicago, to a height of 1,454 ft in 40-mph winds in 7 hours 25 min at the rate of 3.2 ft/min. Goodwin, a professional acrobat and gymnast, used suction cups and T-shaped clamps.

Lead climber Jean-Claude Droyer (b May 8, 1946) of Paris, France, and Pierre Puiseux (b Dec 2, 1953) of Pau, France, climbed up the out-

**PLAYING WITH A FULL
DECK** (below): Actually, John
Sain played with some 300 full
decks when he constructed this
68-story house of cards in South
Bend, Ind. Sain executed the
whole project by himself, using no
adhesives and never creasing the
cards. (*South Bend Tribune*)

HAIRDRESSING for 400 hours
(16+ days) continuously is the
record set by Avi Cohen of
Brooklyn (above). He beat the
previous mark by 34 hours.

GOLF BALL BALANCING
(right): Lang Martin's record of 7
has stood since Feb 1980. Here he
is concentrating so that the
dot-on-dot structure will remain
standing.

side of the Eiffel Tower to a height of 984 ft in 2 hours 18 min on July 21, 1980. They made the climb with no dynamic mechanical assistance.

> Jaromir Wagner (b Czechoslovakia 1941) became the first man to fly the Atlantic standing on the wing of an aircraft. He took off from Aberdeen, Scotland, on Sept 28, 1980.

The name of the masked man who rode atop a DC-8 airliner at 240 mph in Apr 1977 has not been disclosed. It is however believed unlikely that he is a member of the Jet Set.

Joke Telling. T. R. (Tim) Benker (b 1962) of Chicago told jokes unremittingly for 48½ hours while in the window of the Marshall Field store during an Oprah Winfrey TV show in Chicago on Nov 19, 1985.

A claim for a 55-hour marathon has been made by "Ramblin' Rob" McDonald who told jokes before a crowd on May 9–11, 1986 at the Pizza Factory in Oakhurst, Calif.

The duo duration record is 52 hours by Wayne Malton and Mike Hamilton at the Howard Johnson Motor Hotel, Toronto Airport, Canada, Nov 13–16, 1975.

Juggling and Joggling. Joggling is juggling objects while running or jogging. The contestant must juggle every step of the way. If the object is dropped, it must be picked up at the spot of the drop before the runner resumes. Bouncing balls are now allowed. Albert Lucas of Las Vegas,

HUMAN FLY: Already a record holder, Daniel Goodwin, who climbed the outside of the world's tallest building, the Sears Tower in Chicago, has nothing higher to conquer, so he keeps in practice climbing, climbing, climbing. Here he is ascending the Bonaventure Building in LA, using only clamps and suction cups. (*Anne Marie Weber, TKO Images*)

Nev (b May 11, 1960, London of US parents) tied the world juggling records long held by Enrico Rastelli (b Dec 19, 1896, Samara, Russia, d Dec 13, 1931, Bergamo, Italy) when he "flashed"—as opposed to "juggled"—10 balls and then 8 plates, on July 2, 1984 at the Hacienda Resort Hotel, Las Vegas. On the following two days, Lucas gave further evidence that he is the top juggler today by setting these world records: juggling 5 clubs for 37 min 10 sec (beating the former record of 16 min 20 sec); making 7,291 consecutive throws; juggling 7 balls for 2 min 3.48 sec; and juggling 7 rings for 3 min 23.05 sec.

5 objects (while joggling)	Bill Gillen (US) covered 1 mi in 8 min 28 sec, June 25, 1985
5 objects (while joggling)	Bill Gillen (US) covered 3/10ths of a mi without a drop
3 objects while joggling	Owen Morse (US) 100m in 12.34 sec in 1986
	Scott Damgaard (US) 1 mi in an unofficial 4 min 37 sec in 1981
	Kirk Swenson (US) 5 km in 16 min 55 sec in 1986
5 balls (inverted)	Bobby May (US) (since 1953)
3 balls without drop	Tom Martin (US) 3 hours 14 min 24 sec, 1986
16 hoops (hands and feet)	Ala Naite (female, Japan), 1937
7 clubs	Albert Petrovski (USSR), 1963
	Sorin Munteanu (Romania), 1975
	Jack Bremlov (Czech) currently
	Albert Lucas (US) 1985
12 rings	Albert Lucas (US) 1985
Pirouettes with 3 cigar boxes	Kris Kremo (quadruple turn with 3 boxes in midair) 1977
5 table tennis balls with mouth	Gran Picaso (Spain) 1971
79 cigar boxes on chin	Bruce Block (US) 1986

In an unequaled exhibition, 476 jugglers kept 1,067 objects up in the air simultaneously on July 23, 1983 in Purchase, NY, at the SUNY campus on the last day of the International Jugglers Assn's 36th Annual Convention. Each person juggled at least 3 objects.

For spinning 7 basketballs simultaneously on Jan 13, 1986 (on one finger of each hand, knees, toes, head, plus one on a stand), Maxwell Ruppe, Jr, of Fayetteville, NC, claims a record for juggling basketballs. (See *Soccer* in Sports, Chapter 12 for soccer ball balancing.)

Karate Chop. *Note: Claims for breaking bricks and wooden blocks are unsatisfactory because of the lack of any agreed standards upon which comparisons can be made of friability and the spacing of fulcrums.*

Kissing. The most prolonged osculatory marathon in cinematic history is one of 185 sec by Regis Toomey and Jane Wyman (later Mrs. Ronald Reagan) in *You're In the Army Now,* released in 1940.

Eddie Levin, 30, and Delphine Crha, 26, both of Chicago set the

LARGEST KITE (above): The "Thai Snake," flown by two Dutchmen on Aug 11, 1984, is 2,133 ft long, and 8,288 sq ft in area.

CIGAR-BOX BALANCER (above): On his chin, Bruce Block (US) manages to mount 79 "ungimmicked" King Edward cigar boxes. (*Photo by C D Stouffer, courtesy Jugglers Network*)

BALL SPINNER: Maxwell Ruppe shows how he spins 7 basketballs simultaneously, using all parts of his body, even his head.

record for the longest kiss ever of 17 days 10½ hours on Sept 24, 1984, and celebrated with a kiss.

The most protracted kiss underwater was one of 2 min 18 sec by Toshiaki Shirai and Yukiko Nagata on Fuji TV in Tokyo, Japan on Apr 2, 1980.

John McPherson kissed 4,444 women in 8 hours in Newcastle, Eng, on Mar 8, 1985, at a rate of 1 each 6.48 sec.

Kiss of Life. Five members of the St John Ambulance, Pier One, Sydney, Australia, maintained a "Kiss of Life" (mouth-to-mouth resuscitation) for 315 hours with 232,150 inflations Aug 27–Sept 9, 1984. The "patient" was a dummy.

Kite Flying. The longest recorded flight is one of 180 hours 17 min by the Edmonds Community College team at Long Beach, Wash Aug 21–29, 1982. Managing the flight of the J-25 parafoil was Harry N. Osborne.

The classic record is 31,955 ft up by a chain of 8 kites over Lindenberg, (now East) Germany, on Aug 1, 1919. The record altitude for a single kite is 22,500 ft (min)–28,000 ft (max) by Prof Philip R. and Jay P. Kunz of Laramie, Wyo, on Nov 21, 1967, according to *Kite Lines* magazine.

The most kites flown on a single line is 5,581 by Kazuhiko Asaba, 60, at Kamakura, Japan Nov 8, 1983.

The largest kite ever flown (2,133 ft long and 8,288 sq ft in area) was the "Thai Snake" flown by Herman van den Broek and Jan Pieter Kuil for 22 min 50 sec at Uithuizen, The Netherlands, on Aug 11, 1984.

Knitting. The most prolific hand-knitter has been Mrs Gwen Matthewman (b 1927) of Featherstone, W Yorkshire, England, who in 1979 knitted 915 garments involving 11,012 oz of wool (equivalent to the fleece of 89 sheep). She has been timed to average 111 stitches per min in a 30-min test. Her technique has been filmed by the world's only Professor of Knitting—a Japanese.

Knot Tying. The fastest recorded time for tying the six Boy Scout Handbook knots (square knot, sheet bend, sheep shank, clove hitch, round turn and two half hitches and bowline) on individual ropes is 8.1 sec by Clinton R. Bailey Sr, 52, of Pacific City, Ore on Apr 13, 1977.

Leap Frogging. Fourteen members of Phi Gamma Delta fraternity at the University of Seattle, Wash, covered 602 miles in 114 hours 46 min, March 20–25, 1983. (Total leaps 108,463—one every 9.77 yd.)

Life Saving. In Nov 1974, the City of Galveston, Tex and the Noon Optimist Club unveiled a plaque to the deaf-mute lifeguard Leroy Colombo (1905–74), who saved 907 people from drowning in the waters around Galveston Island, 1917–74.

Lightning-Struck. The only man in the world to be struck by lightning 7 times is former Shenandoah Park Ranger Roy C. Sullivan (US), the human lightning-conductor of Virginia. His attraction for lightning began in 1942 (lost big toenail) and was resumed in July 1969 (lost eyebrows), in July 1970 (left shoulder seared), on Apr 16, 1972 (hair set on fire) and, *finally*, he hoped, on Aug 7, 1973: as he was driving along a bolt came out of a small, low-lying cloud, hit him on the head through his hat, set his hair on fire again, knocked him 10 ft out of his car, went through both legs, and knocked his left shoe off. He had to pour a pail of water over his head to cool off. Then, on June 5, 1976, he was struck again for the sixth time, his ankle injured. When he was struck for the *seventh* time on June 25, 1977, while fishing, he was sent to Waynesboro Hospital with chest and stomach burns. He could offer no explanation for his magnetism, but he donated his lightning-burnt Ranger hats to some of the Guinness World Records Exhibit Halls. In Sept 1983, reportedly rejected in love, he died of a self-inflicted gunshot wound.

LIGHTNING STRUCK him 7 times and didn't kill Roy C. Sullivan, Virginia Park Ranger, but finally he died in 1983 by his own hand.

Lion Taming. The greatest number of lions mastered and fed in a cage simultaneously by an unaided lion-tamer was 40, by "Captain" Alfred Schneider in 1925.

Clyde (Raymond) Beatty (b Bainbridge, Ohio, June 10, 1903, d Ventura, Calif, July 19, 1965) likewise handled more than 40 "cats" (mixed lions and tigers) simultaneously. Beatty, top of the bill for 40 years, insisted on being called a lion-trainer. More than 20 lion-tamers have died of injuries since 1900.

Log Rolling. The record number of International Championships is 10 by Jubiel Wickheim (of Shawnigan Lake, BC, Canada) between 1956 and 1969. At Albany, Ore, on July 4, 1956, Wickheim rolled on a 14-in log against Chuck Harris of Kelso, Wash for 2 hours 40 min before losing.

The youngest international log-rolling champion is Cari Ann Hayer (b June 23, 1977) who won her first championship July 15, 1984 at Hayward, Wis.

Magician, Most Versatile. Under the surveillance of two officers of the British Magical Society, Paul Scott (b 1937) performed 49 separate tricks in 4 min at the National Agricultural Centre, Stoneleigh, Eng, on Sept 9, 1984.

Merry-Go-Round. The longest marathon ride on record is one of 312 hours 43 min by Gary Mandau, Chris Lyons and Dana Dover in Portland, Ore, Aug 20–Sept 2, 1976.

Message in a Bottle. The longest recorded interval between drop and pick-up is 72 years in the case of a message thrown from the *SS Arawatta* out of Cairns, Aust, on June 9, 1910, in a lotion bottle and reported to be found on Moreton Is, Aust, June 6, 1983.

A bottle apparently bearing a message written on Nov 19, 1899, by Capt Charles Weieerishen of the SS *Crown Princess Cecilia* off Varberg, Sweden, was reportedly picked up on the coast of Victoria, BC, Canada, on Dec 9, 1936.

Milk Bottle Balancing. The greatest distance walked by a person while continuously balancing a full pint milk bottle on his head is now 24 miles, set by Ashrita Furman of Jamaica, NY, July 10, 1983.

Morse Code. The highest recorded speed at which anyone has received Morse code is 75.2 wpm—over 17 symbols per sec. This was achieved by Ted R. McElroy (US) in a tournament at Asheville, NC, July 2, 1939. The highest speed recorded for hand key transmitting is 475 symbols per min by Harry A. Turner of the US Army Signal Corps at Camp Crowder, Mo, Nov 9, 1942.

Motorcycle and Car Stunting. The longest distance ever achieved for motorcycle long jumping is 212 ft over 16 buses by Alain Jean Prieur (b July 4, 1939) of France at Montlhéry near Paris, on Feb 6, 1977.

The pioneer of this form of exhibition—Evel Knievel (b Oct 17, 1938, Butte, Mont)—suffered 433 bone fractures in his career.

Terry McGauren motorcycled up the outdoor 1,760 steps of the CN Tower, Toronto, Canada, on June 26, 1984.

Doug Domokos went 145 mi on the back wheel of his motorcycle without stop or touching down on the 2.66-mi tri-oval paved track at Alabama International Motor Speedway in Talladega, Ala, on June 27, 1984. His average speed was in excess of 50 mph, and he stopped only because he ran out of gas on the 146th mi.

The first recorded case of bettering 100 mph on the back wheel only of a motorcycle was by Ottis Lance at Penwell Raceway Park, Tex when he sped 112 mph over 440 yd on a Suzuki GS-1000.

Driving 2,945 mi from NYC to San Francisco is the record set by Dwight B. Mitchell and Steve Kirkpatrick on a Honda 400 cc motorcycle June 11–15, 1983. They took 74 hours 37 min at an average speed of 39.46 mph.

The longest ramp jump in a car by a professional stunt driver is 232 ft by Jacqueline De Creed (*née* Creedy) in a 1967 Ford Mustang at Santa Pod Raceway, Bedfordshire, Eng, on Apr 3, 1983.

The most on one motorcycle is 35 members of the Police Traffic Branch, Brisbane, Australia, who managed to mount a Yamaha 1100-cc at Surfers Paradise track in Queensland and hang on for 533 yd on June 22, 1984. A claim of 31 French gendarmes on a single machine was received in Nov 1983 and is being verified.

Musical Chairs. The largest game on record was one starting with 5,151 participants and ending with Bill Bronson on the last chair at the Univ of Notre Dame, Indiana, on Sept 6, 1985.

Needle Threading. The record number of strands of cotton threaded through a number 13 needle (eye ½ × 1/16 in) in 2 hours is 3,795 by Brenda Robinson of the College of Further Education, Chippenham, Wiltshire, England, on March 20, 1971.

Omelet Making. The greatest number of 2-egg omelets made in 30 min is 315 by John Elkhay at the City Lights Restaurant in Providence, RI on June 29, 1985. He went on to set an endurance record of 36 hours during which he made 5,247 omelets, all of which were eaten by hungry observers or sent to worthy institutions.

Onion Peeling. The record for onion peeling is 50 lb (52 onions) in 5 min 23 sec by Alfonso Salvo of York, Pa, on Oct 28, 1980. Before the current requirement of having at least 50 onions in the 50 lb, a record of 3 min 18 sec was set by Alain St John of Plainfield, Conn on July 6, 1980.

Organ Marathons. The longest church organ recital ever sustained was one of 110 hours by Angie Thompson of St Stephen's Church, Newport, Humberside, Eng, Apr 16–20, 1985.

The longest recorded electric organ marathon is 411 hours by Vince Bull at the Comet Hotel, Scunthorpe, England June 2–19, 1977.

Paddle Boating. The longest recorded voyage in a paddle boat is 2,226 mi in 103 days by the foot power of Mick Sigrist and Brad Rud down the Mississippi River from the headwaters in Minn to the Gulf of Mexico, Aug 4–Nov 11, 1979.

Parachute, Longest Fall Without Parachute. Vesna Vulovic, 23, a Jugoslavenski Aerotransport hostess, survived when her DC-9 blew up at 33,330 ft over the Czechoslovak village of Serbska Kamenice on Jan 26, 1972. She was hospitalized for 16 months after emerging from a 27-day coma, having broken many bones. She is now Mrs Breka.

It is said that the king of Ayattkaya, Siam, in 1617, was "diverted" by an ingenious athlete parachuting with two large umbrellas. Also in 1617, Faustus Verancis is reputed to have descended in Hungary with a "framed canopy."

Parachute Jumping. In a 24-hour period, July 3–4, 1985, David Huber, a jumpmaster at Issaquah Parachute Center, Wash State, made 250 consecutive parachute jumps. The former recordholder, Alan Jones (236) assisted in the ground crew. At the same time Cece Classon jumped 74 times in 7 hours (before retiring due to nausea and back pain) to claim a women's record.

Party Giving. The most expensive private party ever thrown was that of Mr and Mrs Bradley Martin of Troy, NY. It was staged at the Waldorf-Astoria Hotel, NYC in Feb 1897. The cost to the host and hostess was estimated to be $369,200 in the days when dollars were made of gold.

At the largest party ever, in Hyde Park, London, given by the Royal Family, 160,000 children attended in celebration of the International Year of the Child, May 30–31, 1979.

The largest Christmas Party ever staged was that thrown by the Boeing Co in the 65,000-seat Kingdome, Seattle in two shows before an audience of 103,152 people on Dec 15, 1979. It was managed by general chairman John Mathiasen and produced by Greg Thompson with a cast of 2,506. The floor was decorated with 1,000 Christmas trees, each with 100 lights; 150,000 snow-white balloons; and 3 ice ponds.

During St. Patrick's week of Mar 11–17, 1985, Houlihan's Old Place hosted St. Pat's parties at the 47 Kansas City, Missouri-based Gilbert/Robinson restaurants for a total of 206,854 documented guests.

"WHEELIE KING" Doug Domokos (above) alone on his record-breaking 145-mi ride at Talladega, Ala, in 1984.

MOTORCYCLE ASCENT (right): Riding up stairs is not what bikes were intended for, but Terry McGauran, a professional stuntman, 23, got the idea that he could mount the 1,760 steps of Toronto's CN Tower on his 250-cc Yamaha. So, on the tower's 8th birthday, he did it. (*Toronto Star*)

BIGGEST PARACHUTE CANOPY (left): The 23 parachutists of the "CRW world record crew" who joined in this formation exited from their plane at 15,000 ft over Houston Gulf Airport on June 16, 1985.

PARACHUTING RECORDS

First from Tower	Louis-Sébastian Lenormand (1757–1839)	quasi-parachute	Montpellier, France	1783
First from Balloon	André-Jacques Garnerin (1769–1823)	2,230 ft	Monçeau Park, Paris	Oct 22, 1797
First from Aircraft (man)	"Capt" Albert Berry	aerial exhibitionist	St Louis	Mar 1, 1912
(woman)	Mrs Georgina "Tiny" Broadwick		Griffith Park, Los Angeles	June 21, 1913
Longest Base Jump[3]	Carl Ronald Boenische; Jean K. Campbell Boenische	5,784 ft	Trollveggan Spire, Romsdal, Norway	July 4, 1984
Lowest Escape	Squad Leader T. Spencer, RAF	30–40 ft	Wismar Bay, Baltic Sea	Apr 19, 1945
Longest Duration Fall	Lt Col Wm. H. Rankin, USMC	40 min, due to thermals	North Carolina	July 26, 1956
Highest Escape	Flt Lt J. de Salis and Fg Off P. Lowe, RAF	56,000 ft	Monyash, Derby, Eng	Apr 9, 1958
Longest Delayed Drop (man)	Capt Joseph W. Kittinger	84,700 ft (16.04 miles) from balloon at 102,800 ft	Tularosa, NM	Aug 16, 1960
(woman)	O. Kommissarova (USSR)	46,250 ft	over USSR	Sept 21, 1965
(civilian)	R. W. K. Beckett (GB) Harry Ferguson (GB)	30,000 ft from 32,000 ft	D. F. Malan Airport, Capetown, So Africa	Nov 23, 1969 Nov 25, 1956
Most Southerly	T/Sgt Richard J. Patton (d 1973)	Operation Deep Freeze	South Pole	
Most Northerly	Dr Jack Wheeler (US)	Pilot, Capt Rocky Parsons (−25 °F)	in Lat 90° 00′ N	Apr 15, 1981

Category	Name	Measurement	Location	Date
Career Total (man)	Yuri Baranov (USSR) and Anatolyi Osipov (USSR)	10,000	over USSR	to Sept 1980
(woman)	Valentina Zakoretskaya (USSR)	8,000	over USSR	1964–Sept 1980
Highest Landing	Ten USSR parachutists[2]	23,405 ft	Lenina Peak	May 1969
Heaviest Load	US Space Shuttle *Columbia* (external rocket retrieval)	80 ton capacity triple array each 120 ft dia	Atlantic, off Cape Canaveral, Fla	Apr 12, 1981
Highest from Bridge	Donald R. Boyles	1,053 ft	Royal Gorge, Colo	Sept 7, 1970
Highest Tower Jump	Herbert Leo Schmidtz (US)	KTUL-TV Mast 1,984 ft	Tulsa, Okla	Oct 4, 1970
Connected Free Fall (Biggest Star) (Canopy formation)	99-man team	Formation held 17 sec (US rules)	Freeport, Ill	Apr 3, 1985
Highest Column	23 parachutists	Exited at 15,000 ft	Houston Gulf Airport	June 16, 1985
	28-man US team	United Parachute Club	Gilbertsville, Pa	Dec 17, 1985
Lowest Indoor Jump	Andy Smith and Phil Smith	192 ft	Houston Astrodome, Tex	Jan 16–17, 1982
Most Traveled	Kevin Seaman from a Cessna Skylane (pilot, Charles Merritt)	12,186 miles	Jumps in all 50 US states	July 26–Oct 15, 1972
Oldest Man	Edwin C. Townsend	89 years	Vermillion Bay, La	Feb 6, 1986
Oldest Woman	Mrs Stella Davenport (GB)	75 years 8 mos	Humberside, Eng	June 27, 1981
24-Hour Total	David Huber (US)	250	Issaquah, Wash	July 3–4, 1985

[1] Maximum speed in rarefied air was 625.2 mph at 90,000 ft—marginally supersonic.
[2] Four were killed.
[3] "Base" is an acronym for jumping from fixed objects—*Building, Antenna, Span* and *Earth*. Carl Boenische was killed on July 7, 1984.

PLATE SPINNER Shukuni Sasaki of Takamatsu, Japan, has been setting records since 1980, when he had 55 plates going at the same time. His current record (1981) is 72 as seen here in a 75-plate try. He has to move quickly back and forth as the plates wobble when they lose speed.

POGO STICK DISTANCE CHAMP: Ashrita Furman is intent on setting any number of Guinness records. Not content with holding a world record at somersaulting and another for balancing a milk bottle on his head, Ashrita went to Japan to pogo-jump on Mt Fuji foothills for a record distance of 11.53 mi up and down in 8 hours 21 min in Jan 1986. Then in Mar 1986, he jumped on his pogo 3,303 times in 3 hours 20 min in 8½-ft-DEEP WATER!

Piano Playing. The longest piano-playing marathon has been one of 1,218 hours (50 days 18 hours) by David Scott May 7–June 27, 1982, at Wagga Wagga League's Football Club, Australia.

The women's record is 133 hours non-stop (5 days 13 hours) by 280-lb Mrs Marie Ashton, aged 40, in a theatre at Blyth, Northumberland, England, Aug 18–23, 1958. Her last piece was "Five Minutes More."

In the now-discontinued non-stop category, the longest on record was 176¾ hours (7 days 8¾ hours) by Jim Montecino (b Aug 29, 1903) in the Trocadero Ball Room, Auckland, New Zealand in 1951.

Piano Tuning. The record time for pitch raising (one semi-tone or 100 cents) and then returning a piano to a musically acceptable quality is 4 min 20 sec by Steve Fairchild at the Piano Technicians Guild contest at the Dante Piano Co factory, Ronkonkoma, NY, Feb 5, 1980.

Pipe Smoking. The duration record for keeping a pipe (with 3.3 grams of tobacco) continuously alight with only an initial match under IAPSC (International Association of Pipe Smokers Clubs) rules is 126 min 39 sec by the 5-time champion William Vargo of Swartz Creek, Mich at the 27th World Championships in 1975. The only other 5-time champion is Paul T. Spaniola (US) (1951 66 70 73 77). Joe Oetli achieved 130 min 11 sec at the Iowa State Fair contest on Aug 18, 1984, using *two* matches. Longer durations have been recorded in less rigorously invigilated contests in which the foul practices of "tamping" and "gardening" are not unknown.

Plane Pulling. Dave Gauder, 30, frustrated the takeoff of two Piper Cherokees by holding two tow ropes despite a pull of 1,349 lb at Bobbington, Staffs, Eng, on July 16, 1985.

Plate Spinning. The greatest number of plates spun simultaneously is 72 by Shukuni Sasaki of Takamatsu, Japan, at the Nio Town Taiyo Exhibition, Kagawa, on July 16, 1981.

Pogo Stick Jumping. The greatest number of jumps achieved on a pogo stick is 130,077 by Guy Stewart in Reading, Ohio on Mar 8–9, 1985.

In 8½-ft-deep water, Ashrita Furman (b 1954) of NYC made 3,303 jumps on a pogo stick in 3 hours 20 min on Mar 14, 1986. With each jump his head came up above the surface and he breathed through mask and snorkel.

Furman also set a distance record of 11.53 mi on a pogo stick, going up and down the foothills of Mt Fuji, Japan, on Jan 8, 1986 in 8 hours 21 min.

Pole Sitting. There being no international rules, the "standards of living" atop poles vary widely. The record squat is 488 days by Mark Sutton in Victoria (BC), Canada, ending on July 1, 1985. He was sitting for the local Paraplegic Association.

Modern records do not, however, compare with that of St Simeon the Elder (*c.* 390?–459 AD), called Stylites (Greek, *stylos* = pillar), a monk who spent his last 37 years on a stone pillar on the Hill of Wonders, Syria. This is probably the earliest example of record setting.

Potato Peeling. The greatest amount of potatoes peeled by 5 people to an institutional cookery standard with regular kitchen knives in 45 min is 587 lb 8 oz by J. Mills, M. McDonald, P. Jennings, E. Gardiner and V. McNulty at Bourke Street Hall, Melbourne, Australia, on Mar 17, 1981.

Quizzing. The highest number of participants was 80,977 in the All Japan High School Quiz Championship televised on Dec 31, 1983. The most protracted contest was that lasting 110 hours in Long Hanborough, Eng, Mar 27–Apr 1, 1986 when two teams correctly answered 22,483 out of 37,310 questions.

Quoit Throwing. The world's record for rope quoit throwing is an unbroken sequence of 4,002 pegs by Bill Irby, Sr of Australia in 1968.

Rappeling (or Abseiling). The west face of Thor Peak, Baffin Island, Canada, allowed an abseiling or rappeling record of 3,250 ft by Steve Holmes (US) in July 1982. The longest descent down the side of a sky-scraper is one of 580 ft (52 stories) in Hong Kong by Capt Martin Fuller (GB) on Sept 1, 1984.

Rocking Chair. For 453 hours 40 min (just a few hours short of 19 days), "Ramblin' Rob" McDonald sat and rocked in the window of the Pizza Factory in Mariposa, Calif, Mar 14–Apr 2, 1986.

Roller Coasting. The endurance record for rides on a roller coaster is 503 hours by M. M. Daniel Glada and Normand St-Pierre at Parc Belmont, Montreal, Canada July 18–Aug 10, 1983. The minimum qualifying average speed required is 25 mph.

Roller Skating. The longest recorded continuous roller skating marathon was one of 344 hours 18 min by Isamu Furugen at Naka Roller Skate Land, Okinawa, Japan, Dec 11–27, 1983.

Rolling Pin. The record distance for a woman to throw a 2-lb rolling pin is 175 ft 5 in by Lori La Deane Adams, 21, at the Iowa State Fair, Aug 21, 1979.

Rummage Sale. The largest known rummage sale or "white elephant sale" was held at the Cleveland, O, Convention Center on Oct 18 and 19, 1983. On the first day $294,972.53 was collected, and for the two days, a total of $427,935.21 was raised for the non-profit Garden Center of Greater Cleveland.

Sand Sculpting. The longest sand sculpture on record was an 8,498-ft long representation of a 19th-century train along Virginia Beach, Va, on Oct. 2, 1983.

The world's tallest sand castle, 5 stories or 52.81 ft tall, representing the "Lost City of Atlantis," may also be the largest, weighing an estimated 48,384 tons. Built on Treasure Island, Fla, Apr 19–26, 1986 (and torn down on May 5, 1986), it was constructed by 2,000 enthusiastic volunteers trained by the Sand Sculptures International Group. It was 257.5 ft long and 200 ft wide.

Search, Longest. Walter Edwin Percy Zillwood (b London, Dec 1900) traced his missing sister Lena (Mrs Elizabeth Eleanor Allen, b Nov 1897, d Jan 1982) after 79 years through the agency of the Salvation Army on May 3, 1980.

See-Saw. The most protracted session for see-sawing indoors is one of 1,101 hours 40 min by George Partridge and Tamara Marquez of Auburn High School, Wash, on a suspension see-saw (indoors) on Mar 28–May 13, 1977.

Georgia Chaffin and Tammy Adams of Goodhope Junior High School, Cullman, Ala, completed 730½ hours outdoors, June 25–July 25, 1975.

TALLEST SAND CASTLE is five stories (38.0 ft) high and weighs more than 48,000 tons. Some 2,000 enthusiasts built this "Lost City of Atlantis" on Treasure Island, Fla, in Apr 1986. (*Everett Chimbidis*)

Sermon. The longest sermon on record was delivered by the Rev Ronald Gallagher at the Baptist Temple, Lynchburg, Va, June 26–July 1, 1983 for 120 hours.

From May 31 to June 10, 1969, the 14th Dalai Lama (b July 6, 1935, as Tenzin Gyalto), the exiled ruler of Tibet, preached a sermon on Tantric Buddhism for 5 to 7 hours per day to total 60 hours, in India.

Shaving. The fastest barber on record is Gerry Harley, who shaved 987 men in 60 min with a safety razor in Gillingham, England, on Apr 28, 1983, taking 3.64 sec per volunteer. He shaved 235 even braver volunteers with a cutthroat razor in a less perfunctory 15.3 sec per face on Aug 13, 1984. He drew blood only once.

Shoe Shining. In this category (limited to teams of 4 teenagers, an 8-hour time limit, and all shoes "on the hoof") the record is 6,780 pairs by the Sheffield (England) Citadel Band of the Salvation Army on Feb 27, 1982.

Shorthand, Fastest. The highest recorded speeds ever attained under championship conditions are: 300 words per minute (99.64% accuracy) for 5 minutes and 350 wpm (99.72% accuracy, that is, two insignificant errors) for 2 minutes by Nathan Behrin (US), in NYC in Dec 1922. Behrin (b 1887) used the Pitman system invented in 1837. Morris I. Kligman, official court reporter at the US Court House, NYC has taken 50,000 words in 5 hours (a sustained rate of 166.6 wpm). Rates are dependent upon the nature, complexity, and syllabic density of the material.

G. W. Bunbury of Dublin, Ireland, held the unique distinction of writing at 250 wpm for 10 minutes on Jan 23, 1894.

Arnold Bradley achieved a speed of 309 words per min without error using the Sloan-Duployan system with 1,545 words in 5 minutes in a test in Walsall, England on Nov 9, 1920.

Showering. The most prolonged continuous shower bath on record is one of 340 hours 40 min set by Kevin "Catfish" McCarthy at NY State University (Buffalo) Mar 29–Apr 12, 1985.

The feminine record is 121 hours 1 min by Lisa D'Amato, Nov 5–10, 1981, at Harpur College, Binghamton, NY.

Desquamation can be a positive danger.

Singing. The longest recorded solo singing marathon is one of 200 hours 20 min by Jorge Antonio Hidalgo Chamomo at the Piano Bar, Barcelona, Spain, Nov 7–11, 1985. The marathon record for a choir is 72 hours 2 min by the combined choir of Girls High School and Prince Edward School, Salisbury, Zimbabwe, Sept 7–10, 1979.

Acharya Prem Bhikuji started chanting the Akhand Rama-Dhoon on July 31, 1964 and devotees took this up in rotation continuing their devotions, which were still in progress on Dec 23, 1985 at Jamnagar, India.

Skateboarding. Although no official association exists any longer, "world" championships have been staged intermittently since 1966. David Frank, 25, covered 270.483 mi in 36 hours 43 min 40 sec in Toronto, Canada Aug 11–12, 1985.

The highest speed recorded on a skateboard is 71.79 mph on a course at Mt Baldy, Calif, in a prone position by Richard K. Brown, 33, on June 17, 1979.

The stand-up record is 53.45 mph by John Hutson, 23, at Signal Hill, Long Beach, Calif, June 11, 1978.

The high jump record is 5 ft 5.7 in by Trevor Baxter (b Oct 1, 1962) of Burgess Hill, Sussex, England, at Grenoble, France, Sept 14, 1982. At Signal Hill on Sept 25, 1977, Tony Alva, 19, jumped over 17 barrels (17 ft).

SINGING ALONE (with just his guitar) Jorge Chamomo sang continuously for 200 hours 20 min at the Piano Bar in Barcelona, Spain, in Nov 1985.

Slinging. The greatest distance recorded for a slingshot is 1,434 ft 2 in, using a 51-in-long sling and a 2-oz stone, by Lawrence L. Bray at Loa, Utah, on Aug 21, 1981.

Smoker, Most Voracious. Jim (The Mouth) Purol of Livonia, Mich, broke his own records by simultaneously smoking 140 cigarettes for 5 min on Jan 28, 1983 in Detroit; then on Apr 21, 1983 in Farmington, Mich he simultaneously smoked 40 cigars for 5 min; not content with that, Purol kept 38 pipes in his mouth for 5 min in Hollywood on June 9, 1983. Purol is a non-smoker.

Simon Argevitch of Oakland, Calif, whistled, hummed, gave bird imitations, sang and talked while lighting 17 cigars and smoking them at the same time July 3, 1982 in front of the Guinness Museum of World Records on Fisherman's Wharf, San Francisco, Calif.

George Anastassopoulos (b Patras, Greece Aug 20, 1911) kept account of smoking 40,730 cigars from Jan 1950 to June 1984.

Smoke-Ring Blowing. The highest recorded number of smoke rings formed with the lips from a single pull of a cigarette with cheek tapping disallowed, is 355 by Jan van Deurs Formann of Copenhagen, Denmark, achieved in Switzerland in Aug 1979.

Spinning. The duration record for spinning a clock balance wheel by hand is 5 min 26.8 sec by Philip Ashley, aged 16, of Leigh, Greater Manchester, England, May 20, 1968. The record using 36 in of string with a 7¼ oz top is 58 min 20 sec by Peter Hodgson at Southend-on-Sea, Eng on Feb 4, 1985.

Spitting. The greatest distance achieved at the annual (July) tobacco-spitting classic (instituted 1955) at Raleigh, Miss is 33 ft 7½ in by Jeff Barker on July 25, 1981. (He won his 13th national title in 1985 at Raleigh. In 1980 he reached 45 ft at Fulton, Miss.) In the 3rd International Spittin', Belchin' and Cussin' Triathlon, Harold Fielden reached 34 ft ¼ in at Central City, Colo, July 13, 1973. Distance is dependent on the quality of salivation, absence of cross wind, two-finger pucker and the coordination of the back arch and neck snap. Sprays or wads smaller than a dime are not measured.

Randy Ober of Bentonville, Ark, spat a tobacco wad 47 ft 7 in (without any tail wind) at the Calico 5th Annual Tobacco Chewing and Spitting Championships north of Barstow, Calif, Apr 4, 1982.

The record for projecting a melon seed under WCWSSA (World Championship Watermelon Seed Spitting Association) rules is 65 ft 4 in by John Wilkinson in Luling, Tex, on June 28, 1980. The greatest reported distance for a cherrystone is 65 ft 2 in by Rick Krause, at Eau Claire, Mich on July 5, 1980. Spitters who care about their image wear 12-in block-ended boots so practice spits can be measured without a tape.

Stair Climbing. The 100-story record for stair climbing was set by Dennis W. Martz in the Detroit Plaza Hotel, Detroit, Mich on June 26, 1978, at 11 min 23.8 sec. Dale Neil, 22, ran a vertical mile up and down the stairs of the Peachtree Plaza Hotel, Atlanta, Ga in continuous action of 2 hours 1 min 24 sec on Mar 9, 1984. *These records can only be attempted in buildings with a minimum of 70 stories.*

Pete Squires raced up the 1,575 steps of the Empire State Building, NYC, in 10 min 59 sec on Feb 12, 1981. Janine Aiello of San Francisco set the women's record for the event when she scaled the 1,050 vertical ft in 13 min 14 sec on Feb 14, 1985.

The record for climbing the 1,760 steps in the world's tallest freestanding structure, Toronto's CN Tower, is 8 min 28 sec by George Kepenyes, 22, of Hamilton, Ont, Canada, on Oct 27, 1985, beating 1,300 people in a charity climb. Robert C. Jezequel ran 7 round trips in 6 hours 23 min in 1982 without use of the elevator for a vertical height of 15,708 ft.

In the line of duty, Bill Stevenson has mounted 334 of the 364 steps of the tower in the Houses of Parliament, England, 4,000 times in 15 years (1968–83)—equivalent to 24.9 ascents of Mt Everest.

Standing Up. The longest period on record that anyone has stood up continuously is more than 17 years, from 1955 to Nov 1973, in the case of Swami Maujgiri Maharij while performing the *Tapasya* or penance in Shahjahanpur, Uttar Pradesh, India. When sleeping he would lean against a plank. He died aged 85 in Sept 1980.

Stilt Walking. Even with a safety wire, very high stilts are extremely dangerous—25 steps are deemed to constitute "mastery." Eddy Wolf (also known as Steady Eddy) of Loyal, Wis, mastered stilts measuring 40 ft 6½ in from ground to ankle over a distance of 27 steps without touching his safety handrail wires, at Yokohama Dreamland Park, Japan, on Mar 9, 1986. His aluminum stilts weighed 55 lb each.

Joe Long (b Kenneth Caesar), who has suffered 5 fractures, mastered 56-lb 24-ft stilts at the BBC TV Centre, London on Dec 8, 1978.

Hop pickers use stilts up to 15 ft. In 1892 M. Garisoain of Bayonne, France stilt-walked 4.97 miles into Biarritz in 42 min to average 7.10 mph.

In 1891 Sylvain Dornon stilt-walked from Paris to Moscow *via* Vilno in 50 stages for the 1,830 miles. Another source gives his time as 58 days.

The endurance record is 3,008 miles by Joe Bowen from Los Angeles to Bowen, Ky, Feb 20–July 26, 1980.

Masahami Tatsushiko (Japan), 28, ran 100 meters on 1-ft-high stilts in 14.5 sec in Tokyo on March 30, 1980.

Stowaway. The most rugged stowaway was Socarras Ramirez, who escaped from Cuba June 4, 1969, by stowing away in an unpressurized wheel well in the starboard wing of a Douglas DC-8 in a 5,600-mile Iberia Airlines flight from Havana to Madrid. He survived 8 hours at 30,000 ft where temperatures were −8°F.

String Ball. The largest ball of string on record is one of 12 ft 9 in in diameter, 40 ft in circumference and weighing 10 tons, amassed by Francis A. Johnson of Darwin, Minn, between 1950 and 1978.

Submergence. The longest submergence under water (excluding the use of diving bells) is 147 hours 15 min established by Robert Ingolia in tests in which the US Navy received all the data in 1961.

The *continuous* duration record (*i.e.* no rest breaks) for SCUBA (selfcontained underwater breathing apparatus) without surface air hoses, is 212 hours 30 min by Michael Stevens of Birmingham, Eng, in a Royal Navy tank, Feb 14–23, 1986.

Measures have to be taken to reduce the risk of severe desquamation in such endurance trials.

Swinging. The record duration for continuous swinging in a hammock

ALL TIED UP (above): To make the world's largest string ball, Francis Johnson of Darwin, Minn, has been adding to this ball until now, 40 ft around, it needs its own house. (*Minneapolis Star Tribune*)

LIFTER (right): Tom Owen of The King's Ranch, Chelsea, Ala, shows how he lifted 540 lb off the ground using just his arms and teeth with this platform as his fulcrum.

is 196 hours by Patrick Galvin and Mark Ungar of San Mateo, Calif, July 31–Aug 8, 1984.

Tailoring. The highest speed in making a 3-piece wool suit, starting with shearing the sheep and ending with a finished article, is 1 hour 34 min 33.42 sec by 65 members of the Melbourne College of Textiles, Pascoe Vale, Australia, on June 24, 1982. The catching and fleecing took 2 min 21 sec; the carding, spinning, weaving and tailoring occupied the remaining time.

Talking. The record for non-stop talking has been 7 days 15 min by Hugh Porter at the Queensland Government Travel Center, Brisbane, Australia, Sept 24–Oct 10, 1984.

The women's non-stop talking record was set by Mrs Mary E. Davis, who, Sept 2–7, 1958, started talking at a radio station in Buffalo, NY, and did not draw breath until 110 hours 30 min 5 sec later in Tulsa, Okla.

Dr Donald Thomas, who set the record for longest sermon (93 hours) 5 years ago, set a record of 19 hours 20 min for after-dinner speaking on June 21–22, 1985 at City College, NYC. It was at a catered dinner sponsored by Fmali, Inc, and at no time were fewer than 9 people present, including the press and radio representatives. He spoke about herbs and their history in maintaining physical fitness.

Pulling with Teeth. The "strongest teeth in the world" belong to John "Hercules" Massis (b Wilfried Óscar Morbée, June 4, 1940) of Oostakker, Belgium, who at Evrey, France on March 19, 1977, raised a weight of 513⅜ lb to a height of 6 in from the ground with a bit in his teeth. Massis prevented a helicopter from taking off using only a mouth harness in Los Angeles Apr 7, 1979, for the "Guinness Spectacular" ABC-TV show.

Throwing. (*See Games, Chapter 12.*)

Tightrope and Wire Walkers. In this field, two names stand out—Charles Blondin (1824–97) and Steven McPeak (b Apr 21, 1945). Blondin, born in France (real name Jean-François Gravelet) became famous for his feats of crossing Niagara Falls between the US and Canada on a rope, and McPeak traveled (and still travels) all over the world setting up high cables to cross.

No one had crossed the 165-ft-high Niagara Falls before Blondin in 1859. On June 30, Blondin started out. A short way out, Blondin stopped, lay down on his back full length on the rope, then raised himself on one leg. The crossing took 20 minutes in all.

But his supreme act was to carry his 145-lb friend and manager, Harry Colcord, on his back while crossing. (The photo on the next page testifies to the truth of this.)

McPeak, who makes his home in Las Vegas, Nev, and earns his living as a steel rigger and stage set designer, has now tied Blondin's record for carrying a person on his back. He practiced 300 times across Hoover Dam in Nevada on a 1,620-ft-long cable before carrying his 114-lb fiancée, Carly, on his back in Feb 1983. In the middle of the walk, they sat down on the wire and by intercom radio the pair got married by a minister on the ground. Then they traversed the rest of the cable.

McPeak performed the highest high-wire act by crossing on a thin wire he had rigged between two peaks of the Zugspitze on the W German-Austrian border on June 25, 1981, at a height of 3,150 ft above the ground below, and 9,718 ft above sea level. He needed 181 steps to cross the snow-covered gorge.

On the same day he finished the longest wire walk (beating his previous record set in Rio de Janeiro, Brazil), by walking on a 46.5-cm diameter cable up the Zugspitze cable car lift in 3 stints aggregating 5 hours 4 min for a total of 7,485 ft, with a one-day walk of 3,117 ft. The gradient was above 30°. At his highest, McPeak was 2,313 ft higher than at the cable car base.

The greatest height above street level in a high-wire performance was when Philippe Petit, 24, of Nemours, France crossed on a wire 1,350 ft above the street in NYC between the newly constructed twin towers of the World Trade Center on Aug 7, 1974. He shot the 140-ft-long wire across by bow and arrow. He was charged with criminal trespass after a 75-min display of at least 7 crossings. The police psychiatrist's verdict was, "Anyone who does this 110 stories up can't be entirely right."

The tightrope endurance record is 185 days by Henri Rochetain (b

CABLE CROSSER SUPREME: Steve McPeak (above) performs on the cable that runs from Rio de Janeiro, Brazil, to the top of Sugar Loaf Mt—2,400 ft. (*Franklin Berger photo*)

ROPE-WALKING MARVEL: Charles Blondin was such an intrepid tightrope artist that he crossed Niagara Falls nine times in 1859–60. One time he stopped in the middle, lay down on his back, and raised himself back on one leg. After a few crossings he carried his 145-lb friend and agent, Harry Colcord, on his back (shown left) three times. Colcord had to get down onto the rope several times during the trip which took as long as 50 minutes. (*Francis Petrie*)

TIRE SUPPORTER:
Standing up under 96 tires
piled on top of him like a
clothes tree, Gary
Windebank of Romsey,
Eng, survived under a
total of 1,440 lb.

1926) of France on a wire 394 ft long, 82 ft above a supermarket in St Etienne, France, March 28–Sept 29, 1973. His ability to sleep on the wire has left doctors puzzled.

Steven G. Wallenda, 33, walked 2.36 mi on a wire 250 ft long 32 ft high at North Port, Fla, on Mar 26, 1983 in 3 hours 31 min.

Tire Supporting. The greatest number of car tires supported in a free-standing "lift" at one time is 96 by Gary Windebank of Romsey, England in Feb 1984. The total weight was 1,440 lb. The tires were Michelin XZX 155 × 13.

Tree Climbing. The fastest climb up a 100-ft fir spar pole and return to the ground is one of 27.16 sec by Ed Johnson of Victoria, BC, Canada in July 1982 at the Lumberjack World Championships in Hayward, Wis. The fastest time up a 29.5-ft coconut tree barefoot is 4.88 sec by Fuatai Solo, 17, in Sukuna Park, Fiji, Aug 22, 1980.

Tree Sitting. Timothy Roy entered a tree house in Norwalk, Calif on July 4, 1982, and did not come down for 431 days, on Sept 8, 1983.

Typing, Fastest. The highest recorded speeds attained with a ten-word penalty per error on a manual machine are:
One Minute: 170 words, Margaret Owen (US) (Underwood Standard),

RUNNING WITH A BOTTLE ON A TRAY: Roger Bourban won the full marathon of 26 mi 385 yards in London, after winning all the waiters' marathons in Beverly Hills, Calif. The bottle was open, didn't spill, and he ran the entire way in waiter's uniform, holding the tray in the same hand.

NYC, Oct 21, 1918. Five Minutes: 176 wpm net by Mrs Carole Forristall Waldschlager Bechen in Dixon, Ill, 1959.

One Hour: 147 words (net rate per min), Albert Tangora (US) (Underwood Standard), Oct 22, 1923.

Records on electric and computer-driven typewriters cannot be compared with any accuracy.

Typing, Longest. The longest duration typing marathon on a manual machine is 120 hours 15 min by Mike Howell, a 23-year-old blind office worker from Greenfield, Oldham, Greater Manchester, England, Nov 25–30, 1969, on an Olympia manual typewriter in Liverpool. In aggregating 561,006 strokes he performed a weight movement of 2,780 tons plus a further 174 tons in moving the carriage on line spacing.

Les Stewart of Mudjimba Beach, Queensland, Australia has typed the numbers 1 to 417,000 *in words* on 8,230 long sheets as of Feb 26, 1986.

Underwater Cycling. Thirty-two certified SCUBA divers in 60 hours, Nov 27–29, 1981, rode a submarine tricycle 64.96 miles on the bottom of Amphi High School pool, Tucson, Ariz, to raise money for a charity. A relay team of 32 bicycled underwater for 87.81 miles in 72 hours in Norvik, Norway, Mar 28–31, 1984.

Underwater Violinists. The pioneer violinist to surmount the problems of playing the violin underwater was Mark Gottlieb. Submerged in Evergreen State College swimming pool in Olympia, Wash, in Mar 1975 he gave a submarine rendition of Handel's *Water Music.* His most intractable problem was his underwater *détaché.* On Oct 7, 1979 the first underwater quartet performed in the *Challenge the Guinness* TV show on Channel 7 in Tokyo, Japan.

Waiters' Marathon. Beverly Hills restaurateur Roger Bourban (b May 10, 1948) ran a full marathon of 26 mi 385 yards in full uniform in London, England, May 9, 1982, carrying a free-standing open bottle on a tray (gross weight 3 lb 2 oz) in 2 hours 47 min, using the same hand the whole way.

Walking-on-Hands. The duration record for walking-on-hands is 871 miles by Johann Hurlinger of Austria, who, in 55 daily 10-hour stints, averaged 1.58 mph from Vienna to Paris in 1900.

Thomas P. Hunt of the USAF Academy, Colorado Springs, completed a 50-meter inverted sprint in 18.4 sec in Tokyo, Japan on Sept 22, 1979.

Stunts and Miscellaneous Endeavors ▪ 473

WRAPPING AS AN ART FORM: Christo, the Bulgarian-born sculptor, when he isn't curtaining valleys or draping islands, is wrapping bridges. Here he is adorning Paris' famous Pont Neuf with woven fabric and rope. The French gave him permission. (*Photo © Wolfgang Volz*)

Four men (Bob Sutton, Danny Scannell, Phil Johnson and John Hawkins) relayed a mile in Oak Ridge, Tenn, on Mar 13, 1983 in 31 min 15.8 sec.

Walking on Water. Using outsize shoes-cum-floats Fritz Weber walked on the Main River, W Germany from Bayreuth over 185 mi to Mainz Sept 1 to Oct 15, 1983.

Weather Balloon Blowing. The inflation by lung power of a standard 1,000 gram meteorological balloon to a diameter of 8 ft against time was achieved by Nicholas Berkeley Mason in 57 min 7 sec for a Fuji TV program in Tokyo on Mar 9, 1986.

Wheelbarrow Pushing. The heaviest loaded one-wheeled barrow pushed for a minimum 200 level ft is one loaded with bricks weighing a gross 7,750 lb through 237 ft by Gary Windebank at Romsey, Eng, on Oct 12, 1985.

Wheelbarrow Racing. The fastest time reached for a 1-mile wheelbarrow race is 4 min 50.29 sec by John Coates and Brian Rhodes of Richmond, BC, Canada, at the Ladner Centennial Sports Festival, Delta, BC, July 9, 1983.

Wheelies. See *Motorcycle and Car Stunting,* p. 457.

Whip Cracking. The longest stock whip ever "cracked" (*i.e.,* the end made to travel above the speed of sound—760 mph) is one of 104 ft 5 in (excluding the handle), wielded by Noel Harris at Sunbury, Melbourne, Australia, June 24, 1982.

Whistling Loudest and Longest. Roy Lomas (GB) achieved 122.5 decibels at 2½ meters in the Deadroom at the BBC Manchester (Eng) Studios on Dec 19, 1983. The whistling marathon record is by David Frank of Toronto, Canada, who completed 30 hours 10 min nonstop at the Annapurna Restaurant, Toronto, Nov 23–24, 1985.

Window Cleaning. The fastest time to clean (without a smear) 3 standard 40.94 × 45.39-in office windows with an 11.8-in-long squeegee and 15.83 pints of water was 18.92 sec by Roy Ridley of Sydney, Australia, in a contest on Oct 19, 1984.

Wire Slide. The greatest distance recorded in a wire slide is from a height of 175 ft over a distance of 300 ft by Grant Page with Bob Woodham over his shoulder across the Australian landmark known as "The Gap" for the filmed episode in "The Stunt Men" in 1972.

Wood Cutting. The earliest competitions date from Tasmania in 1874. The records set at the Lumberjack World Championships at Hayward, Wis (founded 1960), are:

Power Saw   8.73 sec.
　by Sven Johnson (US)   1983
One-Man Bucking   21.70 sec.
　by Merv Jensen (NZ) (d Apr 1983)   1982
Standing Block Chop   25.38 sec.
　by Mel Lentz (US)   1982
Underhand Block Chop   18.66 sec.
　by Mel Lentz (US)   1982
Two-Man Bucking   9.44 sec.
　by Merv Jensen (NZ) and Cliff Hughes (NZ)   1982
Hand Splitting a cord into quarters*   53 min 40 sec.
　by Richard Sawyer (US)   1982

* Hardwood (white ash) cord of 128 cu ft using a quartering wedge at Sag Harbor, NY, on July 2 1982.

White pine logs 14 in in diameter are used for chopping and 20 in for sawing.

Worm Charming (see p. 95).

Wrapping. Christo, the sculptor who has made gigantic curtains and draped islands (see pages 349–350), in 1985 wrapped the famous bridge, Pont Neuf, in Paris with 440,000 sq ft of polyamide fabric and 42,900 ft of rope.

Writing Small. In 1926 an account was published of Alfred McEwen's pantograph record in which the 56-word version of the Lord's Prayer was written by diamond point on glass in the space of 0.0016 × 0.0008 in.
　Frank C. Watts of Felmingham, Norfolk, England, demonstrated for photographers, on Jan 24, 1968, the ability, without mechanical or optical aids, to write the Lord's Prayer 34 times (9,452 letters) within the size of a definitive postage stamp (0.84 × 0.71 in).
　In Dec 1980 Michael Isaacson, Associate Professor of the School of Applied and Engineering Physics, Cornell Univ, Ithaca, NY, succeeded in etching the 16 letters in "molecular devices" on a sodium chloride crystal with a 100,000 volt electron beam. The "writing" was 2 nanometers wide.
　Tsotomu Ishii of Tokyo demonstrated his ability to write the names of

44 countries (184 letters) on a single grain of rice, and the words TOKYO JAPAN in Japanese on a human hair in Apr 1983.

Writing Under Handicap. The ultimate feat in "funny writing" would appear to be the ability to write extemporaneously and decipherably backwards, upside down, laterally inverted (mirror-style) while blindfolded, with both hands simultaneously. Three claims to this ability with both hands and feet simultaneously, by Mrs Carolyn Webb of Thirlmere, NSW, Aust, Mrs Judy Hall of Chesterfield, Va, and Robert Gray of Toronto, Canada are outstanding, but have not been witnessed in the act by our staff.

Yodeling. The most protracted yodel on record was that of Errol Bird for 26 hours in Lisburn, N Ireland, Sept 27–28, 1984. Yodeling has been defined as "repeated rapid changes from the chest-voice to falsetto and back again." The most rapid recorded is 5 tones (3 falsetto) in 1.9 sec by Donn Reynolds of Canada on July 25, 1984.

Yo-Yo. Yo-yo was a toy in Grecian times and is depicted on a bowl dated 450 BC. It was also a Filipino jungle fighting weapon recorded in the 16th century weighing 4 lb with a 20-ft thong. The word means "come-come." Though illustrated in a book in 1891 as a bandalore, the yo-yo did not become a craze until it was marketed by Donald F. Duncan of Chicago in 1926. The most difficult modern yo-yo trick is the "Whirlwind," incorporating both inside and outside horizontal loop-the-loops.

The individual continuous endurance record is 120 hours by John Winslow of Gloucester, Va, Nov 23–28, 1977.

Dr Allen Bussey in Waco, Tex on Apr 23, 1977 completed 20,302 loops in 3 hours (including 6,886 in a single 60-min period). He used a Duncan Imperial with a 34½-in nylon string. Spins of 8,000 rpm have been recorded.

The largest yo-yo ever constructed was one by Dr Tom Kuhn weighing 256 lb, test-launched from a 150-ft crane in San Francisco on Oct 13, 1979.

EATING RECORDS

While no healthy person has been reported to have succumbed in any contest for eating non-toxic food or drinking non-alcoholic drinks, such attempts, from a medical point of view, must be regarded as *extremely* inadvisable, particularly among young people. Gastronomic record at-

---

The greatest omnivore is Michel Lotito (b 1950) of Grenoble, France, known as Monsieur Mangetout, who has been eating metal and glass since 1959. Gastroenterologists have X-rayed his stomach and have described his ability to consume 2 lb of metal per day as unique. His diet since 1966 has included 10 bicycles, a supermarket cart (in 4½ days), 7 TV sets, 6 chandeliers and a low-calorie Cessna light aircraft, which he ate in Caracas, Venezuela. He is said to have provided the only example in history of where a coffin (handle and all) ended up inside a man.

---

tempts should aim at improving the *rate* of consumption, rather than the volume. This book will not list any records involving the consumption of more than 2 liters (approximately 2 quarts) of beer or any at all involving liquor. Nor will this book list records for potentially dangerous categories such as consuming live ants, goldfish, quantities of chewing gum or marshmallows, or raw eggs in shells. The ultimate in stupidity—the eating of a bicycle—has, however, been recorded since it is unlikely to attract competition.

Liquidizing, processing or puréeing foodstuffs is not permitted. However, drinking during attempts is permissible.

Specific records have been claimed as follows:

Baked Beans. 2,780 cold beans one by one, with a cocktail stick, in 30 min by Karen Stevenson of Merseyside, Eng, Apr 4, 1981.

Bananas. 17 (edible weight min 4½ oz each) in 2 min by Dr Ronald L. Alkana at the University of California, Irvine on Dec 7, 1973.

Beer. Steven Petrosino drank one liter of beer in 1.3 sec on June 22, 1977, at "The Gingerbreadman," in Carlisle, Pa.
Peter G. Dowdeswell (b London, July 29, 1940) of Earls Barton, Northants, Eng, drank 2 liters in 6 sec on Feb 7, 1975. He also holds the speed record for consuming 2 Imp pints, in 2.3 sec, June 11, 1975, and for 3 Imp pints in 5.0 sec on July 6, 1985.

Champagne. 1,000 bottles per year by Bobby Acland of the "Black Raven," Bishopsgate, London.

Cheese. 16 oz of hard English cheddar in 1 min 13 sec by Peter Dowdeswell (see above) in Earls Barton, England, on July 14, 1978.

Chicken. 27 (2-lb pullets) by "Bozo" Miller at a sitting at Trader Vic's, San Francisco in 1963. Also, 4 lb 10 oz in 10 min 37 sec by Valentin Florentino Muñoz Muñoz, Viacaya, Spain, Apr 27, 1986.

Clams. 424 Little Necks in 8 min by Dave Barnes at Port Townsend Bay, Wash, on May 3, 1975.

Doughnuts. 12¾ (weighing 51 oz) in 5 min 46 sec by James Wirth, and 13 (52 oz) in 6 min 1.5 sec by John Haight, both at the Sheraton Inn, Canandaigua, NY, Mar 3, 1981.

Eels. 1 lb of elvers (1,300) in 13.7 sec by Peter Dowdeswell (see above) at Reeves Club, Bristol, England, on Oct 20, 1978.

Eggs. (Hard-boiled) 14 in 58 sec by Peter Dowdeswell (see above) in Corby, England, on Feb 18, 1977. (Soft-boiled) 38 in 75 sec by Peter Dowdeswell in Kilmarnock, Scotland, on May 28, 1984. (Raw, without shells) 13 in 1.0 sec by Peter Dowdeswell in Kilmarnock on May 16, 1984.

Stunts and Miscellaneous Endeavors ▪ **477**

Frankfurters. 23 (2-oz) without rolls, in 3 min 10 sec by Lynda Kuerth, 21, at Veterans Stadium, Philadelphia, on July 12, 1977.

Gherkins. 1 lb in 41.6 sec by Peter Dowdeswell (see above) at Ronelles Discotheque, Eng, on Feb 8, 1986.

Grapes. 3 lb 1 oz in 34.6 sec by Jim Ellis of Montrose, Mich, on May 30, 1976.

QUEEN OF THE FRANKFURTER EATERS (above left): At a contest in Veterans Stadium, Philadelphia, Lynda Kuerth, 21, won by swallowing 23 hot dogs without rolls in 3 min 10 sec. (*Neil Benson*)

NO ONE EATS as much as fast as Peter Dowdeswell (above right) of London. Here he is showing off his gluttony. A few of the records he holds are: 14 hard-boiled eggs in 58 sec, 21 hamburgers in 9 min 42 sec, and 62 pancakes in less than 7 min!

OYSTER-EATING CHAMP: Displaced as the snail-eating record holder, Thomas (Muskrat) Greene in Annapolis, Md, turning to oysters, swallowed a 6-lb mass of 288 oysters in 1 min 33 sec in July 1985.

Hamburgers. 21 hamburgers (weighing 3½ oz each or 4½ lb of meat) and buns in 9 min 42 sec by Peter Dowdeswell at Birmingham, Eng, on June 30, 1984.

Ice Cream. 3 lb 6 oz of unmelted ice cream in 50.04 sec by Tony Dowdeswell in Surrey, Eng, on Jan 26, 1984.

Jelly. 20 fl but gelatinous oz in 13.11 sec by Peter Dowdeswell (see above) at Stoke Mandeville, Eng, on June 27, 1984.

Lemons. 12 quarters (3 lemons) whole (including skin and seeds) in 15.3 sec by Bobby Kempf of Roanoke, Va on May 2, 1979.

Meat. One whole roast ox in 42 days by Johann Ketzler of Munich, Germany, in 1880.

Milk. One Imperial quart (1.2 US quarts) in 3.2 sec by Peter Dowdeswell (see above) at Dudley Top Rank Club, West Midlands, England on May 31, 1975.

Oysters. Edible mass of 288 (6 lb) in 1 min 33 sec by Tommy "Muskrat" Greene in Annapolis, Md, on July 6, 1985.
The record for opening oysters is 100 in 2 min 45.5 sec by W. G. Heath Jr at Babson Park, Fla on Oct 28, 1983.

Pancakes. 62 (each 6 in in diameter, buttered and with syrup) in 6 min 58.5 sec by Peter Dowdeswell (see above) in Northampton, England on Feb 9, 1977.

Peanuts. 100 (whole, out of the shell) singly in 46 sec by Jim Kornitzcr, 21, at Brighton, England on Aug 1, 1979.

Peas. 7,175 petit pois one by one in 60 min using chopsticks by Mrs Janet Harris, Seal Hotel, Selsey, Eng, on Aug 16, 1984.

Pickled Onions. 91 (total weight 30 oz) in 1 min 8 sec by Pat Donahue in Victoria, BC, Canada, on March 9, 1978.

Pizza. 1.8 lb in 5 min 23 sec by Geir Storvann of Drammen, Norway, on Aug 24, 1984 at Karl Johans Gate, Oslo.

Potato Chips. 30 2-oz bags in 24 min 33.6 sec, without a drink, by Paul G. Tully of Brisbane University, Australia, in May 1969.

Potatoes. 3 lb in 1 min 22 sec by Peter Dowdeswell in Earls Barton, England on Aug 25, 1978.

Prunes. 144 in 34 sec by Peter Dowdeswell in Easy St Nightclub, Nottingham, Eng, on Apr 26, 1985.

Ravioli. 5 lb (170 squares) in 5 min 34 sec by Peter Dowdeswell (see above) in Suffolk, Eng on Sept 25, 1983.

Sandwiches. 40 (jam and butter, 6 × 3¾ × ½ in) in 17 min 53.9 sec by

TREE EATER: Jay Gwaltney eating an 11-ft-tall birch sapling. He ate branches, leaves and the 4.7-in-diameter trunk over a period of 89 hours to win $10,000 as first prize in a WKQX-Chicago radio station contest called "What's the Most Outrageous Thing You Would Do?"

Peter Dowdeswell (see above) on Oct 17, 1977, at the Donut Shop, Reedley, Calif.

Sausage Meat. 5 lb 12¾ oz (96 pieces) in 4 min 29 sec by Peter Dowdeswell on Fuji TV, Tokyo, Japan on Feb 24, 1985. No "Hot Dog" contest results have been remotely comparable.

Shellfish. 100 (unshelled) whelks in 5 min 17 sec by John Fletcher in Liverpool St Station, London on Aug 18, 1983.

Shrimps. 3 lb in 3 min 10 sec by Peter Dowdeswell (see above) at Weymouth, Dorset, Eng, on Aug 7, 1985.

Snails. 38.8 oz in 1 min 5.6 sec by Andoni Basterrechea Dominguez in Vizcaya, Spain on Apr 27, 1986.

Spaghetti. 100 yd in 21.7 sec by Peter Dowdeswell in Weedon, England, Feb 25, 1983.

Sushi. 1½ lb in 1 min 13.5 sec by Peter Dowdeswell in Tokyo on Feb 22, 1985.

Strawberries. 2 lb in 12.95 sec by Peter Dowdeswell at Corby, Eng on July 5, 1985.

Tortillas. 74 (total weight 4 lb 1½ oz) in 30 min by Tom Nall in the 2nd World Championship at Mariano's Mexican Restaurant, Dallas, Tex on Oct 16, 1973.

Tree. 11-ft birch (4.7-in-diameter trunk) in 89 hours by Jay Gwaltney, 19, on WKQX's Outrageous Contest, Chicago, Sept 11–15, 1980. As he finished, he said, about the taste, "as far as trees go, it's not bad."

WEALTH AND POVERTY

The comparison and estimation of extreme personal wealth are beset with intractable difficulties. Quite apart from reticence and the element of approximation in estimating the valuation of assets, as Jean Paul Getty (1892–1976) once said: "If you can count your millions, you are not a billionaire." The term "millionaire" was invented c. 1740 and "billionaire" in 1861.

Cornelius Vanderbilt (1794–1877) left $100 million in 1877. The earliest dollar billionaires were John Davison Rockefeller (1839–1937); Henry Ford (1863–1947); and Andrew William Mellon (1855–1937). In 1937, the last year in which all 3 were alive, a billion dollars was worth about 17 times as much in purchasing power as it is today.

The riches of most of the world's remaining 29 monarchs are national rather than personal assets. The least fettered monarch is H M Sir Muda Hassanal Bolkiah Mu'izzaddin Waddaulah, the Sultan of Brunei (b July 15, 1946). He appointed himself Prime Minister, Finance Minister and Home Affairs Minister on Jan 1, 1984. The annual oil revenue of Brunei is $3,780 million and its foreign reserves are $14,000 million, all of which are effectively at his personal disposal.

Richest People

The US was estimated to have some 832,500 millionaire families in early 1985 with the million mark expected in mid-1987.

The richest person in the US is Gordon Peter Getty (b 1930), fourth son of Jean Paul Getty (by his fourth wife, Ann Rork) and sole trustee of the Sarah C. Getty Trust, valued in Sept 1984 at $4,100 million, but reduced by estate taxes to under $1 billion by 1986.

Forbes Magazine lists 13 billionaires in 1985, headed by Sam Moore Walton, 67, of Wal-Mart Stores, Bentonville, Ark.

The richest man in Great Britain is Sir John Moores (b Jan 25, 1896), the co-founder of football pools, who is estimated to be worth £1,600 million ($2,400,000,000).

Highest Income

The greatest incomes derive from the collection of royalties per barrel by rulers of oil-rich sheikhdoms, who have not abrogated personal entitlement. Shaikh Zayid ibn Sultan an-Nuhayan (b 1918), head of state of the United Arab Emirates, arguably has title to some $9,000 million of the country's annual gross national product.

The highest gross income ever achieved in a single year by a private citizen is an estimated $105 million in 1927 by the Neapolitan-born gangster Alphonse ("Scarface Al") Capone (1899–1947). This was derived from illegal liquor trading and alky-cookers (illicit stills), gambling establishments, dog tracks, dance halls, "protection" rackets and vice. On his business card, Capone described himself as a "Second Hand Furniture Dealer."

Paul McCartney reputedly earned in excess of £25 million ($57.5 million) in the years since 1979, for the highest gross income by a Briton.

Highest Salary

The highest salary in 1985 was reported to be $12.7 million paid to Victor Posner, chairman of the board of DWG Corp of Miami Beach, Fla. The highest salary, bonus and stock option earnings ever reported were paid to the board chairman of Federal Express, Frederick W. Smith, namely $51,544,000 in 1982.

Youngest Millionaire

The youngest person ever to accumulate $1 million dollars was the child film actor Jackie Coogan (b Los Angeles, Oct 26, 1914), co-star with (Sir) Charles Chaplin (1889–1977) in "The Kid," made in 1920.

Child with Most Money

If the dollar in the 1930's was worth 17 times more than it is today, then Shirley Temple (b Apr 23, 1928, Santa Monica, Calif) earned more than $14 million in the movies by the time she was 10 years old.

Millionairesses

The world's wealthiest woman was probably Princess Wilhelmina Helena Pauline Maria of Orange-Nassau (1880–1962), formerly Queen of The Netherlands (from 1890 to her abdication, Sept 4, 1948), with a fortune which was estimated at over $300 million.

The cosmetician Madame Charles Joseph Walker (*née* Sarah Breedlove, 1867–1919), a black woman, is reputed to have become the first self-made millionairess. She was an uneducated orphan whose fortune was founded on a hair straightener. She had been a scrubwoman and a laundress.

Richest Families

It has been tentatively estimated that the combined value of the assets nominally controlled by the Du Pont family of some 1,600 members may be on the order of $150 billion. The family arrived from France on Jan 1, 1800. Capital from Pierre Du Pont (1730–1817) enabled his son Eleuthère Irénée Du Pont to start his explosives company (E. I. Du Pont).

It was estimated in 1984 that both sons and both daughters of H. L. (Haroldson Lafayette) Hunt, the oil man, possessed fortunes in excess of $1 billion each.

Biggest Dowry

The largest recorded dowry was that of Elena Patiño, daughter of Don Simón Iturbi Patiño (1861–1947), the Bolivian tin millionaire, who in 1929 bestowed $22,400,000 from a fortune at one time estimated to be worth $350 million.

Greatest Miser

If meanness is measurable as a ratio between expendable assets and expenditure then Henrietta (Hettie) Howland Green (*née* Robinson) (1835–1916), who kept a balance of over $31,400,000 in one bank alone, was the all-time world champion. She was so stingy that her son had to have his leg amputated because of the delays in finding a *free* medical clinic. She herself lived off cold oatmeal because she was too thrifty to heat it. Her estate proved to be worth $95 million.

Return of Money

Jim Priceman, 44, assistant cashier at Doft & Co Inc, returned an envelope containing $37.1 million in *negotiable* bearer certificates found outside 110 Wall Street to A. G. Becker, Inc, NYC on Apr 6, 1982. In announcing a reward of $250, the Becker Company was acclaimed as being "all heart."

The largest amount of *cash* ever found and returned to its owners was $500,000 found by Lowell Elliott, 61, on his farm in Peru, Ind. It had been dropped in June 1972 by a parachuting hijacker.

Greatest Bequests

The greatest bequests in a lifetime of a millionaire were those of the late John Davison Rockefeller (1839–1937), who gave away sums totaling $750 million.

The Scottish-born US citizen Andrew Carnegie (1835–1919) is estimated to have made benefactions totaling $350 million in the last 18 years of his life. These included 7,689 church organs and 2,811 libraries. He had started in a bobbin factory at $1.20 a week.

The largest bequest made in the history of philanthropy was the $500 million gift, announced on Dec 12, 1955, to 4,157 educational and other institutions by the Ford Foundation (established 1936) of NYC.

MOST MISERLY MISER: Hettie Green in the early 1900's lived on cold oatmeal, and left $95 million when she died in 1916.

2. HONORS, DECORATIONS AND AWARDS

Highest US Decoration

The highest US military decoration is the Congressional Medal of Honor. Five marines received both the Army and Navy Medals of Honor for the same acts in 1918, and 14 officers and men from 1863 to 1915 received the medal on two occasions.

Top Jet Ace

The greatest number of kills in jet-to-jet battles is 16 by Capt Joseph Christopher McConnell, Jr (USAF) (b Dover, NH, Jan 30, 1922) in the Korean War (1950–53). He was killed on Aug 25, 1954. It is possible that an Israeli ace may have surpassed this total in the period 1967–70, but the identity of pilots is subject to strict security.

Top Woman Ace

The record score for any woman fighter pilot is 12 by Jr Lt Lydia Litvak (USSR) in the Eastern Front campaign of 1941–43. She was killed in action on Aug 1, 1943.

Submarine Warfare

The largest target ever sunk by a submarine was the Japanese aircraft carrier *Shinano* (59,000 tons) by the *USS Archerfish* (Commander Joseph F. Enright, USN) Nov 29, 1944.

Most Statues

The record for raising statues to oneself was set by Generalissimo Dr Rafael Leónidas Trujillo y Molina (1891–1961), a former President of the Dominican Republic. In March 1960 a count showed that there were "over 2,000." The country's highest mountain was named Pico Trujillo (now Pico Duarte). One province was called Trujillo and another Trujillo Valdez. The capital was named Ciudad Trujillo (Trujillo City) in 1936, but reverted to its old name of Santo Domingo on Nov 23, 1961. Trujillo was assassinated in a car ambush on May 30, 1961, and May 30 is now celebrated annually as a public holiday.

The man to whom most statues have been raised is undoubtedly Buddha. The 20th century champion is Vladimir Ilyich Ulyanov, *alias* Lenin (1870–1924), busts of whom have been mass-produced. Busts of Mao Tse-tung (1893–1976) and Ho Chi Minh (1890–1969) have also been mass-produced.

Most Decorated Soldier

Maj Audie Murphy (1924–71) was the most decorated soldier in World War II, receiving the Medal of Honor, the Silver Star with 2 oak leaf clusters, the Bronze Star with an oak leaf cluster, the Distinguished Service Cross, the French Croix de Guerre, the Legion of Merit, the Purple Heart with 2 oak leaf clusters, and the French Légion d'Honneur.

Most Honorary Degrees

The greatest number of honorary degrees awarded to any individual is 100, given to Rev Father Theodore M. Hesburgh (b 1918), president of

TOP SCORING AIR ACES

The "scores" of air aces in both wars are still hotly disputed. The highest figures officially attributed have been:

Country	World War I 1914–18	World War II 1939–45
World	75 Col René Paul Fonck (France) Gr Cordon, L. d'H., C. de G. (26 palms) Med. Mil (Belge) (d. 1953)*	352 Major Erich Hartmann (Germany)
US	26 Capt Edward Vernon Rickenbacker M.H., D.S.C. (7 o.l.c.), L. d'H., C. de G.	40 Major Richard I. Bong, M.H., D.S.C., S.S., D.F.C. (6 o.l.c.), A.M. (11 o.l.c.).
Canada	72 Lt-Col William Avery Bishop, V.C., C.B., D.S.O. and bar, M.C., D.F.C., L. d'H., C. de G.	31½ Sq-Ldr George F. Beurling, D.S.O., D.F.C., D.F.M. and bar.

* A total of 80 was attributed to Rittmeister Manfred Freiherr (Baron) von Richthofen (Germany) but fewer than 60 of these could be verified from German records. Col Fonck unofficially has been credited with as high a score as 125. The German high score is 62 by Col-Gen Ernst Udet.

MOST CLUSTERS AND GOLD STARS

Navy Cross	5 gold stars	Lt Gen Lewis B. Puller, USMC
Distinguished Service Cross	7 clusters	Capt Edward Rickenbacker (d 1973)
Silver Star	8 clusters	Col David H. Hackworth, USA
Distinguished Flying Cross	11 clusters 11 gold stars	Col Francis S. Gabreski, USAF Maj Charles Carr
Distinguished Service Medal (Army)	4 clusters	Gen of the Army Douglas MacArthur (also one Naval award)
		Gen of the Army Dwight D. Eisenhower
	3 clusters	Gen Lyman L. Lemnitzer (also one USN and one USAF award)
Distinguished Service Medal (Navy)	3 gold stars	Fleet Adm William F. Halsey Marine Gen Holland M. Smith
Legion of Merit	5 clusters	Maj Gen Richard Steinbach
Purple Heart	9 clusters	Sgt Raymond E. Tirva

the University of Notre Dame, South Bend, Ind. These were accumulated from 1954 through June 1984.

Nobel Prize Winners

The Nobel Foundation of $8,960,000 was set up under the will of Alfred Bernhard Nobel (1833–96), the unmarried Swedish chemist and chemical engineer who invented dynamite in 1866. The Nobel Prizes are presented annually on Dec 10, the anniversary of Nobel's death and the festival day of the Foundation. Since the first Prizes were awarded in 1901, the highest cash value of the award, in each of the six fields of Physics, Chemistry, Medicine and Physiology, Literature, Peace and Economics was $220,000 (approx) in 1985.

The most awards (3) were won by the International Committee for the Red Cross.

Individually, the only person to have won two Prizes outright is Dr Linus Carl Pauling (b Feb 28, 1901), Prof of Chemistry since 1931 at the Calif Institute of Technology, Pasadena, Calif. He was awarded the Chemistry Prize for 1954 and the Peace Prize for 1962. Only three others have won two Prizes. One was Madame Marie Curie (1867–1934), born in Poland as Marja Sklodowska, who shared the 1903 Physics Prize with her husband, Pierre Curie (1859–1906) and Antoine Henri Becquerel (1852–1908), and won the 1911 Chemistry Prize outright. Another was Prof Frederick Sanger (UK) (b Aug 13, 1918) who twice shared the Chemistry Prize (1958 and 1980). The third was Prof John Bardeen (US) (b May 23, 1908) who shared the Physics Prize in 1956 and 1972.

The oldest prizeman was Prof Francis Peyton Rous (b Baltimore, 1879–1970), who worked at the Rockefeller Institute, NYC. He shared the Medicine Prize in 1966, at the age of 87.

The youngest laureate has been Prof Sir William Lawrence Bragg (b Adelaide, South Australia, 1890, d 1971), of the UK, who, at the age of

25, shared the 1915 Physics Prize with his father, Sir William Henry Bragg (1862–1942), for work on X-rays and crystal structures. Bragg and also Theodore William Richards (1868–1928) (US) who won the 1914 Chemistry Prize, carried out their prize work when aged 23. The youngest Literature prizeman was (Joseph) Rudyard Kipling (UK) (1865–1936) at the age of 41, in 1907.

Who's Who

The longest entry of the 66,000 entries in *Who's Who in America* is that of Dr Glenn T. Seaborg (b Apr 19, 1912), whose record listing of 100 lines compares with the 9-line entry for Ronald Reagan.

In the British *Who's Who*, the longest entry was that of Winston Churchill, who appeared in 67 editions from 1899 (18 lines) and had 211 lines by the 1965 edition. When he died he was replaced by the romantic novelist, Barbara Cartland, who has 130 lines. The youngest entry of those who qualify without hereditary title is Yehudi Menuhin (b NYC, Apr 22, 1916), the concert violinist now living in England, who first appeared in the 1932 edition, aged 15.

Chapter 12

Sports, Games and Pastimes

Earliest

The origins of sport stem from the time when self-preservation ceased to be the all-consuming human preoccupation. Archery was a hunting skill in Mesolithic times (by *c.* 8000 BC), but did not become an organized sport until later, certainly by about 300 AD, among the Genoese and possibly as early as the 12th century BC, as an archery competition is described in Homer's *Iliad*. The earliest dated evidence for sport is *c.* 2750–2600 BC for wrestling. Ball games by girls, depicted on Middle Kingdom murals at Beni Hasan, Egypt, have been dated to *c.* 2050 BC.

Fastest

The highest speed reached in a non-mechanical sport is in sky-diving, in which a speed of 185 mph is attained in a head-down free-falling position, even in the lower atmosphere. In delayed drops, a speed of 625 mph has been recorded at high rarefied altitudes. The highest projectile speed in any moving ball game is *c.* 188 mph in pelota (jai-alai). This compares with 170 mph (electronically timed) for a golf ball driven off a tee.

Slowest

In amateur wrestling, before the rules were modified toward "brighter wrestling," contestants could be locked in holds for so long that a single bout once lasted for 11 hours 40 min. In the extreme case of the 2-hour-41-min pull in the regimental tug o'war in Jubbulpore, India, Aug 12, 1889, the winning team moved a net distance of 12 ft at an average speed of 0.00084 mph.

Longest

The most protracted sporting contest was an automobile duration test of 222,621 miles (equivalent to 8.93 times around the equator) by Appaurchaux and others in a Ford Taunus at Miranas, France. This was contested over 142 days (July–Nov) in 1963.

The most protracted non-mechanical sporting event is the *Tour de France* cycling race. In 1926 this was over 3,569 miles, lasting 29 days, but is now reduced to 23 days.

GREATEST EARNER: Muhammad Ali (right) seems to be knocking the stuffing out of Joe Frazier in the "thriller in Manila" when he won $6½ million. Ali's earnings in his 61 fights totaled about $69 million, making him the highest paid in any sport. (*AP*)

MOST VERSATILE ATHLETE (below left): Mildred (Babe) Didrikson Zaharias (US) was tops in basketball, high jump, javelin throwing, hurdling and golf (19 championships), besides having boxing and baseball talent.

1912 OLYMPIC MEDALS RESTORED (below right): Jim Thorpe, the American Indian who was a football star, pole-vaulted to a gold medal in the decathlon of the 1912 Olympics and won a second gold that year, only to have them revoked because he had once received $25 for playing semi-pro baseball, received his medals back postmortem in 1982, seventy years later.

Most Versatile Athletes

Charlotte "Lottie" Dod (1871–1960) won the Wimbledon singles title (1887 to 1893) 5 times, the British Ladies Golf Championship in 1904, an Olympic silver medal for archery in 1908, and represented England at hockey in 1899. She also excelled at skating and tobogganing.

, Mildred (Babe) Didrikson Zaharias (US) (1914–56) was an All-American basketball player, took the silver medal in the high jump, and gold medals in the javelin throw and hurdles in the 1932 Olympics. Turning professional, she first trained as a boxer, and then, switching to golf, eventually won 19 championships, including the US Women's Open and All-American Open. She holds the women's world record also for longest throw of a baseball—296 ft.

Jim Thorpe (US) (1888–1953) excelled at football, baseball, the 10-event decathlon, and the 5-event pentathlon. He won two gold medals in the 1912 Olympics and was declared "the greatest athlete in the world" by King Gustav of Sweden.

Greatest Earnings

The greatest fortune amassed by an individual in sport is an estimated $69 million by the boxer Muhammad Ali Haj (US) to the end of 1981.

The highest-paid woman athlete is tennis player Martina Navratilova (b Prague, Czechoslovakia, Oct 18, 1956) (US) whose career earnings passed $10 million by Mar 8, 1986.

Youngest and Oldest Recordbreakers

The youngest age at which any person has broken a non-mechanical world record is 12 years 298 days for Gertrude Caroline Ederle (b Oct 23, 1906) of the US, who broke the women's 880-yd freestyle swimming world record with 13 min 19.0 sec at Indianapolis, Ind, Aug 17, 1919.

The oldest person to break a world record is Gerhard Weidner (W Germany) (b Mar 15, 1933) who set a 20-mi walk record on May 25, 1974, aged 41 years 71 days.

Youngest and Oldest Champions

The youngest person to have successfully participated in a world title event was a French boy, whose name is not recorded, who coxed the winning Netherlands Olympic pair in rowing at Paris on Aug 26, 1900. He was not more than 10 and may have been as young as 7. The youngest individual Olympic winner was Marjorie Gestring (US) (b Nov 18, 1922), who took the springboard diving title at the age of 13 years 268 days at the Olympic Games in Berlin, Aug 12, 1936. Oscar G. Swahn (see below) was aged 64 years 258 days when he won the gold medal in the 1912 Olympic Running Deer team shooting competition.

Youngest and Oldest Internationals

The youngest age at which any person has won international honors is 8 years in the case of Joy Foster, the Jamaican singles and mixed doubles table tennis champion in 1958. It would appear that the greatest age at which anyone has actively competed for his country is 72 years 280 days in the case of Oscar Gomer Swahn (Sweden) (1847–1927), who won a silver medal for shooting in the Olympic Games at Antwerp on July 26, 1920. He qualified for the 1924 Games, but was unable to participate because of illness.

AUTO RACING

A complete listing of Auto Racing tracks and records, including charts and winners throughout the years, can be found in the "Guinness Sports Record Book."

Earliest Races

There are various conflicting claims, but the first automobile race was the 201-mile Green Bay-to-Madison, Wis, run in 1878, won by an Oshkosh steamer.

In 1887, Count Jules Felix Philippe Albert de Dion de Malfiance (1856–1946) won the *La Velocipede* 19.3-mile race in Paris in a De Dion steam quadricycle in which he is reputed to have exceeded 37 mph.

The first "real" race was from Paris to Bordeaux and back (732 miles) June 11–13, 1895. The winner was Emile Levassor (1844–97) (France) driving a Panhard-Levassor two-seater with a 1.2-liter Daimler engine developing 3¾ hp. His time was 48 hours 47 min (average speed 15.01 mph). The first closed-circuit race was held over 5 laps of a mile dirt track at Narragansett Park, Cranston, RI on Sept 7, 1896. It was won by A. H. Whiting, who drove a Riker electric.

The oldest auto race in the world still being regularly run is the R.A.C. Tourist Trophy, first staged on the Isle of Man on Sept 14, 1905. The oldest continental race is the French Grand Prix, first held June 26–27, 1906. The Coppa Florio, in Sicily, has been irregularly held since 1900.

Fastest Races

The fastest race in the world is the NASCAR Busch Clash, a 125-mile all-out sprint on the 2½-mile 31-degree banked tri-oval at Daytona International Speedway, Daytona Beach, Fla. In the 1979 event, Elzie Wylie "Buddy" Baker (b Jan 25, 1941) of Charlotte, NC, averaged 194.384 mph in an Oldsmobile. Bill Elliott set the world record for a 500 mile race in 1985 when he won at Talladega, Ala at an average speed of 186.288 mph. The NASCAR qualifying record is 212.229 mph by Bill Elliott in a Ford Thunderbird at Alabama International Motor Speedway, Talladega, Ala on May 1, 1986.

Le Mans

The greatest distance ever covered in the 24-hour *Grand Prix d'Endurance* (first held May 26–27, 1923) on the old Sarthe circuit (8 miles 650 yd) at Le Mans, France, is 3,314.222 miles by Dr Helmut Marko (b Graz, Austria, Apr 27, 1943) and Jonkheer Gijs van Lennep (b Bloemendaal, Netherlands, March 16, 1942) driving a 4,907-cc flat-12 Porsche 917K Group 5 sports car June 12–13, 1971. The record for the current circuit is 3,161,928 miles (average speed 131.747 mph) in a Porsche 956 June 15–16, 1985 by Klaus Ludwig (W Ger), Paulo Barilla (Italy), and John Winter (W Ger). The race lap record (8.475-mile lap) is 3 min 25.1 sec (average speed 148.61 mph) by Jackie Ickx (Belgium) in a Porsche 962C in 1985. The practice lap record is 3 min 14.8 sec (av. speed 156.62 mph) by Hans Stuck (W Ger) in a Porsche 962C on June 14, 1985.

The most wins by one man is 6 by Jackie Ickx (Belgium), who won in 1969, 75–77 and 81–82.

LAPPING IT UP: Niki Laudia in a MacLaren TAG set an Austrian Grand Prix race lap record of 143.109 mph on Aug 19, 1984.

LE MANS: Record-breaking crowd of 400,000 watches the start of the 24-hour race for touring cars called the Grand Prix d'Endurance.

Indianapolis 500

The Indianapolis 500-mile race (200 laps) was inaugurated on May 30, 1911. The most successful driver has been Anthony Joseph "A. J." Foyt, Jr (b Houston, Tex, Jan 16, 1935), who won in 1961, 64, 67 and 77.

The record time is 2 hours 55 min 43.48 sec (average speed 170.722 mph) by Bobby Rahal (US) on May 31, 1986, driving a March Cosworth. This was the closest 3-car finish in the 70-year history of the race. Bobby Rahal beat Kevin Cogan by 1.4 sec and beat Rick Mears (b 1952, Calif) by 1.8 sec. He did it with a last lap of 209.152 mph, the fastest race lap in Indy history.

The qualifying 4-lap record average speed is 216.828 mph, including a one-lap record of 217.581 mph by Rick Mears in a Pennzoil Z-7 with a Cosworth engine on May 10, 1986.

The record prize fund is $4,001,450 for the 1986 race, the 70th. The individual prize record is the $581,062.50 won by Bobby Rahal in 1986.

The first and only woman to qualify for and compete in the Indianapolis 500 is Janet Guthrie (b Mar 7, 1938). She passed her rookie test in May 1976, and earned the right to compete in the qualifying rounds, but was unable to win a place on the starting line when the Vollstedt-Offenhauser she drove was withdrawn from the race after repeated mechanical failures. In the 61st running of the Indianapolis 500, in 1977, Guthrie became the first woman to compete, although her car developed mechanical problems which forced her to retire after 27 laps. In 1978, she completed the race, finishing in ninth place after 190 laps.

Fastest Pit Stop

Bobby Unser (US) took 4 sec to take on fuel on lap 10 of the Indianapolis 500 on May 30, 1976.

Most Successful Drivers

Based on the World Drivers' Championships, inaugurated in 1950, the most successful driver is Juan-Manuel Fangio (b Balcarce, Argentina, June 24, 1911), who won five times in 1951, 54–57. He retired in 1958, after having won 24 Grand Prix races (2 shared).

The most successful driver in terms of race wins is Richard Lee Petty (b Randleman, NC, July 2, 1937) with 200 NASCAR Grand National wins, 1958–85. (See also *Stock Car Racing*.) His best season was 1967 with 27 wins. His total earnings reached $5,767,488 to July 28, 1985. Geoff Bodine won 55 races in 1978. The NASCAR career money record is $6,703,305 to June 4, 1986, by Darrell Waltrip (b Feb 1949). Bill Elliott won a year's record $2,044,468 in NASCAR events in 1985.

The most Grand Prix victories is 27 by Jackie Stewart (b June 11, 1939) of Scotland between Sept 12, 1965 and Aug 5, 1973. Jim Clark (1936–68) of Scotland shares the record of Grand Prix victories in one year with 7 in 1963; Alain Prost (France) (b Feb 24, 1955) had 7 in 1984. Clark won 61 Formula One and Formula Libre races between 1959 and 1968. The most Grand Prix starts is 176 (out of a possible 184) between May 18, 1958, and Jan 26, 1975, by (Norman) Graham Hill (1929–75). He took part in 90 *consecutive* Grands Prix between Nov 20, 1960 and Oct 5, 1969.

The most Grand Prix points won is 418½ by Nicki Lauda (Austria) (b Feb 22, 1949) in 171 Grands Prix, with 25 wins from 1971 to 1985.

Oldest and Youngest World Champions

The oldest was Juan-Manuel Fangio, who won his last World Championship Aug 18, 1957, aged 46 years 55 days. The youngest was Emerson Fittipaldi (b São Paulo, Brazil, Dec 12, 1946) who won his first World Championship Sept 10, 1972, aged 25 years 273 days.

Youngest and Oldest Grand Prix Winners and Drivers

The youngest Grand Prix winner was Bruce Leslie McLaren (1937–70) of New Zealand, who won the US Grand Prix at Sebring, Fla, on Dec 12, 1959, aged 22 years 104 days. The oldest Grand Prix winner was Tazio Giorgio Nuvolari (1892–1953) of Italy, who won the Albi Grand Prix at Albi, France, on July 14, 1946, aged 53 years 240 days.

The oldest Grand Prix driver was Louis Alexandre Chiron (Monaco, 1899–1979), who finished 6th in the Monaco Grand Prix on May 22, 1955, aged 55 years 292 days. The youngest Grand Prix driver was Michael Christopher Thackwell (b New Zealand, March 30, 1961) who took part in the Canadian Grand Prix on Sept 28, 1980, aged 19 years 182 days.

Stock Car Racing

Richard Petty was the first stock car driver to attain $1 million lifetime earnings on Aug 1, 1971. Also see *Most Successful Drivers.*

Closest Finishes

The closest finish to a World Championship race occurred when Ayrton Senna (Brazil) beat Nigel Mansell (GB) by 0.014 sec in the Spanish Grand Prix at Jerez de la Frontera Apr 13, 1986.

The closest finish in the Indianapolis 500 was in the 1982 race when the winner, Gordon Johncock, crossed the finish line just 0.16 sec before runner-up Rick Mears.

Manufacturers

Ferraris have won a record eight manufacturers' world championships, 1961, 1964, 1975–7, 1979, 1982–3. Ferraris have 91 race wins in 390 Grands Prix, 1950–85.

Duration Record

The greatest distance ever covered in one year is 400,000 km (248,548.5 miles) by François Lecot (1879–1949), an innkeeper from Rochetaillée, France, in a 1,900-cc 66-bhp Citroën 11 sedan mainly between Paris and Monte Carlo, from July 22, 1935 to July 26, 1936. He drove on 363 of the 370 days allowed.

Pikes Peak Race

The Pikes Peak Auto Hill Climb, Colorado (instituted 1916) has been won by Bobby Unser 13 times between 1956 and 1974 (10 championship, 2 stock and 1 sports car titles). In the 1979 race Dick Dodge set a record time of 11 min 54.18 sec in a Chevrolet-powered Wells Coyote over the 12.42-mile course, rising from 9,402 to 14,110 ft through 157 curves.

Earliest Rally

The earliest long rally was promoted by the Parisian daily *Le Matin* in 1907 from Peking to Paris, over about 7,500 miles on June 10. The winner, Prince Scipione Borghese (1872–1927), arrived in Paris on Aug 10,

1907 in his 40-hp Itala accompanied by his chauffeur, Ettore, and Luigi Barzini.

Indianapolis 500

Winners since 1946 (all US except where stated):

	Driver	Car	Speed (mph)
1946	George Robson	Thorne Engineering	114.820
1947	Mauri Rose	Blue Crown Special	116.338
1948	Mauri Rose	Blue Crown Special	119.814
1949	Bill Holland	Blue Crown Special	121.327
1950	Johnny Parsons	Wynn Kurtis Kraft	124.002
1951	Lee Wallard	Belanger	126.224
1952	Troy Ruttman	Agajanian	128.922
1953	Bill Vukovich	Fuel Injection	128.740
1954	Bill Vukovich	Fuel Injection	130.840
1955	Bob Sweikert	John Zink Special	128.209
1956	Pat Flaherty	John Zink Special	128.490
1957	Sam Hanks	Belond Exhaust	135.601
1958	Jimmy Bryan	Belond A. P.	133.791
1959	Rodger Ward	Leader Card Special	135.857
1960	Jim Rathmann	Ken-Paul Special	138.767
1961	A. J. Foyt	Bowes Seal Fast	139.130
1962	Rodger Ward	Leader Card Special	140.293
1963	Parnelli Jones	Agajanian Special	143.137
1964	A. J. Foyt	Sheraton-Thompson Special	147.350
1965	Jim Clark (GB)	Lotus-Ford	150.686
1966	Graham Hill (GB)	American Red Ball	144.317
1967	A. J. Foyt	Sheraton-Thompson Special	151.207
1968	Bobby Unser	Rislone Special	152.882
1969	Mario Andretti	STP Oil Treatment Special	156.867
1970	Al Unser	Johnny Lightning Special	155.749
1971	Al Unser	Johnny Lightning Special	157.735
1972	Mark Donohue	Sunoco McLaren	162.962
1973	Gordon Johncock	STP Double Oil Filter	159.036
1974	Johnny Rutherford	McLaren	158.589
1975	Bobby Unser	Jorgensen Eagle	149.213
1976	Johnny Rutherford	Hygain McLaren	148.725
1977	A. J. Foyt	Gilmore Coyote-Foyt	161.331
1978	Al Unser	Lola-Chapparal Cosworth	161.363
1979	Rick Mears	Penske-Cosworth	158.899
1980	Johnny Rutherford	Chapparal Cosworth	142.862
1981	Bobby Unser	Penske-Cosworth	139.084
1982	Gordon Johncock	Wildcat-Cosworth	162.025
1983	Tom Sneva	March-Cosworth	162.117
1984	Rick Mears	March-Cosworth	163.612
1985	Danny Sullivan	March-Cosworth	152.982
1986	Bobby Rahal	March-Cosworth	170.722

Longest Rallies

The longest rally ever was the *Singapore Airlines* London-Sydney Rally over 19,329 miles, from Covent Garden, London, on Aug 14, 1977,

DRAGSTER RECORD for terminal velocity was set by "Big Daddy" Don Garlits at 268 mph in Oct 1958 at Pomona, Calif. Drag cars are designed for high speeds over short distances, usually just 440 yd. (*All Sport*)

to the Sydney Opera House, won Sept 28, 1977, by Andrew Cowan, Colin Malkin and Michael Broad in a Mercedes 280E.

The longest rally held annually is the Safari Rally (first run 1953 through Kenya, Tanzania and Uganda, now only Kenya), which has been up to 3,874 miles long, as in the 17th Safari held Apr 8–12, 1971. It has been won a record 5 times by Shekhar Mehta (Uganda) in 1973, 79–82.

Piston-Engined Dragsters

Terminal velocity is the speed attained at the end of a 440-yd run made from a standing start, and elapsed time is the time taken for the run.

The lowest elapsed time recorded by a piston-engined dragster is 5.391 sec from a standing start for 440 yd by Gary Beck (US) in qualifying for the World Finals at Irvine, Calif on Oct 15, 1983.

The highest terminal velocity recorded at the end of a 440-yd run is 268.01 mph by Don Garlits (US) (b 1932) at Pomona, Calif on Oct 17, 1985 in qualifying for the World Finals.

The world record for two runs in opposite directions over 440 yd from a standing start is 6.70 sec by Dennis Victor Priddle (b 1945) of Yeovil, Somerset, England, driving his 6,424-cc supercharged Chrysler dragster, developing 1,700 bhp using nitromethane and methanol, at Elvington Airfield, England, Oct 7, 1972. The faster run took 6.65 sec.

Rocket or Jet-Engined Dragsters

The highest terminal velocity recorded by any dragster is 392.54 mph by Kitty O'Neil (US) at El Mirage Dry Lake, Calif, on July 7, 1977. The lowest elapsed time was 3.72 sec also by Kitty O'Neil on the same occasion.

Land Speed Records

The highest speed attained by any wheeled land vehicle is 739.666

mph or Mach 1.0106 (making it the only land vehicle to break the sound barrier) *in a one-way stretch* by the rocket-engined *Budweiser Rocket,* designed by William Frederick, and driven by Stan Barrett at Edwards Air Force Base, California, on Dec 17, 1979. The vehicle, owned by Hal Needham, has a 48,000-hp rocket engine with 6,000 lb of extra thrust from a sidewinder missile. The rear wheels (100-lb solid discs) lifted 10 in off the ground above Mach 0.95, acting as 7,500-rpm gyroscopes.

The official 1-mi land speed record, which is for the average of a two-way run, was set on Oct 4, 1983 when Richard Noble (GB) drove a jet-powered car, *Thrust 2,* at 633.468 mph at Black Rock Desert, Gerlach, Nev. The previous record, 622.287, was set by Gary Gabelich and had stood for 13 years.

The most successful land speed record breaker was Major Malcolm Campbell (1885–1948) (UK). He broke the official record nine times between Sept 25, 1924, with 146.157 mph in a Sunbeam, and Sept 3, 1935, when he achieved 301.129 mph in the Rolls-Royce-engined *Bluebird.*

The world speed record for compression-ignition-engined cars is 190.344 mph (average of two runs over measured mile) by Robert Havemann of Eureka, Calif, driving his *Corsair* streamliner, powered by a turbocharged 6.981-cc 6-cylinder GMC 6-71 diesel engine developing 746 bhp, at Bonneville Salt Flats, Utah, in Aug, 1971. The faster run was made at 210 mph.

Worst Disaster

Drivers have hit spectators with appalling regularity throughout the history of racing, first place doubtless going to Pierre Levegh, who killed 81 spectators as well as himself at Le Mans in 1955.

BASEBALL

Earliest Games

The Reverend Thomas Wilson, of Maidstone, Kent, England, wrote disapprovingly, in 1700, of baseball being played on Sundays. The earliest game on record under the Cartwright (Alexander Joy Cartwright, Jr, 1820–92) rules was on June 19, 1846, in Hoboken, NJ, where the "New York Nine" defeated the Knickerbockers 23 to 1 in 4 innings. The earliest all-professional team was the Cincinnati Red Stockings in 1869, who had 56 wins and 1 tie that season.

Night Baseball

The first night game was played on June 2, 1883 (M.E. College vs professionals from Quincy, Ill). The major leagues were slow to adopt this change of program, then considered radical. The Cincinnati Reds were the first big-league team to play under lights when they hosted the Philadelphia Phillies on May 24, 1935. President Franklin D. Roosevelt pressed a button at the White House to flick the switch at Crosley Field. Wrigley Field, home of the Chicago Cubs, still remains unlit.

Home Runs

Henry L. (Hank) Aaron (b Feb 5, 1934, Mobile, Ala) broke the major league record set by George H. (Babe) Ruth of 714 home runs in a life-time when he hit No. 715 on Apr 8, 1974. Between 1954 and 1974 he hit 733 home runs for the Milwaukee and Atlanta Braves in the National League. In 1975, he switched to the Milwaukee Brewers in the American League and in that year and 1976, when he finally retired, he hit 22 more, bringing his lifetime total to 755, the major league record.

Mickey Mantle's homer in Detroit on Sept 10, 1960, which ascended over the right field roof and is said to have landed in a lumberyard, was measured trigonometrically in 1985 to have traveled 643 ft.

A North American record of almost 800 in a lifetime has been claimed for Josh Gibson (1911–47), mostly for the Homestead Grays of the Negro National League, who was elected in 1972 to the Baseball Hall of Fame in Cooperstown, NY. Gibson is said to have hit 75 round-trippers in one season, in 1931, but no official records were kept.

The most officially recorded home runs hit by a professional player in the US in one season is 72, by Joe Bauman, of the Roswell, NM team, a minor league club, in 1954. The major league record is 61 in 161 games of a 162-game season by Roger Maris (b Sept 10, 1934), of the NY Yankees, in 1961. George Herman "Babe" Ruth (1895–1948) hit 60 in a 154-game season in 1927.

The longest home run ever measured was one of 618 ft by Roy Edward "Dizzy" Carlyle (1900–56) in a minor league game at Emeryville Ball Park, Calif, July 4, 1929. Babe Ruth hit a 587-ft homer for the Boston Red Sox vs NY Giants in an exhibition game at Tampa, Fla, in 1919. The longest measured home run in a regular-season major league game is 565 ft by Mickey Mantle (b Oct 20, 1931) for the NY Yankees vs Washington Senators on Apr 17, 1953, at Griffith Stadium, Wash DC.

In 1893, there was an important rules change that must be considered when looking at batting records. In the early days of the game, pitching was viewed merely as a matter of trying to get the ball over the plate. Any outfielder might be called upon to pitch. But as managers discovered that there was a decisive advantage to having a pitcher who knew how to throw a knuckleball or a spitball, batting averages declined drastically. Thus in 1893 the distance between home plate and the pitcher's rubber was changed from 50 ft to the current 60 ft 6 in. Batting averages soared.

Shortest and Tallest Players

The shortest major league player was surely Eddie Gaedel, a 3-ft-7-in, 65-lb midget, who pinch hit for the St Louis Browns vs the Detroit Tigers on Aug 19, 1951. Wearing number ⅛, the batter with the smallest ever major league strike zone walked on four pitches. Following the game,

MOST HITS, MOST AT-BATS, MOST GAMES: Pete Rose, spark plug of the Cincinnati Reds (with the Phillies for 5 years), now manager of the Reds, ended the 1985 season with 4,204 hits (13 more than Cobb) in 3,490 games and 13,816 times at the plate.

LONGEST HITTING STREAK (below): Joe DiMaggio, a 3-time MVP, batted safely in 56 straight games, collecting 91 hits over the 2-month stretch in 1941.

MOST HITS: Ty Cobb (above) held the record of 4,191 career hits established in 1928 until Pete Rose broke it in 1985. (*UPI-Bettmann Archives*)

BASE STEALER SUPREME: Rickey Henderson, while with the Oakland A's in 1982, stole 130 bases in 149 games. This record was threatened in 1985 by Vince Coleman (St L NL) before he was injured in a freak accident. (*Steve Babineau photo*)

MOST CONSECUTIVE INNINGS PLAYED: Cal Ripken, Jr, the Baltimore Oriole shortstop, has played all of every inning for 690 games in a unique record of 6,247 innings from June 5, 1982 to the 1986 All-Star break (*Jerry Wachter*)

major league rules were hastily rewritten to prevent the recurrence of such an affair.

The tallest major leaguer was John Alexander Gee (b Dec 7, 1915), a 6-ft-9-in pitcher who spent 6 seasons in the National League: 1939, 41, 43–46.

Fastest Base Runner

Ernest Evar Swanson (1902–73) took only 13.3 sec to circle the bases at Columbus, Ohio, in 1932, averaging 18.45 mph.

Youngest and Oldest Players

The youngest major league player of all time was the Cincinnati pitcher Joe Nuxhall, who started his career in June 1944, aged 15 years 10 months 11 days.

Leroy Satchel Paige (1906?–82) pitched three scoreless innings for the Kansas City Athletics at approximately age 59 in 1965. Baseball's color barrier had kept him out of the major leagues until 1948, when he was a 42-year-old "rookie," and his record of 6 wins and 1 loss helped the Cleveland Indians win the pennant. His birthday is listed as July 7, 1906, but many believe he was born earlier. The Atlanta Braves carried Paige on their roster in 1968 to allow him to qualify for a pension.

Best Day at Bat

John Paciorek of the Houston Colt '45s had a perfect day at bat in 1963 with 3 singles, 2 walks, 4 runs scored, and 3 RBI's, for a 1.000 average.

Most Strikeouts

Bobby Bonds in 1970, while playing right field for the San Francisco Giants, fanned 189 times in 157 games.

Fewest Strikeouts

Joe Sewell in 1929, while playing third base for the Cleveland Indians, played in 115 consecutive games, going to bat 437 times without once striking out. In his career stretching 14 years he only struck out 114 times.

Most Strikeouts in an Inning

Seventeen different pitchers hold the record of 4 in an inning. How? The catcher misses on a third strike and the batter gets on base, so the hurler has to fan another batter. The latest pitcher to have 4 K's (strikeouts) in one inning was Mario Soto of the Reds on May 17, 1984 against the Cubs.

Most Foul-Offs

Luke Appling, shortstop for the White Sox in the 1930's, fouled off 14 consecutive pitches from Dizzy Trout of the Tigers. On the 15th pitch, Trout threw his glove instead of the ball.

Attendances

The World Series record attendance is 420,784 (6 games with total gate receipts of $2,626,973.44) when the Los Angeles Dodgers beat the Chicago White Sox 4 games to 2, Oct 1–8, 1959.

The single game record is 92,706 for the fifth game (gate receipts $552,774.77) at the Memorial Coliseum (no longer used for baseball), LA, Oct 6, 1959.

The highest seating capacity in a baseball stadium is 74,208 in the Cleveland Municipal Stadium.

The all-time season record for attendance for both leagues has been 46,828,819 in 1984–85.

An estimated 114,000 spectators watched a game between Australia and an American serviceman's team in a "demonstration" during the Dec. 1, 1956 Olympics in Melbourne, Australia.

Fastest Pitcher

The fastest recorded pitcher is (Lynn) Nolan Ryan (b Jan 31, 1947) who, on Aug 20, 1974 (then of the California Angels, now of the Houston Astros) at Annaheim Stadium, Calif, was measured to pitch at 100.9 mph.

Do-Nothing Record

Toby Harrah of the Texas Rangers (AL) played an entire double-header at shortstop on June 26, 1976, without having a chance to make any fielding plays, assists or putouts.

Do-Everything Record

Two major league ballplayers, Bert Campaneris (b Mar 12, 1942) and Cesar Tovar (b July 3, 1940), have the distinction of playing each of the nine field positions in a single major league game. Campaneris did it first, on Sept 8, 1965, when his team, the Kansas City Athletics, announced he would. He played one inning at each position, including the full eighth inning as a pitcher, and gave up just one run. Tovar duplicated the feat on Sept 22, 1968, when he played for the Minnesota Twins. He pitched a scoreless first inning and retired the first batter, none other than Campaneris. On June 4, 1983, Mike Ashman, a minor league player for the Albany-Colonie A's of the Eastern League, improved upon the Campaneris-Tovar feat by playing 10 positions, including designated hitter, in a game against Nashua.

Consecutive Innings

Calvin Ripken, Jr (b Aug 24, 1960), of the Baltimore Orioles set what is believed to be a record for playing every inning of consecutive games, stretching his streak that began June 5, 1982 to 690 games (6,247 innings) by the All-Star break in 1986. Ripken played the first six games of the streak at third base, then moved to shortstop. Baseball researchers have found no previous streak longer than 534 games (Buck Freeman, Boston Red Sox, 1901–05).

Playoff Players

Lonnie Smith in 1985 played for the Cardinals and Kansas City, the playoff winners. Al Oliver played for the Dodgers and Blue Jays, the playoff losers.

Hit by Pitch

Ron Hunt, an infielder who played with various National League teams from 1963 to 1974, led the league in getting hit by pitched balls for a record 7 consecutive years. His career total is 243, also a major league record.

Running Bases in Reverse

Herman (Germany) Schaefer of the Washington Senators in 1910 stole first base. This was after he had stolen second with a runner on third. Dissatisfied because the catcher had not thrown to second to allow a double steal to begin, he stole first on the next pitch to try again. A new baseball rule (7.08 i) was instituted at once to prevent this happening again.

MAJOR LEAGUE ALL-TIME RECORDS
(Including 1985, not 1986 season)

Individual Batting

Highest percentage, lifetime (5,000 at-bats)
.367 Tyrus R. Cobb, Det AL, 1905–26; Phil AL, 1927–28

Highest percentage, season (500 at-bats)
.438 Hugh Duffy, Bos NL, 1894

Modern Record
.424 Rogers Hornsby, St L NL, 1924

Most games played
3,490 Peter Rose, Cin NL, 1963–78; Phil NL, 1979–83; Mont NL, 1984; Cin NL, 1984–86

Most consecutive games played
2,130 Henry Louis (Lou) Gehrig, NY AL, June 1, 1925 through Apr 30, 1939

Most runs batted in, season
190 Lewis R. (Hack) Wilson, Chi NL, 155 games, 1930

Most runs batted in, game
12 James L. Bottomley, St L NL, Sept 16, 1924

Most runs batted in, lifetime
2,297 Henry L. (Hank) Aaron, Mil NL, 1954–65, Atl NL, 1966–74; Mil AL, 1975–76

Most runs, lifetime
2,244 Tyrus R. Cobb, Det AL, 1905–26; Phil AL, 1927–28

Most base hits, lifetime
4,204 Peter Rose, Cin NL, 1963–78; Phil NL, 1979–83; Mont NL, 1984; Cin NL 1984–85

Most base hits, season
257 George H. Sisler, St L AL, 154 games, 1920

Most hits in succession
12 M. Frank (Pinky) Higgins, Bos AL, June 19–21 (4 games), 1938
Walter Dropo, Det AL, July 14, July 15, 2 games, 1952

Most base hits, consecutive, game
7 Wilbert Robinson, Balt NL, June 10, 1892, 1st game (7-ab), 6-1b, 1-2b
Renaldo Stennett, Pitt NL, Sept 16, 1975 (7-ab), 4-1b, 2-2b, 1-3b
Cesar Gutierrez, Det AL, June 21, 1970, 2nd game (7-ab) 6-1b, 1-2b (12-inning game)

Most times at bat, lifetime
13,816 Peter Rose, Cin NL, 1963–78; Phil NL, 1979–83; Mont NL, 1984; Cin NL, 1984–85

Most consecutive games batted safely, season
56 Joseph P. DiMaggio, NY AL (91 hits—16-2b, 4-3b, 15 hr), May 15 to July 16, 1941

Most total bases, lifetime
6,856 Henry L. (Hank) Aaron, Mil NL, 1954–65; Atl NL, 1966–74; Mil AL, 1975–76

Most total bases, season
457 George H. (Babe) Ruth, NY AL, 152 gs (85 on 1b, 88 on 2b, 48 on 3b, 236 on hr), 1921

Most total bases, game
18 Joseph W. Adcock, Mil NL (1-2b, 4-hr), July 31, 1954

Most one-base hits (singles), season
202 William H. (Wee Willie) Keeler, Balt NL, 128 games, 1898

Most two-base hits, season
67 Earl W. Webb, Bos AL, 151 games, 1931

Most three-base hits, season
36 J. Owen Wilson, Pitts NL, 152 games, 1912

Most home runs, season
61 Roger E. Maris, NY AL (162-game schedule) (30 home, 31 away), 161 gs, 1961

60 George H. (Babe) Ruth, NY
AL (154-game schedule)
(28 home, 32 away), 151
gs, 1927

Most home runs, lifetime
755 Henry L. Aaron, Mil NL,
1954 (13), 1955 (27), 1956
(26), 1957 (44), 1958 (30),
1959 (39), 1960 (40), 1961
(34), 1962 (45), 1963 (44),
1964 (24), 1965 (32); Atl
NL, 1966 (44), 1967 (39),
1968 (29), 1969 (44), 1970
(38), 1971 (47), 1972 (34),
1973 (40), 1974 (20); Mil
AL, 1975 (12), 1976 (10)

Most home runs, bases filled, lifetime
23 Henry Louis (Lou) Gehrig,
NY AL, 1923–39

Most home runs with bases filled,
season
5 Ernest Banks, Chi NL, May
11, 19, July 17 (1st game),
Aug 2, Sept 19, 1955
James E. Gentile, Balt AL,
May 9 (2), July 2, 7, Sept
22, 1961

Most home runs, with bases filled,
game
2 Anthony M. Lazzeri, NY
AL, May 24, 1936
James R. Tabor, Bos AL
(2nd game), July 4, 1939
Rudolph York, Bos AL, July
27, 1946
James E. Gentile, Balt AL,
May 9, 1961 (consecutive
at-bats)
Tony L. Cloninger, Atl NL,
July 3, 1966
James T. Northrup, Det AL,
June 24, 1968 (consecutive
at-bats)
Frank Robinson, Balt AL,
June 26, 1970 (consecutive
at-bats)

Most consecutive games hitting
home runs
8 R. Dale Long, Pitt NL, May
19–28, 1956

Most home runs, one doubleheader
5 Stanley F. Musial, St L NL,
1st game (3), 2nd game (2),
May 2, 1954
Nathan Colbert, SD NL, 1st

game (2), 2nd game (3),
Aug 1, 1972

Most bases on balls, game
6 James E. Foxx, Bos AL, June
16, 1938
Andre Thornton, Clev AL,
May 2, 1984 (16 inns)

Most bases on balls, season
170 George H. (Babe) Ruth, NY
AL, 152 games, 1923

Most hits, pinch-hitter, lifetime
150 Manuel R. Mota, SF NL,
1962; Pitt NL, 1963–68;
Mont NL, 1969; LA NL,
1969–80

Most consecutive home runs, pinch-
hitter
3 Del Unser, Phil NL, June 30,
July 5, 10, 1979
Lee Lacy, LA NL, May 2, 6,
17, 1978 (one walk in be-
tween)

Most consecutive pinch hits
9 David E. Philley, Phil NL,
Sept 9, 11, 12, 13, 19, 20,
27, 28, 1958; Apr 16, 1959

Base Running

Most stolen bases, lifetime
938 Louis C. Brock, Chi NL,
1961–64; St L NL, 1964–79

Most stolen bases, season since 1900
130 Rickey Henderson, Oak AL,
149 games, 1982

Most stolen bases, game
7 George F. (Piano Legs)
Gore, Chi NL, June 25,
1881
William R. (Sliding Billy)
Hamilton, Phil NL, 2nd
game, 8 inn, Aug 31, 1894

Modern Record

6 Edward T. Collins, Phil AL,
Sept 11 and again Sept 22,
1912

Most times stealing home, lifetime
35 Tyrus R. Cobb, Det AL,
1905–26; Phil AL 1927–28

Fewest times caught stealing, season
(50+ attempts)
2 Max Carey, Pitt NL, 1922
(53 atts)

Pitching

In 1893 the distance from home plate to where the pitcher must stand was changed from 50 feet to the current 60 feet, 6 in.

Most years
25 James Kaat, Minn AL 1959–73; Chi AL 1973–75; Phil NL 1976–79; NY AL 1979–80; St L NL 1980–83

Most games, lifetime
1,070 J. Hoyt Wilhelm, NY-St L-Atl-Chi-LA (448) NL, 1952–57, 69–72; Clev-Balt-Chi-Cal (622) AL, 1957 69

Most complete games, lifetime
751 Denton T. (Cy) Young, Clev-St L-Bos NL (428); Bos-Clev AL (323), 1890–1911

Most games, season
106 Mike Marshall, LA NL, 1974

Most complete games, season
74 William H. White, Cin NL, 1879

Lowest earned run average, season
0.90 Ferdinand M. Schupp, NY NL, 1916 (140 inn)
1.01 Hubert B. (Dutch) Leonard, Bos AL, 1914 (222 inn)
1.12 Robert Gibson, St L NL, 1968 (305 inn)

Most innings pitched, game
26 Leon J. Cadore, Bklyn NL, May 1, 1920
Joseph Oeschger, Bos NL, May 1, 1920

Most games won, lifetime
511 Denton T. (Cy) Young, Clev NL (239) 1890–98; St L NL (46) 1899–1900; Bos AL (193) 1901–08; Clev AL (29) 1909–11; Bos NL (4) 1911

Most games won, season
60 Charles Radbourn, Providence NL, 1884

STRIKEOUT KINGS: Sandy Koufax (left) pitched a record 23 strikeouts in 4 World Series games in 1963 for the LA Dodgers. Nolan Ryan (above), now with Houston, in 1983 was the first to eclipse Walter Johnson's (Wash AL) career record of 3,508 strikeouts (1907–27). By the end of the 1985 season his total had grown to 4,083, and by mid-season 1986 by 116 more.

41 John D. Chesbro, NY AL, 1904

Most consecutive games won, lifetime
24 Carl O. Hubbell, NY NL, 1936 (16); 1937 (8)

Perfect game—9 innings
1880 John Lee Richmond, Worcester vs Clev NL, June 12   1–0
    John M. Ward, Prov vs Buff NL, June 17 AM   5–0
1904 Denton T. (Cy) Young, Bos vs Phil AL, May 5   3–0
1908 Adrian C. Joss, Clev vs Chi AL, Oct 2   1–0
†1917 Ernest G. Shore, Bos vs Wash AL, June 23 (1st g)   4–0
1922 C. C. Robertson, Chi vs Det AL, Apr 30   2–0
*1956 Donald J. Larsen, NY AL vs Bklyn NL, Oct 8   2–0
1964 James P. Bunning, Phil NL vs NY, June 21 (1st g)   6–0
1965 Sanford (Sandy) Koufax, LA NL vs Chi, Sept 9 1–0
1968 James A. (Catfish) Hunter, Oak AL vs Minn, May 8   4–0
1981 Leonard H. Barker II, Cleve AL vs Tor, May 15   3–0
1984 Michael Witt, Cal AL vs Texas, Sept 9, 1984   1–0

Special mention
1959 Harvey Haddix, Jr, Pitt vs Mil NL, May 26, pitched 12 perfect innings, allowed hit in 13th and lost.

Most strikeouts, season
505 Matthew Kilroy, Balt AA, 1886 (Distance 50 ft)
383 L. Nolan Ryan, Cal AL, 1973 (Distance 60 ft 6 in)

†Starting pitcher, "Babe" Ruth, was banished from game by Umpire Brick Owens after an argument. He gave the first batter, Ray Morgan, a base on balls. Shore relieved and while he pitched to second batter, Morgan was caught stealing. Shore then retired next 26 batters to complete the "perfect" game.

*World Series game.

Most strikeouts, career
4,083 L. Nolan Ryan, NY NL, Cal AL, Houston NL, 1968–85

Most strikeouts, game (9 inn) since 1900
19 Steven N. Carlton, St L NL vs NY, Sept 15, 1969 (lost)
    G. Thomas Seaver, NY NL vs SD, Apr 22, 1970
    L. Nolan Ryan, Cal AL vs Bos, Aug 12, 1974

Roger Clemens, Bos AL vs Seat, Apr 29, 1986 struck out 20 batters

Most strikeouts, extra-inning game
21 Thomas E. Cheney, Wash AL vs Balt (16 inns), Sept 12, 1962 (night)

Most no-hit games, lifetime
5 L. Nolan Ryan, Cal AL, 1973 (2)–74–75; Hou NL, 1981

Most consecutive no-hit games
2 John S. Vander Meer, Cin NL, June 11–15, 1938

Most consecutive games won, season
19 Timothy J. Keefe, NY NL, 1888
    Richard W. (Rube) Marquard, NY NL, 1912

Most shutout games, season
16 George W. Bradley, St L NL, 1876
    Grover C. Alexander, Phil NL, 1916

Most shutout games, lifetime
113 Walter P. Johnson, Wash AL, 21 years, 1907–27

Most consecutive shutout games, season
6 Donald S. Drysdale, LA NL, May 14, 18, 22, 26, 31, June 4, 1968

Most consecutive shutout innings
58 Donald S. Drysdale, LA NL, May 14-June 8, 1968

Most saves, season
45 Daniel Quisenberry, KC AL, 1983
    Bruce Sutter, St L NL, 1984

Most saves, lifetime
324 Roland (Rollie) Fingers, Oak AL, 1968–76; SD NL 1977–80; Mil AL 1981–84

Fielding

Best percentage, season, by position

First Base: 1.000
Steven Garvey, SD NL, 1984

Second Base: .9948
Robert Wilfong, Minn AL, 1980

Third Base: .9894
Donald Money, Mil AL, 1974

Shortstop: .9912
Lawrence Bowa, Phil NL, 1979

Outfield: 1.000
Curtis Flood, St L NL, 1966 (based on most chances handled without an error—396)

Catcher: 1.000
Warren (Buddy) Rosar, Phil AL, 1946

Pitcher: 1.000
Randall Jones, SD NL, 1976 (based on most chances handled without an error—112)

Consecutive games, no errors, by position

First Base: 193
Steven Garvey, SD NL, 1983–85

Second Base: 91
Joe Morgan, Cin NL, 1977–78

Third Base: 97
James Davenport, SF NL, 1966–68

Shortstop: 72
Edwin Brinkman, Det AL, 1972

Outfield: 266
Donald Demeter, Phil NL–Det AL, 1962–65

Catcher: 148
Lawrence P. (Yogi) Berra, NY AL, 1957–59

Pitcher: 385
Paul Lindblad, KC–Oak AL, 1966–74

World Series Records

Most series played
14 Lawrence P. (Yogi) Berra, NY, AL, 1947, 49–53, 55–58, 60–63

Highest batting percentage (20 g min.), total series
.391 Louis C. Brock, St L NL, 1964, 67–68 (g-21, ab-87, h-34)

Highest batting percentage, 4 or more games, one series
.625 4-game series, George H. (Babe) Ruth, NY AL, 1928

Most runs, total series
42 Mickey C. Mantle, NY AL, 1951–53, 55–58, 60–64

Most runs, one series
10 Reginald M. Jackson, NY AL, 1977

Most runs batted in, total series
40 Mickey C. Mantle, NY, AL, 1951–53, 55–58, 60–64

Most runs batted in, consecutive times at bat
7 James L. (Dusty) Rhodes, NY NL, first 4 times at bat, 1954

Most base hits, total series
71 Lawrence P. (Yogi) Berra, NY AL, 1947, 49–53, 55–58, 60–63

Most home runs, total series
18 Mickey C. Mantle, NY AL, 1952 (2), 53 (2), 55, 56 (3), 57, 58 (2), 60 (3), 63, 64 (3)

Most home runs, one series
5 Reginald (Reggie) M. Jackson, NY AL, 1977

Most home runs, game
3 George H. (Babe) Ruth, NY AL, Oct 6, 1926; Oct 9, 1928
Reginald (Reggie) M. Jackson, NY AL, Oct 18, 1977

Pitching in most series
11 Edward C. (Whitey) Ford, NY AL, 1950, 53, 55–58, 60–64

Most victories, total series
10 Edward C. (Whitey) Ford, NY AL, 1950 (1), 55 (2), 56

(1), 57 (1), 60 (2), 61 (2), 62 (1)

Most games won, one series
3 games in 5-game series
   Christy Mathewson, NY NL, 1905
   J. W. Coombs, Phil AL, 1910
Many others won 3 games in series of more games.

Most victories, no defeats
6 Vernon L. (Lefty) Gomez, NY AL, 1932 (1), 36 (2), 37 (2), 38 (1)

Most shutout games, total series
4 Christy Mathewson, NY NL, 1905 (3), 1913

Most shutout games, one series
3 Christy Mathewson, NY NL, 1905

Most strikeouts, one pitcher, total series
94 Edward C. (Whitey) Ford, NY AL, 1950, 53, 55–58, 60–64

Most strikeouts, one series
23 in 4 games
   Sanford (Sandy) Koufax, LA NL, 1963
18 in 5 games
   Christy Mathewson, NY NL, 1905
20 in 6 games
   C. A. (Chief) Bender, Phil AL, 1911
35 in 7 games
   Robert Gibson, St L NL, 1968
28 in 8 games
   W. H. Dinneen, Bos AL, 1903

Most strikeouts, one pitcher, game
17 Robert Gibson, St L NL, Oct 2, 1968

Most runs batted in, game
6 Robert C. Richardson, NY AL, (4) 1st inn, (2) 4th inn, Oct 8, 1960

Most Series Won
22 New York AL, 1923, 1927, 1928, 1932, 1936–39, 1941, 1943, 1947, 1949–53, 1956, 1958, 1961, 1962, 1977, 1978

Longest and Shortest Major League Games

The Brooklyn Dodgers and Boston Braves played to a 1–1 tie after 26 innings on May 1, 1920.

The NY Giants needed only 51 min to beat the Philadelphia Phillies, 6–1, in 9 innings on Sept 28, 1919. (A minor league game, Atlanta vs Mobile in the Southern Association on Sept 19, 1910, took only 32 min, it is claimed.)

The Chicago White Sox played the longest ball game in elapsed time—8 hours 6 min—before beating the Milwaukee Brewers, 7–6, in the 25th inning on May 9, 1984 in Chicago. The game was ended with a homer by Harold Baines, making Tom Seaver the winning pitcher for pitching the last inning. The game took 2 days, actually. It started on Tuesday night and was still tied at 3–3 when the 1 A.M. curfew caused suspension until Wednesday night.

Most Strikeouts, Career

Nolan Ryan of the Houston Astros pitched his 4,000th strikeout on July 11, 1985 against the NY Mets, his former team. By the season's end

All Runs Unearned

The Mets scored 16 runs against the Houston Astros on July 27, 1985, winning 16–4, with all the Met runs unearned. Houston made only 5 errors in the game.

his total had risen to 4,083. No other pitcher in the history of baseball has achieved such a record. Ryan was the first to eclipse Walter Johnson's (Wash AL) record of 3,508 which he set between 1907 and 1927 and which stood for 55 years until April 27, 1983.

Dwight Gooden (b Nov 16, 1964) of the Mets in the 1984 All-Star Game in San Francisco struck out 6 consecutive AL batters.

Gooden, in 1985, became the youngest pitcher to win the coveted Cy Young Award. He won it by unanimous vote of the 24 sports writers who make the selection.

Managers

Connie Mack (1892–1956) managed in the major leagues for 53 seasons—3 with Pittsburgh (NL), 1894–96, and 50 with the Philadelphia Athletics (AL), the team he owned, 1901–50. He amassed a record 3,776 regular-season victories (952 victories ahead of John McGraw). Eddie Stanky managed the Texas Rangers (AL) for one day (June 23, 1977) before deciding he did not want the job—even though his team beat Minnesota, 10–8. It is believed to be the shortest term for anyone who signed a managerial contract (that is, excluding interim managers).

Charles D. "Casey" Stengel (1890–1975) set records by managing the NY Yankees (AL) in 10 World Series and winning 7 of them, including 5 in a row (1949–53).

Fly Ball Stays Up

When the architects planned the Metrodome in Minneapolis they didn't know they had to contend with Dave Kingman, the slugger who has played in the American and National Leagues, who has been known previously for his many home runs and many strikeouts. Now Kingman has entered the *Guinness Book* with a record for a fly ball he hit that went straight up and didn't come down. It happened when he came up to bat for the Oakland Athletics against the Minnesota Twins on the night of May 4, 1984.

The ball penetrated the netting of the fabric ceiling of the dome 180 feet up and rolled around. When it didn't drop down for an infielder to catch it, the umpires didn't know what to call it. It wasn't in the rule book, of course. Was Kingman out, on the supposition that the fly ball would have been caught? They decided that the ball park was at fault and ruled it a "ground rule double." P.S. The A's lost the game anyway 3–1. P.S. When the groundskeeper got the ball down, it was sent to the Baseball Hall of Fame in Cooperstown, NY.

Tale of Two Cities Record

Joel Youngblood (b Aug 28, 1951) started a day game at Wrigley Field in Chicago on Aug 4, 1982, as a NY Met, hit a single in the 3rd inning, left the game when he received word that he had been traded to the Montreal Expos, and immediately made plane reservations to Philadelphia where the Expos were playing a night game. He had dinner on the plane, took a taxi from the airport, arrived at the field in the 3rd inning, was substituted for the Expos' right fielder in the 6th inning, and got a single in his one time at bat. His record: playing (and getting a hit) for two different teams in two different cities in the same day. Other major leaguers have played for two teams in one day, but in only one city as they were swapped between games of a doubleheader.

Longest Throw

The longest throw of a 5-5¼-oz (regulation) baseball is 445 ft 10 in by Glen Gorbous (b Canada) Aug 1, 1957. Mildred "Babe" Didrikson (later Mrs George Zaharias) (1914–56) threw a ball 296 ft at Jersey City, NJ, July 25, 1931.

Ball Drop from a Dirigible

Joe Sprinz, later catcher for the Cleveland Indians, in 1939 was playing for the Seals of the Pacific Coast League, when Lefty O'Doul was his manager. The San Francisco World's Fair was drawing crowds to Treasure Island in the Bay when someone dreamed up the stunt of dropping baseballs from a dirigible from 1,200 ft up for the Seals' players to try to catch. Sprinz was the only one who had dared to try.

"I had to shade my eyes, I saw the ball all the way, but it looked the size of an aspirin tablet," he said later. "The ball hit me in the mouth, my lips were lacerated very badly, 12 cracks in my upper jaw, lost 5 teeth, was knocked out." And he dropped the ball.

Rained-Out Game in Covered Stadium

The first time in baseball history a game in a covered stadium was called because of rain was on June 16, 1976, in Houston. Flooding around the Astrodome prevented anyone getting into the stadium and the game between Houston and Pittsburgh was called.

Sadaharu Oh played for 22 years in the Japanese majors after gaining fame as a schoolboy star, starting out as a lefty pitcher (like Babe Ruth), and winding up as a first baseman to keep his bat in the lineup daily. With a strange one-legged stance, he would step into the ball and gain impetus by swinging his bat like a Samurai sword, a discipline he learned from a master of the martial arts. He reveals in his autobiography (Times Books, 1984) that he also practiced Zen for mental strength. He played with and against many US ball players in Japanese leagues, and would have been a star in the US, in the opinion of 30 American players who are quoted in the book's appendix.

BASKETBALL

Origins

Ollamalitzli was a 16th century Aztec precursor of basketball played in Mexico. If the solid rubber ball was put through a fixed stone ring placed high on one side of the stadium, the player was entitled to the clothing of all the spectators. The captain of the losing team often lost his head (by execution). Another game played much earlier, in the 10th century BC by the Olmecs in Mexico, called *Pok-ta-Pok*, also resembled basketball in its concept of a ring through which a round object was passed.

Modern basketball was devised by the Canadian-born Dr James Naismith (1861–1939) at the Training School of the International YMCA College at Springfield, Mass, in Dec 1891. The first game played under modified rules was on Jan 20, 1892. The first public contest was on March 11, 1892.

The International Amateur Basketball Federation (FIBA) was founded in 1932.

Rule Change

In the 1940's coaches devised a new tactic, "freezing the ball," in order to maintain a leading score. It consisted of dribbling the ball and avoiding shooting it at the basket in order to maintain possession. In a short time this strategy became part of the entire game resulting in slow play and low scores. The lowest ever was when the Fort Wayne Pistons beat the Minneapolis Lakers 19–18, Nov 22, 1950. As attendance dropped as a result of boring play, Danny Biasone, a team owner, conceived of the "24-second rule" which requires a team to make a try at a basket within 24 seconds of gaining possession of the ball or turn possession over to the opposing team. In 1954, the NBA adopted the rule and scores increased dramatically—as did attendance. In international amateur play the 30-second rule is enforced. In college play the rule is 45 seconds.

Most Accurate Shooting

The greatest goal-shooting demonstration was made by a professional, Ted St. Martin, now of Jacksonville, Fla, who, on June 25, 1977, scored 2,036 consecutive free throws.

In a 24-hour period, May 31–June 1, 1975, Fred L. Newman of San Jose, Calif, scored 12,874 baskets out of 13,116 attempts (98.15%). Newman has also made 88 consecutive free throws while blindfolded at the Central YMCA, San Jose, Calif, Feb 5, 1978. On May 17, 1985 he made 322 free throws out of 351 attempts in 10 min, using two balls and two retrievers.

In 24 hours, Jeff Liles scored more free throws 15,138 out of 17,862 taken (but with 84.75% accuracy) at Lakeland Christian School, Lakeland, Fla, Apr 11–12, 1986.

The longest reported string of consecutive free throws made at any level of organized game competition is 126 by Daryl Moreau over 2 seasons (Jan 17, 1978–Jan 9, 1979) of high school play for De La Salle in New Orleans, La. The best reported one-game free throw performance was by Chris McMullin who made all 29 of his foul shots for Dixie College (St. George, Utah) in the NJCAA National Finals on March 16, 1982.

Greatest Attendances

The Harlem Globetrotters played an exhibition to 75,000 in the Olympic Stadium, West Berlin, Germany, in 1951. The largest indoor basketball attendance was 67,596, including 64,682 tickets sold at the box office, for the Indiana Olympic Basketball Tribute at the Hoosier Dome, Indianapolis on July 9, 1984. They saw victories by the US men's and women's Olympic teams over all-star opposition. The record for a women's college game is 22,157 in Iowa City between Univ of Iowa and Ohio State Univ, on Feb 3, 1985. The NBA record is 44,180 on Feb 15, 1986 in Pontiac, Mich, with the Philadelphia 76ers vs Detroit Pistons.

Marathon

The longest game is 102 hours by two teams of five from the Sigma Nu fraternity at Indiana Univ of Pennsylvania, Indiana, Penn, April 13–17, 1983.

Tallest Players

The tallest player of all time is reputed to be Suleiman Ali Nashnush (b 1943) who played for the Libyan team in 1962 when he measured 8 ft tall. Aleksandr Sizonenko of the USSR national team is 7 ft 10 in tall. The tallest woman player is Iuliana Semenova (USSR) who played in the 1976 Olympics and is reputed to stand 7 ft 2 in tall and weigh 281 lb.

OLYMPIC CROWD (above): At the Hoosier Dome in Indianapolis 67,596 people gathered on July 9, 1984 to witness the Olympic tryouts in which the Olympic choices beat all-star opposition.

FOOLING AROUND draws the biggest crowds, Meadowlark Lemon and the Harlem Globetrotters found out many years ago.

NBA REGULAR SEASON RECORDS
(Including 1985–86)

The National Basketball Association's Championship series was established in 1947. Prior to 1949, when it joined with the National Basketball League, the professional circuit was known as the Basketball Association of America.

SERVICE

Most Games, Lifetime
1,328 Kareem Abdul-Jabbar, Mil 1970–75, LA Lakers 1976–86

Most Games, Consecutive, Lifetime
906 Randy Smith, Buf-SD-Cleve-NY 1972–83

Most Complete Games, Season
79 Wilt Chamberlain, Phil 1962

Most Minutes, Lifetime
51,002 Kareem Abdul-Jabbar, Mil 1970–75, LA Lakers 1976–86

Most Minutes, Season
3,882 Wilt Chamberlain, Phil 1962

SCORING

Most Seasons Leading League
7 Wilt Chamberlain, Phil 1960–62; SF 1963–64; SF-Phil 1965; Phil 1966

Most Points, Lifetime
35,108 Kareem Abdul-Jabbar, Mil 1970–75, LA Lakers 1976–86

Most Points, Season
4,029 Wilt Chamberlain, Phil 1962

Most Points, Game
100 Wilt Chamberlain, Phil vs NY, Mar 2, 1962

Most Points, Half
59 Wilt Chamberlain, Phil vs NY, Mar 2, 1962

NBA Championships

The most National Basketball Association titles have been won by the Boston Celtics with 16 championships from 1957 to 1986. The Celtics also hold the record for consecutive championships with 8 (1959–66).

Most Points, Quarter
33 George Gervin, SA vs NO, Apr 9, 1978

Most Points, Overtime Period
14 Butch Carter, Ind vs Bos, March 20, 1984

Highest Scoring Average, Lifetime (400+ games)
30.1 Wilt Chamberlain, Phil-SF-LA 1960–73

Highest Scoring Average, Season
50.4 Wilt Chamberlain, Phil 1962

Field Goals Made

Most Field Goals, Lifetime
14,404 Kareem Abdul-Jabbar, Mil 1970–75; LA Lakers 1976–86

Most Field Goals, Season
1,597 Wilt Chamberlain, Phil 1962

Most Field Goals, Game
36 Wilt Chamberlain, Phil vs NY, Mar 2, 1962

Most Field Goals, Half
22 Wilt Chamberlain, Phil vs NY, Mar 2, 1962

Most Field Goals, Quarter
13 David Thompson, Den vs Det, Apr 9, 1978

Most 3-Point Field Goals, Game
   8   Rick Barry, Hou vs Utah,
       Feb 9, 1980
       John Roche, Den vs Sea,
       Jan 9, 1982

Most 3-Point Field Goals, Season
   92   Darrell Griffith, Utah 1985

Field Goal Percentage

Most Seasons Leading League
   9   Wilt Chamberlain, Phil
       1961; SF 1963; SF-Phil
       1965; Phil 1966–68; LA
       1969, 72–73

Highest Percentage, Lifetime
   .600   Artis Gilmore, Chi
          1977–82; SA 1983–86

Highest Percentage, Season
   .727   Wilt Chamberlain, LA 1973

Free Throws Made

Most Free Throws Made, Lifetime
7,694   Oscar Robertson, Cin-Mil
        1961–74

Most Free Throws Made, Season
   840   Jerry West, LA 1966

Most Free Throws Made, Consecutive, Season
   78   Calvin Murphy, Hou Dec
        27, 1980–Feb 28, 1981

Most Free Throws Made, Game
   28   Wilt Chamberlain, Phil vs
        NY, Mar 2, 1962
        Adrian Dentley, Utah vs
        Hou, Jan 5, 1984

Most Free Throws Made (No Misses), Game
   19   Bob Pettit, St L vs Bos, Nov
        22, 1961
        Bill Cartwright, NY vs KC,
        Nov 17, 1981

Most Free Throws Made, Half
   19   Oscar Robertson, Cin vs
        Balt, Dec 27, 1964

Most Free Throws Made, Quarter
   14   Rick Barry, SF vs NY, Dec
        6, 1966
        Pete Maravich, At vs Buff,
        Nov 28, 1973

Free Throw Percentage

Most Seasons Leading League
   7   Bill Sharman, Bos 1953–57,
       59, 61

Highest Percentage, Lifetime
   .900   Rick Barry, SF-GS-Hou
          1966–67, 73–80

Highest Percentage, Season
   .958   Calvin Murphy, Hou 1981

REBOUNDS

Most Seasons Leading League
   11   Wilt Chamberlain, Phil
        1960–62; SF 1963; Phil
        1966–68; LA 1969, 71–73

Most Rebounds, Lifetime
23,924   Wilt Chamberlain, Phil-
         SF-LA 1960–73

Most Rebounds, Season
2,149   Wilt Chamberlain, Phil
        1961

Most Rebounds, Game
   55   Wilt Chamberlain, Phil vs
        Bos, Nov 24, 1960

Most Rebounds, Half
   32   Bill Russell, Bos vs Phil,
        Nov 16, 1957

Most Rebounds, Quarter
   18   Nate Thurmond, SF vs
        Balt, Feb 28, 1965

Highest Average (per game), Lifetime
   22.9   Wilt Chamberlain, Phil-
          SF-LA 1960–73

Highest Average (per game), Season
   27.2   Wilt Chamberlain, Phil
          1961

ASSISTS

Most Seasons Leading League
   8   Bob Cousy, Bos 1953–60

Most Assists, Lifetime
9,887   Oscar Robertson, Cin-Mil
        1961–74

Most Assists, Season
1,123   Isiah Thomas, Det 1985

Most Assists, Game
   29   Kevin Porter, NJ vs Hou,
        Feb 24, 1978

MAKING A POINT: Kareem Abdul-Jabbar (left) (Mil-LA) compiled 35,108 points with 14,484 field goals, 1970–86. Pearl Moore (below) (#12) scored a record 4,061 during her college career (1975–79) at Francis Marion College (SC), 16 more than the men's college record held by Travis Grant of Kentucky State.

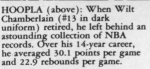

HOOPLA (above): When Wilt Chamberlain (#13 in dark uniform) retired, he left behind an astounding collection of NBA records. Over his 14-year career, he averaged 30.1 points per game and 22.9 rebounds per game.

BULL'S EYE (right): Artis Gilmore of the Chicago Bulls leads the NBA with a .600 field goal percentage. The 7-ft-2-in center has raised his percentage by 23 points in 5 years.

Most Assists, Half
    19 Bob Cousy, Bos vs Minn,
        Feb 27, 1959

Highest Average (per game), Lifetime
    10.68 Earvin (Magic) Johnson,
           LA Lakers 1979–86

Highest Average (per game), Season
    13.86 Isiah Thomas, Detroit
           1985

PERSONAL FOULS

Most Personal Fouls, Lifetime
    4,193 Elvin Hayes, SD-Hou-
           Balt/Wash-Hou 1969–84

Most Personal Fouls, Season
    386 Darryl Dawkins, NJ 1984

Most Personal Fouls, Game
    8 Don Otten, TC vs Sheb,
       Nov 24, 1949

STEALS

Most Steals, Season
    301 Alvin Robertson, SA, 1986

Highest Steals Average, Season, per game
    3.67 Alvin Robertson, SA, 1986

Most Steals, Game
    11 Larry Kenon, SA vs KC,
        Dec 26, 1976

DISQUALIFICATIONS
(Fouling Out of Game)

Most Disqualifications, Lifetime
    127 Vern Mikkelsen, Minn,
         1950–59

Most Disqualifications, Season
    26 Don Meineke, Ft W 1953

Most Games, No Disqualifications, Lifetime
    1,045 Wilt Chamberlain, Phil-
           SF-LA 1960–73 (Entire
           Career)

NBA PLAYOFF RECORDS
(Through 1986)

Most games played, lifetime
    180 Kareem Abdul-Jabbar,
         Mil-LA Lakers, 15 years

Most points scored, lifetime
    4,912 Kareem Abdul-Jabbar,
           Mil-LA Lakers, 15 years

Most points, game
    63 Michael Jordan, Chi vs Bos,
        Apr 20, 1986 (2 overtimes)
    61 Elgin Baylor, LA Lakers vs
        Bos, Apr 14, 1962

Best scoring average, lifetime
    29.1 Jerry West, LA Lakers, 13
          years

Most field goals, game
    24 Wilt Chamberlain, Phil vs
        Syr, March 14, 1960
        John Havlicek, Bos vs Atl,
        Apr 1, 1973

Most free throws, lifetime
    1,213 Jerry West, LA Lakers, 13
           years

Most free throws, game
    30 Bob Cousy, Bos vs Syr,
        March 21, 1953 (4 overtimes)
    21 Oscar Robertson, Cin vs
        Bos, Apr 10, 1963

Most rebounds, lifetime
    4,104 Bill Russell, Bos, 13 years

Most rebounds, game
    41 Wilt Chamberlain, Phil vs
        Bos, Apr 5, 1967

Most assists, lifetime
    1,278 Earvin (Magic) Johnson, LA
           Lakers, 7 years

Most assists, game
    24 Earvin (Magic) Johnson,
        LA Lakers vs Phoenix,
        May 15, 1984

Olympic Champions

The US won all 7 Olympic titles from the time the sport was introduced to the Games in 1936 until 1972, without losing a single contest. In 1972, in Munich, the US run of 63 consecutive victories was broken when its team lost, 51–50, to the USSR in a much-disputed final game. The US regained the Olympic title in Montreal in 1976, again without losing a game. In 1980 Yugoslavia took the Olympic gold, but the US came back once more in 1984 for a record 9th title.

In women's Olympics, the USSR won in 1976 and 1980, but the US took the gold in 1984.

Individual Scoring

Marie Boyd (now Eichler) scored 156 points in a girls' high school basketball game for Central HS, Lonaconing, Md, in a 163–3 victory over Ursuline Academy, on Feb 25, 1924. The boys' high school record is 135 points by Danny Heater of Burnsville, W Va, on Jan 26, 1960.

In college play, Clarence (Bevo) Francis of Rio Grande College, Ohio, scored 113 points against Hillsdale on Feb 2, 1954. One year earlier, Francis scored 116 points in a game, but the record was disallowed because the competition was with a two-year school. In women's college basketball, Annette Kennedy of State Univ at Purchase, NY, scored 70 points vs Pratt Institute on Jan 22, 1984, with 34 field goals in 43 attempts.

Wilton Norman (Wilt) Chamberlain (b Aug 21, 1936) holds the professional record with 100 points for the Philadelphia Warriors vs NY Knicks, scored in one game on Mar 2, 1962. During the same season, Wilt set the record for points in a season (4,029).

Kareem Abdul-Jabbar (formerly Lewis Ferdinand Alcindor) (b Apr 16, 1947) has scored a professional career record of 35,108 points from 1969 through the 1986 season for the Milwaukee Bucks and Los Angeles Lakers. Wilt Chamberlain holds the record average of 30.1 points per game for his total of 31,419.

Pearl Moore of Francis Marion College, Florence, SC, scored a record 4,061 points during her college career, 1975–79. The men's college career scoring record is 4,045 points by Travis Grant for Kentucky State, 1969–72.

Mats Wermelin (Sweden), 13, scored all 272 points in a 272–0 win in a regional boys' tournament in Stockholm, Sweden, on Feb 5, 1974.

Longest Field Goal

The longest *measured* field goal in a college game was made from a distance of 89 ft 10 in by Bruce Morris for Marshall Univ vs Appalachian St, Feb 7, 1985. In an AAU game at Pacific Lutheran University on Jan 16, 1970, Steve Myers sank a shot while standing out of bounds at the other end of the court. Though the basket was illegal, the officials gave in to crowd sentiment and allowed the points to count. The distance is claimed to be 92 ft 3½ in from measurements made 10 years later. The longest for a woman is one of 72 ft 6 in by Annette Alverson of Ohio Northern Univ vs Northern Kentucky, Jan 11, 1985.

Team Scoring

The highest game total in the NBA is 370 points in the Detroit Pistons' victory over the Denver Nuggets 186–184 in 1983. The highest in college play is 282, Univ of Nevada–Las Vegas vs Utah State, 1985. Nevada won, 142–140.

World Champions

The USSR has won most titles at both the Men's World Championships (inst. 1950) with three (1967, 1974 and 1982) and Women's (inst. 1953) with six (1959, 1964, 1967, 1971, 1975 and 1983).

Youngest and Oldest

Bill Willoughby (b May 20, 1957) made his NBA debut for the Atlanta Hawks on Oct 23, 1975, when he was 18 years 5 months 3 days old. The oldest NBA player was Bob Cousy (b Aug 9, 1928), who was 41 years 6 months 2 days old when he appeared in the last of seven games he played for the team he was coaching (Cincinnati Royals) during 1969–70.

BIATHLON   See Skiing

BOWLING

Origins

Bowling can be traced to articles found in the tomb of an Egyptian child of 5200 BC where there were nine pieces of stone to be set up as pins at which a stone "ball" was rolled. The ball first had to roll through an archway made of three pieces of marble. In the Italian Alps about 2,000 years ago, the underhand tossing of stones at an object is believed the beginnings of *bocci,* a game still widely played in Italy and similar to bowling. Martin Luther is credited with the statement that nine was the ideal number of pins. In the British Isles, lawn bowls was preferred to bowling at pins. In the 16th century, bowling at pins was the national sport in Scotland. Early British settlers probably brought lawn bowls to the US and set up what is known as Bowling Green at the tip of Manhattan Island in NY but perhaps the Dutch under Henry Hudson were the ones to be credited.

In 1841, the Connecticut state legislature prohibited the game and other states followed. Eventually, a tenth pin was added to what had all along been a 9-pin game, to evade the ban.

Organizations

The American Bowling Congress (ABC), established in NY on Sept 9, 1895, was the first body to standardize rules, and the organization now comprises 3,656,928 men who bowl in leagues and tournaments. The Women's International Bowling Congress (WIBC), founded 1916, has a membership of 3,713,751. The Professional Bowlers Association (PBA), formed in 1958, comprises more than 2,800 of the world's best male bowlers. The Ladies Professional Bowlers Tour has 170 members.

Lanes

In the US there were 8,629 bowling establishments with 159,394 lanes in 1985 and about 68 million bowlers.

The world's largest bowling center (now closed) was the Tokyo World Lanes Center, Japan, with 252 lanes. Currently the largest center is Fukuyana Bowl, Osaka, Japan, which has 144 lanes.

Marathons

Donnie Moore (b 1960), a US Navy petty officer stationed at the Jacksonville, Fla Naval Air Station, bowled 2,028 games in 217 hours, 55 min, July 15–24, 1985, for an average of 9.3 games per hour. He was under medical surveillance, stopping for blood pressure and vital sign checks regularly and on July 22 stopped for 24½ hours for hospital rest and oxygen intake per doctor's orders.

Dorothy Meinecke of Detroit, Mich, bowled 130 games in 16 hours 30 min, non-stop, Jan 24, 1926 for an average of 7.9 games per hour.

ABC LEAGUE RECORDS

Highest Scores

The highest individual score for three games is 886 by Albert "Allie" Brandt of Lockport, NY, on Oct 25, 1939. Glenn Allison (b 1930) rolled a perfect 900 in a 3-game series in league play on July 1, 1982, at La Habra Bowl, LA, Calif, but the ABC refused to recognize the record when an ABC inspector examined the lanes and determined they had been illegally oiled (for other 900 series see *Most Perfect Scores,* below). Highest team score is 3,858 by Budweisers of St Louis on March 12, 1958.

The highest season average attained in sanctioned competition is 242 by John Ragard of Susquehanna, Pa, for 66 games in 1981–82.

In a 2-man ABC sanctioned game, the record is 599 by Toby Contreras (299) and Tim McClure (300), both of Kansas City, Mo, on June 9, 1982. The 2-man team series record is 1,635 by the same team.

Consecutive Strikes

The record for consecutive strikes in sanctioned match play is 33 by John Pezzin (b 1930) at Toledo, Ohio, on March 4, 1976.

Most Perfect Scores

The highest number of sanctioned 300 games is 27 (through 1985) by Elvin Mesger of Sullivan, Mo. The maximum 900 for a three-game series has been recorded five times in unsanctioned games—by Leon Bentley at Lorain, Ohio, on March 26, 1931; by Joe Sargent at Rochester, NY, in 1934; by Jim Margie in Philadelphia, on Feb 4, 1937; by Bob Brown at Roseville Bowl, Calif, on Apr 12, 1980; and by Glenn Allison (see above) at Whittier, Calif, on July 1, 1982.

ABC TOURNAMENT RECORDS

Highest Individual

Highest three-game series in singles is 801 by Mickey Higham of Kansas City, Mo, in 1977. Best three-game total in any ABC event is 833 by Fran Bax of Niagara Falls, NY, in team in 1983. Jim Godman of Lorain,

Ohio, holds the record for a nine-game All-Events total with 2,184 (731–749–704) set in Indianapolis, Ind, in 1974. ABC Hall of Famers Fred Bujack of Detroit, Bill Lillard of Houston, and Nelson Burton Jr of St Louis, have won the most championships with 8 each. Bujack shared in 3-team and 4-team All-Events titles between 1949 and 1955, and also won the individual All-Events title in 1955. Lillard bowled on Regular and team All-Events champions in 1955 and 1956, the Classic team champions in 1962 and 1971, and won regular doubles and All-Events titles in 1956. Burton shared in 3 Classic team titles, 2 Classic doubles titles and has won Classic singles twice and Classic All-Events.

Highest Doubles

The ABC national tournament record of 558 was set in 1976 by Les Zikes of Chicago and Tommy Hudson of Akron, Ohio. The record score in a doubles series is 1,453, set in 1952 by John Klares (755) and Steve Nagy (698) of Cleveland.

Perfect Scores

Les Schissler of Denver scored 300 in the Classic team event in 1967, and Ray Williams of Detroit scored 300 in Regular team play in 1974. In all, there have been only forty-two 300 games in the ABC tournament through 1985. There have been 23 perfect games in singles, 15 in doubles, and four in team play.

Best Finishes in One Tournament

Les Schissler of Denver won the singles, All-Events, and was on the winning team in 1966 to tie Ed Lubanski of Detroit and Bill Lillard of Houston as the only men to win three ABC crowns in one year. The best four finishes in one ABC tournament were third in singles, second in doubles, third in team and first in All-Events by Bob Strampe, Detroit, in 1967, and first in singles, third in team and doubles and second in All-Events by Paul Kulbaga, Cleveland, in 1960.

Strikes and Spares in a Row

In the greatest finish to win an ABC title, Ed Shay set a record of 12 strikes in a row in 1958, when he scored a perfect game for a total of 733 in singles. Most strikes in a row is 20 by Lou Viet of Milwaukee in 1977.

The most spares in a row is 23, a record set by Lt Hazen Sweet of Battle Creek, Mich, in 1950.

Most Tournament Appearances

Bill Doehrman of Fort Wayne, Ind, competed in 71 consecutive ABC tournaments, beginning in 1908. (No tournaments were held 1943–45.)

Attendance

Largest spectator attendance on one day for an ABC Tournament was 5,257 in Milwaukee in 1952. The total attendance record was set at Reno, Nev, in 1977 with 174,953 in 89 days.

Youngest and Oldest Winners

The youngest champion was Ronnie Knapp of New London, Ohio, who was a member of the 1963 Booster team champions when he was 16 years old. The oldest champion was Joe Detloff of Chicago, Ill, who, at the age of 72, was a winner in the 1965 Booster team event. The oldest doubles team in ABC competition totaled 165 years in 1955: Jerry Ameling (83) and Joseph Lehnbeutter (82), both from St Louis. The youngest bowler to score 300 is said to be John Jaszkowski of S Milwaukee, Wis, who performed this feat at age 11, on Mar 13, 1982.

WIBC RECORDS

Highest Scores

Patty Ann of New Ulm, Minn, had a record 232 average in league play in the 1983–84 season, and a record 5-year composite average of 225.6 through 1985. She also holds the women's record for the highest total in a three-game series, 859.

The highest 5-woman team score for a 3-game series is 3,379 by Freeway Washer of Cleveland in 1960. The highest game score by a 5-woman team is 1,210 by Sheraton Inn, Scranton, Pa in 1981–82.

Championship Tournaments

The highest score for a 3-game series in the annual WIBC Championship Tournament is 737 by D. D. Jacobson in the 1972 singles competition. The record for one game is 300 (the only perfect game) by Lori Gensch in the 1979 doubles event. The WIBC sanctioned 153,435 leagues in the 1985 season.

Mary Covell of Chicago participated in her 54th WIBC tournament in 1985, tying the late Myrtle Schulte, St Louis, for most appearances. The

MOST PERFECT SCORES by a woman: In WIBC competition, Jeanne Maiden of Solon, Ohio rolled 300 nine times.

oldest participant was Ethel Brunnick (b Aug 30, 1887) of Santa Monica, Calif, at age 97 in 1985. Mary Ann Keiper of St Louis was only 5 years old when she participated in the 1952 tournament. The youngest champion was Leila Wagner (b July 12, 1960) of Seattle, Wash, who was 18 when she was a member of the championship 5-woman team in 1979.

Millie Martorella is the only one to win three, 1967, 1970, and 1971.

The highest lifetime average is 199.14 by Dorothy Fothergill of Lincoln, RI, who has bowled for 10 years but is now inactive.

The 1983 tournament in Las Vegas drew 14,430 teams attracted by a record $1,627,815 in prize money.

Consecutive Strikes, Spares and Splits

The record for most consecutive strikes is 26 by Robin Romeo of Beverly Hills, Calif. Joan Taylor of Syracuse, NY, made 27 consecutive spares. Shirley Tophigh of Las Vegas, Nev, holds the unenviable record of rolling 14 consecutive splits.

Perfect Games

The most 300 games rolled in a career is 9 by Jeanne Maiden of Solon, Ohio. The oldest woman to bowl a perfect game was Helen Duval of Berkeley, Calif, at age 66 in 1982. Of all the women who rolled a perfect game, the one with the lowest average was Diane Ponza of Santa Cruz, Calif, who had a 112 average in the 1977–78 season.

PBA RECORDS

Perfect Games

A total of 119 perfect (300-pin) games were bowled in PBA tournaments in 1979. Dick Weber rolled 3 perfect games in one tournament (Houston) in 1965, as did Billy Hardwick of Louisville, Ky (in the Japan Gold Cup competition) in 1968, Roy Buckley of Columbus, Ohio (at

FRAME AND FORTUNE: Earl Anthony of Dublin, Calif, is the PBA champion with a lifetime total of 42 titles and earnings of more than $1¼ million.

Chagrin Falls, Ohio) in 1971, John Wilcox (at Detroit), Norm Meyers of St Louis (at Peoria, Ill) in 1979, and Shawn Christensen of Denver (at Denver) in 1984.

Don Johnson of Las Vegas, Nev, bowled at least one perfect game in 11 consecutive seasons (1965–75). Guppy Troup, of Savannah, Ga, rolled 6 perfect games on the 1979 tour.

Most Titles

Earl Anthony of Dublin, Calif, has won a lifetime total of 41 PBA titles through Oct 1986. The record number of titles won in one PBA season is 8, by Mark Roth of North Arlington, NJ, in 1978.

Consecutive Titles

Only three bowlers have ever won three consecutive professional tournaments—Dick Weber in 1961, Johnny Petraglia in 1971, and Mark Roth in 1977.

Highest Earnings

The greatest lifetime earnings on the Professional Bowlers Association circuit have been won by Earl Anthony who has taken home $1,257,021 to Oct 15, 1984. Anthony also holds the season earnings record with $164,735 in 1981.

Highest Score in 24 Hours

A team of 6 from Portsmouth Polytechnic scored 37,934 in 24 hours at AMF Humber Bowling Center, Portsmouth, Eng, Mar 1–2, 1986.

Television Bowling

Nelson Burton Jr, St Louis, rolled the best series, 1,050, for four games (278-279-257-236) at Dick Weber Lanes in Florissant, Mo, Feb 11, 1984.

BOXING

Boxing with gloves was depicted on a fresco from the Isle of Thera, Greece, which has been dated to 1520 BC. The earliest prize-fighting code of rules was formulated in England, Aug 16, 1743, by the champion pugilist Jack Broughton (1704–89), who reigned from 1729 to 1750. Boxing, which had in 1867 come under the Queensberry Rules, formulated for John Sholto Douglas, 9th Marquess of Queensberry, was not established as a legal sport in Britain until after a ruling of Mr Justice Grantham following the death of Billy Smith (Murray Livingstone) due to a fight on Apr 24, 1901, at Covent Garden, London.

There are two governing bodies, the World Boxing Association (formed as the National Boxing Association in the US in 1920) and the World Boxing Council (formed in 1963). At most weights separate champions are recognized by these two organizations.

Longest Fights

The longest recorded fight with gloves was between Andy Bowen of New Orleans and Jack Burke in New Orleans, Apr 6–7, 1893. The fight lasted 110 rounds (7 hours 19 min from 9:15 P.M. to 4:34 A.M.) but was

HEAVYWEIGHT CHAMPION in the making: Mike Tyson, unbeaten 220-lb, 20-year-old, knocked out 21 of his first 24 opponents, 1984–86, 14 of them in the first round. Here he is smashing a left hook to the chin.

declared no contest (later changed to a draw) when both men were unable to continue. The longest recorded bare knuckle fight was one of 6 hours 15 min between James Kelly and Jack Smith at Fiery Creek, Dalesford, Australia, Dec 3, 1855. The greatest recorded number of rounds is 276 in 4 hours 30 min, when Jack Jones beat Patsy Tunney in Cheshire, England, in 1825. The longest world title fight was in 1906 when Joe Gans (US) beat Battling Nelson (Den) when Nelson was disqualified in the 42nd round of a scheduled 45-round contest.

Shortest Fights

There is a distinction between the quickest knockout and the shortest fight. A knockout in 10½ sec (including a 10-sec count) occurred on Sept 23, 1946, when Al Couture struck Ralph Walton while the latter was adjusting his mouthpiece in his corner at Lewiston, Me. If the time was accurately taken it is clear that Couture must have been more than halfway across the ring from his own corner at the opening bell.

The shortest fight on record appears to be one in a Golden Gloves tournament in Minneapolis, Minn, Nov 4, 1947, when Mike Collins floored Pat Brownson with his first punch and the contest was stopped, without a count, 4 sec after the bell.

The shortest world title fight was the James J. Jeffries (1875–1953) vs Jack Finnegan heavyweight bout on Apr 6, 1900, won by Jeffries in 55 sec.

The shortest *professional* bout occurred Apr 3, 1936 when Al Carr (Alfred Tramantano) stopped Lew Massey in 7 sec with one punch in New Haven, Conn.

Longest Career

The heavyweight Jem Mace (GB) (1831–1910), known as "the Gypsy," had a career lasting 50 years from 1855 to 1905, when he put on an exhibition bout with Tug Wilson, but his career is not fully documented. Kid Azteca (b Louis Villanueva Parano, 1915, Mexico City) started boxing professionally in 1929 and has a published record that includes at least one bout per year, 1932–61.

Tallest Boxer

The tallest boxer to fight professionally was Gogea Mitu (b 1914) of Rumania in 1935. He was 7 ft 4 in and weighed 327 lb. John Rankin, who won a fight in New Orleans in Nov 1967, also claimed 7 ft 4 in.

WORLD HEAVYWEIGHT CHAMPIONS

Earliest Title Fight

The first world heavyweight title fight, with 3-oz gloves and 3-minute rounds, was between John L. Sullivan (1858–1918) and Dominick McCaffrey on Aug 29, 1885 in Cincinnati, O. It went 6 rounds and Sullivan won.

Longest and Shortest Reigns

The longest reign of any world heavyweight champion is 11 years 252 days by Joe Louis (b Joseph Louis Barrow, 1914–81), from June 22, 1937, when he knocked out James J. Braddock in the 8th round at Chicago until announcing his retirement on March 1, 1949. During his reign Louis made a record 25 defenses of his title. The shortest reign was by Greg Page (US) (b Oct 25, 1958) for 150 days, Dec 1984 to Apr 29, 1985. Ken Norton (US) (b Aug 6, 1945) was recognized by the WBC as champion for 83 days, Mar 18–June 9, 1978.

The longest-lived heavyweight champion was Jack Dempsey, who died May 31, 1983 aged 87 years 341 days.

Heavyweight Champions through the Years

1882 John L. Sullivan (US)
1892 James J. Corbett (US)
1897 Bob Fitzsimmons (GB)
1899 James J. Jeffries (US)
1905 Marvin Hart (US)
1906 Tommy Burns (Can)
1908 Jack Johnson (US)
1915 Jess Willard (US)
1919 Jack Dempsey (US)
1926 Gene Tunney (US)
1930 Max Schmeling (Ger)
1932 Jack Sharkey (US)
1933 Primo Carnera (Ita)
1934 Max Baer (US)
1935 James J. Braddock (US)
1937 Joe Louis (US)
1949 Ezzard Charles (US)
1951 Jersey Joe Walcott (US)
1952 Rocky Marciano (US)
1956 Floyd Patterson (US)

1959 Ingemar Johansson (Swe)
1960 Floyd Patterson (US)
1962 Sonny Liston (US)
1964 Cassius Clay/Muhammad Ali (US)
1965 Ernie Terrell (US)—WBA only till 1967
1968 Joe Frazier (US)—NY State
1968 Jimmy Ellis (US)—WBA
1970 Joe Frazier (US)—undisputed
1973 George Foreman (US)
1974 Muhammad Ali (US)
1978 Leon Spinks (US)
1978 Ken Norton (US)—WBC
1978 Muhammad Ali (US)—WBA
1978 Larry Holmes (US)—WBC, IBF from 1983
1979 John Tate (US)—WBA
1980 Mike Weaver (US)—WBA
1982 Mike Dokes (US)—WBA
1983 Gerry Coetzee (So Afr)—WBA
1984 Tim Witherspoon (US)—WBC
1984 Pinklon Thomas—WBC
1984 Greg Page—WBA
1985 Tony Tubbs (US) WBA
1985 Michael Spinks (US)—WBC, IBF
1986 Trevor Berbick (Canada) WBC
1986 Tim Witherspoon (US) WBA

WBC—World Boxing Council, headquartered in Mexico City. President: Jose Sulaiman, who has devoted himself to boxing for 20 years. A substantial portion of WBC's income has been spent furthering the sport, protecting the athletes and improving medical facilities. This is the most highly regarded organization.

WBA—World Boxing Association, headquartered in Panama City, Panama. President: Gilberto Mendoza.

IBF—International Boxing Federation, headquartered in NJ. President: Bob Lee.

These 3 bodies represent national federations of boxing commissions throughout the world, and have a variety of financial and political connections.

Oldest and Youngest

The oldest man to win the heavyweight crown was Jersey Joe Walcott (b Arnold Raymond Cream, Jan 31, 1914, at Merchantville, NJ), who knocked out Ezzard Charles on July 18, 1951, in Pittsburgh, when aged 37 years 5 months 18 days. Walcott was the oldest title holder at 38 years 7 months 23 days when he lost to Rocky Marciano on Sept 23, 1952. The youngest age at which the world heavyweight title has been won is 21 years 331 days by Floyd Patterson (b Waco, NC, Jan 4, 1935), who won the vacant title by beating Archie Moore in 5 rounds in Chicago on Nov 30, 1956.

Undefeated

Rocky Marciano (b Rocco Francis Marchegiano) (1923–69) is the only heavyweight champion to have been undefeated in his entire professional career (1947–1956). His record was 49 wins (43 by KO) and no losses or draws.

Most Recaptures

Muhammad Ali Haj (b Cassius Marcellus Clay, in Louisville, Ky, Jan 17, 1942) is the only man to regain the heavyweight title twice. Ali first won the title on Feb 25, 1964, defeating Sonny Liston. He defeated George Foreman on Oct 30, 1974, having been stripped of his title by the world boxing authorities on Apr 28, 1967. He lost his title to Leon Spinks on Feb 15, 1978, but regained it on Sept 15, 1978 by defeating Spinks in New Orleans.

Heaviest and Lightest

The heaviest world champion was Primo Carnera (Italy) (1906–67), the "Ambling Alp," who won the title from Jack Sharkey in 6 rounds in NYC, on June 29, 1933. He scaled 267 lb for this fight. He had the longest reach at 85½ in (finger tip to finger tip) and an expanded chest measurement of 53 in.

The lightest was Robert James Fitzsimmons (1863–1917), (b Helston, Cornwall, England) who, at a weight of 167 lb, won the title by knocking out James J. Corbett in 14 rounds at Carson City, Nev, March 17, 1897.

The greatest differential in a world title fight was 86 lb between Carnera (270 lb) and Tommy Loughran (184 lb) of the US, when the former won on points at Miami, Fla, March 1, 1934.

OLDEST HEAVYWEIGHT CHAMP: Joe Walcott, 37, knocks out Ezzard Charles, in a 1951 upset, to win the crown in Pittsburgh. (*AP London*)

Tallest and Shortest

The tallest world champion was Primo Carnera, who was measured at 6 ft 5.4 in by the Physical Education Director at the Hemingway Gymnasium of Harvard, although he was widely reported and believed in 1933 to be 6 ft 8½ in tall. Jess Willard (1881–1968), who won the title in 1915, was often described as being 6 ft 6¼ in tall, but was in fact 6 ft 5¼ in. The shortest was Tommy Burns (1881–1955) of Canada, world champion from Feb 23, 1906, to Dec 26, 1908, who stood 5 ft 7 in and weighed between 168 and 180 lb.

Knockout Percentage

George Foreman (b Jan 10, 1949) had the highest career knockout percentage of any heavyweight champion. In his 47 professional fights, Foreman KO'd 42 opponents, thus winning 89.36% of his bouts by knockout.

George Foreman is the only US champion in any weight class to have won, defended, and lost his crown all outside the US. To win his title he defeated Joe Frazier in Kingston, Jamaica, Jan 22, 1973. He defended it against Jose Roman in Tokyo, Japan, Sept 1, 1973, and against Ken Norton in Caracas, Venezuela, Mar 26, 1974. He lost it to Muhammad Ali in Kinshasa, Zaire, Oct 30, 1974. As world champion, this native of Marshall, Tex never fought in his own country.

WORLD CHAMPIONS (ANY WEIGHT)

Longest Reign

Joe Louis's heavyweight duration record of 11 years 252 days stands for all divisions.

Youngest and Oldest

The youngest at which any world championship has been won is 17 years 176 days by Wilfredo Benitez (b Sept 12, 1958) of Puerto Rico, who won the WBA light-welterweight title in San Juan, March 6, 1976.

The oldest world champion was Archie Moore (b Archibald Lee Wright, Collinsville, Ill, Dec 13, 1913 or 1916), who was recognized as a light-heavyweight champion up to Feb 10, 1962, when his title was removed. He was then between 45 and 48. Bob Fitzsimmons (1863–1917) had the longest career of any official world titleholder with over 31 years from 1883 to 1914. He had his last world title bout on Dec 20, 1905 at the age of 42 years 208 days.

Greatest "Tonnage"

The greatest "tonnage" in a world title fight was 488¾ lb when Primo Carnera (259½ lb) fought Paolino Uzcudun (229¼ lb) of Spain, in Rome, Italy, Oct 22, 1933.

The greatest "tonnage" recorded in any fight is 700 lb, when Claude "Humphrey" McBride of Okla at 340 lb knocked out Jimmy Black of Houston at 360 lb in the 3rd round at Oklahoma City, June 1, 1971.

Smallest Champions

The smallest man to win any world title has been Netranoi Vorsingh (b Apr 22, 1959) (Thailand), WBC light-flyweight champion from May to Sept 1978, at 4 ft 11 in tall. Jimmy Wilde (b Merthyr Tydfil, 1892, d 1969, UK), who held the flyweight title from 1916 to 1923, was reputed never to have fought above 108 lb.

Longest Title Fight

The longest world title fight (under Queensberry Rules) was between the lightweights Joe Gans (1874–1910), of the US, and Oscar "Battling" Nelson (1882–1954), the "Durable Dane," at Goldfield, Nev, Sept 3, 1906. It was terminated in the 42nd round when Gans was declared the winner on a foul.

Most Title Bouts

The record number of title bouts in a career is 37, of which 18 ended in

TITLE DEEDS: Joe Louis (left) kept the heavyweight title for over 11 years, the longest reign at any weight class. Known as "The Brown Bomber," Louis successfully defended his title a record 25 times. Louis' largest purse, earned in his 8th round KO of Billy Conn in 1946, was $625,916—a far cry from today's high-priced bouts. Ringside seats cost a then-record $100.

"no decision," by 3-time world welterweight champion Jack Britton (US) (1885–1962), from 1915 to 1922.

Most Titles Simultaneously

The only man to hold world titles at three weights simultaneously was Henry "Homicide Hank" Armstrong (b Dec 12, 1912) of the US, at featherweight, lightweight and welterweight from Aug to Dec 1938.

Most Knockdowns in Title Fights

Vic Toweel (South Africa) knocked down Danny O'Sullivan of London 14 times in 10 rounds in their world bantamweight fight at Johannesburg, Dec 2, 1950, before the latter retired.

Most Recaptures

The only boxer to win a world title five times at one weight is Sugar Ray Robinson (b Walker Smith, Jr, in Detroit, May 3, 1921) who beat Carmen Basilio (US) in the Chicago Stadium on March 25, 1958, to regain the world middleweight title for the fourth time. The other title wins were over Jake LaMotta (US) in Chicago on Feb 14, 1951; Randy Turpin (UK) in NYC on Sept 12, 1951; Carl "Bobo" Olson (US) in Chicago on Dec 9, 1955; and Gene Fullmer (US) in Chicago on May 1, 1957.

Amateur World Championships

Two boxers have won three world championships (instituted 1974): Teofilo Stevenson (Cuba), heavyweight 1974, 1978 and 1986, and Adolfo Horta (b Oct 3, 1957) (Cuba), bantam 1978, feather 1982 and lightweight 1986.

ALL FIGHTS

Highest Earnings in Career

The largest known fortune ever made in a fighting career (or any sports career) is an estimated $69 million (including exhibitions) amassed by Muhammad Ali from Oct 1960 to Dec 1981, in 61 fights comprising 549 rounds.

Largest Purse

The greatest purse for one boxer is $12 million by Sugar Ray Leonard (US) (b May 17, 1956) when he beat Thomas Hearns (US) for the undisputed world welterweight title at Las Vegas, Nev, on Sept 16, 1981. The total purse for both fighters was a record $17.1 million. The purse for the Gerry Cooney vs Larry Holmes heavyweight championship fight, June 11, 1982 in Las Vegas, was over $18 million which was split equally.

The largest stake ever fought for in the bare-knuckle era was $22,500 in a 27-round fight when Jack Cooper beat Wolf Bendoff at Port Elizabeth, South Africa, July 26, 1889.

Most Knockouts

The greatest number of knockouts in a career is 145 (129 in professional bouts) by Archie Moore (1936 to 1963). The record for consecutive KO's is 44, set by Lamar Clark of Utah at Las Vegas, Nev, Jan 11, 1960. He knocked out 6 in one night (5 in the first round) in Bingham Canyon, Utah, on Dec 1, 1958.

Highest and Lowest Attendances

The greatest paid attendance at any boxing fight has been 120,757 (with a ringside price of $27.50) for the Tunney vs Dempsey world heavyweight title fight at the Sesquicentennial Stadium, Philadelphia, Sept 23, 1926. The indoor record is 63,360 for the Spinks vs Ali world heavyweight title fight at the Louisiana Superdome in New Orleans, Sept 15, 1978. The record for live gate receipts is $7,293,600 for the Larry Holmes vs Gerry Cooney WBC heavyweight title bout in Las Vegas, Nev, on June 11, 1982. The highest non-paying attendance is 135,132 at the Tony Zale vs Billy Pryor fight at Juneau Park, Milwaukee, Wis, Aug 18, 1941.

The smallest attendance at a world heavyweight title fight was 2,434 at the Ali vs Liston fight at Lewiston, Me, May 25, 1965.

Most Fights

The greatest recorded number of fights in a career is 1,024 by Bobby Dobbs (US) (1858–1930), who is reported to have fought from 1875 to 1914, a period of 39 years. Abraham Hollandersky, *alias* Abe the Newsboy (US), is reputed to have had 1,309 fights in the 14 years from 1905 to 1918, but many of them were one-round exhibition bouts. Len Wickwar, an English lightweight who fought between 1928–47, had 463 documented fights.

Most Fights Without Loss

Edward Henry (Harry) Greb (US) (1894–1926) was unbeaten in 178 bouts, but these included 117 "no decisions" 1916–23 and 5 were unofficial losses. Of boxers with complete records Packey McFarland (US)

BIGGEST PURSE: Sugar Ray Leonard (left) and Thomas Hearns set the world's record for the largest total purse for both fighters of $17.1 million, of which Leonard earned a record share with $12 million (almost three times greater than Joe Louis's lifetime earnings of $3.8 million for 71 fights). (*All-Sport*)

MUHAMMAD ALI (right) shows his vaunted right smash to Ken Norton. Ali made $69 million, the most in any sport.

(1888–1936) had 97 fights (five draws) in 1905–15 without a defeat. Pedro Carrasco (b Spain, Nov 7, 1943) won 83 consecutive fights from Apr 22, 1964 to Sept 3, 1970, and then drew once and had a further nine wins before his loss to Armando Ramos in a WBC lightweight contest on Feb 18, 1972.

Most Consecutive KO's

Mike Tyson, 20 years old, 220 lb, is the youngest heavyweight fighter in boxing history to have won all but 2 of his first 24 fights by knockout, 15 of them in the 1st round (including 6 in a row in the initial round) in 1984–86, beating Rocky Marciano's record of 16, on the way to winning the world heavyweight crown. Tyson is managed by Bill Cayton and Jim Jacobs, the managers of Wilfred Benitez, who won 3 world titles, and of Edwin Rosario, who won the lightweight title.

At the age of 13, Tyson moved from a reformatory where he had spent two years, to the home and tutelage of prominent boxing teacher Cus D'Amato (d 1985), who had previously brought Floyd Patterson from reformatory to the world heavyweight championship, and Jose Torres to the light-heavyweight championship.

Olympic Gold Medals

In the 1984 Olympics, US boxers won a record total of 9 of the 12 gold medals.

Only two boxers have won three Olympic gold medals: southpaw László Papp (b 1926, Hungary), who took the middleweight (1948) and the light-middleweight titles (1952 and 56), and Cuban heavyweight Teofilo Stevenson (b Mar 23, 1952), who won the gold medal in his division for three successive Games (1972, 76 and 80). The only man to win two titles in one meeting was Oliver L. Kirk (US), who took both the bantam and featherweight titles at St Louis, Mo, in 1904, but he only needed one bout in each class.

The oldest man to win an Olympic gold medal in boxing was Richard K. Gunn (1871–1961) (GB), who won the featherweight title on Oct 27, 1908, in London, aged 38.

Time-Keeping

There is a little known variable in the sport of boxing. While all rule books agree that, under the Queensberry rules, a round lasts 3 min, in fact they often do not. At the Gerrie Coetzee-Michael Dokes heavyweight championship fight (Sept 23, 1984) the rounds were about 3 min, 2 sec. If the correct time had been kept the fighters would have been in their corners when Coetzee knocked out Dokes at 2:58 of round 10. It is not unusual for a timekeeper to be off by as much as a minute. The chairman of the NY State Athletic Commission explained it this way: "With all the excitement, it's sometimes hard to keep exact time."

CYCLING

Earliest Race

The earliest recorded bicycle race was a velocipede race over 2 km (1.24 miles) at the Parc de St Cloud, Paris, on May 31, 1868, won by Dr James Moore (GB) (1847–1935).

The time-trial was devised in 1889–90 by F. T. Bidlake to avoid the congestion caused by ordinary mass road racing.

Highest Speed

Fred Markham recorded an unofficial unpaced 6.832 sec for 200 m (65.484 mph) on a streamlined bicycle on Highway 120, Calif, on May 11, 1986.

The greatest distance ever covered in one hour is 76 miles 604 yd by Leon Vanderstuyft (Belgium) on the Montlhéry Motor Circuit, France, Sept 30, 1928. This was achieved from a standing start paced by a motorcycle ahead. (Cycling rules permit a motorcycle to precede a bicycle in an event of over 10 km.) The 24-hour record behind pace is 860 miles 367 yd by Sir Hubert Ferdinand Opperman (b May 29, 1904) in Melbourne, Australia on May 23, 1932.

The greatest distance covered in 60 min unpaced is 31 mi 1,381 yd by Francesco Moser (Italy) at Mexico City on Jan 23, 1984. The 24-hour record on the road is 515.8 miles by Teuvo Louhivouri of Finland on Sept 10, 1974.

Indoors, unpaced, the 24-hour record is 516 mi 427 yd by Michael Secrest (b Jan 20, 1953) of Flint, Mich, who cycled this distance at the Montreal (Canada) Olympic Velodrome Mar 13–14, 1985.

John Howard, 37, of Encinitas, Calif, achieved 152.284 mph on July 20, 1985, riding a specially designed bicycle at Bonneville Salt Flats, Utah. A former Olympic cyclist, he rode behind a car modified with a large tail section designed to cut down on air resistance.

Most World Titles

World championships, contested annually, were first staged for amateurs in 1893 and for professionals in 1895. The most wins at a particular event is 9 by Koichi Nakano (Japan) (b Nov 14, 1955), professional sprint 1977–85. The most wins at a men's amateur event is 7 by Daniel Morelon (France) (b July 28, 1944), sprint 1966–7, 69–71, 73, 75; and Leon Meredith (UK) (1882–1930), 100-km motor-paced 1904–5, 1907–9, 11, 13.

The most women's titles is 7 by Beryl Burton (UK) (b May 12, 1937), pursuit 1959–60, 62–63, 66 and road 1960, 67; and by Yvonne Reynders (Belgium) pursuit 1961, 64–65 and road 1959, 61, 63, 66.

Tour de France

For the first time in 83 years the Tour de France was won by a non-European, Greg LeMond (b June 26, 1961) of Reno, Nevada. He beat the field, including his teammate Bernard Hinault (b Nov 14, 1954) (France) who won in 1978, 79, 81, 82 and 85. This race takes about 23 days to stage annually. The longest ever was in 1926 when it lasted for 29

CROSS-AMERICA IN
RECORD TIME (above): On
a tandem bike, Cheryl Marek
and Estelle Gray in 1985
crossed the US, cycling 2,925
mi in 10 days 22 hours 48
min, for an average of 267 mi
per day.

OLYMPIC WINNER: Alexi
Grewal (US) is elated as he
crosses the finish line,
victorious in the Individual
Road Race.

SPEEDIEST BIKER: John Howard, riding in the vacuum created behind a large-tail racing car on a specially designed bicycle, sped more than 152 mph on Bonneville Salt Flats in July 1985. (*Al Gross*)

days. It is estimated that as many as 10 million people watch some part of it.

The greatest number of wins in the Tour de France (inaugurated 1903) is 5 by Jacques Anquetil (b Jan 8, 1934) (France), who won in 1957, 1961–64; Eddy Merckx (b June 17, 1945) (Belgium) who won five titles (1969–72, 1974); and Bernard Hinault (see above) who also won 5 times.

The closest race ever was in 1968 when after 2,898.7 mi over 25 days (June 27–July 21) Jan Jannssen (Netherlands) (b May 19, 1940) beat Herman van Springel (Belgium) in Paris by 38 sec. The longest course was 3,569 miles on June 20 to July 18, 1926. The length of the course is usually about 3,000 miles, but varies from year to year.

The fastest average speed was 23.51 mph by Bernard Hinault in 1981. The greatest number of participants were 170 starters in 1982 and 1984.

Six-Day Races

The greatest number of wins in six-day races is 88 out of 233 events by Patrick Sercu (b June 27, 1944), of Belgium, 1964–83.

Longest One-Day Race

The longest single-day "massed start" road race is the Bordeaux-to-Paris, France, event of 342 to 385 miles. Paced over all or part of the route, the highest average speed in 1981 was 29.32 mph by Herman van Springel (Belgium) (b Aug 14, 1943) for 363.1 mi in 13 hours 35 min 18 sec.

Most Olympic Titles

The greatest number of gold medals ever won is 3 by Paul Masson (France) in 1896, Francisco Verri (Italy) in 1906 and Robert Charpentier (France) in 1936. Daniel Morelon (France) won two in 1968 and a third in 1972. He also won a bronze medal in 1964. Marcus Hurley (US) (1884–1950) won 4 events in the "unofficial" cycling competition in the 1904 Games.

Endurance

Tommy Godwin (1912–75) (GB) in the 365 days of 1939 covered

75,065 miles or an average of 205.65 miles per day. He then completed 100,000 miles in 500 days to May 14, 1940. Jay Aldous and Matt DeWaal cycled 14,290 miles on a round trip from Place Monument, Salt Lake City, Utah, in 106 days, Apr 2–July 16, 1984.

Nicholas Mark Sanders (b Nov 26, 1957) of Glossop, Eng, circumnavigated the world (13,035 road miles) in 78 days, 3 hours 30 min between July 5 and Sept 21, 1985.

Jonathan Boyer cycled across America in a record 9 days 2 hours 6 min in July 1985. Cheryl Marek and Estelle Gray completed a tandem ride across the US from Santa Monica Pier, Calif, to NYC, 2,925 mi, in 10 days 22 hours 48 min in 1985. Wayne Phillips of Richmond, BC, rode across Canada from Vancouver, BC, to Halifax, Nova Scotia, covering the 3,800 miles in 14 days 22 hours 47 min June 13–28, 1982.

Carlos Vieira cycled for 191 hours "non-stop" at Leiria, Portugal June 8–16, 1983. The distance covered was 1,496.04 mi, and he was moving 98.7% of the time.

Highest Altitude

Nicholas and Richard Crane cycled their mountain bikes to the summit of Mount Kilimanjaro, Tanzania, 19,340 ft, on Dec 31, 1984.

Touring

The most participants in a bicycle tour were 27,220 in the 56-mile London-to-Brighton Bike Ride on June 15, 1986.

The longest cycle tour on record is the more than 402,000 miles amassed by Walter Stolle (b Sudetenland, 1926), an itinerant lecturer. From Jan 24, 1959 to Dec 12, 1976, he covered 159 countries, had 5 bicycles stolen and suffered 231 other robberies, along with over 1,000 flat tires. From 1922 to Dec 25, 1973, Tommy Chambers (1903–84) of Glasgow, Scotland, rode a verified total of 799,405 miles.

John Hathaway of Vancouver, Canada, covered 50,600 miles, visiting every continent, from Nov 10, 1974 to Oct 6, 1976.

Veronica and Colin Scargill, of Bedford, England, traveled 18,020 miles around the world, on a tandem, Feb 25, 1974–Aug 27, 1975.

Roller Cycling

The greatest distance achieved in 24 hours is 1,560.73 mi by Piet Vitten (Neth) at Midden, Beemster, The Netherlands on Mar 8–9, 1980. Paul Swinnerton (GB) achieved a record 102 mph for 200 meters on rollers on Feb 12, 1982, at Stoke-on-Trent, England.

Unicycle Records

The tallest unicycle ever mastered is one 101 ft 9 in tall ridden by Steve McPeak (with a safety wire or mechanic suspended to an overhead crane) for a distance of 376 ft in Las Vegas in Oct 1980. The freestyle riding of even taller unicycles must inevitably lead to serious injury or fatality.

Deepak Lele of Maharashtra, India, unicycled 3,963 mi from NYC to LA, June 6–Sept 25, 1984. Brian Davis of Tillicoultry, Scotland rode 901 mi from Land's End to John O'Groats May 16–June 4, 1980 in 19 days 1¾ hours. Takayuki Koika of Kanagawa, Japan set a record for 100 mi in 7 hours 49 min 12 sec on Sept 16, 1985. The sprint record from a standing start over 100 meters is 14.89 sec by Floyd Grandall of Pontiac, Mich, in Tokyo, Japan on Mar 24, 1980.

Stationary Cycling

Rudi Jan Jozef De Greef (b Dec 28, 1955) stayed stationary without support for 10 hours at Meensel-Kiezegem, Belgium, Nov 19, 1982. David Steed of Tucson, Ariz, former recordholder at 9½ hours, claims to have stayed for 24 hours.

FISHING

Origins

From time immemorial men have fished the seas and rivers of the world for food, but fishing for pleasure and leisure seems to have been practiced in Egypt, according to wall paintings, from the 5th Dynasty, 2470–2320 BC. On tomb inscriptions, Amenemhat, a prince of Beni Hasan, is described as "overseer of the swamps of enjoyment," a reference interpreted as fishing grounds.

Freshwater Casting

The longest freshwater cast ratified under ICF (International Casting Federation) rules is 574 ft 2 in by Walter Kummerow (W Germany), for the Bait Distance Double-Handed 30-g event held at Lenzerheide, Switzerland, in the 1968 Championships.

The longest Fly Distance Double-Handed cast is 257 ft 2 in by Sverne Scheen (Norway) also set at Lenzerheide in Sept 1968.

Longest Fight

The longest recorded fight between a fisherman and a fish is 32 hours 5 min by Donal Heatley (NZ) (b 1938) with a black marlin (estimated length 20 ft and weight 1,500 lb) off Mayor Island off Tauranga, New Zealand, Jan 21–22, 1968. It towed the 12-ton launch 50 miles before breaking the line.

CAUGHT 3,001 BASS in a season: David Romeo of East Meadow, NY found the right fresh-water spots.

World Championships

The *Confédération Internationale de la Pêche Sportive* championships were inaugurated as European championships in 1953. They were recognized as World Championships in 1957. France won 12 times between 1956 and 1981 and Robert Tesse (France) took the individual title uniquely three times, 1959–60, 65. The record weight (team) is 76 lb 8 oz in 3 hours by W Germany in the Neckar at Mannheim, W Germany on Sept 21, 1980. The individual record is 37 lb 7 oz by Wolf-Rüdiger Kremkus (W Germany) at Mannheim on Sept 20, 1980. The most fish caught is 652 by Jacques Isenbaert (Belgium) at Dunajvaros, Yugoslavia on Aug 27, 1967.

Spear-Fishing

The largest fish ever taken underwater was an 804-lb giant black grouper by Don Pinder of the Miami Triton Club, Fla, in 1955.

Bass, Anyone?

If you're a bass-fisher, you should check into Indiana State University at Terre Haute, where 10,000 enrollees from ten states take courses sponsored by the school's Bass Fishing Institute.

Most Valuable Fish

It was a modern version of an old fairy tale. When Al McReynolds went fishing one stormy night, the fish he caught brought fame and fortune. In this case, the magic was supplied by ABU-Garcia, a leading manufacturer of fishing tackle, through a contest that offered a $250,000 reward for landing an all-tackle world record fish in one of four categories.

McReynolds, 36, and his friend Pat Erdman were fishing from a jetty in their hometown, Atlantic City, NJ, on the night of Sept 21, 1982, when McReynolds hooked and, after a 2-hour fight, landed a 78-lb-8-oz striped bass—a world record for rod and reel. As one ordeal had ended, another began. McReynolds had to wait for the IGFA and ABU-Garcia to determine that the record was legitimate—a process that took nearly 5 months. Testing even included having the fish x-rayed to determine no stones or weights had been added to make the fish heavier.

It all ended happily on Feb 11, 1983, at the Explorers Club in NYC when McReynolds received a check for $250,000—the most money ever paid for a fish.

A claim has been made that two fishermen won $500,000 each in a fishing contest in Puget Sound, Wash in 1983. The objective was to catch one of 8 tagged fish. The two reportedly succeeded and split the $1 million prize.

Largest Catches

The largest fish ever caught on a rod is an officially ratified man-eating great white shark (*Carcharodon carcharias*) weighing 2,664 lb, and measuring 16 ft 10 in long, caught by Alf Dean at Denial Bay, near Ceduna, South Australia, on Apr 21, 1959. In June 1978 a great white shark measuring 29 ft 6 in in length and weighing over 10,000 lb was harpooned and landed by fishermen in the harbor of San Miguel, Azores.

A white pointer shark weighing 3,388 lb was caught on a rod by Clive Green off Albany, W Australia, on Apr 26, 1976, but this will remain unratified as whale meat was used as bait.

The largest marine animal ever killed by *hand* harpoon was a blue whale 97 ft in length by Archer Davidson in Twofold Bay, NSW, Australia, in 1910. Its tail flukes measured 20 ft across and its jaw bone 23 ft 4 in.

The biggest single freshwater catch ever ratified was on the Snake River, Idaho, in 1956 when Willard Cravens caught a white sturgeon weighing 360 lb. However, that may not be the last word as two years previously, in the same river, Glenn Howard claims to have caught one which weighed 394 lb.

Caught on line but not on rod, the heaviest is a 468-lb sturgeon by Joey Pallotta on July 9, 1983 off Benicia, Calif. An 834-lb freshwater sturgeon was *landed* by Garry Oling from the Fraser River, Albion, Brit Columbia, on Aug 11, 1981.

Smallest Catch

The smallest fish ever to win a competition was a smelt weighing 1/16 of an oz, caught by Peter Christian at Buckenham Ferry, Norfolk, England, on Jan 9, 1977. This beat 107 other competitors who failed to catch anything.

MOST VALUABLE FISH: A prize of $250,000, the most money ever paid for a fish, awaited Al McReynolds of Atlantic City, NJ, when he caught this 78-lb-8-oz striped bass off a jetty after a 2-hour fight in Sept 1982.

FISHING WORLD RECORDS

Selected Sea and Freshwater fish records taken by tackle as ratified by the International Game Fish Association to June 1986. For a more complete listing of IGFA all-tackle records, see the *Guinness Sports Record Book (1986–87)* (Sterling).

Species	Weight in lb oz		Name of Angler	Location	Date
Amberjack	155	10	Joseph Dawson	Challenger Bank, Bermuda	June 24, 1981
Barracuda††	83	0	K. J. W. Hackett §§	Lagos, Nigeria	Jan 13, 1952
Bass (Giant Sea)	563	8	James D. McAdam, Jr	Anacapa Island, Calif	Aug 20, 1968
Bass (Striped)	78	8	Albert J. McReynolds	Atlantic City, NJ	Sept 21, 1982
Bluefish	31	12	James M. Hussey	Hatteras, NC	Jan 30, 1972
Carp†	57	13	David Nikolow	Potomac, Wash, DC	June 19, 1983
Cod	98	12	Alphonse J. Bielevich	Isle of Shoals, NH	June 8, 1969
Mackerel, Spanish	10	15	Heather J. Wadsworth	Oak Bluffs, Mass	Sept 18, 1983
Marlin (Black)	1,560	0	Alfred C. Glassell, Jr	Cabo Blanco, Peru	Aug 4, 1953
Marlin (Atlantic Blue)	1,282	0	Larry Martin	St Thomas, US VI	Aug 6, 1977
Marlin (Pacific Blue)	1,376	0	Jay Wm. deBeaubien	Kaaiwi Point, Kona, Hawaii	May 31, 1982
Marlin (Striped)	455	4	Bruce Jenkinson	Mayor Island, NZ	Mar 8, 1982
Marlin (White)	181	14	Evando Luiz Coser	Vitoria, Brazil	Dec 8, 1979
Pike (Northern)	46	2	Peter Dubuc	Sacandaga Reservoir, NY	Sept 15, 1940
Sailfish (Atlantic)	128	1	Harm Steyn	Luanda, Angola	Mar 27, 1974
Sailfish (Pacific)	221	0	C. W. Stewart	Santa Cruz I, Galapagos, Ecuador	Feb 12, 1947
Salmon (Chinook)§	97	4	Les Anderson	Kenai River, Alaska	May 17, 1985
Salmon, Sockeye	12	8	Mike Boswell	Yakutat, Alaska	June 23, 1983
Shark (Blue)	437	0	Peter Hyde	Catherine Bay, NSW, Aust	Oct 2, 1976
Shark (Hammerhead)	991	0	Allen Ogle	Sarasota, Fla	May 30, 1982
Shark (Mako)**	1,080	0	James L. Melanson	Montauk, NY	Aug 26, 1979
Shark (White or Man-eating)	2,664	0	Alfred Dean	Ceduna, S Aust	Apr 21, 1959
Shark (Porbeagle)	465	0	Jorge Potier	Cornwall, England	July 23, 1976

Shark (Thresher)‡	802	Dianne North	Tutukaka, NZ	Feb 8, 1981
Shark (Tiger)	1,780	Walter Maxwell	Cherry Grove, SC	June 14, 1964
Sturgeon‡‡	468	Joey Pallotta, III	Benicia, Calif	July 9, 1983
Swordfish	1,182	L. E. Marron	Iquique, Chile	May 17, 1953
Tarpon	283	M. Salazar	Lago de Maracaibo, Venez	Mar 19, 1956
Trout (Brook)	14	Dr. W. J. Cook	Nipigon R, Ont, Can	July 1916
Trout (Lake)¶	65	Larry Daunis	Great Bear Lake, Can	Aug 8, 1970
Tuna (Allison or Yellowfin)	388	Curt Wiesenhutter	San Benedicto Is, Mex	Apr 1, 1977
Tuna (Atlantic Big-eyed)	375	Cecil Browne	Ocean City, Md	Aug 26, 1977
Tuna (Pacific Big-eyed)	435	Dr Russel V. A. Lee	Cabo Blanco, Peru	Apr 17, 1957
Tuna (Bluefin)	1,496	Ken Fraser	Aulds Cove, Nova Scotia	Oct 26, 1979
Wahoo	149	John Pirovano	Cat Cay, Bahamas	June 15, 1962
Weakfish	19	Philip W. Halstead	Chesapeake Bay, Va	May 19, 1983

†† A barracuda weighing 103 lb 4 oz was caught on an untested line by Chester Benet at West End, Bahamas, on Aug 11, 1932. Another weighing 48 lb 6 oz was caught barehanded by Thomas B. Pace at Panama City Beach, Fla, on Apr 19, 1974.

§§ Hackett was only 11 years 137 days old at the time.

† A carp weighing 83 lb 8 oz was taken (not by rod) near Pretoria, South Africa. A 60-lb specimen was taken by bow and arrow by Ben A. Topham in Wythe Co, Va, on July 5, 1970.

§ A salmon weighing 126 lb 8 oz was taken (not by rod) near Petersburg, Alaska.

** A 1,295-lb specimen was taken by two anglers off Natal, South Africa, on March 17, 1939, and a 1,500 lb specimen harpooned inside Durban Harbour, South Africa, in 1933.

‡ W. W. Dowding caught a 922-lb thresher shark in 1937 on an untested line.

‡‡ An 834-lb sturgeon was landed (not by a rod) by Garry Oiling at Albion, BC, Canada, from the Fraser River on Aug 11, 1981.

¶ A 102-lb trout was taken from Lake Athabasca, northern Saskatchewan, Canada, on Aug 8, 1961.

Most Fish Caught in a Season

In 77 days of fishing from Apr 1 to Oct 31, 1984, David Romeo of East Meadow, NY, caught on rod and reel 3,001 largemouth bass in the fresh waters of NY State and Florida, the most ever caught in a season. Mr. Romeo, who doesn't like eating fish but enjoys catching them, threw back all but 24 of them for this and legal reasons. His log books helped the environment conservation people to make "informed bass management decisions."

FOOTBALL

Origins

The origin of modern football stems from the "Boston Game" as played at Harvard. Harvard declined to participate in the inaugural meeting of the Intercollegiate Football Association in NYC in Oct 1873, on the grounds that the proposed rules were based on the non-handling "Association" code of English football. Instead, Harvard accepted a proposal from McGill University of Montreal, which played the more closely akin English Rugby Football. The first football match under the Harvard Rules was thus played against McGill at Cambridge, Mass, in May 1874. Most sports historians point to a contest between Rutgers and Princeton at New Brunswick, NJ, on Nov 6, 1869, as the first football game, but many American soccer historians regard this contest as the first intercollegiate *soccer* game. (Rutgers won the game, 6 goals to 4, and there were 25 players to a side.) In Nov 1876, a new Intercollegiate Football Association, with a pioneer membership of 5 colleges, was inaugurated at Springfield, Mass, to reconcile the conflicting versions of the sport. It was not until 1880 that the game, because of the organizational genius of Walter Camp of Yale, began to take its modern form. Among other things, he reduced the number of players on a side to 11, which it is today (and defined their positions), and also replaced the scrum with the line of scrimmage.

Professional football dates from the Latrobe, Pa vs Jeannette, Pa match at Latrobe, in Aug 1895. The National Football League was founded in Canton, Ohio, in 1920, although it did not adopt its present name until 1922. The year 1969 was the final year in which professional football was divided into separate National and American Leagues, for record purposes.

Most Prolific Recordbreaker

After he finished his 4-year career at Portland State U in 1980, Neil Lomax held 90 NCAA football records and was tied for two other records, mostly on the basis of his passing feats. No other football player, past or present, has been remotely close to holding that many records—in any college sport.

College Series Records

The oldest collegiate series still contested is that between Yale and Princeton dating from 1873, or 3 years before the passing of the Springfield rules, with 108 games played through the 1985 season. The most regularly contested series is between Lafayette and Lehigh, who have met 121 times, 1884 to 1985.

Yale University became the only college to win more than 700 games when it finished the 1979 season with a total of 701 victories in 107 seasons. Yale has 733 wins in 113 seasons to the end of 1985.

All-America Brothers

Twice have three brothers made All-America at the same school. The first trio were the Wistert brothers at Mich, all of whom were tackles. Francis was honored in 1933, Albert in 1942, Alvin in 1948–49. At Oklahoma, defensive lineman Lucious Selmon was an All-America in 1973 and he was followed by his brothers Leroy, a defensive tackle, and Dewey, an offensive guard, in 1975.

Jim Thorpe vs Dwight D. Eisenhower

The two met in 1912 when Thorpe was playing for the Carlisle School for Indians (Pa) and Eisenhower was playing for Army (West Point, NY). Eisenhower and another back were instructed to follow Thorpe wherever he went. In the third quarter of the game they both hit Thorpe so hard that the pair of them were dazed and were taken out of the game by their coach. Thorpe played to the end.

SUPER BOWL RECORD: When the Chicago Bears beat the New Eng Patriots 46–10 in Jan 1986, it was the biggest margin of victory ever in the annual classic. This is how play looked at ground level. (*All Sport*)

ALL-TIME NATIONAL
FOOTBALL LEAGUE RECORDS
(Through 1985 Season)

SERVICE

Most Seasons, Active Player
26 George Blanda, Chi Bears, 1949–58; Balt, 1950; AFL: Hou, 1960–66; Oak, 1967–75

Most Games Played, Lifetime
340 George Blanda, Chi Bears, 1949–58; Balt, 1950; AFL: Hou, 1960–66; Oak, 1967–75

Most Consecutive Games Played, Lifetime
282 Jim Marshall, Cleve, 1960; Minn, 1961–79

Most Seasons, Head Coach
40 George Halas, Chi Bears, 1920–29, 33–42, 46–55, 58–67

SCORING

Most Seasons Leading League
5 Don Hutson, GB, 1940–44 Gino Cappelletti, Bos, 1961, 63–66 (AFL)

Most Points, Lifetime
2,002 George Blanda, Chi Bears, 1949–58; Balt, 1950; AFL: Hou, 1960–66; Oak, 1967–75 (9-td, 943-pat, 335-fg)

Most Points, Season
176 Paul Hornung, GB, 1960 (15-td, 41-pat, 15-fg)

Most Points, Rookie Season
132 Gale Sayers, Chi Bears, 1965 (22-td)

Most Points, Game
40 Ernie Nevers, Chi Cards vs Chi Bears, Nov 28, 1929 (6-td, 4-pat)

Most Consecutive Games, Scoring
151 Fred Cox, Minn 1963–73

Touchdowns

Most Seasons Leading League
8 Don Hutson, GB, 1935–38, 41–44

Most Touchdowns, Lifetime
126 Jim Brown, Cleve, 1957–65 (106-r, 20-p)

Most Touchdowns, Season
24 John Riggins, Wash (24 r), 1983

Most Touchdowns, Rookie Season
22 Gale Sayers, Chi Bears, 1965 (14-r, 6-p, 1-prb, 1-krb)

Most Touchdowns, Game
6 Ernie Nevers, Chi Cards vs Chi Bears, Nov 28, 1929 (6-r)
William (Dub) Jones, Cleve vs Chi Bears, Nov 25, 1951 (4-r, 2-p)
Gale Sayers, Chi Bears vs SF, Dec 12, 1965 (4-r, 1-p, 1-prb)

Most Consecutive Games Scoring Touchdowns
18 Lenny Moore, Balt, 1963–65

Points After Touchdown

Most Seasons Leading League
8 George Blanda, Chi Bears, 1956; AFL: Hou, 1961–62; Oak, 1967–69, 72, 74

Most Points After Touchdown, Lifetime
959 George Blanda, Chi Bears, 1949–58; Balt, 1950; AFL: Hou, 1960–66; Oak, 1967–69, 72, 74

Most Points After Touchdown, Season
66 Uwe von Schamann, Miami 1984–85

Most Points After Touchdown, Game
9 Marlin (Pat) Harder, Chi Cards vs NY, Oct 17, 1948

Bob Waterfield, LA vs Balt,
Oct 22, 1950
Charlie Gogolak, Wash vs
NY Giants, Nov 27, 1966

**Most Consecutive Points After
Touchdown**
234 Tommy Davis, SF, 1959–65

**Most Points After Touchdown (no
misses), Game**
9 Marlin (Pat) Harder, Chi
Cards vs NY Giants, Oct
17, 1948
Bob Waterfield, LA Rams vs
Balt, Oct 22, 1950

Field Goals

Most Seasons Leading League
5 Lou Groza, Cleve, 1950,
52–54, 57

Most Field Goals, Lifetime
373 Jan Stenerud, KC, 1967–69;
Gr Bay 1980–83, Minn
1984–85

Most Field Goals, Season
35 Ali Haji-Sheikh, NY Giants,
1983

Most Field Goals, Game
7 Jim Bakken, St L vs Pitt,
Sept 24, 1967

**Most Consecutive Games, Field
Goals**
31 Fred Cox, Minn, 1968–70

Highest Field Goal Percentage, Season
95.24 Mark Mosely, Wash, 1982
(20–21)

Most Consecutive Field Goals
23 Mark Mosely, Wash,
1981–82

Longest Field Goal
63 yd Tom Dempsey, NO vs
Det, Nov 8, 1970

RUSHING

Most Seasons Leading League
8 Jim Brown, Cleve, 1957–61,
63–65

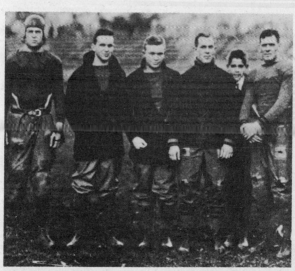

FAMOUS FOOTBALLER: The man who played for Army and
went on to become President is the third from the left in this
photo—Dwight D. Eisenhower.

NEW RUSHING RECORD of 2,105 yds in one season was set by Eric Dickerson (LA Rams) in 1984, eclipsing O.J. Simpson's record of 2,003 which held for 11 years. (*UPI—Bettmann Archive*)

RUSHING RECORDHOLDER: Walter Payton of the Super-Bowl Champion Chicago Bears on his way through the Dallas Cowboy defense to setting a record in 1984 for 58 games with 100 yds or more gained. In 1977 he broke the record for yds gained in one game (275). (*UPI—Bettmann Archive*)

Most Yards Gained, Lifetime
14,860 Walter Payton, Chi Bears,
1975–85

Most Yards Gained, Season
2,105 Eric Dickerson, LA Rams,
1984

Most Yards Gained, Game
275 Walter Payton, Chi Bears
vs Minn, Nov 20, 1977

Longest Run from Scrimmage
99 Tony Dorsett, Dall vs
Minn, Jan 3, 1983 (td)

Highest Average Gain, Lifetime
(799 att)
5.2 Jim Brown, Cleve, 1957–65
(2,359–12,312)

Highest Average Gain, Game (10
att)
17.1 Marion Motley, Cleve vs
Pitt, Oct 29, 1950
(11–188)

Most Touchdowns Rushing, Lifetime
106 Jim Brown, Cleve, 1957–65

Most Touchdowns Rushing, Season
24 John Riggins, Wash, 1983

Most Touchdowns Rushing, Game
6 Ernie Nevers, Chi Cards vs
Chi Bears, Nov 28, 1929

PASSING

Most Seasons Leading League
6 Sammy Baugh, Wash, 1937,
40, 43, 45, 47, 49

Most Passes Attempted, Lifetime
6,467 Fran Tarkenton, Minn,
1961–66, 72–78; NY
Giants, 1967–71
(3,686 completions)

Most Passes Attempted, Season
609 Dan Fouts, SD, 1981 (360
completions)

Most Passes Attempted, Game
68 George Blanda, Hou vs Buff,
Nov 1, 1964 (AFL) (37
completions)

Most Passes Completed, Lifetime
3,686 Fran Tarkenton, Minn,

1961–66, 72–78; NY Giants,
1967–71 (6,467 attempts)

Most Passes Completed, Season
362 Dan Marino, Miami, 1984
(564 attempts)

Most Passes Completed, Game
42 Richard Todd, NY Jets vs
SF, Sept 21, 1980 (59 attempts)

Most Consecutive Passes Completed
20 Ken Anderson, Cin vs Hou,
Jan 2, 1983

Longest Pass Completion (all tds)
99 Frank Filchock (to Farkas),
Wash vs Pitt, Oct 15,
1939
George Izo (to Mitchell),
Wash vs Cleve, Sept 15,
1963
Karl Sweetan (to Studstill)
Det vs Balt, Oct 16, 1966
C. A. Jurgensen (to Allen),
Wash vs Chi Bears, Sept
15, 1968
Jim Plunkett (to Branch),
LA Raiders vs Wash,
Oct 2, 1983
Ron Jaworski (to Quick)
Phil vs Atl, Nov 10, 1985

Most Yards Gained Passing,
Lifetime
47,003 Fran Tarkenton,
Minn, 1961–66,
72–78; NY Giants,
1967–71

Most Yards Gained Passing, Game
554 Norm Van Brocklin, LA vs
NY Yanks, Sept 28, 1951
(41–27)

Most Yards Gained Passing, Season
5,084 Dan Marino, Miami, 1984

Most Touchdown Passes, Lifetime
342 Fran Tarkenton, Minn,
1961–66, 72–78; NY
Giants, 1967–71

Most Touchdown Passes, Season
48 Dan Marino, Miami, 1984

Most Touchdown Passes, Game
7 Sid Luckman, Chi Bears vs
NY Giants, Nov 14, 1943
Adrian Burk, Phil vs Wash,
Oct 17, 1954

George Blanda, Hou vs NY Titans, Nov 19, 1961 (AFL)

Y. A. Tittle, NY vs Wash, Oct 28, 1962

Joe Kapp, Minn vs Balt, Sept 28, 1969

Most Touchdown Passes, Consecutive Games
47 John Unitas, Balt, 1956–60

Passing Efficiency, Lifetime (1,500 att)
63.3 Joe Montana, SF 1979–85; (1,627–2,571)

Passing Efficiency, Season (100 att)
70.55 Ken Anderson, Cin, 1982 (309–218)

Passing Efficiency, Game (20 att)
90.9 Ken Anderson, Cin vs Pitt, Nov 10, 1974 (22–20)

Passes Had Intercepted

Most Passes Intercepted, Game
8 Jim Hardy, Chi Cards vs Phil, Sept 24, 1950 (39 attempts)

Most Consecutive Passes Attempted, None Intercepted
294 Bryan (Bart) Starr, GB, 1964–65

Fewest Passes Intercepted, Season (Qualifiers)
1 Joe Ferguson, Buff, 1976 (151 attempts)

Lowest Percentage Passes Intercepted, Lifetime (1,500 att)
2.61 Joe Montana, SF 1979–85 (2,571–67)

Lowest Percentage Passes Intercepted, Season (Qualifiers)
0.66 Joe Ferguson, Buff, 1976 (151–1)

PASS RECEPTIONS

Most Seasons Leading League
8 Don Hutson, GB, 1936–37, 39, 41–45

Most Pass Receptions, Lifetime
716 Charley Joiner, Hou 1969–72, Cinc 1972–75, SD 1976–85

Most Pass Receptions, Season
106 Art Monk, Wash, 1984

Most Pass Receptions, Game
18 Tom Fears, LA Rams vs GB, Dec 3, 1950 (189 yd)

Longest Pass Reception (all tds)
99 Andy Farkas (Filchock), Wash vs Pitt, Oct 15, 1939

Bobby Mitchell (Izo), Wash vs Cleve, Sept 15, 1963

Pat Studstill (Sweetan), Det vs Balt, Oct 16, 1966

Gerry Allen (Jurgensen), Wash vs Chi Bears, Sept 15, 1968

Cliff Branch (Plunkett), LA Raiders vs Wash, Oct 2, 1983

Mike Quick (Jaworski), Phil vs Atl, Nov 10, 1985

Most Consecutive Games, Pass Receptions
127 Harold Carmichael, Phil, 1972–1980

Most Pass Receptions by a Running Back, Game
17 Clark Gaines, NY Jets vs SF, Sept 21, 1980

Most Yards Gained Pass Receptions, Game
309 Stephone Paige, KC vs SD, Dec 22, 1985

Touchdowns Receiving

Most Touchdown Passes, Lifetime
99 Don Hutson, GB, 1935–45

Most Touchdown Passes, Season
18 Mark Clayton, Miami, 1984

Most Touchdown Passes, Game
5 Bob Shaw, Chi Cards vs Balt, Oct 2, 1950

Kellen Winslow, SD vs Oak, Nov 22, 1981

Most Consecutive Games, Touchdown Passes
11 Elroy (Crazy Legs) Hirsch, LA Rams, 1950–51

Gilbert (Buddy) Dial, Pitt, 1959–60

PASS INTERCEPTIONS

Most Interceptions by, Lifetime
  81 Paul Krause, Wash (28),
      1964–67; Minn (53),
      1968–79

Most Interceptions by, Season
  14 Richard (Night Train)
      Lane, LA Rams, 1952

Most Interceptions by, Game
  4 By 17 players, twice by
      Jerry Norton St L vs
      Wash, Nov 20, 1960; St L
      vs Pitt, Nov 26, 1961

Most Touchdowns Interception Returns, Lifetime
  9 Ken Houston, Hou
      1967–79; Wash 1973–80

PUNTING

Most Seasons Leading League
  4 Sammy Baugh, Wash,
      1940–43
    Jerrel Wilson, AFL: KC,
      1965, 68; NFL: KC,
      1972–73

Most Punts, Season
  114 Bob Parsons, Chi, 1981

Most Punts, Game
  14 Dick Nesbitt, Chi Cards vs
      Chi Bears, Nov 30, 1933
    Keith Molesworth, Chi
      Bears vs GB, Dec 10,
      1933
    Sammy Baugh, Wash vs
      Phil, Nov 5, 1939
    John Kinscherf, NY Giants
      vs Det, Nov 7, 1943
    George Taliaferro, NY
      Yanks vs LA Rams, Sept
      28, 1951

Most Punts, Lifetime
  1,083 John James, Atl 1972–81,
        Det 1982, Hou 1982–84

Longest Punt
  98 yd Steve O'Neal, NY Jets vs
        Den, Sept 21, 1969
        (AFL)

Average Yardage Punting

Highest Punting Average, Lifetime
(300 punts)
  45.1 yd Sammy Baugh, Wash,
          1937–52 (338)

Highest Punting Average, Season
(20 punts)
  51.4 yd Sammy Baugh, Wash,
          1940 (35)

Highest Punting Average, Game (4 punts)
  61.8 yd Bob Cifers, Det vs Chi
          Bears, Nov 24, 1946

KICKOFF RETURNS

Yardage Returning Kickoffs

Most Yards Gained, Lifetime
  6,922 Ron Smith, Chi Bears,
        1965, 70–72; Atl,
        1966–67; LA, 1968–69;
        SD, 1973; Oak, 1974

Most Yards Gained, Season
  1,345 George (Buster) Rhymes,
        Minn 1985

Most Yards Gained, Game
  294 Wally Triplett, Det vs LA,
      Oct 29, 1950 (4)

Longest Kickoff Return for Touchdown
  106 Al Carmichael, GB vs Chi
      Bears, Oct 7, 1956
    Noland Smith, KC vs Den,
      Dec 17, 1967 (AFL)
    Roy Green, St L vs Dall,
      Oct 21, 1979

Highest Average, Lifetime (75 returns)
  30.6 Gale Sayers, Chi Bears,
        1965–71

Average Yardage Returning Kickoffs

Highest Average, Season (15 returns)
  41.1 Travis Williams, GB, 1967
        (18)

Highest Average, Game (3 returns)
  73.5 Wally Triplett, Det vs LA
        Rams, Oct 29, 1950
        (4–294)

Touchdowns Returning Kickoffs

Most Touchdowns, Lifetime
  6 Ollie Matson, Chi Cards,
      1952 (2), 54, 56, 58 (2)
    Gale Sayers, Chi Bears,
      1965, 66 (2), 67 (3)
    Travis Williams, GB, 1967
      (4), 69, 71

Most Touchdowns, Season
    4 Travis Williams, GB, 1967
       Cecil Turner, Chi Bears,
       1970

Most Touchdowns, Game
    2 Thomas (Tim) Brown, Phil
       vs Dall, Nov 6, 1966
       Travis Williams, GB vs
       Cleve, Nov 12, 1967

PUNT RETURNS

Yardage Returning Punts

Most Yards Gained, Lifetime
3,036 Billy Johnson, Hou
       1974–80, Atl 1982–85

Most Yards Gained, Season
  692 Fulton Walker, LA Raiders
       1985

Most Yards Gained, Game
  207 Le Roy Irvin, LA Rams vs
       Atl, Oct 11, 1981

Longest Punt Return (all tds)
   98 Gil LeFebvre, Cin vs Brk,
       Dec 3, 1933
       Charlie West, Minn vs
       Wash, Nov 3, 1968
       Dennis Morgan, Dall vs St
       L, Oct 13, 1974

Highest Average, Lifetime (75 or
more returns)
12.78 George McAfee, Chi Bears,
       1940–41, 1945–50

Highest Average, Season (Qualifiers)
 23.0 Herb Rich, Balt, 1950

Highest Average, Game (3 returns)
 47.7 Chuck Latourette, St L vs
       NO, Sept 29, 1968

Touchdowns Returning Punts

Most Touchdowns, Lifetime
    8 Jack Christiansen, Det,
       1951–58

Rick Upchurch, Den,
1975–83

Most Touchdowns, Season
    4 Jack Christiansen, Det,
       1951
       Rick Upchurch, Den, 1976

Most Touchdowns, Game
    2 Jack Christiansen, Det vs
       LA Rams, Oct 14, 1951;
       vs GB, Nov 22, 1951
       Dick Christy, NY Titans vs
       Den, Sept 24, 1961
       Rick Upchurch, Den vs
       Cleve, Sept 26, 1976
       LeRoy Irvin, LA Rams vs
       Atl, Oct 11, 1981

FUMBLES

Most Fumbles, Lifetime
  105 Roman Gabriel, LA Rams,
       1962–72; Phil, 1973–77

Most Fumbles, Season
   17 Dan Pastorini, Hou, 1973
       Warren Moon, Hou 1984

Most Fumbles, Game
    7 Len Dawson, KC vs SD,
       Nov 15, 1964 (AFL)

Longest Fumble Ruturn
  104 Jack Tatum, Oak vs GB,
       Sept 24, 1972

Most Opponents' Fumbles Recovered, Lifetime
   29 Jim Marshall, Cleve, 1960;
       Minn, 1961–79

Most Opponents' Fumbles Recovered, Season
    9 Don Hultz, Minn, 1963

Most Opponents' Fumbles Recovered, Game
    3 by 8 players 1949–81

Ban Football!

Although remembered as one of the most athletic of presidents, Theodore Roosevelt threatened to ban college football in 1905. Eighteen players had died of injuries that year and 73 were seriously hurt. One of Roosevelt's sons, a freshman at Harvard, came home from the first day of practice with a black eye. At the President's urging, the flying wedge

SUPER BOWL RECORDS
(Through 1986 Game)

Most points, lifetime
24 Franco Harris, Pitt, 4 games (4 td)

Most points, game
18 Roger Craig, SF vs Miami, Jan 20, 1985 (3 td)

Most field goals, game
4 Don Chandler, GB vs. Oak, Jan 14, 1968
Ray Wersching, SF vs Cin, Jan 24, 1982

Most field goals, lifetime
5 Ray Wersching, SF, 2 games

Longest field goal
48 Jan Stenerud, KC vs Minn, Jan 11, 1970

Most yards rushing, lifetime
354 Franco Harris, Pitt, 4 games

Most yards rushing, game
191 Marcus Allen, LA Raiders vs Wash, Jan 22, 1984

Most yards passing, lifetime
932 Terry Bradshaw, Pitt, 4 games

Most yards, passing, game
331 Joe Montana, SF vs Miami, Jan 20, 1985

Most passes completed, lifetime
61 Roger Staubach, Dallas, 4 games

Most passes completed, game
29 Dan Marino, Miami vs SF, Jan 20, 1985

Most touchdown passes, lifetime
9 Terry Bradshaw, Pitt, 4 games

Most touchdown passes, game
4 Terry Bradshaw, Pitt vs Dallas, Jan 21, 1979

Longest completed pass
80 Jim Plunkett to Kenny King, Oak Raiders vs Phil, Jan 25, 1981

Most yards receiving, lifetime
364 Lynn Swann, Pitt, 4 games

Most yards receiving, game
161 Lynn Swann, Pitt vs Dallas, Jan 18, 1976

Most receptions, lifetime
16 Lynn Swann, Pitt, 4 games

Most receptions, game
11 Dan Rose, Cin vs SF, Jan 24, 1982

Most interceptions, game
3 Rod Martin, Oak Raiders vs Phil, Jan 25, 1981

Longest punt
62 Rich Camarillo, NE Patriots vs Chi Bears, Jan 26, 1986

Longest punt return
34 Darrell Green, Wash vs LA Raiders, Jan 22, 1984

Longest kickoff return
98 Fulton Walker, Miami vs Wash, Jan 30, 1983

---

was outlawed as a move, and a neutral zone between opposing lines was instituted. Roosevelt's demands to outlaw rough play led to the Rules Committee legalizing the forward pass in 1906.

First Televised Football Game

Fordham U, NYC, was the host to Waynesburg, a Pa school, in the first football game ever televised—in 1939. Fordham won, 34–7.

Longest Streaks

The longest collegiate winning streak is 47 straight by Oklahoma. The longest unbeaten streak is 63 games (59 won, 4 tied) by Washington from 1907 to 1917. Macalaster University of St Paul, Minn, ended a record 50-game losing streak when, with 11 sec remaining in the game, a 23-yd field goal beat Mount Senario, 17–14, on Sept 6, 1980. It was Macalaster's first victory since Oct 11, 1974.

Highest Score

The most points ever scored (by one team and both teams) in a college football game was 222 by Georgia Tech, Atlanta, Ga, against Cumberland University of Lebanon, Tenn on Oct 7, 1916. Tech also set records for the most points scored in one quarter (63), most touchdowns (32) and points after touchdown (30) in a game, and the largest victory margin (Cumberland did not score).

NFL Champions

The Green Bay Packers have won a record 11 NFL titles from 1929 through 1967. The Packers also won the first two Super Bowls (instituted Jan 1967), when the games were a competition between NFL and AFL champions. The Pittsburgh Steelers have the most Super Bowl victories with 4 (1975–76, 79–80). The 1972 Miami Dolphins had the best record for one season, including playoffs and Super Bowl (played Jan 1973), with 17 wins and no losses or ties.

Coaching Records

The longest-serving head coach was Amos Alonzo Stagg (1862–1965), who served Springfield in 1890–91, Chicago from 1892 to 1932 and College of the Pacific from 1933 to 1946, making a total of 57 years. He later served as an assistant coach to his son.

The record for most victories by a coach of a professional team is 325, by George Halas (1895–1983), who coached the Chicago Bears, 1920–29, 33–42, 46–55, 58–67.

In 1948, Bennie Oosterbaan, an assistant coach at Mich, his alma mater, was elevated to head coach. He won all 9 games and the national championship, becoming the first and only man to do that as a first-year head coach.

In 1985, Eddie Robinson of Grambling State University (Louisiana) won his 324th game, all at Grambling, in his 43 years there, to become the winningest coach in college football history. The previous record of 323 had been set by Paul "Bear" Bryant in 1982. Bryant had coached at Maryland (1945), Kentucky (1946–53), Texas A&M (1954–57) and Alabama (1958–82). Robinson finished 1985 with 329 victories.

College Record Passer

Doug Flutie of Boston College became the first major college player to pass for more than 10,000 yards in a career. His next-to-last game of the 1984 season on Nov 23 saw him complete 34 of 46 passes for 472 yards and 3 touchdowns with no interceptions in a victory over the University of Miami, 47–45. The winning touchdown pass of 64 yards came in the last seconds of play in the Orange Bowl before 30,235 spectators and

MODERN MAJOR-COLLEGE
INDIVIDUAL RECORDS
(Through 1985 Season)

Points

Most in a Game	43	Jim Brown (Syracuse)	1956
Most in a Season	174	Lydell Mitchell (Penn State)	1971
	174	Mike Rozier (Nebraska)	1983
Most in a Career	368	Luis Zendejas (Ariz State)	1981–84

Touchdowns

Most in a Game	7	Arnold Boykin (Mississippi)	1951
Most in a Season	29	Lydell Mitchell (Penn State)	1971
	29	Mike Rozier (Nebraska)	1983
Most in a Career	59	Glenn Davis (Army)	1943–46
	59	Tony Dorsett (Pittsburgh)	1973–76

Field Goals

Most in a Game	7	Mike Prindle ('W Mich)	1904
Most in a Season	29	John Lee (UCLA)	1984
Most in a Career	79	John Lee (UCLA)	1982–85
Most Consecutively (Career)	30	Chuck Nelson (Washington)	
			1981–82

Other Season Records

Yards Gained Rushing	2,342 yd	Marcus Allen (So Cal)	1981
Highest Average Gain per Rush (min. 150 attempts)	9.35 yd	Greg Pruitt (Oklahoma)	1971
Most Passes Attempted	511	Robbie Bosco (Brigham Young)	1985
Most Passes Completed	338	Robbie Bosco (Brigham Young)	1985
Most Touchdown Passes	47	Jim McMahon (Brigham Young)	1980
Most Yards Gained Passing	4,571 yd	Jim McMahon (Brigham Young)	1980
Most Passes Caught	134	Howard Twilley (Tulsa)	1965
Most Yards Gained on Catches	1,779 yd	Howard Twilley (Tulsa)	1965
Most Touchdown Passes Caught	18	Tom Reynolds (San Diego St)	1969
Most Passes Intercepted by	14	Al Worley (Washington)	1968
Highest Punting Average (min. 30 punts)	49.8 yd	Reggie Roby (Iowa)	1981

millions on a national TV hookup. The receiver of the final pass and many others of Flutie's passes was Gerald Phelan, his roommate.

Shortest Touchdown Pass

When the Dallas Cowboys had only 2 inches to go for a touchdown against the Washington Redskins on Oct 9, 1960, quarterback Eddie Le-Baron did the unexpected. Knowing that everyone was looking to a powerful thrust at the line by the heaviest plunging back on his team, Le-Baron took the ball from center and instead of handing it off to his fullback, slipped into the pocket and unleashed a short pass over the left side to his left end Bielski to set a world record for the shortest distance gained by a pass for a touchdown—2 inches.

U.S. Presidents Who Played College Football

Eisenhower at West Point.
Kennedy tried out for the team at Harvard.
Nixon at Whittier College, in California.
Ford at Michigan, where he played on a national championship team and later captained the varsity.
Reagan at Eureka College, in Illinois.

Worst Attendance

The worst attendance for a college football game was recorded on Nov 12, 1955 at Pullman, Washington. The game was between Wash State and San Jose State. It was played in spite of high winds and a temperature of 0°F. Total paid attendance: 1.

Super Bowl Winners

1967 Green Bay Packers (NFL)
1968 Green Bay Packers (NFL)
1969 New York Jets (AFL)
1970 Kansas City Chiefs (AFL)
1971 Baltimore Colts (AFC)
1972 Dallas Cowboys (NFC)
1973 Miami Dolphins (AFC)
1974 Miami Dolphins (AFC)
1975 Pittsburgh Steelers (AFC)
1976 Pittsburgh Steelers (AFC)
1977 Oakland Raiders (AFC)
1978 Dallas Cowboys (NFC)
1979 Pittsburgh Steelers (AFC)
1980 Pittsburgh Steelers (AFC)
1981 Oakland Raiders (AFC)
1982 San Francisco 49ers (NFC)
1983 Washington Redskins (NFC)
1984 Los Angeles Raiders (AFC)
1985 San Francisco 49ers (NFC)
1986 Chicago Bears (NFC)

The highest victory margin was in 1986 when the Bears beat the New England Patriots by 36 points, 46-10. This was also the most points scored by a winning team.

A record $550,000 per 30 sec was charged by NBC for advertising on the telecast.

GAMES AND PASTIMES

BRIDGE (CONTRACT)

Bridge (corruption of Biritch) is thought to be either of Levantine origin, similar games having been played there in the early 1870's, or to have come from the East—probably India.

Auction bridge (highest bidder names trump) was invented *c.* 1902. The contract principle, present in several games (notably the French game *Plafond, c.* 1917), was introduced to bridge by Harold S. Vanderbilt (US) on Nov 1, 1925, during a Caribbean voyage aboard the SS *Finland.* The new version became a worldwide craze after the US vs GB challenge match between Rumanian-born Ely Culbertson (1891–1955) and Lt-Col Walter Thomas More Buller (1887–1938) at Almack's Club, London, Sept 1930. The US won the 200-hand match by 4,845 points.

On June 14, 1986, for the first time, a tournament was simultaneously held worldwide sponsored by the Epsom Computer Corp with about 50,000 pairs participating.

Most World Titles

The World Championship (Bermuda Bowl) has been won most often by Italy's Blue Team (*Squadra Azzura*), 1957–9, 61–3, 65–7, 69, 73–5. Italy also won the Olympiad in 1964, 68 and 72. Giorgio Belladonna (b 1923) was on all these winning teams.

MOST DURABLE BRIDGE PLAYER: Oswald Jacoby was a world-rank competitor for 52 years. (ACBL)

Most Durable Player

Oswald Jacoby (b Dec 8, 1902, Dallas, Tex, d 1984) was a world-rank competitor for 52 years after winning his first world title in 1931. In Oct 1967, he became the first player to amass 10,000 master points. He retired in July 1983 but came back in Nov 1983 to be part of a team that won the North America team championship. (He also won the World Backgammon title.)

The bridge player with the longest unbroken record of competition in an ACBL annual is Jay T. Feigus (b 1892) of Middleton, NJ, who in 1985 played in his 56th consecutive Goldman Trophy contest. He twice finished in second place.

Most Master Points

In the latest ranking list based on Master Points awarded by the World Bridge Federation, the leading male player in the world was Giorgio Belladonna, a member of Italy's Blue Team, with 1,821¼ points, followed by four more Italians. The world's leading woman player is Dorothy Hayden Truscott (US) with 331¼ points.

As for master points awarded by the American Contract Bridge League, the leader was Barry Crane of Los Angeles (b 1927 Detroit, d July 5, 1985) who won a total of 35,137.6 points just before he died. Only 4 other players have even reached 25,000. The leader now is Paul Soloway with 26,119.41 points.

Most Players

Most competitors in play simultaneously: 4,444 at 1,111 tables during the 1979 Summer North American Championships at Las Vegas, Nev. Largest bridge tournament on record: 1979 Summer North American Championships with 18,517½ in ten days at the Las Vegas Hilton hotel.

Youngest Life Masters

Dougie Hsieh (NYC) was 11 years 306 days when he reached the rank of Life Master in the ACBL, and youngest ever to win a regional championship.

Adair Gellman of Bethesda, Md, became the youngest-ever female life master at age 14 years 6 months 4 days on Oct 24, 1983, breaking a record that had stood for 6 years. Then on Nov 5, 1983, just 12 days later, she was toppled from her peak by a still younger lady, Patricia Thomas of Las Cruces, NM, who was 14 years and 28 days. According to bridge columnist Alan Truscott of *The NY Times,* Miss Thomas joined the ACBL when barely 10 and became a senior master at the age of 11.

Marathon

The longest recorded session is one of 180 hours by four students at Edinburgh University, Scotland, Apr 21–28, 1972.

CHESS

The game originated in ancient India under the name Chaturanga (literally "four-corps")— an army game. The name chess is derived from the Persian word *shah.* The earliest reference is from the Middle Persian Karnamak (c. 590–628), though there are grounds for believing its origins are from the 2nd century, owing to the discovery, announced in Dec 1972, of two ivory chessmen in the Uzbek Soviet Republic, datable to

LARGEST CLAY CHESS SET: The King and Queen are 49 inches high, but the Knight is 53 inches.

that century. The *Fédération Internationale des Eschecs* was established in 1924. There were an estimated 7 million registered players in the USSR in 1973.

Most Opponents

Vlastimil Hort (b Jan 12, 1944) (Czechoslovakia), in Seltjarnes, Iceland, Apr 23–24, 1977, played 550 opponents, including a record 201 simultaneously. He only lost ten games.

Dimitrije Bjelica (Yugoslavia) played 301 opponents simultaneously (258 wins, 36 draws, 7 losses) in 9 hours on Sept 18, 1982, at Sarajevo, Yugoslavia. Bjelica's weight dropped by 4½ lb as he walked a total of 12.4 miles.

Eric Knoppert (W Germany) played 500 games of 10-min chess against opponents averaging 2,002 on the Elo scale Sept 13–16, 1985. He scored 413 points (1 for win, ½ for draw), a success rate of 82.6%.

The record for most consecutive games played is 660 by Vlastimil Hort over 32½ hours at Porz, W Germany on Oct 5–6, 1984. He played 60–100 opponents at a time, scoring over 80% and averaging 30 moves per game.

George Koltanowski (Belgium, later of US) tackled 56 opponents "blindfold" and won 50, drew 6, lost 0 in 9¾ hours at the Fairmont Hotel, San Francisco, on Dec 13, 1960.

Longest Games

The master game with the most moves on record was when Yedael Stepak (b Aug 21, 1940) (Israel) beat Yaakov Mashian (b Dec 17, 1943) (Iran, later Israel) in 193 moves in Tel Aviv, Israel, March 23–Apr 16, 1980. The total playing time was 24½ hours.

The slowest reported move (before modern rules) in an official event is reputed to have been played by Louis Paulsen (1833–91) (Germany) against Paul Charles Morphy (1837–84) (US) on Oct 29, 1857. The game ended in a draw on move 56 after 15 hours of play, of which Paulsen used most of the allotted time. Grandmaster Friedrich Sämisch (1896–1975) (Germany) ran out of the allotted time (2½ hours for 45 moves) after only 12 moves, in Prague, Czechoslovakia, in 1938.

World Champions

World champions have been generally recognized since 1886. The longest undisputed tenure was 27 years by Dr Emanuel Lasker (1868–1941) of Germany, from 1894 to 1921. Robert J. (Bobby) Fischer (b Chicago, March 9, 1943) is reckoned on the officially adopted Elo system to be the greatest Grandmaster of all time at 2,785. Anatoliy Karpov (USSR) (b May 23, 1951) was world champion 1975–85, with a rating lower than that of Gary Kasparov (USSR) (b Apr 13, 1963), rated 2,715, to whom he lost his title in Nov 1985. In a prior match in early 1985, the two set a record for draws in a championship match, 40. Kasparov at 2,720 is currently the highest-ranked player.

The women's world championship was held by Vera Menchik-Stevenson (1906–44) (USSR, later GB) from 1927 till her death, and was successfully defended a record 7 times. Nona Gaprindashvili (USSR) (b May 3, 1941) held the title from 1962 to 1978, and defended successfully 4 times. The highest-rated woman player is Maya Chiburdanidze (USSR) at 2,455.

The youngest world champion is Gary Kasparov who, at 22 years 210 days on Nov 9, 1985, beat Anatoliy Karpov (see above). Maya Chiburdanidze (b Jan 17, 1961) of Tbilisi (USSR) won the women's title in 1978 in a women-only match at the age of 17. The oldest was Wilhelm Steinitz (1836–1900) (Czech) who was 58 years old when he lost his title to Lasker in 1894.

José Raúl Capablanca (1888–1942) (Cuba) lost only 34 games in his adult career, 1909–39, for the fewest games lost by a world champion. He was unbeaten from Feb 10, 1916, to Mar 21, 1924, and was world champion from 1921 to 1927.

Marathon

The longest recorded session is one of 200 hours by Roger Long and Graham Croft in Bristol, Eng, May 11–19, 1984.

MONOPOLY®

The patentee of Monopoly, the world's most popular proprietary board game of which Parker Brothers has sold in excess of 80 million copies, was Charles Darrow (1889–1967). He invented the patented version of the game in 1933, while an unemployed heating engineer, using the street names of Atlantic City, NJ, where he spent his vacations.

Marathon

The longest game by four players ratified by Parker Brothers is 660 hours by Caara Fritz, Randy Smith, Phil Bennett, and Terry Sweatt in Atlanta, Ga July 12–Aug 8, 1981.

POKER

In the 1983 World Series of Poker held in Las Vegas, Nev, Tom McEvoy, a former Mich accountant, topped 107 other contestants, and with a $100 buy-in won the $540,000 top prize.

Joe Marquis dealt for 109 hours in a 7-card stud game at the Nevada Club in Laughlin, Nev, July 5–9, 1985, for the longest poker game on record.

SCRABBLE® CROSSWORD GAME

The crossword game was invented by Alfred M. Butts in 1931 and was developed, refined and trademarked as Scrabble Crossword Game by James Brunot in 1948. He sold the North American rights to Selchow & Righter Company, NY, the European rights to J. W. Spears & Sons, London, and the Australian rights to Murfett Pty Ltd, Melbourne.

The longest Scrabble Crossword Game is 153 hours by Peter Finan and Neil Smith at St Anselm's College, Merseyside, Eng, Aug 18–24, 1984.

THROWING

The greatest distance any inert object heavier than air has been thrown is 1,298 ft (433 yd) in the case of the Skyro flying ring by Tom McRann (b Jan 17, 1950) of Menlo Park, Calif on May 21, 1986 at Great America Park, Santa Clara, Calif.

In Frisbee (flying disc) throwing. Don Cain of East Brunswick, NJ set the record for maximum time aloft by keeping a flying disc in the air for 16.72 sec in Phila, Pa, on May 26, 1984. For women, the time-aloft record is 11.47 sec, set in Sonoma, Calif, by Denise Garfield on Oct 5, 1980.

The greatest distance achieved for throwing a flying disc, running, and catching it is 272.6 ft by Steve Bentley on Apr 8, 1982, at Sacramento, Calif. The women's record is 196.9 ft by Judy Horowitz of NYC on June 29, 1985 at LaMirada, Calif.

The world record for outdoor distance is 550.8 ft by Frank Aquilera of LaPuente, Calif at Las Vegas, Nev, Feb 4, 1984. The indoor distance

FASTEST DISC THROW: Alan Bonopane holds the record for tossing a Frisbee—74 mph—and for throwing discs for 250 mi in 24 hours with his partner Dan Roddick. (*Donnell A. Tate Photography*)

record is held by Van Miller of Tempe, Ariz, with a 399-ft toss at Flagstaff, Ariz, on Sept 18, 1982.

Liz Reeves holds the women's outdoor distance record (401.5 ft, set in Surrey, England, June 14, 1980), while the women's indoor distance record belongs to Suzanne Fields, of Boston, who threw 229.6 ft in Cedar Falls, Iowa, Apr 26, 1981.

The 24-hour group distance record is 428.02 miles set in Vernon, Conn, by the South Windsor Ultimate Frisbee Disc Team, July 8–9, 1977. Dan Roddick and Alan Bonopane of Pasadena, Calif, hold the outdoor world record for 24-hour pair distance with 250.02 miles, Dec 30–31, 1979. Jamie Knerr and Keith Biery set the indoor 24-hour pair distance mark with 298.37 miles, Aug 14–15, 1982, at Allentown, Pa.

The Prince George's Community College Flying High Club set the group marathon mark with 1,198 hours, June 1–July 22, 1983. The two-person marathon record is held by Jamie Knerr and Keith Biery, who played 110 hours 40 min in Allentown, Pa, Aug 23–27, 1981.

Alan Bonopane threw a professional model Frisbee disc at a speed of 74 mph and his teammate Tim Selinske made a clean catch of the throw on Aug 25, 1980 in San Marino, Calif.

LARGEST TWISTER: This aerial view of the Albany campus shows all 4,034 NY State Univ players in their record-setting game.

TWISTER

Twister is played on a mat of 24 colored dots. Players place their hands and feet on the dots and move them to other dots according to the results of an arrow spun on a board. As hands and feet become twisted, players fall and are eliminated. The last one to remain on all fours is the winner.

Mass Twister games are played with contestants starting with three players per mat and consolidating as some are eliminated. The record for the greatest number of participants in one game was set on Apr 19, 1986 by 4,034 students at the State Univ of NY at Albany. The winner was Jennifer Ratcliff of Wellesley, Mass.

VIDEO GAME CONTEST RESULTS

Highest score records are meaningless because of the tremendous variance between the games and cassettes available for play at home and in arcades. Each machine, each joy stick setting, each environment is different so that skill and endurance cannot be measured and compared with precision. Therefore the only records worth publishing are those of contest winners.

To ascertain what scores in video games are actually world records, competitions have been held, the latest being in June–July, 1986 by the US National Video Game Team, with Steve Harris as project director. World records, set in this contest and others in previous years, are as follows by game with winners' birth dates included:

Game	Score	Player's Name/Hometown	Birth Date
Alpine Ski	241,525	John T. Gordon, College Station, Tex	07/31/59
Arm Wrestling	781,030	Mark Haber, Pacific Palisades, Calif	08/25/66
Baby Pac-Man	1,220,800	Tim Uyeda, Los Angeles, Calif	10/11/69
Badlands	146,080	Gary Hatt, Monrovia, Calif	06/27/61
Battlezone	10,000,000	David Palmer, Auburn, Calif	05/01/58
Berzerk (Fast)	104,680	Ron K. Bailey, Shelby, NC	Not Available
Bosconian	615,490	Frank Rion, Anchorage, Alaska	09/25/59
Bubbles	1,365,970	Joe Malasarte, Anchorage, Alaska	01/26/68
Bump-N-Jump	421,760	Chris Cummins, Oil City, Pa	02/28/68
Burgertime	4,978,550	Bill Mitchell, Ft Lauderdale, Fla	07/16/65
Catch-22 (Combat)	4,532,950	Douglas DePirro, Anderson, Ind	04/05/63
Centipede	5,500,000	G. Ben Carter Jr, Fremont, Neb	04/04/58
Circus	101,600	Robert Hawkins, Seattle, Wash	02/08/57
Cheyenne	319,209,350	Donn Nauert, Austin, Tex	03/21/65
Choplifter	1,781,000	Charles Collins, Madison, Wis	06/29/64
Commando	835,700	Jeff Wakefield, Loveland, Colo	10/10/70
Congo Bongo	379,500	Steve Harris, Kansas City, Mo	11/07/66
Crackshot	4,885,140	Pat Harmon, Auburn, Ala	11/29/67
Crossbow	9,212,500	Donn Nauert, Austin, Tex	03/21/65
Crystal Castles	881,306	Mark Alpiger, Louisville, Ky	04/06/63
Defender	230,125	Gino Yoo, Anchorage, Alaska	Not Available
Dig Dug	1,847,960	Ken Eshtiaghi, Victoria, BC, Can	05/15/66
Discs of Tron	418,200	David Bagenski, Syracuse, NY	11/30/64

Game	Score	Player's Name/Hometown	Birth Date
Donkey Kong	874,300	Bill Mitchell, Ft Lauderdale, Fla	07/16/65
Donkey Kong, Jr	957,300	Bill Mitchell, Ft Lauderdale, Fla	07/16/65
Donkey Kong 3	2,132,100	Lloyd Bromola, Honolulu, Hawaii	12/24/66
Elevator Action	143,450	G. Ben Carter Jr, Fremont, Neb	04/04/58
Empire Strikes Back	1,345,049	David Palmer, Auburn, Calif	05/01/58
Excitebike	398,730	James Hillard, Upland, Calif	12/26/68
Express Raider	197,200	Gary Hatt, Monrovia, Calif	06/27/61
Firefox (9000 Mile)	707,790	David Palmer, Auburn, Calif	05/01/58
Flicky	4,548,540	Jonathan Long, Asheboro, NC	10/07/67
Food Fight	3,216,100	Gregory Jew, Sepulveda, Calif	04/13/58
Frogger	86,880	Todd Walker, Milpitas, Calif	Not Available
Frontline	268,000	William Joyce, Kansas City, Mo	12/14/67
Future Spy	276,950	Joey Wisniewski, Wausau, Wis	03/15/73
Galaga	2,278,190	Jim Vollandt, La Verue, Calif	08/20/66
Galaga 3 (Gaplus)	1,320,500	Bill Bradham, Dublin, Ga	08/27/66
Galaxian	186,770	Lloyd Dahling, Anchorage, Alaska	12/08/61
Ghosts & Goblins	510,500	Richard Webb, Cedar Rapids, Iowa	03/01/72
Gimme A Break	599	Carlos G. Gonzales, San Jose, Calif	03/23/61
Gunsmoke	1,348,850	Richie Paul Woodward, San Jose, Calif	11/07/64
Gyruss	14,009,300	Luke Rodgers, Denver, Colo	11/03/69
Hang-On (Simulator)	40,715,030	Don Novak, Wichita, Kans	08/05/42
Hogan's Alley	2,738,100	Jack Gale, N Miami Beach, Fla	06/20/66
Hyper Sports	538,340	Kelly Kobashigawa, Los Angeles, Calif	11/15/68
Indiana Jones	1,176,520	Ronald Mangio, Azusa, Calif	05/21/60
I, Robot	1,383,959	Dave Ryan, N Little Rock, Ark	07/31/67
Joust	1,537,500	Brett Watt, Citrus Heights, Calif	12/24/69
Junior Pac-Man	331,000	Kevin Fischer, Silver Springs, Md	10/01/53
Jungle King	198,280	Andy Noriega, Paramount, Calif	02/01/63
Karate Champ	239,900	George Weller, League City, Tex	10/08/67
Krull	323,780	Mark Rodobaugh, Lakewood, Calif	07/10/64
Kung-Fu Master	1,349,040	Mike Sullivan, Riverside, Calif	09/09/65

Game	Score	Player's Name/Hometown	Birth Date
Lode Runner	162,340	David Leicht, Honolulu, Hawaii	Not Available
MACH 3 (Bomber)	361,900	Sur Baycroft, Victoria, BC, Canada	03/26/68
MACH 3 (Fighter)	455,600	Randy Albright, Anchorage, Alaska	Not Available
Mad Crasher	844,988	Jack Gale, N Miami Beach, Fla	06/20/66
Mad Planets	129,714	Janice Rose, Winston-Salem, NC	02/22/52
Major Havoc	1,940,078	Ettore Ciaffi, Staten Is, NYC	05/20/64
Make Trax	1,358,120	James Delorme, Dawson Creek, BC, Can	01/20/65
Mappy	573,450	Mike Reynolds, Seattle, Wash	11/27/51
Marble Madness	187,880	Stan Szczepanski, Beverly Hills, Calif	08/04/50
Mario Bros	1,758,800	Perry Rodgers, Redondo Beach, Calif	06/17/62
Mat Mania	3,722,600	Jon Sitzman, Hixson, Tenn	10/03/70
Mayhem 2002	10,200	David Leicht, Honolulu, Hawaii	Not Available
Megazone	973,190	Stephen Joseph, Tarzana, Calif	07/27/56
Millipede	4,822,800	James Schneider, Oakland, Calif	01/24/60
Mini Golf	60,500	Stan Szczepanski, Beverly Hills, Calif	08/04/50
Missile Command	1,695,265	Roy Shildt, Los Angeles, Calif	07/02/55
Moon Patrol	366,700	Carl Lierman, Seattle, Wash	06/04/64
Mr Do!	1,390,350	Desiree McCrorey, San Jose, Calif	Not Available
Mr Do!'s Castle	370,520	Roy Sidor, Anchorage, Alaska	05/20/31
Ms Pac-Man	874,530	Chris Ayra, Miami, Fla	09/24/63
Nibbler	390,156,320	Marc Wertheim, N Bergen, NJ	10/09/64
Pack Rat	630,157	Bill Carmichael, Cheyenne, Wyo	10/27/68
Pacland	874,330	Scott Hilty, Wintersville, Ohio	03/18/70
Pac-Man	3,155,320	Patrice Corbell, Montreal, Quebec, Can	08/20/67
Paperboy	1,136,435	John Philip Britt, Riverside, Calif	11/21/65
Pengo	460,650	Terry Tanaka, Honolulu, Hawaii	08/31/60
Pole Position I	67,260	Les Lagier, Sunnyvale, Calif	Not Available
Pole Position II (Test Track)	79,890	Jeff Peters, Etiwanda, Calif	05/17/66
Pole Position II (Fuji)	78,020	Michael Klug, Sunnyvale, Calif	12/01/65
Pole Position II (Sazuka)	44,150	George Fabela, Farmer's Branch, Tex	12/08/66
Pole Position II (Seaside)	75,390	Jeff Peters, Etiwanda, Calif	05/17/66

Game	Score	Player's Name/Hometown	Birth Date
Popeye	351,150	Steve Harris, Kansas City, Mo	11/07/66
Punch-Out!!	15,019,240	Dale Klaus, Houston, Tex	07/17/70
Q*Bert	1,895,565	Tom Gault, Duluth, Minn	Not Available
Rally-X	51,660	Tad Perry, Seattle, Wash	02/02/64
Red Baron	214,230	David Palmer, Auburn, Calif	05/01/58
Return of the Jedi	1,938,010	Mike Sullivan, Riverside, Calif	09/09/65
Robotron	960,350	Robert (Bonney) Griffin, Kirkland, Wash	12/08/64
Rush-N-Attack	447,140	Dave Lopez, Casper, Wyo	04/26/69
Sarge	137,575	Dale Klaus, Houston, Tex	07/17/70
Satan's Hollow	18,098,450	Michael Ward, Madison, Wis	11/27/64
SiniStar	282,225	Jeff Peters, Etiwanda, Calif	05/17/66
Space Harrier	31,077,900	Richard Hunter, Compton, Calif	08/21/63
Space Invaders	29,090	Sonny Shum, Victoria, BC, Canada	05/11/64
Speed Buggy (Off-Road)	101,440	Tim Mereno, Virginia Beach, Va	12/20/67
Speed Buggy (North)	151,870	Danny Carranza, Culver City, Calif	04/10/68
Speed Buggy (South)	177,480	Mark Foster, Santa Monica, Calif	07/17/57
Speed Buggy (East)	57,890	Scott Jung, Maryland Heights, Mo	01/27/67
Speed Buggy (West)	83,990	Tim Mereno, Virginia Beach, Va	12/20/67
Spy Hunter	9,512,590	Paul Dean, Riverside, Calif	10/01/64
Star Gate	194,200	Scott Heyano, Seattle, Wash	Not Available
Star Rider	339,015	David Palmer, Auburn, Calif	05/01/58
Star Trek	1,723,175	Maurice Disciullo, Ft Lauderdale, Fla	Not Available
Star Wars	31,660,614	David Palmer, Auburn, Calif	05/01/58
Stocker	53,970	Cody Joens, Rochester, Miss	12/26/49
Super Basketball	1,394,930	Tim McGuire, Anchorage, Alaska	10/09/66
Super Mario Bros	2,229,350	Michael Perring, San Francisco, Calif	08/25/65
Super Pac-Man	855,940	Bill Deluca, Colonia, NJ	11/21/66
Super Punch-Out!!	182,980	Sean Jensen, Anchorage, Alaska	12/29/71
Tapper	9,068,625	Michael Ward, Madison, Wis	11/27/64
Tempest	822,852	Jeff Seymour, Sacramento, Calif	12/25/59
Ten-Yard Fight	295,100	Mike Macy, Salina, Kans	03/07/67
Tiger-Heli	659,960	George Cifrancis III, Steubenville, Ohio	06/22/66
Time Pilot	5,197,100	Jeff Peters, Etiwanda, Calif	05/17/66
Time Pilot '84	463,300	Samantha Johanik, Des Moines, Iowa	08/11/65

Game	Score	Player's Name/Hometown	Birth Date
Track & Field	95,040	Kelly Kobashigawa, Los Angeles, Calif	11/15/68
Tron	1,695,463	David Palmer, Auburn, Calif	05/01/58
Turbo	53,179	Wish Stuckey, Laurel, Miss	08/07/69
Turkey Shoot	74,650	Stefan Pare Delisle, Montreal, Quebec, Can	08/28/66
Tutankham	205,780	Jorge Matsufuji, College Station, Tex	06/29/65
Vanguard	317,330	Thomas Chaka, Wharton, Tex	08/17/65
Vertigo	595,028	Donn Nauert, Austin, Tex	03/21/65
Wizard of Wor	80,300	Marc Longridge, Oshawa, Ont, Canada	10/01/65
Zaxxon	804,150	Dave Ander, Anchorage, Alaska	12/12/62
Zoo Keeper	20,063,920	Jack Gale, N Miami, Fla	06/20/66

GOLF

Origins

It has been suggested that golf originated with Scottish shepherds using their crooks to knock pebbles into rabbit holes. This may be apocryphal, but somewhat firmer evidence exists. A stained glass window in Gloucester Cathedral, dating from 1350, portrays a golfer-like figure, but the earliest mention of golf occurs in a prohibiting law passed by the Scottish Parliament in March 1457, under which "golff be utterly cryit doune and not usit."

The Romans had a cognate game called *paganica,* which may have been carried to Britain before 400 AD. The Chinese National Golf Association claims the game is of Chinese origin ("*Ch'ui Wan*—the ball-hitting game") from the 3rd or 2nd century BC. There were official ordinances prohibiting a ball game while states in Belgium and Holland from 1360. Gutta-percha balls succeeded feather balls in 1848, and were in turn succeeded in 1902 by rubber-cored balls, invented in 1899 by Coburn Haskell (US). Steel shafts were authorized in the US in 1925.

Golf was first played on the moon in Feb 1971 by Capt Alan Shepard (US), commander of the *Apollo XIV* spacecraft.

Oldest Clubs

The oldest club of which there is written evidence is the Gentleman Golfers (now the Honourable Company of Edinburgh Golfers) formed in March 1744—10 years prior to the institution of the Royal and Ancient Club of St Andrews, Fife, Scotland. However, the Royal Burgess Golfing Society of Edinburgh claims to have been founded in 1735. The oldest existing club in North America is the Royal Montreal Club (Nov 1873) and the oldest in the US is St Andrews, Westchester County, NY (1888). An older claim is by the Foxbury Country Club, Clarion County, Pa (1887).

LOWEST TOURNAMENT SCORE (above): Sam Snead carded a 59 for 18 holes in the 1959 Greenbrier Open. "Slammin' Sam" won a record 84 US PGA tournaments in his career, and 134 altogether. Snead shot a 12-under-par 60 (11 strokes under his age) in July 1983. The crowds still follow him. (*Radio Times Hulton Picture Library*)

WINNINGEST AMATEUR (left): Bobby Jones won the US Open 4 times and the US Amateur 5 times. He never turned pro.

Highest and Lowest Courses

The highest golf course in the world is the Tuctu Golf Club in Morococha, Peru, which is 14,335 ft above sea level at its lowest point. Golf has, however, been played in Tibet at an altitude of over 16,000 ft.

The lowest golf course in the world was that of the now defunct Sodom and Gomorrah Golfing Society at Kallia (Qulya), on the northern shores of the Dead Sea, 1,250 ft below sea level. Currently the lowest is the par-70 Furnace Creek Golf Course, Death Valley, Calif, at a disputed average of 178–272 ft below sea level.

Longest Course

The world's longest course is the par-77, 8,325-yd International GC, Bolton, Mass, from the "Tiger" tees, remodeled in 1969 by Robert Trent Jones.

Biggest Bunker

The world's biggest trap is Hell's Half Acre on the 585-yd 7th hole of the Pine Valley course, Clementon, NJ, built in 1912 and generally regarded as the world's most trying course.

Longest Hole

The longest hole in the world is the 7th hole (par 7) of 909 yd at the Sano Course, Satsuki GC, Japan.

Largest Green

Probably the largest green in the world is that of the par-6, 695-yd 5th hole at International GC, Bolton, Mass, with an area greater than 28,000 sq ft.

MOST WINS IN MAJOR TOURNAMENTS

US Open	Willie Anderson (1880–1910)	4	1901–03–04–05
	Robert Tyre Jones, Jr (1902–71)	4	1923–26–29–30
	W. Ben Hogan (b Aug 13, 1912)	4	1948–50–51–53
	Jack William Nicklaus (b Jan 21, 1940)	4	1962–67–72–80
US Amateur	R. T. Jones, Jr	5	1924–25–27–28–30
British Open	Harry Vardon (1870–1937)	6	1896–98–99, 1903–11–14
British Amateur	John Ball (1861–1940)	8	1888–90–92–94–99, 1907–10–12
PGA Championship (US)	Walter C. Hagen (1892–1969)	5	1921–24–25–26–27
	Jack W. Nicklaus	5	1963–71–73–75–80
Masters Championship (US)	Jack W. Nicklaus	6	1963–65–66–72–75–86
US Women's Open	Elizabeth (Betsy) Earle-Rawls (b May 4, 1928)	4	1951–53–57–60
	"Mickey" Wright (b Feb 14, 1935)	4	1958–59–61–64
US Women's Amateur	Mrs Glenna Vare (née Collett) (b June 20, 1903)	6	1922–25–28–29–30–35

Lowest Scores for 9 and 18 Holes

Three professional players are recorded to have played a long course (over 6,000 yd) for a score of 57: Bill Burke at the Normandie Golf Club, St Louis (6,389 yds, par 71) on May 20, 1970; Tom Ward at the Searcy (Ark) Country Club (6,098 yds, par 70) in 1981; Augie Navarro at the Sim Park Golf Course (Wichita, Kans) in 1982.

Alfred Edward Smith (1903–85), the English professional at Woolacombe, achieved an 18-hole score of 55 (15 under bogey 70) on his home course on Jan 1, 1936.

Nine holes in 25 (4, 3, 3, 2, 3, 3, 1, 4, 2) was recorded by A. J. "Bill" Burke in his round of 57 (32 + 25) (see above), and by teenager Douglas Beecher at the Pitman (NJ) Country Club (3,150 yd, par 35) in 1976. The tournament record is 27 by Mike Souchak (US) (b May 1927) for the second nine (par 35) first round of the 1955 Texas Open; Andy North (US) (b Mar 9, 1950) second nine (par 34), first round, 1975 BC Open at En-Joie GC, Endicott, NY; and Jose Maria Canizares (Spain) (b Feb 18, 1947), first nine, third round, in the 1978 Swiss Open on the 6,811-yd Crans-Sur course, and by Robert Lee (GB) (b Oct 12, 1961) first nine, first round, in the Monte Carlo Open on the 6,249 yd Mont Agel course on June 28, 1985.

The US PGA tournament record for 18 holes is 59 (30 + 29) by Al Geiberger (b Sept 1, 1937) in the second round of the Danny Thomas Classic, on the 72-par, 7,249-yd Colonial CC course, Memphis, Tenn, June 10, 1977.

In non-PGA tournaments, Samuel Jackson Snead (b May 27, 1912) had 59 in the Greenbrier Open (now called the Sam Snead Festival), at White Sulphur Springs, W Va, on May 16, 1959; Gary Player (South Africa) (b Nov 1, 1935) carded 59 in the second round of the Brazilian Open in Rio de Janeiro on Nov 29, 1974; and David Jagger (GB) also had 59 in a Pro-Am tournament prior to the 1973 Nigerian Open at Ikoyi Golf Club, Lagos.

Lowest Scores for 36 Holes

The record for 36 holes is 122 (59 + 63) by Sam Snead in the 1959 Greenbrier Open (now called the Sam Snead Festival) (non-PGA) (see above), May 16–17, 1959. Horton Smith (see below) scored 121 (63 + 58) on a short course on Dec 21, 1928.

Floyd Satterlee Rood used the entire United States as a course, when he played from the Pacific surf to the Atlantic surf from Sept 14, 1963 to Oct 3, 1964 in 114,737 strokes. He lost 3,511 balls on the 3,397.7-mi trail.

Women's Lowest Scores

The lowest recorded score on an 18-hole course (over 6,000 yd) for a woman is 62 (30 + 32) by Mary (Mickey) Kathryn Wright (b Feb 14, 1935), of Dallas, on the Hogan Park Course (6,286 yd) at Midland, Tex, in Nov 1964.

Wanda Morgan (b March 22, 1910) recorded a score of 60 (31 + 29) on the Westgate and Birchington Golf Club course, Kent, England, over 18 holes (5,002 yd) on July 11, 1929.

The LPGA record for 9 holes is held by Pat Bradley who scored 28 in Denver, Colo, Aug 24, 1984.

Lowest Scores for 72 Holes

The lowest recorded score on a first-class course is 255 (29 under par) by Leonard Peter Tupling (b Apr 6, 1950) (GB) in the Nigerian Open at Ikoyi Golf Club, Lagos, in Feb 1981, made up of 63, 66, 62 and 64 (average 63.75 per round). Horton Smith (1908–63), twice US Masters Champion, scored 245 (63, 58, 61 and 63) for 72 holes on the 4,700-yd course (par 64) at Catalina Country Club, Calif, to win the Catalina Open, Dec 21–23, 1928.

The lowest 72 holes in a US professional event is 257 (60, 68, 64 and 65) by Mike Souchak in the 1955 Texas Open at San Antonio.

The lowest 72 holes in an Open championship in Europe is 262 by Percy Alliss (1897–1975) of Britain, with 67, 66, 66 and 63 in the Italian Open Championship at San Remo in 1932, and by Lu Liang Huan (b Dec 10, 1935) (Taiwan) in the 1971 French Open at Biarritz. Kelvin D. G. Nagle (b Dec 21, 1920) of Australia shot 261 in the Hong Kong Open in 1961.

Longest Drive

In long-driving contests 330 yd is rarely surpassed at sea level.

In officially regulated long-driving contests over level ground the greatest distance recorded is 392 yd by Tommie Campbell (b July 24, 1927) (Foxrock Golf Club), a member of the Irish PGA, made at Dun Laoghaire, Co Dublin, in July 1964.

The USPGA record is 341 yd by Jack William Nicklaus (b Columbus, Ohio, Jan 21, 1940), then weighing 206 lb, in July 1963.

Liam Higgins (Ireland) drove a Spalding Top Flite ball 634.1 yd on an airport runway at Baldonnel Military Airport, Dublin, Ireland, Sept 25, 1984.

The longest on an ordinary course is 515 yd by Michael Hoke Austin (b Feb 17, 1910) of Los Angeles, in the US National Seniors Open Championship at Las Vegas, Nev, Sept 25, 1974. Aided by an estimated 35-mph tailwind, the 6-ft-2-in 210-lb golfer drove the ball on the fly to within a yard of the green on the par-4, 450-yd 5th hole of the Winterwood Course. The ball rolled 65 yd past the flagstick.

Arthur Lynskey claimed a drive of 200 yd out and 2 miles down off Pikes Peak, Colo (14,110 ft), June 28, 1968.

A drive of 2,640 yd (1½ miles) across ice was achieved by an Australian meteorologist named Nils Lied at Mawson Base, Antarctica, in 1962. On the moon, the energy expended on a mundane 300-yd drive would achieve, craters permitting, a distance of a mile.

Longest Hitter

The golfer regarded as the longest consistent hitter the game has ever known is the 6-ft-5-in-tall, 230-lb George Bayer (US) (b Sept 17, 1925), the 1957 Canadian Open Champion. His longest measured drive was one of 420 yd at the fourth in the Las Vegas Invitational in 1953. It was measured as a precaution against litigation since the ball struck a spectator. Bayer also drove a ball pin high on a 426-yd hole in Tucson, Ariz. Radar measurements show that an 87-mph impact velocity for a golf ball falls to 46 mph in 3.0 sec.

MOST TOURNAMENT VICTORIES: Kathy Whitworth (below) has won 88 LPGA contests in 23 touring years through 1985.

18 TOURNAMENT WINS in a year is the record Byron Nelson (above) set in 1945.

Most Tournament Wins

The record for winning tournaments in a single season is 18 (plus one unofficial), including a record 11 consecutively, by Byron Nelson (b Feb 4, 1912) (US), March 8–Aug 4, 1945.

Sam Snead has won 84 official USPGA tour events to Dec 1979, and has been credited with a total 134 tournament victories since 1934.

Kathy Whitworth (b Sept 27, 1939) (US) topped this with her 88th LPGA victory through 1985, her 23nd year on the tour. Mickey Wright (US) won a record 13 tournaments in one year, 1963.

Jack Nicklaus (US) is the only golfer who has won all five major titles (British Open, US Open, Masters, PGA and US Amateur) twice, while setting a record total of 20 major tournament victories (1959–86). His remarkable record in the US Open is 4 firsts, 8 seconds and 2 thirds. Nicklaus has accumulated 71 PGA tournament wins in all.

In 1930 Bobby Jones achieved a unique "Grand Slam" of the US and British Open and British and US Amateur titles.

Biggest Winning Margin

The greatest margin of victory in a major tournament is 21 strokes by Jerry Pate (b Sept 15, 1953) (US) in the Colombian Open with 262 on Dec 10–13, 1981.

Cecilia Leitch won the Canadian Ladies Open Championship in 1921 by the highest margin for a major title, 17 up and 15 to play.

Longest Putt

The longest recorded holed putt in a major tournament was one of 86 ft on the vast 13th green at the Augusta National, Ga, by Cary Middlecoff (b Jan 1921) in the 1955 Masters Tournament.

Bobby Jones was reputed to have holed a putt in excess of 100 ft on the 5th green in the first round of the 1927 British Open at St Andrews, Scotland.

Bob Cook (US) sank a putt measured at 140 ft 2¾ in on the 18th at St Andrew's, Scotland, in the International Fourball Pro-Am Tournament on Oct. 1, 1976.

Highest Earnings

The greatest amount ever won in official USPGA golf prizes is $4,857,494 by Jack Nicklaus through May 1986.

The record for a year is $530,808 by Tom Watson (US) in 1980.

The highest LPGA career earnings by a woman is $2,096,497 by Pat Bradley (b Mar 24, 1951) to July 8, 1986. Nancy Lopez (b Jan 6, 1957) holds the record for earnings in one season, $416,472 in 1985.

US Open

This championship was inaugurated in 1895. The lowest 72-hole aggregate is 272 (63, 71, 70, 68) by Jack Nicklaus on the Lower Course (7,015 yd) at Baltusrol Golf Club, Springfield, NJ, June 12–15, 1980. The lowest score for 18 holes is 63 by Johnny Miller (b Apr 29, 1947) of Calif on the 6,921-yd, par-71 Oakmont, Pa, course on June 17, 1973, and Jack Nicklaus and Tom Weiskopf (b Nov 9, 1942), both on June 12, 1980.

US Masters

The lowest score in the US Masters (instituted at the 6,980-yd Augusta National Golf Course, Ga, in 1934) was 271 by Jack Nicklaus in 1965 and Raymond Floyd (b Sept 4, 1942) in 1976. Jack Nicklaus has won most often—6 times. The lowest round is 63 by Nick Price (b Jan 28, 1957) (Zimbabwe) in 1986. The oldest champion was Jack Nicklaus at 46 years 114 days in 1986, and the youngest was Severiano Ballesteros (Spain) aged 23 years 4 days in 1980.

British Open

The Open Championship was inaugurated in 1860 at Prestwick, Strathclyde, Scotland. The lowest score for 9 holes is 28 by Denis Durnian (b June 30, 1950) at Royal Birdale, Southport, Eng, in the second round on July 15, 1983.

The lowest scoring round in the Open itself is 63 by Mark Hayes (US, b July 12, 1949) at Turnberry, Strathclyde, Scotland, in the second round on July 7, 1977, and by Isao Aoki (Japan) (b Aug 31, 1942) in the third round in Muirfield, July 19, 1980. Henry Cotton (GB) at Royal St George's, Sandwich, Kent, England, completed the first 36 holes in 132 (67 + 65) on June 27, 1934.

The lowest 72-hole aggregate is 268 (68, 70, 65, 65) by Tom Watson (US) (b Sept 4, 1949) at Turnberry, Scotland, ending on July 9, 1977.

US PGA Championship

The Professional Golfers' Association championship was first held in 1916 as a match play tournament but since 1958 it has been contested

BIGGEST PRIZE WINNER: Johnny Miller (above left) captured the $500,000 prize offered by Sun City, a course in an enclave in S Africa in 1982.

U S MASTER (above right): Bernhard Langer (W Ger) surprised American golf enthusiasts when he won the US Masters tournament, Apr 14, 1985. The tournament had been won by non-Americans only five times in its 51-year history.

HIGHEST EARNINGS (below): Besides winning 20 major tournaments (71 in all) for a record, Jack Nicklaus has earned more than $4,800,000 to June 1986 in prize money. Nicklaus is the only golfer who has won all 5 major titles twice. (*E. D. Lacey*)

over 72 holes of stroke play. It has been won a record five times by Walter Hagen between 1921 and 1927, and Jack Nicklaus between 1963 and 1980. The oldest champion was Julius Boros at 48 years 18 days in 1968 and the youngest was Gene Sarazen aged 20 years 5 months 20 days in 1922. Since 1958 the greatest margin of victory has been the seven-stroke lead by Nicklaus in 1980. The lowest aggregate was 271 by Bobby Nichols at Columbus, Ohio in 1964, and the lowest round was 63 by Bruce Crampton in 1975 and Ray Floyd in 1982. The lowest score for 36 holes has been 131 by Hal Sutton (65, 66) in 1983. The 54-hole mark is 202 (69, 66, 67) by Raymond Floyd in 1969.

US Amateur

Initially held in the same week and at the same venue as the first US Open in 1895. Bobby Jones won a record five times between 1924 and 1930, having first qualified for the tournament in 1916, aged 14 yr 5½ months, the youngest ever to do so. The oldest player to win the title was Jack Westland, aged 47 years 8 months 9 days in 1952, while the youngest was Robert Gardner at 19 years 5 months in 1909. (Three years later, in 1912, Gardner broke the world pole vault record becoming the first to clear 13 ft.)

Biggest Prize Putt

Jack Nicklaus' total earnings went up by $240,000 when he sank an 8-foot putt on the 18th green of the Desert Highlands course in Scottsdale, Ariz, on Nov 25, 1984 in a "Skins" match against Arnold Palmer, Gary Player and Tom Watson. All three of his opponents missed their birdie putts from further distances and Nicklaus won the accumulated prize money.

US Women's Open

This tournament was first held in 1946, and currently is played over 72 holes of stroke play. Betsy Rawls won a record four times between 1951 and 1960, and this was equalled by Mickey Wright between 1958 and 1964. The oldest champion was Fay Crocker (Uru) at 40 years 11 months in 1955, while the youngest was Catherine Lacoste (France) at 22 years 5 days in 1967, when she became the only amateur player to win the title. The greatest margin of victory was by Babe Didrikson Zaharias who beat Betty Hicks by 12 strokes in 1954. The lowest aggregate score has been 280 (70, 70, 68, 72) by Amy Alcott in 1980, and the lowest round was 65 by Sally Little in 1978. The record for 36 holes is 139 by Carol Mann and Donna Caponi in 1970, the latter going on to a 54-hole score of 210.

Most Rounds in a Day

The greatest number of rounds played on foot in 24 hours is 22 rounds plus 5 holes (401 holes) by Ian Colston, 35, at Bendigo GC, Victoria, Australia (73 par, 6,061 yd), Nov 27–28, 1971. He covered more than 100 miles.

Using golf carts for transport, Charles Stock played 702 holes in 24 hours at an average 72.12 min per round at Boston Hills Country Club, Hudson, O, July 7–8, 1985. Terry Zachary played 391 holes in 12 hours on the 6,706-yd course at Connaught Golf Club, Alberta, Canada on June 16, 1986. Dr. R. C. "Dick" Hardison, aged 61, played 236 holes under USGA rules in 12 hours at Sea Mountain GC, Punaluu, Hawaii July 31, 1984, maintaining an average score of 76 per round, with an average time per hole of 3.05 min. His best round was a 68, achieved in 49 min 58 sec, including a second nine of 30 in 24 min 28 sec. He used seven fore caddies and 26 electric golf carts, which he drove himself.

The most holes played on foot in a week (168 hours) is 1,128 by Steve Hylton at the Mason Rudolph Golf Club (6,060 yd), Clarksville, Tenn, Aug 25–31, 1980.

Most Shots One Hole

The highest number of strokes taken at a single hole in a major tournament was achieved in the inaugural Open Championship at Prestwick, Scotland, in 1860, when an unnamed player took 21. In the 1938 US Open, Ray Ainsley achieved instant fame when he took 19 strokes at the par-4 16th hole. Most of them were in an attempt to hit the ball out of a fast-moving brook. Hans Merrell of Mogadore, Ohio, took 19 strokes on the par-3, 222-yd 16th during the Bing Crosby tournament at Cypress Point Club, Del Monte, Calif, on Jan 17, 1959. At Biarritz, France in 1888 it was reported that Chevalier von Cittern took 316 for 18 holes, thus averaging 17.55 strokes per hole.

The story to top them all concerns a lady player in the qualifying round of a tournament in Shawnee-on-Delaware, Pa in the early part of the century. Her card showed she took 166 strokes for the short 130-yd 16th hole. Her tee shot landed and floated in a nearby river, and, with her meticulous husband, she set out in a boat and eventually beached the ball 1½ mi downstream. From there she had to play through a forest until finally she holed the ball. A. J. Lewis, playing at Peacehaven, Sussex, Eng, in 1890 had 156 putts on one green without holing the ball.

Fastest Rounds

With such variations in lengths of courses, speed records, even for rounds under par, are of little comparative value. Rick Baker completed 18 holes (6,142 yd) in 25 min 48.47 sec at Surfer's Paradise, Queensland, Australia, Sept 4, 1982, but this test permitted striking the ball while it was still moving. The record for a still ball is 28.09 min by Gary Wright (b Nov 27, 1946) at Tewantin-Noosa Golf Club, Queensland, Australia (18 holes, 6,039 yd), on Dec 9, 1980.

Seventy-seven players completed the 18-hole 6,502 yd Kern City course, Calif. in 10 min 30 sec on Aug 24, 1984 using only one ball. They scored 80!

Richest Prize

The greatest first-place prize money was $500,000 (total purse $1.1 million) won by Johnny Miller (US) (b Apr 29, 1947) in 1982, and by Raymond Floyd (b Sept 4, 1942) in 1983 at Sun City, Bophuthatswana, S Africa. After 72-hole scores of 277, Miller beat Severiano Ballesteros (Spain) (who won $160,000 for second place) and Floyd beat Craig Stadler in playoffs.

US Women's Amateur Championship

Instituted in Nov 1895, and currently 36 final holes of match play after 36 qualifying holes of stroke play. Glenna Collett Vare won a record 6 titles between 1922 and 1935. The oldest champion was Dorothy Campbell-Hurd (GB) aged 41 years 4 months when winning her third title in 1924, and the youngest was Laura Baugh at 16 years 2 months 21 days in 1971. Margaret Curtis beat her sister, Harriot, in the 1907 final—they later presented the Curtis Cup for competition between the US and GB.

IN THE CUP. Arnold Palmer prepares to putt as his many followers, known as Arnie's Army, look on. Palmer won the Masters 4 times and played on 6 winning teams in World Cup play. He was the first golfer to reach $1 million in career earnings.

Ryder Cup

The biennial Ryder Cup (instituted 1927) professional match between the US and GB (Europe since 1979) has been won by the US 21½–4½. In 1985, GB-Europe won 16½ to US 11½ in Eng. William Earl "Billy" Casper (b San Diego, Calif, June 24, 1931) has the record of winning most matches, with 20 won out of 37 (1961–75). Neil Cales (GB) played in a record 40 matches (1961–77).

World Cup (formerly Canada Cup)

The World Cup (instituted 1953), contested over 72 holes of stroke play by teams of two with scores aggregated, has been won most often by the US with 16 victories between 1955 and 1983. In 1985, the winning team was Canada with a score of 559 for Dan Halldorson and Dave Barr, combined. The only men on six winning teams have been Arnold Palmer (b Sept 10, 1929) (1960, 62–64, 66–67) and Jack Nicklaus (1963–64, 66–67, 71, 73). The only man to take the individual title three times is Jack Nicklaus (US) in 1963–64, 1971. The lowest aggregate score for 144 holes is 545 by Australia, Bruce Devlin (b Oct 10, 1937) and David Graham (b May 23, 1946) at San Isidro, Buenos Aires, Argentina, Nov 12–15, 1970, and the lowest score by an individual winner was 269 by Roberto de Vicenzo (b Buenos Aires, Argentina, Apr 14, 1923) on the same occasion.

Walker Cup

The US versus Great Britain–Ireland series instituted in 1921 (for the Walker Cup since 1922), now biennial, has been won by the US 27½–2½ to date. In 1985, the US won 13-11 in NJ. Joe Carr (GB–I) played in 10 contests (1947–67).

Youngest and Oldest Champions

The youngest winner of the British Open was Tom Morris, Jr (1851–75) at Prestwick, Ayrshire, Scotland, in 1868, aged 17 years 249 days. The oldest British Open champion was "Old Tom" Morris (1821–1908) who was aged 46 years 99 days when he won in 1867. In modern times, the oldest was 1967 champion Roberto de Vicenzo (Argentina), when aged 44 years 93 days.

The oldest US Amateur Champion was Jack Westland (b Dec 14, 1904) at Seattle, Wash, on Aug 23, 1952, aged 47 years 253 days. The oldest US Open Champion was Raymond Floyd at 43 years 284 days on June 15, 1986. Isabella "Belle" Robertson (b Apr 11, 1936) won the 1986 Scottish Women's Championship aged 50 years 43 days.

Longest Span

Jacqueline Ann Mercer (*née* Smith) (b Apr 5, 1929) won her first South African title at Humewood GC, Port Elizabeth, in 1948, and her fourth title at Port Elizabeth GC on May 4, 1979, 31 years later.

HOLES-IN-ONE

Golf Digest was notified in 1984 of 39,828 holes-in-one, and in 1985 of 43,386, so averaging 119 per day.

Longest

The longest straight hole shot in one is the 10th hole (447 yd) at Miracle Hills GC, Omaha, Neb. Robert Mitera achieved a hole-in-one there on Oct 7, 1965. Mitera, aged 21 and 5 ft 6 in tall, weighed 165 lb. A two-handicap player, he normally drove 245 yd. A 50-mph gust carried his shot over a 290-yd drop-off. The group in front testified to the remaining distance.

The longest dogleg achieved in one is the 480-yd 5th hole at Hope CC, Ark, by Larry Bruce on Nov 15, 1962.

The women's record is 393 yd by Marie Robie of Wollaston, Mass, on the first hole of the Furnace Brook GC, Sept 4, 1949.

Consecutive

There is no recorded instance of a golfer performing three consecutive holes-in-one, but there are at least 16 cases of "aces" being achieved in two consecutive holes, of which the greatest was Norman L. Manley's unique "double albatross" on two par-4 holes (330-yd 7th and 290-yd 8th) on the Del Valle CC course, Saugus, Calif, on Sept 2, 1964.

The first woman ever to card consecutive aces is Sue Prell, on the 13th and 14th holes at Chatswood GC, Sydney, Australia, on May 29, 1977.

The closest recorded instances of a golfer getting 3 consecutive holes-in-one were by the Rev Harold Snider (b July 4, 1900) who aced the 8th, 13th and 14th holes of the par-3 Ironwood course in Phoenix, Ariz, on June 9, 1976, and the late Dr Joseph Boydstone on the 3rd, 4th and 9th at Bakersfield GC, Calif on Oct 10, 1962.

Most Aces

The greatest number of holes-in-one in a career is 68 by Harry Lee Bonner 1967 to 1985, most at his home 9-hole course of Las Gallinas, San Rafael, Calif.

The most aces in one year is 30 by Scott Palmer June 5, 1983–May 31,

1984, all on holes between 130 and 260 yd in length at Balboa Park, San Diego, Calif. He also made 4 aces in 4 consecutive rounds, Oct 9–12, 1983.

Douglas Porteous, 28, aced 4 holes over 39 consecutive holes—the 3rd and 6th on Sept 26, and the 5th on Sept 28 at Ruchill GC, Glasgow, Scotland, and the 6th at the Clydebank and District GC Course on Sept 30, 1974. Robert Taylor holed the 188-yd 16th hole at Hunstanton, Norfolk, England, on three successive days—May 31, June 1 and 2, 1974. On May 12, 1984, Joe Lucius of Tiffin, Ohio, aced for the 13th time the par-3, 141-yd 15th hole at the Mohawk Golf Club. Lucius has 10 aces for the 10th hole on the same course, and 31 aces in all.

Youngest and Oldest

The youngest golfer recorded to have shot a hole-in-one was Coby Orr (aged 5) of Littleton, Colo, on the 103-yd fifth hole at the Riverside GC, San Antonio, Tex, in 1975. *Golf Digest* credits Tommy Moore (6 yrs 1 month 7 days) of Hagerstown, Md with being the youngest for an ace he shot on a 145-yd hole in 1969.

The oldest golfer to have performed the feat is Otto Bucher (Switz) (b May 12, 1885) aged 99 years 244 days on Jan 13, 1985 when he aced the 130-yd 12th hole at La Manga GC, Spain.

The oldest woman to score an ace is Erna Ross, 96, who holed-in-one on the 112-yd 17th hole of the Everglades Club, Palm Beach, Fla, on May 25, 1986.

The oldest player to score his age is C. Arthur Thompson (1869–1975) of Victoria, BC, Canada, who scored 103 on the Uplands course of 6,215 yd when age 103 in 1973.

Largest Tournament

The Volkswagen Grand Prix Open Amateur Championship in the UK attracted a record 321,778 (206,820 men and 114,958 women) competitors in 1984.

GYMNASTICS

Earliest References

Tumbling and similar exercises were performed *c.* 2600 BC as religious rituals in China, but it was the Greeks who coined the word gymnastics. A primitive form was practiced in the ancient Olympic Games, but it was not until Johann Friedrich Simon began to teach at Basedow's Gymnasium in Dessau, Germany, in 1776 that the foundations of the modern sport were laid. The first national federation was formed in Germany in 1860 and the International Gymnastics Federation was founded in Liège, Belgium in 1881. The sport was included at the first modern Olympic Games at Athens in 1896.

Current events for men are: floor exercises, horse vault, rings, pommel horse, parallel bars and horizontal bar, while for women they are: floor exercises, horse vault, asymmetrical bars, and balance beam.

BEST ALL-ROUND OLYMPIC
GYMNAST (above): Mary Lou
Retton (US) won the gold medal
in this category, silver medal in
the vault, and bronze medal in the
uneven parallel bars in the 1984
Games.

HANDSTAND PUSH-UP CHAMPION (above right): 8-year-old
Chung Kwun Ying pushed-up 2,750 times consecutively like this in
Hong Kong, May 18, 1986.

MOVING TOWER (below): A record 5-story pyramid on roller skates
was achieved by the NSA Roller Gymnastics Team on July 3, 1986 in
Madison Sq Garden, NYC.

World Championships

In Olympic years, the Olympic title is the World Championship title.

The greatest number of individual titles won by a man in the World Championships including Olympics is 10 by Boris Shakhlin (USSR) between 1954 and 1964. He was also on three winning teams. The women's record is 12 individual wins and 5 team titles by Larissa Semyonovna Latynina (b Dec 27, 1934, retired 1966) of the USSR, between 1956 and 1964. She has the most medals, 31, of which 18 are Olympic medals. Japan has won the men's team title a record 5 times (1962, 66, 70, 74, 78) and the USSR the women's team title on 9 occasions (1954, 58, 62, 70, 74, 78, 81, 83 and 85).

Olympic Medalists

Japan has won 5 men's team titles (1960, 64, 68, 72, 76) and the USSR has won the women's title 8 times (1952–80).

The only men to win 6 individual gold medals are Boris Shakhlin (b Jan 21, 1932) (USSR), with one in 1956, 4 (2 shared) in 1960 and one in 1964; and Nikolai Andrianov (b Oct 14, 1952) (USSR) with one in 1972, 4 in 1976 and one in 1980.

The most successful woman has been Vera Caslavska-Odlozil (b May 3, 1942) (Czechoslovakia), with 7 individual gold medals, 3 in 1964 and 4 (one shared) in 1968. Larissa Latynina of the USSR won 6 individual and 3 team gold medals for a total of 9. She also won 5 silver and 4 bronze for an all-time record total of 18 Olympic medals.

Ecaterina Szabo (Romania) won 4 gold medals and a silver—the most in the 1984 Games at any sport.

The most medals for a male gymnast is 15 by Nikolai Andrianov (USSR), 7 gold, 5 silver and 3 bronze, 1972–80. Aleksandr Ditiatin (USSR) (b Aug 7, 1957) is the only man to win a medal in all eight categories in the same Games, with 3 gold, 4 silver and 1 bronze at Moscow in 1980.

Nadia Comaneci (b Nov 12, 1961) (Romania) was the first gymnast to be awarded a perfect score of 10.00 in the Olympic Games, in the 1976 Montreal Olympics. She ended the competition with a total of 7 such marks (4 on the uneven parallel bars, 3 on the balance beam). Since then Nelli Kim (USSR) in the same Games and a number of others have received marks of 10.00.

In the 1984 Olympics a record 10 perfect marks of 10.00 were awarded.

Modern Rhythmic Gymnastics

This recent addition to the female side of the sport incorporates exercises with different hand-held apparatus, including ribbons, balls, ropes, hoops and Indian clubs. The most overall titles won in world championships is 3 by Maria Gigova (Bulgaria) in 1969, 71, and 73 (shared), while the most individual apparatus titles is 9 by Gigova and Galina Shugurova (USSR). The latter has also won a record total of 14 medals. This category of the sport was included in the Olympic Games for the first time in 1984.

Largest Gymnasium

The world's largest gymnasium is Yale University's 9-story Payne Whitney Gymnasium at New Haven, Conn, completed in 1932 and valued at $18 million.

Youngest International Competitors

Pasakevi "Voula" Kouna (b Dec 6, 1971) was aged 9 years 299 days at the start of the Balkan Games at Serres, Greece on Oct 1–4, 1981, when she represented Greece. Olga Bicherova (b Oct 26, 1966) won the women's world title at 15 years 33 days in Nov 1981. The youngest men's champion was Dmitri Relozerchev (USSR) at 16 years 315 days at Budapest, Hungary in 1983.

World Cup Titles

In the first World Cup competition, in London in 1975, Ludmilla Tourischeva (now Mrs. Valeriy Borzov) (b Oct 7, 1952) (USSR) won all 5 gold medals.

American Cup Titles

Olympic gold medalist Mary Lou Retton (b 1968) of Fairmont, W Va won her first American Cup in 1983 in NYC and has not relinquished the title since that competition. She is the only female gymnast to hold the title for three straight years. US gymnast Kurt Thomas won the title three years in a row from 1978 to 1980.

Chinning the Bar

The greatest number of continuous chin-ups (from a dead hang position) is 170 by Lee Chin Yong (b Aug 15, 1925) at Backyon Gymnasium, Seoul, Korea on May 10, 1983. Robert Chisnall (b Dec 9, 1952) performed 22 one-arm (his right) chin-ups, from a ring, 18 two-finger chins and 12 one-finger chins, from a nylon strap on Dec 3, 1982 at Queen's Univ, Kingston, Ont, Canada.

Sit-Ups

Tim Kides of West NY, NJ, a 21-year-old sophomore at Glassboro (NJ) State College, set a record of 72,746 sit-ups with his legs straight, with no weights or anyone holding his legs, in 64 hours Nov 13–15, 1985, beating the former record of 45,005 set in July 1985.

Louis Scripa, Jr, did 43,418 sit-ups within 24 hours in Sacramento, Calif, on Oct 6–7, 1984. As for leg raises, Scripa did 21,598 in 6 hours in Fairfield, Calif on Dec 8, 1983.

Rope Climbing

The US Amateur Athletic Union (AAU) records are tantamount to world records: 20 ft (hands alone), 2.8 sec, by Don Perry, at Champaign, Ill, on Apr 3, 1954; 25 ft (hands alone), 4.7 sec, by Garvin S. Smith at Los Angeles, on Apr 19, 1947.

Moving Human Tower

The NSA Roller Gymnastics Team built a tower of 120 gymnasts 5 stories high, and it moved to music 30 ft in 20 sec on July 3, 1986 at Madison Sq Garden, NYC, before 18,000 spectators. It was part of the NSA (Nichiren Shoshu Soka Gakkai) of America 2nd Youth Music Festival.

Parallel Bar Dips

Roger Perez (b July 11, 1962) of Sacramento, Calif, performed a record 718 parallel bar dips in an hour on Dec 14, 1983. Jack LaLanne (b 1914) is reported to have done 1,000 in Oakland, Calif, in 1945.

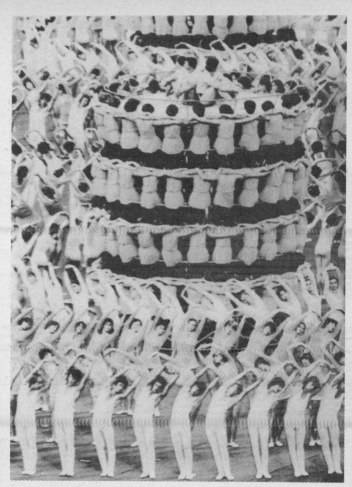

OLYMPIC CENTERPIECE: Americans never saw this Russian gymnastic display on TV as it happened in Moscow in 1980 when the Americans boycotted the Games.

ROPE JUMPING

The longest recorded non-stop rope-jumping marathon was one of 12 hours 34 min by Randall Schneider in Janesville, Wis on Aug 2, 1985.

Other rope-jumping records made without a break:

Most turns in 1 minute	418	Tyrone Krohn	Midcletown (NY) HS	July 10, 1984
Most turns in 10 seconds	128	Albert Rayner	Birmingham, Eng	Nov 19, 1982
Most turns in 1 hour	8,320	Tyrone Krohn	WAEC-TV, NY	Dec 20, 1985
Most doubles (with cross)	1,664	Sean Birch	Kerr, Ireland	Apr 27, 1984
Double turns	10,133	Katsumi Suzuki (Japan)	Saitama	Sept 29, 1979
Treble turns	381	Katsumi Suzuki (Japan)	Saitama	May 29, 1975
Quadruple turns	51	Katsumi Suzuki (Japan)	Saitama	May 29, 1975
Quintuple turns	6	Hideyuki Takeda (Japan)	Aomori	June 19, 1982
Duration	1,264 miles	Tom Morris (Aust)	Brisbane-Cairns	1963
Most on a single rope (minimum 12 turns obligatory)	160	(50 m rope) Shimizu Iida Junior High School	Shizuoka-ken, Japan	Dec 10, 1982
Most turns on single rope (team of 90)	97	Erimomisaki School	Hokkaido, Japan	May 28, 1983
On a tightrope (consecutive)	58	Bryan Andrew (né Dewhurst)	TROS TV, Holland	Aug 6, 1981

ROPE-JUMP CHAMP: Katsumi Suzuki (Japan) amazes spectators when he performs a quadruple turn in which he jumps about 4 ft in the air and turns the rope 4 times under his feet and around his body before landing back on the floor. (*Photo by Dean Moon*)

Sargent Jump

Devised by, and named after, an eminent American professor of physical education in the 1920s, this exercise measures the differential between the height reached by a person's fingertips with feet flat on the ground, and that reached by jumping. The record is 48 in by Darrell Griffith (US) of the University of Louisville in 1976. Olympic Pentathlon champion Mary E. Peters (GB) reportedly jumped 30 in in Calif in 1972.

Push-Ups

Paul Lynch (GB) did 25,573 push-ups in 24 hours at the Hippodrome Club, London, Eng, on July 18, 1985.

Colin Hewick (GB) did 3,836 one-arm push-ups in 5 hours at Bodyworld Health Club, Hull, Eng, on June 13, 1986.

Chung Kwun Ying (Hong Kong) did 2,750 handstand push-ups at Government City Hall, Hong Kong, on May 18, 1986. John Deckert (GB) did 4,500 fingertip push-ups at the Congleton Leisure Centre, Cheshire, Eng, June 28, 1986 in 5 hours. Harry Lee Welch completed 100 one-finger push-ups in Durham, NC, Mar 31, 1985.

Somersaults

Ashrita Furman (US) performed 7,400 forward rolls over 12 miles 390 yards from Boston to Lexington, Mass, in Apr 1986.

Corporal Wayne Wright (GB) of the Royal Engineers made a successful dive-and-tucked somersault over 37 men at Old Park Barracks, Dover, Kent, England on July 30, 1980.

Shigeru Iwasaki (b 1960) backwards somersaulted over 50 m (54.68 yd) in 10.8 sec in Tokyo, March 30, 1980.

Jumping Jacks

The greatest number of consecutive side-straddle hops is 40,014 in 24 hours by August John Hoffman Jr at Van Nuys, Calif, on Dec 4, 1982.

HOCKEY

Origins

There is pictorial evidence of a hockey-like game (Kalv) being played on ice in The Netherlands in the early 16th century. The game probably was first played in North America on Dec 25, 1855, at Kingston, Ontario, Canada, but Halifax also lays claim to priority.

The International Ice Hockey Federation was founded in 1908. The National Hockey League was inaugurated in 1917. The World Hockey Association was formed in 1971 and disbanded in 1979 when 4 of its teams joined the NHL.

World Championships and Olympic Games

World Championships were first held for amateurs in 1920 in conjunction with the Olympic Games, which were also considered as World Championships up to 1968. From 1977 World Championships have been open to professionals. The USSR has won 20 world titles between 1954 and 1986, including the Olympic titles of 1956, 64 and 68. They have won 3 further Olympic titles in 1972, 76 and 84. Canada won 19 titles between 1920 and 1961, including 6 Olympic titles (1920, 24, 32, 48 and 52). The longest Olympic career is that of Richard Torriani (b Oct 1, 1911) (Switzerland) from 1928 to 1948. The most gold medals won by any player is 3; this was achieved by 4 USSR players in the 1964, 68 and 72 Games—Vitaliy Davidov, Aleksandr Ragulin, Anatoliy Firssov and Viktor Kuzkin. Goalie Vladimir Tretiak (USSR) won 3 golds (1972, 1976 and 1984) as well as a silver in 1980.

Longest Season

The only man ever to play 82 games in a 78-game season is Ross Lonsberry. He began the 1971–72 season with the Los Angeles Kings where he played 50 games. Then, in January, he was traded to the Philadelphia Flyers (who had played only 46 games at the time) where he finished out the season (32 more games).

Brad Marsh (b Mar 31, 1958) played 83 games (17 with Calgary and 66 with Philadelphia) during an 80-game season in 1981–82.

Fastest Player

The highest speed measured for any player is 29.7 mph (without the puck) for Bobby Hull (then of the Chicago Black Hawks) (b Jan 3, 1939). The highest puck speed is also attributed to Hull, whose left-handed slap shot has been measured at 118.3 mph. Also known as the "Golden Jet," Hull is the only player besides Gordie Howe to score over 1,000 goals in NHL and WHA play.

MOST 3-GOAL GAMES: Phil Esposito, in his 18-year NHL career (with Chi-NY-Bos) scored 3 goals or more in 32 games. (*Al Ruelle*)

Longest Game

The longest game was 2 hours 56 min 30 sec (playing time) when the Detroit Red Wings eventually beat the Montreal Maroons 1-0 in the 17th minute of the sixth period of overtime at the Forum, Montreal, at 2:25 A.M. on March 25, 1936, 5 hours 51 min after the opening faceoff. Norm Smith, goaltender for the Red Wings, turned aside 92 shots in registering the NHL's longest single shutout.

Stanley Cup

This cup, presented by the Governor-General Lord Stanley (original cost $48.67), became emblematic of world professional team supremacy 33 years after the first contest at Montreal in 1893. It has been won most often by the Montreal Canadiens, with 23 wins in 1916, 24, 30–31, 44, 46, 53, 56–60 (a record 5 straight), 65–66, 68–69, 71, 73, 76–79, 86. Henri Richard played in his eleventh finals in 1973.

Winners from 1970 are:

1970 Boston Bruins	1979 Montreal Canadiens
1971 Montreal Canadiens	1980 New York Islanders
1972 Boston Bruins	1981 New York Islanders
1973 Montreal Canadiens	1982 New York Islanders
1974 Philadelphia Flyers	1983 New York Islanders
1975 Philadelphia Flyers	1984 Edmonton Oilers
1976 Montreal Canadiens	1985 Edmonton Oilers
1977 Montreal Canadiens	1986 Montreal Canadiens
1978 Montreal Canadiens	

REGULAR SEASON

Service

Most Seasons
26 Gordie Howe, Det, 1947–71; Hart, 1980

Most Games, Lifetime
1,767 Gordie Howe, Det, 1947–71; Hart, 1980

Consecutive Games Played
914 Gary Unger, Tor-Det-St L-Atl, Feb 24, 1968–Dec 21, 1979

Scoring

Most Points, Lifetime
1,850 Gordie Howe, Det, 1947–71; Hart, 1980

Most Points, Season
215 Wayne Gretzky, Edm, 1986

Most Points, Game
10 Darryl Sittler, Tor vs Bos, Feb 7, 1976

Most Points, Period
6 Bryan Trottier, NY Isl vs NY Ran, Dec 23, 1978

Consecutive Games Scoring Points
51 Wayne Gretzky, Edm, Oct 5, 1983–Jan 27, 1984

Most Goals, Lifetime
801 Gordie Howe, Det, 1947–71; Hart, 1980

Most Goals, Season
92 Wayne Gretzky, Edm, 1982

Most Goals, Game
7 Joe Malone, Que Bulldogs vs Tor St Pat, Jan 31, 1920

Most Goals, One Period
4 Harvey Jackson, Tor vs St L, Nov 20, 1934
   Max Bentley, Chi vs NY Ran, Jan 28, 1943
   Clint Smith, Chi vs Mont, Mar 4, 1945

Red Berenson, St L vs Phil, Nov 7, 1968
Wayne Gretzky, Edm vs St L, Feb 18, 1981
Grant Mulvey, Chi vs St L, Feb 3, 1982
Bryan Trottier, NY Isl vs Phil, Feb 13, 1982

Most Hat Tricks (3 or more goals in a game), Lifetime
37 Wayne Gretzky, Edm, 1980–86
   Mike Bossy, NY Isl 1978–86

Most Hat Tricks, Season
10 Wayne Gretzky, Edm, 1982, 1984

Consecutive Games Scoring Goals
16 Harry Broadbent, Ottawa, 1921–22

Most Assists, Lifetime
1,049 Gordie Howe, Det, 1947–71; Hart, 1980

Most Assists, Season
163 Wayne Gretzky, Edm, 1986

Most Assists, Game
7 Billy Taylor, Det vs Chi, Mar 16, 1947
   Wayne Gretzky, Edm vs Wash, Feb 15, 1982; vs Chi Dec 11, 1985

Most Assists, Period
5 Dale Hawerchuk, Win vs LA, Mar 6, 1984

Goaltending

Games Played, Lifetime
971 Terry Sawchuk, Det-Bos-Tor-LA-NY Ran, 1950–70

Shutouts, Lifetime
103 Terry Sawchuk, Det-Bos-Tor-LA-NY Ran, 1950–70

Shutouts, Season
22 George Hainsworth, Mont, 1929

Consecutive Scoreless Streak
461 min 29 sec Alex Connell, Ottawa, 1927–28

FASTEST SKATER (left): Bobby Hull was timed at 29.7 mph. His slap shot went screaming at goaltenders at 118.3 mph. Hull was the only player besides Gordie Howe to score 1,000 NHL and WHA goals.

GOAL ORIENTED (above right): Wayne Gretzky showed he was no flash-in-the-pan when, in 1982, he began breaking assist and most-points records and also set a goal-scoring record by netting 92 goals, including a record 10 hat tricks. In 1984, he scored 10 hat tricks again (total of 37 to the end of the 1986 season) and in 1986, a point record of 215 and an assist record of 163 in a season. (*Edmonton Oilers*)

LONGEST CAREER: Gordie Howe played in the NHL for 26 seasons and collected career records for most games (1,767), goals (801), assists (1,049), and points (1,850), was selected as an all-star a record 21 times, and also collected 500 stitches in his face.

Consecutive Games Without Defeat
32 Gerry Cheevers, Bos, Nov
14, 1971–Mar 27, 1972

Most Saves, One Game
70 Roy Worters, Pitt Pirates vs
NY Americans, Dec 24,
1925

Penalties

Most Minutes Penalized, Lifetime
3,515 David (Tiger) Williams,
Tor-Van-Det-LA, 1975–86

Most Minutes Penalized, Season
472 Dave Schultz, Phil, 1975

Most Minutes Penalized, Game
67 Randy Holt, LA vs Phil, Mar
11, 1979

STANLEY CUP

Most Games, Lifetime
180 Henri Richard, Mont,
1956–69, 1971–75

Most Points, Lifetime
176 Jean Beliveau, Mont
1954–69, 1971

Most Points, Season
47 Wayne Gretzky, Edm, 1985

Most Points, Game
7 Wayne Gretzky, Edm, vs
Calg, Apr 17, 1983
Wayne Gretzky, Edm vs
Win, Apr 25, 1985

Most Goals, Lifetime
83 Mike Bossy, NY Isl, 1978–86

Most Goals, Season
19 Reggie Leach, Phil, 1976

Most Goals, Game
5 Maurice Richard, Mont vs
Tor, Mar 23, 1944
Darryl Sittler, Tor vs Phil,
Apr 22, 1976
Reggie Leach, Phil vs Bos,
May 6, 1976

Most Assists, Lifetime
111 Wayne Gretzky, Edm,
1980–86

Most Assists, Season
30 Wayne Gretzky, Edm, 1985

Most Assists, Game
6 Mikko Leinonen, NY Ran vs
Phil, Apr 8, 1982

Most Shutouts by Goalie, Lifetime
14 Jacques Plante, Mont,
1953–63; St L, 1969–70

Most Victories by Goalie, Lifetime
88 Billy Smith, NY Isl, 1975–85

Longest Streaks

In the 1981–82 season, the NY Islanders won 15 consecutive games, Jan 21–Feb 20, 1982. The longest a team has ever gone without a defeat is 35 games, set by the Philadelphia Flyers with 25 wins and 10 ties from Oct 14, 1979, to Jan 6, 1980.

Longest Career

Gordie Howe (b March 31, 1928, Floral, Saskatchewan, Canada) skated 25 years for the Detroit Red Wings from 1946–47 through the 1970–71 season, playing in a total of 1,687 NHL regular-season games.

After leaving the Red Wings, he ended a 2-year retirement to skate with his two sons as teammates and played for 6 more seasons with the Houston Aeros and the New England Whalers of the World Hockey Association, participating in 497 games.

With the incorporation of the (now Hartford) Whalers into the NHL for the 1979–80 season, Gordie Howe skated in all 80 regular season games (for a record total of 1,767) in his record 26th year in that league. The remarkable 52-year-old grandfather was again selected as an NHL all-star, more times than any other player. Including Howe's 157 NHL playoff appearances, he skated in 2,421 "major league" games in all.

Team Scoring

The greatest number of goals recorded in a World Championship match has been 47-0 when Canada beat Denmark on Feb 12, 1949.

The Edmonton Oilers set an NHL record of 446 goals in the 1983–84 season.

The NHL record for both teams is 21 goals, scored when the Montreal Canadiens beat the Toronto St Patricks at Montreal 14-7 on Jan 10, 1920. The most goals ever scored by one team in a single game was set by

THE PUCK STOPS HERE: Gerry Cheevers (left) who drew stitch marks on his mask whenever it protected him from injury, went 32 straight games without a loss for the Bruins in 1971–72. As the Bruins' coach in 1982–83, he found himself rooting for his goalie, Pete Peeters, to break the record, but Peeters' streak ended at 31 consecutive undefeated games. (*Boston Bruins*)

ROCKET MAN: Maurice "Rocket" Richard (below) beats the Boston goaltender to score one of his record 82 Stanley Cup goals, this one in the 1953 finals. Of those 82 goals, 18 were game winners with 6 coming in overtime. Maurice Richard's brother, Henri "Pocket Rocket" Richard, played in and won 11 finals as part of his record 180 playoff-game appearances.

the Canadiens, when they defeated the Quebec Bulldogs on March 3, 1920 by a score of 16-3.

The most goals in a period is 9 by the Buffalo Sabres in the second period of their 14-4 victory over Toronto on March 19, 1981.

The Detroit Red Wings scored 15 consecutive goals without an answering tally when they defeated the NY Rangers 15-0 on Jan 23, 1944.

Fastest Scoring

Toronto scored 8 goals against the NY Americans in 4 min 52 sec on March 19, 1938.

The fastest goal ever scored from the opening whistle came at 5 sec of the first period. This occurred twice, most recently by Bryan Trottier of the NY Islanders vs Boston Bruins on Mar 22, 1984. The previous time was by Doug Smail of the Winnipeg Jets against St Louis on Dec 20, 1981. Claude Provost of the Canadiens scored a goal against Boston after 4 sec of the opening of the second period on Nov 9, 1957.

The Boston Bruins set an NHL record with three goals in a span of 20 sec against the Vancouver Canucks on Feb 25, 1971. Left winger John Bucyk began the record-breaking feat with a goal at the 4 min 50 sec mark of the third period. Center Ed Westfall scored 12 sec later at 5 min 2 sec, while defenseman Ted Green rounded out the surge with a goal at the 5 min 10 sec mark.

The fastest scoring record is held by Bill Mosienko (Chicago) who scored 3 goals in 21 sec against the NY Rangers on March 23, 1952. In a playoff game Pat LaFontaine of the NY Islanders scored 2 goals in 22 sec vs Edmonton Oilers, May 19, 1984.

Gus Bodnar (Toronto Maple Leafs) scored a goal against the NY Rangers at 15 sec of the first period of *his first NHL game* on Oct 30, 1943. Later in his career, while with Chicago, Bodnar again entered the record book when he assisted on all 3 of Bill Mosienko's quick goals.

Several fast scoring feats have been reported from non-NHL competition: Kim D. Miles scored in 3 sec for Univ of Guelph vs Univ of W Ontario on Feb 11, 1975; Steve D'Innocenzo scored 3 goals in 12 sec for Holliston vs Westwood in a high school game in Mass on Jan 9, 1982; Clifford "Fido" Purpur, 38, scored 4 goals in 25 sec for the Grand Forks AMerks vs Winnipeg All Stars in Grand Forks, ND, on Jan 29, 1950. In team play, the Skara Ishockeyclubb, Sweden, scored 3 goals in 11 sec against Orebro IK at Skara on Oct 18, 1981; the Vernon Cougars scored 5 goals in 56 sec against Salmon Arm Aces at Vernon, BC, Canada, on Aug 6, 1982; the Kamloops Knights of Columbus scored 7 goals in 2 min 22 sec vs Prince George Vikings on Jan 25, 1980.

Goaltender's Goal

The only goaltender to score a goal in an NHL game is Billy Smith (NY Islanders), against the Colorado Rockies in Denver, Nov 28, 1979. After the Rockies had removed their goaltender in favor of an extra skater during a delayed penalty, a Colorado defenseman's errant centering pass sent the puck skidding nearly the full length of the ice and into his own untended goal. Goalie Smith was the last Islander to touch the puck and was credited with the goal even though he did not take the actual "shot."

Penalties

The most any team has been penalized in one season is the 2,621 min assessed against the Philadelphia Flyers in 1980–81. The most penalty-filled game was a contest between Boston and Minnesota in Boston on Feb 26, 1981, with a total of 84 penalties (42 by each team) for 406 min (211 min by Minnesota).

HORSE RACING

Origins

There is evidence that men were riding horses, as distinct from riding in chariots pulled by horses, in Assyria and Egypt c 1400 BC. However, early organized racing appears to have been confined to chariots, for which the Roman method used riders with a foot on each of two horses. The first racing on horseback was by the Greeks in the 33rd Olympic Games in 648 BC. The earliest recorded race in Britain was at Netherby, Cumbria in 210 AD between Arabian horses brought to Britain by the Roman Emperor, Lucius Septimius Severus. The first recognizable regular race meeting was that held at Smithfield, London at the weekly horse fairs on Fridays in 1174. The first known prize money was a purse of gold presented by Richard I (the Lion-heart) in 1195 for a race between knights over a distance of 3 mi.

Organized horse racing began in New York State at least as early as March 1668. The original Charleston (Va) Jockey Club, organized in 1734, was the world's first.

· Racing colors (silks) became compulsory in 1889.

All thoroughbred horses in the world today are descended from at least one of three great stallions, which were imported into Britain in the 17th and 18th centuries. The "Darley Arabian" was brought from Aleppo, Syria by the British Consul Richard Darley of Yorkshire c 1704; the "Byerley Turk" was brought to England from Turkey c 1685 and used by Captain Byerley as a charger in Ireland; and the Godolphin Barb—the latter word derived from the Barbary Coast of North Africa—was originally brought from France by Edward Coke in about 1735 and then acquired by the Earl of Godolphin.

Largest Prizes

The richest races ever held were the Breeders' Cup 7-race meetings, run at Hollywood Park, Calif, on Nov 10, 1984 and at Aqueduct, NYC, on Nov 2, 1985, which paid $10 million total in prize money. This included $3 million to the winner of the 1¼-mi Breeders' Cup Classic.

Victories

The horse with the best win-loss record was "Kincsem," a Hungarian mare foaled in 1874, who was unbeaten in 54 races (1876–79), including the English Goodwood Cup of 1878.

The longest winning sequence is 56 races, in Puerto Rico 1953–5, by "Camarero," foaled in 1951. He had 73 wins in 77 starts altogether. The most wins in a career is 137 from 159 starts by "Galgo Jr" (foaled 1928) in Puerto Rico between 1930 and 1936; in 1931 he won a record 30 races in one year. The only horse to win the same race in 7 successive years was "Doctor Syntax" (foaled 1811) in the Preston Gold Cup, 1815–21.

HORSE CENTS: "John Henry" (#1A, in foreground), with Bill Shoemaker up, is first to the wire for the $600,000 first prize in the 1½-mile 1981 Arlington Million. The first horse ever to pass $6 million in purses, "John Henry" was purchased as a yearling for only $1,100 and changed hands seven times before Sam Rubin bought him for $25,000 in 1978. He retired in July 1985.

MOST
SUCCESSFUL
JOCKEY: Bill
(Willie) Shoemaker,
94 lb and 4 ft 11 in
tall, has made over
$103 million for the
owners of the 38,201
mounts he has
ridden.
(*Gerry Cranham*)

Dead Heats

There is no recorded case in turf history of a quintuple dead heat. The nearest approach was in the Astley Stakes at Lewes, England, on Aug 6, 1880, when "Mazurka," "Wandering Nun" and "Scobell" triple dead-heated for first place, just ahead of "Cumberland" and "Thora," who dead-heated for fourth place. Each of the five jockeys thought he had won. The only three known examples of a quadruple dead heat were between "Honest Harry," "Miss Decoy," "Young Daffodil" and "Peteria" at Bogside, England, on June 7, 1808; between "Defaulter," "The Squire of Malton," "Reindeer" and "Pulcherrima" in the Omnibus Stakes at The Hoo, England, on Apr 26, 1851; and between "Overreach," "Lady Go-Lightly," "Gamester" and "The Unexpected" at Newmarket, England, on Oct 22, 1855.

Since the introduction of the photo-finish, the highest number of horses in a dead heat has been three, on several occasions.

Greatest Winnings

The most won in a single race is $2.6 million by "Spend a Buck" on May 27, 1985 at Garden State Park in Cherry Hill, NJ. This included a $2 million bonus for also winning the Kentucky Derby and 2 preparatory races at Garden State Park.

The greatest amount ever won by a horse is $6,597,947 by the gelding "John Henry" (foaled 1975) from 1977 to July 1985, when he was retired.

"All Along" (foaled 1979) won $3,018,420 in France and the US 1981–84 to become the leading money winner among mares.

Topmost Tipster

The only recorded instance of a racing correspondent forecasting ten out of ten winners on a race card was at Delaware Park, Wilmington, Del, on July 28, 1974, by Charles Lamb of the *Baltimore News American*.

Greatest Pay-Out

Three bettors shared the Sweep Six pool at Exhibition Park, Vancouver, BC, on July 10, 1982, each winning $579,129 (US) for a $2 (Canadian) ticket in what is believed to be the biggest single payoff in racing history.

Most Valuable Horses

The most expensive horse ever is the 1983 Irish Derby winner "Shareef Dancer." Reportedly 40 shares in the horse were sold at $1 million each in 1983 by his owner, Sheikh Mohammed Bin Rashid al Maktoum.

The highest price for a yearling is $13.1 million for "Seattle Dancer" on July 23, 1985, in Keeneland, Ky, by Robert Sangster and partners.

Triple Crown

Eleven horses have won all three races in one season which constitute the American Triple Crown (Kentucky Derby, Preakness Stakes and the Belmont Stakes). This feat was first achieved by "Sir Barton" in 1919, and most recently by "Seattle Slew" in 1977 and "Affirmed" in 1978.

The only Triple Crown winner to sire another winner was "Gallant Fox," the 1930 winner, who sired "Omaha," who won in 1935. The only jockey to ride two Triple Crown winners is Eddie Arcaro (b Feb 19, 1916), on "Whirlaway" (1941) and "Citation" (1948).

Most Horses in a Race

In the Grand National (England) on Mar 22, 1929, there were 66 horses.

Trainers

The greatest number of wins by a trainer is 496 in one year by Jack Van Berg in 1976, and 4,400 in his career to 1986. The greatest amount won in a year is $11,802,701 by D. Wayne Lucas (US) in 1985. The only trainer to saddle the first 5 finishers in a championship race is Michael

Dickinson in the 1983 Cheltenham Gold Cup. On Dec 27, 1982, he won a record 12 races in one day.

Jockeys

The most successful jockey of all time is William Lee (Bill or Willie) Shoemaker (b at 2½ lb on Aug 19, 1931) now weighing 94 lb and standing 4 ft 11 in. (His wife is nearly 1 ft taller than he is.) From Mar 1949 to Jan 29, 1986, he rode 8,514 winners from 38,201 mounts, earning $103,848,268. Laffitt Pincay, Jr (b Dec 29, 1946, Panama City, Panama) has earned a record $106,595,202 in over 6,000 wins, 1966–86.

Chris McCarron (US), (b 1955), won a total of 546 races in 1974 out of 2,199 mounts, an average of 6 races a day. He earned $12,038,213 in 1984, the greatest amount ever won by any jockey in a year.

The most winners ridden on one card is 8 by Hubert S. Jones, 17, out of 13 mounts at Caliente, Calif, on June 11, 1944 (of which 5 were photo-finishes); by Oscar Barattuci at Rosario, Argentina, on Dec 15, 1957; by Dave Gall from 10 mounts at Cahokia Downs, East St Louis, Ill, on Oct 18, 1978; and by Chris Loseth, 29, out of 10 mounts at Exhibition Park in Vancouver, BC, Canada on Apr 9, 1984.

Owners

The most lifetime wins by an owner is 4,775 by Marion Van Berg in N America in the 35 years up to his death in 1971.

The most winners by an owner in one year is 494 by Dan R. Lasater (US) in 1974. The greatest amount won in a year is $3,070,225 by John Franks in 1984.

Largest Grandstand

The largest at a racecourse is at Belmont Park, Long Island, NY, which seats 30,000 and is 440 yd long.

Longest Race

The longest recorded horse race was one of 1,200 miles in Portugal, won by "Emir," a horse bred from Egyptian-bred Blunt Arab stock. The holder of the world record for long distance racing and speed is "Champion Crabbet," who covered 300 miles in 52 hours 33 min, carrying 245 lb, in 1920.

ICE SKATING

Origins

The earliest skates were made of animal bones, such as those found in France and thought to be 20,000 years old. The first reference to skating is in early Norse literature c 200 AD but the earliest report of skating as a sport or pastime is in a British chronicle by William Fitzstephen of 1180. The first club was founded in Edinburgh in 1744, and the earliest artificial ice rink was opened in London in 1876.

Speed skating or racing must have taken place from the earliest times, although curved rinks, especially for racing, did not appear until the 1880s. Two Americans developed figure skating into an art. E. W. Bushnell invented steel blades in 1848 and thereby provided the precision skate needed for ever more intricate figures, and the first true innovator and teacher was Jackson Haines. He was a ballet master who transferred the artistry of the dance to the ice when he went to Vienna in 1864. Louis Rubinstein was a founder of the Amateur Skating Association of Canada in 1878, the first national governing body in the world. In 1892 the International Skating Union was set up at Scheveningen, The Netherlands.

Longest Race

The longest race regularly held was the "Elfstedentocht" ("Tour of the Eleven Towns") in The Netherlands, covering 200 km (124 miles 483 yd). The fastest time was 6 hours 5 min 12 sec by Jan-Roelof Kruithof (Neth) on Feb 25, 1979 at Oulu, Finland. Kruithof won the race 8 times, 1974, 76–77, 79–83. The race was transferred to Finland in 1964 and subsequently to Canada, but it was returned to The Netherlands in 1985. An estimated 16,000 skaters took part in 1986.

Largest Rink

The world's largest indoor artificial ice rink is in the Moscow Olympic arena which has an ice area of 86,800 sq ft. The largest outdoors is the Fujikyu Highland Promenade Rink complex in Japan with 285,243 sq ft.

Marathon

The longest recorded skating marathon is 109 hours 5 min by Austin McKinley of Christchurch, NZ, June 21–25, 1977.

FIGURE SKATING

Most Difficult Jumps

Many of the most difficult jumps in skating are named after their originators, such as the Axel (after Axel Paulsen of Norway) and the Salchow (after Ulrich Salchow of Sweden).

The first woman to attempt a jump in major competition is said to have been Theresa Weld (US) who was reprimanded for her "unfeminine behavior" in the 1920 Olympic events. Cecilia Colledge (GB) was the first woman to achieve two turns in the air a few years later. In the 1962 World Championships Donald Jackson (Can) performed the first triple Lutz in a major competition and in the 1978 championships Vern Taylor, another Canadian, achieved the first triple Axel. Among women, the first triple Salchow was done by Sonja Morgenstern (E Ger) in 1972, and the first triple Lutz by Denise Beilmann (Switz) in the 1978 European championships. Incidentally, the latter has a spin named after her.

The first quadruple twist was performed by Marina Tcherkasova and Sergei Shakrai (USSR) in a pairs competition in Helsinki in 1977. They were able to achieve this because of the unusual difference in size between the tiny 12-year-old girl and her tall male partner.

A backward somersault jump was successfully negotiated by Terry Kubicka (US) in the 1976 world championships but it was immediately banned as being too dangerous.

Highest Marks

The highest score from a single set of marks in any world figure skating competition was gained by Jayne Torvill (b Oct 7, 1957) and Christopher Dean (b July 27, 1958) of Great Britain when awarded maximum

THE ONLY AMERICAN to win a gold in figure skating in the 1984 Olympics was Scott Hamilton (above).

ON THE WAY TO STARDOM (left): Dorothy Hamill (US) started by winning the Olympic figure skating gold in 1976 and the World title that year too. She went on to star in ice shows. (*UPI*)

sixes by all 9 judges for artistic presentation of their free dance "Barnum-on-ice" routine in the World Ice-Dance championships at Helsinki, Finland, Mar 12, 1983.

The highest number of maximum sixes awarded for one performance in an international championship was 13 to Torvill and Dean in the World Ice Dancing Competition in Ottawa, Canada, on Mar 24, 1984.

Donald Jackson (Canada) was awarded 7 "sixes" (the most by a soloist) in the world men's championship at Prague, Czechoslovakia, in 1962.

World Titles

The greatest number of individual world men's figure skating titles (instituted 1896) is 10 by Ulrich Salchow (1877–1949), of Sweden, in 1901–05, 07–11. The women's record (instituted 1906) is also 10 individual titles, by Sonja Henie (Apr 8, 1912–Oct 12, 1969), of Norway, between 1927 and 1936. Irina Rodnina (b Sept 12, 1949), of the USSR, has won 10 pairs titles (instituted 1908)—four with Aleksiy Ulanov (1969–72) and six with her husband Aleksandr Zaitsev (1973–78). The most ice dance titles (instituted 1952) won is 6 by Aleksandr Gorshkov (b Oct 8, 1946) and his wife, Ludmilla Pakhomova (1946–86), both of the USSR, in 1970–74 and 76.

MOVIE STAR Sonja Henie (Norway) earned an estimated $47 million in ice shows and films after winning 3 golds in the 1928–32–36 Olympics.

HIGHEST FIGURE SKATING MARKS (below): Jayne Torvill and Christopher Dean (GB) have been leading all competition with maximum sixes from all 9 judges since 1983.

Olympic Titles in Figure Skating

The most Olympic gold medals won by a figure skater is 3 by Gillis Grafström (1893–1938), of Sweden, in 1920, 24 and 28 (also silver medal in 1932); by Sonja Henie (see *World Titles*) in 1928, 32 and 36; and by Irina Rodnina (see *World Titles*) in the pairs event in 1972, 76 and 80.

Distance

Robin Cousins (GB) (b Mar 17, 1957) achieved 19 ft 1 in in an Axel jump and 18 ft with a back flip at Richmond Ice Rink, Surrey, Eng on Nov 16, 1983.

Barrel Jumping (on ice skates)

The official distance record is 29 ft 5 in over 18 barrels by Yvon Jolin at Terrebonne, Quebec, Canada, in 1981. The feminine record is 20 ft 4½ in over 11 barrels by Janet Hainstock in Mich on Mar 15, 1980.

SPEED SKATING

World Titles

The greatest number of world overall titles (instituted 1893) won by any skater is 5 by Oscar Mathisen (Norway) (1888–1954) in 1908–09, 12–14, and Clas Thunberg (1893–1973) of Finland, in 1923, 25, 28–29 and 31. The most titles won by a woman is 4 by Mrs Inga Voronina, *née* Artomonova (1936–66) of Moscow, USSR, in 1957–58, 62 and 65, and Mrs Atje Keulen-Deelstra of The Netherlands (b Dec 31, 1938) in 1970, 72–74.

WORLD SPEED SKATING RECORDS
(Ratified by the I.S.U.)

Distance	min:sec	Name and Nationality	Place	Date
MEN				
500 m	36.49*	Igor Zhelezovsky (USSR)	Moscow, USSR	Dec 21, 1985
1000 m	1:12.58	Pavel Pegov (USSR)	Medeo, USSR	Mar 25, 1983
1500 m	1:53.00	Igor Zhelezovsky (USSR)	Medeo, USSR	Dec 15, 1985
3000 m	4:03.22	Viktor Shasherin (USSR)	Davos, Switzerland	Jan 19, 1986
5000 m	6:49.15	Viktor Shasherin (USSR)	Medeo, USSR	Mar 23, 1984
10,000 m	14:12.14	Geir Karlstad (Norway)	Inzell, W Ger	Feb 16, 1986
WOMEN				
500 m	39.52	Karin Kania (*née* Enke) (E Ger)	Medeo, USSR	Mar 21, 1986
1000 m	1:18.84	Karin Kania (E Ger)	Karulzawa, Japan	Feb 23, 1986
1500 m	1:59.30	Karin Kania (E Ger)	Medeo, USSR	Mar 22, 1986
3000 m	4:18.02	Karin Kania (E Ger)	Medeo, USSR	Mar 21, 1986
5000 m	7:20.99	Andrea Ehrig (*née* Schöne) (E Ger)	Medeo, USSR	Mar 22, 1986

* Represents an average speed of 30.65 mph. Note that Medeo, Alma Ata, USSR is situated at an altitude of 1,691 m.

The record score achieved in the world overall title is 162.973 points by Eric Heiden (US) at Oslo, Norway, Feb 10–11, 1979. The record by a woman is 171.760 points by Andrea Schöne of E Germany at Medeo, USSR Mar 23–24, 1984.

Olympic Titles

The most Olympic gold medals won in speed skating is 6 by Lidia Skoblikova (b March 8, 1939), of Chelyabinsk, USSR, in 1960 (2) and 1964 (4). The male record is held by Clas Thunberg (see above) with 5 gold (including 1 tied gold) and also 1 silver and 1 tied bronze in 1924–28; and by Eric Heiden (US) (b June 14, 1958) who won 5 gold medals, all at Lake Placid, NY, in 1980.

24 Hours

Ton Smits (Neth) skated 314.65 mi in 24 hours in Eindhoven, Neth, Dec 15–16, 1984.

SPEED SKATING DOUBLE GOLD MEDALIST (above): At the 1985 Winter Olympics, Karin Kania (E Ger) won 2 golds and in 1986 regained 4 of her world records.

ERIC HEIDEN (US) swept all 5 speed skating events in the 1980 Winter Olympics to set a mark for the most individual golds won at one Games. (*UPI*)

MARATHONS (Running)

The inaugural marathon races were staged in Greece in 1896. There were two trial races before the first Olympic marathon at Athens. The race commemorated the legendary run of an unknown Greek courier, possibly Pheidippides, who in 490 BC ran some 24 miles from the Plain of Marathon to Athens with the news of a Greek victory over the numerically superior Persian army. Delivering his message—"Rejoice! We have won."—he collapsed and died. The Olympic races were run over varying distances until 1924 when the distance was standardized at 26 miles 385 yd, the distance first instituted in the 1908 Games in London.

Marathon Progressive Record

Men

2:55:18.4	Johnny Hayes (US)	1908
2:52:45.4	Robert Fowler (US)	1909
2:46:52.6	James Clark (US)	1909
2:46:04.6	Albert Raines (US)	1909
2:42:31.0	Fred Barrett (GB)	1909
2:40:34.2	Thore Johansson (Swed)	1909
2:38:16.2	Harry Green (GB)	1913
2:36:06.6	Alexis Ahlgren (Swed)	1913
2:32:35.8	Hannes Kolehmainen (Fin)	1920
2:29:01.8	Albert Michelsen (US)	1925
2:27:49.0	Fusashige Suzuki (Japan)	1925
2:26:44.0	Yasao Ikenaka (Japan)	1935
2:26:42.0	Kitei Son (Japan)	1935
2:25:39.0	Yun Bok Suh (S Korea)	1947
2:20:42.2	Jim Peters (GB)	1952
2:18:40.2	Jim Peters (GB)	1953
2:18:34.8	Jim Peters (GB)	1953
2:17:39.4	Jim Peters (GB)	1954
2:15:17.0	Sergey Popov (USSR)	1958
2:15:16.2	Abebe Bikila (Ethiopia)	1960
2:15:15.8	Toru Terasawa (Japan)	1963
2:14:28.0*	Buddy Edelen (US)	1963
2:13:55.0	Basil Heatley (GB)	1964
2:12:11.2	Abebe Bikila (Ethiopia)	1964
2:12:00.0	Morio Shigematsu (Japan)	1965
2:09:36.4	Derek Clayton (Australia)	1967
2:08:33.6	Derek Clayton (Australia)	1969
2:08:05.2	Alberto Salazar (US)	1982
2:08:05.0	Stephen Jones (GB)	1984
2:07:12.0	Carlos Lopes (Port)	1985

Women

3:40:22.0	Violet Piercy (GB)	1926
3:27:45.0	Dale Greig (GB)	1966
3:19:33.0	Mildred Sampson (NZ)	1964
3:15:22.0	Maureen Wilton (Can)	1967

* 36 yd (about 6 sec) under standard distance.

3:07:26.0	Anni Pede (W Ger)	1967
3:02:53.0	Caroline Walker (US)	1970
3:01:42.0	Elizabeth Bonner (US)	1971
2:46:30.0	Adrienne Beames (Australia)	1971
2:46:24.0	Chantal Langlace (France)	1974
2:43:54.5	Jackie Hansen (US)	1974
2:42:24.0	Liane Winter (W Ger)	1975
2:40:15.8	Christa Vahlensieck (W Ger)	1975
12:38:19.0	Jackie Hansen (US)	1975
2:35:15.4	Chantal Langlace (France)	1977
2:34:47.5	Christa Vahlensieck (W Ger)	1977
2:32:30.0	Grete Waitz (Nor)	1978
2:27:33.0	Grete Waitz (Nor)	1979
2:25:42.0	Grete Waitz (Nor)	1980
2:25:29.0	Allison Roe (NZ)	1981
2:25:29.0	Grete Waitz (Nor)	1983
2:22:43.0	Joan Benoit (US)	1984
2:21:06.0	Ingrid Kristiansen (Nor)	1985

There are no official records for the distance due to the variety of courses used and their varying severity, but the above figures are generally accepted to be the progressive best-known times on record.

The NYC Marathon regularly draws the largest number of spectators to any sporting event—an estimated 2,500,000 people who line the route through city streets each year.

MOTORCYCLING

Earliest Motorcycle

On Nov 10, 1885, a single-track vehicle, powered by an internal-combustion engine designed by Gottlieb Daimler, was ridden a little over 7 mi from Canstatt to Unterturkheim, Germany. Daimler's vehicle, due to its engine location and basic design features which remain current today, is universally acknowledged as the world's first motorcycle, predating the first automobile—also by Daimler—by several months.

Earliest Races and Circuits

The first motorcycle race was held on an oval track of 1 mi at Sheen House, Richmond, Surrey, England, on Nov 29, 1897, won by Charles Jarrott (1877–1944) on a Fournier.

In the early days many races were for both motorcycles and cars, and often took the form of long-distance inter-city or inter-country events. These were heavily criticized following the aborted Paris to Madrid race of 1903 which resulted in a number of deaths of competitors and spectators. In 1904 the International Cup Race was held in France for motorcycles only, and on a closed road circuit. However, in 1905 the race was held again, and this is recognized as the first international motorcycling event. The venue was Dourdon near Paris, and it was organized by the newly formed Fédération Internationale des Clubs Motocyclistes (FICM), the predecessor of the Fédération Internationale Motocycliste

SIMULTANEOUS HOLDER OF 4 WORLD TITLES: Erik Gunderson (Sweden) became the first person to capture championships at singles, pairs, team and long track. (*All Sport*)

QUICK AS A VINK: Henk Vink of The Netherlands set world records in 1977 for 1 kilometer and for 440 yds on his Kawasaki in 2-way runs from standing starts.

(FIM). The race was a success and was won by an Austrian named Wondrick.

The Auto-Cycle Union Tourist Trophy (TT) series was first held on the 15.81-mile "Peel" ("St John's") course on the Isle of Man on May 28, 1907, and is still run on the island, on the "Mountain" circuit.

Longest Circuit

The 37.73-mile "Mountain" circuit on the Isle of Man, over which the two main TT races have been run since 1911, has 264 curves and corners and is the longest used for any motorcycle race.

Fastest Circuits

The highest average lap speed attained on any closed circuit is 160.288 mph by Yvon du Hamel (Canada) (b 1941) on a modified 903-cc four-cylinder Kawasaki Z1 on the 31-degree banked 2.5-mile Daytona International Speedway, Fla, in March 1973. His lap time was 56.149 sec.

The fastest road circuit has been the Francorchamps circuit near Spa, Belgium. It is 14.12 km (8 miles 1,340 yd) in length and was lapped in 3 min 50.3 sec (average speed of 137.150 mph) by Barry S. F. Sheene (b Holborn, London, England, Sept 11, 1950) on a 495-cc four-cylinder Suzuki during the Belgian Grand Prix on July 3, 1977.

The TT circuit (Isle of Man) speed record is 118.47 mph by Joey Dunlop on a Honda on June 4, 1984.

Fastest Race

The fastest track race in the world was held at Grenzlandring, W Germany, in 1939. It was won by Georg "Schorsh" Meier (b Germany Nov 9, 1910) at an average speed of 134 mph on a supercharged 495-cc flat-twin BMW.

The fastest road race is the 500-cc Belgian Grand Prix on the Francorchamps circuit (see above). The record time for this 10-lap 87.74-mile race is 38 min 58.5 sec (average speed of 135.068 mph) by Barry Sheene (UK) on a 495-cc four-cylinder Suzuki on July 3, 1977.

Longest Race

The longest race is the Liège 24 Hours, run on the Francorchamps circuit. The greatest distance ever covered is 2,761.9 miles (average speed 115.08 mph) by Jean-Claude Chemarin and Christian Leon of France on a 941-cc four-cylinder Honda on the Francorchamps circuit on Aug 14–15, 1976 (see above).

DOUBLE WINNER: World champion Barry Sheene (UK) holds both the lap and race records for the Belgian Grand Prix, the road race held at Francorchamps.

Most Successful Machines

Italian MV-Agusta motorcycles won 37 world championships between 1952 and 1973 and 276 world championship races between 1952 and 1976. Japanese Honda machines won 29 world championship races and 5 world championships in 1966. In the 7 years Honda contested the championship (1961–67) its annual average was 20 race wins. In the side-car class BMW machines won an unprecedented 19 consecutive championships between 1955 and 1973.

Speed Records

Official world speed records must be set with two runs over a measured distance within a time limit (one hour for FIM records, two hours for AMA records).

Donald Vesco (b Loma Linda, Calif, Apr 8, 1939) riding his 21-ft-long *Lightning Bolt* streamliner, powered by two 1,016-cc Kawasaki engines on Bonneville Salt Flats, Utah, on Aug 28, 1978, set AMA and FIM absolute records with an overall average of 318.598 mph and had a fastest run at an average of 318.66 mph.

The world record average speed for two runs over 1 km (1,093.6 yd) from a standing start is 16.68 sec by Henk Vink (b July 24, 1939) (The Netherlands) on his supercharged 984-cc 4-cylinder Kawasaki, at Elvington Airfield, Yorkshire, England, on July 24, 1977. The faster run was made in 16.09 sec.

The world record for two runs over 440 yd from a standing start is 8.805 sec by Henk Vink on his supercharged 1,132-cc 4-cylinder Kawasaki, at Elvington Airfield, Yorkshire, England, on July 23, 1977. The faster run was made in 8.55 sec.

The fastest time for a single run over 440 yd from a standing start is 7.08 sec by Bo O'Brechta (US) riding a supercharged 1,200-cc Kawasaki-based machine at Ontario, Calif, in 1980. The highest terminal velocity recorded at the end of a 440-yd run from a standing start is 201.34 mph by Elmer Trett at Indianapolis, on Sept 5, 1983.

World Championships

Races are currently held for the following classes of motorcycles: 50 cc, 125 cc, 250 cc, 350 cc, 500 cc, and sidecars.

Most world championship titles (instituted by the *Fédération Internationale Motocycliste* in 1949) won are 15 by Giacomo Agostini (b Lovere, Italy, June 16, 1942) in the 350-cc class 1968–74 and in the 500-cc class 1966–72 and 75. Agostini is the only man to win two world championships in five consecutive years (350 and 500 cc titles 1968–72). Freddie Spencer (US) in 1985 became the first ever to win world titles at both 250 and 500 cc in the same year. Agostini won 122 races in the world championship series between Apr 24, 1965, and Aug 29, 1976, including a record 19 in 1970, also achieved by Stanley Michael "Mike" Hailwood, (b Oxford, England, 1940, d 1981) in 1966.

A record 3 world trials championships have been won by Yrjö Vesterinen (Finland) (1976–8) and by Eddie Lejeune (Belgium).

Klaus Enders (Germany) (b 1937) won 6 world sidecar titles, 1967, 69–70, 72–74.

Alberto "Johnny" Cecotto (b Caracas, Venezuela, Jan 25, 1956) was the youngest person to win a world championship. He was aged 19 years 211 days when he won the 350-cc title on Aug 24, 1975. The oldest was Hermann-Peter Müller (1909–76) of W Germany, who won the 250-cc title in 1955, aged 46.

Cross-US Trek

Joseph Railton (b 1920) of Park City, Utah, rode a motorcycle from San Francisco to NYC in 64 hours June 1–4, 1985 for the fastest transcontinental trip, averaging 45.84 mph over the 2,934-mi distance.

Matthew P. Guzzetta, 31, of Don Vesco Products, Spring Valley, Calif claims to have ridden a 260-lb, 125-cc revised Suzuki motorcycle whose shell he designed and built, from San Diego, Calif, to Daytona Beach, Fla, without refueling, Mar 3–17, 1984. With a writer-friend, Gerald Foster, he covered the 2,443 mi on 11.83 gallons, for a record consumption of 214.37 mpg. In a snowstorm, they had to put the motorcycle in a van for 36 mi.

Moto-Cross (Scrambling)

This is a very specialized sport in which the competitors race over rough country including steep climbs and drops, sharp turns, sand, mud and water. The sport originated in England in 1924 when some riders competed in "a rare old scramble." Until the Second World War it remained mainly a British interest but the Moto-Cross des Nations was inaugurated in 1947, and became an annual event, with the current rules formulated in 1963. In 1961 the Trophée des Nations, for 250 cc machines, was introduced by the FIM. World championships had been instituted in 1957.

Joël Robert (b Chatelet, Belgium, Nov 11, 1943) has won six 250-cc moto-cross (also known as "scrambles") world championships (1964, 68–72). Between Apr 25, 1964, and June 18, 1972, he won a record fifty 250-cc Grands Prix. He became the youngest moto-cross world champion on July 12, 1964, when he won the 250-cc championship aged 20 years 244 days.

MOTO-CROSS RACE in progress. André Malherbe (Belgium) almost takes flight on his way to victory in the 500-cc contest in 1980.

RODEO

Origins

While there is no known "first rodeo," as early as 1860 cowboys were competing at railheads and on trails for unofficial titles for bronc riding and other skills of their trade. After the great cattle drives were eliminated, due to the introduction of more and more railroads, large ranches began to "give a rodeo." As towns developed, they adopted the rodeo with Cheyenne, Wyo, claiming to have had the first in 1872.

A rodeo has been held each year in Prescott, Ariz, on the Fourth of July since 1888.

The sport was not organized until 1936 when a group of rodeo contes-

6-TIME ALL-ROUND CHAMPS: Tom Ferguson (above) is tied with Larry Mahan (below), seen here aboard the bucking "Moon Rocket" at Calgary.

YOUNGEST CHAMP: When Metha Brorsen of Okla was only 11 years old, she won the barrel-racing event. (*IRA*)

tants founded the Cowboys Turtle Association (now the Professional Rodeo Cowboys Association) to standardize the sport. The official events now are saddle bronc riding, bareback riding, bull riding, calf roping, steer wrestling, and, in some states, team roping.

Largest Prize Money

The largest rodeo in the world is the U.S. National Finals Rodeo, held annually in Dec by the PRCA. The total prize money for the 1985 rodeo held in Las Vegas was $1,790,000.

The top 24 cowboys in the 1984 championship standings were invited to compete in the Winston Tour during which $1 million was awarded in prizes for calf roping, saddle bronc riding, bareback riding, steer wrestling, bull riding, barrel racing and team roping.

Most World Titles

The record number of all-round titles in the Professional Rodeo Cowboys Association world championships is 6 by Larry Mahan (US) (b Nov 21, 1943) in 1966–70 and 1973 and, consecutively, 1974–9 by Tom Ferguson (b Dec 20, 1950). Jim Shoulders (b 1928) of Henryetta, Okla, won a record 16 world championships between 1949 and 1959.

THREE IN ONE YEAR: Roy Cooper not only earned more than $150,000 in prizes in 1983, but his world championships were in steer roping, calf roping and all-round cowboy work.

KNOWS THE ROPES: Chris Lybbert parlayed his calf-roping and steer-wrestling skills into a then record $123,709 in the 1982 All-Around Championship on the Professional Rodeo Cowboys Association (PRCA) circuit. Since Lybbert joined the PRCA in 1976, total prize money has nearly doubled with over $13 million to be divided up nowadays.

Highest Earnings

The record figure for prize money in a single season is $153,391 by Roy Cooper (b 1956) in 1983. The greatest earnings in a rodeo career is $978,809 by Tom Ferguson through 1985. The record for the most money won at one rodeo is $30,677 by Dee Pickett at the National Finals Rodeo in Oklahoma City in Dec 1984.

Champion Bull

The top bucking bull was probably "Tornado," who bucked out of the chute 220 times before Freckles Brown in 1967 became the first cowboy to ride him to the 8-sec bell. "Tornado" retired a year later after a 14-year career.

Champion Bronc

Traditionally a bronc called "Midnight" owned by Jim McNab of Alberta, Canada, was never ridden in 12 appearances at the Calgary Stampede.

Youngest Champion

The youngest winner of a world title is Metha Brorsen of Okla, who was only 11 years old when she won the International Rodeo Association Cowgirls barrel-racing event in 1975.

The youngest women's champion in the female division of the Professional Rodeo Cowboys Association competition is Jackie Jo Perrin of Antlers, Okla, who won the barrel-racing title in 1977 at age 13.

Time Records

Records for timed events, such as calf roping and steer wrestling, are not always comparable, because of the widely varying conditions due to the size of arenas and amount of start given the stock. The fastest time recently recorded for roping a calf is 5.7 sec by Lee Phillips in Assiniboia, Saskatchewan, Canada, in 1978, and the fastest time for overcoming a steer is 2.4 sec by James Bynum at Marietta, Okla, in 1955; by Carl Deaton at Tulsa, Okla, in 1976; and by Gene Melton at Pecatonica, Ill, in 1976.

The standard required time to stay on in bareback, saddle bronc and bull riding events is 8 sec. In the now discontinued ride-to-a-finish events, rodeo riders have been recorded to have survived 15 min or more, until the mount had not a buck left in it.

The highest score in bull riding was 98 points out of a possible 100 by Denny Flynn on "Red Lightning" at Palestine, Ill, in 1979.

SKIING

Origins

The most ancient ski in existence was found well preserved in a peat bog at Höting, Sweden, dating from c. 2500 BC. However, in 1934 a Russian archaeologist discovered a rock carving of a skier at Bessovysledki, USSR, which dates from c. 6000 BC. These early skiers used the bones of animals whereas wooden skis appear to have been introduced to Europe from Asia. The first reference in literature is in a work by Procopius c. 550 AD who referred to "Gliding Finns." Additionally in the Scandinavian sagas there occur gods of skiing. By 1199, the Danish historian Saxo was reporting the military use of troops on skis by Sigurdsson Sverrir, the Norwegian King.

The modern sport did not develop until 1843 when the first known competition for civilians took place at Tromsó, Norway. The first ski club, named the Trysil Shooting and Skiing Club, was founded in Norway in 1861. Twenty years later ski bindings were invented by Sondre Nordheim, from Morgedal in the Telemark area, and the people of this region were the pioneers of the sport. The legendary "Snowshoe" Thompson, whose parents were Norwegian, was the earliest well-known skier in the US (1856) although skiing took place here in the 1840s. It was not until Olaf Kjeldsberg went to Switzerland in 1881 that the sport began to take hold in that country, and in 1889 one of the earliest of British exponents, Arthur Conan Doyle, began skiing at Davos, Switz. The first downhill race—as opposed to the Scandinavian races across country—was held at Kitzbuhel, Austria in 1908. The International Ski Federation (FIS) was founded on Feb 2, 1924. The Winter Olympics were inaugurated on Jan 25, 1924, and Alpine events have been included since 1936. The FIS recognizes both the Winter Olympics and the separate World Ski Championships as world championships.

Most Alpine World Titles

The World Alpine Championships were inaugurated at Mürren, Switzerland, in 1931. The greatest number of titles won has been 13 by

TRIPLE WINNER IN 1984 OLYMPICS: Marja-Liisa Haemaelainen (Fin) dominated the women's cross-country skiing events, taking all three individual gold medals.

AMERICAN TWINS WON gold and silver in Slalom in 1984 Olympics: Phil Mahre (above) beat his twin brother Steve by 21/100ths of a second.

Christel Cranz (b July 1, 1914), of Germany, with 7 individual—4 Slalom (1934, 37–39) and 3 Downhill (1935, 37, 39); and 5 Combined (1934–35, 37–39). She also won the gold medal for the Combined in the 1936 Olympics. The most titles won by a man is 7 by Anton "Toni" Sailer (b Nov 17, 1935), of Austria, who won all 4 in 1956 (Giant Slalom, Slalom, Downhill and the non-Olympic Alpine Combination) and the Downhill, Giant Slalom and Combined in 1958.

Most Olympic Victories

Marja-Liisa Haemaelainen (Fin), after having twice won the women's World Cup title in Nordic, 1983–84, won all 3 individual gold medals in the 1984 Olympics.

The most Olympic gold medals won by a man for skiing is 4 by Sixten Jernberg (b Feb 6, 1929), of Sweden, in 1956–64 (including one for a relay). In addition, Jernberg has won 3 silver and 2 bronze medals for a record 9 Olympic medals. Four were also won by Nikolai Zimjatov (b June 28, 1955) (USSR) in 1980 (30 km, 50 km and on the team for 4 × 10-km relay) and in 1984 (30 km).

The only woman to win 4 gold medals is Galina Koulakova (b Apr 29, 1942) of USSR who won the 5 km and 10 km (1972) and was a member of the winning 3 × 5-km relay team in 1972 and the 4 × 5-km team in 1976. Koulakova also has won 2 silver and 2 bronze medals, 1968–80.

The most Olympic gold medals won in men's Alpine skiing is 3, by Anton "Toni" Sailer in 1956 and Jean-Claude Killy in 1968.

Most Nordic World Titles

The first world Nordic championships were those of the 1924 Winter Olympics at Chamonix, France. The greatest number of titles won is 9 by Galina Koulakova (b Apr 29, 1942) (USSR), 1968–78. She also won 4 silver and 4 bronze medals for a record total of 17. The most won by a man is 8, including relays, by Sixten Jernberg (b Feb 6, 1929) (Sweden), 1956–64. Johan Grottumsbraaten (1899–1942), of Norway, won 6 individual titles (2 at 18 km cross-country and 4 Nordic Combined) in 1926–32. The record for a jumper is 5 by Birger Ruud (b Aug 23, 1911), of Norway, in 1931–32 and 1935–37. Ruud is the only person to win Olympic titles in each of the dissimilar Alpine and Nordic disciplines. In 1936 he won the ski-jumping and the Alpine downhill (which was not then a separate event, but only a segment of the Combined event).

World Cup

The Alpine World Cup, instituted in 1967, and extended to include Nordic in 1981, has been won 4 times by Gustavo Thoeni (Italy) (b Feb 28, 1951) in 1971–73, and 75. The women's cup has been won 6 times by the 5-ft-6-in 150-lb Annemarie Moser (née Pröll) (Austria) in 1971–75 and 79. From Dec 1972 to Jan 1974 she completed a record sequence of 11 consecutive downhill victories. She holds the women's record of 62 individual event wins (1970–79). The most by a man is 83 by Ingemar Stenmark (b Mar 18, 1956) (Sweden), 1974–86, including a record 14 in one season in 1979. Franz Klammer (Austria) (b Dec 3, 1953) won a record 35 downhill races, 1974–85.

Alexander Zavialov (USSR) (b June 2, 1955) has two wins, 1981 and 1983, in the cross-country or Nordic World Cup (inst 1979). Also with two wins are Marja-Liisa Hamalainen (Finland) in 1983 and 1984, and Gunde Svan (Sweden) in 1984 and 1985. The jumping World Cup (inst

SLALOM STAR (left): Ingemar Stenmark (Sweden) has won 83 World Cup events and 2 Olympic gold medals, far surpassing anyone else, but unusually, he has never raced downhill. (*All Sport*)

WINTER WONDER: Jean-Claude Killy (France) (right) thrilled his countrymen when he swept all 3 Olympic gold medals in the 1968 Winter Olympics in Grenoble, France. Killy also won the Alpine Combination world title that year and 2 other world titles in 1966.

1980) has been twice won by Armin Kogler (Austria) (b Sept 4, 1959) 1981–2, and by Matti Nykanen (Finland) 1983 and 1985.

Duration

The record distance covered in 48 hours of Nordic skiing is 319 mi 205 yd by Bjorn Lokken (Norway) (b Nov 27, 1937) Mar 11–13, 1982.

In 24 hours Teuvo Rantanen covered 195 miles at Jyväskylä, Finland Mar 24–25, 1984. The women's record is 122.9 miles by Marlene Severs at East Burke, Vt, Mar 7–8, 1985.

The longest time spent in downhill skiing under regulated conditions is 82 hours 9 min by two members of the Canadian Ski Patrol, Andrew Hempel and John Nicholas Rutter at Silverwood Winter Park, Fredericton, New Brunswick, Jan 25–28, 1984. The ski lift was exclusively confined to the record attempt and no time was wasted waiting for the lift, nor did the skiers sit down on the lift (no seats), but they did take the allowed rest breaks of 5 min after each hour of skiing.

Luc Labrie at Daie Comeau, Quebec, Canada, skied alone for 138 hours, Feb 20–25, 1984.

Highest Speed—Cross Country

Bill Koch (US) (b Apr 13, 1943) on Mar 26, 1981 skied ten times around a 5-km (3.11-mi) loop on Marlborough Pond, near Putney, Vt. He completed the 50 km in 1 hour 59 min 47 sec, an average speed of 15.57 mph. A race includes uphill and downhill sections; the record time for a 50-km race is 2 hours 10 min 49.9 sec by Gunde Svan in the 1985 World Championships, an average speed of 14.25 mph. The record for a 15-km Olympic or World Championship race is 38 min 52.5 sec by Oddvar Braa (Nor) (b Mar 16, 1951) at the 1982 World Championships, an average speed of 14.38 mph.

Closest Verdict

The narrowest winning margin in a championship ski race was one hundredth of a second by Thomas Wassberg (Sweden) (b March 23, 1956) over Juha Mieto (Finland) in the Olympic 15 km cross-country race at Lake Placid, NY on Feb 17, 1980. His winning time was 41 min 57.63 sec.

The narrowest margin of victory in an Olympic Alpine event was 2/100ths of a sec by Barbara Cochran (US) over Daniele De Bernard (France) in the 1972 slalom at Sapporo, Japan.

Highest Speed

The highest speed ever achieved by any skier is 129.827 mph by Franz Weber (b Austria 1957) on Apr 21, 1984 at Les Arcs, France. The fastest by a woman is 124.759 mph by Melissa Dimino (US) Apr 19, 1984 at Les Arcs, France.

The highest average race speed in the Olympic downhill was 64.95 mph by Bill Johnson (US) (b Mar 30, 1960) at Sarajevo, Yugoslavia, on Feb 16, 1984. The fastest in a World Cup downhill is 67.00 mph by Harti Weirather (Austria) (b Jan 25, 1958) at Kitzbuhl, Austria on Jan 15, 1982.

Highest Altitude

Jean Atanassieff and Nicolas Jaeger (both France) skied down from 26,900 ft to 20,340 ft on Mt Everest in 1978.

AERODYNAMICALLY ATTIRED for speed, Franz Weber (Austria) (left) holds the downhill skiing record at 129,827 mph set in 1984.

RECORDHOLDER: Gunde Svan (Sweden) (right) won the 1984 Olympic gold for 15,000 m. In setting the 50-km Nordic uphill and downhill record, his average time was 14.25 mph. (*All Sport*)

Longest Run

The longest all-downhill ski run in the world is the Weissfluhjoch-Küblis Parsenn course (7.6 miles long), near Davos, Switzerland. The run from the Aiguille du Midi top of the Chamonix lift (vertical lift 9,052 ft) across the Vallée Blanche is 13 miles.

Longest Jump

The longest ski jump ever recorded is one of 626 ft by Matti Nykänen (Fin) (b July 17, 1963) at Planica, Yugoslavia on Mar 15, 1985, and by Andreas Felder (Aust) at Bad Mitterndorf, Austria, on Mar 6, 1986.

The women's record is 110 m (361 ft) by Tiina Lehtola (Fin) (b Aug 3, 1962) at Ruka, Finland, on Mar 29, 1981.

The longest dry ski jump is 92 m (301 ft 10 in) by Hubert Schwarz (W Germany) at Berchtesgaden, W Germany, on June 30, 1981.

Steepest Descent

Sylvain Saudan (b Lausanne, Switzerland, Sept 23, 1936) achieved a descent of Mt Blanc on the northeast side down the Couloir Gervasutti from 13,937 ft on Oct 17, 1967, skiing gradients· of about 60 degrees.

Longest Races

The world's longest ski races are the Grenader, run just north of Oslo, Norway, and the König Ludwig Lauf in Oberammergau, W Germany. Both are 90 km (55.9 miles). The Canadian Ski Marathon at 160 km (99 miles) is longer, but is run in two parts on consecutive days.

The world's greatest Nordic ski race is the Vasaloppet, which commemorates an event in 1521 when Gustavus Vasa (1496–1560), later King of Sweden, fled 85.8 km (53.3 miles) from Mora to Sälen, Sweden. He was overtaken by loyal, speedy scouts on skis, who persuaded him to return eastwards to Mora to lead a rebellion and become the king of Sweden. The re-enactment of this return journey is now an annual event at 89 km (55.3 mi), contested by about 12,000 skiers. The fastest time is 3 hours 48 min 55 sec by Bengt Hassis (Swe) on Mar 2, 1986.

The Vasaloppet is now the longest of 10 long distance races, constituting the world loppet, staged in 10 countries.

The longest downhill race is the *Inferno* in Switzerland, 8.7 miles from the top of the Schilthorn to Lauterbrunnen. In 1981 there was a record entry of 1,401, with Heinz Fringen (Switz) winning in a record 15 min 44.57 sec.

Longest Lift

The longest gondola ski lift is 3.88 mi long at Grindelwald-Männlichen, Switzerland (in two sections, but one gondola). The longest chair lift was the Alpine Way to Kosciusko Châlet lift above Thredbo, near the Snowy Mountains, NSW, Australia. It took from 45 to 75 min to ascend the 3.5 mi, according to the weather. It has now collapsed. The highest is at Chacaltaya, Bolivia, rising to 16,500 ft.

Backflip on Skis

The greatest number of skiers to perform a back layout flip while holding hands is 28 at Bromont, Quebec, Canada, on Feb 10, 1982.

Ski Parachuting

The greatest recorded vertical descent in parachute ski-jumping is

BACKFLIP: The record for this popular stunt (sometimes called "hotdogging") has increased from 19 (as shown here) to 28 in just a few years. (*Gary McMillin*)

3,300 ft by Rick Sylvester (b Apr 3, 1942) (US), who on July 28, 1976, skied off the 6,600-ft summit of Mt Asgard in Auyuittuq National Park, Baffin Island, Canada, landing on the Turner Glacier. The jump was made for a sequence in the James Bond film *The Spy Who Loved Me.*

Ski-Bob

The ski-bob was invented by J. C. Stevenson of Hartford, Conn in 1891, and patented (No. 47334) on Apr 19, 1892 as a "bicycle with ski-runners." The Fédération Internationale de Skibob was founded on Jan 14, 1961 in Innsbruck, Austria, and the first world championships were held at Bad Hofgastein, Austria in 1967. The highest speed attained is 103.4 mph by Erich Brenter (b 1940) (Austria) at Cervinia, Italy, 1964.

The only ski-bobbers to retain a world championship are: men—Alois Fischbauer (Austria) (b Oct 6, 1951), 1973 and 1975, Robert Mühlberger (W Germany), 1979, and 1981; women—Gerhilde Schiffkorn (Austria) (b Mar 22, 1950), 1967 and 1969, Gertrude Geberth (Austria) (b Oct 18, 1951), 1971 and 1973.

Grass Skiing

Grass skis were first manufactured by Josef Kaiser (W Ger) in 1963. World Championships (awarded for giant slalom, slalom and combined) were first held in 1979. The most titles won is 5 by Ingrid Hirschhofer (Austria) to 1985. The most by a man is 4 by Erwin Gansner (Switzerland), two each in 1981 and 1983. The speed record is 53.99 mph by Erwin Gansner on Sept 5, 1982.

BIATHLON

The biathlon, which combines cross-country skiing and rifle shooting, was first included in the Olympic Games in 1960, and world championships were first held in 1958.

The biathlon is now competed over 10 km, 20 km and a 4 × 7.5 km relay.

Most Olympic Titles

Magnar Solberg (Norway) (b Feb 4, 1937), in 1968 and 1972, is the only man to have won two Olympic individual titles. The USSR has won all five 4 × 7.5 km relay titles, 1968–84. Aleksandr Tikhonov (b Jan 2,

1947) who was a member of the first 4 teams also won a silver in the 1968 20 km.

Most World Championships

Frank Ullrich (E Ger) (b Jan 24, 1958) has won a record six individual world titles, at 10 km, 1978–81, including the 1980 Olympics, and at 20 km 1982–83. Aleksandr Tikhonov was in ten winning USSR relay teams, 1968–80 and won four individual titles. Ullrich has also won the world cup (inst 1979) three times, 1980–82.

BIATHLON CHAMP: Frank Ullrich (E Ger), who has won 6 titles including Olympics, shows how he handles the gun while on a ski run.

SOCCER

Origins

Ball-kicking games were played very early in human history.

A game with some similarities termed *Tsu-chu* was played in China in the 3rd and 4th centuries BC. One of the earliest references to the game in England is a Royal Proclamation by Edward II in 1314 banning the game in the City of London. A soccer-type game called Calcio was played in Italy in 1410. The earliest clear representation of the game is in a print from Edinburgh, Scotland, dated 1672–73. The game became standardized with the formation of the Football Association in England on Oct 26, 1863. Eleven players on a side was standardized in 1870.

The sport is nationally governed by the US Soccer Federation with headquarters in NYC, which is affiliated with the *Fédération Internationale de Football Association*. The North American Soccer League is affiliated with the USSF.

Highest Team Scores

The highest score recorded in any first-class match is 36. This occurred in the Scottish Cup match between Arbroath and Bon Accord on Sept 12, 1885, when Arbroath won 36–0 on their home ground. But for the lack of nets and the consequent waste of retrieval time, the score might have been even higher. Seven goals were disallowed for offside.

The highest margin recorded in an international match is 17, when

England beat Australia 17–0 at Sydney June 30, 1951. This match is not listed as a *full* international.

Individual Scoring

The most goals scored by one player in a first-class match is 16 by Stephan Stanis (*né* Stanikowski, b Poland, July 15, 1913) for Racing Club de Lens vs Aubry-Asturies, in Lens, France, on Dec 13, 1942.

The record number of goals scored by one player in an international match is 10 by Sofus Nielsen (1888–1963) for Denmark vs France (17–1) in the 1908 Olympics and by Gottfried Fuchs for Germany, which beat Russia 16–0 in the 1912 Olympic tournament (consolation event) in Sweden.

The most goals scored in a specified period is 1,216 by Edson Arantes do Nascimento (b Baurú, Brazil, Oct 23, 1940), known as Pelé, the Brazilian inside left, in the period Sept 7, 1956 to Oct 2, 1974 (1,254 games). His best year was 1959 with 126 goals. His *milesimo* (1,000th) came in a penalty for his club, Santos, in the Maracaña Stadium, Rio de Janeiro, on Nov 19, 1969, when he was playing in his 909th first-class match. He came out of retirement in 1975 to add to his total with the New York Cosmos of the North American Soccer League. By his retirement on Oct 1, 1977 his total had reached 1,281 in 1,363 games. He added 4 more goals later in special appearances.

Franz ("Bimbo") Binder (b Dec 1, 1911) scored 1,006 goals in 756 games in Austria and Germany between 1930 and 1950.

Goalkeeping

The longest that any goalkeeper has succeeded in preventing any goals being scored past him in international matches is 1,142 min for Dino Zoff (Italy) from Sept 1972 to June 1974.

The biggest goalie on record was Willie J. ("Fatty") Foulke of England (1874–1916) who stood 6 ft 3 in and weighed 311 lb. By the time he died, he tipped the scales at 364 lb. He once stopped a game by snapping the cross bar.

Longest Matches

The world duration record for a first-class match is 3 hours 30 min (with interruptions), in the Copa Libertadores championship in Santos, Brazil, Aug 2, 3, 1962, when Santos drew 3–3 with Peñarol FC of Montevideo, Uruguay.

A match between St Ignatius College Preparatory of San Francisco and Bellarmine College Preparatory of San Jose lasted 4 hours 56 min (230 min playing time) at San Francisco on Feb 6, 1982.

Most Postponements

In the winter of 1978–79, the tie-breaking match for the Scottish Cup between Inverness Thistle and Falkirk had to be postponed 29 times due to weather conditions. Falkirk finally won 4–0.

Fastest Goals

The record for an international match is 3 goals in 3½ min by Willie Hall (Tottenham Hotspur) for England against Ireland on Nov 16, 1938, at Old Trafford, Manchester, England.

The fastest authenticated time for a goal from kickoff is 6 sec by Albert Mundy (1958), Barnie Jones (1962), Keith Smith (1964) and

BALL JUGGLERS: The Brazilian youngster (left) in the street in Rio dreams of being a star soccer player like his fellow countryman Pelé. Mikael Palmquist (Sweden) (below) has kept a soccer ball in midair for 14 hours 14 min non-stop.

ATHLETE OF THE CENTURY (above left): Pelé celebrates one of his 1,285 goals, this one with the NY Cosmos of the NASL. In a seemingly premature poll of 20 international newspapers, the tremendously popular Brazilian soccer star was named "Athlete of the Century" by the French sports magazine "L'Equipe." Jesse Owens was runner-up.

NET WEIGHT: At 6 ft 3 in and 311 lb, Fatty Foulke (below) was the most massive goalkeeper ever. One of his greatest exploits came off the field, however, when, appearing at the dinner table early one evening, Foulke ate the team's entire meal before any of his teammates arrived.

Tommy Langley (1980). Wind-aided goals in 3 sec after kickoff have been scored by a number of players.

In amateur soccer, Tony Bacon, of Schalmont HS, scored three goals vs Ichabod Crane HS in 63 sec at Schenectady, NY on Oct 8, 1975.

Ball Control

Mikael Palmquist (Sweden) juggled a regulation soccer ball for 14 hours 14 min non-stop with feet, legs and head without the ball ever touching the ground at Göteborg, Sweden, on Apr 6, 1986. He also headed a regulation soccer ball non-stop for 4½ hours at Göteborg, Sweden in 1984.

Radoslav Metdiev Nikolov juggled a ball with his feet for 2 hours 57 min 3 sec while covering a distance of 11.15 mi around a running track at Plovdiv, Bulgaria on Aug 18, 1984. He kicked the ball 18,110 times.

The greatest distance covered while juggling a soccer ball is 13.11 mi by Uno Lindstrom of Boden, Sweden, on May 10, 1985.

World Cup

The 1986 World Cup Competition, the 13th tournament, was held in Mexico May 31–Jun 29. The *Fédération Internationale de Football Association (FIFA)*, which was founded on May 21, 1904, instituted the first World Cup on July 13, 1930, in Montevideo, Uruguay. Thirteen nations took part then, playing for a trophy named after Jules Rimet, the late Honorary President of FIFA from 1921–1954. The first team to win the competition three times was to keep the trophy, a feat achieved by Brazil in 1970.

The only countries to win three times have been Brazil (1958, 62, 70) and Italy (1934, 38, 82). Brazil was also second in 1950, and third in 1938 and 1978, and is the only one of the 47 participating countries to have played in all 12 competitions, losing only 10 of a total of 57 matches.

Antonio Carbajal (b 1923) played for Mexico in goal in a record 5 competitions, in 1950, 54, 58, 62 and 66. Uwe Seeler (W Ger) (b Nov 5, 1936) shares the record for the most appearances in final tournaments, playing as a center forward in 21 games in the 1958–70 events, while Pelé is the only player to have been with 3 World Cup winning teams. The youngest World Cup player ever was Norman Whiteside, who played for N Ireland vs Yugoslavia, aged 17 years 42 days on June 17, 1982.

The record goal scorer has been Just Fontaine (France) with 13 goals in 6 games in the final stages of the 1958 competition. Gerd Müller (W Ger) (b Nov 3, 1945) scored 10 goals in 1970 and 4 in 1974 for the highest aggregate of 14 goals. Fontaine and Jairzinho (Brazil) are the only two players to have scored in every game in a final series, as Jairzinho scored 7 in 6 games in 1970. The most goals scored in the final game is 3 by Geoffrey Hurst (b Dec 8, 1941) for England vs W Germany in 1966. Three players have scored in 2 finals: Vava (real name, Edwaldo Izito Neto) (Brazil) in 1958 and 62, Pelé in 1958 and 70, and Paul Breitner (W Ger) in 1974 and 82.

The highest score in a World Cup match is New Zealand's 13–0 defeat of Fiji in a qualifying match at Auckland on Aug 16, 1981. The highest score in the Finals Tournament is Hungary's 10–1 win over El Salvador at Elche, Spain, on June 15, 1982. The highest match aggregate in the Finals Tournament is 12 when Austria beat Switzerland in 1954.

The highest-scoring team in a Finals Tournament has been W Germany, which scored 25 in 6 games in 1954 for the highest average of 4.17 goals per game. England has the best defensive record, conceding only 3 goals in 6 games in 1966. Curiously, no team has ever failed to score in a World Cup Final.

The fastest goal scored in World Cup competition was one in 27 sec by Bryan Robson for England vs France in Bilbao, Spain, on June 16, 1982.

World Cup Winners

	Winner	Locale
1930	Uruguay	Uruguay
1934	Italy	Italy
1938	Italy	France
1950	Uruguay	Brazil
1954	W Germany	Switzerland
1958	Brazil	Sweden
1962	Brazil	Chile
1966	England	England
1970	Brazil	Mexico
1974	W Germany	W Germany
1978	Argentina	Argentina
1982	Italy	Spain
1986	Argentina	Mexico

Largest Tournament

In the Metropolitan Police 5-a-side Youth Competition in 1981 a record 7,008 teams entered.

Marathons

The longest outdoor game played was 74½ hours by two teams trying to establish a record at Liswerry Leisure Centre, Gwent, Wales, June 23–26, 1983. The indoor soccer record is 104 hours 10 min set by two teams of students at Summerhill College, Sligo, Ireland, Mar 27–31, 1983.

Penalties

All 11 players and 2 substitutes were "booked" before the start of a game played by Glencraig United (UK) because the referee took exception to the chant which greeted his arrival.

Crowds

The greatest recorded crowd at any soccer match was 205,000 (199,854 paid) for the Brazil vs Uruguay World Cup final in Rio de Janeiro, Brazil, on July 16, 1950.

The greatest crowd to see a soccer game in the US and Canada was the 77,691 spectators at Giants Stadium, NJ, who watched an NASL playoff game between the NY Cosmos and Ft Lauderdale Strikers on Aug 14, 1977.

The highest attendance at any amateur match is 120,000 at Senayan Stadium, Djakarta, Indonesia, on Feb 26, 1976, for the Pre-Olympic Group II Final between North Korea and Indonesia.

SOFTBALL

Origins

Softball, as an indoor derivative of baseball, was invented by George Hancock at the Farragut Boat Club of Chicago, in 1887. Rules were first codified in Minneapolis in 1895 as Kitten Ball. The name Softball was introduced by Walter Hakanson at a meeting of the National Recreation Congress in 1926. The name was adopted throughout the US in 1930. Rules were formalized in 1933 by the International Joint Rules Committee for Softball and adopted by the Amateur Softball Association of America. The International Softball Federation was formed in 1950 as governing body for both fast pitch and slow pitch, and reorganized in 1965.

Marathons

The longest fast pitch marathon is 61 hours 36 min 33 sec by two teams of 9 (no substitutes) belonging to the Marines of the 2nd Radio Battalion at Camp Lejeune, NC, May 3–5, 1984. The game went 266 innings and the score was 343-296.

The longest slow pitch softball game took exactly 100 hours June

DOMINATING SOFTBALL: (left) Ty Stofflet (US) has struck out 33 in one game and 98 in a year. (Right) Joan Joyce (US) has pitched 2 perfect games and fanned 76 batters in a season.

WORLD CHAMPIONSHIP
FAST PITCH SOFTBALL RECORDS

MEN
Batting

Highest batting average:	.583	Takayuki Ietke, Japan	1984
Most hits in a game:	17	Basil McLean, New Zealand	1976
Most runs scored in a game:	14	Takayuki Ietke, Japan	1984
Most runs batted in in a game:	14	Chuck Teuscher, US	1966
	14	Bob Burrows, Canada	1976
Most doubles in a game:	5	Hector Serranto, Puerto Rico	1966
	5	Luis Delgado, Mexico	1966
	5	Frank Hurtt, US	1968
	5	Filomeno Codinera, Philippines	1968
Most triples in a game:	3	Akira Nakagawa, Japan	1976
	3	Jesus Augon, Guam	1976
Most home runs in a game:	4	Bob Burrows, Canada	1976

Pitching (in a year)

Most wins:	6	Owen Walford, New Zealand	1976
	6	Owen Walford, US	1980
Most strikeouts, total:	99	Kevin Herlihy, New Zealand	1972
	98	Ty Stofflet, US	1976
Most strikeouts in one game:	33	Ty Stofflet, US in 20 innings 1–0 win over New Zealand	1976
Most innings pitched in a year:	59	Ty Stofflet, US	1976
	58⅔	Kevin Herlihy, New Zealand	1972
Lowest earned run average:			
(59 innings pitched)	0.00	Ty Stofflet, US	1976
(32⅓ innings pitched)	0.00	Chuck Richard, US	1966
(34⅔ innings pitched)	0.00	Owen Walford, US	1980
Most consecutive wins:	15	Owen Walford, US and New Zealand	1976, 80, 84
Perfect games:	7	tied	1968–84

WOMEN
Batting

Highest batting average:	.550	Tamara Bryce, Panama	1978
Most hits in a game:	17	Miyoko Naruse, Japan	1974
Most runs scored in a game:	13	Kathy Elliott, US	1974
Most runs batted in in a game:	11	Miyoko Naruse, Japan	1974
	11	Keiko Uoul, Japan	1974
	11	Kathy Elliott, US	1974
Most doubles in a game:	4	Vicki Murray, NZ	1983
	4	Suh-Chiung Ju, Taiwan	1983
Most triples in a game:	6	Miyoko Naruse, Japan	1974
	6	Yug-Feng Yang, Taiwan	1982

Most wins:	6 Lorraine Wooley, Australia	1965
	6 Nancy Welborn, US	1970
Most innings pitched:	50 Nancy Welborn, US	1970
Most strikeouts in a year:	76 Joan Joyce, US	1974
Most no-hitters:	3 Joan Joyce, US	1974
	3 Kathy Arendsen, US	1978
Most perfect games:	2 Joan Joyce, US	1974

20–24, 1986 at Bun Ryan Field, County of Los Alamos, N Mex. Twenty students in 2 teams of 10 (without substitutes) played for 390 consecutive innings, with umpiring duties shared by 48 volunteers, while 20 volunteers kept time.

Exhibition Softball

Using only 4 players against teams of 9, the team led by pitcher Rosie Black called "The Queen and Her Court" has traveled around the US for 21 years challenging all comers. The reason they win almost all of their games is that Rosie can throw a softball 100 mph, and has a variety of risers, drops and knuckleballs, as well as the usual assortment of curves, fastballs and change-ups.

World Championships

The US has won the men's world championship (instituted in 1966) four times, 1966, 68, 76 (shared) and 80. The US has also won the women's title (instituted in 1965) twice, in 1974 and 78.

(See previous page for chart of record performances.)

SWIMMING

Earliest References

Egyptian hieroglyphics, c. 3000 BC, indicate swimming figures, and a bronze of a diver dating from c. 510 BC was found near Perugia, Italy. Both Julius Caesar and Charlemagne were known to be good swimmers. Competitions took place in Japan in 36 BC, and that country was the first to take to the sport in a major way with an Imperial edict by the Emperor G-Yozei decreeing its introduction in schools. In Britain, sea bathing was practiced as early as 1660 at Scarborough, but competitive swimming was not introduced until 1837, when competitions were held in London's artificial pools organized by the National Swimming Society, founded in that year. Australia was in the forefront of modern developments and an unofficial world 100-yd championship was held in Melbourne in 1858. With the foundation in Britain of the Amateur Swimming Association (though not known by this name till later) in 1869 came the distinction between amateurs and professionals.

The first recognizable stroke style seems to have been the breaststroke, although the "dog-paddle" technique may well have preceded it. From this developed the sidestroke, which is the breaststroke performed sideways, a style which was last used by an Olympic champion in 1904, when Emil Rausch (Ger) won the 1-mi event. About the middle of the 19th century, some American Indians had swum in London exhibiting a style resembling the crawl. An Englishman, John Trudgen, noted a variation of this style while on a trip to South America in the 1870s. His forerunner to the modern crawl used the legs in basically a breaststroke way. However, from ancient carvings and wall paintings it would seem that the trudgen stroke was in use in early times.

Another "throwback" was the front or Australian crawl which is credited to a British emigrant to Australia, Frederick Cavill, and his sons, who noticed the unusual style of South Sea Island natives, and modified it to their own use. American swimmers developed this even further by variations of the kicking action of the legs. At the beginning of the 20th century some had shown their prowess by attempting the breaststroke on their backs, and later the crawl action was tried in the same position. Thus the backstroke was born. In the 1930s the idea of recovering the arms over the water in the breaststroke was developed, and led to a drastic revision of the record book, until the new style was recognized as a separate stroke, the butterfly, in 1952. Also in the 1930s came the introduction, mainly in the US, of medley events in which swimmers use all four major strokes during one event, a real test of all-around ability.

World Titles

In the world swimming championships (instituted in 1973), the greatest number of medals won is 10 by Kornelia Ender of E Germany (8 gold, 2 silver) in 1973 and 75. The most by a man is 8 (5 gold, 3 silver) by Ambrose "Rowdy" Gaines (US, b Feb 17, 1959) in 1978 and 1982. The most gold medals is 6 by James Montgomery (b Jan 24, 1955) in 1973 and 1975.

The most medals in a single championship is 6 by Tracy Caulkins (US) (b Jan 11, 1963) in 1978 with 5 gold and a silver. She has won a record 48 US titles before she retired in 1984.

The most successful country in the championships has been the US with a total of 50 swimming, 9 diving and 8 synchronized swimming titles. However, in women's swimming events alone E Germany has a record total of 31 victories.

Other than relays, the only gold medalist in the same event at three championships is Phil Boggs (US) in springboard diving.

Most World Records

Men: 32, Arne Borg (Sweden) (b 1901), 1921–29. Women: 42, Ragnhild Hveger (Denmark) (b Dec 10, 1920), 1936–42. Under modern conditions (only metric distances in 50-meter pools) the most is 26 by Mark Spitz (US, b Feb 10, 1950), 1967–72, and 23 by Kornelia Ender (now Matthes) (E Germany, b Oct 25, 1958), 1973–76.

Hveger's record of 42 gained for her the name "Golden Torpedo." Her records came in 18 different events. She was a virtual certainty to win at the 1940 Olympic Games, but, of course, war intervened. Retiring in 1945, she made a comeback for the 1952 Games and placed fifth in the 400 m freestyle.

Most Individual Gold Medals

The record number of individual gold medals won is 4 shared by four swimmers: Charles M. Daniels (US) (1884–1973) (100 m freestyle 1906 and 1908, 220 yd freestyle 1904, 440 yd freestyle 1904); Roland Matthes

(E Germany) (b Nov 17, 1950) with 100 m and 200 m backstroke 1968 and 1972; and Mark Spitz and Mrs Patricia McCormick (see next item).

Most Olympic Gold Medals

The greatest number of Olympic gold medals won is 9 by Mark Andrew Spitz (US) (b Feb 10, 1950), as follows:

100 m freestyle	1972
200 m freestyle	1972
100 m butterfly	1972
200 m butterfly	1972
4 × 100 m freestyle relay	1968 and 1972
4 × 200 m freestyle relay	1968 and 1972
4 × 100 m medley relay	1972

All but one of these performances (the 4 × 200 m relay of 1968) were also world records at the time. He also won a silver (100 m butterfly) and a bronze (100 m freestyle) in 1968 for a record 11 medals.

The record number of gold medals won by a woman is 4 shared by Mrs Patricia McCormick (*née* Keller) (US) (b May 12, 1930) with the high and springboard diving double in 1952 and 1956 (also the women's record for individual golds); by Dawn Fraser (Australia) (b Sept 4, 1937) with the 100 m freestyle (1956, 60, 64) and the 4 × 100 m freestyle relay (1956); and by Kornelia Ender (E Germany) with the 100 and 200 m freestyle (1976), the 100 m butterfly (1976) and the 4 × 100 m medley relay (1976). Dawn Fraser is the only swimmer to win the same event on three successive Olympic occasions.

MOST RECORDS: A young Mark Spitz (17 years old in this photo) is congratulated after setting a world record early in his career. Spitz might be considered the most successful swimmer ever. Of his 9 Olympic gold medals (including the unequaled haul of 7 in 1972), 8 were won in world record time. In his 6-year career, Spitz set a total of 26 world records.

SWIMMING WORLD RECORDS (MEN)

At distances recognized by the Fédération Internationale de Natation Amateur as of July 16, 1983. FINA no longer recognizes any records made for non-metric distances. Only performances in 50-m pools are recognized as World Records.

Distance	min:sec	Name and Nationality	Place	Date
		FREESTYLE		
50 m	22.33	Matthew Biondi (US)	Orlando, Fla	June 26, 1986
100 m	48.74	Matthew Biondi (US)	Orlando, Fla	June 24, 1986
200 m	1:47.44	Michael Gross (W Ger)	Los Angeles	July 29, 1984
400 m	3:47.80	Michael Gross (W Ger)	Remscheid, W Ger	June 27, 1985
800 m	7:50.64	Vladimir Salnikov (USSR)	Moscow, USSR	July 4, 1986
1,500 m	14:54.76	Vladimir Salnikov (USSR)	Moscow	Feb 22, 1983
4 × 100 m Relay	3:17.08	US National Team	Tokyo	Aug 17, 1985
		(Scott McCadam, Michael Heath, Paul Wallace, Matthew Biondi)		
4 × 200 m Relay	7:15.69	US National Team	Los Angeles	July 30, 1984
		(Michael Heath, David Larson, Jeff Float, Bruce Hayes)		
		BREASTSTROKE		
100 m	1:01.65	Steve Lundquist (US)	Los Angeles	July 29, 1984
200 m	2:13.34	Victor Davis (Canada)	Los Angeles	Aug 2, 1984
		BUTTERFLY STROKE		
100 m	52.84	Pedro Pablo Morales (US)	Orlando, Fla	June 23, 1986
200 m	1:56.24	Michael Gross (W Ger)	Hanover, W Ger	June 27, 1986
		BACKSTROKE		
100 m	55.19	Richard (Rick) Carey (US)	Caracas, Venezuela	Aug 21, 1983
200 m	1:58.14	Igor Polyansky (USSR)	Erfurt, E Ger	Mar 3, 1985

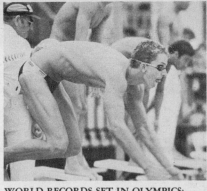

WORLD RECORDS SET IN OLYMPICS:
Michael Gross (above) (W Ger) who set the 200-m freestyle and 100-m butterfly records in the 1984 Games, went on to new records in the 400-m freestyle (1985) and 200-m butterfly (1986). Steve Lundquist (below) (US) set the 100-m breaststroke world mark in the 1984 Olympics that still prevails.

INDIVIDUAL MEDLEY

200 m	2:01.42	Alex Baumann (Canada)	Los Angeles	Aug 4, 1984
400 m	4:17.41	Alex Baumann (Canada)	Los Angeles	July 30, 1984

Montreal, Canada — Mar 4, 1986

MEDLEY RELAY
Backstroke, Breaststroke, Butterfly Stroke, Freestyle

4 × 100 m	3:38.28	US National Team (Richard "Rick" Carey, John Moffett, Pablo Morales, Matthew Biondi)

Tokyo — Aug 18, 1985

SWIMMING WORLD RECORDS (WOMEN)

FREESTYLE

Distance	min:sec	Name and Nationality	Place	Date
50 m	25.34	Tamara Costache (Romania)	Bucharest, Romania	June 14, 1986
100 m	54.79	Barbara Krause (E Ger)	Moscow	July 21, 1980
200 m	1:57.55	Heike Friedrich (E Ger)	E Berlin	June 18, 1986
400 m	4:06.28	Tracey Wickham (Aust)	W Berlin	Aug 24, 1978
800 m	8:24.62	Tracey Wickham (Aust)	Edmonton, Canada	Aug 5, 1978
1,500 m	16:04.49	Kim Linehan (US)	Ft Lauderdale	Aug 19, 1979
4 × 100 m Relay	3:42.41	East German National Team (Kristin Otto, Karen Konig, Heike Friedrich, Birgit Meineke)	Moscow	Aug 21, 1984
4 × 200 m Relay	8:02.27	E Germany (Kristin Otto, Karen Konig, Heike Friedrich, Birgit Meineke)	Moscow	Aug 21, 1984

BREASTSTROKE

Distance	min:sec	Name and Nationality	Place	Date
100 m	1:08.29	Sylvia Gerasch (E Ger)	Moscow	Aug 22, 1984
200 m	2:28.20	Sylvia Gerasch (E Ger)	Leningrad	Mar 1, 1986

BUTTERFLY STROKE

Distance	min:sec	Name and Nationality	Place	Date
100 m	57.93	Mary Meagher (US)	Milwaukee	Aug 16, 1981
200 m	2:05.96	Mary Meagher (US)	Milwaukee	Aug 13, 1981

BACKSTROKE

Distance	min:sec	Name and Nationality	Place	Date
100 m	1:00.59	Ina Kleber (E Ger)	Moscow	Aug 24, 1984
200 m	2:08.60	Betsy Mitchell (US)	Orlando, Fla	June 27, 1986

INDIVIDUAL MEDLEY

200 m	2:11.73	Ute Geweniger (E Ger)	E Berlin	July 4, 1981
400 m	4:36.10	Petra Schneider (E Ger)	Guayaquil, Ecuador	Aug 1, 1982

MEDLEY RELAY

(Backstroke, Breaststroke, Butterfly Stroke, Freestyle)

4 × 100 m Relay	4:03.69	E German National Team	Moscow	Aug 24, 1984
		(Ina Kleber, Sylvia Gerasch, Ines Geissler, Birgit Meineke)		

BUTTERFLY CHAMPION: Mary Meagher (US) set 100 m and 200 m butterfly records in 1981 that still stand. She also holds the Olympic records in these events.

LONG-TIME CHAMPION: No one has been able to beat the record of Petra Schneider of E Germany in the 400 m individual medley since 1982.

Most Olympic Medals

The most medals won is 11 by Spitz, who in addition to his 9 golds (see above), won a silver (100 m butterfly) and a bronze (100 m freestyle), both in 1968.

The most medals won by a woman is 8 by Dawn Fraser, who in addition to her 4 golds (see above) won 4 silvers (400 m freestyle 1956, 4 × 100 m freestyle relay 1960 and 1964, 4 × 100 m medley relay 1960); by Shirley Babashoff (US) who won 2 golds (4 × 100 m freestyle relay 1972 and 1976) and 6 silvers (100 m freestyle 1972, 200 m freestyle 1972 and 1976, 400 m and 800 m freestyle 1976, and 400 m medley 1976); and by Kornelia Ender (E Germany) who, in addition to her 4 golds (see above), won 4 silvers (200 m individual medley 1972, 4 × 100 m medley 1972, 4 × 100 m freestyle 1972 and 1976).

Swimming into the Movies

The ability to move well in water has been the key to a movie career for a number of champion swimmers. The first star was Australian Annette Kellerman who made a number of silent films, and was the first woman to wear a one-piece bathing suit. However, it was the 1924 and 1928 Olympic gold medalist, Johnny Weissmuller (US), who became the first major box-office attraction from the swimming world, playing the role of Tarzan in a dozen films. His 1928 Olympic teammate, Clarence "Buster" Crabbe, who later won the 1932 400 m freestyle title, also went to Hollywood, where he was the hero in the long-running Buck Rogers and Flash Gordon serials.

Another 1932 Olympic champion, the glamorous Eleanor Holm (US) made several movies, although she did not go to Hollywood until she was dropped from the 1936 team for disciplinary reasons. Perhaps the best-known swimming star was Esther Williams, American 100 m champion in 1939 and favorite for the cancelled Olympics of 1940. Turning professional she created a new vogue in the cinema, the swimming musical, in which she was supreme throughout the 1940s. One of her co-stars was Fernando Lamas, who had been a national swimming champion in his native Argentina, and whom she later married.

Synchronized Swimming

Started in 1904 by Annette Kellerman when she swam underwater and performed water ballets on the stage of the NYC Hippodrome, this did not become an Olympic event for women until 1984 at Los Angeles. The contestants are judged on presentation and showmanship as well as the athlete's skill and technique.

Closest Race

In the women's 100 m freestyle final in the 1984 Olympics, Carrie Steinseifer (US) and Nancy Hogshead (US) won in a tie at 55.92 sec, and were both awarded gold medals. It was not in record time, but it was the first dead heat in Olympic swimming history.

Fastest Swimmers

The fastest 50 m in a 50-m pool is 22.33 sec by Matthew Biondi (US) in Orlando, Fla, June 26, 1986.

The fastest by a woman is 25.34 sec by Tamara Costache (Rom), averaging 4.41 mph at Bucharest, Romania, June 14, 1986.

Largest Pools

The largest swimming pool in the world is the salt-water Orthlieb Pool in Casablanca, Morocco. It is 480 m (1,574 ft) long, 75 m (246 ft) wide, and has an area of 8.9 acres.

The world's largest competition pool is at Osaka, Japan. It accommodates 13,614 spectators.

24-Hour Swim

David Goch (US) swam 55.682 mi in a 25-yd pool at Univ of Mich, May 17–18, 1986. In a 50-yd pool, Bertrand Malegue swam 54.39 mi at St Étienne, France, May 31–June 1, 1980.

Greatest Lifetime Distance

Gustave Bricker (b Feb 10, 1912) of Charleroi, Pa, in 58 years to Nov 1985 recorded 38,162 mi of swimming.

Underwater Swimming

Paul Cryne (UK) and Samir Sawan al Aw swam 49.04 mi underwater in a 24-hour period at Doha, Qatar on Feb 21–22, 1985 using sub-aqua equipment. They were swimming underwater for 95.5% of the time.

The first underwater cross-Channel swim was achieved by Fred Baldasare (US), aged 38, who completed a 42-mile swim from France to England with SCUBA in 18 hours 1 min, July 10–11, 1962.

Treading Water

The duration record for treading water (vertical posture in an 8-ft square without touching the pool sides or bottom or lane markers) is 98½ hours set by Reginald (Moon) Huffstetler of Belmont, NC, at The Reef in Myrtle Beach, SC, May 20–24, 1986.

Albert Rizzu trod water in the sea at Qawra, Malta, for 100 hours 9 min, Sept 7–12, 1983.

Diving Titles

Klaus Dibiasi (Italy, b Austria, Oct 6, 1947) won a total of 5 Olympic diving medals (3 gold, 2 silver) in 4 Games from 1964 to 1976. He is also the only diver to win the same event (highboard) at 3 successive Games (1968, 72 and 76). He also won 4 medals (2 gold, 2 silver) in world events in 1973 and 1975.

Irina Kalinina (USSR) (b Feb 8, 1959) has won 5 medals (3 gold, one silver, one bronze) in 1973, 1975 and 1978.

Greg Louganis (US) (b Jan 29, 1960), won one gold in 1978 and 2 in the 1982 world championships at Guayaquil, Ecuador, where he became the first to score over 700 points for the 11-dive springboard event with 752.67 on Aug 1, 1982. He went on to be awarded a score of 10.0 by all 7 judges for his highboard inward 1½ somersault in the pike position. In the 1984 Olympics, Louganis won two gold medals and set record totals of 754.41 for springboard and 710.91 for highboard.

DIVING RECORDS (left): Pat McCormick (US) won 4 diving events in the 1952 and 1956 Olympics, for the most golds won by a woman.

DIVING CHAMPION (right): Greg Louganis (US), considered by many to be the best diver in the world in the 1980's is one of two divers to earn perfect 10's from all 7 judges for one dive. He achieved the feat while winning his 2nd and 3rd world championships. In the 1984 Olympics he won 2 gold medals and set new world records for springboard and highboard.

Perfect Dive

In the 1972 US Olympic Trials, held in Chicago, Michael Finneran (b Sept 21, 1948) was awarded a score of 10 by all seven judges for a backward 1½ somersault 2½ twist (free) from the 10-m platform, an achievement then without precedent. Greg Louganis matched this feat in 1982.

Long Distance Swimming

A unique achievement in long distance swimming was established in 1966 by Mihir Sen of Calcutta, India. He swam the Palk Strait from Sri Lanka to India (in 25 hours 36 min, Apr 5–6); the Straits of Gibraltar (Europe to Africa in 8 hours 1 min on Aug 24); the Dardanelles (Gallipoli, Europe, to Sedulbahir, Asia Minor, in 13 hours 55 min on Sept 12); the Bosphorus (in 4 hours on Sept 21) and the entire length of the Panama Canal (in 34 hours 15 min, Oct 29–31). He had earlier swum the English Channel in 14 hours 45 min on Sept 27, 1958.

The longest ocean swim was one of 128.8 miles by Walter Poenisch (US) (b 1914), who started from Havana, Cuba, and arrived at Little Duck Key, Fla (in a shark cage and wearing flippers) 34 hours 15 min later, July 11–13, 1978.

The greatest recorded distance ever swum is 1,826 miles down the Mississippi from Ford Dam, near Minneapolis, to Carrollton Avenue, New Orleans, July 6 to Dec 29, 1930, by Fred P. Newton, then 27, of Clinton, Okla. He was in the water a total of 742 hours, and the water temperature fell as low as 47° F. He protected himself with petroleum jelly.

The longest swim using the highly exhausting butterfly stroke exclusively was 40.6 miles from Gun Cay, the Bahamas to near Florida by twins James and Jonathan di Donato (b Oct 24, 1953) (US) June 23, 1985. They were stopped by foul weather after 20 hours 6 min.

The fastest swim around Manhattan was made by a woman, Shelley Taylor of Australia (b 1961) who set a record of 6 hours 12 min 29 sec on Oct 15, 1985. The men's record was set by Drury J. Gallagher in 6 hours 41 min 35 sec on Sept 7, 1983. The longest swim around Manhattan was done over a period of 6 days in a row—Aug 15–20, 1985—28½ mi each day (except for the first day—20 mi) by Julie Ridge of NYC, who was an actress in the cast of a Broadway show.

The longest duration swim ever achieved was one of 168 continuous hours, ending on Feb 24, 1941, by the legless Charles Zibbelman, *alias* Zimmy (b 1894), of the US, in a pool in Honolulu, Hawaii.

The longest duration swim by a woman was 87 hours 27 min in a salt water pool at Raven Hall, Coney Island, NY by Mrs Myrtle Huddleston of NYC, in 1931.

The greatest distance covered in a continuous swim is 299 miles by Ricardo Hoffmann (b Oct 5, 1941) from Corrientes to Santa Elena, Argentina, in the River Paraná in 84 hours 37 min, Mar 3–6, 1981.

Jon Hestoy (Iceland) swam 55.41 mi in a 25-m pool at Aarhus, Denmark on May 29–30, 1982. The record in a 50-m pool is 54.39 mi by Bertrand Malègue at St. Etienne, France on May 31–June 1, 1980.

Gustave Brickner (b Feb 10, 1912) of Charleroi, Pa in 57 years to Nov 1985 had recorded 38,162 mi for the greatest lifetime distance.

Earliest Channel Swimmers

The first to swim the English Channel (without a life jacket) was the merchant navy captain Matthew Webb (1848–83) (GB), who swam breaststroke from Dover, England, to Calais Sands, France, in 21 hours 45 min, Aug 24–25, 1875. Webb swam an estimated 38 miles to make the 21-mile crossing. Paul Boyton (US) had swum from Cap Gris Nez to the South Foreland in his patented lifesaving suit in 23 hours 30 min, May 28–29, 1875. There is good evidence that Jean-Marie Saletti, a French soldier, escaped from a British prison hulk off Dover by swimming to Boulogne in July or Aug 1815. The first crossing from France to England was made by Enrico Tiraboschi, a wealthy Italian living in Argentina, who crossed in 16 hours 33 min on Aug 12, 1923, to win a $5,000 prize. By the end of 1981 the English Channel had been swum by 228 persons on 366 occasions.

The first woman to succeed was Gertrude Ederle (b Oct 23, 1906) (US) who swam from Cap Gris Nez, France, to Deal, England, on Aug 6, 1926, in the then record time of 14 hours 39 min. The first woman to swim from England to France was Florence Chadwick of California, in 16 hours 19 min on Sept 11, 1951.

Youngest and Oldest Channel Swimmers

The youngest conqueror is Marcus Hooper (b June 14, 1967) of Eltham, England, who swam from Dover to Sangatte, France, in 14 hours 37 min, when he was aged 12 years 53 days. The youngest woman was Samantha Claire Druce (b Apr 21, 1971) aged 12 years 119 days when she swam from England to France in 15 hours 27 min on Aug 18, 1983.

The oldest is Ashby Harper (b Oct 1, 1916) of Albuquerque, N Mex, at 65 years 332 days. He swam from Dover to Cap Blanc Nez in 13 hours 52 min on Aug 28, 1983. He also held the record as the oldest person to swim around Manhattan before that record was broken on Aug 26, 1984 by the 73-year-old Dr Adrian Kanaar of Poughkeepsie, NY.

The oldest woman to conquer the Channel is Stella Ada Rosina Taylor (b Bristol, Avon, England, Dec 20, 1929), aged 45 years 350 days when she swam it in 18 hours 15 min on Aug 26, 1975.

Most Conquests of the English Channel

The greatest number of Channel conquests is 31 by Michael Read (GB), to Aug 19, 1984, including a record 6 in one year. Cindy Nicholas made her first crossing of the Channel on July 29, 1975, and her 19th (and fifth 2-way) on Sept 14, 1982.

Double Crossings of the Channel

Antonio Abertondo (Argentina), aged 42, swam from England to France in 18 hours 50 min (8:35 a.m. on Sept 20 to 3:25 a.m. on Sept 21, 1961) and after about 4 minutes' rest returned to England in 24 hours 16 min, landing at St Margaret's Bay at 3:45 a.m. on Sept 22, 1961, to complete the first "double crossing" in 43 hours 10 min.

The fastest double crossing was in 18 hours 15 min by Irene van der Laan (Neth) (b Dec 27, 1960) on Aug 18, 1983.

The fastest by a relay team is 15 hours 36 min 30 sec by the West One International Team on Sept 24, 1985.

Triple Crossing of the Channel

The first triple crossing of the English Channel was by Jon Erikson (b Sept 6, 1954) (US) in 38 hours 27 min, Aug 11–12, 1981.

Fastest Channel Crossings

The official Channel Swimming Association record is 7 hours 40 min by Penny Dean (b March 21, 1955) of California, who swam from Shakespeare Beach, Dover, England to Cap Gris Nez, France on July 29, 1978.

The fastest crossing by a relay team is 7 hours 17 min by 6 Dover (Eng) lifeguards from England to France on Aug 9, 1981.

Relay Records

The New Zealand national relay team of 20 swimmers swam a record 113.59 mi in Lower Hutt, NZ in 24 hours, passing 100 mi in 20 hours 47 min 13 sec on Dec 9–10, 1983.

The most participants in a one-day swim relay is 2,135, each swimming a length, organized by the Syracuse (NY) YMCA, Apr 11, 1986. A team of 4 from Capalaba State Primary School, Kim Wilson, Tanya Obstoj, Paul Giles, Daren Sheldrick, set an endurance record of 168 hours with one of the team in the water at any time, covering 336 mi on Dec 12–19, 1983 at Sheldon, Queensland, Australia.

The fastest time recorded for 100 miles in a pool by a team of 20 swimmers is 21 hours 41 min 4 sec by the Dropped Sports Swim Club of Indiana State University at Terre Haute, Ind, Mar 12–13, 1982. Four swimmers from the Darien YMCA, Conn, covered 300 miles in relay in 122 hours 59 min 40 sec, Nov 25–30, 1980.

Tony Boyle, Eddie McGettigan, Laurence Thermes and Gearoid

Murphy swam a relay of 332.88 mi underwater in 168 hours using sub-aqua equipment at the Mosney Holiday Centre, Co. Meath, Ireland, June 22–29, 1985.

LONGEST TOUGH SWIM (above): Using the exhausting butterfly stroke exclusively, the di Donato twins, James and Jonathan, swam 40.6 miles in 20 hours 6 min from Gun Cay, Bahamas, to near the Fla coast before foul weather stopped them. They also swam the 28+ miles around Manhattan Island in 9 hours 42 min using the butterfly stroke.

LONG-TIME CHAMPION: Cindy Nicholas of Canada (right) was the first woman to make a double crossing of the English Channel in 1977, knocking 10 hours off the men's mark. She beat this by an hour in 1982.

TENNIS

Origins

The modern game of lawn tennis is generally agreed to have evolved as an outdoor form of the French Royal Tennis or *Jeu de Paume* from the 11th century. "Field Tennis" was mentioned in an English magazine (*Sporting Magazine*) on Sept 29, 1793. In 1858 Major Harry Gem laid out a "court" on the lawn of a friend in Birmingham, Eng, and in 1872 he founded the Leamington Club. In Feb 1874, Major Walter Clopton Wingfield of England (1833–1912) patented a form called "sphairistike," which was nicknamed "sticky," but the game soon became known as lawn tennis. The US Lawn Tennis Association (USLTA) was founded in 1881.

Amateurs were permitted to play with and against professionals in Open tournaments starting in 1968.

"Grand Slams"

The "grand slam" is to hold at the same time all four of the world's major championship titles: Wimbledon, the US Open, Australian and French championships. The first time this occurred was in 1935 when Frederick John Perry (GB) (b 1909) won the French title, having won Wimbledon (1934), the US title (1933–34) and the Australian title (1934).

The first player to hold all four titles simultaneously was J. Donald Budge (US) (b June 13, 1915), who won the championships of Wimbledon (1937), the US (1937), Australia (1938), and France (1938). He sub-

"GRAND SLAM" WINNER: Rod Laver (Australia) was the last man to win all 4 major tournaments, 1962 and 1969.

HIGHEST EARNINGS: Martina Navratilova, easily the top money-winning woman athlete in the world, is one of 3 women who have won the "grand slam" (1983–84). She had a streak of 74 singles victories in 1984 and 109 doubles victories 1983–85. (*USTA*)

sequently retained Wimbledon (1938) and the US (1938). Rodney George Laver (Australia) (b Aug 9, 1938) achieved this grand slam in 1962 as an amateur and repeated as a professional in 1969 to become the first two-time grand slammer.

Three women players also have won all these four titles in the same tennis year. The first was Maureen Catherine Connolly (US). She won the US title in 1951, Wimbledon in 1952, retained the US title in 1952, won the Australian in 1953, the French in 1953, and Wimbledon again in 1953. She won her third US title in 1953, her second French title in 1954, and her third Wimbledon title in 1954. Miss Connolly (later Mrs Norman Brinker) was seriously injured in a riding accident shortly before the 1954 US championships; she died in June 1969, aged only 34.

The second woman to win the "grand slam" was Margaret Smith Court (Australia) (b July 16, 1942) in 1970. Martina Navratilova (US) (b Prague, Oct 18, 1956) became the most recent "grand slam" winner on June 9, 1984 when she won the French title, beating Christine Evert Lloyd (US), after winning the other three titles in 1983. She won 6 successive "grand slam" singles titles 1983-June 1984, and with her partner Pamela Howard Shriver (US) (b July 4, 1962) won 8 successive "grand slam" tournament women's doubles titles, and 109 successive doubles matches from Apr 24, 1983 through July 6, 1985.

The most singles championships in "grand slam" tournaments is 24 by Margaret Court (11 Australian, 5 French, 5 US, 3 Wimbledon), 1960–73. The men's record is 12 by Roy Emerson (Australia) (b Nov 3, 1936) (6 Australian, 2 each French, US, Wimbledon), 1961–67.

In doubles, the only men to win a "grand slam" are Frank Sedgman (Aust) and Ken McGregor (Aust) in 1951. Margaret Smith Court (Aust) and Ken Fletcher (Aust) won it in mixed doubles in 1961. Martina Navratilova (US) and Pam Shriver (US) managed a "grand slam" in doubles in 1983–84, the same year Martina got her "grand slam" in singles. (*See* "Grand Slams")

Wimbledon Tournament Winners

Men's Singles

1919 Gerald Patterson (Aus)
1920 Bill Tilden (US)
1921 Bill Tilden (US)
1922 Gerald Patterson (Aus)
1923 William Johnston (US)
1924 Jean Borotra (Fra)
1925 René Lacoste (Fra)
1926 Jean Borotra (Fra)
1927 Henri Cochet (Fra)
1928 René Lacoste (Fra)
1929 Henri Cochet (Fra)
1930 Bill Tilden (US)
1931 Sidney Wood (US)
1932 Ellsworth Vines (US)
1933 Jack Crawford (Aus)
1934 Fred Perry (GB)
1935 Fred Perry (GB)
1936 Fred Perry (GB)
1937 Donald Budge (US)
1938 Donald Budge (US)
1939 Bobby Riggs (US)
1940–45 not held
1946 Yvon Petra (Fra)
1947 Jack Kramer (US)
1948 Bob Falkenburg (US)
1949 Ted Schroeder (US)
1950 Budge Patty (US)
1951 Dick Savitt (US)
1952 Frank Sedgman (Aus)
1953 Vic Seixas (US)
1954 Jaroslav Drobny (Cze)
1955 Tony Trabert (US)
1956 Lew Hoad (Aus)
1957 Lew Hoad (Aus)
1958 Ashley Cooper (Aus)
1959 Alex Olmedo (US)
1960 Neale Fraser (Aus)
1961 Rod Laver (Aus)
1962 Rod Laver (Aus)
1963 Chuck McKinley (US)
1964 Roy Emerson (Aus)
1965 Roy Emerson (Aus)
1966 Manuel Santana (Spa)
1967 John Newcombe (Aus)
1968 Rod Laver (Aus)
1969 Rod Laver (Aus)
1970 John Newcombe (Aus)
1971 John Newcombe (Aus)
1972 Stan Smith (US)
1973 Jan Kodes (Cze)
1974 Jimmy Connors (US)
1975 Arthur Ashe (US)
1976 Bjorn Borg (Swe)
1977 Bjorn Borg (Swe)
1978 Bjorn Borg (Swe)
1979 Bjorn Borg (Swe)
1980 Bjorn Borg (Swe)
1981 John McEnroe (US)
1982 Jimmy Connors (US)
1983 Jimmy Connors (US)
1984 John McEnroe (US)
1985 Boris Becker (W Ger)
1986 Boris Becker (W Ger)

Women's Singles

1919 Suzanne Lenglen (Fra)
1920 Suzanne Lenglen (Fra)
1921 Suzanne Lenglen (Fra)
1922 Suzanne Lenglen (Fra)
1923 Suzanne Lenglen (Fra)
1924 Kathleen McKane (GB)
1925 Suzanne Lenglen (Fra)
1926 Kathleen Godfree (GB)
1927 Helen Wills (US)
1928 Helen Wills (US)
1929 Helen Wills (US)
1930 Helen Wills Moody (US)
1931 Cilly Aussem (Ger)
1932 Helen Wills Moody (US)
1933 Helen Wills Moody (US)
1934 Dorothy Round (GB)
1935 Helen Wills Moody (US)
1936 Helen Jacobs (US)
1937 Dorothy Round (GB)
1938 Helen Wills Moody (US)
1939 Alice Marble (US)
1940–45 not held
1946 Pauline Betz (US)
1947 Margaret Osborne (US)
1948 Louise Brough (US)
1949 Louise Brough (US)
1950 Louise Brough (US)
1951 Doris Hart (US)
1952 Maureen Connolly (US)
1953 Maureen Connolly (US)
1954 Maureen Connolly (US)
1955 Louise Brough (US)
1956 Shirley Fry (US)
1957 Althea Gibson (US)
1958 Althea Gibson (US)

1959 Maria Bueno (Bra)
1960 Maria Bueno (Bra)
1961 Angela Mortimer (GB)
1962 Karen Susman (US)
1963 Margaret Smith (Aus)
1964 Maria Bueno (Bra)
1965 Margaret Smith (Aus)
1966 Billie Jean King (US)
1967 Billie Jean King (US)
1968 Billie Jean King (US)
1969 Ann Jones (GB)
1970 Margaret Smith Court (Aus)
1971 Evonne Goolagong (Aus)
1972 Billie Jean King (US)
1973 Billie Jean King (US)
1974 Christine Evert (US)
1975 Billie Jean King (US)
1976 Christine Evert (US)
1977 Virginia Wade (GB)
1978 Martina Navratilova (Cze)
1979 Martina Navratilova (Cze)
1980 Evonne Goolagong Cawley (Aus)
1981 Christine Evert Lloyd (US)
1982 Christine Evert Lloyd (US)
1983 Martina Navratilova (US)
1984 Martina Navratilova (US)
1985 Martina Navratilova (US)
1986 Martina Navratilova (US)

Men's Doubles
First held 1884.

Most wins: 8 Laurence Doherty and Reginald Doherty (GB): 1897–1901, 1903–05

Winners since 1965:
1965 John Newcombe, Tony Roche (Aus)
1966 Ken Fletcher, John Newcombe (Aus)
1967 Bob Hewitt, Frew McMillan (S Af)
1968 John Newcombe, Tony Roche (Aus)
1969 John Newcombe, Tony Roche (Aus)
1970 John Newcombe, Tony Roche (Aus)
1971 Roy Emerson, Rod Laver (Aus)
1972 Bob Hewitt, Frew McMillan (S Af)
1973 Jimmy Connors (US), Ilie Nastase (Rom)
1974 John Newcombe, Tony Roche (Aus)
1975 Vitas Gerulaitis, Sandy Mayer (US)
1976 Brian Gottfried (US), Raul Ramirez (Mex)
1977 Ross Case, Geoff Masters (Aus)
1978 Bob Hewitt, Frew McMillan (S Af)
1979 Peter Fleming, John McEnroe (US)
1980 Peter McNamara, Paul McNamee (Aus)
1981 Peter Fleming, John McEnroe (US)
1982 Peter McNamara, Paul McNamee (Aus)
1983 Peter Fleming, John McEnroe (US)
1984 Peter Fleming, John McEnroe (US)
1985 Heinz Gunthardt (Switz), Bela Taroczi (Hungary)
1986 Mats Wilander (Swe), Joakim Nystram (Swe)

Women's Doubles
First held 1899, but not a championship event until 1913.

Most wins: 12 Elizabeth (Bunny) Ryan (US): 1 with Agatha Morton 1914; 6 with Suzanne Lenglen 1919–23, 1925; 1 with Mary Browne 1926; 2 with Helen Wills Moody 1927, 1930; 2 with Simone Mathieu 1933–34

Winners since 1965:

1965 Maria Bueno (Bra), Billie Jean Moffitt (US)
1966 Maria Bueno (Bra), Nancy Richey (US)
1967 Rosemary Casals, Billie Jean King (née Moffitt) (US)
1968 Rosemary Casals, Billie Jean King (US)
1969 Margaret Court, Judy Tegart (Aus)
1970 Rosemary Casals, Billie Jean King (US)
1971 Rosemary Casals, Billie Jean King (US)
1972 Billie Jean King (US), Betty Stove (Hol)
1973 Rosemary Casals, Billie Jean King (US)
1974 Evonne Goolagong (Aus), Peggy Michel (US)
1975 Ann Kiyomura (US), Kazuko Sawamatsu (Japan)
1976 Christine Evert (US), Martina Navratilova (Cze)
1977 Helen Cawley (Aus), Joanne Russell (US)
1978 Kerr Reid, Wendy Turnbull (Aus)
1979 Billie Jean King (US), Martina Navratilova (Cze)
1980 Kathy Jordan, Anne Smith (US)
1981 Martina Navratilova (Cze), Pam Shriver (US)
1982 Martina Navratilova (US), Pam Shriver (US)
1983 Martina Navratilova (US), Pam Shriver (US)
1984 Martina Navratilova (US), Pam Shriver (US)
1985 Kathy Jordan (US), Liz Smylie (Aus)
1986 Martina Navratilova (US), Pam Shriver (US)

WIMBLEDON RECORDS

The first Championship was in 1877. Professionals first played in 1968. From 1971 the tie-break system was introduced, which effectually prevents sets proceeding beyond a 17th game, i.e., 9–8.

Most Wins

Six-time singles champion Billie Jean King (née Moffitt) has also won 10 women's doubles and 4 mixed doubles during the period 1961 to 1979, to total a record 20 titles.

The greatest number of singles wins was 8 by Helen N. Moody (née Wills) (b Oct 6, 1905) (US), who won in 1927–30, 32–33, 35 and 38.

The greatest number of singles wins by a man since the Challenge Round (wherein the defending champion was given a bye until the final round) was abolished in 1922 is 5 consecutively by Bjorn Borg (Sweden) in 1976–80. The all-time men's record was seven by William C. Renshaw, 1881–86 and 1889.

The greatest number of doubles wins by men was 8 by the brothers Doherty (GB)—Reginald Frank (1872–1910) and Hugh Lawrence (1875–1919). They won each year from 1897 to 1905 except for 1902. Hugh Doherty also won 5 singles titles (1902–06) and holds the record for most men's titles with 13.

The most wins in women's doubles was 12 by Elizabeth "Bunny" Ryan (US) (1894–1979). The greatest number of mixed doubles wins was 7 by Elizabeth Ryan, giving her a record total of 19 doubles wins 1914–34.

The men's mixed doubles record is 4 wins: by Elias Victor Seixas (b Aug 30, 1923) (US) in 1953–56; by Kenneth N. Fletcher (b June 15,

YOUNGEST WIMBLEDON WINNER (above): Boris Becker (W Ger) was not yet 18 when he was victorious in 1985. A year later he won again. (*Photo by David L. Boehm/Tamron*)

QUEEN AT WIMBLEDON (above left): Billie Jean King holds a record 20 titles in that famous tournament. A great contributor to the advancement of women's sports, she made news at Wimbledon in 1982 and 1983 by reaching the semi-finals at ages 38 and 39. In the 1983 mixed doubles final she lost a close match in a bid for her 21st title. In 1986, she was given a Guinness award. (*Leon Serchuk*)

1940) (Australia) in 1963, 65–66 and 68; and by Owen Keir Davidson (Australia) (b Oct 4, 1943) in 1967, 71 and 73–74.

Youngest Champions

The youngest champion ever at Wimbledon was Charlotte (Lottie) Dod (1871–1960), who was 15 years 285 days old when she won in 1887.

The youngest male champion was Boris Becker (W Ger) (b Nov 22, 1967) who won the men's singles title in 1985 at 17 years 227 days.

The youngest-ever player at Wimbledon is reputedly Miss Mita Klima (Austria), who was 13 years old in the 1907 singles competition. The youngest player to win a match at Wimbledon is Kathy Rinaldi (b March 24, 1967) (US), who was 14 years 91 days old on June 23, 1981.

Oldest Champions

The oldest champion was Margaret Evelyn du Pont (*née* Osborne) (b Mar 4, 1918) (US) who was 44 years 125 days old when she won the mixed doubles in 1962 with Neale Fraser (Aust). The oldest singles champion was Arthur Gore (GB) at 41 years 182 days in 1909.

Most Appearances

Arthur W. Gore (1868–1928) (GB) made 36 appearances between 1888 and 1927, and was in 1909 at 41 years the oldest singles winner ever.

In 1964 Jean Borotra (b Aug 13, 1898) of France made his 35th appearance since 1922. In 1977 he appeared in the Veterans' Doubles, aged 78. In Nov 1985, at the age of 87, Borotra played for the 100th time in the match between the International Clubs of France and GB at Wimbledon. Twice yearly he participated in every match since it was first staged in 1929.

Greatest Attendance

The record crowd for one day at Wimbledon is 39,813 on June 26, 1986. The total attendance record was set at the 1986 Championships with 400,032.

Tennis Olympics

Tennis was part of the Olympic program up until 1924 and it was also a demonstration sport at Mexico City in 1968 and LA in 1984. It is likely to be reinstated to the Games proper in 1988.

The most gold and total medals won was by 1911 Wimbledon doubles champion Max Decugis (Fra) with 4 gold, one silver and one bronze in 1900, 1906 and 1920. Kitty McKane Godfree (GB) set a women's record with one gold, 2 silver and 2 bronze in 1920 and 1924. In the latter year she won the first of her two Wimbledon singles championships. The 1908 Olympic tennis was played at the All-England Club, Wimbledon.

US CHAMPIONSHIPS

Most Wins

Margaret Evelyn du Pont (*née* Osborne) won a record 25 titles between 1936 and 1962. She won a record 13 women's doubles (12 with Althea Louise Brough), 8 mixed doubles and 3 singles. The men's record is 16 by William Tatem Tilden, including 7 men's singles, 1920–25, 1929—a record for singles shared with Richard Dudley Sears (1861–1943), 1881–87; William A Larned (1872–1926), 1901–02, 1907–11; and at women's singles by Molla Mallory (*née* Bjurstedt) (1892–1959), 1915–16, 1918, 1920–22, 1926 and Helen Moody (*née* Wills), 1923–25, 1927–29, 1931.

Youngest and Oldest

The youngest champion was Vincent Richards (1903–59) who was 15 years 139 days when he won the doubles with Bill Tilden in 1918. The youngest singles champion was Tracy Ann Austin (b Dec 12, 1962) who was 16 years 271 days when she won the women's singles in 1979.

The oldest champion was Margaret du Pont who won the mixed doubles at 42 years 166 days in 1960. The oldest singles champion was William Larned at 38 years 242 days in 1911.

US Open Champions

The USTA Championships were first held in 1881 and continued until 1969. The Tournament was superseded in 1970 by the US Open Championships which had first been held in 1968, and is now held at Flushing Meadow, New York.

Highest Earnings

(*Earnings from special restricted events and team tennis are not included.*)

FOR OPENERS: Christine Evert Lloyd has had more wins in the US Open, 78, than any other player—man or woman—through 1986. (*Leon Serchuk*)

The greatest reward for playing a single match is the $500,000 won by James Scott (Jimmy) Connors (US) (b Sept 2, 1952) when he beat John Newcombe (Australia) (b May 23, 1944) in a challenge match at Caesars Palace Hotel, Las Vegas, Nev, Apr 26, 1975. The highest total prize money is $3,450,800 for the 1986 US Championships.

The record for career earnings is held by Martina Navratilova, who won $10,881,986 by July 8, 1986.

The single season record for men is $2,028,850 by Ivan Lendl (Czechoslovakia) in 1982 (and including the Volvo Masters tournament held in January 1983). The women's record is $2,173,556 in 1984 (including a $1 million "Grand Slam" bonus) by Martina Navratilova in 1984.

Fastest Service

The fastest service ever *measured* was one of 163.6 mph by William Tatem Tilden (1893–1953) (US) in 1931.

A serve by Steve Denton (US) (b Sept 5, 1956) was timed at 138 mph at Beaver Creek, Colo on July 29, 1984, and is the record for fastest service timed with modern equipment.

Longest Game

The longest known singles game was one of 37 deuces (80 points) between Anthony Fawcett (Rhodesia) and Keith Glass (GB) in the first round of the Surrey championships at Surbiton, Surrey, England, on May 26, 1975. It lasted 31 min.

· A junior game lasted 52 min (9 deuces) between Noelle Van Lottum and Sandra Begijn in the semi-finals of the under-13 Dutch National Indoor Championships in Ede, Gelderland, Holland on Feb 12, 1984.

The longest rally in tournament play is one of 643 times over the net between Vicky Nelson and Jean Hepner at Richmond, Va in October 1984. The 6 hour 22 min match was won by Nelson 6–4, 7–6. It concluded with a 1 hour 47 min tiebreaker, 13–11, for which one point took 29 min.

The longest tiebreaker was the 26–24 for the fourth and decisive set of a first round men's doubles at the Wimbledon Championship on July 1, 1985. Jan Gunnarsson (Sweden) and Michael Morterven (Denmark) defeated John Frawley (Australia) and Victor Pecci (Paraguay) 6–3, 6–4, 3–6, 7–6.

NO. 1 SEED: Ivan Lendl (below), the Czech who now lives in the US, is top ranking star, having succeeded to that role by beating John McEnroe (left) (US) on numerous occasions (inheriting his annoying vocal tactics to some extent as well). (*Photos by David L. Boehm/Tamron*)

US OPEN CHAMPIONSHIPS:
Jimmy Connors (left) and John
McEnroe dominated the
tournament between 1974 and
1984, Connors winning in
1974–76–78–82–83 and McEnroe
in 1979–80–81–84. Bill Tilden
(above) in his time, won 6 years
in a row, 1920–25, and 1929.
(*Connors photo by David L. Boehm*)

Tennis Marathons

The longest recorded tennis singles match is one of 117 hours by Mark
and Jim Pinchoff at the Fitness Resort, Lafayette, La, May 14–19, 1985.

The duration record for doubles is 96 hours 25 minutes by Ann Wilkinson, Peter Allsopp, John Thorpe, and David Dicks at Mansfield
Lawn Tennis Club, Nottingham, Eng, August 17–21, 1983.

Grand Prix Masters

The first WCT Masters Championships were staged in Tokyo, Japan
in 1971 and have been held annually in NYC since 1977. Qualification to
this annual event is by relative success in the preceding year's Grand
Prix tournaments. John Patrick McEnroe (US) (b Feb 16, 1959) has won
a record five titles, 1979, 1981, 1983–5. James Scott Connors (US) (b Sept
7, 1952) uniquely qualified for 14 consecutive years, 1972–85. He chose
not to play in 1975, 1976 and 1985 and won in 1977.

Greatest Crowd

The greatest crowd at a tennis match was the 30,472 who came to the
Houston Astrodome in Houston, Tex, on Sept 20, 1973, to watch Billie

Jean King (US, b Nov 22, 1943) beat Robert Larimore (Bobby) Riggs (US, b Feb 25, 1918), over 25 years her senior, in straight sets in the so-called "Tennis Match of the Century."

The record for an orthodox match is 25,578 at Sydney, Australia, on Dec 27, 1954, in the Davis Cup Challenge Round vs the US (1st day).

Davis Cup

The most wins in the Davis Cup (instituted 1900), the men's international team championship, have been (inclusive of 1982) by the US with 28.

Roy Emerson (b Nov 3, 1936) (Australia) played on 8 Cup-winning teams, 1959–62, 1964–67.

Nicola Pietrangeli (Italy) (b Sept 11, 1933) played a record 163 rubbers, 1954 to 1972, winning 120. He played 109 singles (winning 78) and 54 doubles (winning 42). He took part in 66 ties.

Wightman Cup

The most wins in the Wightman Cup, contested annually by women's teams from the US and GB (instituted 1923) have been 47 by the US through 1985. Virginia Wade (b July 10, 1945) (GB) played in a record 21 ties and 56 rubbers between 1965 and 1985. Christine Evert Lloyd (b Dec 21, 1954) (US) won all 26 of her singles matches, 1971–85. Mrs Lloyd was selected by the Women's Sports Foundation in 1985 as the "greatest American Woman Athlete of the last 25 years."

Federation Cup

The most wins in the Federation Cup (instituted 1963), the women's international team championship, is 11 by the US. Virginia Wade (GB) played each year from 1967 to 1983, in a record 55 ties, playing 100 rubbers, including 56 singles (winning 36) and 44 doubles (winning 30). Christine Evert Lloyd won all of her 28 singles matches and 14 of 15 doubles, 1977–82.

TRACK AND FIELD

Earliest References

There is evidence that running was involved in early Egyptian rituals at Memphis c. 3800 BC, but usually track and field athletics date from the ancient Olympic Games. The earliest accurately known Olympiad dates from July 776 BC, at which celebration Coroibos won the foot race of 164–169 yd. The oldest surviving measurements are a long jump of 23 ft 1½ in by Chionis of Sparta c. 656 BC, and a discus throw of 100 cubits (c. 152 ft) by Protesilaus.

Earliest Landmarks

The first time 10 sec ("even time") was bettered for 100 yd under championship conditions was when John Owen, then 30 years old, recorded 9 4/5 sec in the AAU Championships at Wash, DC, on Oct 11, 1890. The first recorded instance of 6 ft being cleared in the high jump was when Marshall Jones Brooks (1855–1944) jumped 6 ft 0⅛ in at Marston, near Oxford, England, on March 17, 1876. (He is reputed to have done much of his jumping while wearing a high hat.) The first man over 7 ft was Charlie Dumas (US) who jumped 7 ft 0½ in in June 1956. The breaking of the "4-minute barrier" in the one mile was first achieved by Dr Roger Gilbert Bannister (b Harrow, England, March 23, 1929), when he recorded 3 min 59.4 sec on the Iffley Road track, Oxford, at 6:10 p.m. on May 6, 1954. John Walker (NZ) became the first man to run the mile in less than 4 min 100 times by Feb 17, 1985, in Auckland, NZ. His time in that race was 3:54.57.

Most Records

The greatest number of official world records (in events on the current schedule) broken by one athlete is 14, by Paavo Nurmi (Fin) at various events between 1921 and 1931, and by Iolanda Balas (Rom) in the high jump from 1956 to 1961. Nurmi also set eight marks in events no longer recognized, giving him a grand total of 22.

The only athlete to have his name entered in the record book 6 times in one day (in fact, within one hour) was J. C. "Jesse" Owens (US) (1913–80) who at Ann Arbor, Mich, on May 25, 1935, equaled the 100-yd running record with 9.4 sec at 3:15 p.m.; long-jumped 26 ft 8¼ in at 3:25 p.m.; ran 220 yd (straight away) in 20.3 sec at 3:45 p.m.; and 220 yd over low hurdles in 22.6 sec at 4 p.m. The two 220-yd runs were also ratified as 200-m world records.

World Championships

The first-ever track and field world championships were staged at Helsinki, Finland, Aug 7–14, 1983. The most gold medals won was 3 by Carl Lewis (US) in the 100 m dash, long jump, and 4 × 100 m relay; and by Marita Koch (E Ger) in the 200 m dash, 4 × 100 m relay, and 4 × 400 m relay. With a silver medal in the 100 m dash, Koch was the top medal winner with 4.

Standing High Jump

The best high jump from a standing (as opposed to a running) position is 6 ft 2¾ in by Rune Almen (b Oct 20, 1952) (Sweden) at Karlstad, Sweden, on May 30, 1980. The best jump by a woman is 4 ft 11 in by Grete Bjørdalsbakke (b June 23, 1960) (Norway) at Orsta, Norway on Dec 12, 1979.

Fastest Speed

The fastest speed recorded in an individual world record is 22.69 mph, but this does not allow for the effects of the delay in reaching peak speed from a standing start. Maximum speeds exceeding 25 mph for men and 22.5 mph for women have been measured; for instance, for Carl Lewis and Evelyn Ashford, respectively, for their final 10 meters in the 1984 Olympic sprint relays.

One-Legged High Jump

Arnie Boldt (b 1958), of Saskatchewan, Canada, cleared a height of 6 ft 8¼ in in Rome, Italy, on Apr 3, 1981, in spite of the fact that he has only one leg.

Standing Long Jump

Joe Darby (1861–1937), the famous Victorian professional jumper from Dudley, Worcestershire, England, jumped a measured 12 ft 1½ in

LONG WINNING STREAK: Edwin Moses (US) has not been beaten in the 400 m hurdles since 1977. By Aug 1986, he had won 101 consecutive times in finals.

CLASSIC LONG JUMP (above): Bob Beamon's 29-ft-2½-in leap in Mexico City in 1968 has not been broken since. (*E. D. Lacey*)

MOST RECORDS IN ONE DAY (above left): Jesse Owens, rated by many as the greatest athlete of the 20th century, not only won 4 Olympic golds in one meet (1936), but set 6 world records in one hour at Ann Arbor, Mich (3 to 4 PM, May 25, 1935). Here he shows his hurdling style. He was also a supreme runner and jumper. (*Photo, courtesy Atlantic Richfield Co—ARCO Jesse Owens Games*) *without* weights at Dudley Castle, on May 28, 1890. Arne Tverrvaag (Norway) jumped 12 ft 2¼ in in 1968. The best long jump by a woman is 9 ft 7 in by Annelin Mannes (Norway) at Flisa, Norway on March 7, 1981.

Oldest and Youngest Record Breakers

The greatest age at which anyone has broken a world track and field record is 41 years 196 days in the case of John J. Flanagan (1868–1938), who set a world record in the hammer throw on July 24, 1909. The female record is 35 years 255 days for Dana Zátopkova (*née* Ingrova) (b Sept 19, 1922) of Czechoslovakia, who broke the women's javelin record with 182 ft 10 in at Prague, Czechoslovakia, on June 1, 1958.

The youngest individual record breaker is 15-year-old Wang Yang (b 1971) (China) who set a women's 3,000 m walk record in 21 min 33.8 sec at Jian, China on Mar 9, 1986. The male record is 17 years 198 days by Thomas Ray (1862–1904) when he pole-vaulted 11 ft 2¼ in on Sept 19, 1879.

Longest Winning Sequence

Iolanda Balas (Romania) (b Dec 12, 1936) won 140 successive high jump competitions from 1956 to 1967. The record for track races is 116 (including 101 finals) at 400-meter hurdles by Edwin Corley Moses (US) (b July 31, 1955) from 1977 to Aug 1986.

Most Olympic Gold Medals in Field and Track

The most Olympic gold medals won in field events is 10 individual medals by Ray C. Ewry (US) (1874–1937) with:

Standing High Jump	1900, 1904, 1906, 1908
Standing Long Jump	1900, 1904, 1906, 1908
Standing Triple Jump	1900, 1904

The most gold medals won by a woman is 4, a record shared by Francina E. Blankers-Koen (Netherlands) (b Apr 26, 1918) with 100 m, 200 m, 80 m hurdles and 4 × 100 m relay (1948); Betty Cuthbert (Australia) (b Apr 20, 1938) with 100 m, 200 m, 4 × 100 m relay (1956) and 400 m (1964); and Barbel Wöckel (*née* Eckert) (b March 21, 1955) (E Germany) with 200 m and 4 × 100 m relay in 1976 and 1980.

The most gold medals at one Olympic celebration is 5 by Nurmi in 1924 and the most individual is 4 by Alvin C. Kraenzlein (US) (1876–1928) in 1900 with 60 m, 110 m hurdles, 200 m hurdles and long jump.

Longest Race

The longest races ever staged were the 1928 (3,422 miles) and 1929 (3,-665 miles) transcontinental races from NYC to Los Angeles. The Finnish-born Johnny Salo (1893–1931) was the winner in 1929 in 79 days, from March 31 to June 18. His elapsed time of 525 hours 57 min 20 sec gave a running average of 6.97 mph. His margin of victory was only 2 min 47 sec.

WORLD TRACK AND FIELD RECORDS (MEN)

World Records for the 32 men's events (excluding the walking records) scheduled by the International Amateur Athletic Federation. Note: On July 27, 1976, IAAF eliminated all records for races measured in yards, except for the mile (for sentimental reasons). All distances up to (and including) 400 m must be electrically timed to be records. When a time is given to one-hundredth of a second, it represents the official electrically-timed record.

RUNNING

Event	min:sec	Name and Nationality	Place	Date
100 m	9.93A	Calvin Smith (US)	Colorado Springs	July 3, 1983
200 m	19.72A	Pietro Mennea (Italy)	Mexico City	Sept 12, 1979
400 m	43.86A	Lee Edward Evans (US)	Mexico City	Oct 18, 1968
800 m	1:41.73	Sebastian Coe (GB)	Florence, Italy	June 10, 1981
1,000 m	2:12.18	Sebastian Coe (GB)	Oslo	July 11, 1981
1,500 m	3:29.45	Said Aouita (Morocco)	W Berlin	Aug 23, 1985
1 mile	3:46.32	Steve Cram (GB)	Oslo	July 27, 1985
2,000 m	4:51.39	Steve Cram (GB)	Budapest, Hungary	Aug 4, 1985
3,000 m	7:32.1	Henry Rono (Kenya)	Oslo	June 27, 1978
5,000 m	13:00.40	Said Aouita (Morocco)	Oslo	July 27, 1985
10,000 m	27:13.81	Fernando Mamede (Portugal)	Stockholm	July 2, 1984
20,000 m	57:24.2	Jos Hermens (Neth)	Papendal, Neth	May 1, 1976
25,000 m	1 hr. 13:55.8	Toshihiko Seko (Japan)	Christchurch, NZ	Mar 22, 1981
30,000 m	1 hr. 29:18.8	Toshihiko Seko (Japan)	Christchurch, NZ	Mar 22, 1981
1 hour	13 miles 24 yd 2 ft	Jos Hermens (Neth)	Papendal, Neth	May 1, 1976

FIELD EVENTS

Event	ft	in	Name and Nationality	Place	Date
High Jump	7	10¾	Igor Paklin (USSR)	Kobe, Japan	Sept 4, 1985
Pole Vault	19	8¾	Sergei Bubka (USSR)	Moscow	July 8, 1986
Long Jump	29	2½A	Robert Beamon (US)	Mexico City	Oct 18, 1968
Triple Jump	58	11½	Willie Banks (US)	Indianapolis, Ind	June 16, 1985
Shot Put	74	2½	Ulf Timmerman (E Ger)	Berlin	Sept 22, 1985
Discus Throw	243	0	Jurgen Schult (E Ger)	Neubrandenburg, E Ger	June 6, 1986

| Hammer Throw | 284 4 | Tallin, USSR | Yuri Sedykh (USSR) | June 22, 1986 |
| Javelin Throw* | 343 10 | East Berlin | Uwe Hohn (E Ger) | July 20, 1984 |

Note: One professional performance which was equal or superior to the IAAF marks, but where the same highly rigorous rules as to timing, measuring and weighing were not necessarily applied, was the Shot Put of 75 ft by Brian Ray Oldfield (US), at El Paso, Tex, on May 10, 1975. *Old javelin

RELAYS

4 × 100 m	37.83	US Team (Sam Graddy, Ron Brown, Calvin Smith, Carl Lewis)	Los Angeles	Aug 11, 1984
4 × 200 m	1:20.26†	University of Southern California (US) (Joel Andrews, James Sanford, William Mullins, Clancy Edwards)	Tempe, Ariz	May 27, 1978
4 × 400 m	2:56.16	US Olympic Team (Vincent Matthews, Ronald Freeman, G. Lawrence James, Lee Edward Evans)	Mexico City	Oct 20, 1968
4 × 800 m	7:03.89	Great Britain Team (Peter Elliott, Garry Cook, Steve Cram, Sebastian Coe)	London	Aug 30, 1982
4 × 1,500 m	14:38.8	W German Team (Thomas Wessinghage, Harald Hudak, Michael Lederer, Karl Fleschen)	Cologne, W Ger	Aug 17, 1977

† The time of 1:20.2 achieved by the Tobias Striders at Tempe, Ariz on May 27, 1978 was not ratified as the team was composed of varied nationalities.

NOTE: Records marked A were set at high altitude—Mexico City 7,349 ft, Colorado Springs 7,201 ft. Best marks at low altitude have been: Carl Lewis (US) (b July 1, 1961) 200 m—19.75 and long jump—28 ft 10¼ in, both at Indianapolis, June 19, 1983. Ben Johnson (Canada) 100 m—9.95, Moscow, July 2, 1986. Alberto Juantorena (Cuba) (b Nov 21, 1950) 400 m—44.26, Montreal, July 29, 1976, and the US 4 × 100 m relay team—2:56.65, Montreal, July 31, 1976.

(continued)

HURDLING

Event	Name and Nationality	min:sec	Place	Date
110 m (3'6")	Renaldo Nehemiah (US)	12.93	Zurich	Aug 19, 1981
400 m (3'0")	Edwin Corley Moses (US)	47.02	Coblenz, W Ger	Aug 31, 1983
3,000 m Steeplechase	Henry Rono (Kenya)	8:05.4	Seattle, Wash	May 13, 1978

DECATHLON

Event	Name and Nationality	Place	Date
8,847 points (1985 scoring)	Francis Morgan "Daley" Thompson (GB)	Los Angeles	Aug 8–9, 1984

WORLD TRACK AND FIELD RECORDS (WOMEN)

RUNNING

Event	Name and Nationality	min:sec	Place	Date
100 m	Evelyn Ashford (US)	10.76	Zurich	Aug 22, 1984
200 m	Marita Koch (E Ger)	21.71	Potsdam, E Ger	July 21, 1984
200 m	Heike Dreschler (E Ger)	21.71	Jena, E Ger	June 29, 1986
400 m	Marita Koch (E Ger)	47.60	Canberra, Australia	Oct 6, 1985
800 m	Jarmila Kratochvilova (Czech)	1:53.28	Munich	July 26, 1983
1,000 m	Tanyana Providokhina (USSR)	2:30.6	Podolsk, USSR	Aug 20, 1978
1,500 m	Tatyana Kazankina (USSR)	3:52.47	Zurich, Switz	Aug 13, 1980
1 mile	Mary Decker Slaney (US)	4:16.71	Zurich, Switz	Aug 21, 1985
2,000 m	Maricica Puica (Romania)	5:28.69	London, Eng	July 11, 1986
3,000 m	Tatyana Kazankina (USSR)	8:22.62	Leningrad	Aug 26, 1984
5,000 m	Zola Budd (GB)	14:48.07	London	Aug 26, 1985
10,000 m	Ingrid Kristiansen (Norway)	30:13.74	Oslo, Norway	July 5, 1986

FIELD EVENTS

Event	ft	in	Name and Nationality	Place	Date
High Jump	6	9¾	Stefka Kosadinova (Bulgaria)	Sofia, Bulgaria	May 31, 1986
Long Jump	24	5½	Heike Drechsler (E Ger)	Dresden, E Ger	July 3, 1986
Shot Put	73	11	Natalya Lisovskaya (USSR)	Sochi, USSR	May 27, 1984
Discus Throw	244	7	Zdena Silhava (Czech)	Nitra, Czech	Aug 26, 1984
Javelin Throw	247	4	Petra Felke (E Ger)	Schwerin, E Ger	June 4, 1985

HEPTATHLON

	Name and Nationality	Place	Date
7,161 points	Jackie Joyner (US)	Houston, Tex	July 1–2, 1986

HURDLES

Event	min:sec	Name and Nationality	Place	Date
100 m (2′9″)	12.36	Grazyna Rabsztyn (Poland)	Warsaw	June 13, 1980
400 m (2′6″)	53.55	Sabine Busch (E Ger)	E Berlin	Sept 22, 1985

RELAYS

Event	min:sec	Name and Nationality	Place	Date
4 × 100 m	41.37	E Germany (Silke Gladisch, Sabine Rieger, Ingrid Auerswold, Marlies Göhr)	Canberra, Australia	Oct 6, 1985
4 × 200 m	1:28.15	E Germany (Marlies Göhr, Romy Miller, Barbel Wöckel, Marita Koch)	Jena, E Ger	Aug 10, 1980
4 × 400 m	3:15.92	E Germany (Gesine Walther, Sabine Busch, Dagmar Ruebsam, Marita Koch)	Erfurt, E Ger	June 3, 1984
4 × 800 m	7:50.17	USSR (Nadezha Olizarenko, Lyubov Gunina, Lyudmila Borisova, Irina Padyalowskaya)	Moscow, USSR	Aug 7, 1984

TRIPLE JUMPING has never been as popular as today. A major reason is the ebullient enthusiasm and popularity of Willie Banks (left) (US), who holds the world record. LONG DISTANCE RUNNER Said Aouita (right) (Morocco) is the first person in 30 years to hold concurrent world records at 1,500 and 5,000 m. (*All Sport*)

Greatest Mileage

Jay F. Helgerson (b Feb 3, 1955) of Foster City, Calif, ran a certified marathon (26 miles 385 yd) or longer, each week for 52 weeks from Jan 28, 1979 to Jan 19, 1980, totalling 1,418 racing miles.

Sy Mah (1926–), an instructor at Toledo University (Ohio), has run 374 "marathons" of 26.2 mi or longer since 1966 for a total of 9,800 mi. He paces himself to take 3½ hours for each run.

Douglas Alistair Gordon Pirie (b Feb 10, 1931) (GB), who set 5 world records in the 1950s, estimated that he had run a total distance of 216,000 miles in 40 years to 1981.

The greatest distance run in one year is 15,472 miles by Tina Maria Stone (b Naples, Italy, Apr 5, 1934) of Irvine, Calif, in 1983.

POLE-VAULT RECORD HOLDER Sergei Bubka (USSR) (left) keeps breaking his own record every time he leaps. By July 1986, he had reached 19 ft 8¾ in.

THREE WORLD RECORDS IN 20 DAYS (below): Steve Cram (GB) set a new record in running 1500 m on July 16, 1985 (3:29.67), in the mile run on July 27 (3:46.32), and 2000 m race on Aug 4 (4:51.39). On Aug 10 he came in with the world's second best time in 1000 m, against a head wind. Shown here, he exults over his victory in the mile. He set a better mark in the 1500 m in 1985. (*IAAF Mobile Grand Prix*)

HURDLER Sabine Busch (E Ger) (left) became invincible at 400 m hurdles after being converted from a 400 m runner. She broke the world record in her first year in only her eighth race. (*All Sport*)

244-LB SHOT PUT CHAMP (below): Center of attention was Tamara Andreyevna (Fatty) Tyshkyevich (USSR), the gold medal winner in the 1956 Olympics.

The longest-ever solo run is 10,608 miles by Robert J. Sweetgall (US) (b Dec 8, 1947) around the perimeter of the 48 states, starting and finishing in Wash, DC, Oct 9, 1982–July 15, 1983.

Ron Grant (Aust) (b Feb 15, 1943) ran around Australia, 8,316 miles in 217 days 3 hours 45 min, running every day Mar 28–Oct 31, 1983.

Ernst Mensen (1799–1846) (Norway), a former seaman in the British Navy, is reputed to have run from Istanbul, Turkey, to Calcutta, in West Bengal, India, and back in 59 days in 1836, so averaging an improbable 92.4 miles per day.

Max Telford (b Hawick, Scotland, Feb 2, 1935) of New Zealand ran 5,110 miles from Anchorage, Alaska, to Halifax, Nova Scotia, in 106 days 18 hours 45 min from July 25 to Nov 9, 1977.

The greatest non-stop run recorded is 352.9 miles in 121 hours 54 min by Bertil Järlåker (Sweden) at Norrköping, Sweden, May 26–31, 1980. He was moving 95.04% of the time.

Fastest 100 Miles

The fastest recorded time for 100 miles is 11 hours 30 min 51 sec by Donald Ritchie (b July 6, 1944) at Crystal Palace, London, on Oct 15, 1977. The best by a woman is 15 hours 31 min 56 sec by Donna Hudson (US) at Shea Stadium, NYC, June 17–18, 1983.

Trans-America Run

The fastest time for the cross-US run is 46 days, 8 hours 36 min by Frank Giannino Jr (b 1952) (US) for the 3,100 miles from San Francisco to NYC, Sept 1–Oct 17, 1980.

When Johnny Salo won the 1929 Trans-America race from NYC to LA, his total elapsed time of 525 hours 57 min 20 sec gave him a margin of only 2 min 47 sec over second-place Peter Gavuzzi—after 3,665 miles.

Nicki Lewis, 50, of Santa Monica, Calif, is the first American woman to run across the continent, setting a speed record of 3,224 miles in 75 days, Aug 16, 1983–Oct 30, 1983, running an average of 42.8 miles per day from Santa Monica to NYC. She was escorted by David Hermilage (Eng). She wore out one pair of shoes and had two other pairs sent by Nike to her, enroute.

In an attempt to beat the record, three women sponsored by The Greyhound Corporation set out from Boston, Mass in the summer of 1984 for San Francisco. Two of the women finished, Caroline Merrill, 42, and Annabel Marsh, 61, after 130 days and 3,261 miles. They wore out 12 pairs of shoes each.

Running unaccompanied, Sandy Goldstein, 38, ran from Sacramento, Calif to Hyannis, Mass, her hometown, also in 1984 in 130 days, but covering 3,328 miles.

Trans-Canada Run

The only woman to have run across Canada from Victoria, BC, to Halifax, Nova Scotia, a distance of 3,824 mi in 6½ months, touching all 10 provinces, is Kanchan Beryl Stott of Ottawa, Ont. It was probably the longest run ever made by a woman.

Six-Day Race

The greatest distance covered by a man in six days (*i.e.* the 144 permissible hours between Sundays in Victorian times) was 635 miles 1,385 yards by Yiannis Kouros (Greece) (b Feb 13, 1956) at Colac, Australia on Nov 26–Dec 1, 1984. On the same occasion Eleanor Adams (UK) (b Nov 20, 1947) set the women's record at 500 mi 1,452 yds.

Downhill Mile

Mike Boit (Kenya) ran what is believed to be the fastest mile ever when he won the Molenberg Mile in 3 min 28.36 sec over a carefully measured downhill course along Queen Street, Auckland, NZ, on Apr 16, 1983. The course had an overall vertical drop of nearly 208 yd.

GREATEST DISTANCE run in one year is 15,472 mi by Tina María Stone, born in Italy, but now running in Irvine, Calif.

Mass Relay Record

The record for 100 miles by 100 runners belonging to one club is 7 hours 53 min 52.1 sec by Baltimore Road Runners Club of Towson, Md, on May 17, 1981. The women's mark is 10 hours 47 min 9.3 sec by a team from the San Francisco Dolphins Southend Running Club, on Apr 3, 1977.

The best club time for a 100 × 400 m relay is 1 hour 29 min 11.8 sec (average 53.5 sec) by the Physical Training Institute, Leuven, Belgium, on Apr 19, 1978. The best women's club time for 100 × 100 meters relay is 23 min 28 sec by Amsterdanse dames athletiekvereniging, on Sept 26, 1981, in Amsterdam, Netherlands.

The longest relay ever run was 10,524 mi by 2,660 runners at Trondheim, Norway, Aug 26–Oct 20, 1985. Twenty members of the Melbourne Fire Brigade ran around Australia on Highway No. 1 in 43 days 23 hours 58 min, July 10–Aug 23, 1983. The most participants is 4,800 (192 teams of 25), in the Batavierenrace, 103.89 mi from Nijmegen to Enschede, The Netherlands, won in 9 hours 30 min 44 sec on Apr 23, 1983.

Running Backwards

The fastest time recorded for running 100 yd backwards is 12.8 sec by Ferdie Adoboe (Kenya, now US) in Amherst, Mass, on July 28, 1983.

Anthony "Scott" Weiland, 27, ran the Detroit marathon backwards in 4 hours 7 min 54 sec on Oct 3, 1982.

Donald Davis (b Feb 10, 1960) (US) ran 1 mi backwards in 6 min 7.1 sec at the University of Hawaii on Feb 21, 1983.

Arvind Pandya (India) ran LA-NY in 107 days, Aug 18–Dec 3, 1984.

Blind 100 Meters

The fastest time recorded for 100 m by a blind man is 11.4 sec by Graham Henry Salmon (b Sept 5, 1952) of Loughton, Essex, England, at Grangemouth, Scotland, on Sept 2, 1978.

Fastest 100 Kilometers

Donald Ritchie ran 100 km in a record 6 hours 10 min 20 sec at Crystal Palace, London, on Oct 28, 1978. The women's best, run on the road, is 7 hours 27 min 22 sec by Chantal Langlace (b Jan 6, 1955) (France) at Amiens, France on Sept 6, 1980.

Three-Legged Race

The fastest recorded time for a 100-yd three-legged race is 11.0 sec by Olympic medalists Harry L. Hillman (1881–1945) and Lawson Robertson (1883–1951) in Brooklyn, NYC, on Apr 24, 1909.

Pancake Race Record

The annual "Housewives" Pancake Race at Olney, Buckinghamshire, England, was first mentioned in 1445. The record for the winding 415-yd

OLDEST RACE RECORD: The 3-legged race record of 100 yards in 11 seconds was set 76 years ago by Harry Hillman (left) and Lawson Robertson (right), both Olympic medalists in 1904.

course (three tosses mandatory) is 61.0 sec, set by Sally Ann Faulkner, 16, on Feb 26, 1974. The record for the counterpart race at Liberal, Kansas, is 58.5 sec by Sheila Turner (b July 9, 1953) in 1975.

Dale R. Lyons (b Feb 26, 1937) (GB) has run several marathons during which he tosses a 2-oz pancake repeatedly en route in a 1½ lb pan. His fastest time is 3 hours 6 min 48 sec in London, Apr 20, 1986.

TRIATHLON

A new type of competition, the Triathlon, began in Feb 1978 in Hawaii when two Navy men challenged each other to a particularly strenuous test of all the major muscles of the body in strength and endurance: a swim of 2.4 miles in the ocean, followed immediately by a 112-mile bike race, and then a full marathon run of 26 miles 385 yd, with no time-outs.

They were joined by 13 others in the first two Triathlons in Feb 1978 and Feb 1979. Then, in 1980 ABC on its "Wide World of Sports" began televising what began to be called the Ironman Triathlon and 108 com-

TRIATHLON WINNERS: (Left) Scott Tinley of San Diego set a world record of 8 hours 50 min 54 sec in Oct 1985 in winning his second Ironman. (*Photo by Reggie David*) (Right): Joanne Ernst of Palo Alto, Calif, won the women's championship in the same event. (*Photo by Noel Black*) The race comprises a 2.4-mi swim followed by a 112-mi bike race followed by a 26.2-mi marathon run.

peted. Now there are hundreds of triathlons—but not all are Ironman Triathlons. The "tinman" races cut the distances in half or less.

In Oct 1985, in the Bud Light Ironman Triathlon in Kona, Hawaii, Scott Tinley, 29, of San Diego, Calif, won his second Ironman in the men's division with a record time 8 hours 50 min 54 sec, shaving 3 min 8 sec off the previous record set by Dave Scott of Davis, Calif, in 1984.

In the women's division a new record was set in 1984. Sylviane Puntous (Montreal, Canada) finished in 10 hours 25 min 13 sec. Patricia, her identical twin sister, finished right behind her in 10 hours 27 min 28 sec.

The largest field in a triathlon of any kind has been 2,060 finishers in the US Triathlon (swim 1500 m, bike 40 km and run 10 km) in Chicago in July 1985.

VOLLEYBALL

Origins

The game was invented as Mintonette in 1895 by William G. Morgan at the YMCA gymnasium at Holyoke, Mass. The International Volleyball Association was formed in Paris in Apr 1947. The ball travels at a speed of up to 70 mph when smashed over the net, which stands 7 ft 11½ in high. In the women's game it is 7 ft 4¼ in high.

World Titles

World Championships were instituted in 1949 for men and 1952 for women. The USSR has won 6 men's titles (1949, 52, 60, 62, 78, and 82). The USSR won the women's championship in 1952, 56, 60, and 70. The record crowd is 90,000 for the 1983 world title matches in Brazil.

Most Olympic Medals

In the 1984 Olympics the US won the gold medal in the men's game, and China won in the women's.

The sport was introduced to the Olympic Games for both men and women in 1964. The only volleyball player to win four medals is Inna Ryskal (USSR) (b June 15, 1944), who won silver medals in 1964 and 76 and golds in 1968 and 72.

The record for medals for men is held jointly by Yuriy Poyarkov (USSR), who won gold medals in 1964 and 68, and a bronze in 1972, and Katsutoshi Nekoda (Japan) (b Feb 1, 1944) who won a gold in 1972, silver in 1968, and a bronze in 1964.

Marathon

The longest recorded volleyball marathon by two teams of six is 84 hours by players from Beta Theta Pi fraternity, Bethany College, Bethany, W Va, Sept 27–30, 1984.

WALKING

Longest Race

The Paris-Colmar event (until 1980 it was the Strasbourg-Paris event, instituted in 1926 in the reverse direction), now 322 miles, is the world's longest annual walk event. Gilbert Roger (France) has won 6 times (1949, 53–54, 56–58). The fastest performance is by Robert Pietquin (b 1938) (Belgium) who walked 315 miles in the 1980 race in 60 hours 1 min 10 sec (deducting 4 hours of compulsory stops), averaging 5.25 mph. The first woman to complete the race was Annie van den Meer (Neth) (b Feb 24, 1947) who was 10th in 1983 in 82 hours 10 min.

Dumitru Dan (1890–1978) of Romania was the only man of 200 entrants to succeed in walking 100,000 km (62,137 miles), in a contest organized by the Touring Club de France on Apr 1, 1910. By March 24, 1916, he had covered 96,000 km (59,651 miles), averaging 27.24 miles per day.

Longest in 24 Hours

The greatest distance walked in 24 hours is 140 mi, 1,229 yd by Paul Forthomme (Belgium), on a road course at Woluwé, Belgium Oct 13–14, 1984. The best by a woman is 125.7 miles by Annie van den Meer (Netherlands) at Rouen, France, Apr 30–May 1, 1984, over a 1.185-km-lap road course.

Most Olympic Medals

Walking races have been included in the Olympic schedule since 1906, but walking matches have been known since 1589. The only walker to win 3 gold medals has been Ugo Frigerio (Italy) (1901–68) with the 3,000 m in 1920 and the 10,000 m in 1920 and 1924. He also holds the record of most medals with 4 (having additionally won the bronze medal in the 50,000 m in 1932), a total shared with Vladimir Golubnichiy (USSR) (b June 2, 1936), who won gold medals for the 20,000 m in 1960 and 1968, the silver in 1972 and the bronze in 1964.

In the 1984 Olympics Ernesto Canto (Mex) won the 20,000 m in 1 hour 23 min 13 sec. Raul Gonzalez (Mex) won the 50,000 m walk in 3 hours 47 min 26 sec. Canto's world record at 20,000 m set May 5, 1984 in Fana, Norway, is 1 hour 18 min 39.9 sec. Gonzalez' world record at 50,000 m set May 25, 1979 at Fana, Norway, is 3 hours 41 min 38.4 sec.

Walking Across the Americas

George Meegen (GB) walked 19,017 mi from Ushuaia, Argentina, at the southern tip of S America to the Beaufort Sea in northern Alaska, taking 2,426 days from Jan 26, 1977 to Sept 18, 1983.

Longest Non-Stop Walk

Tom Benson (GB) walked 414.74 miles in 6 days 12 hours 45 min at

WALKING THE DOG: When Sean Maguire says he's taking his dog "Sweden" for a walk, he means it. They set out from the Yukon River, Alaska, and arrived at their destination (Key West, Fla) 10 months and 7,327 miles later.

Moor Park, Preston, Eng Apr 29–May 5, 1986. This was 233 laps of a 1.78-mi closed circuit. He was not permitted any stops for rest and was moving 98.78 percent of the time.

Most Titles

Four-time Olympian Ronald Owen Laird (b May 31, 1938) of the NYAC won a total of 65 US National titles from 1958 to 1976, plus 4 Canadian championships.

Walking Backwards

The greatest exponent of reverse pedestrianism has been Plennie L. Wingo (b Jan 24, 1895) then of Abilene, Tex, who started on his 8,000-mile transcontinental walk on Apr 15, 1931, from Santa Monica, Calif, to Istanbul, Turkey, and arrived on Oct 24, 1932. He celebrated the walk's 45th anniversary by covering the 452 miles from Santa Monica to San Francisco, Calif, backwards, in 85 days, aged 81 years.

The longest distance recorded for walking backwards in 24 hours is 84 mi by Anthony Thornton in Minneapolis Dec 31, 1985–Jan 1, 1986.

Walking Around the World

The first person reported to have "walked around the world" is George M. Schilling (US), Aug 3, 1897–1904, but the first verified achievement was by David Kunst (b 1939), who started with his brother John from Waseca, Minn, on June 10, 1970. John was killed in 1972 by Afghan bandits who thought they were carrying UNICEF funds they were soliciting. David was wounded, so another brother, Pete, joined him. David arrived home, after walking 14,500 miles, on Oct 5, 1974.

Tomas Carlos Pereira (b Argentina, Nov 16, 1942) spent 10 years, Apr 6, 1968, through Apr 8, 1978, walking 29,825 miles around all 5 continents.

John Lees, 27, of Brighton, England, Apr 11–June 3, 1972, walked 2,876 miles across the US from City Hall, Los Angeles, to City Hall, NYC, in 53 days 12 hours 15 min (53.746 miles per day).

Sean Eugene Maguire (b Sept 15, 1956) (US) walked 7,327 miles from the Yukon River, north of Livengood, Alaska, to Key West, Fla, in 307 days, from June 6, 1978 to Apr 9, 1979.

The record for the trans-Canada (Halifax to Vancouver) walk of 3,764 miles is 96 days by Clyde McRae, 23, from May 1 to Aug 4, 1973.

WATER SKIING

Origins

The sport originated with people walking on water with planks attached to their feet, possibly as early as the 14th century. A 19th century treatise on sorcerers refers to Eliseo of Tarentum who, in the 14th century, "walks and dances" on the water. The first report of aquaplaning on large boards behind a motorboat was from the Pacific coast of the US in the early 1900's. A photograph exists of a "plank-riding" contest in a regatta won by a Mr H. Storry at Scarborough, Yorkshire, England, on July 15, 1914. Competitors were towed on a *single* plank by a motor launch.

The present-day sport of water skiing was pioneered by Ralph W. Samuelson on Lake Pepin, Minn, on two curved pine boards in the summer of 1922, though claims have been made for the birth of the sport on Lake Annecy (Haute-Savoie), France, in 1920. The first world organization, the United Internationale de Ski Nautique, was formed in Geneva, Switz on July 27, 1946.

Slalom

The world record for slalom is 5 buoys on a 10.75-m line by Bob La-Point (US) at Shreveport, Fla, 1984. Andy Mapple (GB) tied this record in Sept 1985.

The women's record is 4 buoys, on a 11.25-m line, on Oct 2, 1983, by Deena Brush (US) at Okeechellee Record Classic, W Palm Beach, Fla. This was tied in Aug 1985 by Jennifer Leachman.

Highest Speed

The fastest water skiing speed recorded is 143.08 mph by Christopher Michael Massey (Australia) on the Hawkesbury River, NSW, Australia, Mar 6, 1983. His drag-boat driver was Stanley Charles Sainty. Donna Patterson Brice (US) (b 1953) set a feminine record of 111.11 mph at Long Beach, Calif, on Aug 21, 1977.

Most Titles

World overall championships (instituted 1949) have been won three times by Sammy Duvall (US) in 1981, 1983 and 1985. The women's title has been won three times by Mrs Willa McGuire (*née* Worthington) of the US, in 1949–50 and 55, and Elizabeth Allan-Shetter (US) in 1965, 69, and 75. Allan-Shetter has also won a record 8 individual championship events and is the only person to win all 4 titles (slalom, jumping, tricks and overall) in one year, at Copenhagen, Denmark, in 1969. The US has won the team championship on 15 successive occasions, 1957–85.

Jumps

The first recorded jump on water skis was 50 ft by Ralph W. Samuelson, off a greased ramp at Lake Pepin, Wis, in 1925, and this was not exceeded officially until 1947.

The longest jump recorded is one of 203 ft by Michael Hazelwood (GB) at Birmingham, Ala, on June 30, 1986. The women's record is 150 ft 2 in by Sue Lipplegoes (Australia) at Reading, Eng, on July 31, 1983.

SLALOM TWISTSTER (above): Deena Brush (US) rounding 4 buoys at 11.25-m line set a women's world record in Oct 1983 in Florida.

"TRICKS" SPECIALIST Patrice Martin (right) outpointed Cory Pickos to win the World Championship in 1985. Pickos then took the world record score, while Martin's 10,370 points in Florida in May 1986 is probably ineligible for a world record. (*All Sport*).

Barefoot

The first person to water ski barefoot is reported to be Dick Pope, Jr, at Lake Eloise, Fla, on March 6, 1947. The barefoot duration record is 2 hours 42 min 39 sec by Billy Nichols (US) (b 1964) on Lake Weir, Fla, on Nov 19, 1978. The backwards barefoot record is 39 min by Paul McManus (Australia). The barefoot jump record is 65 ft 11¼ in by Mike Siepel in 1984. The official barefoot speed record (two runs) is 110.02 mph by Lee Kirk (US) at Firebird Lake, Phoenix, Ariz, on June 11, 1977. His fastest run was 113.67 mph. The fastest by a woman is 73.67 mph by Karen Toms (Australia) on Mar 31, 1984 in New South Wales, Australia. The fastest official speed backward and barefoot is 62 mph by Robert Wing (Australia) on Apr 3, 1982.

Tricks

The tricks or freestyle event involves various maneuvers for which points are awarded according to the degree of difficulty and the speed at which they are performed.

The tricks record is 10,370 points by Patrice Martin (France) in Florida in May 1986, but probably is ineligible for a world record, in which case the record is 10,300 points by Cory Pickos (US), set in Sept 1985.

The women's record is 8,350 points by Ana Maria Carrasco (Venezuela) at McCormick, Fla, on Sept 14, 1984.

Longest Run

The greatest distance traveled is 1,304.6 miles by Will Coughey on Feb 18–19, 1984 on Lake Tikitapu, New Zealand.

VENEZUELAN RECORDHOLDER: Ana Maria Carrasco scored 8,350 points in water ski tricks in 1984, and her world record still stands.

NEWLY VERIFIED RECORDS

The following pages include records which were received and verified too late to be included in the main sections of this book.

Fire-Eating (p 44). Roberto Kalin (b 1961) of Bregenz, Austria, extinguished 14,468 torches of flame successively in his mouth in 2 hours on May 29, 1986 in Ried, Austria.

Longest Frog Jump (p 84). "Rosie the Riveter," owned and trained by Lee Guidici of Santa Clara, Calif, jumped 21 ft 5¾ in on May 18, 1986 at the annual Calaveras Jumping Jubilee.

Cucumber (p 100). Eileen Chappel has grown a larger specimen—48½ lb on May 13, 1986.

Wreath (p 108). A wreath 100 ft 8 in in diameter was constructed in Nov 1985 by the Farm Stand at Walworth, NY.

Hailstones (p 142). Hailstones of up to 2½ lb are reported to have killed 92 people in the Gopalganj district of Bangladesh on Apr 14, 1986.

Perfume Shower (p 162). 198 gallons of jasmine essence perfume were sprayed over 140,000 people who attended a local carnival in Rio de Janeiro, Brazil, on Feb 9, 1986, as arranged by Carlos Norberto Varaldo of Chiero da Terra Perfumes.

Longest Sentence (p 193 in 1986 edition). Jack McClintock of the Univ of Miami, Fla, wrote a one-sentence article for the May 26, 1985 edition of the *Miami Herald* that had 2,403 words, not counting numbers and counting hyphenated words as only one.

Largest Orchestra (p 212). 6,179 musicians congregated at Bay Shore Mall, Milwaukee, Wis, for the playing of John's "Stars and Stripes Forever." Originally, our editors withheld recognition of the event because not all played musical instruments, but instead played kazoos, bongo drums, bottles, coffee cans, and all types of thumpers.

Most Durable Leading Actors (p 221). Ranzaburo Nakamura, 77, of Tokyo, Japan, has played 803 leading roles on stage in Kabuki theatre, Nov 1926–Sept 1985, an estimated total of 20,075 performances.
David Raven played the part of Major Metcalf in *The Mousetrap* in London on 4,557 occasions July 22, 1957–Nov 23, 1968.

Highest-Paid TV Performer (p 229). Bill Cosby was reported in July 1986 to have earned about $9 million in the previous 12 months from TV appearances, ads and cassettes, besides book royalties.

Most Watched Performer on TV (p 230). Lucille Ball has been clocked on television in the US and 85 other countries at over 300,000

LARGEST CLASSICAL CONCERT CROWD (p 212): As part of the Miss Liberty weekend celebration in Central Park, July 5, 1986, the NY Philharmonic Orchestra attracted an estimated 800,000 people. This shot was taken from a helicopter in the early evening. (*Newsday*)

hours, including network first runs, reruns and syndication, in the 35 years she has been performing.

Road Tunnel (p 263). Traffic in the Yerba Buena Island Tunnel reached 80 million vehicles annually in 1986.

Most Expensive Used Car (p 293). A 1931 Bugatti Royale from the Harrah Collection was sold for $6.5 million at auction in Reno, Nev, on June 27, 1986.

Two-Wheel Driving (p 294). A speed of 83.8 mph was achieved in a standard Volvo 760 at Anderstrop, Sweden, on May 18, 1986 by Goran Eliason of Boras, Sweden.

Unicycles (p 302). Hanspeter Beck of Jindabyne, S Australia rode 3,876.08 mi in 51 days, 23 hours, 25 min, June 30–Aug 20, 1985, going from W Australia to Melbourne.

Flight Duration (p 316). The longest flight without refueling was 110 hours and 11,857 mi by "The Voyager," an experimental, mostly plastic feather-light plane flying over Mojave, Calif, July 11–15, 1986. It was piloted by Richard Rutan and designed by him and his brother Burt.

Fastest Helicopter (p 319). Trevor Eggington, 53, averaged 249.10 mph over Somerset, Eng, on Aug 11, 1986, in a Westland Lynx Co demonstration helicopter.

BEARD OF BEES (p 439): Unstung Maxwell J. Beck 21, of Arcola, Pa. had his entire body (except his face and bare arms) covered by bees on Aug 24, 1985 at the Eastern Apiaries Society Convention. About 70,000 bees weighing 20 lb were attached to him.

Tallest Windmill (p 323). A taller windmill, the De Noord, 109 ft 4 in, exists in Schiedam, The Netherlands.

Longest Watch (p 335). A "Swatch" 531 ft 6 in long and 65 ft 7½ in in diameter, made by D. Tomas Feliu, was set up in the Bank of Bilbao Building, Madrid, Spain, Dec 7–12, 1985.

Candle (p 348). A candle 89 ft 1 in high was constructed on June 1, 1986 by the Atletiek-en Trimvereniging Tegelen Sports Club of Holland.

Jig-Saw Puzzle (p 353). A puzzle 84 ft 10½ in x 15 ft 2½ in with 15,520 pieces was constructed by the Monadnock United Way of Keene, NH at the Keene College gym, Sept 21–23, 1985.

Largest Pies (p 405). A pecan pie 12½ ft in diameter, 3 in thick and weighing 3,015 lb was baked in 8 hours in Okmulgee, Okla at the Pecan Festival there on June 21, 1986. Every piece was sold.

North Pole Conquests (p 428). The first to reach the Pole, solo and without dogs, was Dr Jean-Louis Etienne, 39, on May 11, 1986, after 63 days.

Marine Records (p 434). Fastest W–E Atlantic crossing, 3 days 8 hours 31 min, was made by the 72-ft *Virgin Atlantic Challenger II*, a monohull owned by Richard Branson with a crew of 6, June 26–29, 1986.

Band Marathon (p 437). A 6-piece rock band played continuously for 100 hours 25 min, Apr 7–11, 1986, sponsored by WROC, Cleveland, O.

LARGEST PAINTING (p 181): Seen from the air, this 18-paneled 32,-400-sq-ft painting by Rey Hernandez (US, b Puerto Rico) was painted with oil-based paint on vinyl canvas with the help of only one assistant, Canadian artist Diane St Laurent. It was unveiled on July 9, 1986 in Van Cortlandt Park with NYC officials, headed by Mayor Koch, present. (*Photo by M. Danza*, NYPD)

Crochet (p 443). A longer chain 38.83 mi long has been completed by Miss Ria van der Honing of Wormerveer, The Netherlands, on July 14, 1986.

Dancing, Ballroom (p 444). For 126 hours non-stop Scott Michael, 31, dancing instructor of Huntington Beach, Calif, danced with 27 partners June 20–25, 1986, at the Dance Masters Ballroom Studio, Stanton, Calif.

Dancing, Tap (p 444). Macy's beat its own record by having 3,783 dancers tapping simultaneously on Aug 17, 1986.

Flute Marathons (p 448). Playing for 61 hours continuously, Joseph Shury of Sri Chinmoy Marathon Team, Toronto, Canada, set a new record.

Hula-Hooping (p 450). Tonya Lynn Mistal, 15, of Cottonwood, Calif, went 88 hours without a drop of the hoop, July 9–14, 1986, beating her 1983 world record of 60 and topping the later record of 72 hours set by Kym Coberly.

Juggling (p 452). Kirk Swenson of Philadelphia ran 5 km joggling in 16 min 55 sec, and also ran 1 mi joggling in 4 min 43 sec (a new *official* record). Owen Morse of Tustin, Calif, ran 100 m joggling in 12.34 sec. These events took place on July 24, 1986 at the International Jugglers Convention in San Jose, Calif.

Parachuting (p 460). During the National Skydiving Championships at Davis Field, Muskogee, Okla, a team of 100 led by Guy Manos and Tom Piras of Deland, Fla, linked in a cluster formation for 7.67 sec on July 5, 1986. They jumped at 15,000 ft and took 61 sec to make the formation.

Talking (p 469). Andy Page, 23, a Methodist lay preacher at Woolton, Liverpool, Eng, gave an after-dinner speech lasting 24 hours July 1–2, 1986, at the city's St George Hotel.

Eggs (p 477). Peter Dowdeswell beat his own time by consuming 14 hard-boiled eggs in 41.57 sec on July 17, 1986, on TV in NYC on "The Morning Show."

Ice Cream (p 479). Tony Dowdeswell beat his own time by swallowing 3 lb 6 oz of unmelted ice cream in 31.67 sec at the Guinness Museum, NYC, on July 15, 1986.

Jelly (p 479). Peter Dowdeswell beat his own time by eating 20 oz in 8.25 sec at the Royal Oak, Eng, on July 5, 1986.

Spaghetti (p 480). Peter Dowdeswell beat his own record by consuming 100 yd in 12.02 sec at 42nd St Disco, Halesowen, Eng, on July 3, 1986.

Greatest Bequests (p 483). The Chairman of the Japanese Shipbuilding Industry Foundation, Ryoichi Sasakawa, is reported to have made donations totaling more than $2.6 billion between 1962 and 1984.

Golf, British Open (p 571). Greg Norman (Aust) equaled the record of 62 at Turnberry for the lowest-scoring round, July 18, 1986.

Golf, Most Rounds in a Day (p 573). Charles Stock topped his own record by playing 711 holes in 24 hours (averaging 36.5 shots per 9 holes) at the same course on July 7, 1986. Also Bill Ridge (US) played on foot 504 holes (28 rounds) in 24 hours on June 26, 1986, at the Bob-O-Link Country Club.

Golf, Hole-in-One (p 576). Jim Cobb, 69, of Craig, Colo, aced 3 holes in 30 hours, Aug 8, 1986, according to *USA Today*.

Gymnastics, Rope Jumping (p 582). John Baber skip-ran the 10-mi People Classic road race at Williamstown, Mass, in 78 min 40 sec on Apr 27, 1986.

Gymnastics, Push-Ups (p 583). Jack Atherton did 29,601 in 24 hours, July 11–12, 1986, at HMP Featherstone, Eng.

Skiing, Duration (p 612). With no waiting for lifts, Dave Phillips and Gerry O'Neill skied for 83 hours at Grouse Mt, N Vancouver, Canada, Feb 20–23, 1986.

Softball, Marathon (p 621). A second 100-hour record was set for a slow-pitch game by Alpha Gamma Chi fraternity, Lee College, Cleveland, Tenn, Apr 1–5, 1986 with 20 players participating.

Swimming, Freestyle (p 628). Tamara Costache beat her own record by swimming 50m in 25.31 sec on Aug 2, 1986, in Sofia, Bulgaria.

Swimming, Double Crossing of Channel (p 634). Philip Rush (NZ) (b Nov 6, 1963) swam the fastest, 17 hours 56 min, beating the 18 hours 15 min set in 1983.

Tennis, Federation Cup (p 646). The US won for the 12th time, but Chris Lloyd's unbroken sequence of success ended after 29 singles victories.

Track and Field (p 650). In the 5000-mi run Ingrid Kristiansen of Norway set a new record of 14 min 17.37 sec in Stockholm on Aug 5, 1986, beating Zola Budd's record of 1985 by more than 10 sec.

Water Skiing, Tricks (p 666). Patrice Martin scored 10,440 points on July 27, 1986, at Giffaumont, France.

INDEX

Descent, whales 52, pinnipeds 56, diving, ocean, salvage 430–31, parachute 460–61, rappeling 464, skiing 614, parachute skijumping 614–15
Desert 140
Destroyer 283
Destructive war 379
Detectable sound 40–41
Diamonds 169, 170, 172, 173, 361, synthetic 170
Diary 196
Dictionaries 191, 197, 202
Diesel-engined car 289
Dik-dik 61
Dinosaurs 98
Director, movie 235
Dirigible, ball drop from 510
Disaster 119–20, 422–25, sports 497
Disco dancing 444
Discomfort humidity and 141
Discrete object, largest 155–56
Discs, see **Records**
Diseases 34–35, 422
Disguises 224
Dish, food 409
Dish telescopes 168
Distance to city centers, airport 319
Distant object 156, visible 156
Distilleries 340
Diving, animal 52, 56, bird 76, depth, salvage by 431, shallow, high 445, 447; see also **Swimming**
Divorces 374, 386, 434
Doctorates 417
Doctors 33, 34, 38, 375, 417
Document 198
Dogs 50, 65–70, 72, 362
Dog sled race 66
Dolls 349–50, 359
Dolphins 52, 117
Domes 266
Domesticated animals, mammals 64–73, birds 78–79
Domino toppling 446, 447
Donor, blood 36
Doors 267, 346
Doughnuts, eating 477
Dow Jones average 345
Dowry 482
Dragline excavator 327
Dragonfly 92
Dragsters, automobile 496
Draping, islands 349, 350, bridge 474, 475
Drawbridge 257, 258
Drawing 184
Dream 43
Dredger 284
Dress 350
Drilling and mines 276–78
Drink 163–65
Drivers 413, licenses 415, 413, racing 491–94
Drives, golf 569
Driving, two-wheel 294, 295, round-the-world 294–95, in reverse 296, longest trip 300, carriage 440
Drought 145

Drugs 162–63, sniffing by dogs 68–69, prescription 163, hauls 393–94
Drum 210
Drumming 446, 447
Drydock 267
Dryness 145
Duck, laying 364
Ducks and drakes 447
Dump truck 298
Dunes, sand 132
Durability, light bulb 177, advertiser 207, musicians 209, actors 221, TV shows and performers 230, car 294, railroad station 305–6, batteries 326, driver 415, professor 416, bridge player 556
Dwarfs 5–10
Dwellings, elevation 372–73

E

Eagles 75, 77
Earnings 481–82, blurb writer 201–2, musicians 215, singers 215–16, 222, 229, 481, sports people 222, 489, 490, 493, 522, 523, 529, 530, 531, 571, 572, 573, 574, 575, 597, 607, 608, 637, 642–43, TV stars 222, 229–30 movie actors 235, 482, 597, stuntman 234, 235
Earrings 360
Ear 73
Earth 123, 140, 153, rotation 174, land area 368
Earth mover 298
Earthquakes 119–20, 422
Earthworms 95, attracting 95
Easter egg 402
Eaters 51, human 476–81
Eating records 476–81
Eclipses 150
Economic records 394–416
Education 416–18
Eels 87, 88, eating 477
Eggplant 100
Eggs, animal 50–51, bird 50, 76, 77, heaviest 76, 77, 364, fish 88, insect 91, laying rate, yolks, goose, duck 364, Easter 402, stunts with 447–48, omelet making 457, eating 477
Eisenhower, D.D. 545, vs Jim Thorpe 543
Eland 61
Elections 377, 378, papal 421
Electric current 175
Electric fish 87, 88
Electric shock 44
Elements 123, 161
Elephant bird 50, 76
Elephants 50, 52, 53, 54, 62
Elephant seal 56
Elevators, grain 246, passenger 328, involuntary entrapment 328, fatalities 424
Embassy 246
Embroidery, see **Tapestries**